DYNAMICS OF GROUP PSYCHOTHERAPY

DYNAMICS OF GROUP PSYCHOTHERAPY

S.R. Slavson

*edited in consultation
with the author by*
Mortimer Schiffer

NEW YORK • JASON ARONSON • LONDON

ISBN: 0-87668-372-3

Library of Congress Catalog Number: 79-51903

Manufactured in the United States of America

CONTENTS

PART TWO: GROUP PSYCHOTHERAPY: CHILDREN AND
ADOLESCENTS

PART THREE: AN S.R. SLAVSON BIBLIOGRAPHY

THE GENEALOGY OF GROUP PSYCHOTHERAPY

S.R. Slavson pioneered in group psychotherapy, and his contributions to this specialized modality of treatment during more than four decades would be difficult to assess in their entirety. Among other things, he was undoubtedly the most prolific writer on the subject. This is testified by perusal of these Selected Papers and the extensive bibliography in Part III of this volume. His numerous books and articles on analytical group psychotherapy and related topics established the foundations of this relatively new approach in treatment.

The task of selecting from a total of 194 publications those that adequately delineate the breadth of Slavson's seminal conceptions is formidable. From the bulk of his written works we finally chose eighty-two substantive papers deemed representative of Slavson's fundamental theses anent the dynamics and practices of analytical and analytically oriented group psychotherapies. However, for practical reasons it was necessary to limit this present collection to forty-nine; the others have been transferred to the bibliography and are noted by asterisks.

The present collection consists of three major parts: Parts I and II are composed of a number of basic articles groups under two headings: Adults, and Children and Adolescents; five of these articles were heretofore unpublished [1, 2, 4, 33, 48]. Part III is a completed bibliography of the bulk of his other publications in several fields. A significant feature of this volume is that all entries in Parts I, II, and III are identified by bracketed numbers which have been used extensively in cross-referencing to serve readers and students who may desire further elaboration on specific topics.

Much of Slavson's written material was also used by him didactically in his extensive teaching and consultative roles both in the United States and in seven European countries. He maintained communication with literally hundreds of psychiatrists and other clinicians in his unremitting efforts to spread group therapy and monitor its appropriate use. To do this he served as consultant to numerous clinics and community agencies, and conducted seminars on clinical analyses of practices in various therapeutic projects. It is inevitable during the development of a new clinical procedure that original writings and teaching procedures would have some repetition of concepts. In the case of Slavson, this occurred mainly in articles dealing with children's group therapy, which was the first group treatment method that Slavson originated, in 1934. Because of this, some minor editing has been done in these papers. Additional articles on children's, adolescents', and adults' therapy groups have been annotated in the bibliography.

The forty-nine basic papers are intact except for the addition of bracketed cross-reference numbers. Their content are their own message, and required no editorial deletions, additions, or modifications. Readers and students will discover for themselves the illuminating clarity of exposition that distinguishes all of Slavson's writings. These papers constitute an exposition of basic theories, principles, and practices of group psychotherapy. Rather than present them in chronological sequence, they have been arranged in order of sequential relevance. The introductory essay, "Psychotherapy and the Human Condition" [1], was written by Slavson specifically for this volume. It is a probing, psychophilosophical distillation of a lifetime's occupation with individuals of all ages in groups of various design developed by Slavson. Global in perspective, it integrates the experiences and reflections of an active, creative mind ever concerned with the welfare of man. The essay explores man's basic nature; his biological and psychological attributes and drives; his attempts to synthesize the conflicting demands of innate needs and the dictates of uncompromising social (group) realities and the successes and failures attending these efforts, including the psychomalignancies that are the invariable consequences of inadequate resolution of emotional conflicts. Slavson identifies man's individual and universal dilemmas, his tensions, anxieties, irrationalities, confusions, and accomplishments, projecting all these against the panoply of natural and social forces that constitute life's arena.

This formidable essay is a retrospective, integral assessment of the current state of human personality and the resulting social conditions by an acute observer and analyst. Embodied in it is a measure of philosophy but, in addition, and more concretely, are predictions of impending social crises of universal dimensions, with serious portents as to the survival of mankind as a whole. Whatever may be prescient in the content of this essay, Slavson attempts to validate with observations and analyses of man's typical responses to phenomenological events. Slavson deems man capable of sublimity—but sublimity yet to be acquired following a global struggle which man will himself eventually precipitate because of his *essential psychosis*. An original, startling psychological concept, the essential psychosis is a crystallization of numerous observations and intuitions, and is defined and illuminated with actual human events. Also included in the essay is Slavson's estimation of the responsibilities and potentials of psychotherapy in palliating and correcting the individual and group stresses which accompany man's compromises and adjustments. Emphasized are the unique contributions of group psychotherapy for problems in which failures in social interaction figure prominently.

Against the theme of this introductory essay, in the second presentation, "The Essence of Psychotherapy" [2], he further elaborates the psychological elements involved in psychotherapy. Analytical and individual group psychotherapy are delineated and evaluated on the basis of nosology and other clinical desiderata. And, following the background frame of reference established in the first two essays, the succeeding papers describe in progressive detail the foundational concepts of intra- and interindividual dynamics, and specific group methodologies for children, adolescents, and adults. In the bulk of these presentations the serious student will discover pertinent descriptions of technical elements that will expand his understanding of analytical group psychotherapy and also enhance the technical skills required for the various group methods. In his clinical writings, Slavson was at all times concerned with the need to delineate clearly the considerations involved in actual practice [*viz.* 5, 11, 19, 22, 34, 49, 56]. He stressed the importance of first ascertaining the *nuclear problems* of each patient and then the selection of patients for whom analytical group psychotherapy is indicated, and finally, the proper composition of groups. The student can only profit from such a determinate, instructive exposition.

Part III of this volume is a complete listing of Slavson's books and articles in addition to those of Parts I and II. These are classified under six categories: books, books in other languages, chapters in books, chapters in books and journals in other languages, psychotherapy articles in periodicals, and education, recreation and group work. All articles on group psychotherapy that were not selected for use in Part I are included in this section, which reveals Slavson's catholic interests and records his multifarious activities during the past more than sixty years.

Since its beginnings with latency children in 1934, the practice of analytical and analytically oriented group psychotherapies experienced extraordinary growth, to the extent that today it has numerous practitioners in this country and in many countries abroad.[1] In conformity with the principle of *specificity*, first formulated by Slavson, group psychotherapies have been evolved by him for patients of various ages and clinical categories which are now accepted as essential modalities for treating patients with neurotic and character disorders. Of course, many individuals with accredited status have participated in these developments. However, it is the extraordinary achievements of Slavson that entitles him to the epithet "father of group psychotherapy," bestowed upon him in 1972 by the journal *Family Health* in its listing of the one hundred most important leaders in the world of health [191].

Slavson designed the first experimental small therapy groups for children [53] and in later years devised other analytical group methods for them as well as for adolescents and adults [55, 56, 61]. Slavson's

---

1. The total membership of the American Group Psychotherapy Association, the primary organization representing the field of group psychotherapy which Slavson initiated in 1942, is more than 3,000. Affiliated are 22 local societies in this country and nine in other countries.

inventive use of psychotherapy groups did *not* evolve from preexisting methods of treatment nor from the theoretical constructs upon which these methods are based.[2] To the contrary, his discoveries of the corrective, therapeutic potentiality which is inherent in groups, when they are properly constituted and managed, came from entirely different sources. Initially, from 1911 to 1930, Slavson was engrossed with "Self-Culture Clubs" (which he initiated), social group work, and progressive education with children and teenagers. These earlier groups were concerned primarily with the personal enrichment of individuals through active participation in creative pursuits. The generative beginnings of Slavson's clinical groups, which occurred much later, followed upon these unusual preceding experiences with groups whose activities and purposes were remote from traditional theories and practices. The historical events that led to his original discoveries in group psychotherapy will be detailed presently.

Slavson was not the first, of course, to stress the formative influences of groups on the individual's personality, starting with the family group. His fundamental contributions stem from his passionate conviction of the inherent creativity of every individual and the effects of interaction on character development and social adjustment. His later discovery of the corrective potency of specially designed groups in treating emotional disturbances and social maladjustments stemmed from his basic humanism and preoccupation with the welfare of mankind generally.

Voluminous writings in psychoanalysis emphasized the inseparability of human development from the family. Yet, they were notably devoid of references to the utilization of extrafamiliar groups as therapeutic instrumentalities. In all of Sigmund Freud's massive contributions to psychoanalytical thought and practice only one small book, *Group Psychology and the Analysis of the Ego*, is concerned primarily with the "group."[3] Despite his acknowledgment of its

2. See ten papers in the series "Theoretical Basis of Analytical Group Psychotherapy" in Vols. 4, 5, 6, 9, 10, 11, 12, 16, 19, 22, *International Journal of Group Psychotherapy*.

3. In his writings Slavson repeatedly indicated the misuse of the term "group," probably through faulty translation. The terms "crowds," or "masses" would have been more accurate for the monolithic, artificial "groups" Freud used in his analysis, i.e., the church and the army. Slavson suggested that one of the major therapeutic dynamics in group psychotherapy is the *mutual interpenetration* of patients, which in his experience (later confirmed by a study by the American Psychological Association) cannot occur among more than eight interacting persons.

primacy and its relation to individual psychology, Freud's therapeutic theories and practices remained entirely oriented to individual patients, as did those of his contemporaries and followers. They had failed to recognize the clinical potentials of groups and their capacity to reconstruct psyches and behaviors in patients whose disorders are in a large measure intransigent to traditional psychoanalytical treatment.

Slavson discriminates between emotional disorders that *should* be treated by individual psychoanalysis while others can best be reached through the medium of the group. In his view, intensive psychoneuroses can require traditional psychoanalysis, for the group does not allow the degree of regression through free association because of the interference from other members. The group also dilutes the transference attitudes toward the therapist and the inevitable group transactions alter the positive image of the therapist essential in psychoanalysis. The interruptions in the free association of a psychoneurotic patient by other group members increase frustrations which have been his lot in the past.

In essence, it was the discovery of the use of the group as a therapeutic instrumentality that was Slavson's. Equally important was his inventiveness in formulating distinct types of group methods for treating children, adolescents, and adults [6, 7, 23, 24, 43, 46, 55, 56, 59, 60, 64], and the selection of suitable patients and proper groupings [34, 39].

It is of significance for later developments that in Slavson's earliest books and in other of his publications—which were devoted at the time to the subjects of creative recreation, progressive education and character development—there are embodied concepts of social and interactional groups. These were the germs of what, decades later, were the building blocks of group psychotherapy. Witness his careful elaboration in 1938 of basic "group dynamics" in *Character Education in a Democracy* [52, chap. 4]. Even today, in their precise formulation, these "group dynamics" represent substantially the generally accepted, psychological principles governing interactions in analytical group psychotherapy in addition to other characteristics of therapy groups.

Slavson's historical involvement with groups of various ages and

---

He suggested the mathematical formula: $s = n(n-1)(n-2)(n-3)...(n-n+1)$ for the maximum number of interactions possible in the group. Thus, the number (n) of persons in an analytical group should not exceed eight. Five or six may be even more effective.

types merits further attention if we are to discern how he eventually came upon the therapeutic potentials of the group. It is not the editor's intention to describe here the personal development of a pioneer, but rather to emphasize his seminal concepts and theories about individuals, groups, and society as they appeared in the course of his work and to understand how these became permuted to clinical forms. Retrospective knowledge of the transmutations that took place during later years deepens our understanding of the fundamental principles and practices of group psychotherapy as these evolved. It also enables us to discriminate between methods whose validity and reliability have withstood the test of time and other, purported group procedures that are ill-founded in theory and/or methodology.

In 1911 Slavson formed the coeducational groups for adolescents which came to be known as "Self-Culture Clubs" in Brooklyn, New York, where he resided. These groups provided enriching experiences in the various art forms—painting, music, dance, and poetry—and also opportunities for group discussions of topics meaningful to the members. He introduced the young people to symphony concerts as well as the more literary theatre performances that led to their own productions from time to time. In the late 1920s he expanded this work to wider social activities for youth programs in neighborhood settlements in Manhattan. Slavson later initiated similar activities under labor union auspices. During this period Slavson's professional engagement was in civil engineering for which he had received training at the evening school of Cooper Union.

The psychology of human development had always fascinated Slavson and it was this interest that brought him to the relatively new field of progressive education of children—first, at the prestigious Walden School in New York and later at the famous Malting Housing School for small children in Cambridge, England. He had, by that time, already devised an unusual program in education which he termed "Search-Discovery" and which he applied some years later with postgraduate students at Springfield College. His first published book, in 1937, *Science in the New Education* [50] is a record of these early activities in education beginning in 1918.

It was at the Walden School that he came upon a discovery of significant implications with respect to his subsequent involvements with group psychotherapy. He observed in a seriously disturbed young girl of eleven how success in creative activities and the increased feelings of self-worth and the social recognition she received from the peer group were instrumental in effecting dramatic changes in her personality and behavior [4].

Some time thereafter, in 1934, he experimented along similar lines with a group of emotionally disturbed girls who were being seen individually by volunteer Big Sisters as part of the program of the Jewish Board of Guardians in New York, a clinical agency engaged in treating children and their parents. These girls had proven intractable and resistive despite the best efforts of their Big Sisters. Slavson's involvement in this project resulted from a casual conversation with several friends, in which they described the difficulties they were experiencing with these girls. Slavson spontaneously suggested that intrinsically creative outlets in a group setting might influence the girls and help them modify their maladaptive behavior. When he was asked to formulate such an experiment he arranged a summer program of planned weekly excursions to places of interest for one group led by a Big Sister which always ended with a snack.

The Big Sisters involved in this experiment reported decided improvements in the attitudes, behavior, and responses of their young charges, whom they continued to see on an individual basis. Emboldened by these observations, Slavson started additional small groups for troubled latency age children. These new groups, whose composition was more carefully monitored, were conducted on a continuing, weekly basis in meeting rooms equipped with a variety of crafts media and games. A *permissive* adult worker helped create a climate of freedom where the children were allowed to use the materials as they wished and to interact with each other without interference from the adult. The children improved in these activity groups, without the use of interpretations of behavior which was characteristic of individual therapy.

As described to the editor by Slavson, after a year's experimentation with one of these groups, he closeted himself with the weekly detailed written protocols of the sessions which he used in the supervision conferences, to fathom the meaning of the material and discover the psychological elements responsible for the surprising changes observed in the children. He finally confirmed his original premise: it was the element of *compresence*, the actuality of being and interacting one with the other in the peer group, the sense of self-worth gained from newly acquired skills, the self-selected, completed craft and art projects, fortified by the spontaneous praise of fellow members, and the improved social status that were responsible for the corrective effects on personality and character.[4] As a result the name of the project was altered from "The Therapeutics of Creative Activity" to "Group Therapy," and later to "Activity Group Therapy." Slavson then became engaged further in clinical experimentation with groups, as the first director of group therapy of the Jewish Board of Guardians and in many other therapeutic or helping agencies.

It had been noted that some children, more emotionally conflicted, who had resisted or did not respond to individual therapy, did accept exclusive Activity Group Therapy but did not respond as well as expected. Another method was devised by Slavson, *Activity-Interview Group Psychotherapy*, which combined both activities and individual and group discussions. A similar analytical approach, titled *Play Group Therapy* was used with young, preschool children. Finally, *Transitional Groups* for patients who had been in activity and activity-interview groups were employed with children being terminated from these treatments, to help them progress as groups into settlement house programs.

While this comprehensive group program with children was expanding, Slavson introduced analytical treatment groups for selected parents of children receiving treatment. For other parents, group guidance was created [60]. It is important to note that he was the first to train and supervise all the therapists at the Jewish Board of Guardians and in a number of community clinics in three states. He was also the first to conduct continuous seminars for some twelve years. Gradually attention was drawn nationally to these programs of group treatment, and such projects have spread widely throughout the United States and in some European countries and, lately, to other continents. In 1957, Slavson spent sixteen weeks in seven countries teaching and lecturing on group psychotherapy as well as presenting papers at

---

4. In a brief summary of his extensive, evaluative study, the late Dr. Lawson G. Lowrey said: "In my study a total of 176 children [of 500–550 who had been in groups] were identified in reading 19 of 72 available group records... In a total of 101 cases there were data enough in the records read to permit a 'personal' judgment of the results of the group therapy. There were 74 cases with good results and 27 with poor or no results."

numerous international conferences on clinical and mental health subjects since 1948. The latter were stimulated by reports published first by Slavson and later by others, and by Slavson's books, some of which had been translated into six languages.

Perhaps because of the burgeoning group treatment programs for children and the widespread response, the implications of Slavson's early analytical treatment groups for adults and adolescents tend to be overlooked. The experiences with these analytical groups and the many permutations in techniques that have grown out of them had a definite relation to the subsequent development of analytical group psychotherapy for adults and para-analytical groups for adolescents. Some decades later Slavson evolved a unique and most effective type of *Vita-Erg Therapy* for mental hospitals [25, 63].

Slavson also recognized that some parents of child patients did not require intensive probing of unconscious motivations in their parenting which had negatively affected their children. He felt that these parents could gain sufficient understanding through "guided discussions" in groups and thus acquire alternative ways of dealing with and relating to their children. This guidance group method for parents [60] led Slavson to further refine the variables in presenting problems, which resulted in favorable management by parents.

Slavson evolved significant differentiations in diagnostic findings and their utilization in different group approaches with adults. These important variables are found in the various forms of analytical and analytically oriented group psychotherapy and counseling and guidance in use today. He also concretized the particular value of group psychotherapy for ego-syntonic, character problems, for which individual treatment is usually ineffective.

Slavson was responsible for still another para-analytical method that proved eminently successful with a patient population that had always proved uniquely intransigent to the interventions of psychotherapy— institutionalized, hardened delinquent adolescents. This method, *Para-analytic Group Psychotherapy and the Inversion Technique* [58, 62], proved to be a treatment of choice for some nonpsychotic adolescent patients.

Slavson has referred to his discovery of children's group therapy as a serendipitous occurrence, averring that it originated in his experiences with the emotionally troubled girl referred to earlier [4]. The possibility of the relationship of an "accidental" event to the discovery of a technical, psychological procedure cannot be denied. However, when one weighs Slavson's background, his social, political, economic, and humanistic roots, his extensive engagement in creative group enterprises of various types, what is discernible is the inevitable transition of his concern for the welfare of mankind to an all-encompassing involvement for more than four decades in group psychotherapy. There is an unmistakable thread of continuity linking Slavson's work with individuals in groups that illuminates a deeper meaning. The common factor was his basic regard for the needs of individuals, his recognition of the creative potentialities of every human, given the opportunities for their actualization, and an overriding conviction that troubled individuals can derive sustenance in constructive group participation. These basic elements are implicit in all of Slavson's work and embodied in his philosophical conceptions of the nature of man. Subsequently these developed into consciously planned clinical designs. All of Slavson's endeavors are rooted in his firm belief in man's innate gregariousness. He coined the terms "groupism" and "social hunger" to describe this uncompromising need of man for the company of man.

Thus, group psychotherapy, as conceived by Slavson, was not solely the result of a serendipitous occurrence, as were the original few groups. It was, rather, the inevitable consequence of a compelling social philosophy which became pragmatically employed with individuals of all ages in many forms of groups.

Any new movement, including group psychotherapy, which was in the beginning entirely novel in the field of clinical treatment, usually generates differences of opinion as to theory and practice with polemical exchanges among proponents holding varying views. Slavson remained an ever-vigilant surveyor of these developments, defending clinical integrity and protecting it when necessary from the potentially weakening effects of unproved, uncritical and, at times, unfounded group procedures. He labored indefatigably to establish the validity of group psychotherapy, not committing himself to any clinical procedure—his own or another's—until convinced of its merits by empirical results.

Two fundamental considerations seem to have guided his efforts: the absolute rights of patients to proper treatment by thoroughly trained therapists under adequate supervision and/or consultation; a strong conviction that all procedures professing to be psychotherapy be founded on tested psychological foundations validated through objective experimentation under clinical controls. Where he questioned theories and practices, it was because they failed to adhere to these basic desiderata. He decried pronouncements of purportedly "new" procedures prematurely communicated in publications and in conferences with so-called "findings" based on limited experiences.

Even in the early stages of group psychotherapy, Slavson, in his various capacities in the American Group Psychotherapy Association, warned of future "invasions" by superficial, nonclinical group procedures and practitioners that would endanger group psychotherapy and threaten the professional identity of the association he constantly sought to safeguard. Subsequent events confirmed his prescience. Recently someone assessed that *more than 301* group procedures claim to help emotionally troubled individuals!

It was not Slavson's aim to defend the past, to delimit practice, or to discourage honest experimentation. Repetitively through the years he pointed out to this editor and to others his belief in the value of modifying traditional techniques in both individual and group psychotherapy according to the needs of specific patients at appropriate times, which he characterized as "strategies." In his estimation, there were proper uses for unique interventions as confrontation, assertiveness procedures, and other directive, manipulative, exhortatory techniques provided basic tested assumptions are maintained. He conceded to the intuitive, practiced therapist the right to employ skills and to know when and how to depart from fundamental techniques to meet episodic, situational needs of patients and groups. "The expert knows when to break the rules," he often asserted.

What Slavson did find questionable was—and, to a certain extent, still is—the growing tendency of some therapists to institutionalize a single technique or strategy, employing it in a gross, undifferentiated fashion as a total form of psychotherapy for *all* patients. However, his uncanny perceptions of the uniqueness of patients' personalities and characters, including their deviant aspects, rejected the possibility that any one technique is suitable in all situations or serves the global needs of total therapy [29, 30, 154, 187].

Slavson was a pioneer in analytical group psychotherapy, the originator of tested group treatment modalities of carefully selected patients, the founder of the American Group Psychotherapy Association and its first president (later President Emeritus), founder of the Association's official publication, the *International Journal of Group Psychotherapy*, and its editor for many years, and the initiator of what became the International Association of Group Psychotherapy. Slavson was, therefore, the logical person to assume responsibility for insuring the orderly, progressive growth of the field. While a vigorous and tireless advocate of group treatment and its defender, it is significant that all his voluminous writings, covering a span of more than half a century, are devoid of polemical content. All of his publications in the clinical area consist of definitive formulations of group psychotherapy—its theory, principles, and practices—and are free of argumentativeness or subjectivity. In a remark to the editor, Slavson stated that he felt it would have been totally unproductive, perhaps self-destructive, for him to use his energies in writing defensively or critically of the views of others or exposing their inaccuracies, subjectivity, and sometimes irrational claims. He remained confident that these would in the future be surely identified and eliminated, and that the basic concepts on which group psychotherapy is founded would prevail and would determine its valid, enduring methods [30].

However, under other circumstances, such as when Slavson served as discussant or respondent on panels and symposia at professional conferences, he never hesitated to discharge his obligation by questioning, examining, and evaluating the presentations of others and assessing their clinical probity. His real "threat" was to obscurantism, faulty psychology, illogical methods, and always to unethical practices. He had little sufferance for "bright" ideas which lacked substance and pragmatic value. Practiced "theoreticians" who tended to expound abstruse concepts in psychotherapy without demonstrating their applicability in sound practice, failed to impress him. Slavson, who was not lacking as a seminal thinker, was always impelled by the pressing realities of human need toward practical applications of theories and conceptions to alleviate the emotional burdens of patients. This inclination, almost a compulsion, is revealed in the following from a presentation in London at the International Conference on Medical Psychotherapy in 1948.

"It is rather important that therapy groups should not be relegated to the realm of mysticism and that transcendental concepts should be eliminated from discussions of them... I have taken the opportunity [55] to indicate both the semantic discrepancy as well as the epistemological unsuitability of such terms as 'group symptom' and 'group emotion'.... 'Group culture,' for example, implies staticism, while psychotherapy is dynamic both in its inherent process and in terms of intrapsychic activity.... The foundations of group psychotherapy lie in clinical, not in sociological or philosophical concepts. Clinical and diagnostic understandings must be dominant here as in any other branch of psychiatry; especially important is clinical diagnosis...."

It has been said, and it is true, that Slavson would not make accommodations with ideas and methods with which he could not agree after sober evaluation. There were times, especially during the early days, when some individuals took umbrage with his assiduous resistance to methods he considered questionable. They viewed him as "uncompromising." It was a "fault" that eventually inured to the benefit of group psychotherapy which, at the time, was experiencing the unavoidable trials of any innovative treatment procedure. Slavson's criticisms were invariably directed to the context of clinical presentations and issue, never *ad hominem*. If he displayed unusual zealousness in exposing ignorance it was only to establish truths. On the other hand, he eagerly participated in all objective analyses of errors or failures in therapeutic endeavors of his own and those of others to discover the causes, because according to him this represented the road to new learnings and improved methods. But, in his estimation, ignorance tended to be negative, unproductive and static, unworthy of indulgence. Freud had expressed exactly the same conviction and logical intolerance in a pithy statement: "Ignorance is ignorance; no right to believe anything is derived from it."[5]

Slavson was driven by infinite sensitivity for the welfare of patients and as a result of this emphasis there are numerous practitioners whom he had trained directly and who studied his writings who are all indebted to him for their professional excellence and growth. They all testify to his open, honest questioning of technical procedures and his

5. Freud, S. (1927). *The Future of an Illusion, Standard Edition* 21, p. 40.

continuous helpful suggestions. Slavson was always available to everyone as advisor and consultant, motivated solely by his desire to extend and purify professional skills and thereby improve the welfare of patients.

This editor, who had the good fortune to have been associated with Slavson for four decades, starting as one of his students, offers personal testimony to the foregoing. As a trainer Slavson displayed great tolerance for errors of his trainees. There is no gainsaying the supportive, even paternalistic attitude he exhibited toward those who labored as novices with the complex and subtle elements both of theory and practice of group psychotherapy. His attitude was sometimes reminiscent of Freud's toward Jung before events separated them, when the latter was rather overenthusiastically regaling Freud with his views on occultism, his new interest. Freud wrote to Jung: "It is better not to understand something than to make such great sacrifices to understanding."[6] Slavson's attitude toward practitioners who abandoned the sound bases of psychotherapy parallels that of Freud who eventually terminated his relationships with his disciples when their work assaulted his psychological convictions. Slavson, too, would sever professional ties with any individual who, in his judgment, continued being inimical to the welfare of patients. His overriding preoccupation was always patients and their therapeutic needs. This he has repeatedly emphasized in his teaching, writings and supervisory conferences.

One of the amazing facts is that this man, whose only professional training was as a civil engineer, was entirely self-trained in the wide gamut of all his various group endeavors and in human relations. Years before he heard the name of Freud he was actively involved with individuals and social problems as well as in creative pursuits. Decades passed before he learned the nature and meanings of psychoanalytical psychology. It was two personal analyses by a former trainee of Freud that illuminated for Slavson the deeper unconscious motivants of the human psyche. It was after his discovery of Activity Group Therapy and the other methods of treatment he later formulated that the relevance of psychoanalytical principles became clear to him.

6. McGuire, W., ed. (1974). *The Freud-Jung Letters*. Princeton, N.J.: Princeton University Press, p. 219.

There seems to be much in the precise training and discipline of engineering that served him well through the years of explorations in clinical procedures. This precision is exemplified in both the quality of his work and in his numerous publications, which are models of clarity and succinctness, and also in the rigorous standards he set for study and experimentation.

Slavson can be numbered among the select group of explorers who, acting as their own guides, were capable of discovering entirely new dimensions. For such inventiveness and creativity formal training is unavailable. Imagination, purposeful drive, and a high level of integrity are the elements capable of translating germinal ideas into major formulations. These are the compass and sextant for such individuals.

A fitting conclusion to this Preface is the following, first, an extract from an unpublished paper. Implicit is his personal conviction that the propelling force behind his lifetime's creative output is the enduring belief in the pervasive influence of social forces in the lives of men, and his unremitting faith in the essentiality of truth:

"Truth need not be proved; it needs only be stated, for time and events demonstrate its veracity. He who strains to prove the validity of his assertions reveals the uncertainty of his beliefs. Truth cannot be—and has never been—blocked; it was only retarded and delayed. The annunciation from ancient Greece that 'Man without the work of man is nothing' and 'that which is human in us is given us by other humans' [as Slavson put it]—this needs no proof. It is only the *ways* in which this occurs that need to be studied, not the fact of it. One corollary is that man's fulfillment and his redemption lie in his society and his relation to it; another is that the group is the milieu from which man's health and unhealth flow."

His own deep humanitarian convictions are embraced, finally, in the poem which he had written in his twenties and included in a brief address in 1969 on the occasion of receiving one of his seven awards from the American Academy of Psychotherapists:

> Can you not hear the mothers weep,
> Can you not hear the children cry,
> Can you not see humanity asleep
> As life and opportunities fleet by?

Can you not feel man's pain and woe,
Can you not feel rent hopes and hearts,
Can you not see humanity's foe
When the giant mass slowly starts?

Can you not taste the bitterness of life,
Can you not taste your life's bitter cup,
Can you not see war and strife
Whenever masses hopefully look up?

Can you not smell the pestiferous past,
Can you not smell the cadaverous present,
Can you not see Life at last
In the vista of the Future so pleasant?

Decades after this was written, in 1971, in his second award from the American Group Psychotherapy Association, who knew Slavson's work best, the phrase is included "... and his dedicated and selfless service to troubled people."

Mortimer Schiffer
May 1978

PART ONE

Group Psychotherapy: Adults

CHAPTER 1

PSYCHOTHERAPY AND THE HUMAN CONDITION
(1976)

Man's *Misplace* in Nature

Unlike the definitive term *psychotherapy*, the concept of the *human condition* is not as clear. The phrase evokes in the mind of the average person the socioeconomic climate and the pressures under which one lives at a given time in history. This understandable reaction is only partially, perhaps minimally true, for the major dynamics that form the human condition, which pattern the life and struggles of man, are deeply rooted in his biological and psychological heritage that fashions the social setting in a given geographic milieu.

While environment determines gross adaptations, it is the biopsychological needs and urges that determine the use to which the milieu is employed. It is, therefore, necessary to recognize in the concept of "human condition" the interplay of these two operational forces and that the resultant product mirrors the basic nature of man as affected by external circumstances.

As we shall presently see, much of the current environment, even in nature itself, is the outcome of man's anomalous, latent attributes and their fruition through education, culture, technology, civilization, and his creative genius. Although the present impasse is threatening the very survival of the human race, reconciliation of the two forces—the order of nature and man's creative achievements—thus establishing much needed harmony, is not at present in sight, despite efforts to bring into alignment the implacable demands of nature and the conflicting and confusing impulsions of man. In his effort to bring social order and individual equanimity in his life, various devices have been attempted: laws, religion, ethics, and philosophy; but so far to no avail. What is required is to abandon the antiquated social instrumentalities and to recreate society on the basis of new human relationships and values.

Despite this crisis in human evolution, it should be the policy of the clinician to strictly keep apart clinical from philosophical approaches, lest clinical practice be confounded with philosophy and mysticism. It is too easy to fall prey to theory and abstraction at the cost of confronting reality and the implacable tasks psychotherapy imposes. Everyone is susceptible to a vestigial, infantile hope for the magical and the esoteric and everyone employs language as the wand for achievement. To evade these temptations requires building objectivity, courage, fearlessness of reality, and the willingness to exert effort confronting oneself and life itself. This requires constant alertness against the escapism into verbalization and overrigid conceptualization, instead of dealing with the frequently crass and tedious demands of one's life, work, and actuality.

However, despite our distrust of abstraction and mysticism, we cannot resist the temptation to speculate why, among the myriads of nature's creations, man stands alone in the overwhelming current of inner conflict; why he alone has for eons floundered in the sea of life, seeking a path toward the millenium, sometimes by direct, but more often by devious means, only everlastingly to be defeated; why he alone among the multifarious forms of inert and sentient life is hopelessly confused, unable to fathom the riddle of existence which he alone, among the all the species, forever tries to solve; and why he, despite all efforts, is incapable of finding an effective and satisfying *modus vivendi*.

Why is it that man, though a biologic entity and an integral part of nature and subject to all its laws, finds himself in an endlessly losing struggle *against* nature and, despite this failure, is still unable to conform to its comparatively simple laws and demands? Since the dawn of thought, man's mind has formulated numerous simple and intricate explanations and in this pursuit resorted to schemes ranging from magic to science, from hypothesis to experimentation, from superstition to agnosticism, from myth to exploration, from God to atheism. He has set up fetishes and invented deities, conceived sin, become addicted to guilt and prey to ambivalence and conflict.

Many of these conflicting streams of thought can be explained in terms of the inherent inconsistency between man's biological and moral natures; between his intellect and irrationality; between his narcissistic and allotropic needs. His psyche is the battleground of innumerable opposing forces, some conscious but most unconscious, which he attempts with little success to understand, to harmonize, and to control. Instrumentally, these efforts constitute the root of the total educative procedures in the score or so of the diverse cultures through which mankind has passed during its social development under various conditions and localities.

The multitudinous theories to explain man's nature, his condition, and his existence—all of them at once adequate and inadequate, disharmonious, and conflicting on every point—reveal the basic disharmony of the human animal in the context of nature and his place or misplace in it. Why should this be the lot of man alone while all other creatures adapt to their particular state in life? In the sequential stages of the evolution of most organisms, suitable provisions are found in nature to assure their survival without the conflict and turmoil that is imposed upon man. Man's discord with nature and his drive to explore, control, and modify it generate fascinating challenges but at the same time also great difficulties for him, difficulties that mandate specific efforts on his part to bring harmony within himself and to his milieu.[1]

Psychically, man stands alone in nature. On the one hand, he is the unique creature with the basic attributes of other species, but he possesses, in addition, the singular capacities for fantasy, projection, distortion, symbolization, and displacement. On the other hand, he is prey to these and other psychic mechanisms, unknown to others, that confuse and overburden him. The basic disharmony between man and nature is made palpable and ominous in his drive toward self-destruction, the destruction of members of his own and other species and his physical environment—a trend that is inconsistent with nature and alien to all others in the animal kingdom.

There are many conflicting forces that flow from biological and

---

1. This anomaly can be explained by the fact that unlike his soma, his brain is a mutation, thus rendering the human species *extranatural*.

economic sources, the elaboration of which falls outside the scope of this thesis. An impelling source of the difficulties in the human species is a biopsychological duality, *viz.*, man's atavistic animalism and his capacity for moralism, the latter being unavoidably imposed by society to assure its own welfare and survival. The need to repress atavistic urges is a potent and inescapable source of maladjustments within the individual and also in his relations with others. While man's "divinity" derives from his morality and creativity, they are essentially oppositional to raw nature whose basic law is physical survival of the species.

Another source of disturbance in man lies within his inner structure: the opposing functions of different parts of his brain. The cerebrum is the source of control and cognition, whereas impulse, "irrational" and socially unacceptable conduct flow from deeper, primitive layers. The autonomic and central nervous systems are in constant interaction, with the actualities of life favoring the latter, but at the same time seeking to bring the two into harmony and balance, though never fully succeeding with any degree of permanence.

Man: The Quarrelsome Animal

Man is considered the most quarrelsome species among all animals. (Second to man in this respect is an Antarctic subspecies of the seal.) Both human prehistory and history are replete with unending incidences of struggles—intergroup, intertribal, and interindividual. The human tendency for quarreling and fighting is close to the surface even in civilized man and can be set off at the slightest provocation, as in common parlance "at the drop of a hat." The quarreling urge is probably a derivative of the atavistic, biologically inherent hostility of prehuman and savage man. It was the major tool for existence and the resulting engrams became ingrained in the neuroglandular system of homo sapiens today.

Over the ages, various strategies such as laws, mores, and morals have been evolved to assure effective community life by controlling these primal urges. Such controls have been systematized and integrated in the cultural climate of communities and nations that vary in minor respects in different areas on the globe as determined by the imperatives for survival: climatic conditions, soil fertility, and geophysical structure of the locality. The quarreling urge assumes more "civilized" forms in more evolved cultures such as planned debates ostensibly for clarifying ideas, outbursts at community meetings, and more subtle forms such as political strategies, gossip, spreading of rumors, conflicts among individuals, and other such avenues of emotional discharge.

The disharmonies in the nature of man are set off also with respect to survival. While all other animals operate by adaptation, man from his earliest stages has utilized *active* adjustment, as differentiated from the *passive* adaptation by which other animal species live. These original active adjustments increased when man discovered primitive tools such as the club, the bow and arrow, and the utilization of fire. Such simplistic techniques have in time evolved into patterns of planned controls, manipulations, and alterations of the environment not only to meet survival needs but also, as is the case today, in aberrant fantasies and grandiose wishes. By and large, these are distortive processes with the qualities of a psychotic's perceptions of the life about him. His proclivities to aggress against nature and to convert it to his concepts and will can be viewed as a form of psychosis which is, in our view, basic to and inherent in the human species.

Essential Psychosis

This characteristic potential in homo sapiens is, in our view, the *essential psychosis* (as differentiated from clinical psychosis), confirmation of which abounds in the lives of individuals in contemporary societies as well as in man's history. For example: no other mammal kills its own species for food, while cannibalism has been widespread at certain stages in the development of man and still is practiced in isolated and remote regions on the globe. The extraordinary capacity in man for torturing his fellow creatures, nonexistent among other animals (except in cats), is another illustration of his essential psychosis. A report issued by the Geneva-based International Commission of Jurists describes events in Chile following the overthrow of the Marxist government of President Allende:

A substantial number of those arrested have been subjected to torture. Methods employed have included electric shock, blows, beatings, burning with acid and cigarettes, prolonged standing, prolonged hosing and isolation in solitary confinement, extraction of nails, crushing of testicles, physical assault, immersion in water, hanging, simulated executions, insults, threats, and the compelling attendance at the torture of others.

These are not isolated instances which could be passed off as the work of real psychotics or temporarily deranged individuals. Following the Russian Revolution, similar and worse indignities were visited upon millions of opponents to the new regime and still are, and in other countries, as well, great numbers were subjected to atrocities and executions for dissident views. Reports of indignities, brutalities, rapings, killings, and tortures filled the pages of newspapers during and following the second world war. The appalling brutalities in Vietnam during the recent war, inconceivable to the sane mind, included hanging naked women by their feet and beating them. And more recently we are plagued by reports of bombings, killings, tortures and rapings in cities, towns, and villages in many parts of the world.

Such acts are not products of what may seem to be mere aberrations. The tendency and the need for them in the human cannot be blithely dismissed for they are inherent in man's psychic nature. These brutalities are committed by so-called "normal" humans; areas of the brain are responsible for what we characterize as essential psychosis in man. In a report in *Newsweek* (September 30, 1974) we read:

> Since last May, more than 100 cattle have been found dead and gruesomely mutilated in Nebraska, Kansas and Iowa.... On one farm, a cow was killed with a blunt instrument... and her udder and sexual organs were cut off. When a veterinarian examined the corpse, he found that all of the animal's blood had been drained. On a nearby ranch... a month-old bull calf was clubbed to death. Its blood was drained off, too, and someone cut a hole in the calf's side, removing the intestines and coiling them neatly next to the head.

Possible witchcraft was given as the explanation, but the very capacity of man to evolve such witchcraft, if witchcraft it is, is itself a form of essential psychosis.

The fact that there are thousands of children every year in the United States alone who are battered by their seemingly "normal" parents through maiming, burning, and scalding with hot water, cannot but be the manifestation of suppressed essential psychosis present in the ordinary person. While it was established that such maltreatment of children is committed by parents who had themselves been victims of parental brutality, nonetheless the fact that parents are susceptible to this type of behavior attests to an irrationality which is part of essential psychosis. Infanticides and patricides are not rare phenomena. In the poem, "Daddy" by Sylvia Plath (who finally did commit suicide), the following passage appears: "Daddy, I have had to kill you. / You died before I had time... I tried to die / And get back... to you." Such fantasies are not uncommon and testify to the verity of the assumption of a basic or essential psychosis which manifests itself in other relations as well.

The thesis of essential psychosis in man is further confirmed in the content of dreams and nightmares. While Freud believed that the function of dreams is to protect sleep from outside disturbances, my own conclusion is that these nocturnal aberrations are also the effulgence of suppressed psychotic trends and the anxieties in daily "civilized" living. The cumulative frustrations with and inevitable controls upon events of the day, are stored up in the unconscious and appear in phantasmagoric guise of the dream and, especially, in nightmares. In full-blown psychotics this phenomenon appears as *daymares*. Both are cathartic in nature against suppressed hostilities and frustrations and often have wishful intent as well as at times prophetic content.

Another universal phenomenon in human history that can be attributed to essential psychosis is the belief in miracles and superstitions. While in recent times these have grown less compelling and less intense largely due to scientific knowledge and the weakening of religiosity, there are still many residues even in the more advanced Western cultures. The widespread belief (which stems from man's overwhelming insecurity and loneliness) in the effectiveness of prayer to a personal deity, for example, is related to man's lurking faith in miracles.

The Greek mythologies confirm the hypothesis of a psychotic element in man. The birth and trials of Dionysius, for example, run parallel to those of Jesus Christ. Dionysius was also born of a human mother and was fathered by a god, Zeus. He, too, displayed supernatural powers. Spirits, good and evil, permeated Greek religious beliefs, some of which survive to this day throughout the world. Polls reveal that fifty-two percent of Americans believe in the existence of evil spirits which can and do "take over" individuals. Witness the reaction to the motion picture, *The Exorcist*, as well as the currently spreading cults of Holy Rollers, demonologists, witchcrafters and others. Likewise, there still persists belief in the existence of monsters such as the Abominable Snowman of the Himalayas and "Big Foot" in the state of Washington—the latter purported to be an eight hundred pound, hairy, humanlike figure whose footprints are fifteen inches long and nine inches wide.

A recital of the numerous manifestations of essential psychosis, even among the most advanced nations of the Western world, could fill many volumes. In a film called *Snuff* a woman is supposedly tortured, murdered and dismembered on screen "for sexual effect." Made in lurid color, the film grossed $66,456 in one week. Tickets sell for four dollars. The victim is literally butchered—starting with the lopping off of a finger and ending with evisceration.

Of course it's not real, we're told. (Animal entrails provide the sport, one hears.) What shocks one is not the fact that a pack of ghouls and degenerates made this film, but that thousands of people are paying their four dollars to watch this bloody exercise.

Even contemplating such films as *Snuff* is a little terrifying. This is not simply kinky sex, or Grand Guignol horror or Gothic thrills. There are screaming nerves, madness, a terrible social sickness on display here. So many events in our daily lives oblige us to ask, "What sort of people are we?" And where does this sort of depravity lead?

A few of so-called "amusement" spectacles: professional wrestling, involving mutual, brutal pummeling; high wire walking and bicycle riding (at times even backwards and sometimes with another acrobat standing on the rider's shoulders or a third poised on a narrow strip of wood between two cyclists); trapeze acrobatics as performed by the "Flying Ferraras," in which a family with a seven-year-old boy as the star oscillate great distances apart and exchange places in the air via bloodcurdling acrobatics, to the screams of frightened and at the same time delighted throngs; hundred-foot dives into a body of water or, what is more risky, diving forty feet into a tub of four feet of water; roller-coasting at great speeds and heights; "rock" theatrical performances replete with violence such as those by the male performer, Alice Cooper, resulting in serious bodily injuries to the participants; the antics of Evel Kneivel; *Monty Python's Flying Circus* with its irrational dialogues, grotesque faces, rolling heads, and dismembered bodies; and the Hilarious House of Freightenstein and its distorted faces and strange characters on television that cannot but give disturbed nights and nightmares to young and old. Alice in Wonderland could have been conceived and written only by a person with an active essential psychosis, which, however, did not interfere with his prowess in mathematics, which he taught on the university level.

This applies also to Pirandello and Genet, whose conceptions of life, especially the dialogues of their plays, have an unmistakable stamp of essential psychosis, compared, for example, with the plays of Ibsen, whose plots and dialogues are earthy and strictly rational. A remark by Richard Condon, whose fiction writings bears the mark of essential psychosis, is significant in this respect. Speaking of his own writing style, he states, "Without paranoia you wouldn't have good storytelling." He characterized his own style as "a kind of illusory hyper-realism. You approach it as realism but it's *on a tilt* all the time" (*Newsweek*, June 9, 1975, p. 83; italics mine). The arts are replete with works that emanate from essential psychosis. This is especially true of modern paintings and sculpture that reflect the disorder of contemporary society as well as the pathology of their creators. Dali and Picasso in his later years, are the most prominent in this art genre. This is not to say that all the performers, writers, and artists themselves possess a greater quantum of essential psychosis. Rather, the point emphasized here is that the widespread and intense appeal of these works is symptomatic of its prevalence in all mortals.

The monstrous headgear, masks, and attire devised by primitive African tribes and American Indians for their bizarre rituals and celebrations, and the grotesque drawings, paintings, and statuary, while symbolic representations of animals and birds, ancestors, ghosts and gods, cannot but be the phantasmagoric products of the essential psychosis inherent in the mind of man.

The widespread prevalence of essential psychosis even among the comparatively enlightened in current societies is reflected in a review of *The Power of Evil* by Richard Cavendish in *Newsweek* (August 18, 1975) by Margo Jefferson, who writes:

Trolls, witches, vampires, bad fairies and the Devil himself are just a few of the everyday demons who have haunted mankind from the fall of Adam and Eve to "Jaws"... most cultures have developed elaborate systems of evil, which they then tried to sabotage with counter-systems of good. But Cavendish clearly finds evil more engaging. ...

According to one Greek legend, Night's home is "deep under the earth at the root of things, where she cradles in her arms Sleep and his brother Death." Irish priests have been famous for their occasional meetings with fairies, and Cavendish conjures up one such reported encounter with spirits who were "fair and small, with long, luxuriant hair (and who) disapproved of human beings as a lying, inconstant, ambitious race...."

Time and again, in civilizations across the map, evil has been found lurking in sex; in apprehension over being devoured or sucked dry by "other beings"; in a fascination with the dead's hold over the living. These fears have had political impact; Julius Caesar, after a dream of sleeping with his mother, crossed the Rubicon and invaded his motherland. No sooner had European traders returned from their first explorations of Africa and established the slave trade than demons at home suddenly began appearing as Africans...

In 1969, a Swiss court found five men and a woman guilty of murdering a young woman in an exorcism rite during which they beat her with walking sticks, a riding crop, and a rubber truncheon, and made her eat her own excrement.

But, perversely, what has been most compelling about evil—and what is most compellingly recounted in the book—is its power to inspire legend-makers with images of great, if chilling beauty. One of the most vivid characters in Celtic mythology is the hag who in wartime can be seen "washing the bloodstained clothes and weapons of men soon to die in battle." And according to old Norse legend, the world will end when "an ice winter will seize the earth in its grip, a great wolf will devour the sun."

Rock performances, meeting as they do the irrational cravings of so many people, earn Alice Cooper seventeen million dollars a year. Whenever the hairy, ape-like "rock actor" Sly Stone gave his bizarre performances (with a "bloodied" face) they were always sold out. When Stone was married in no less an edifice than New York's

Madison Square Garden, twenty-two thousand persons paid admission to witness the event.

The prevalent *pernicious fascination* of psychotics was what drew thousands of paying spectators to Bethel (from which the word "bedlam" was derived), a building in which psychotics in London, England, were confined and chained. For many years, many thousands paid admission to watch the behavior and antics of the deteriorated residents. The pleasure of witnessing public quarterings and beheadings of criminals in medieval England is another manifestation of essential psychosis. The fascination for psychosis is manifested by the "thrill" students even now experience in the more or less regular visits to mental hospitals to observe the deterioration of which the human personality is capable. Actually, in our society, due to unconscious empathy, latent or nuclear schizophrenics attract more attention than do well-constituted persons.

Very few species in the order of nature resort to self- or species destruction and when it does occur, its usefulness in terms of survival and ecology is apparent. Not so with man. Man's tendency to self, species, and global destruction is universal and inherent in his primary nature and is part of his essential psychosis.

Essential psychosis is present in varying degrees and levels in different individuals. In nearly everyone, even in civilized societies, it manifests itself in thoughts such as in the poem quoted above by Sylvia Plath. In some it is closer to the surface than in others; in Miss Plath it was quite close and dominated her life, for she committed suicide. This was also the case among members of the Manson "family" who in 1969 committed multiple murders of persons whom they did not even know. None of the group were found legally or clinically insane, but the brutal coldbloodedness with which these murders had been carried out could have occurred only in a state of so-called "temporary insanity" (which is nothing less than the breakthrough of essential psychosis). This was unmistakably verbalized by Susan Atkins, who murdered the pregnant actress, Sharon Tate, repeatedly stabbing her. She said: "It felt so good the first time I stabbed her, and when she screamed at me, it did something to me, sent a rush through me, and I stabbed her again." "How many times?" the interviewer inquired, "I don't remember. I just kept stabbing her until she stopped screaming.... It's like a sexual release. . . . Especially when you see the blood spurting out. It's better than a climax."[2]

We can also hypothesize that essential psychosis is present in different quanta in different individuals, that is, some exposed to the same external stresses may break down into clinical psychosis while others may endure them with moderate or no effects. A most pervasive phenomenon of differential quanta of essential psychosis in individuals is the effect on them of the intense anxiety and fear aroused by battles in a war. Some apparently normal individuals break down into permanent insanity, others can be rehabilitated by psychiatric means in field hospitals, while the vast majority remain undamaged.[3]

There is the possibility that what psychological tests indicate in some patients such as "schizoid characters," "latent or nuclear schizo-phrenia," "borderline psychosis," and "temporary insanity"[4] are actually manifestations of essential psychosis. One can also hazard the prognostication that once this assumption is accepted, tests may be developed to ascertain the quanta of essential psychosis in different individuals and means found for preventing its development into clinical psychosis, which is now the case in patients who have been subjected to prolonged stress or to the shock of a *precipitating event.*

Essential psychosis is not always canalized in gross forms such as those described above; it is often revealed as idiosyncrasies or irrationality in everyday acts and relationships. Biologically inherent, it is not accessible to direct therapy. The experience of everyone who has encountered it in others in the form of defensive rigidity, unstable transilience, or "extreme stubbornness" is that reasoning and marshalling evidence to the contrary is of little or no avail. Latent essential psychosis is usually surfaced by tensions, emotional disturbance, and overintense anxiety and the more massive these are, the greater is its quantum aroused, often overwhelming the individual's ego and resulting in clinical psychosis. In this way essential psychosis is transformed into clinical psychosis.

2. Bugliosi, V. (with Curt Gentry) (1974). *Helter Skelter: The True Story of the Manson Murders.* New York: W. W. Norton, p. 95.

3. See "The Bio-Quantum Theory of the Ego and Its Application to Group Psychotherapy" [61, chap. 5].

4. In terms of our theory "temporary insanity" occurs when the ego, under the stress of an extraordinary event, is overwhelmed and no longer able to control behavior with the result that inherent psychosis takes over.

As psychotherapy reduces patients' emotional vulnerability by improving self-image and strengthening ego controls, essential psychosis is held in check, normalizing behavior and responses. The processes involved in this are sloughing off and/or working through hostilities, anxieties, and fears. The therapist may also employ direct explanations, interpretations and, when indicated, benign confrontation. These enhance patients' reality testing.

The relation of essential psychosis and the ego is convincingly demonstrated in the mind-boggling and tragic developments in Jonestown in Guyana in November 1978, where a great many of the 911 victims committed "voluntary" suicide and poisoned their children. The members of this commune relegated their personal egos to their leader, the Reverend James Jones, permitting him to manage their lives, even relinquishing all their worldly possessions including their incomes, in many instances social security checks. In the pattern of contemporary Western societies these material elements are the primary instruments by which the lives of individuals are managed and which represent major functions of the ego. When the individual's ego is weakened the instinctive (id) urges come into prominence and the essential psychosis asserts itself. It was this dynamic that rendered the communards susceptible to self-destruction and the murder of their children. The communal (group) ego was thus invested in the person of the leader and caused the ego-less individuals to follow his order to "die with dignity" for the cause.

The survival of all groups is conditioned by cohesiveness, which emerges from the relinquishing of all or part of the egos of their constituents, for without cooperation and cohesiveness the essential effectiveness and survival of groups cannot be achieved. This inevitable dynamic—relegating part of the egos of group members—is counterindicated in psychotherapy groups (except in Activity Group Therapy of latency children). One of the major aims of psychotherapy is *strengthening* the egos of patients by eliminating conscious and unconscious psychic tensions that overload ego capacities. Note has to be taken that in the holocaust in Jonestown a comparatively small number escaped into the surrounding jungles. These were individuals who retained either partially or totally their ego defenses.

The Ubiquitous Natures of Anxiety and Aggression

Anxiety is basic to all sentient beings and in man it is a propelling dynamic behind all effort and creativity. Atypical persons such as mental defectives and the autistic may be free of it or contain it to a minimal degree, but in the ordinary person even a lowered blood sugar level generates anxiety that propels action toward assuaging it by eating. The homo sapiens is unique also in that he is subject to innumerable hungers—physical, psychological, and spiritual—which are essential both to physical homeostasis and intellectual and spiritual fulfillment. Such anxieties are not only useful but essential for personality effectiveness and growth. A state of pervasive or overintense anxiety, however, does not serve these constructive ends. Under these conditions it is deleterious and destructive. It is this *neurotic anxiety* which the psychotherapist serves to eliminate or reduce in his patients.

Another factor inherent in the human (internal) condition is *aggression*. Aggression is not as simple a concept as at first appears. Assertiveness, enterprise, determination, and adherence to conviction are often misinterpreted as aggression. They are rather valuable assets in the human personality, provided they do not proceed from, or are not tinged with, hostility. Aggression is operative everywhere in nature. The means by which even vegetables and insects, not to speak of higher animals, survive both as individuals and as a species is aggression against their environment. The survival of animal life in nature would be impossible without it [35, 61]. However, while aggression in animals is directed solely for individual and species survival, in man it assumes the character of a random weapon against others, his environment, nature, and even against himself.

The displacement of the philosophical and religious guides to life by materialistic science, technology, and commercialism with their competition and profit motives in contemporary civilization have alienated man from nature, from himself, and from his fellow man. Some types of aggression, erroneously taken for creativity have altered nature's aims, disturbed its balance, and in man also engendered distortions of actuality and values in life that have led to the events which beset mankind today. Man's views of life and his aims, perceived in the light of his altered psyche, are threatening the survival of the species itself. This condition can best be understood as a form of essential psychosis.

The widespread feelings of apprehension, anxiety, and insecurity, and the realities of poverty, starvation, disease, warfare and rampant criminality are the cumulative results of man's failure to apply in time his rationality to direct events and bring them under control, to utilize his positive endowments for counteracting his "irrationality." The failure to create a lifepattern conducive to health and happiness is, in the last analysis, the outcome of the ascendancy of irrationality over wisdom and higher purpose which allowed the expansion of materialism and technology to the levels they have now reached.

In a real sense the problems that now plague mankind are all but irreversible and no small role may be assigned to the irresponsibility of overexpanding science in the past two centuries. Had the potentially destructive trends been recognized in time and checked, the current near-fatal conditions of mankind could have been avoided

The Problem of Death

Death is an eternally disturbing awareness in man. The statement that "Death always walks beside you," reflects his inescapable conscious and unconscious preoccupation with it. While before the onset of old age, this awareness remains latent within the individual, the reality of death is inescapable. It is repetitively recalled in the demise of friends, relatives, neighbors and in the community generally, and in the media which daily report murders and accidents in great detail, thus perpetuating awareness of death in the population. This imposed awareness of dying generates imperceptive anxiety from which humans are never free. Much of the individual's effort is aimed at offsetting the threat of death by clinging to the miraculous expectation that he alone will be spared.

Man is the only animal that is aware of death, but his rational mind cannot *conceive* the cessation of being: being cannot conceive of *not* being. In past generations death's sting was meliorated by beliefs in life after death and reincarnation. Prehistoric tribes consoled themselves by the reality of living spirits around them. Such consolations are no longer available to most modern men. As is characteristic of the pervasive commercialism, books, lectures and seminars on death and dying now attempt to take the place of these consolations of the past. The current "educational" enterprises are damagingly involving even young people in high schools, colleges, and the community at the ages when awareness of the inevitability of death is still minimal.

Nature is inexorably cruel in its provisions for the struggle for existence in all living creatures. The one area of nature's "kindness" is that the normal process of dying is made gradual by diminishing urges and appetites with advances in age. Eventually death comes to man as a welcome release. The actual act of dying is a pleasant one and it is said that all who die a natural death do so with a smile on their lips.

The theory that death produces a sensation of release, my own longstanding conviction, received unexpected, objective confirmation in a study by Dr. Elisabeth Kubler-Ross[5] of one hundred persons who had been revived by "heroic medical efforts." Most "were angry" at the rescue teams that brought them back to life. They revealed details that "startled" the investigator. All found the transition from life to death an indescribably "pleasant, wonderful sensation" and would have preferred to remain dead. What puzzled Dr. Kubler-Ross was that the dying individuals felt that "something left their bodies and rose upward," and that some of the religious saw figures like Moses or Christ, while others had visions of relatives and close friends.

Contemplating these extraordinary phenomena—something rising from the body, seeing friends and relatives—an explanation occurred to me. Being a nonbeliever in a soul apart from the summation of bodily and psychic functions, I was constrained, willy-nilly, to come to some conclusion. I thus speculate that the deeply implanted and universally accepted belief that man has a soul, emphasized by all religions and perpetuated by common conviction, resulted in the strange feeling of levitation by the subjects studied. As to clearly seeing dear ones at the instant of dying, this can be explained by the confirmed fact that the dying individual recapitulates his past in a briefest moment before he expires. This information has been obtained from many revived drowning victims.

Psychotherapy facilitates the reduction of the discomfort relative to death by (a) diminution of anxiety generally, (b) enhancement of the capacity to accept the inevitable in life (reality testing), and (c) by the

5. Kubler-Ross, E. (1969). *On Death and Dying.* New York: Macmillan.

general rise in philosophical objectivity which always follows in the wake of relaxation and increased frustration tolerance. Another mechanism of greatest importance is that a person who has had a fulfilling life can accept the fact of death with greater equanimity than one who was subjected to frustration, quarrelsomeness, conflict, and general unhappiness. This relation of life and death is analogous to the feeling of a person who is satiated with food and no longer craves for more, as compared to one who, because of hunger, is driven by perpetual torment for more. Fulfillment in life is the preparation for death and psychotherapy ipso facto helps to acquire that fulfillment.

Sex and Romanticism

Adequate consideration of somatopsychological and social implications of human sexuality would be opening a veritable Pandora's box. In no animal are the manifestations and convolutions of the sex urge simple, but in none are they as complex as in the human species. Innumerable contradictory trends and forces operate in this complex in man and the most troublesome among them are the resulting societal attitudes, taboos, guilt feelings, conflicts, and shame. In addition, inescapable feelings of possessiveness and jealousy beget interpersonal rifts, suffering and, at times, even homicide.

Romanticism, a potent factor in engendering insuperable stress in humans, is not known to other animals and is a comparatively recent attribute in intersexual relations even in man. Originating as it does in sexuality and determined by early fixations, romanticism has become widespread in the last few centuries and more so among the "cultured." The guilt and hostility aroused by the sexual act stem from the social taboos and the unresolved oedipal and incestuous feelings, which only too often cause marital discord and extramarital sexual acting out. Having been nurtured in close family relations during childhood and latency, and later in adolescence when the sex urge is most intense and rigidly tabooed, these feelings are converted into fantasies and play a part in the phenomenon of romanticism. Also, consider Freud's sagacious remark that "every act of intimacy leaves a residue of aggression (hostility)" which is converted into sadism in many individuals.

The urge for adventure—the need for new stimuli to realize untapped resources and powers which is impellingly operative in homo sapiens— leads to a constantly expanding chain of relationships and activities that in all but a few modern societies is frustrated. One of them is extramarital sexual involvement. Madames of brothels and call girls testify that the vast majority of their "clients" are married men. The researches of sexologists attest to this fact as well. As pleasant as these sexual indulgences seem to appear on the surface, they cannot but create guilt feelings even in the callous, feelings that are transformed into hostility toward one's marital partner and also discharged in numerous ways such as dreams, irascibility, quarrelsomeness, prolonged silences, noncooperativeness, spitefulness, excessive out-of-home interests, lack of tenderness and, in increasing instances, in impotence, frigidity, separation and divorce.

The increasing number of rapes accompanied by futile sex murders and other forms of sexual sadism (which are reaching epidemic proportions in many countries) are aberrations of the procreative intent in nature and may be included in the category of "disharmony of nature," a term Metchnikoff employed to characterize behavior oppositional to nature's order and aims.

The Multiplicity of Human Appetites

It is common for physicians to inquire from their patients whether they have good "appetites." This is invariably understood as the appetite for food (which is often an indication of good health). This particularity ignores the critical fact that homo sapiens is driven by a multitude of real and fantasied appetites or hungers: physical, intellectual, social, emotional. Appetites in humans comprise food, sex, possession, power, recognition, acceptance, adventure, and numerous others in various combinaions and concatenations differing in different individuals. Appetites or hungers are felt as needs, drives, desires, and urges, many of which are repressed from childhood on and form part of the unconscious, adding to the total of one's intrapsychic difficulties. When the conscious and unconscious dynamisms remain unfulfilled, impoverishment not only of one's life and personality occurs, but the individual becomes the victim of discomfort, suffering and frustrations in the midst of an immensely enriched technological, industrial, artistic and spiritual environment. In a simple pastoral culture, desires and expectations were simple and limited and the environment offered ready gratifications. Warm interpersonal and community relations and simple pleasures were at hand.

Technological-industrial societies, with their deification of success and achievement, drive everyone beyond the limit of natural inclinations and capacities. As a result many are doomed to failure, frustration, and depression and disappointment. Feeling oneself a failure causes most painful inner reactions for it connotes weakness and worthlessness. Few have the wisdom to differentiate between "success" and being "successful." The need to succeed in whatever one undertakes is ipso facto natural and healthy, except for the type of psychoneurotic who compulsively and unconsciously seeks to defeat himself. One needs to clearly contrast the values inherent in being a success and of being successful in whatever one undertakes. Success as understood in contemporary societal terms is achievement of power, fame and/or wealth rather than attaining inner peace, tranquility, and self-acceptance. In this, good psychotherapy is most successful.

The Rift Between Pleasure and Purpose

One of the great difficulties in man's basic condition is his automatic divorcement of *pleasure* from *purpose*. The meaning of, and the use made of money is an example. Money has no intrinsic value; it is merely a symbol, a means for acquiring and exchanging necessities of life in a fiduciary civilization and in the mature mind it is so viewed. However, for the immature and for some types of neurotics, money assumes an intensely intrinsic value to the point of a pathologic drive for amassing it in amounts beyond one's needs. Thus, it ceases to be of utilitarian value and assumes quintessential meanings beyond the bounds of reality.

This dynamic of separation of pleasure from purpose is operative in man's biological functions as well, with even more deleterious results. Individual and species' survival require four basic functions. They are eating, evacuation, physical exercise, and sex. To assure their fulfillment, nature had endowed them with the capacity for intense pleasure. The first three serve survival of the individual, the fourth perpetuates the species. All animals but man preserve the unity of function and pleasure of these essential biologic constraints. Other animals eat only when hungry and only foods suitable to their particular natures. Man, on the other hand, has evolved multifarious complex food and drink preparations that appeal to taste, not necessarily beneficial to health and survival. In fact, many of these are injurious and cause numerous illnesses, including cancer and death itself. Other animals evacuate normally and without difficulty when the byproducts of food digestion make them feel uncomfortable. This is quite unlike the condition of mankind which is plagued by diverse disorders in stomach and bowel functions. Similarly in the case of sex as well, single, periodic, or seasonal copulation serves in all other animals only the end of procreation, but in homo sapiens, whose sex drive is omnipresent, copulation is indulged for pleasure without the purpose designed by nature, namely, procreation.

Man's Urge for Variety and Adventure

As already indicated, man's warring tendencies, though primordially essential in his quest for survival but which no longer serve these ends in "civilized" societies, still persist. In fact, they rather impede his tranquility and happiness, but the basic imprints and the gratification they have yielded during the eons of savagery and barbarism still continue. This is also true of the longing in all humans for pursuit in the form of movement, travel, and excitement which in primitive stages yielded the rewards of hunting game and capturing a mate, and which in modern man is extended to research and exploration. These remain engrammatically imprinted in the human nervous and motor systems and give rise to instinctive rocking, swinging, jogging and running to be found in all races and climes and also in travel of modern man. The wasteful killings of animals as a form of "sport" is attributable as well to the atavistic residues of survival experiences in primordial man. It is noteworthy how quarrelsomeness and cruelty are diminished and often completely subside as a result of good psychotherapy.

The Inevitability of Prejudice

The dictionary definition of "prejudice" is "an unfavorable opinion or feeling . . . especially of a hostile nature . . . ." The word itself is derived from the Latin, meaning prejudgment. One of the traits that has held sway over man from time immemorial is prejudice. Prejudice against people is particularly unsuitable in the present world that requires tolerance, collectivity, and cohesion. Even when it is directed against things and the environment it limits ethnic, national, spiritual and experiential scope and personality expansion. Nonetheless, this attitude dominates a widespread portion of mankind for it has its roots in biology and is present in rudimentary state in other animals as well. In man it is vastly elaborated, more complex and more injurious.

Sociologists hold that "difference increases distance" which fact can be observed in some animals. In a chicken run on our farm, for example, the ordinary species of birds, which greatly outnumbered the six little black guinea hens, savagely attacked the latter whenever they attempted to join their unfriendly neighbors. It was necessary for us to scatter grain at a considerable distance from the others as well as provide water troughs for them apart from the majority.

Teleologically, the roots of prejudice serve the ends of survival and are a channel for discharge of innate hostility as well as being a defense against threat and danger. When viewed from this stance, prejudice stems from primary fear. One can posit that for humans, and to a lesser extent in other animals, nature has provided what can be characterized as three psychic efficiency devices: *memory* (through alterations in brain cells), *habit* (by establishing neuronic, conditioned reflexes— engrams) and *preference* (through acquiring more or less permanent choices).

Memory saves man from perpetually rediscovering and relearning the multitudinous facts that make up the content of his life; *habit* renders it unnecessary to relearn *ab novo* each time each of the processes involved in performing the multitude of daily acts and behaviors; and *preference* eliminates the need to reevaluate and make decisions on the even greater volume of matters and occurrences that confront the individual at every moment of his life. One maintains preferences in foods, people, and physical and interpersonal lifestyles.

The difficulty with homo sapiens, however, is that preferences are cathected, highly emotionalized, and serve to discharge aggression and hostility. *It is these factors that transmute preference into prejudice*, particularly when it is reinforced by group or national consensus. Thus, prejudice in humans generates hate, discrimination, conflict, atrocities, scapegoating, and not infrequently, is the *causus belli*.

All the socializing devices in modern cultures—family, school, church and education—are mobilized (but seldom successfully) against the transmutations of preferences (to which an individual is entitled in a civilized society) into virulence. The cultural level of an individual can be measured by the quantity of his preference manifestations and their quality and intensity. One of the disconcerting native universal characteristics of homo sapiens is readiness to succumb to feelings of hatred. Hatred unifies people much more readily than does love and facilitates scapegoating in groups and in society. Witness the contemporary response of the Arab nations who had been traditionally at odds with each other and in perpetual states of near war. Having found in Israel a common object of hatred, they overcame their centuries-old antagonisms and formed an almost unitary phalanx against that country. This psychic mechanism operates on a smaller scale also in the life of communities even among the most "civilized" nations and in all individuals. Psychotherapy has a major role in this area for its two chief aims are (1) to dissolve feelings of hostility lodged in the preconscious and unconscious, and (2) remove the anxieties and guilts bound up in the unconscious. Patients present also many other difficulties peculiar to each, but all suffer from these major two: hostility and guilt.

The Stress of Ambivalence

One of the most stressful characteristics of the human psyche is its potential for *ambivalence*. Being torn between two or more oppositional urges and the resulting state of indecision is a source of great stress and turmoil that debilitates one and often causes physical and psychic illness. The destructive effects of ambivalence are commensurate with the significance of the matter on which decision is to be made and the complexity of modern cultures and civilizations have greatly enhanced ambivalent states in individuals. There are myriads of situations in the complex world created for us that beset everyone with numerous problems and choices for which solutions are not readily clear in marital, filial and other interpersonal relations, in social choices, and in philosophical and doctrinal guides to life.

Essentially, adult patients who seek psychological help are torn between distressing conflictual emotions that arise from many of these sources. The simultaneous presence of sadism and masochism, primitive animalism and cultural humanism, love and hate, as well as the multiple choices demanded in everyday life are sources of great discomfort and stress. There are comparatively few situations in the life of modern man that yield to ready solutions. In marital relations, for example, which are always fraught with guilt, and may have easy resolutions, they are instead transmuted into mutual neglect, quarrelsomeness, and cruelty between the involved partners. Similar ambivalences inhere in parent-child relations with accompanying guilt feelings. Punishments meted out by parents to children often proceed from guilt. Just as the basic emotion of children is fear, the root emotion of parents is guilt. Ambivalence of love and hate dominates attitudes toward persons beyond the family as well. This atavistic binary nature of the human inner condition, peculiar to the human species, is generated and reinforced by phylogenetic and ontogenetic morals and ethics, and are in perpetual struggle or supremacy throughout the span of one's life.

The "Emptiness" Syndrome

In addition to this brief foregoing enumeration of some elements of the internal human condition, of personality and of social disorders with which psychotherapy is concerned, are numerous others, some equally and some less imperative. One of these is what is referred to as the "emptiness" syndrome (boredom)—the state of being, a sequela to the absence of sustaining interests and occupations that could assuage the potentials of the human personality. Such interests and occupations can be said to give *content to human life*. In the absence of such content, restlessness and depression take over, which is especially pronounced in women after their grown children leave their homes, creating a void in the mothers' psyches. Through enforced idleness by retirement, while their energies and drives are still intact, men become victims of the emptiness syndrome. They grow lethargic, irritable and subject to depression. Retirement should not be only *from* something but *to* something. The wise woman, freed from her customary routines, engages in volunteer community services, in political activities, or acquires a new work career. Many men and women turn to hobbies such as painting and crafts or pursue educational courses which give content to their lives. Some adopt or offer their homes to children in need while others find life content and affectional gratifications in caring for domestic pets. Numerous men fill the void in their lives by becoming addicted to sports as actors or spectators and compulsively follow results in the reports of the media, while as many women turn to fineries, cosmetics, and to appearance.

To counteract the emptiness syndrome, psychotherapists and counselors often steer patients to sustaining interests. In fact, much of womens' rebelliousness can be laid to the monotony and isolation involved in homemaking and the lack of variety in stimulation.

Immaturity and Social Parapathology

One of "the differences between men and boys is the size and cost of their toys" is one of the folk adages pointing up the basic immaturity of the predominant majority of adults in contemporary societies. This was also sagaciously expressed by a television humorist who quipped, "This program is unsuitable for adults because it is mature." Another scoffed: "Now there is a show for those who cannot grow up."

Psychologic immaturity is the root of most personality and especially behavior difficulties that create interpersonal, communal, political, and social problems which are habitually attributed to external conditions. Many social malignancies and psychological disturbances result from misleading values and misdirected strivings fostered by the hedonism of profit-motivated, consumer-oriented societies and family relations that arrest development of predominate numbers of individuals. These malignant conditionings are furthered by monotony, social rigidities and overemphasis on competitive sports and competition generally. Even colleges and universities deny intellectual independence and self-reliance to students who are required to accept curricula prepared for them without relevance to their needs and interests. They are also subjected to grades and evaluations as though they were still children.

Some fifty years ago the late Professor Horace Kallen of the New School for Social Research published a pamphlet entitled "Colleges Prolong Infancy," which had created a stir in the educational circles at the time. Only at the graduate level are students given some leeway in choosing topics for their theses (subject to approval by "advisors") and to carry on research on their own and writing (again subject to the approval by a "committee of the faculty"). Spontaneity, originality and self-determination have been by that time almost completely snuffed out by antecedent schooling which the doctoral candidates can no longer rekindle. That a few occasionally stumble upon something original later in life is usually the result of serendipity or, in some rare instances, the miraculous survival from the past repressive, soul-impoverishing life patterns and school regimens.

However, the scourge from which contemporary communities suffer most (in addition to antiquated economic and political systems), is the emotional immaturity of their leaders and the masses whose lives and works are motivated by infantile cravings for power, fame, and possession that arraign man against man. This is contrary to the laws of nature where, in the last analysis, survival depends on mutual aid and interdependence. In addition, this self-encapsulating climate begets loneliness and morbidity which is growing increasingly more pathological and widespread in "civilized" man, causing a variety of personality dislocations and aberrant behavior. In a study of the emotional motivations in delinquency in adolescents [62] I have found that the major elements that triggered their antisocial acts were their infantile characters, the infantile quality of their pleasure urges, their strivings and desires seeking immediate gratifications, and the belief in miracles (that they will not be discovered, which is common to all criminals)—all characteristic of childhood.

While riots with fire setting, pillage, horrendous brutality, torture, and other revolting acts are closely related to essential psychosis, the uniform responses and behavior of audiences at give-away television game shows, their uncontrolled jumping and screaming, so inappropriate for adults, unmistakably reveal the basic infantile character of the masses. The buffoonery of the "emcees" of these performances and the abuse and discomfiture of "willing victims" who volunteer to participate in these performances poignantly reveal immaturity. The vociferous pleasure displayed when an unsuspecting victim is suddenly plunged into a hidden pool of water or having his face splashed by a custard pie, or the laughter evoked by a pedestrian who slips and falls are not so much "negative identifications" or unconscious sadism; they are, rather, infantile reactions.

All patients of whatever category have various character disorders.

Our concern here, however, is with immaturity of a special type of character structure that is not accessible by ordinary therapeutic interventions. In all sound psychotherapies character changes inevitably do occur as a part of the "secondary process" with improved emotions and behavior, though in adult patients there always remain residues of the tenacious basic character traits, or the "primary process."

The community climate generated by widespread psychic immaturity, however, together with other individual and group pathologies, constitute the prevailing *social parapathology* of contemporary cultures. Freud emphasized the psychopathology of everyday life in individuals. This significant concept needs, in the light of current conditions, to be extended to the body *sociale* as a whole and we, therefore, suggest the term *social parapathology* to depict this phenomenon. This concept is embraced in the nascent profession of "social psychiatry," which is as yet perfunctory in its practices and still inadequately defined. Social psychiatry cannot be conducted in isolation as is the case in clinical psychiatry, which is willy-nilly included in the former. Its setting must be the vast and confusingly complex canvas of the community and nation and this will require new and hitherto untapped insights and procedures as yet alien to academically trained psychiatrists, psychologists, and social service practitioners. But a beginning has been made and hopefully beneficial outcomes will result from all this in the future.

Of the many crucial neglects and oversights in the management of community, national, and world affairs as well as in other areas of the workaday life, the most virulent is the blind unawareness of the psychological and parapathological forces that affect individual, group, mass, national, and international behavior. The scope and the complexity of the infinite variety of irrational human reactions and ideas (essential psychosis) present quandaries so vast and challenges so great that it will take extended time and great effort on the part of the best minds to integrate psychological understanding in social management of contemporary societies. The present practice of teaching or demonstrating to groups and communities "principles" of mental health, for example, will not suffice. What is necessary is to interweave them with sociology, economics, industry, schooling, and many other knowledges and practices involved in the complex societies of today out of which completely new economic and governmental patterns will evolve. The total climate of rampant individualism and material hedonism will then give way to a humanistic culture.

Everyone in modern times can understand and accept the need for fusing economics and sociology, which until recently have been disparate concerns. Recent developments have uncovered the ineffectiveness of these two disciplines operating separately, for neither one nor even their combination can explain or control contemporary events. Economists have finally come to admit defeat in "understanding" the fluctuations of the economies in the world today and sociologists are bewildered by the immense problems of the world. The missing links in this combination are psychology and a heroic recognition and acceptance of men's vital needs, suppressed strivings, and the capriciousness of the human psyche. When these "sciences" will be finally orchestrated, mankind will be closer to salvation.

The teachings and practices of both economics and, to a somewhat lesser degree, of sociology, at present overlook the pivotal human elements in societal events. Just as schooling, problems of administration, fiduciary preoccupations, and teaching devices are the major concerns of "educators" while students are the last concern, so is it in social management that the rights and needs of people are subordinated to materialistic considerations. Both children and society are victims of this purblindness of the persons in authority and are continued in a state of primary process in the service of the self.

Man's Potentials for Sublimity

While it may appear from the preceding discussion, which centered on pathology depicting man as though he were all evil, this is not the case in fact. The content of this essay, geared as it is toward psychotherapy, required that aspects of the human personality in need of change and correction be emphasized. Man has the potential for sublimity as well. His urgent needs for association with others, his potential for sympathy, empathy, compassions, and succor raise him far above all other species. Man could not have survived without cooperation; his basic disposition and capacities led him to evolve under specific conditions: patterns of mutual aid, kindliness, helpfulness, justice and morality (in fact, the word civilization is derived from the Latin "civos," city) and that which is spiritual and esthetic in his life arose from proximity and interaction with others, with nature and with groups.

Unfortunately, specified nationalities, organized religions with their separate rituals, on the one hand, and individualistic, profit-motivated economic patterns on the other, characteristic of contemporary societies, decimated mankind and pitted individuals in competitive roles, submerging love, trust, compassion, and honesty. Impersonal philanthropy and other perfunctory efforts at helpfulness flow more from feelings of guilt rather than from empathy. Having abandoned ideals and the virtues that set humans apart from other animals, they unavoidably succumb to *necessity* and have become dominated only by expediency; ideals no longer regulate life and values, at the cost of inner peace and outer harmony. It is, therefore, erroneous to consider "the human condition" in terms of outer conditions alone. The outer world created by man is a reflection of man's *inner condition* at any point in time, which requires nurture on the one hand and guidance on the other.

Autocreativity of the Self

The preceding is far from being a complete inventory of the inner life of homo sapiens and the forces that propel both his growth and his degeneration. Rather, it is a free-associative product of more than sixty years of intimate work with people of all ages and conditions—forty years of which were spent with emotionally disturbed and socially maladjusted individuals, including full-blown chronic psychotics. The contents of this partial inventory are involved in or causative of pathology in man; they are also the materials and instruments from which sentient life flows. They were enumerated here as they came to mind during intellectual rumination and memories of events, experiences, and observations stored up during a long life and a variety of works. But these inner forces, with numerous others, are the stuff of which human life is forged; these are the elements of man's greatness and nobility—even his partial divinity—if adequately nurtured and molded, as well as the sources of tragedy and degradation when neglected or malshaped by life's conditions.

I am mindful that the human condition can be viewed from many approaches: teleology, metaphysics, metapsychology, existentialism, among others. While these knowledges and formulations widen intellectual and emotional horizons, expand consciousness, and enrich the meaning of life and events, they cannot serve as instruments for shaping and controlling life. The pragmatic workers in the arena of forging human life—parents, educators, counselors or therapists— must have the knowledge and know the procedures to mold and correct the malformed human personality when this is indicated, in conformity with the actualities of the outer world, its prospects for the future and the inherences of the inner world of each individual. These two elements need to be appropriately and sensitively guided if health and serenity are to be achieved. Everyone must *be* in the world, but not necessarily *of* this world.

The psychotherapist's aims have to be particularly directed toward an accommodation of the inner and outer complementary forces by considering all the factors that inhere in this extraordinary complex. For the psychotherapist to allow himself to be drawn into subliminal, esoteric or futuristic areas at the neglect of world actualities and inner realities of the self, would maximize personality malformation and perpetuate, if not increase, pathology.

I am informed at this writing that a book is being published in the United States describing "301 types of psychotherapy." Obviously, the vast majority of these cannot properly belong under the classification of "psychotherapy," though some of them may have transient therapeutic effects. Procedures such as behavior modification and conditioning, raising the level of consciousness, reeducation, altering values, counseling and guidance—all of these and many others have their place in modern, complex society for persons who are uncomfortable, unhappy, or maladjusted. These types of helping procedures are as old as human societies and have been employed for millenia.

When Homo Erectus observed the fear of fire in predatory animals (probably set off by lightning), he descended from his isolated, individualistic arboreal domicile and settled on the surface of the earth in various localities. Others who observed this joined him. This was the origin of social life as we find it today. It was inevitable that cooperation and rivalry in hunting and gathering of food should emerge. It is out of these conditions that modern nations and societies ultimately evolved. It was equally inevitable that this cooperation would result in communities such as hamlets, villages, town and, later, cities.

Wherever there is cohabitation among humans, organization inevitably and naturally emerges with resultant institutions and controls of individual conduct essential to orderly group living. In humans, these dynamics are what we know as morals, laws, and ethics, which in turn generate anxiety and guilt. To deal with these imperative conflictual conditions, members of primitive groups turned for solace or relief to specific individuals such as chiefs, shamans, magicians, as well as various gods during the periods of pantheism.

In evolved societies these special relief sources were replaced by clergy as definite systems of religion appeared. In later years, physicians, psychologists, social workers and others in the so-called "helping" professions were resorted to in order to solve inner conflicts, personality problems and social maladjustments. The emergence of these professionals was stimulated by the work of Sigmund Freud, who gave content and direction to the otherwise haphazard, variegated, more or less superficial approaches. The basic contributions common to psychotherapy (as differentiated from procedures that have "therapeutic" effects), the fundamental elements of Freud's revolutionary formulations, are his constructs of id, ego, and superego, infantile sexuality, sibling rivalry, and the oedipal complex.

Homo sapiens is extremely complex; his sensitivity and his superlative reactivity and creativity render him vulnerable and subject to pathogeneses. The super-numerous stimuli and demands and massive tensions of the complex technological world of today constantly disturb his homeostasis. Together with these, his compelling tendency to quarrelsomeness, a vestige of animal combat for survival and for achieving procreation, produces behavior inconsistent with the values and mores of organized society, causing further maladjustments to fellow men and society as a whole. But what is even more disturbing are the internal conflicts, ambivalences, stressful feelings, or, in Freudian terms, the demands of the id and the superego. Masses of people consequently turn for relief of their suffering and discomfort to psychotherapy and other techniques that, hopefully, give them temporary surcease.

It was recently, in fact in 1934, when the present author concluded that since most of the difficulties of many individuals arise in the setting of group life, many of them can consequently be corrected in a group setting. Thus appeared what is now widespread and known as *group psychotherapy* or *group therapy*, depending upon the depth of the personality problems presented. However, intensive and full-blown *psychoneurosis*, which means the conflict between the id and the superego with which the ego cannot deal, can be reached only by traditional Freudian psychoanalysis.

CHAPTER 2

THE ESSENCE OF PSYCHOTHERAPY
(1964)

In the innermost recesses of the temple there dwelt the oracle. To him men turned to seek solution to the dilemmas of their lives and to find solace and hope for it was he who knew what was hidden from man. The high priests served only the oracle and even they did not understand the secrets of living and the portent of events. As lofty as their stations were, the priests could not be the ultimate source of wisdom and knowledge; they, too, had to turn to the oracle for enlightenment, to interpret events and prognosticate the future. This relation is symbolic of man's place in eternity and in the riddle of his existence. It is not given to man to perceive or understand the *ultimate truth* and the essence of his own life and the life around him.

For eons man had struggled to understand what seemed to him the immutable, irrational and brutal forces that directed his fate. Superstitions begotten by fear, then religion, then philosophy, and finally science—all have attempted to penetrate the impenetrable secret of life and of living. In its forward thrust toward understanding the structure of the universe and the basic forces that operate in it, science can only reveal processes and causes of phenomena, even to the point of creating matter and life itself; but still the *absence* of the riddle of nature remains closed to his understanding. When Einstein was asked what the basic aim of his work was, his cryptic, profound, as well as puzzling response was, "I am trying to find God."

But God is unattainable to man. Man can only project upon him his own images, urges, unfulfilled wishes, and dilemmas. Only God holds the key to essence. We who are mortal and finite must be satisfied with the striving for this knowledge as a limit—as is the case with all infinity—but never quite reaching the ultimate cause.

When, in the light of this understanding, and perhaps also wisdom, we turn to psychotherapy and attempt to find its essence, we are also faced with the same impediments, for the essence of psychotherapy is as obscure as the essence of all human endeavor. How shall we approach the quest for this essence? Shall we seek it in terms of definition, in terms of aims, or process or results? Or shall we set forth into the uncharted seas of abstraction, philosophy, and mysticism? Some who are either frightened or discouraged have done so. They have departed from the sound and sustaining soil of clinical guides and practices into the volatile regions of metaphysics, transcendentalism, and the mysticisms of oriental philosophies. Thus we find practitioners who closely resemble faith healers. Whether they are known as "existential therapists," "Zen Buddhist analysts," or by other designations, they have abandoned the sound bases of diagnostic classification, psychodynamic guides, and the tested therapeutic techniques that have been so far evolved.

Herein lies the greatest of all dangers for a craft (which psychotherapy is): sailing forth into the realms of generalizations, philosophy, and metaphysics. Because of the anarchic nature of man's mind and its limitations, it is prone to stray into abstractions and create jungles of ideas as soon as definitive and finite base lines or references are given up.

As do all other workers in the fertile expanse of the intellect, it is of utmost importance that we, too, continue our pursuit of higher meanings for our work and its relation to the total area of man's life; but we must not stray so far afield from our base lines as to lose sight of them. Rather, it would be safer at this juncture that our efforts be bent on attaining higher reaches in the light of, and as an extension of, what is *knowable* and understandable by our finite intellects. Above all, it is necessary that we do not substitute abstractions for tools, and philosophy for insightful understanding of the minutiae that are indispensible for the effective practice of psychotherapy

I hope that the above will not be construed as a negative reflection on philosophies. Together with the poet, the philosopher exercises the license of excursion into unrestricted thought and speculation. The dilemmas of nature and of man's existence permit much flexibility, many avenues of approach, and a variety of constructs. It is only in relation to the *practice* of the craft, and art, of psychotherapy that we must hew as far as posible to the lines of experiential and tested knowledge. This is not suggested with an attitude unmindful of the irrational and suprarational nature of man's psyche. We need to be fully aware of this and of the vagaries of the responses and strivings in man; but to be of help to patients we had better deal with these scientifically. We should not reinforce them by our flights from actualities and thus render patients even less capable of dealing with the realities of their lives.

May I also suggest a corollary thought. Stimulated by the periods of Scholasticism and the Renaissance, Western man's deification of intellect and his belief in the omnipotence of thought and words have inevitably led him to blind alleys of frustration. When thought is too detached from empiricism, and fantasy from pragmatism, we alienate ourselves from nature and fall into the fatal error of considering obscurity as profundity, venerating the complex and the incomprehensible as superior to the simple and the obvious, forgetting that all greatness in ideas and persons is essentially simple. It would be of interest to speculate about the escape value of such views and practices as defenses against ego fragility and their significance to the psychic economy of their adherents. But this excursion would take us too far from the central task of this presentation.

With these warnings in mind, let us attempt to examine our subject from several diverse approaches. Let us attempt to define psychotherapy. Of the plethora of definitions, I would like to suggest two. One is that psychotherapy is the process through which the structure of the psyche is corrected and/or reconstructed so that an individual can function most efficiently, within the limits of his native capacities, conditioned by his native equipment and as defined by the mores of the culture in which he lives. The other definition is based upon a more specific concept: psychotherapy is the process through which an individual who has rejected or was made inaccessible to the educational influences exerted upon him, is rendered accessible to these influences.

This definition posits two concepts. One is that the individual is psychically formed by the innumerable influences, relations, and experiences with his environment, both animate and inanimate. The other is that the patient has been so conditioned that he is prevented from assimilating the healthy formative influences, that is, education in its widest sense. When an individual, because of early frustrations and anxiety, is fixated at specific stages of psychosocial development, he becomes impervious or resistive to the expanding and maturing educational opportunities of life. In this connection, education has to be understood to have a broader meaning than schooling. It encompasses the totality of stimuli, experiences, influences, and relationships that pattern the character and forge the personality of the individual in time and setting.

The first definition, that psychotherapy is a reconstructive process, implies the assumption derived from Freud's topological structure of the psyche; namely, the system and relations of the id, ego, and superego, pathology consisting in their inappropriate development and their imbalance. If there is a recognizable essence in psychotherapy, it consists of correcting psychic forces and giving each of them its appropriate place, both in the progressive development of the individual and in his final maturation, thus achieving the balance necessary for the patient's health and functioning.

This instrumental definition of psychotherapy delineates process and aim rather than identifying an essence. Further analysis reveals another unavoidable dilemma: Can this definition and this aim be applied to all types of patients that come for treatment? Are they equally applicable to all clinical categories encountered in practice, such as the psychoneuroses, the character disorders, the schizophrenias, and the psychoses? In terms of instrumental practice we are forced to recognize that there are different aims in the different categories, beyond the general one; namely, to make patients healthy. By and large the objective in treatment of the psychoneuroses, for example, is to eliminate the internal conflicts arising from oppositional strivings of the id and the superego which the ego is unable to resolve. The aid with this type of patient is to detach his libido from some internal and external foci or fixations so as to free it for the service of personal expansion, inner freedom, and better interpersonal adjustment. The aim includes also a reduction of the rigid superego demands that generate guilt and tensions, vitiate orderly function and prevent satisfactions that properly belong in the process of living.

In psychotherapy of patients with character disorders, the focus shifts to the reconditioning of the ego and its functioning. Our efforts are directed here toward the patient's character and conduct unsuitable to his own best interests and to the interests of those around him. The chief though not the exclusive aim, is not ego reintegration, but an alteration of ego functioning and of ego defenses. Unlike in the psychoneurotic, in whom new values emerge as a result of increased inner freedom, in the character disorder we aim to alter his value system through objective evaluation, as well as through improved identifications and by internalization of the therapist's ego.

As to the schizophrenic, the aim is to strengthen the reserves of the ego and its defenses, and to improve his capacity for reality testing (in conjunction with convulsive and chemotherapies, when so indicated).

So far, we have viewed the essence of psychotherapy mainly from the standpoint of aims. When essence of psychotherapy is viewed in terms of process, differences make it difficult to formulate a unitary principle applicable to all types of psychotherapy. In the treatment of neuroses, for example, the fundamental element is the transference of the patient upon the therapist by means of which the patient, through displacement, transference, and projection, can relive the traumata and the accompanying affects lodged in his unconscious and free himself from the guilt and anxiety that are bound up in them. The patient's fantasy allows him to regressively react to the therapist, with hostility at times and affection at other times. It is this *living over* libidinal relations in a new context and with a new understanding, aided by the therapist's as well as the patient's interpretations, that the reconstructive process in the psychoneurotic occurs.

In the patient with a character disorder, the therapeutic process is considerably different. Since the procedure here aims at a new and different way of ego functioning, the patient has to be helped to become *aware* of his characteristic behavior, responses, and values in relation to his milieu. The central point of therapy here is not uncovering and exploration (though these are used as subsidiary strategies), but rather confronting him with his reactions and behaviors so that he may view them critically, through the eyes of the therapist, or a group of fellow patients, whom he accepts as a teacher and support. As this is taking place, the patient internalizes the ego of the therapist and models himself by the latter's patterns of response, behavior, and value system. It is largely, though not entirely, through imitation, identification, and internalization that changes occur. The central characteristic of therapy with character disorders is that it is reality oriented. As the patient lives and acts in his natural setting or in a therapy group he is helped to perceive critically his reactions and behavior in a new light. What has been ego-syntonic in the past must become ego-alien and a new syntonicity needs to be evolved.

Experience shows that the reconstruction of ego functioning with adults is an extremely difficult task. It is by far more difficult than with children in whom the ego has not as yet been rigidized and in whom defenses are still fluid. With children the task is comparably easier and changes in ego structure often can be achieved very effectively even by nonverbal types of therapy, such as Activity Group Therapy. With adults the task is made considerably more difficult, not only because the defenses have been ingrained in the personality and engrams established in the psychic and neuronic structures, but also because the ego, upon whose alliance psychotherapy relies for its effectiveness, is itself involved. Thus, the ego has to work upon itself to change itself; and since it has already an ingrained pattern with its rigid defenses, it is extremely difficult to involve it in its own reconstruction. In the treatment of psychoneuroses a therapist can remain largely passive, but in treatment of character disorders the therapist's activity is essential. In the psychologic treatment of schizophrenics there are four elements to which psychotherapy, as differentiated from convulsive—and chemotherapies, has to address itself: (1) the element of orality, (2) the element of hostility, (3) ego deficiency, and (4) retreat from reality.

In his interpersonal orientation, the schizophrenic *substitutes*, as do child patients, the therapist (and others *in loco parentis*) for his parents and entertains the same hostile, homicidal, and infantile (cannibalistic) oral incorporation drives toward him as he did toward his parents. In order to lay a basis for emotional growth, these urges must be satisfied first, before the patient can establish ego boundaries and move toward progressive development and integration of his personality, which is at all times limited by his constitutional resources. Thus, the patient has to "ingest" the therapist symbolically, as a baby does its mother. This very complex process is at least partially achieved by the therapist's unconditional acceptance of the patient's aggression (within the boundaries of his inner controls) and by permission to be used by him at will. One of the ways to do so is to be available at all times. The therapist has to display affection to the patient also in more tangible ways, including feeding. A patient in private individual treatment once bitterly complained that she was not "loved" by the therapist. One of her complaints was: "You never even gave me anything to eat!"

The patient constantly seeks to involve the therapist in his psychotic network of feeling and hallucination, which should be allowed with the therapist aware of the patient's maneuvers and of his own behavior and response. (It is a task that few can achieve with real success!) It is through his own awareness and skill at pulling the patient back to reality that the therapist helps him become more reality oriented.

The second task or function of the therapist with a schizophrenic patient is to deal with his overt hostilities without any trace of counterhostility, which the patient invariably experienced nearly all of his life. It is this element more than any other that makes for strain and difficulties in the treatment. In the therapy of schizophrenics, therapists fall in two categories: those who respond to their hostility and those who respond to their utter helplessness; and only the latter can be successful in treating them. A psychotherapist who feels counterhostility (very easily aroused under the circumstances) should not attempt to treat schizophrenics.

Important as gratifying orality and accepting hostility are, the actual therapeutic dynamics that operate in the improvement of the schizophrenic are ego strengthening and defense building on the one hand, and evoking a sense of reality and reality testing on the other. The first of these processes—the structuring of the ego—occurs automatically, as the patient orally internalizes the therapist. Ego *reinforcement* is the pivot of the treatment, but it takes place only after the patient accepts the therapist as the good parent, which he can do after a prolonged period of the therapist's acceptance of his orality and hostility. It is this *good* parent that the patient incorporates, together with his ego. At the same time, the therapist needs to build a bridge between the patient's ego and reality subtly holding him down to reality, by introducing realistic values, and above all, by experiences and activities that involve actual situations.

As the ego is strengthened by these various techniques of reinforcement, it abandons its former defenses of violence and of retreat from reality and in their stead appear more normal defenses. At this point the patient is introduced to more demanding conditions in which he finds himself successful, first with the help of the therapist and other helpful persons, and later as he functions on his own. However, one must forever keep in mind that the newly acquired or reinforced defenses can never be as strong in a "cured" or improved true schizophrenic (as differentiated from induced schizophrenia) as in a nonschizophrenic. In the former the *foundations* of the personality structure will forever be weaker than in the ordinary person and its maximal capacities for withstanding stress is always at a low level. One should always keep in mind the dictum: once a schizophrenic, always a schizophrenic.

As the young child, so does the psychotic operate on his *perception* rather than on testing of reality and its validation through experience. The psychotic's perceptions are determined by his (a) development, which is arrested at levels of primitivism, (b) the phantoms which populate his psyche, and (c) the perception of his own identity, or lack of it.

The levels of his development are orality, hostility, homicide, and incest. He, therefore, perceives the world as hostile, threatening, and destructive. These feelings have to be overcome through the discovery that in actuality the world is not as he perceives it. Such a change can be achieved only by testing that world and by testing oneself against it, which the psychotic can do at first only with the support of the therapist's (borrowed) ego. He can venture on this exploration, only in a setting that is commensurate with his current, though growing, strengths; that is, in an environment which *does not overload his ego* at any given stage of his development.

This complicated task is best achieved through exposing the patient to *graded reality*, that is, to an environment which is graded in complexity and demands as the patient's ego is strengthened and his psychic resources are enhanced [63].

Clinical categories alone are not sufficient marks by which to chart our therapeutic sights, however. Each patient within each of these categories presents a personality and a set of problems peculiar to him. The type and nature of his traumata and his reactions to it are characteristically different and peculiar to each. Not all psychoneurotics, for example, have experienced precisely the same disturbing or distorting relations. Nor are patients with character disorders identical. Neither are the drives, hallucinatory content, or the paranoid systems of schizophrenics identical. Each and every one of the patients in all clinical categories have reacted to a different set of stimuli in their past which resulted in a specific complex of reactions and distortions, because of differences in constitutional dispositions and external circumstances.

To be most effective, psychotherapy has to be directed toward the *nuclear problem* of each patient. Thus, while the psychodynamic *structure* of the disease entity may be alike in patients of a given clinical category, the specific nosological problems of each patient need to be recognized and therapeutic effort directed toward them.

On many occasions, both medically and nonmedically trained psychotherapists have come to me for guidance with patients whom they described as "criminals," "delinquents," "addicts," various kinds of psychosomatic complaints, etc. It was not always easy to convince the consultees that patients cannot be categorized by behavior or symptoms; that patients need to be viewed as *people*, whose observable responses are hardly ever unicausal. There are different reasons why individuals manifest a specific behavioral symptom. There are no "criminals," but individuals who commit criminal acts; there are no "addicts," but persons who seek escape from difficulties through alcohol or narcotics; and so on.

This doctrine has its logical corollary; namely, that regardless of complaint, each patient needs to be diagnosed individually as to his past life situation, his trauma and his current psychodynamics manifest in the symptoms. This is what we mean by the term "nuclear problem." Thus individualization must go hand in hand with categorization. I cannot go along with therapists who castigate clinical diagnoses and extol descriptive phenomena as sufficient by themselves. I believe that both are necessary; each yielding complementary understanding to the other.

The further we attempt to identify the elements that enter into the complex of psychotherapy, the further we move from the holistic picture into the elementaristic. While we cannot escape the holistic approach to the understanding of the patient as the result of biological, constitutional, environmental, and relational backgrounds and experiences, the practice of corrective psychotherapy cannot be a holistic consideration alone; it is also elementaristic, which the patient through his own improved health fuses into a unitary whole and integrates into his life process.

Despite the apparent discreteness and specificity in the psychotherapeutic process, there are also some univerals present, which bring us closer to the essence of psychotherapy *as a limit* to which we have referred earlier.

What are these universals? Briefly, they are:

1. First and foremost is the presence of a *positive basic transference,* so characterized because in the transference relation there are always negative phases. For psychotherapy to be effective, the latter must be temporary and transient.

2. The nonpsychotic patient must feel *completely free* to discharge his thoughts, feelings, and hostilities, and act them out within permissible limits and within the patient's boundaries of his ego controls. This catharsis is essential in analytically oriented psychotherapy. Vigilance in this regard is particularly essential with psychotic patients where psychoanalytic techniques should be avoided.

3. The therapist must be clear as to clinical diagnoses and the *nuclear problem* of each patient and possess the skill and experience to deal with them.

4. Except in cases of schizophrenia, psychotherapy aims to facilitate communication between the conscious (ego) and the unconscious. This is especially essential in the treatment of adults.

5. As the patient, in whatever category, discharges through therapy his hostilities (in the transference relation), thereby diminishing their intensity, he still needs help to reconcile himself to the *hostile residue* with which his ego must deal throughout life.

This list can be expanded; however, these five universals are paramount, and perhaps by stretching somewhat the meaning of the word, they can be considered as constituting the "essence" of psychotherapy. However, I for one would not be happy with such a formulation. Essence is defined in the Platonic sense as "form-giving cause." It is viewed by others as "the quintessence," the fundamental intrinsic being; "the prime character"; "the ultimate or intrinsic nature." As a clinician, one who adheres strictly to clinical practice cannot discern any such "ultimate," unitary, quintessential principles in psychotherapy. Perhaps if one were to venture into the precincts of philosophy, one might evolve many constructs and elaborations as others have done, but this would only mislead one into mysticism and speculation which inevitably prove to be detrimental to any instrumental art or science. While there are many areas in human life requiring the aid of philosophic postulates and interpretations, to apply them to psychotherapy is gratuitous and incorrect.

It has always been my conviction that a glimpse of basic truths and of the essence of life and phenomena is vouchsafed to some extent to artists and not to the scientist. The scientist would be hard put to formulate the essence of the sun setting beyond the sea, as does the painter and poet; or the essence of loneliness and yearning, as did Heine; or the essence of human relationships with the vividness of Walt Whitman; or the human tragedy, as did Dostoeyvsky; or the essential nature of people and objects, as depicted by an abstractionist artist like Picasso; or the rhythm and conflict, the harmony and discord in nature, as interpreted by Stravinsky or Malipieri.

It is the great artists who are the high priests and in communication with the oracle. The scientist's arena is the never-ending exploration of facts and interpretation of phenomena, and he should be content with this perhaps limited, but important function. As my friend, Dr. Maurice E. Linden stated:

> We are not physicians of the psyche through some armchair pondering on the vagaries of existence, the indestructableness of matter and energy, and the ambiguous and the inconsistent acceptance of a divinity.
>
> If we are effective, it is because we are realists. Just as physicists, chemists, internists, and surgeons deal with tangible and finite things, so do we also deal with hard tangible realities.
>
> For us, the derivatives of the unconscious, the ego defense mechanisms, the qualitative and quantitative nature of conscience, the instinctual vectors and the resultants of all their interactions are hard, cold, observable, demonstrable facts. The mere fact that we work with elusive energies and gossamer dynamisms does not make us less scientific or less realistic. We have simply assigned ourselves a difficult task. It is easy to work with things that have gravitational mass. It's hard to work with forces all the laws of whose behavior are not yet known and whose very substance is surmised through indirect observation.[1]

Hence the essentiality of keen perception and, above all, practiced intuition.

1. Linden, M. (1960). Our heritage in prospect. *International Journal of Group Psychotherapy* 10:131-135.

CHAPTER 3

THE ERA OF GROUP PSYCHOTHERAPY
(1959)

The Emergence of "Groupism"

It was not so long ago when all of us were greatly disturbed by the fact that the physical and technological discoveries and developments have outdistanced the humanities and the social sciences. There are signs now that this hiatus is rapidly being closed and some telling results should be noted in the not too distant future. Man's attention can be turned onto himself only when his life and survival are secure; or when he is overcome by great catastrophe. Both these conflicting conditions are now in operation.

The staggering developments in business and industry, their vast production and distribution, and the comparative stability and material security, at least for Western nations, have released man's creative genius toward understanding himself, his motivations, and his behavior. His attention and interest are unmistakably turning inward, as it were. As man masters his outer environment and feels increasingly secure in it, his preoccupations are directed toward understanding his relation to it and toward mastery of himself.

The upheaval in the last two generations set off by the two great world wars and the consequent social turmoil so widespread and disturbing in its current and historic imperatives, can no longer be reasonably attributed to social catastrophe and to external circumstances and conditions alone. Even the most intellectually humble and unschooled no longer can ignore the fact that much of what has been and is going on in the world today proceeds as much from man as it does from the conditions of his life. Science and psychology are no longer ignored, nor are they scoffed at, or treated semihumorously, as they had been only in the recent past.

But mankind, and especially its intellectual vanguard, is aware not only of the past and current dilemmas. The leaders of man are cognizant of the slowly but unmistakably evolving crisis that Western man will soon have to face and solve if he is to maintain his status in the world or to survive altogether. There are many such crises, but it will be possible to touch only upon a few of them in this paper.

All are aware of the pernicious virility of the destructive social forces abroad. These forces in their blindness and vigor are making their mark in many parts of the world and seem to be gaining momentum rather than receding. The current social regression makes us pause in reflection and fear. We are also aware of the problems that will face us as a result of automation and the resulting idleness of many millions without inner resources to fill their leisure with constructive and ego-integrating interests and occupations. Disorganizing indulgences, dissipation, and moral deterioration are the alternatives. Automation will also shift the demand from physical labor to technically trained professional workers and to a lesser extent to mechanically skilled craftsmen. Since the majority of participants in our industrial life are in occupations requiring comparatively little intellectual or technical training, the dislocation in the world's social economy could be catastrophic.

Idleness is destructive to personality, and an effortless life is subject to all the evil that man fell heir to. This situation will require the very best insights into the nature, cravings, and needs of man and concerted planning and doing will be necessary to find means for adequate sublimations and substitute gratifications.

Enforced idleness and excessive leisure will be further enhanced by the atomic age that is impending. Nearly all the unskilled labor in mining and the oil industries, in the production of electric power, in services and allied occupations and trades will no longer be needed, or certainly a vastly decreased number will be required. The millions engaged in these pursuits who, to a large extent, may be unfit for more intellectual and skilled occupations will not only constitute a glut upon the labor market, but unless proper planning is instituted, many even offer a menace to our constituted social order, for the devil has many works for idle hands.

The impending atomic age presages even more dire possibilities. The prospect of destruction and the ravaging effects of the atomic weapons have created consternation not only in the man on the street, but have pricked the consciences of the scientists themselves and have instilled fear in the hearts of even the military leaders of the world. No one who is to any extent aware of life's currents can remain unmoved or untouched by the impending catastrophe from this direction and no thinking person can escape the inevitable conclusion that it can be prevented only through concerted and unified effort of *groups* of peoples and of nations. It is clear that such weapons of destruction cannot be allowed to remain in the control of individual persons or even individual nations.

It is becoming increasingly evident to everyone, in fact, that the solution of these and other pressing problems, current and impending, are no longer within the scope of individuals. They can be solved with any degree of adequacy, if at all, by *groups* of interested people acting in concert or through constituted and representative authority. The essential difference between the authoritarian social matrix and democracy is that in the one the autocrat is looked to for solutions of social problems while in the other the individuals involved or affected combine in a common effort to deal with their concerns. In one the attitude is "let the top man do it," in the other it is "let's do it together."

The aftermath of the two world wars, especially the second, clearly demonstrated how dangerously power can be used by unscrupulous and pathologic individuals to the detriment and near-destruction of mankind itself. Thus the awareness of the importance of group effort and group control, which has been in the past limited to some professional workers and a small number of social scientists, has spread far and wide.

There have been, however, more tangible evidences of the power of the group and of the mass impressed on our minds. This is the skillful and most effective uses that have been made of the group by the leading totalitarian countries such as Russia and, especially, Hitler's Germany. They have palpably demonstrated the irresistible power of the Mass, its susceptibility to emotional contagion, its blindness to rationality, its avidity for submission and its capacity for destructiveness and brutality. The effectiveness of the youth groups upon which both Soviet Russia and Nazi Germany have leaned so heavily demonstrated to us their importance and have made us more aware than ever of the potentialities of the group for good and for evil. In the hands of the demagogues, the group or mass becomes a dangerous instrument of destruction and barbarism, and thinking people in democratic countries stopped short in their habitual complacency to examine the verity of their assumptions. Is individualism run rampant without social and community controls safe? Can it happen here?

It is in this atmosphere that the *era of the group* has made its appearance.

Lester Ward, in my estimation the greatest sociologist America has produced, has suggested the stages of the development in nature as chemism, bathmism, zoism, and psychism. In a seminar on "group work" I conducted in 1939, I have suggested that the next stage in the evolutionary development of man is *groupism*. This concept I have elaborated in my book *Child Psychotherapy* which appeared in 1952 [57].

Although some neurologists believe that imperceptible evolutionary changes in man's nervous system are occurring, they also aver that these changes are so slight as to take perhaps millions of years before any telling effects can be expected and thereby man's behavior and feelings altered. Meanwhile the social changes that are occurring before our very eyes differ from biological evolution in that they are within the power of man to direct and control. If mankind can find means of determining the direction and content of social development a wonderful world can be envisaged for our progeny. But members of our profession know full-well that the unconscious, disruptive, and destructive drives of man, individually and collectively, will always subordinate his knowledge and rationality. It is the task of the best thinkers and most ardent of activists to evolve ways for guiding the masses of people toward a healthier life and self-fullfillment.

This is not the task for the philosopher or the theoretician alone, but rather for those rare individuals who have the foresight and operational capacity to transform theory into a living practice. What I am suggesting is a new profession, that of "social engineering." The members of this new profession will have to have the same type of scientific training and facilities as do the industrial and construction engineers, but they would be vastly more imaginative and flexible. The engineers I envisage will have to be drawn from the human sciences who would understand the vagaries, instabilities, and irrationalities of the material with which they are to deal, namely, man. Especially will they have to be expert at understanding and directing group behavior. Such scientists will have to be recruited from the fields of sociology, psychology, psychiatry and psychotherapy, as well as economics and industry.

I am aware that such reliance on technology has been dubbed somewhat cynically by writers such as Gabriel Marcel as "optimism of the technique." We must recognize, however, that much is contributed to our social tensions by the fact that though we live in a highly scientific and technologic era and at the threshold of the atomic age, our politics and governments have still many of the characteristics of the horse and buggy period. It is high time that this anomaly be corrected and that the affairs of the world be placed in the hands of trained intelligence rather than conscienceless manipulators.

We have learned to direct and control the forces in the realm of chemism, and to understand, train, and utilize animals in the realms of zoism. In recent years man, in his desperation and bewilderment, turned to trying to understand and direct *himself* through the science of psychology. He shall be forced in the near future to turn to the study of the nature and potentials of the group. For it is through groups that man's greatest effectiveness is achieved and in groups does he find the instruments of social assertiveness and influence.

The new *science of groupism* now in the process of development and its instrumental application to life is the only hope mankind has for escaping inevitable catastrophies. We cannot agree entirely with H. G. Wells' statement that man's future history is a race between education and catastrophe. Education alone cannot meet the needs of mankind nor prevent the tragedy Wells so prophetically envisaged; that is, unless we include in the term education the influences of man's total environment, economic demands, and his value systems. We rather need to find procedures that would place man in a different relation to his fellowmen. Further, we have to find means for forging his unconscious in a way that his hostilities and aggressions toward others and himself can be either eliminated or at least sublimated. Obviously this can be achieved only through human relationships and through groups with their power to sanction, prohibit, control, accept and reject.

That the *era of groupism* is in the making is evident from the vast quantity of experimentation in group dynamics and group management, and in the literature that has been appearing in the last decade or so. The group has been the central theme of numerous publications in various fields. Although the profession that is most concerned with it is understandably sociology, educators, psychologists, and psychiatrists are increasingly turning their attention to this subject as well. The American Group Psychotherapy Association with more than 850[1] members drawn from the fields of psychiatry, psychotherapy, and case work with its fourteen local affiliated organizations in various parts of the United States, is only one development to bear witness to this fact. There are similar associations already in existence in Holland, England, Japan, and in Argentina and smaller groups scattered throughout the world. The International Committee on Group Psychotherapy now has a representation of twenty-nine nations. It held its first international congress in 1954, in Toronto, Canada, at which many countries were represented. The second congress was held in August 1957 in Zurich, Switzerland. Translations of our books have been made into Japanese, German, French, Hebrew, and Italian and an ever-growing indigenous literature is being produced in a great many countries. I have personally received inquiries, corresponded with and had visitors in my office from the following forty-eight countries: Africa, Australia, Austria, Belgium, Bulgaria, Canada, Czechoslovakia, Bahamas, Virgin Islands, West Indies, Ceylon, China, Hong Kong, Cuba, Denmark, England, Finland, France, Germany, Greece, Hawaii, Holland, India, Indochina, Indonesia, Iran, Israel, Italy, Japan, Mexico, New Zealand, Norway, Portugal, Puerto Rico, Scotland, Argentina, Brazil, Chile, Peru, Venezuela, Guatemala, Spain, Sweden, Switzerland, Turkey, U.S.S.R., Yugoslavia. The *International Journal of Group Psychotherapy* which I have the privilege of editing has readers in twenty-nine countries on all the continents of the world.

1. More than 3,000 in 1974 [ed.].

But this expanding preoccupation with the group as a tool in social and professional function is not limited to our field alone. In a symposium which I have had the privilege to edit, an imposing number of the fields are represented in which group techniques are being employed. These included government, industry, education, radio communication, community mental health and others. In another contribution on the subject even wider application of these techniques have been noted [105]. Group methods have been steadily expanding in the fields of education, interracial relations, management and labor, industrial and commercial activities, family counseling, parent guidance and education, student mental health, training for medicine and psychiatry, hospital management, delinquency prevention and correction, prison management, treatment of addictions, and other management, therapeutic, and prophylactic activities too numerous to list here.

Groupism and Psychiatry

It is understandable and entirely inevitable that psychiatry should have been caught up in this evolving era of *groupism*. Society has many characteristics of an organism and is subject to reflex and referred reactions to all important developments and changes that occur in the body politic. It is well known that no significant development can occur in any area of the social organism without affecting to varying degrees the nature and functions of other areas.

Actually, groups were used in medical practice in America long before the developments delineated above took place. One Dr. Ingersol conducted a small home in upstate New York in the middle of the last century for "nervous" ailments in which the treatment consisted of a group living process and the resultant personality interactions, bible reading, religious devotionals, and, strangely enough, conditioning the patients so that the men and women could, and did, walk about this small sanitarium stark naked. Considering the fact that this development took place in the pre-Freudian era, it is indeed a significant, though isolated, precursor of the awareness that had come much later in the field of psychiatry.

Groups have been used in primitive miracle treatment. Group hypnotism and hysteria were employed by shamans and medicine men from time immemorial. One is not too certain that the late Dr. Joseph K. Pratt of Boston was fully aware of the group as a factor in his "class method" which he conducted for tubercular patients at the turn of this century. His aim was to encourage patients to carry out the medical regimen prescribed. This may have been a time saving device as well as a technique to motivate submission to the instructions of the doctor. Later the "class method" was extended by Dr. Pratt and his pupils to patients with peptic ulcers and other partially psychogenic illnesses, and to psychotics and neurotics.

Neither are we convinced that the group as such was the prime consideration of the very talented and original pioneer, Dr. Trigand Burrow. His patients lived together with the doctors and they did "work through" their attitudes and conflicts toward one another, undoubtedly with great benefit. But here as well the group was not used as a consciously scientifically planned instrument of psychotherapy. The emphasis in Dr. Burrow's work was upon the individual interactions and the spontaneous group tensions that inevitably arise in the course of daily intimate living in close proximity.

The early stages of Dr. Louis Wender's work with large groups as well does not carry the stamp of group psychotherapy as we understand it today. His work falls in the didactic category, though his explanations to patients of psychic phenomena and their difficulties were derived from Freudian psychology. Dr. Wender either lectured to comparatively large audiences consisting of sanatoria patients, conducted discussions on psychiatric and mental hygiene topics, or presented cases of the patients present, anonymously, for reaction and discussion by the others present.

The first psychiatrist who used a *small group* of adult patients for deep analytical treatment that I am personally aware of was Dr. Paul Schilder at Bellevue Hospital in New York City, who started this work in 1937. Dr. Schilder worked with small groups of eight or ten psychotic and neurotic patients who had been under treatment by him individually. His work was psychoanalytically oriented and his procedure followed technically that of psychoanalysis, or as much of it as can be used in a group situation.

Group Psychotherapy with Children

In 1934, three years before Schilder, our work in group psychotherapy with small groups was started. At first we concentrated on the treatment of children in latency, between the ages of eight and twelve, through a technique later to become known as *Activity Group Therapy* [53]. In this method *carefully selected children* according to special clinical considerations with personality and maladjustment difficulties are placed in groups of six to eight in a specially designed physical environment in which they are free to act out their impulses, as aggressive as they may be. Out of the apparent chaotic environment prevalent at first, there gradually and usually imperceptibly emerges a degree of order and group norms that reflect the order within the children and the integration of their psychic forces.

This technique, which is now rather widespread not only in the United States but in many other countries, is deceptively simple. The physical environment set for the groups consists of rough furniture, some of it designed for arts and crafts and carpentry work, table tennis, and other simple team and individual games, with free space for movement, for running about and for acting out. One small table is set aside for children who are unready for direct interaction with others and who may have a need to isolate themselves. This table is known as the "isolate table," which serves the requirements of the children whom we designate as "isolates." The other types of children included in the groups are those who can serve either as "instigators" or as "neutralizers."

The materials for work supplied to boys are simple. They are almost always within the scope of the children's past experience at home and at school or through their ordinary hobbies. These consist of simple carpentry tools and wood, pewter and copper discs with molds for hammering out ashtrays and the necessary tools, copper foil for making plaques, plasticine for simple sculpture (which boys use more often to make pellets for their "clay wars"), water colors and paper for drawing and painting, boat and airplane models, occasionally small electrical toys, and a few magnets with iron filings. The equipment for girls includes some of the items used by boys but in addition materials for doll-making, simple sewing, small weaving looms, and the makings of jewelry.

A visitor observing an activity therapy group through a screen would see somewhat of the following. A few boys may be busily engaged in work with tools at the tables and benches, two may be playing table tennis with a third watching them or waiting to play the "winner," one engaged in drawing at the isolate table, two wrestling or fighting. The scene soon changes and tumult suddenly ensues. Four or five of the boys who had been quietly occupied only a few moments ago are now galvanized into action of a more or less violent nature. They run about, push each other, scream, laugh and have a hilarious time. Soon a conflict arises among a few of the participants which has to be resolved by themselves, since the therapist is enjoined from interfering with the children's spontaneous outbursts. After an interlude of this, all return to quieter occupations.

This "activity catharsis" serves to discharge pent-up feelings and the energy potentials built up through the normal metabolic processes, the accumulated hostility and tensions as a reaction to frustration and rejection by parents, siblings and teachers, as well as the needs for constructive social experimentation.

Of even greater importance is the testing of the therapist. Will he react as the accustomed adult stereotype by disapproval, punishment, and rejection; or will he respond unlike all other adults in their past experience? This is the pivotal test and upon its outcome depends the success or failure of the therapeutic process. The role of the therapist is described as one of "neutrality." He remains unresponsive to the so-called "good" and "bad" in the children's reactions and interactions. He always responds when called upon, he meets all demands, gives whatever is asked of him, helps when help is needed. But beyond that the responsibility for the atmosphere and conduct of the group is on the shoulders of the members.

Unlike the leader in ordinary groups, the therapist here does not usurp the patients' ego and superego functions. Because he does not judge or restrain, the children's own superego is finally activated; and because he does not restrain or control, their ego functions are brought into operation. *He reacts in a manner unlike any other adult.* The children discover for the first time in their lives what real responsibility is, not only the duties of performing tasks in the home and at school, but inner responsibility for their own behavior. This discovery usually sets off considerable anxiety in most of the children for there is no greater task one can assume than freedom, but the therapist knows full well that only freedom leads to inner control and true maturity. Through the setting of the environment and the role of the therapist, a reeducation of the total personality takes place. Impulse is brought under control, better judgment of reality emerges and the attitude toward people and to what seems to our children as a hostile world grows more sanguine.

The sessions that last two full hours once or twice a week always end with a period of refreshments. Here the various anxieties are reactivated in the children and the habitual conflicts and negativism reassert themselves, but the therapist's tolerant and accepting attitude forces the children to inhibit and control their impulses and evolve a new and more suitable pattern of behavior.

With the sharpening of clinical judgment in the selection of patients for this type of "situational therapy," we were able to achieve improvement in 82 percent of our youngsters. In this therapy where no verbal interpretation is given, no restraints are exerted, and the transference is unilateral, the choice and grouping of patients is of paramount, in fact crucial, importance. The highest degree of skill on the part of the therapist is of no avail where a wrong child is included in a group. A thorough understanding of the psychodynamics and ego functioning of each of the patients, as well as a reliable anticipation of the possible interactions among them is essential.

Since the group is the instrument of treatment, its proper constitution, especially its balance, has to receive special and painstaking attention. Criteria for selection, grouping and group balance have been formulated and validated in countless situations and can now be found in the literature. Because of their importance to an understanding of the specificity of group psychotherapy we shall briefly delineate the criteria for selection for this and other types of therapy groups.

The basic requirements for inclusion in these groups is that the prospective young patient must have minimal ego and superego development; he must have had a moderately satisfactory relation with some adult in the past that would have engendered in him a need and the capacity for object relations and group acceptance, or what we term *social hunger*. For the sake of brevity we present the indications and counterindications in a tabular form (Table 1).

TABLE 1

Indications and Counterindications for
Activity Therapy Groups for Children in Latency

Indications	Counterindications*
Clinical	*Clinical*
Oedipal primary behavior disorders	Severe psychoneuroses
Some preoedipal primary behavior disorders	Psychoses
	Psychopathy
Character disorders	Neurotic characters
Mild neuroses	Severe anxiety states
Situational anxiety (anxiety hysteria)	Latent homosexuality
Some latent schizophrenics	Disturbances in libido development
Some schizoid personalities	
Characterological	*Characterological*
Confused sexual identification	Absence of minimal ego development
Effeminacy (in boys)	Absence of minimal superego development
Masculinity (in girls)	
Infantilization	Inadequate capacity for object relationships
Overprotection	
Nonpathological withdrawal	Regressive infantilism
Inadequate ego development	Castration anxiety
Social hunger	Excessive generalized aggression
Only children	Excessive aggression toward adults
	Physical handicaps and deformities
	Stigmatizations
	Mental deficiency

*Children included in this category of counterindications cannot be placed in groups even when they receive individual treatment. They can be referred to groups only after the basic personality problems have been corrected through individual treatment and may require a period of "socialization."

Unlike other therapies, in activity groups children are grouped together not in accordance with clinical criteria, or similarity of syndrome or pathology, but according to their behavioral patterns, that is, some of the patients assigned to a group are aggressive, others are shy, the behavior of still others approximates the average.[2]

2. The terms "instigators," "neuters," and "neutralizers" are applied to these respectively to designate their effect upon the group.

Because acting out is prevalent in these groups, neither continuous chaotic hyperactivity (nodal behavior) nor continuous hypoactivity (antinodal behavior) can be tolerated. These two modes of reaction must alternate and this alternation is achieved through group balance [128]. Where verbal communication and interpretation are the matrix of the therapeutic process, whether with children or adults, the interpretations serve to control and inhibit excessive behavior. In activity groups these controls must come from the patients themselves; therefore, the balancing of the group in terms of behavior of the participating members, their effect upon each other, and the total group atmosphere, are the prime considerations.

As we continued our work for a number of years the fact was brought to bear on us that the children who had failed in this type of treatment needed more analytically oriented therapy groups. We have, therefore, experimented with such groups and have finally evolved two other types to suit the requirements of children of different ages. The essential difference between these groups and the activity therapy groups is that the children's obviously hostile and anxiety reducing, as well as anxiety producing, verbalizations and acts are interpreted to them either by the therapist or by fellow group members. In the analytic therapy groups for children, namely, *play group psychotherapy* and *activity-interview group psychotherapy*, the latent content, that is, the emotional significance of their behavior and statements in terms of transference and displacement are made manifest to them. Thus even the young child of four and five can become aware of his feelings provided they are interpreted to him on his own level and in a language comprehensible and meaningful to him [64].

The analytic groups for children consisting of five or six members are divided into two categories: the "play groups" for preschool children between the ages of four and six, and "activity-interview" for children between eight and twelve—all grouped with an age span not more than one year. The setting for these groups is similar to that of Activity Group Therapy insofar as materials and tools for appropriately simple occupations are supplied and space for free movement provided. It differs from the latter, however, in most important respects. In the analytic groups additional material is added that would activate the children to reveal their sexual and nonsexual libidinal preoccupations and anxieties which are the core of their symptomatic and behavioral difficulties. These we term "nuclear problems."[3] To do this, objects such as the following are to be found in the room in addition to some already enumerated for activity groups: water, rubber tubing, masks of people and animals, toy animals, dolls, including castration dolls of children and of men and women, doll house with furniture for the various rooms—dining room and especially bedroom and bathroom furnishings and fixtures. With these the children play out their sexual, anal and urethral fantasies and preoccupations, their attitudes toward food (which they have a chance to do also during the refreshment period), and their feelings about hostilities toward siblings and parents. It is fascinating to observe how truly the little patients' fantasy play mirrors and reproduces the problems with which they come to us.

Patients selected for these groups are more disturbed than those which we include in activity groups. They also differ clinically. Here we place children with defective capacities for object relations (who may require concurrent individual therapy), definite psychoneuroses with full-blown symptomatology, schizoid personalities and some latent schizophrenics, the latter two types requiring activating experiences with centrifugal relations and activities.

Children in latency with massive psychoneurotic symptomatology, the seriously disturbed, and the anxious require, as do adults, a period of individual psychotherapy before assignment to a group, and most of them benefit from parallel individual and group treatment. More than do adults, children benefit from association and interaction with peers, and group therapy should be used with them more extensively than is being done at the present time.

Here, as well, it is essential that before he is placed in a group, the degree of libidinal distortion and sexual attachment the child has for his parents, especially the parent of the opposite sex, is ascertained. Children whose parents or siblings had been seductive, sexually provocative and overstimulating, who slept with their parents in the same bed or in the same room, or who witnessed or overheard the primal scene, require play therapy in an individual transference relation, interpretation and insight as well as release and cathexis displacement.

3. This term is applied by me in the diagnosis of all patients, children and adults, not only in the cases under discussion.

Even more than in the case of adults, antagonisms toward a sibling may preclude placement of a child in a group. While in most instances sibling hostility can be dissolved by groups, we have found instances where the intensive acting out of these feelings rendered continuing the child patient in a group inadvisable.

Among the children for whom individual therapy is preferred are those who have been subjected to a serious trauma, either a sudden catastrophe, prolonged exposure to a series of traumatic occurrences, or a totally traumatic environment in the family. The anxiety bound up as a result of these exposures has to be released in the security of a positive transference, and treatment has to be focused toward the dissolution of the bound-up anxiety. This can best be done in individual therapy through free association, interpretation, and insight. Children in such straits require the security of a relationship with a therapeutically oriented adult with whom they feel comfortable and free. This removes the burden their still weak and unformed ego has to carry.

The criteria for selection for these groups are shown in Table 2.

TABLE 2

Indications and Counterindications
for Analytic Therapy Groups for Children

Indications	Counterindications*
Clinical	*Clinical*
Reactive behavior disorders	Massive psychoneurotic symptomatology
Character disorders	Libido fixations and distortions
Neurotic traits	Neurotic characters
Neurotic reactions	Diffuse fears and anxiety
Anxiety states	Reactions to trauma
	Psychoses
Characterological	*Characterological*
Only Children	Intense sibling rivalry
Aggressiveness toward adults Excessive submissiveness	Lack of impulse control

*In most of these cases parallel individual and group treatment are indicated.

Group Psychotherapy with Adolescents and Adults

The early work in the field that predated group psychotherapy, or better still, "analytic group psychotherapy," which some therapists call, after Trigand Burrow, "group analysis," and even a smaller number, "group psychoanalysis," cannot justifiably be claimed as being a direct antecedent of the latter. Our own work dating to 1934, Dr. Paul Schilder in 1937, Dr. John Levy at about 1939 or 1940, can be viewed as the legitimate progenitors of psychotherapy with *small groups* of nonpsychotic adults. I would like to underscore the modifying phrase, "small groups," for it is this element that differentiates it from what we designate "mass therapy," if such a thing is possible.

When therapy began to be applied to small groups of five to eight patients, the beginnings of group psychotherapy were made. It is not possible to enter here into the theses of the importance of small numbers. We shall have to be content by suggesting that the web of interactions in a group follows the permutation formula,

$$S = n \, (n\text{-}1) \, (n\text{-}2) \, (n\text{-}3) \ldots (n\text{-}n\text{-}1)$$

It is clear from this formula that a large group in which its members are in intense and continued interaction, such as in a therapy group, would turn into an unmanageable violent mob. The factor of numbers is, therefore, of pivotal consideration. I submit, therefore, that historically group psychotherapy has its beginnings at the point when the idea of the small group was introduced.

There is still another and equally important factor that has determined the nature of true group psychotherapy, and this is the *process*. The *forerunners* of group psychotherapy have employed didactic teaching and lectures. Some, like the late Dr. A. A. Low of Chicago, have employed definite authoritarian and repressive techniques. In fact, in classifying the various techniques that are employed I have named it "the authoritarian-repressive method." There are also the "authoritarian-repressive methods," a phrase used by Dr. Giles W. Thomas in describing Dr. Pratt's way of dealing with his patients.[4] Various quasi-educational approaches, persuasion, release,

4. Thomas, G. W. (1943). Group psychotherapy: reviews, abstracts, notes and correspondence. *Psychosomatic Medicine*, April.

dramaturgic, and relationship techniques are also employed by some therapists exclusively and by others when they are indicated.

There is fair unanimity among practitioners that the therapeutic process in groups most worthy of being considered psychotherapy are those that involve free-association or catharsis, interpretation of resistance and transference, and the acquisition of insight by the patient of his motives, defenses and projections. In other words, the therapeutic process in groups does not differ in essentials from sound individual psychotherapy. The group, however, is an aid in reducing resistance, in modifying and diluting transferences, in supplying vicarious or spectator catharsis; it serves as a catalyzer, and as a matrix for reality testing. As only one example of the effect of the group upon the therapeutic process, I should like to list what I term "catharsis accelerators" in groups. These are: Target Multiplicity, Catalysis, Mutual Induction, Mutual Support, Identification and Universalization [9, 56].

There is less unanimity as to the degree of personality involvement necessary for therapeutic results and as to the content of the group interviews, the production by the patients, and the role and function of the therapist. These are only a few of the elements under consideration at the moment.

Unlike in some other countries, the disputants in the field have not as yet reached a high pitch of acrimony in the United States largely because the contending individuals have been brought and kept together for sixteen years in a common bond of cooperative venture through the American Group Psychotherapy Association founded in 1942 and by its official organ, the *International Journal of Group Psychotherapy* which made its appearance in 1951. Both these instruments supply a full unrestricted forum for expression and interchange. Conflicting ideas and convictions are welcome and are aired. We have operated on the assumption that current and future patients can benefit more from the guidance and learnings that may accrue to the therapists from such exchange rather than by limiting their perspective and skill through isolated sectarianism. The leaders in both of these enterprises have been more sensitive to the best interests of current and future patients than to the claims of special "schools." They hope that truth will more readily come from the impact of ideas and exchange of experience than from the inurement of each in his own and, therefore, necessarily limited convictions.

The differences in ideas and convictions is not limited or inherent to group psychotherapy. They stem from and reflect the state of individual psychotherapy. Some years ago I have had the privilege of addressing an audience of psychotherapists on the topic of "Common Sources of Errors and Confusion in Group Psychotherapy" [5]. On that occasion I made some remarks in this connection that can still stand repeating today. I said:

> Much of the confusion is not in relation to group psychotherapy but in relation to what *is* psychotherapy.... The fault lies with the lack of knowledge of generic psychotherapy rather than that of the specific, group psychotherapy.... Patients... are for the most part not in acute states of disturbance. They have lived with their problems for long periods and grappled with them perhaps throughout their lives. The difficulties do not arise from a specific threat or situation... but rather are a result of inadequate psychic reserves to deal with the total life situation. The need, therefore, is not to change attitudes and feelings in relation to a specific problem... but rather to alter the equipment of the patient so that he can deal more adequately with his inner problems and as a result also with the demands of outer reality. When an individual finds himself in a quandary with respect to a *specific* problem we may help him with it. This is variously referred to as counseling and guidance. In psychotherapy, on the other hand, our focus is to equip the individual with the strength to deal with *any* problem, now and in the future, by reorganizing and reweighting the quantum of emotionality in the unconscious and by establishing a balance in the functioning of the id, ego and superego.

Criteria for selection of patients for analytical group psychotherapy are given in Table 3.

The directive group therapies present by far a greater variety than the psychoanalytically oriented groups. We find among them a number of what came to be designated as inspirational, didactic, recreational, and others. Some are derivatives from the analytic and activity groups, others are of independent origin.

The chief characteristic of the directive groups is that the leader or therapist is an active agent who either activates, directs, stimulates, or

TABLE 3

Indications and Counterindications for
Therapy Groups for Adults and Adolescents

Indications	Counterindications*
Clinical	*Clinical*
Some psychoneuroses	Anxiety neuroses
Character disorders	Neurotic character
Some borderline ambulatory	Compulsive-obsessional
schizophrenics	Psychopaths
Schizoid personalities	Cyclothymic personalities
Psychic masochists	Active psychotics**
	Paranoiacs
	Depressives
	Perverts
	Active homosexuals
	Hypochondriacs
Characterological	*Characterological*
Defensive projection	Inadequate primary relations
Character resistances	Inadequate ego development
Confused identifications	Inadequate superego development
Defective sibling relations	Intense sexual disturbances
Only children	Extreme narcissism
Drive to defeat therapist	

*Many patients included in this category of counterindications can be treated in groups provided they also receive parallel individual treatment. The selection of patients for such parallel treatment may depend entirely upon the clinical judgment of the therapist.

**This category refers here to the inclusion of psychotic patients in groups with nonpsychotics.

guides the patients toward certain specific discussions or activities in accordance with his judgment as to patients' needs. Thus, catharsis is directed, induced, and sometimes forced. Some of the techniques employed are classroom teaching, lectures and discussions based upon verbal and visual material and free activities. In some, the therapist uses direct or subtle authority or activates specific reactions in the patients. In one or two, definite directive or repressive measures are employed. Free association is at a minimum and when encouraged, it is focused on a topic or problem usually suggested by the leader. In the category of directive group therapies are included also the guidance and counseling types which, as already indicated, are aimed at dealing with the *top realities* of the participants. None of the methods grouped in this category results in a basic intrapsychic change of more or less permanent nature. They result rather in corrected attitudes and values, improved self-awareness, and a more wholesome view of self and the outer world. The aim of these techniques is to strengthen the participants through support, give them methods for dealing more adequately with specific personal problems, help them toward a newly developed awareness and an outlook that facilitate in bearing up under stress and dealing with situations with less fear and strain.

Despite the fact that this work does not involve strictly psychiatric tools and techniques, nonetheless to be effective within their limits, they should be conducted by persons who are psychiatrically oriented. It is important that the leaders or directors of these groups be aware of the deeper implications and possible pathology in the members. This is necessary to prevent activation of tensions and anxieties beyond permissible intensity.

I believe that the above describes faithfully the situation as it now exists and has existed for some time in the field of psychotherapy and it evidences that fundamentally the conflict stems from two areas—one is ego therapy, namely, dealing with current problems on a conscious or preconscious level in a blanket fashion for all patients, irrespective of clinical consideration as against the deeper, regressive type of psychotherapy in which early memories, infantile sexuality, oedipal guilt, primary and derivative hostilities, transference and other feelings incorporated in the unconscious are worked through and are reduced or eliminated. This is particularly indicated for the psychoneurotic patient.

The other point of difference is the lack of proper recognition between *symptom improvement* and improvement as a result of *personality restructuring*. The one can be achieved by many therapeutic as well as nontherapeutic procedures and experiences; the other, through regressive living over of early traumata in a transference relation with resulting insight.

Perhaps the contrast in approaches can be more pointedly described as follows. In the ego therapies, in counseling and in guidance, the focus is upon release, advice, identification and understanding (cognition). In what is considered as more basic psychotherapy, the anxiety bound up in the unconscious is released and worked through, which can be achieved only through regression. This, in my opinion, is the pivotal difference in the psychotherapies now in practice under whatever name or school they may be known. Obviously it is inevitable that this difference should permeate group psychotherapy, as well, since the same persons practice both individual and group psychotherapy. My own position is that *all practices are valid when used with patients for whom they are suited.* The future of all psychotherapy, in my opinion, is intelligent, discriminative and informed eclecticism for no one method can be universally effective. If one were to generalize, one can say that the uncovering, exploratory, and regressive therapy is indicated for the full-blown and massive psychoneuroses, while the various ego therapies are suitable for character and behavior disorders with or without slight neurotic symptoms or traits.

Some of the other aspects upon which there are differing opinions specific to group psychotherapy is the use of co-therapists or auxiliary therapists, observers, recorders, and visitors: nonpatients who are present at the group interviews and serve in the various capacities as indicated by their titles. Some therapists favor this practice while others believe that it interferes with the development of transference attitudes in the group members. In dispute are also such devices as "going around," where patients are called upon to speak in rotation; encouragement of acting out by adult patients; the question of anonymity of patients who belong to the same group; "alternate meetings," that is, meetings between regular sessions held by the group without the therapist present; clinical indications for group psychotherapy; the grouping of patients of different clinical categories, and the indications for parallel individual and group psychotherapy.

These and some other questions will not be settled until adequate resources for controlled experimentation and research are made available to qualified, nonbiased therapeutic agencies and individuals. Meanwhile, reports reach us from all parts of the world that even at its present state, group psychotherapy is effective and that it is spreading by leaps and bounds.

My own major interest in addition to the work with children is in *analytic group psychotherapy* with adults which is based upon Freudian psychoanalytic theory and practices. It was possible for us with little effort to apply these basic principles in some instances and modify them in others as the group situation demanded without diminishing or losing their dynamic nature and significance. This development I have set forth in several books and in more than sixty articles and papers. More than two decades of work has been invested in this enterprise and one of the results of these studies and researches are criteria for the selection of nonpsychotic patients for analytic group psychotherapy [6].

Group Therapy with Psychotics

Group psychotherapy with psychotics presents a less clear picture than with the nonpsychotic. This, indeed, is equally true of other types of psychotherapy as well. The diagnosis of psychosis is not as definitive as in other clinical categories. Organic involvements, hereditary factors, degree of contact with reality, and other elements and dynamics makes this category of patients less clear clinically. If we consider the most prevalent and perhaps most puzzling of the psychoses, schizophrenia, as a possibility for treatment by groups, many factors have to be taken into consideration.

First, one must ascertain the intensity of the illness; one must know whether the patient is a potential, borderline, or an active, full-blown schizophrenic. It is obvious that the latter would be unsuitable for any psychotherapy during an active episode and one would have to time it with periods of remission that occur either spontaneously or brought about through chemotherapy or convulsive therapies. Many psychiatrists report good results with borderline schizophrenics placed with other types of patients, in combination with individual treatment, while potential schizophrenics who function almost normally (though a trained eye can recognize their basic ego weakness and deficiencies) can be placed in groups.

The chief consideration in group treatment of schizophrenics are the limitations in their ego strengths and the possibility of causing ego fragmentation through the impact of the group. I adhere to the theory that real schizophrenia is a symptom of organic or constitutional deficiencies with massive or striking psychological concomitants. Because of the lacks in endocrinological balance, the ego reserves are low and unable to deal with pressures, criticism, and attack which are unavoidable in groups. The therapist, therefore, has to be ever on the alert to prevent stress to the one or two schizophrenics in a group that would prove beyond his capacity to bear. The need to protect a patient for whatever reason, alters the required neutral role of the therapist and of necessity affects the transference from the other patients.[5]

Of greatest service that group psychotherapy has been to the hospital treatment of psychotics is a derivative one. Group psychotherapy has reinforced and validated the few and widely scattered efforts at hospital community treatment of patients. In recent years patients have been involved in planning and participation, work and recreation, didactic teaching and group discussions as well as modified group psychotherapy for the less regressed and the more reality-oriented patients. These efforts have received impetus from the growing recognition of the value of interpersonal and group interaction that group psychotherapy has fostered.

By way of summarizing the preceding discussion I would like to present Table 4 and Figure 1 (See pp. 70-71.) One is a graphic presentation of the various types of groups we have either discussed or listed; the other lists the variation in the basic therapeutic dynamics or elements in these groups.

Summary

Groupism is a phenomenon in the evolution of society and is a direct extension of the stages of chemism, bathmism, zoism and psychism. The survival of man, especially in the era of expanding technology, automation, and atomic developments can no longer be assured by individualism and uncontrolled competition. Cooperation for the benefit of the community and mankind as a whole is no longer an ideal to be hoped for, but an essential practice if mankind is to survive. The group as a concept and as an operational instrument has come to the fore out of historic and evolutionary imperatives and has been applied with increasing frequency and skill in many of our social functions. It was, therefore, inevitable that it should also become a tool in efforts at correcting as well as educating and reeducating the human personality.

5. Spotnitz, H. (1957). The borderline in group psychotherapy. *International Journal of Group Psychotherapy* 7:155-174.

TABLE 4

Differential Dynamics in Group Therapy

Type of Group	Transference	Catharsis	Insight	Reality Testing	Sublimation	Resistance
Activity	Sibling Identification Multilateral Unilateral Group	Activity Induced Vicarious	Derivative	In Situ	In Situ	Absenteeism Lateness Passivity
Play	Libidinal Sibling Identification Multilateral Group	Activity Verbal Activity-verbal Free association Induced Vicarious	Direct Derivative	In Situ	In Situ Ex Situ	Irrelevancy* Silence Passivity
Activity Interview	Libidinal Sibling Identification Multilateral Group	Associative Free association Activity Verbal Activity-verbal Induced Vicarious	Direct Derivative	In Situ	In Situ Ex Situ	Irrelevancy Silence Lateness Absenteeism Passivity
Interview	Libidinal Sibling Identification Multilateral Group	Associative Free Association Verbal Directed Induced Vicarious	Direct Derivative	Ex Situ In Situ	Ex Situ	Displacement Deflection Distraction Abruptness Planned communication Associative thinking Irrelevancy Silence Absenteeism Lateness Acting Out

*Absenteeism and lateness are omitted since parents bring children under school age for treatment.

FIGURE I

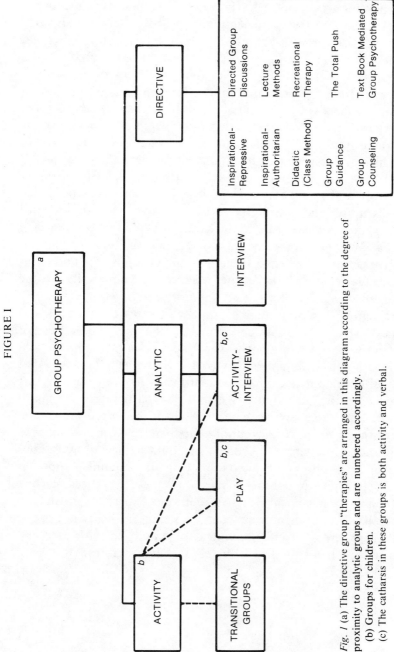

Fig. 1 (a) The directive group "therapies" are arranged in this diagram according to the degree of proximity to analytic groups and are numbered accordingly.
(b) Groups for children.
(c) The catharsis in these groups is both activity and verbal.

Group psychotherapy has been the outcome of these dynamic forces. In its present stage it is experiencing an era of flux, error, and some confusion which is derived from the unclarity prevalent in individual psychotherapy.

Group psychotherapy has implications far beyond the clinical frontiers, for just as the individual cannot develop and survive without the group, society's health and survival as well depends upon adequately functioning and healthy groups. Group psychotherapy has demonstrated that the hostile, aggressive, and destructive forces inherent in man's psyche can be employed in the interest of mental health and the welfare of society. It is only when society learns to accept, direct, and sublimate man's basic hostility that it can be turned from its disruptive and destructive course toward the enhancement of human happiness and security. In the words of Voltaire: "Nothing is so powerful as an idea whose time has come," and the time for unitary, cooperative action is at hand. The era of the group is here and let us hope that mankind will have the wisdom to employ it for the enhancement of man's security and happiness.

Unfortunately in recent years a number of short-cut theories and techniques which do not conform to the best practices of psychotherapy have found their way. While no one can claim to hold the final truth in any human endeavor, it is of utmost importance that we view all developments in our field critically and with the highest degree of scientific objectivity. We must be particularly on guard against the ambitious, self-seeking and self-promoting persons who because of their egotistic drives cannot but do much harm and injury to the thousands of patients who otherwise could be helped by various group techniques if properly suited to patients. It is incumbent upon us to be careful not to confuse issues and these practices. Group psychotherapy is a clinical practice requiring expert diagnosis and trained skill. The imposition of techniques that are really not group psychotherapy must be either avoided or employed with care and discrimination when so indicated by clinical considerations.

CHAPTER 4

DOLORES: THE PROTOTYPE
(1975)

There are those who date group psychotherapy from biblical days and some see group psychotherapy in the practices of the miracle men and shamans in primitive tribes. Bach and Illing attribute the origins of group psychotherapy to Germany, and more recent writers set it in the socioeconomic maelstrom of the twentieth century. Some have even attempted to correlate psychodrama and group psychotherapy. In recent years E. Mansel Pattison has attempted to establish the roots of group psychotherapy in the spread of the democratic principles in self-determination. A book published by a Russian psychiatrist, S. S. Libich, draws liberally from social psychology, the sciences and the philosophies of many countries through the Middle Ages, the Greek philosophers, and hundreds of writers in the last centuries to establish background for group psychotherapy.

The notions of sociologically-oriented interpreters of group psychotherapy, writing retrospectively, that it is a product of the weltanschaung of the times when it appeared may be considered intellectual rambling and a scientific irresponsibility. Following in the footsteps of Pattison, Helen Durkin, for example, writing on the "historical context" of group psychotherapy, states, "Slavson, who earned the title of 'father of group therapy' may be seen as the product of the war for democracy and its aftermath of economic distress and Marxian idealism which stirred the social conscience of many professionals." She further avers complimentarily that "the conclusion seems fair that it is talent, experience and determination of a man which makes him an effective spokesman and agent of his time."[1]

The latter statement is unquestionably applicable to all historical developments for it is the *mood* and *necessity* of the times that project individuals into sponsorship of an idea or social plan. But this applies to social growth generally and to its major essential components such as labor unionism, religion, and education. Such forces are not the causes of minor and subsidiary functions in society such as clinical practice, for example. These functions are affected, some more, some less, *within the primary elements* and fostered by "talent, experience, etc." of individuals.

My own work with groups dates back several decades before the events Dr. Durkin attributed to me. My lifelong compelling interest and love for children led me to organize groups of youngsters in a Brooklyn ghetto in 1911. One of these groups of ten-year-olds grew into the famous Self-Culture Club that continued meeting weekly all day Sunday and one or two evenings during the week until 1918, when I was compelled to terminate it due to my status as a conscientious objector to World War I. This group produced individuals like the noted artist Ben Shahn; Helen Tamaris, the nationally acclaimed modern dancer; former Columbia University Dean and visiting professor at Oxford University, Louis Hacker,[2] and his wife, a former Club member, who taught in one of the university's colleges; Max Gold, who collaborated with Trotsky in writing *The History of the Russian Revolution*; Joseph Freeman, poet and author of *An American Testament* (in which he extolled the influence of the Club and its leader upon his life) and other books; Lena Gurr, who initially acquired her interest in art in the Club, who, though continuing to teach in New York public schools, devoted her life to painting and held a number of noted one-woman shows. Finally, Dan Golenpaul, who originated the immensely popular program, *Information Please*, and later the widely read almanac of the same name, had drawn his inspiration from the Self-Culture Club, of which he had been a member for many years. By following the pattern

1. Durkin, H. (1974). Current problems in group psychotherapy in historical context. In *Group Therapy*. New York: Stratton Intercontinental Medical Books.

2. Fifty years after the termination of the club, Hacker wrote in a letter to my brother: "Some day I want to talk to you about your brother, who gave direction to my life when I was young."

of discussions in that organization, he became the only one who turned his experience into a vastly popular enterprise.

Other Club members entered the professions, and still others became labor leaders and one became a manager of the clothing manufacturers' association in New York. On the Lower East Side of New York, the city erected the Tanya Towers, an extensive residence for elderly men and women and needy deaf in honor of the woman whose surname is Tanya, who is still living, and who had devoted her life to help and instruct the deaf. She attributes the direction she has taken in life to her membership in the Self-Culture Club. Another former member of our group, a woman, directed a rehabilitation home for the blind for many years.

The principles underlying the work with this and other groups were based on free inquiry, open discussions, group interaction and decent human relations [51, 58]. The programs did not consist of intellectual activities alone. We listened together to music, some girls did interpretive dancing to the accompaniment of both classical music and poetry, readings of good literature, discussions of scientific and philosophical subjects, and attended as a group symphony concerts and modern dances performed by Isadora Duncan and groups of other dancers, arts and science museums, and held outdoor picnics. It is interesting to note that the relationships of the members in the Club led to six marriages among them.

When the Club members felt ready for dramatic presentations they chose on their own Gerhard Hauptman's *The Weavers* as their first production. (It is significant that this play, originated in Germany, was one of the forerunners of the workers' rebellion against the conditions of their lives.) The young people, without any professional assistance, planned the scenery, the staging, and the total presentation to which they charged an admission fee. The money earned was used to meet expenses of the art center. During the latter years we had an art studio in charge of a prominent artist one evening a week, for the growing youths who were inclined in that direction.

In no way did I attempt to indoctrinate the Club members toward any specific convictions or beliefs. Our aim was to expose them to life's possibilities and for themselves to find outlets for their energies and talents. The social events of the time were in no way involved in or influenced our work, though throughout those years I have clung to the socialist ideals and revolutionary thought and have spent much time in work for the labor movement and for impoverished tenants who were mercilessly exploited by greedy landlords. I was scrupulously careful not to impose my own convictions upon children and young people who, I believed, had an inherent right to find their own way in life under sensitive guidance.

When I was invited in 1918 to join the famous pioneer in progressive education, Walden School, I continued in my conviction of the need to free children to discover by themselves through Search and Discovery and by exposure to aesthetic and culturalizing interests and activities [50, 161, 167, 168, 175, 178].

When I turned to clinical practice in 1934, I continued to apply the basic principles described above which gave rise to Activity Group Therapy. Despite the recent claims that group psychotherapy had its roots in the emerging social turmoil of the times, I saw no direct connection between the social phenomena and clinical practice.

Activity Group Therapy had its origins in three distince areas: psychoanalysis, progressive education, and social groupwork in neighborhood centers in the ghettos of New York City early in this century.

The pattern of free acting out in Activity Group Therapy by a small group of latency children in a conditioned environment designed in 1934 had no social basis. It was intended (1) to afford satisfactions from *creative activity* to *individuals* through suitable supplies, implements and materials; (2) to fixate their libidos, thereby preventing hyperactivity that a group of disturbed youngsters would generate to their detriment; (3) to activate interpersonal interactions and group cohesion;[3] and (4) to evolve a sense of group belonging and friendly attitudes. Originally, the chief assumption that dominated our clinical work was rooted in the belief of inherent creativity of all people of all ages—in different forms and media, idiosyncratic to each individual— seldom appreciated or encouraged by parents, schools, and society generally. The creative urge, or the *drive to be the cause* [50, chap. 8], is particularly intense in all children. I was convinced from previous experiences in free progressive education and in neighborhood center

---

3. Group cohesion is an essential outcome of group therapy of children which is counterindicated in analytic group psychotherapy with adults.

groups that children with problems would automatically achieve improved self-identities, heightened self-confidence, as well as ego satisfactions from creative work, thereby normalizing their attitudes and conduct.

Of major importance was the interaction that inevitably ensues among youngsters in a climate of freedom and uninhibited, purposeful activity, which inevitably give rise to mutual helpfulness and cooperation among the members of a group. In addition, neglected capacities for constructive relationships and selective friendships (ego supports) are evoked which are unwittingly limited or suppressed in homes and schools. This was particularly important for the sixteen teenage girls first involved in the original experiment in 1934, who were reported to be profoundly socially maladjusted. Some were "lonely," others in irrevocable conflict with their families, at school, and in the community. Because of these considerations our project was originally called the "Therapeutics of Creative Activity." Also, because I have always viewed the periods at meals and retiring for the night the two significantly critical events in the lives of children (and to a lesser degree also in adults), we introduced simple group repasts as part of the sessions. This practice had no precedent in any therapeutic plan in vogue at that time and I was not surprised but much gratified at the salutary effect of this "social" experience in generating commonality and relationships.[4]

It was some time later, after viewing the products of the girls' manual work with arts and crafts in a small exhibit, that I concluded that activity alone could not have been responsible for the impressive improvements in the girls which their Big Sisters enthusiastically reported. After spending a full year analyzing the detailed weekly protocols from the two volunteer "workers" with groups (which we required from them for the weekly supervision sessions), I was able to identify eight "group dynamics" that produced the surprising results reported by the Big Sisters, who initially had reported "insurmountable" difficulties with them. Thus, our assumptions were confirmed.

---

4. Unfortunately, the idea of feeding patients was taken up by group therapists with adults and adolescents where it is strongly counterindicated. One of the tasks of the therapy of patients in these age categories is to help them overcome or to deal with their hostilities which they can do in negative transference with the therapist *in loco parentis* and other patients as sibling substitutes. This they cannot achieve with someone who feeds them, in this instance the therapist.

The idea of our plan for the treatment of the girls was, however, conceived many years before through a unique and very telling episode with a twelve-year-old pupil, Dolores, at the Walden School (on whose staff I was between the years of 1918 and 1927, when I was invited to join an experiment in the intellectual development of young children in Cambridge, England).

Dolores came to the Walden School from a public school where she had been held back for three years because of academic underachievement. She was tall, thin, scrawny, ungainly, with a pale, drawn face, sunken eyes, appearing exceedingly tense and sleepy all the time. She was lethargic and slow in responding when addressed or when asked a question and gave the general impression of being angry and intellectually dull, though there was probability that her intellect was about normal. She seemed terribly frightened and was inordinately withdrawn at the beginning, but as she became more secure in the friendly group in her class of thirteen boys and girls, she displayed her customary violent irascibility and disagreeableness that took the form of general negativism as well as verbal attacks against her fellow classmates. The latter, who came mostly from well-to-do homes and some from affluent environments, were abashed and puzzled by her conduct. Once, after some months, when Dolores was absent, the class decided to have a meeting about her and how to deal with her unpleasant and disturbing behavior. After a lengthy discussion, presided over by a member of the class (with no participation from the teacher), the group concluded that "Dolores must be very unhappy and we must be very nice to her."

After an investigation by the school psychologist, it was ascertained that Dolores' mother had completely rejected her. The mother was critical, and negated and denigrated Dolores in favor of a very beautiful and very charming younger sister. As a result of this continuous rejecting treatment, Dolores apparently became convinced of her worthlessness and lack of ability in any respect; hence, her backwardness in school. It is quite understandable that Dolores would be afraid, distrustful of people, and hostile toward her peers and teachers who had contact with her.

In the Walden School pupils were free individually and as a group to choose occupations and activities. Much creative writing of fiction and poetry was produced and many plays written and staged, almost of professional quality, by the pupils. However, the school, as progressive and liberal as it was, had to defer to the parents in the matters of the three R's and other basics. These were taught in a nonrepressive manner in keeping with the general spirit of the institution. One of my responsibilities (I was in charge of the "science laboratory," the variegated manual arts workshop, and consulted with all the classes whenever scientific and constructional needs arose) was to teach arithmetic to the class of which Dolores was a member. At that period of "educational liberalism," cards were distributed to children with numbers for addition, subtraction, multiplication, and division which were then returned to the teachers for correction. No grades were meted out anywhere in the school; all traces of competition or open evidences of failure or excellence were strictly eschewed. Promotion to higher classes was automatic.

Dolores usually turned in the most absurd answers to the arithmetic exercises. If she had to add 568 and 79, for example, 129 would be her answer. She neither completed nor attempted to correct her answers, but lethargically, as though sleep-walking, turned in her cards.

Although this transpired at a period long before my understanding of psychological problems, it was obvious to me that though she did not particularly possess mathematical brilliance and had been three years behind at public school to boot, she could not have been quite so dull as to arrive at such absurd results. I could not avoid the feeling that she was testing me to find out whether I would react to her as did all other adults in her past. I would accept her in a manner that I later characterized as "unconditional acceptance." My strategy was, therefore, to mark all her results with a "C" (correct) in red pencil. I kept doing it for some time until she finally began turning in correct answers.

One of the several important centers at the school which were open to the children in all grades on a free-choice basis was art, under the direction of an unusually gifted artist teacher with thorough psychoanalytic training, which I lacked at the time. She was able to understand the children's personalities and affect their problems through the medium of art. Another such center was a "research" science laboratory with a multitude of equipment, some on the level of high schools and colleges. However, a variety of scientific toys and materials were also supplied and devised to activate curiosity and play experimentation. We also had a "biology room" in which several types of small animals resided and which the children took care of and observed, studied and generally delighted in. There were also plants to be studied and cared for. The workshop contained numerous possibilities for woodwork, metalwork, printing with two real presses, type to be set and linoleum blocks to cut and print. Here, too, all kinds of investigatory projects were undertaken by the boys and girls. For example, one boy (who many years later became a psychiatrist) had independently evolved a method of printing multicolored reproductions of linoleum blocks done by fellow classmates. Linoleum block cutting was a popular occupation for the girls in the shop. Many of these products were of a very high quality, artistically, worthy of professional artists, and many of them were printed in multiple colors by the future psychiatrist who had gleefully discovered the process.

Dolores came to the workshop regularly and was enticed by linoleum block cutting. She also etched glass in the science laboratory by using the dangerous hydrofluoric acid, which she then colored by filling the grooves with different powdered colorings. It became quite obvious to me that her major interest was art. I therefore discussed her with the art person and suggested to her that she develop a relationship with Dolores to see what could be done for her in terms of exploiting her genuine creative talent which might enhance what I later called her "self-image."

Dolores did surprisingly well in oil painting, as she did also in applying rather original scientific materials for artistic ends·in the laboratory. Soon Dolores was the acknowledged outstanding artist in the school, though many other girls were gifted in painting and sculpture. We made it a point to display Dolores' productions all over the three connected buildings the school occupied so that she could see for herself how her works and talents were appreciated. As a result, her personality changed in time: sour disposition disappeared as did her facial pallor, her eyes grew clear and open, and her original lethargic mien changed considerably; her movements grew more purposeful and her behavior much more normal.

Dolores continued her close relationship with me throughout. One of the policies of the school inaugurated by the psychologist was that those children who displayed problems and who gravitated to a specific teacher should become his or her psychologic "wards" as it were. This consisted of intensifying the relation with the child, seeing parents on occasion, and visiting homes to "get a feel" of the climate in which the children were living. Dolores was therefore assigned to me among several other boys and girls.

I did not see these parents individually as was the case in some of the other families. Dolores' father was an enlightened man but subservient to his autocratic, self-centered wife, whose chief preoccupation (and problem) was social climbing. She seemed to me inaccessible by direct contact. However, appreciating the improvement in Dolores, for which the parents gave me credit, they had invited me on a number of occasions to visit their home and share meals with them. One Sunday when I visited the family, I walked into the living room and was startled by a very beautiful painting. Thinking that it was done by some renowned artist, I impulsively exclaimed, "Who painted this beautiful thing?" The mother gleefully volunteered, "This is *Dolores' painting,* Slavie. Don't you remember she made this frame in your shop?" Dolores was standing next to me as we viewed the painting. I put my arm around her shoulder and, with genuine affection, said, "Dolores, I guess you don't care very much about math any more, do you?" Her smiling, self-satisfied response was, "I don't give a damn." Though belatedly, Dolores had learned to smile!

I left for England in 1927, approximately three years after Dolores joined our school. Decades later, one of the teachers told me that Dolores had earned a scholarship to study art in Vienna. On her return, she had become an art teacher, was married and had two children.

In 1934, when I was faced with the troubled young girls at the Jewish Board of Guardians, who in many respects resembled my old friend Dolores, the memories of the earlier events led me to reproduce in the clinic what had worked so well with many pupils at Walden, and particularly with this one girl. Without being aware of it at the time, I have relied in my dealing with this seriously disturbed and extremely difficult girl upon procedures which decades later proved so effective with clinical patients and what came to be known as Activity Group Therapy. The dominant elements in Activity Group Therapy which later came to be known as "permissive environment," "unconditioned acceptance," "libido-binding" (through self-selected motoric and esthetic activity), "activity catharsis," "dynamic passivity" and "neutrality" (of the therapist), "improved self-image," "social mobility," etc., were present in my dealing with Dolores.

The "group codes" in the school and clinical settings, however, required specific modifications due to their differing objectives. The basic aims of a good *education*, as was the case at Walden School (as differentiated from schooling), were to free intellectual, esthetic, and social creative drives in addition to acquiring basic tools and knowledge essential in life of our culture. We also sought to sharpen curiosity in our pupils, develop individuality (as differentiated from individualism) and allocentricity instead of competition and self-service. On the behavioral dimension, the home and school are duty-bound to implant responsibility, self-control, and self-discipline essential for a full life and adequate social adjustment. Total permissiveness such as we employ in Activity Group Therapy would, therefore, be counterproductive in the ordinary course of education through the home and school. It is only when the treatment of, and demands on, the child have raised havoc with his emotional development that unbridled permissiveness and unconditioned acceptance can be employed as "medicine," as it were, in therapy. These counteract the virulent effects of a disturbed child's past when carefully selected and suitably grouped with other children with problems. In the instance of such children, therapy must seek to evolve channels for healthy object relations and inner controls which earlier life experiences failed to do. Parents and teachers cannot allow absolute permissiveness to the ordinary child without weakening his ego. Discipline, tactfully applied and sensitively dosaged to the child's age, capacities, and development levels beget ego strengths and wholesome identities.

In the creative segments of a school such as art, manual crafts, play and free experimentation, the nonassertiveness of "teachers" should approximate, but never completely be identical with the role of the therapist in Activity Group Therapy. Even in the freest educational processes, children need guidance and sometimes help and direction, not useful in the setting of Activity Group Therapy where they automatically evolve in the climate of the group itself (see [188]). Some demands have to be imposed on pupils to the ends of character training and social responsibility which are counterproductive in our group setting. Pupils must *learn* to be responsible for the tools and materials they use, by returning them to their assigned places (for the convenience of others who may need to use them later on), etc. This, too, occurs in Activity Group Therapy without the therapist's instructions or demands. Serious conflicts among children in the school setting that may lead to violence need attention of the adult in charge. All of these, and similar matters, are not imposed on patients in Activity Group Therapy who must *experience* the consequences of their acts and find for themselves means for dealing with such situations. These lend to ego strength, personality integration, and maturity. The overriding differences between education and the "corrective experiences" of therapy consist of these and other differentials.

CHAPTER 5

COMMON SOURCES OF ERROR AND CONFUSION
(1953)

I do not believe that there is cause for concern in the fact that there now exists so great a variety in the theory and practice of group psychotherapy. This sanguine attitude is not unfounded optimism, for a perusal of any intellectual endeavor, with no exception, reveals a similar history and the same state of affairs. "Honest men differ on all matters of importance," and it would be folly to think that we in group psychotherapy can escape a period of error and confusion before an authoritative body of knowledge emerges. I am fully aware of the danger of unfounded optimism, which has ever plagued mankind. History is replete with tragedy that could have been avoided were it not for the self-deceptive and reality-denying hopefulness and optimism of people and their leaders. Reality can be mastered by realistic means only.

It is therefore not with the motive of escape nor in an effort to deny that the above is said. It is rather the recognition of the fact that all human achievement, in whatever field, must be an emergent process and the result of the endeavors of many differing men. Error has always been the parent of truth, for it is only through the elimination of error that truth is uncovered. Mistakes ought not discourage us but rather spur us on to even greater activity toward uncovering more facts that would lead to a common base for practice and understanding. There are a number of efforts operating at the present time that contribute toward the eventual clarification of the issues involved and in the building of both a broad and a sound base for our work.

One cannot be unaware of the many obvious errors in the theory and practice of group psychotherapy now extant. But a study of this situation reveals that most misconceptions are the result of confusion as to clinical assumptions, patterns of practice, possibilities and limitations. One is also impressed with the fact that much of the confusion and error does not stem from group psychotherapy per se, but rather from inadequate clarity as to psychodynamics, the nature of psychopathology, and the processes of psychotherapy generally. Frequently—in the vast majority of instances—one discovers that misconceptions in the former actually stem from the unclarity as to what constitutes psychotherapy generally, how it occurs and how it is affected.

Truth can be begotten from error, but seldom, if ever, from confusion. Group psychotherapy cannot be held responsible for the confusion that exists in psychiatry and psychotherapy, from which it stems. In the opinion of the present writer, group psychotherapy is not (and probably never will be) an independent discipline. Its foundation is individual therapy, readapted to a specific situation, namely, the compresence of a number of patients. It is my aim in this article to point out some of the more common sources of error and confusion as they are reflected in practice and in the literature dealing with group psychotherapy.

Selection and Grouping

Clinical criteria. A true psychotherapeutic group presupposes the planful choice of patients and grouping of them on the basis of clinical diagnosis and on the known or assumed effect they may have upon one another. That our knowledge in this area is still in its initial stages is indisputable. But this fact does not eliminate it as an essential consideration to be applied and experimented with until it becomes more reliable, leading to definite criteria. The assumption that some practitioners make that *any* patients at all can be grouped together, or that all patients are suitable for group treatment, is a serious misconception as to what constitutes psychotherapy and what its essential process is. One of the common sources of error, therefore, is the prevalent misunderstanding of what a therapeutic group is in contrast to the ordinary social, recreational, or discussion group, and the assumption that a group is *ipso facto* therapeutically valid simply because its members are patients in treatment.

A perusal of the literature which is regularly abstracted and reviewed in the annual volumes of *Progress in Neurology and Psychiatry*[1] by this writer [82-90] and the basic paper by Giles W. Thomas[2] reveals a miasma of points of view and much variation in practice. One must confess a degree of disappointment because results are not always given or substantiated. There is still little awareness of the need for selection of patients in points of age, sex, and clinical diagnoses, and one finds that schizophrenics and manic-depressives are grouped with anxiety hysterias and other neuroses, with psychopaths, convulsives, and other neurological conditions as well as with other types of mentally and emotionally disturbed patients. One should expect very little in common among this variety of syndromes and pathology and therefore little that the patients can do for one another. It is also inevitable that anxiety neurotics would become even more anxious in the presence of psychotics and convulsive patients and that their basic trauma could not be worked through in the presence of others who cannot identify themselves with their special problems and experiences.

A few specific examples of the difficulties that can arise from improper selection and grouping may illustrate our thesis. In the course of my work I am frequently consulted by group psychotherapists on problems as they arise in their practice. On one occasion several psychiatrists pooled some of their patients to form a therapy group. They consulted me before the second session and I found that the criterion for selection of patients for the group they used was the fact that all the patients suffered from "anxiety." They did not, however, evaluate the source of the anxiety or the determining psychologic syndromes or pathology. They were guided by the *symptom* only. As a result anxiety neurotics, anxiety hysterics, hysterical personalities, and compulsive neurotics found themselves together, much to their own and the therapists' distress. When the group was reorganized on a more

1. Spiegel, E., (ed.) (1946-1952). *Progress in Neurology and Psychiatry*, vols. 1-7. New York: Grune & Stratton.

2. Thomas, Giles W. (1943). Group psychotherapy: reviews, abstracts, notes and correspondence. *Psychosomatic Medicine*, April.

clinically homogeneous basis, progress in the group and patients was immediately observed.

Another psychiatrist who attempted to treat a number of alcoholics by the group method got into a similar difficulty because he placed psychoneurotics together with patients having character disorders. When I called this to his attention, he separated the two groups of patients and reported a "startling change" in the nature of the interviews and in the results obtained.

Sex. Grouping of patients in relation to other factors such as sex is another area in which considerable divergence is found. Some therapists eschew mixing of sexes, while others claim that the presence of men and women is advantageous since they stimulate one another and reveal their attitudes toward the opposite sex. The presence of patients of the two sexes, it is claimed by some, supplies stimulation for father and mother and sister and brother transferences to be brought out, which patients in one-sex groups can do only in fantasy. Others, on the other hand, believe that patients in such groups inhibit one another because of their need to impress persons of the other sex. The men tend to build up their potency while the women exhibit their female characteristics and charm. This, according to some, blocks free association and catharsis and vitiates the therapeutic process. In some mixed groups, discussions of sex are overemphasized while in others the subject is shunned because of self-consciousness of the men and women. This is not the case to the same degree in one-sex groups. Inhibitions are not as likely to occur in such groups.

Another situation that is likely to arise from mixed groups of adults is the sexual attraction that patients may develop for one another and act out their impulses. Instances of this have been reported with varying frequency. Some cases of promiscuity were noted. This type of acting out can have serious consequences in terms of the progress and effectiveness of the therapeutic effort, for one must assume that it takes place before positive changes had occurred in the patients as a result of the group treatment. This acting out prevents the treatment from taking root, especially when it is not disclosed and discussed by the group. One group of therapists who encourage full social interrelation among their patients declare that no patients who would not otherwise be promiscuous would be so during the course of treatment. This seems like small consolation.

This situation must be viewed as part of the transference phenomenon. During certain stages the patients develop libidinal desires for the therapist as a parent substitute which for obvious reasons they cannot satisfy. They displace (or retransfer) them upon a fellow patient who may resemble either the natural parent or the newly evolved desirable parental image with which the patient invests the therapist. The activation of the libidinal drives and the proximity of an object for its gratification in the group favor the tendency to act out.

Age. Though not as commonly encountered, there is also some variation in practice in reference to the age range of patients. One group psychotherapist includes, in his mixed groups, persons with an age differential of thirty and more years. He allows parents and their grown children, and even grandparents, in his groups and encourages them to bring out their family difficulties at the sessions. It must be noted that these groups were not organized for parents and children only; they were open to all patients and if they happened to be a parent and offspring, inclusion in the groups was not denied them.

While there is no discussion to be found in the literature of either the question of mixed groups, age ranges, or parent-child patients in groups beyond what I have written on the first two topics, most group therapists adhere to a narrow age range among their patients and only few include parents and children.

Catharsis

Still another error that many psychotherapists make is to consider that communication by itself is therapeutic regardless of its free-associative nature, emotional regression, or concomitant affect. Some psychotherapists consider all communications therapeutically valid as long as their content is personal and generally proscribed. They do not give adequate consideration to whether the material is emotionally significant at the time and whether it is produced through a slow, regressive process in a transference relation; nor is sufficient attention given to the feelings accompanying statements. It is well known that ego tensions can be relieved by "unloading" guilt producing thoughts and memories and that as a result one can temporarily improve in function and adjustment. What is overlooked here is that the aim of psychotherapy is to establish a more adequate psychic balance which should result in a new emotional and intellectual orientation. This can be achieved through the therapeutic dynamics inherent in *all* psychotherapy.

The mistaken idea of *forced* confession stems from the misconception of what psychotherapy is. The fault lies with the lack of knowledge of generic psychotherapy rather than of that of its derivative, group psychotherapy. While patients in groups do tend to diminish resistance and remove restraint in each other by reducing superego demands through universalization, mutual support, and identification, there are limits where communication becomes of little value and even meaningless.

The literature reveals multitudinous devices and artifices employed by group therapists. "The gamut runs from the authoritarian approach of Low to the didactic and inspirational method of Pratt and his followers, the aesthetic activation of Altschuller, the use of drama by Moreno, the social-educational method of Bierer, and the group-analytical approach of Wender, to the psychoanalytic method of Schilder."[3] Many others have been added since the above was written.

To a great extent much of this confusion has been stimulated by army practices during World War II where many methods for relieving acute states of emotional disturbances were flounderingly employed. Patients presented, for the most part, acute and temporary disturbances and the therapeutic efforts were directed toward rehabilitating them as quickly as possible for further military service. Directed group discussions, visual aids, and inspirational methods have undoubtedly helped many soldiers to overcome emotional strain and to prevent serious mental disturbances, but there is no evidence that they permanently changed the patterning of their psychologic structure or function, which is the objective of good psychotherapy.

These methods, though effective in the setting of an army hospital with their limited aims, cannot but be misleading when transplanted into civilian psychiatry and psychotherapy, which was in fact the case. Patients in psychotherapy are for the most part not in acute stages of disturbance. They have lived with their problems for long periods and have grappled with them perhaps throughout their lives. The

---

3. *Progress in Neurology and Psychiatry*, vol. I, 1946, *loc. cit.*

difficulties do not arise from a specific threat or situation, such as the battlefield (though there are some cases of "situational neuroses"), but are rather a result of inadequate psychic reserves to deal with the total life situation. The need, therefore, is not to change attitudes or feelings in relation to a specific problem, as is the case in the armed forces, but rather to alter the equipment of the patient so that he can deal more adequately with his inner problems and, therefore, also with the demands of outer reality. When an individual finds himself in a quandary with respect to a specific problem, we may help him with it. This we refer to variously as counseling or guidance.[4] In psychotherapy, on the other hand, our focus is not to find another way to deal with a problem, but to equip the individual with the strength to deal with any difficulty, now and in the future, by reorganizing and reweighting the quantum of emotionality in the unconscious and establishing a balance in the functioning of id, ego, and superego. This difference in area or focus must, of necessity, alter the process along the lines indicated.

Role of the Therapist

The literature reveals also considerably varying points of view with regard to the role of the therapist. Some view his function as being very much like that of a teacher, in the belief that explanation (as differentiated from interpretation) of concepts, dynamics, and personal reactions has therapeutic (as differentiated from counseling and guidance) value. Others assume a passive role in the expectation that the patients in the group can carry the entire therapeutic burden and that through their interaction and interstimulation unravel and correct each others' unconscious. Still others follow the middle ground and, as in individual psychotherapy, participate in the group interviews or remain silent according to therapeutic indications or necessity. There are therapists who advocate so-called "leaderless groups," though the psychotherapist may be present. A number of group psychotherapists even encourage groups to meet in the absence of the therapist. Some psychotherapists conduct their groups alone while others share this

4. In his presidential address at the Twenty-ninth annual conference of the American Group Psychotherapy Association in 1972, Dr. Jay W. Fidler suggested the term *group psycheducation* for work of this category. See *International Journal of Group Psychotherapy* 23:287-305.

responsibility with another therapist. Usually the team consists of a male psychiatrist and a female caseworker, though in some instances both may be males, a psychiatrist and a psychologist, or both of the same specialty.

There is no unanimity as to what part the additional therapist is to play at the group sessions. In some instances the two play an equal role; in others, the junior of the team remains silent and nonparticipating or as a "participating observer," who is brought into the discussion by the senior member at specific points when he either does not wish to assert himself or when he feels threatened or uncertain. In one case the male analyst who treats groups of adolescents correlative to individual treatment always has a female therapist present and invites adult visitors. To them he turns on occasion for an expression of an opinion, as well as to his assistant, in situations where he does not wish to be involved or where his comment may be taken as being authoritarian. This strategy safeguards his analytic role of comparative neutrality and passivity.

There are psychotherapists who employ the additional person as an "observer." An observer's duties are to make either mental notes or to take them down in writing for the purpose of evaluating or analyzing the process in the group, the responses of the patients and the actions and comments of the therapist. Usually the therapist and the observer discuss and evaluate each session after its termination in order to determine both the correctness of the psychotherapist's function and comments as well as the trend in the group, and to plan future interviews on the basis of that trend.

As far as one can understand the intentions of having in the group such observers, auxiliary therapists, and co-therapists, they fall into two categories. One is the assumption that patients react more realistically and their oedipal conflicts are more easily activated by a family constellation which the presence of a male and female therapist creates. It is assumed that male and female patients in the group are activated to convey their unresolved oedipal feelings and bring out their hostilities to parental figures more easily in this setting where one therapist, of either sex, is present. The other reason one finds expressed, sometimes directly and at other times tacitly, is that the psychotherapist is diffident to face a group alone and needs the support and assurance of a person who, he knows, is on his side. Because the training and experience of psychotherapists is usually limited to work with individuals, a group is inevitably a source of anxiety and insecurity. This brings us to the subject of countertransference, which must remain unexplored here since it merits a fuller discussion [see 19].

Since the above was written, I have received the following from a correspondent who is a practicing group psychotherapist of long standing: "Since speaking to you about the pros and cons of a second therapist in a group, I have come to feel, like you do, that the disadvantages outweigh whatever stimulating and recording values might be obtained by this approach. I have, since February of this year, conducted my weekly therapy groups alone. It is my impression that this has resulted in the group being able to go deeper and work more intensively together. I would, therefore, like to use this occasion to thank you sincerely for your comments and suggestions."

Transference

The problem of transference being pertinent to our discussion here, we shall briefly turn our attention to it at this point and I would like to quote from my communication to a psychiatrist who was assisted in his work with groups by a female caseworker and who submitted to me, for my evaluation, the report on his work. I wrote to him in part:

"The question to which I wish to address myself in my comments grows out of your stated intention, namely, to describe the transference involved in your technique [using a male and female therapist simultaneously] . . .

"I am aware that some psychotherapists attempt, by doing this, to reproduce the family constellation in which the putative siblings can live out and act out their feelings toward their parents and others in the family constellations of their childhood. It seems to me that this setting rather favors *acting out* of feelings, which, I am convinced, retards the treatment process. In a recent discussion by members of the American Group Psychotherapy Association there was unanimity that acting out by adults is a form of resistance. This is contrary to acting out by children for whom it is true catharsis. Acting out is an effort on the part of adults to escape catharsis leading to traumata that arouse anxiety or guilt. By this I mean that instead of continuing, by free association, to regress to the traumatic anxiety and guilt-laden experiences, the patient acts out impulsively. This deflects him from free association. If we accept this assumption, we see how this is demonstrated in your manuscript. Because of the presence of the female therapist the men act out various emotions toward her as a woman, not necessarily as a mother. They use four-letter words and flirt with her. One of them acts out his hostility by being violent to his wife when the female therapist goes on vacation. He refuses to recognize his attitudes toward women generally which we can assume have their origin in his feelings toward his mother, and perhaps sisters.

"Some of the patients act out their feelings toward the male therapist as a father surrogate by denouncing him to the female therapist in his absence. This is an act of ingratiation and a desire to seduce her by conveying to her that they are more loyal to her than to the male therapist.

"These and similar developments I have described as 'induced regression' which occurs here through the presence of a male and female therapist. Feelings are *expressed* rather than *worked through*. Feelings toward women are brought out by male patients also where there is only a male therapist. It takes considerably longer to achieve it, but it is achieved through a slow, free-associative articulation of the stages in the emotional development of the individual so that he finally reaches the points of trauma. The presence of a woman, on the other hand, activates feelings much more quickly, but they do not affect the personality as deeply, since they have not been arrived at through the devolutionary process that I described.

"My third question would be: 'Do not some of these patients play one therapist against the other, as they had done in their own families as children?' Again their acting out here, in my opinion, is not as conducive to emotional growth as if they had come to recognize that they had played their parents against one another and analyzed it in the treatment interviews.

"My fourth question is: 'Is there no possibility for confusion in the libidinal reintegration these patients have in the therapeutic situation?' By supplying a male and female figure they can oscillate between them in *reality* rather than clarifying emotionally their projections of male-female images upon the person of the one therapist. When both are present, patients act out such feelings toward real people and thus continue in their ambivalent state.

"I do not doubt that the technique you describe produces much verbalization, and the preoccupations of the patients are quickly brought to the surface because the reality in the therapeutic setting so closely resembles their childhood-problem-producing environment. But the subjectum is, in my opinion, not as profoundly and as deeply involved as in the case when one therapist is present and no acting out toward a *real* person is possible. . . .

"As I look down the pages I see the following: 'This episode also produced *different* [italics mine] reactions to the fantasied role that the female therapist played in response to the outbursts.' This, in my opinion, confirms the idea that the presence of two therapists confuses the members of the group."

Anonymity

The question of anonymity of patients in therapy groups has been brought forward in a paper presented at a recent conference of the American Group Psychotherapy Association which stimulated considerable discussion. The question of whether there is any disadvantage in patients having extrasessional contacts with one another individually (or in groups) was not viewed with any degree of unanimity as well. Evidence was presented in that paper based on actual events to show that socialization outside the group had serious negative effects.[5] Psychotherapists whose groups meet in their absence and whose patients have, therefore, easy access to one another, have not reported similar undesirable consequences. A number have indicated that while their patients are not encouraged to see one another individually, their groups frequently gather after sessions for a snack at which time, the therapists knew, the discussions of the official sessions are continued. These include also the evaluation of the therapists' personalities, behavior, skill, and effectiveness. One stated that he does not prohibit his patients to fraternize, but they are *directed* to report to the group the nature and conduct at these contacts at the next session.

5. Lindt, H. and Sherman, Max A. (1952). " 'Social incognito' in analytically oriented group psychotherapy," *International Journal of Group Psychotherapy* 2:209-220.

One discussant made the point that outside relationships among patients are a part of reality testing. The patients' interactions and friendships can be considered as an integral part of the treatment effort, since testing themselves in various relations is a part of emotional maturity. This argument can be countered with the fact that patients may not be sufficiently improved at a given time to utilize this reality constructively. Before they had become free of the traumatic memories and unwholesome attitudes, the patients may act out their problems with one another with undesirable results. This situation is somewhat akin to that of acting out among patients of different sexes.

The problem of anonymity in therapy groups requires a great deal of consideration, for acting out in the absence of the therapist and the group usually prolongs and intensifies problems. When patients act out one against the other during the interviews, it is treated as a form of regressive behavior or as resistance, and is interpreted as such. The interpretation and resulting insight aid personality maturity. When acting out by patients with or against each other occurs elsewhere, it serves only to prolong and possibly even to further entrench the problem. Just what the therapist can do to preserve anonymity among his patients is an uncharted area. One suspects, however, that unless it is in some direct or indirect way encouraged by the therapist few patients tend to carry over relationships from the group. At least this was my experience and that of a number of my associates. There exists among patients a degree of reserve in relation to one another; in fact one suspects that there is a degree of antagonism toward one another, as sibling substitutes.

The problem of anonymity also arises in small communities where patients may encounter each another in their daily lives. The revelations in the interviews may be embarrassing to them and one can expect that they would withhold intimate facts of their lives and thus prevent free association and catharsis. Difficulties in this area also arise from cultural mores and religious sanctions. This subject requires further elaboration that would at this point take us too far afield.

Uses of Group Psychotherapy

Differences also exist with regard to the use to which group psychotherapy is put in the scheme of treatment. The use made of groups can be classified as *exclusive, preparatory, correlative,* and *tapering off.* Some psychotherapists believe that groups can be employed as the sole treatment of all, or nearly all, adult patients as well as children. In some instances, group psychotherapy of varying periods precedes assignment to individual treatment while in other cases patients are offered individual treatment initially before they are placed in groups. In the correlative plan, patients are exposed to both group and individual therapy, usually by the same therapist, but sometimes by different therapists. This plan, it is believed, is effective because patients are stimulated through the group toward better productivity in individual interviews, and they also bring forward, in the group, matters which they are unable or unwilling to present when alone with the psychotherapist. Resistances seem to dissolve more readily in the group situation which accelerates catharsis and aids the treatment process. On the other hand, the group serves, it is claimed, as a reality situation in which the patient finds reflected his own difficulties and which also activates his intrapsychic problems such as anxieties, fears, hostilities, oedipal, sibling, and other transference feelings. The patient can then deal with them in individual sessions which furnishes productive therapeutic material. However, one psychiatrist believes that parallel individual interviews vitiate the group treatment.

In tapering-off groups, the essential therapy is accomplished through individual treatment. Group sessions are employed as a testing ground of patients' readiness and ability to deal with a group situation and the frequently strenuous and threatening emotional network with which a group always presents one. The number of tapering-off sessions varies. Some expose their patients to this experience for as little as six sessions; others require them to attend a group for comparatively long periods. Tapering-off groups are usually, though not always, conducted.by the therapist who has had the patient in individual treatment. When another therapist conducts these groups, or the correlative groups, frequent exchanges of information and impressions between the two therapists is the rule. These are part of the routine which aids them both in better utilization of the patients' communications in the interviews and the sounder consolidation of the treatment effort.

"Depth" of Therapy

"Depth" of therapy as a concept and a term is the subject of intense controversy. This controversy is not limited to group psychotherapy. It has been a topic of opposing views for many years and stems from individual psychotherapy and psychoanalysis. It is not, therefore, the concern of the group therapist alone, but of all those who are engaged in the field of mental treatment. There are those who reject the concept of "depth" in treatment. Their position is that treatment is carried on in accordance with the needs of the patient and that what is superficial therapy for one is deep treatment for another. The concept of "depth" is not absolute; rather it is relative and conditioned by the specific circumstances and indications for a specific patient. Contrariwise, the opponents of this thesis view depth in psychotherapy as an absolute value that implies the degree of regression, the extent of recall from memory of traumata and the intensity of affect stimulated. To them depth of therapy connotes the involvement of the sexual libido, of deeply repressed memories and defensive ego mechanisms, the effect of which is freeing the individual from the throes of inhibiting and limiting states of mind. It also means to them that the psychic economy of the patient is reorganized so that the id, ego, and superego function more harmoniously toward a more efficient and more satisfying set of adaptive patterns and responses.

Even the latter can be achieved to different degrees of intensity and levels of depth. Most psychotherapists differentiate the depth in personality changes in psychoanalysis and in the less thoroughgoing psychotherapies, of which there are now quite a number. These psychotherapies also aim at improvement in attitudes, in adjustment, and in function. Some affect "symptom improvement" only, that is, the elimination of the symptom without basic changes in the personality organization or the relation of the intrapsychic forces and dynamics. Unfortunately there are no devices for measuring alterations in the psyche; nor are there determinants as to the possibility in change in function and attitudes without some basic changes in personality structure. Some tend to wonder whether "symptom improvement" is possible without some improvement in the psyche that used the symptom as a defense, as a channel for discharging energies, or as a means for resolving inner conflicts. We have not yet established quantitatively the validity of dealing, in psychotherapy, with the "representative in consciousness" of the intrapsychic conflict rather than the deep-rooted conflict itself [57]. Even though observation points to an affirmative answer, it is unknown whether improvements are lasting or permanent.

The answers to these important questions are still to be derived and upon them depends much of our current practive in the field. Group psychotherapists need not feel that finding these answers is their special responsibility. They are rather generic problems of psychotherapy with which psychiatry will have to wrestle in the future. One cannot take too seriously assertions like "group psychotherapy is more psychoanalytical than psychoanalysis" from whatever source they may come. Nor can the claim that nothing that can be achieved by individual psychotherapy cannot be achieved by group psychotherapy. Such claims which appear at the present state of development as extravagant must await confirmation. Until tools for comparison are at hand, such comparison cannot be considered valid.

The terms "guidance" and "counseling" are frequently employed to describe work, both individually and in groups, where minimal results are sought and only specific problems are to be resolved. Clinical diagnoses are not employed in this work, since the intention is to focus on some specific conflict situation or situational stress which the individual is unable to resolve or solve by himself. The discussions in these groups are canalized toward specific situations rather than toward unraveling inner confusions, or toward changing conditioning and removing emotional cathexes. In practice such palliatives are very helpful to a great many people who are frightened and feel lost in the face of their difficulties.

A major source of confusion in discussions of group psychotherapy, and psychotherapy in general, stems from this very source. No sharp demarcation has as yet been established between psychotherapy and other techniques of helping people in trouble who cannot or are not ready to submit to a more or less radical change within themselves. One is under the distinct and well-founded impression that much of the work that is described as group psychotherapy is actually group guidance or the less "deep" group counseling. One also gains the impression that a good part of the confusion in the communications from group psychotherapists, their inability to find common ground or to understand one another fully, lies in this fact. Only in unanimity as to what constitutes psychotherapy as differentiated from schooling, education, counseling, and guidance will this confusion be unraveled.

In fact, so indistinct is the understanding of the term that recreational activities are considered psychotherapy. Thus the literature describes playing in a band, group reading, singing, hand clapping, ballroom dancing and parties as group psychotherapy. Included in this category are also automobile repairing, lectures, movies, slides, and various classroom work. These and similar occupations are "therapeutic"; that is, they are helpful in various ways and for different reasons in keeping patients less unhappy and occupied with and more aware of reality. However, they do not constitute psychotherapy, as it is defined here. Perhaps the cause of this confusion of terms arises from the fact that to be helpful and effective, activities with patients have to be carried out by leaders and directors with some knowledge of psychiatry and under the supervision of psychiatrists and other qualified psychotherapists. This fact alone may not, however, place the activities in the category of psychotherapy.

Open vs. Closed Groups

Another question about which considerable variance exists in practice and in theory is that of the open, or continuous, as against the closed group. In open or continuous groups patients are introduced during the process of treatment, whereas in closed groups patients are assigned to groups simultaneously and no new members are allowed to join the group during its existence.

Some therapists believe that for a number of reasons the addition of patients interferes with those who have been in treatment for some time. One of these is the fact that they are further advanced in the therapeutic level and the inevitable need to repeat some of the problems and ideas with which the older patients have already dealt is annoying to them. On the other hand, not to go over this material with the new entrants deprives the latter of the therapeutic benefits that would accrue from it. In addition, there is the question of sibling rivalry which arises here and the inevitable hostility activated toward the newcomers. Frequently, almost universally, the new members are exposed to aggression by the former members which creates tensions in them. Of course, this situation can be used as part of the therapeutic process by leading the members to understand these reactions which are in major respects the same as those to newborn siblings. However, there are those who find that this interference with the movement in the group is undesirable, because it creates embarrassment to the newcomers and to the older members and frequently retards the flow of therapy.

On the other hand there are those who believe that this very situation presents the group and the members in it with a realistic setting which is a replica of their childhood reactions. This is beneficial as a part of the therapeutic process and especially for reality testing. Psychotherapists have found that closing cases during the group's life also creates difficulties. The patients in the group seem to go through a brief period of "mourning" for the departed patients and refer to them in the interviews after such departure. Of course, this situation, as well, can be used in the therapeutic grist since life seems to consist of a series of separations which to the child are always threatening and seem even catastrophic. Hence, the separation of a patient who had become emotionally integrated into the group (family) Gestalt does present the others with an emotional problem which is useful to discuss, evaluate and interpret.

Despite some of these advantages, I believe that new patients should not be introduced into groups after the preliminary period during which time there has been a working through of some of the basic attitudes and transferences among the members of the group. Adding new patients in the early stages of the life of the group is permissible.

Visitors

Still another practice in which considerable difference exists is that of visitors to groups. It would seem that the largest number of group psychotherapists do not favor visitors during the group sessions. However, there are others who permit visitors indiscriminately. Opinions in this area would not be too valuable. Rather, a definitive study of the meanings of visitors and patients' reactions to them would be of immense value. One author reported on the fantasies of three different patients in a group to the presence of a female visitor that "all women belong to the therapist (father)." This is in conformity with Freud's original conception of the primal horde in which all women belong to the father, which led to killing the father and resulting guilt feelings.

However, the disadvantage of the presence of such a visitor lies in the fact that it would require intensive and psychoanalytic delving into the individual and tribal unconscious to bring out this fact in the patients. Ordinarily the patients in group psychotherapy are not led to such profound uncovering of the primitive unconscious. But the result is that considerable hostility is generated toward the therapist which would be difficult, if not impossible, to explore and interpret during the treatment situation. One therapist who employs groups in treating adolescents encourages visitors to his groups and it has been reported to me that the youngsters seriously resent this. In fact, a friend of one of the patients in the group told her mother that "Dr. ——— could not be a good therapist. He allows visitors to come to the group." Apparently, at least one of the patients complained to her friend concerning this. In a group of adults which had a male therapist and an auxiliary female therapist, where a woman visitor was present, a male patient exclaimed: "It isn't enough that we have to put up with a woman as a leader, they have to annoy us by sending other women to our meetings!"

My own experience as a visitor to two different groups of mixed nonpsychotic men and women proved very unpleasant, both for the patients and for myself. I attended these groups at the invitation of the therapists in a clinic other than my own where I have never "visited" groups. In one group I was attacked as being indifferent to what was going on (because I apparently maintained a poker face). In the other group I was accused of being "a spy."

No material has come to my attention so far in which beneficial effects from the presence of visitors has been reported. The question of permitting visitors in groups requires further observation and perhaps planful investigation.

Ordinary vs. Therapy Groups

Commonness vs. sameness of aims. Among the most common sources of error in interpretation of the process in therapy groups is the tendency to apply to them the dynamics of ordinary social, political, or recreational groups. The natural group which gathers because of interest or social homogeneity is in every respect different from that of the planned or *structured* group with a therapeutic aim. In the first, grouping occurs spontaneously because of a *common interest* and the members carry out a defined aim or set of aims. To achieve this, the group, which is a deliberative one, adopts *means* for carrying out the common objective and the defined aim. The major procedure (in a democratic group) is free discussion by the members under the direction and guidance of a leader or "central person" (Redl). There is direct interaction among the participants arising from differences of opinion, differences in emphasis, attempts at exerting suasion to change the views of fellow members, submission of some of the members and domination by others, and finally *compromise* and to varying degrees of *unanimity.* In the social groups there exists also the *expectation of pleasure* in each other's presence, the sharing and enjoyment of reciprocal good will and friendship.

As we analyze the parallel elements in a therapy group we see quite a different picture. The group is not a spontaneous phenomenon. It is *planned* and the members are *selected* and assigned by a psychotherapist. The group does not come into existence, rather it is organized and structured. The members in it do not have a common aim; they all have the *same* aim, but not a *common* aim. The aim is a personal one in each of the members, namely, to rid himself of his difficulties, that is, improving or being cured. Despite the fact of this similarity or sameness, the objective is entirely an individual one. It is not common to the group as such but rather particular to each patient, even though it is the same.

"Common" and "same" are sometimes confounded and frequently used synonymously. This closeness in meaning has given rise to confusion in interpretation, though the difference is of utmost importance for sound psychotherapy. If a therapist views his group as his therapeutic object rather than each patient in it, much can go wrong. The therapist must be ever aware of each one of the members of his group, the psychologic effect the interviews have on him, the changes that occur in him, and plan steps in treatment that will benefit each patient.

Not having common aims, there is therefore no planning in a therapy group as to means for carrying them out and the discussions are not aimed at reaching a compromise. Rather the incentive for conversation stems from the suffering of each member. When a patient initiates one, he does not do so for the purpose of clarification of ideas, objectives, or means, but rather with a conscious or unconscious view to alleviating his discomfort. While there are domination and submission trends here—as there are in all situations where people are actively participating—they are not accepted as desirable phenomena in group formation and action. They are rather considered undesirable traits in the patients, the elimination of which is one of the objectives of psychotherapy. Since they are not *action groups*, psychotherapeutic groups do not work toward compromise or unanimity. Rather the communications are part of the process by which inner confusion and tensions are ultimately affected through the reorganization of psychic energies.[6]

Contrasts in dynamics. Many dynamics of interaction observed in ordinary groups never find their way into therapeutic groups, while those that are common to both as a result of the compresence of people assume different form and serve different ends. The dynamic of induction, for example, operates at a high rate of intensity in these groups because of the high degree of susceptibility and empathy due to the similarity of the psychologic syndromes in the patients. Infection, on the other hand, is probably less likely to occur because of the greater narcissism among the patients than in the average population. Intensification of emotions can be expected here at a much higher rate while neutralization on a lesser scale than in ordinary groups. However, the chief factor that differentiates therapeutic from ordinary groups is the retention of each member's individuality and the resulting low rate of so-called "group interaction," and the complete difference in aims.

6. For a fuller discussion of the various types of groups, see (61, pp. 71-94).

Group membership. Only a brief word can be said here about the difference in the personnel or constituency of the two types of groups. In ordinary groups the members are representative of the general population. This means that among them are persons with adequate ego and superego development for function in a group and in social relations. They possess sufficient frustration tolerance to inhibit their impulses and self-indulgent cravings which are in a condition acceptable and assimilable by the group. While anxieties and tensions are always present to a degree, the ego can deal with them adequately and they are under the control of the ego; that is, they are *ego-syntonic* rather than *ego-alien*. As a result of this *comparative* balance and health in its members, the group has a "collective superego," a "we" feeling that makes constructive action possible. This inherent health produces an equally healthy "group ego" for mobilizing power and carrying out the group's intention, that is, a "let's do it" attitude.

It is inevitable that all groups have disturbed and even pathological individuals among them. But the basic health of the group, as a derivative of the health of the majority of its constituents, can absorb them. By this is meant that the influence of the small number of disturbed members neither distorts the "group superego" nor weakens the group's power for action, or its "ego." These crippling results occur when the pathoplastic forces are greater than the healthy portion of the group can resist or assimilate; then the group goes off its constructive course and soon disintegrates. This occurs when the number of emotionally disturbed or pathologic members is large or when the leading or central persons, though small in number, are both disturbed and assertive. All groups are disturbed when the destructive forces overbalance the constructive forces. Under such circumstances the group can (1) either change its course to a destructive one, (2) continue in a state of conflict, turmoil and strife among subgroups or cliques, or (3) disintegrate. There is conflict between constructive and destructive forces in all groups. All groups contain hostile and aggressive members and this is, up to a point, understandable, for healthy groups, like healthy families, must provide for discharge of hostility and aggression. It is only when the quantum exceeds the group's capacity to absorb it that this becomes destructive. We should note in passing that the limit in the capacity for absorbing hostility and pathology is *specific* to each group and depends on a number of factors which we shall not attempt to describe here.

The situation is vastly different in this regard in therapy groups. The members in these groups all have, to varying degrees, defective ego and superego organization. Their anxieties and tensions are intense;their frustration tolerance low, and their hostilities are near the surface and readily acted out. Fear, diffidence, and withdrawal mark some of the members; other are openly aggressive, rivalrous, quarrelsome, assertive, domineering. The patterns of displacement and projection are dominant on the one hand, while on the other, there is overintense identification and empathy. There is little or no "we" feeling and no incentive for "group action."

Many of the pathologic trends in the individual tend to be intensified. Unless they have some well-integrated persons in their midst, groups like these can become seriously pathogenic, a fact that is attested to by the violent behavior and riots in mental institutions, prisons and reform schools, and the difficulties in management of therapy groups in private and agency settings. Therapy groups in a clinical setting frequently become deteriorated, therapeutically speaking, if their members act out their difficulties. To a very large degree the therapist acts as the "group's superego" and "ego" at least in its early stages. As the patients become emotionally more integrated and their psychic forces better organized, inner controls emerge as a result of healthier collective responses.

Leader vs. therapist. We see even from this brief delineation how vastly the forces in ordinary groups in a democratic society differ when compared with those of therapy groups. This oppositeness is also operative in the function of the "leader" and his relation to the group members. In ordinary groups the leader, whether professional or indigenous, is the central person who represents and personifies the needs and aims of the group. Thus a special interest club such as golfing would have for a leader one who is proficient in the game. A scientific body chooses the most productive or the most prominent person in the field. A religious society elevates to leadership the most pious, though a practical man may become director of its fiscal affairs, while the toughest and the most violent become dominant in a gang. The leader's personality and functions are in the service of the common aims and ideals of the members constituting it. To him are assigned, or he relegates to himself, special duties and responsibilities which he is expected to discharge to the advantage and satisfaction of all or most of the members. Failing in this, he is deposed and another is chosen in his place.

Leaders in such groups can be authoritative or democratic, though in some specific and rare instances they can assume a laissez faire role. The latter is so uncommon, since it can occur only in an educational group and never in a planning or action group, that we shall omit it from our discussion. Whether the leader or central person intends it or not, he sets the stage and determines the course and quality of action. In a democratic group he reflects the *will* of the members and sets the pace and pattern of the group. He is the center around whom the group is integrated in a unified and single-purpose entity. The emotional and conative forces of each member radiate toward him rather than toward other members of the group. He is, therefore, the recipient of both conscious and symbolic projections much as a father is in a family. Since the members are individuals, the leader supplies the cementing factor producing unitary and integrative possibilities. He receives their common and several attitudes and is the single unifying symbol among them. He is the one who both integrates the psychic forces of the group members and gives them direction and expression.

This picture is quite different from a therapy group which is neither an action nor a planning group, and since it does not engage in planned, orderly discussion, it requires neither formality nor direction from a special leader. The objective being the unraveling of each person's problems through free association rather than logical, focused discussion, need for "leadership," as described, does not exist. The propelling force here is not an external objective, aim, or interest, but rather the inner necessity arising from discomfort and suffering that serves as the motive power. As already indicated, patients come to the group not to accomplish an objective aim, but to rid themselves of their conflicts and tensions which they perceive as "unhappiness" and suffering.

This situation greatly alters the leader's (therapist's) role. Without going too far into the dynamics of psychotherapy, one can say that the therapist is one who permits expression of hitherto prohibited thoughts and strivings; he is the recipient of love and hate characteristic of transference, represents a parental figure with whom each patient can establish a new and satisfying parent-child relation, the person who both allays and prevents fear and guilt, and he reintegrates inner and outer reality in a new light and with a new emphasis. The symbolic significance of the psychotherapist in a group is that he is a parent substitute on whom the sexual and hostile wishes which the patients had felt toward their parents can be projected and displaced. He is also the person who, while not punishing, will protect the patients from each other's rivalry feelings, anger, and wrath. At the same time he is the person against whom the group can unite in common hostility as a parent substitute. The therapist does not aim to "unify" the group toward a "common purpose" and "activate" them for "group action." His role, function, symbolic meaning and aim are different in every respect from those of a leader in a social or action group.

Intermember relations. A similar contrast in relationship exists also among the individual members of the group to each other. The ordinary group, for example, cannot tolerate the expression and acting out of sibling hostility to the degree that it occurs in therapy groups; nor can it survive the direct expression of the content of the members' unconscious. Matters that are brought to surface in a therapy group *must* be withheld in an ordinary group if it is to survive. The sexual attractions and antipathies inevitably brought out in these groups openly would prove ruinous to other types of groups where intense feelings must be held in abeyance or be subordinated to group aims. Ordinary groups can exist only when morale and unity exist. Without these they disintegrate. This is not the case with psychotherapeutic groups. Here the conscious and unconscious, positive and negative feelings must be laid open and the chips let fly where they may. Considerateness and fear of offending are at a minimum and at times nonexistent. It is this complete emotional abandon or free-associative regression that is the woof and warp of the psychotherapeutic process. Obviously it cannot be permitted in other groups where mutual respect and consideration are prime requirements and where limits must be imposed to the laying bare of one's instinctive impulses and desires. Spontaneity must be controlled or denied.

Group fixity vs. group mobility. Another important dynamic that differentiates the two types of groups is the comparative rigidity of status and relationships of leader and member and among the members themselves. Wherever there is association among men there must be organization. Nothing can be accomplished by a group without some planning, rudimentary though it may be. In such plans function and status are unavoidably assigned or assumed by members that serve in the achievement of the group's objectives. The nature and quality of this organization will, of course, vary with the nature and purpose of the group. However, in all cases, the status of members is more or less definitely fixed and in some instances castes or gradations arise. The latter development is more evident in large organizations, but it exists in less observable forms in all formal and informal groups. I have described this phenomenon before and have designated it as *group fixity.*

When we view therapeutic groups from this vantage point, on the other hand, we find such fixity does not occur here, nor can it be permitted when it does. Patients do assume certain roles, or better still, relations toward other members of the group on a transference basis, but these are self-assumed and not assigned. They are also temporary because as the patient changes, his relations with the other members of the group and with the psychotherapist inevitably change, too. During the group interviews there arise leaders and followers according to the content at a particular time. Thus, when a subject or situation is discussed, a patient who had been hitherto quiet becomes assertive. These and other similar developments give rise in the group to a process which I have characterized as *group mobility.* Group mobility is a characteristic of all democratic free-associative groups, but in them the mobility is limited and predetermined by the common group aim and is quite different in its nature than it is in therapy groups.

Children's vs. Adult Groups

As one leaves the subject of the dynamic processes in search of other matters that need clarification, one is impressed with the fact that there is inadequate differentiation between group treatment of prepubertal and postpubertal patients. The differences, contrasts and contradictions of these two chronologically diverse patients are as obvious as they are important [56, 57].

The contrasts in the superego and ego structures of these two categories of patients are so vast that what applies to one cannot be applied to the other. The child still derives much of his ego strength from the adults about him. His superego is unformed and criteria of right and wrong are set for him by these adults. He is still in the throes of the id, and the pleasure drives are less under control at this age than later in life. His identifications and therefore also his character are fluid and changeable. The ego defenses are only in the process of formation and are still to be organized into a definite pattern and function. These and other conditions of the child make his personality flexible and malleable and when appropriate means are used, he is more easily accessible to corrective measures than adolescents or adults.

The child's unconscious, not having sustained prolonged repression and less subject to defensive measures of the ego, is in greater proximity to the conscious. The child is also less "self-conscious" because of the state of his superego; communication, when appropriate channels are provided, is easy, and resistances are less powerful. Another basic fact that must be taken into consideration is that a child's means of communication are more through action and less through language. The powers of conceptualization and verbal language are in a lower state of development as compared with those of adults. More frequently than we suspect conflict among children and adults stems from their inability to understand each other. A man I knew was impressed when his little girl told him: "I try to be good, but I can't." What she actually meant was: "I try to be good in a way you want me to be good, but being a child, not an adult, I cannot live up to adult standards." Such misunderstanding in our communication with children is not infrequently a source of much unhappiness for both them and the adults, and later for the children when they grow into adulthood.

The language barrier between children and adults makes our work in education and therapy very difficult and greatly reduces their effectiveness. Active education and play therapy are an important outgrowth of this recognition. The language of the child is action and not words and those who deal with children, and this includes nearly all of us, must learn to understand the *language of behavior* and respond to it appropriately. It is for this reason that in my work with children I found it necessary to devise group techniques in which action is the child's means of communication of his difficulties. Activity Group Therapy, Play Group Therapy and Activity-Interview Group Therapy intended for children of different ages and clinical categories have this one thing in common: the catharsis occurs either entirely or partially through acting out.

Once the character of children is contrasted with that of postpubertal persons, especially adults, it becomes cleaɪ that we cannot speak of group psychotherapy for children and adults in the same breath. The basic and deeply affecting differences in the personalities of the two make therapies appropriate to each of them a categorical imperative, not only as far as practice is concerned, but also in theory and interpretation. One cannot escape an awareness, however, that adults who become patients retain to varying degrees many of the characteristics attributed to childhood. Nonetheless the process of living itself establishes even in such adults certain states in the ego and superego that are distinctly different from those of a child. An adult who retains an infantile psychic structure is psychotic.

Groups for Psychotic and Nonpsychotic Adults

This brings us to another area that requires clarification. In the literature on group psychotherapy, one frequently encounters reports of practices with psychotic patients without reference to the fact that these patients fall within that special category. Principles are applied and deductions made without an awareness or emphasis, at least, that what is suitable for psychotics does not necessarily apply to nonpsychotics. A large number of articles have been published on experiences with psychotics in and out of mental hospitals in which are defended practices and theoretic formulations as though they were applicable to the general field of group psychotherapy. There seems to be little reflected in these papers of the fundamental difference in the therapeutic needs of these two types of patients. This situation has produced no end of misunderstanding. Conference audiences who do not keep in mind this basic differentiation are baffled by the divergence and differences of techniques, aims, and principles. While there are other sources of confusion, some of which I have attempted to indicate here, this is one of the most serious.

No one disagrees that the personality structure of psychotic adults differs greatly from that of the nonpsychotic. The ego development of the former is particularly defective and his perception of reality is different from other types of patients. While there is variation in the id urges and superego development, the ego and sense of reality are qualitatively, and not only quantitatively, damaged. In the neurotic or character disordered patient the ego may be defective, but this is a quantitative defect. The ego may distort reality as a defensive measure. It may even deny certain aspects of reality that are too painful for it to face. The psychotic ego on the other hand retreats from reality and creates an illusory world of its own. Thus the capacity for reality testing may be very limited or nonexistent.

This situation obviously presents the therapist with a different task. The problem here is not redistribution and balancing of the psychic forces, but rather activating these forces in some and bringing them under control in others. The objective here has many points in common with the education of the normal child. In the child the sense of reality perception and ego strength, as judged by the adult standards, bring him into conflict with the world. Similarly, the narcissistic retreat into the self unfits the psychotic for living in a world patterned by and for the average person. Treatment of psychotics, therefore, consists of developing of the ego so that its reality testing powers are increased, as is also the case in work with normal children. This is accomplished largely by identification with the therapist's ego and by dealing with reality of progressively increased complexity and demand. I have elsewhere applied to such a conditioned reality the term "graded reality" which is also the essence of childhood education, and education generally. It is because of this awareness that patients are transferred from rigidly controlled wards to less supervised, and later to open wards. This is followed by temporary or occasional parole and finally by full parole and release from the hospital. Here the reality with which the patient has to cope is *graded* in complexity.

When we view psychotherapy with psychotics in the light of this knowledge, the suitability of educational and didactic methods becomes clear, though their effectiveness with nonpsychotics is questionable. Occupational and recreational activities, classroom teaching, didactic lectures, music and group discussions are thus appropriate techniques in group treatment of patients in regressive stages such as psychotics present. Their validity with patients whose "sanity" is intact, but who are emotionally disturbed would be very difficult to defend beyond the fact that some of them may serve as a field for reality testing. The ego deviations and the other intrapsychic disturbances, however, have to be corrected by other therapeutic measures.

The omission of a definitive differentiation between the psychodynamics, pathology, and the therapeutic needs of psychotic and nonpsychotic patients has caused more confusion than any other one factor. Writers will do well and help the growing profession of group psychotherapy if they define the field of their work, whether it is with psychotic or nonpsychotic patients, and clearly indicate the extent to which their formulations apply to each. Such a definitive approach would indeed be of great help.

CHAPTER 6

CRITERIA FOR SELECTION AND
REJECTION OF PATIENTS
(1955)

The Importance of Specificity

Every type of psychotherapy is self-selective, and the therapist's greatest skill and keenest judgment is required to choose for each patient the type of treatment most suitable for him. Conversely, the selection of suitable patients for the type of therapy one employs calls upon an equal degree of knowledge and experience. The proper matching of patient and therapy makes the greatest demand upon the therapist's knowledge, experience, judgment, objectivity, and integrity, but at the same time assures the greatest possibility for good results.

A patient can be helped only if he receives the type of therapy specific for his particular type of illness. Just as blanket practice of medicine wherein a specific remedy indicated for an illness is ignored results in failure and sometimes even in disaster, a uniform and blanket technique applied in the treatment of emotionally disturbed and socially disoriented persons is equally unsuccessful. In psychic disturbances as in somatic illnesses specific remedies are essential. Similarly, as in the practice of medicine, so also in psychotherapy, the nature and dynamics of the illness, that is, diagnosis, has to be established in order that the proper remedies can be applied. To impose upon patients indiscriminately *a treatment of preference* of the therapist's rather than *a treatment of choice* to suit the needs of the patient cannot but yield negative results.

It is not sufficient, as some suggest, that only "clinical judgment" is required in the selection and assignment of patients. In fact, reliance solely on judgment may be quite dangerous. Such a criterion would place the patient at a great disadvantage, because the appropriateness of the decision would be contingent upon the training, length, and nature of the experience, the degree of perspicacity, and other assets and limitations of the therapist. Reliance on "judgment" entails risks especially when beginning practitioners are concerned. A science and a practice prosper only when they evolve transmittable information. Prescribing a suitable psychotherapy must be based on verifiable knowledge of psychodynamics, clinical diagnosis, and the understanding of the processes of various types of mental treatment extant, for nearly all of them are suitable for some patients. To rely on judgment alone is to encourage the untutored, the unskilled, and the untalented.

No one who has participated in any human endeavor can quarrel with the emphasis on judgment. Judgment is the height of wisdom and of knowledge; but appropriate instrumental judgment is derived only from tested and pragmatic experience. However, even under most favorable conditions it cannot be used apart from the essential information and learning upon which sound practice is based. Thus, knowledge and judgment go hand in hand, in which the former should predominate because judgment is reliable only when it is derived from and superimposed upon knowledge and experience.

The fact that there have been evolved a variety of types of psychotherapy and a number of borderline and derivative practices, such as ego support, counseling, and guidance, attests to the specificity of psychotherapy. They also bear witness to the fact that there is awareness of the different needs of specific patients both clinically considered and practically exigent. It was because of this recognition that in my own practice I found it necessary to evolve a variety of group techniques. As we found a particular method of treatment to be unsuited for some patients, adaptations or revisions were made, or new methods evolved. Thus, the original Activity Group Therapy for children in latency was modified to meet the needs of children of different ages and different types and clinical entities and personality problems. "Play Group Psychotherapy" was designed for very young children, because they were too disturbed and too young to utilize constructively a permissive environment. "Activity Interview" groups met the needs of psychoneurotic children of the same age as those in activity groups, but who could not achieve personality integration in a free acting-out milieu, while the less disturbed and the less socially maladjusted were placed in "transitional" or protected groups in neighborhood centers under the leadership of a trained group therapist. Similarly, the original psychoanalytically oriented groups for parents, as patients, had been modified for the less disturbed parents out of which emerged the "child-centered group guidance of parents."

A common example of the application of clinical knowledge to the choice of appropriate therapeutic measures is the borderline psychotic. As effective as standard psychoanalysis is with psychoneurotics, responsible psychoanalysts will not subject these patients to psychoanalysis at the initial stages of treatment, if at all. The indicated treatment for them is an ego-reinforcement psychotherapy and the establishment of corrective identifications with the analyst. Uncovering of the unconscious is counterindicated. Such patients who had been exposed to psychoanalysis had sustained deleterious effects. In some instances they hallucinated during the sessions as they lay on the couch. Their ego, being weak and easily overwhelmed by the unconscious material uncovered through free association and regression, retreated from reality.

On the other hand, psychoneurotic patients with libidinal fixations and distortions and all-pervasive anxiety stemming from unconscious sexual conflicts and unresolved guilts and ego-alien urges are sometimes treated by psychotherapies that deal exclusively with the conscious and preconscious, or by those that emphasize sociological and interpersonal factors instead of psychoanalysis. There are, on the other hand, also nonpsychotic patients with defective ego organization for whom depth therapies are counterindicated either altogether or at the outset of treatment. There are persons with consitutional weaknesses and organic deficiencies who should not be exposed to the unraveling of the unconscious, because they can become so disturbed and disorganized as to be unable to reestablish psychic equilibrium or to require a prolonged recuperative period to do so.

The threshold of psychic break varies with the individual's ego strengths which often have an organic, not exclusively a psychological base. Recovery from temporary pathological regression is also determined by constitutional as well as psychological resources. Patients from the first world war in Veterans hospitals still remain in a state of regression. Some of them might have carried on adequately under normal conditions all their lives, had they not been exposed to the trauma of a battlefield. A patient who continues in therapy under conditions of too great a stress may also break down. Fortunately, patients usually withdraw when their anxieties become too great.

Before a patient gets too far into treatment, it is essential that his ego organization and strengths, as well as the severity of his problem, are understood. Most often this is not possible in advance, especially is this the case in private practice where the anamneses are not always available. In such instances therapy must proceed at a level of least stress until sufficient information is elicited to determine the nature of the pathology and the depth and type of treatment most suitable for a particular patient. In group psychotherapy, there are certain safeguards in that the therapist does not become active early in treatment and that patients have at hand "escape" devices such as silence, evasion, and even absenteeism [19]. We have found a considerable number of adults and children to whom groups proved too anxiety-provoking and who therefore had to be removed. These considerations have important implications for the selection of patients for the various types of group psychotherapy, group guidance and counseling.

Four General Criteria

It would be helpful if we could lay down some general principles for selecting patients for group psychotherapy, even though individualization is the key to our problem. There are only four such principles that I can suggest.[1]

(1) One is that the patient must have experienced *minimal satisfaction* in his primary relations sometime during his childhood. Group treatment as an initial or sole treatment method is

---

1. The Criteria suggested in this paper were derived from screening and treatment of about 5,500 patients of different ages, races, and nationalities, in the last twenty years in various types of clinics and social agencies.

counterindicated for patients whose relations, especially those with parents and siblings, had been extremely destructive. Their unsuitability arises from the fact that they possess only a minimal capacity for object relationships which should be established in childhood and because they are unable to give up their egocentricity. Since relationships in groups are multilateral, the social demands are greater than they are in a person-to-person relationship. It is, therefore, necessary to determine in advance of assigning patients to group treatment whether they have the capacity to fit into a group without deleterious effects on the other members and upon themselves. Frequently, early interpersonal deprivations are revealed in the very first interview. The ways in which a patient had been treated by his parents and his antagonism toward siblings are among the first subjects he brings forth, for these relationships are among the two central problems of all who seek psychotherapy. The other is sex. Patients usually reveal themselves as lonely, emotionally isolated, socially uncomfortable persons with difficulties in relation to mates, offspring, people on the job, and in other situations. Children show a general incapacity for relationships at school, in the street, and at home. Usually a single interview with the mothers of children uncovers a history of destructive parent-child relationships. Obviously, neither an adult nor a child with an intense emotional void could adapt himself to a group.

(2) The second general psychologic vector for determining a patient's adequacy for group psychotherapy is the *degree of sexual disturbance.* A child whose symptomatology stems directly from the oedipal relation, or who had been exposed to sexual overstimulation and the seductiveness of a parent or parents, requires a transference relation and interpretive therapy. Because children's groups address themselves predominantly to ego functioning, the libidinal distortions can be corrected through displacement of cathexis upon another person who would deal with the aberrant drives therapeutically. Adults whose *vita sexualis* is deviant, or charged with anxiety and guilt, are best helped with their libido distortions in a transference relation in individual treatment where the id urges can be worked through and become accessible to the ego in a regressive and insight-evoking process. In some instances a patient may require a period of individual analysis or psychotherapy before assignment to a group.

There are, on the other hand, patients who are for a variety of reasons unable to enter into a person-to-person relation with a therapist but can accept group psychotherapy as an entry to individual treatment.

(3) The third consideration is the *ego strength* of the prospective group member. Although groups offer definite protection in some respects, they also expose patients to stresses and make demands that some may find too difficult to meet. Particularly is this true of therapeutic groups. Patients, of whatever clinical category or adaptive patterns, are therefore acceptable only when their ego is strong enough to withstand the exposure to which they and fellow patients are subjected. Unlike individual treatment where the therapist can control the interviews and select therapeutically indicated content, in a group he can seldom exercise this prerogative. The subjects discussed, the course the interviews take, and the emotional activation, are in the hands of the group which may *overload the ego* of some of the participants. The anxieties, fears, and guilts they induce may be more than some of the patients should be exposed to at a given stage. This is an especially important consideration when interviews are held infrequently, as in the case of one or two weekly sessions and patients are thus compelled to live under such stress in the interim.

(4) In addition to ego sufficiency, it is essential that patients in group psychotherapy have a *minimal superego development*. Individuals devoid of feelings of right and wrong, who are at the mercy of their anarchic impulses and id urges, cannot attain these social criteria solely through group participation. This is our fourth qualification. The superego (as is also the ego though to a somewhat lesser extent) is derived from identifications resulting in the incorporation of the images and standards set by parents or their surrogates. The basic superego cannot be derived from group mores, though they reinforce and modify the parental superego. Conscienceless and id-determined acts on the part of one member evoke anxiety and, therefore, resentment in the others in the group, with little or no benefit to either. The foundations for superego development are derived from relations with individuals, and correction of its malformation has to come from identification with an individual therapist.

On the other hand, an overstrict superego can be relaxed through the permissiveness of a group climate and the support it gives to expression of impulsiveness and aggression. However, in the case of anxiety-ridden, obsessional-compulsive patients, this may have the effect of intensifying feelings of guilt and increase the quantum of anxiety. The criterion of superego sufficiency eliminates from groups certain types of regressive infantile characters, psychopathic personalities, and some psychotics, who are deficient in superego development.

Reasons for Lack of Unanimity

There is currently considerable diversity of opinion as to indications of group psychotherapy for patients. This lack of unanimity stems from a number of sources. First, the practice is comparatively new. The techniques that were forerunners of group psychotherapy had been employed in a blanket manner; that is, all types of patients were lumped together and were submitted to a didactic-lecture or class-discussion method. Repression, inspiration, and conceptualization were the rule. While these groups, which were large enough to be classed as masses, helped both somatic and some types of hysterical and psychotic patients *temporarily* to mobilize ego strengths (self-control) sufficiently to hold in abeyance or repress symptoms, no permanent results could be expected from such techniques in cases of true psychoneuroses and in the various types of anxiety and character syndromes. While direct methods can alter behavior for a time in some types of disorders, basic intrapsychic changes are not affected by these means. The indiscriminate grouping of patients can be attributed at least in part to the traditional lag originating in these pretherapeutic groups.

Another reason for the lack of criteria is the fact that psychoanalytical psychiatry and depth psychology were only recently introduced in the practice of group psychotherapy. The didactic, repressive, and inspirational techniques were perpetuated by physicians in the armed services during the Second World War, many of whom had not had psychiatric training but because of the emergency had been assigned to psychiatric wards. It is understandable that direct methods would be the first to be adopted and in many instances were suitable to the situation since the aim was not to cure the acute psychoneurotic casualties, but rather to prevent further breakdowns and to restore personnel to the ranks as quickly as possible. Because of the recency of these events and because some of the physicians took up the practice of group psychotherapy after their war experience, the trend toward clinical miscellany continued.

The third reason for the lack of criteria is the theoretical bias of psychotherapists. An example of this are adherents of the school of psychotherapy which assumes that because the roots of personality disturbances are in interpersonal relations, their correction as well lies in such relations. Another school of psychotherapy emphasizes the social conditions of patients and underplays the intrapsychic. Other therapists adhere to the principle of active therapy and minimize the importance of free association and regression. Adherents of such schools of thought would obviously tend to rely less on diagnosis and the criteria of psychodynamics than those who view that once a problem had been internalized and had become charged with massive affect, interpersonal experiences in the community can no longer undo the damage. Only transference and interpretive therapy with regressive catharsis and insight are the solvents of such pathological states.

A fourth reason can be found in the comparatively small number of patients a private practitioner usually has that does not allow for detailed choice of patients for groups and for grouping them. Community and hospital clinics, or private practitioners who conduct clinics have at their disposal the required numbers from which to form groups in accordance with specific criteria.

Lastly, the absence of adequate and validated research facilities for establishing scientifically reliable criteria is an important contributing factor to the retardation of this development. There are still lacking in the field of psychiatry sufficient basic data and verified experience and information from which can be drawn scientifically reliable conclusions. As the situation is today, individual subjective reactions are the source of opinion in most instances.

Despite these lacks a survey of the literature and one's own experience justify the opinion that criteria for selection of patients for group psychotherapy fall within three general categories: (1) positive, (2) negative, and (3) positive-negative.

Positive indications appear where a clinical study of a patient's treatment needs show that they can be best met by a group and it is, therefore, the sole treatment of choice. Where a clinical study of a patient reveals that he would be traumatized by a group experience or that his specific difficulty could not be reached through the multirelational experience in the group, we have a complex of negative indications. However, where the decision is that a patient, though essentially requiring individual treatment, is unable to respond to or gain from it because of blockings in the transference relation due to fear and distrust, or because of an uncontrollable need to resist and dominate authority figures, group psychotherapy is recommended as a preliminary stage in therapy with a view of eventually treating him individually either exclusively or parallel with group psychotherapy. Such indications we characterize as positive-negative.

Among the "indications" suggested by some writers is that of "social neurosis." Presumably the term designates a condition that arises from reactions in relation to people and groups by anxiety, fear, or panic. Clinically, it would be difficult to justify such a diagnosis. A social or group situation may precipitate neurotic reactions, but this occurs only where a neurosis already exists. It would be difficult to prove that an individual would react pathologically to groups and to social situations without the presence of an internalized neurotic state that affects his personality and other reactions. Social reactions cannot be divorced from prevailing inner conditions. Responses to interpersonal and social situations are only symptoms of an inner state. It would seem correct to assume that patients with this specific symptom should sometime during their treatment have a group experience as a reality-testing device in a "tapering off" process, but the assumption that anxiety panics in social situations can be treated through group interpersonal reactions may in some cases not be justified.

Positive Indications for Analytic Groups

Among the patients suitable, that is, those with positive indications for analytic group psychotherapy for nonpsychotic adults, are patients with the *defensive mechanism of projection*. These are the patients who persistently blame others for their inadequacies, failures and liabilities. Projective defenses are very difficult to deal with in individual therapy because the therapist, as a parent substitute, is part of the patient's fantasies as well as a target of his projections and blame. In a group this trend is dealt with by the other members naturally and with ease and, as experience indicates, very effectively. Because they do not represent authority this mechanism is more accessible to the interpretation by fellow patients than by an individual therapist. The group, by its reactions, activates the patient to associate freely and to recall early traumatic situations that resulted in his defensive and self-protective pattern. The group's reactions are tangible and real; they are direct, firm and instantaneous. The effectiveness of group treatment of the self-defensive projective pattern has been amply demonstrated by clinical experience.

Many patients come for treatment whose central need is *reinforcement of their biological destinies*, the attitudes toward which have been distorted through inadequate or unfavorable identifications during formative years. They are confused in their sexual identifications or are at odds with the role they have to play in life. The values of the reinforcement by groups of socially defined roles for an individual have been observed in all groups, educational as well as therapeutic. Unless the situation involves massive pathology or perversion, the group support of the individual's own unconscious wish to conform with social demands and mores is most effective. This has been observed by many group therapists. Women patients and adolescents who dressed carelessly or in a masculine fashion quickly change their mode of attire. Others who had habitually neglected their persons grew clean, comely, and trim. This self-improvement may be attributed to the fear of being stigmatized and unacceptable to fellow members or to activation of homosexuality or a corrected feminine identification. In any case, the group has supported the trend toward womanhood which had favorable repercussions in their relations to their mates, offspring, relatives, and associates.

Similar effects occur also in men. Through identification, imitation and ego-reinforcement that accrue from intimate group relations, universalization and improved self-image, the masculine traits that had been held in abeyance come to the fore first cautiously and experimentally, later with more assurance and security. The patients then proceed to test reality against their newly emerging strengths, and they soon take a more appropriate place in the family, on the job, and in other relations.

The difficulties alluded to here stem from characterological deficiencies, though they may also be caused by deep-rooted psychoneuroses and even sexual abnormalities. When the latter is the case group psychotherapy must be used with caution. No proof exists that it can be effective in such situations. There is, however, sufficient evidence of its effectiveness on character malformations that have arisen from past accommodations to unfavorable conditions. *Character disorders* generally yield to the ministrations of therapy groups. The group milieu is a new type of (substitute) family to which accommodations have to be made of an altogether different kind than in the past. This is aided by the fact that what had to be guarded and covered over can be released and exposed to the rays of feeling and understanding; what one had to be ashamed of, one can now reveal with impunity. While in the past one had to watch and control conduct, now one can fling care and caution to the winds.

All this is significant because it can all be done with compunction, without fear of punishment, criticism, or rejection. The therapist as a parental figure is permissive, tolerant, and understanding, so are, by and large, the fellow patients, the new siblings. The latter may take one to task at times, criticize and correct, but for the most part it is all done with an honest intent to help and not to hinder or debase. When a situation gets tight for one the therapist casts the light of understanding. He gives it meaning and significance, thus reducing the burden on the ego. Most often, however, it is one's friends, the patients, that explain and interpret. They not only help one to uncover memories and feelings of early childhood, but also demonstrate and teach one how to react to situations in a different way. But what is even more significant is that they make one react differently than in the past and thus alter the patterning of adaptations and responses.

All groups, whether therapeutic, guidance, educational, or communal, have the effect of modifying behavior, temporarily or permanently, as the case may be. Therapy groups alone, however, alter intrapsychic states and balance. Conditioned only by hereditary resources, character is a result of the native, instinctual interaction with conditions and with life. It is the result of these and of impingement of the demands during the formative years. A new type of adaptation, therefore, aided by a new awareness and favorable conditions can alter personality. The aggressive person, for example, becomes aware of his aggressiveness because others in the group refuse to tolerate it, but the reactions to this behavior are not rejecting or punitive; they are rather aimed to help, even if they are couched in firm and disapproving terms.

The compliant and the diffident are supported by the group to become more outgoing and more reacting. Due to the fact that inherent in all organisms is the trend toward centrifugal responses and aggressive effort, such patients gain more quickly from group experience than do the aggressive. Movement is the basis of life and survival, and unless it is inhibited or distorted at early stages, it automatically grows and evolves. Psychotherapy, and especially group psychotherapy, encourages the natural *centrifugal flow of the libido.*

Patients with one of the forms of character malformation that respond to group treatment are those who act out. Where the acting out is *ego-alien,* there is obviously a neurotic conflict present. Such patients may or may not be accessible to group psychotherapy, depending upon other noxious conditions present, and the intensity and the nature of the pathology. Where acting out is ego syntonic, however, the patient presents *character resistances* to change that are very difficult to reach by ordinary insight therapy. Such patients put up very strong defenses against change and battle, as it were, with the therapist. They deny the existence of a problem, since their difficulties are not alien to their ego and they are therefore devoid of conflict or guilt. Even though at times such patients feel discomfort about the reaction of others, being symptom free this discomfort is not so intense that they cannot mobilize defensive and self-justifying blame against them and external circumstances. They always fall back on the defense of projection.

This picture changes where the acting out is part of a neurotic syndrome as in the anxiety neuroses, or where it is in itself the neurotic symptom, as in the case of a neurotic character. Here the need to act out is a resolution of deep-rooted anxiety of long standing; in fact, its origin is in the preverbal and preconceptual stages. Such compulsive acting out both disturbs the group, and its reactions prove traumatic to the offending patient.

To be affected by group psychotherapy, *impulse must be accessible to the ego,* even if it requires the help of the therapist and fellow patients. When impulses are inaccessible to or overwhelm the ego, and anxiety results, intensive individual therapy is indicated, because in such cases the group's criticism and disapproval can cause great harm. The struggle of an individual so afflicted to control himself only adds to the quantum of his anxiety, and the load his ego has to carry is increased which gives rise to even greater disturbance. One should note, in passing, that the prognosis for adults with neurotic characters is poor in any type of psychotherapy, including psychoanalysis, since the beginnings of the problem predate the verbal stage of development and are structured into the personality. When acting out, however, proceeds from inadequately formed ego, infantile omnipotence, when it serves as a mechanism of control, a source of secondary gains, or a method of testing reality to these patterns, the group is of definite effectiveness.

Patients who present character resistances fare better in groups than in individual treatment. The analysis of character resistance as differentiated from superego and id resistances[2] is a difficult and frequently an insurmountable problem to the psychoanalyst and the psychotherapist. These difficulties are analogous in many respects to ego defenses we have described. Interpretations of these resistances are seldom fruitful since they are ego-syntonic. The patient's ego refuses to recognize or accept the interpretations. Because the ego is a part of the character structure itself, it is itself involved in the process and, therefore, cannot examine itself. A patient can, however, be made aware of his behavior and attitudes through the reactions of fellow group members as they are discussed and mirrored by them. These reactions have proven very effective, and when the resistances are repeatedly assailed and interpreted by a group, their dissolution is more likely to occur than in person-to-person interviews. His craving to be accepted by a group, his social hunger, motivates the patient to modify his conduct and reactions. One should always take into consideration the fact that character resistances are much more tenacious than are neurotic resistances and present a challenge to group psychotherapy as well.

Closely related to character resistance is the need on the part of the

2. Spotnitz, H. (1952). A psychoanalytic view of resistance in groups. *International Journal of Group Psychotherapy*, 2:3-9.

patient to challenge and defeat the therapist as authority. This may be a form of character resistance, but is more likely a transference resistance. This type can be treated adequately in psychoanalysis. In the less intensive psychotherapies, however, in which the patient and therapist are in a face-to-face position, transference resistances present greater difficulties. There is every possibility that the interviews may assume the nature of haggling dialogues and degenerate into contentiousness between patient and therapist. In groups the status of the therapist is much less prominent and, therefore, arouses challenge to a lesser extent. The urge for the infantile oedipal struggle with him on the part of patients is diminished, since transference reactions are divided and diluted in groups; also, due to the fact that there are in groups a multiplicity of targets for hostile feelings (target multiplicity), this particular type of resistance (stemming as it does from an unresolved oedipal situation) can therefore be dealt with by a group more easily.

All patients present *transference resistances* to varying degrees, since all have hostile attitudes toward their parents and suffer from inadequately resolved oedipal struggles. However, the intensity of the remnants of hostility varies, and patients who are less involved call to attention the offending, resistive, or challenging behavior of a fellow member. More often, patients who easily identify with the offending member interpret his mechanism. Here again universalization, identification, and mirror reactions, and sometimes sibling hostility favor therapeutic ends. The meaning of the reactions to the therapist may become the topic of discussion for a time, and by association memories and current attitudes toward parents and siblings are brought out and the connection with the attitudes and feelings toward the therapist and toward other members of the group is established.

Another dynamic that operates in this group syndrome is the protectiveness some patients feel toward the therapist during the phases of their positive transference, when he is challenged or attacked by a fellow patient. In others the childhood fears and anxieties are reawakened when a parental figure is openly attacked, and to allay these anxieties, they either defend the therapist or turn upon the aggressive member.

There are some patients whose nuclear problem is rooted in sibling relationships, even though these may stem in some way from the conduct of their parents. There are many advantages in placing such patients in a situation where they can act out feelings toward substitute siblings in the conditioned environment of a therapy group that offers appropriate emotional reactions, suitable insight, and objective understanding. The tangible reality of other persons in a group activates in a more telling way the patient's conscious and unconscious difficulties than can be done by reconstructing them only verbally. The replica of earlier tensions induced by a (substitute) family setting provided by a group activates the partially repressed feelings associated with that setting. These are then dealt with and worked through by the members of the group. While this situation may set off considerable group tension, it is therapeutically very profitable when analyzed and interpreted by the group as a whole with the planned help of the therapist, if necessary. We have encountered patients, however, whose hostilities toward siblings had been so overwhelmingly intense that they were unable to tolerate a group without disturbing its climate by their aggression or causing great stress to themselves. A few left the groups because their feelings of hostility became intolerable.

Next to sexual urges, sibling antagonisms are perhaps the greatest activators of group tensions. They constitute a fertile field for analytic group psychotherapy where accumulated resentments and hostilities are discharged and appropriately worked through. While with adults the light of understanding and the healing effect of insight are involved, the analysis of group tensions cannot be made the sole therapeutic tool, as some therapists tend to do. Rather, the analysis of the multiple transference relations that exist in every group should be brought out in the light of the patients' emotional backgrounds.

Some patients who had been only children in their families expect and sometimes demand the narcissistic gratifications they had received from that source. They expect to occupy the center of attention in situations where it cannot be realistically achieved. The estate of only childhood also produces definite character traits in which narcissism and faulty object relations predominate. Only children who have not had the need or the opportunity for sharing are frequently deficient in this regard. Sharing and relating on a more mature base are imposed by groups, which may prove difficult and even distressing to individuals without antecedent conditioning in these respects. Even when other problems of patients who had been only children require individual psychotherapy for their resolution, group psychotherapy is indicated for them and a reality situation in sharing and relating.

By and large, patients with *schizoid personalities* are, on theoretical grounds, at least, suitable for group treatment. The activation they require can best be supplied by groups. Special consideration, however, must be given to the nature of the problem and ego strengths. Not every patient with a schizoid personality structure should be exposed to a situation where profoundly disturbing emotions can always be touched off. It would seem that patients in this category are better placed in guidance groups, the discussions of which consist of current events and day-to-day interests or "top realities." The schizoid person tends to remain apart from the flux of life, and he responds to it selectively, remaining for the most part as what appears to be impassive. Mulling over occurrences and practical events of daily living would be helpful, for the more the schizoid patient is activated to participation, the narrower grows the schism between his mental preoccupations and reality.

Schizoid patients remain, for the most part, quiet and withdrawn in groups. They participate little. They are, however, usually among the more observant, the more astute and insightful members, for despite their seeming indifference they actually register everything that goes on in the discussions and their nonverbalized and latent implications. Their remarks, though infrequent and brief, are usually.penetrating and reveal a high level of reflective thought. They well confirm the adage: "Still waters run deep."

Since the true schizoid personality has a constitutional base, therapeutic expectations must of necessity be limited. The capacity for reactivity is comparatively low and the resources small. However, despite these limitations, group association is indicated for the schizoid. Since they are not initiators and have to be stimulated by an outside agency, in a person-to-person relation they remain for the most part uncommunicative. It is this characteristic that makes them more promising candidates for group treatment.

We found that *psychic masochists* gain from groups. Our experience in this regard has been limited to women, and we found that masochistic submissiveness to mothers, husbands, and children was given up by them with surprising rapidity. The interpretation by fellow members, their encouragement, ego reinforcement and support have stood in good stead for the psychic masochists in their efforts toward a new orientation and new ways of relating. Patients reported with great satisfaction, and often with glee, their successes with self-assertiveness, firmness, and independence. They were able to recall childhood situations, the family climate, and individual relationships that resulted in their special type of adaptation, and were rather quickly helped to see the invalidity and ineffectiveness of their attitudes and behavior. The support of the group, as a mother substitute, helped them overcome fears and encouraged them to challenge the persons to whom they submitted implicitly before. We have no evidence at this time as to the effectiveness of group psychotherapy on sexual masochists. However, it is unlikely that groups could correct this condition.

Borderline schizophrenic and other types of psychoses to be described presently as part of the discussion of counterindications have to be placed in groups guardedly. The measure of ego sufficiency of such patients, as, indeed, in other patients as well, has to be ascertained in advance of assignment.

Counterindications for Analytic Groups

The counterindications for group psychotherapy are by far more clearly definable than are the positive indications. We have already noted that as a general principle patients lacking a minimal capacity for object relationships, ego and superego sufficiency, and those with serious sexual disturbances are unsuitable for groups before their basic difficulties have been corrected by individual treatment as a preparation for group therapy.

Obviously, active or disturbed psychotics are unsuitable for outpatient analytic group psychotherapy where the analysis of intrapsychic attitudes and of the unconscious form the body of the interviews.[3] Especially are to be eliminated patients who hallucinate

---

3. Other types of groups and participation in social, recreational, arts and crafts and occupational groups are recommended for them.

or are delusional, and who fragmentize ideas and reality. Among unsuitable patients are the nonpsychotic with very intensive and diffuse anxiety, full-blown anxiety neurotics, the intensely narcissistic, the obsessional-compulsives, depressives, cyclothymic personalities, the suicidal, perverts, active homosexuals, compulsive talkers, also patients who for a variety of reasons cannot refrain from monopolizing the stage. Depending upon the nature and etiology of the narcissism, however, some patients in this last category can gain from intimate group interaction. Among the character disturbances that make patients unsuitable for groups are the neurotic characters, the origin of whose anxiety occurred in the preverbal period. Such anxiety is not within the control of the ego and criticism and disapproval of the group have the effect of increasing rather than allaying their already excessive anxiety.

The hypochondriacs have to be excluded because of their compulsive need repeatedly and sometimes continually to speak about their symptoms without any constructive focus or direction. Repeated reference to their ailments and interpretation of all events and reality in terms of physical pain and discomfort, blocks the group process, prevents therapeutic effectiveness, and causes annoyance and discomfort to the others in the group. An even more important counterindication lies in the fact that the cause of this somatization is not accessible to the group method. The degree of narcissism and the libidinal investment in the physical symptoms are such that if they can be reached at all, it can be done only through a libidinal transference relation in a regressive process that individual psychoanalysis provides. Of major consideration is the fact that hypochondriac symptomatology is in many instances a defense against psychosis which, as already indicated, has to be considered for groups with great care. The reality sense of the hypochondriac is greatly distorted, since events and occurrences are seen in the coloring of his physical discomfort or a pervasive fear or expectation of physical catastrophes. He is a difficult patient for any type of treatment and would be inaccessible to group treatment and, in addition, would provoke anxiety in the others.

True hysteria is still another counterindication for exclusive group treatment of adults. Hysteria, being the result of the oedipal complex operating on the genital level and rooted in guilt concerning past activity or thoughts related to sex, requires a psychoanalytic type of individual libidinal transference psychotherapy. In addition, since the hysteric's attitude toward people is transilient and unpredictable, momentarily assuming extremes of affection and hatred with no apparent reason, his participation in a group may cause much stress and anxiety to others. Still another factor to be considered is the susceptibility to suggestion on the part of the hysteric which may turn the group into a source of pathogenic infection to the patient himself.

Concerning Grouping

Because the central theme of this paper is selection, only a brief statement on the question of grouping needs to be made here. The ideal criterion of grouping patients is their similarity of psychological syndrome and pathology. The degree of identification is at its highest where the *nuclear* or *central problem* is the same in all patients. This not only accelerates therapeutic results, but also reaches the problem of each participant more deeply and more effectively. Identification accelerates cartharsis, helps understanding and empathy, and produces pertinent and effective interpretation. It also renders the therapy a genuine group process. Because each patient's unconscious is similarly involved, the group can be treated as one patient, for the communications of any one represent or reflect those of all, and interpretation given to one applies to all. Vicarious catharsis and spectator therapy are as a result enhanced, and the effectiveness of the group's and the therapist's efforts are therefore multiplied many times. When there is divergence of pathology in a group of patients, identification is considerably less frequent, vicarious catharsis is at its minimum, and the indirect benefits from interpretation and insight are at a low level. It therefore becomes necessary on too frequent occasions for the therapist and the group members to turn their attention to individuals and work through their problems. This is what is referred to as *therapy in a group* as differentiated from *therapy through the group*.

Common problems on which group psychotherapy can always count are the personality problems and neurotic syndromes that emanate from attitudes toward and pathogenic influences of parents. All patients present difficulties in this area; all have unpleasant childhood memories in this regard. In this respect patients in any group are similar and they help each other greatly as a result. Still another common presenting problem is that which proceeds from *vita sexualis*. Seldom, if ever, does one come upon a patient without difficulty in this area. Even when patients claim normal and satisfactory sexual adjustment, further uncovering nearly always reveals traumatic or distortive influences, attitudes, practices, and experiences. These two common denominators—feelings stemming from relations with parents and problems in the area of sex—which are universal sources of difficulty for civilized man, give the group psychotherapist considerable freedom of choice for grouping. There are, however, definite counterindications for combining some patients which I hope to discuss in a later paper.[4]

Despite theoretically established and empirically tested rules for selection and grouping, in practice one finds that these are never ironclad criteria. One finds that patients who by all indications should fit into therapy groups and gain from that treatment, do not respond as expected. Then, again, patients for whom group therapy seems to be counterindicated by known standards do surprisingly well. This can be explained (1) by an error in diagnosis or understanding of the problem by the therapist; (2) by the presence of *unknowable factors* in the psychopathology of the patient; (3) by the presence of other patients in the group who either aid or block the patient's progress, as the case may be; and (4) by the fact that patients show *partial improvement*, that is, improvement in some respects while remaining unaffected in others.

One of the sanguine aspects of group treatment is that it presents definite safeguards against injury to its members. One safeguard is that patients can and do readily withdraw from a group when they find it unsuitable or too disturbing. Patients' self-protective trends and their natural avoidance of pain is to a definite extent a safeguard against traumatization. Another preventive is a patient's escape from

---

4. A word of caution should be offered in the matter of grouping. Sometimes similarity of symptoms is employed as a criterion for grouping. The fact must be kept in mind that a symptom can be produced by a variety of etiological, nosological, and psychopathological factors that form the nucleus of the problem. Since sound psychotherapy addresses itself to the covert cause and not to manifest symptoms, the former, the pathology, needs to be considered as paramount in grouping and not the symptoms.

injury through the many resistance possibilities such as silence, absenteeism and other devices favored by the group situation. [9] The only type of patient that may be injured by an unsuitable therapy group placement is the borderline schizophrenic. Because of their intense dependence these patients may continue to come to groups despite the disturbance and turmoil created in them, and the group psychotherapist must be vigilant with regard to such developments.

TABLE 1

*Shows Indications and Counterindications for
Therapy Groups for Adults and Adolescents*

INDICATIONS	COUNTERINDICATIONS*
Clinical	*Clinical*
Some psychoneuroses	Anxiety neuroses
Character disorders	Neurotic character
Some borderline ambulatory schizophrenics	Compulsive-obsessional
Schizoid personalities	Psychopaths
Psychic masochists	Cyclothymic personalities
	Active psychotics**
	Paranoiacs
	Depressives
	Perverts
	Active homosexuals
	Hypochondriacs
	True hysterics
Characterological	*Characterological*
Defensive projection	Inadequate primary relations
Character resistances	Inadequate ego development
Confused identifications	Inadequate superego development
Defective sibling relations	Intense sexual disturbances
Only children	Regressive infantile characters
Drive to defeat therapist	Extreme narcissism

* Many patients included in this category of counterindications can be treated in groups provided they also receive parallel individual treatment. The selection of patients for such parallel treatment may depend entirely upon the clinical judgment of the therapist.

** This category refers here to the inclusion of psychotic patients in groups with nonpsychotics.

Criteria for Children's Analytic Groups

The criteria for assignment of children to analytic groups—Play Therapy groups and Activity-Interview groups—are considerably less rigid than they are for adults or adolescents. Grouping them is therefore also less exacting. In play groups the children are either in the preoedipal stage or in the midst of the oedipal conflict. Their neuroses, if any, are structurally and dynamically different from the postpubertal neuroses [57]. We have found that children under six years of age of various clinical categories, such as reactive (primary) behavior disorders, character disorders, neurotic traits, and with neurotic reactions, can be treated in groups and can be placed together. Among the other conditions for which groups are the treatment of preference are only children, children who are antagonistic to and aggressive toward adults and children with diffuse anxiety and a lack of minimal impulse controls.

Children in latency with massive psychoneurotic symptomatology, the seriously disturbed and the anxious require, as do adults, a period of individual psychotherapy before assignment to a group, and most of them benefit from parallel individual and group treatment. More than do adults, children benefit from association and interaction with peers, and group therapy should be used with them more extensively than is being done at the present time.

Here, as well, it is essential that before he is placed in groups, the degree of libidinal distortion and sexual attachment the child has for his parents, especially the parent of the opposite sex, is ascertained. Children whose parents or siblings had been seductive, sexually provocative and overstimulating, who slept with their parents in the same bed or in the same room, or who witnessed or overheard the primal scene, require play therapy in an individual transference relation, interpretation and insight as well as release and cathexis displacement [57].

Even more than in the case of adults antagonisms toward a sibling may preclude placement of a child in a group. While in most instances sibling hostility can be dissolved by groups, we have found instances where the intensive acting out of these feelings made continuing the child patient in a group inadvisable.

Among the children for whom individual therapy is preferred are those who have been subjected to a serious trauma, either a sudden catastrophe, prolonged exposure to a series of traumatic occurrences, or a totally traumatic environment in the family. The anxiety bound up as a result of these exposures has to be released in the security of a positive transference and treatment has to be focused toward the dissolution of the bound-up anxiety. This can best be done in individual treatment through free association, interpretation, and insight. Children in such straits require the security of a relationship with a therapeutically oriented adult with whom they feel comfortable and free. This removes the burden their still weak and unformed ego has to carry.

We have found that children even with such intense problems gain immeasurably from participation in appropriate therapeutic groups, skillfully conducted. Since the children's ego organization is still in a rudimentary state and because the catharsis in children's analytic groups is both one of activity and verbalization, the skills and vigilance required in conducting such groups are by far more exacting than in directing groups of nonpsychotic adults [18, 34]. Because acting out is the rule in these groups, children with intense anxiety, particularly if it originates from preverbal and preconceptual stages, that is, children who can be classed as having neurotic characters, should be avoided. They do not meet the requirement of minimal ego development for therapy groups.

Because of the small child's tendency to *substitute* the therapist for his real parents and attach to (displace on) him the latter's attributes, resistances may be so intense as to block the individual therapist's treatment efforts. It was found that a preliminary course of group treatment reduces defenses and the distrust of the adult in such instances. Here as well the communications of fellow group members support and catalyze the child so that he can enter into a therapeutic relation. Thus groups can be used as an exclusive treatment tool, to intensify, to taper off, and as preparation for individual psychotherapy.

Barring those with serious libidinal disturbances, ego insufficiencies, and psychotics, there are large numbers of maladjusted children for whom analytic group psychotherapy is sufficient in itself.

TABLE 2

*Indications and Counterindications
for Analytic Therapy Groups for Children*

INDICATIONS	COUNTERINDICATIONS*
Clinical	*Clinical*
Reactive behavior disorders	Massive psychoneurotic
Character disorders	symptomatology
Neurotic traits	Libido fixations and distortions
Neurotic reactions	Neurotic characters
Anxiety states	Diffuse fears and anxiety
	Reactions to trauma
	Psychoses
Characterological	*Characterological*
Only children	Intense sibling rivalry
Aggressiveness toward adults	Lack of impulse control
Excessive submissiveness	

* In most of these cases parallel individual and group treatment are indicated.

Criteria for Children's Activity Therapy Groups

By far the largest number of children in latency referred for treatment to clinics are devoid of massive symptomatology or intense psychoneuroses. They are the generally maladjusted, rebellious, the disobedient, mild neurotics, mild anxiety (situational) hysteria, and character disorders. Such children's adjustment can be improved and their difficulties overcome through corrective interpersonal relations in a conditioned environment such as activity therapy groups provide.

The chief requirement is that the young patients have a basic desire to belong to a group and be part of it. This minimal desire for and ability to establish object relations is essential. Even though a child may currently present serious adjustment difficulties, he must have *potential capacity* to give up his undesirable behavior in return for the acceptance by the group. This we term *social hunger* and it stems from at least a moderately satisfactory earlier relationship with some person or persons. Lacking such a relationship, the child cannot give up his narcissistic self-centered patterns of feeling and action and is, therefore, inaccessible to group influences.

Assignment to activity groups as well requires at least a minimal development of ego strength and superego organization so that impulses can be brought under control through reactions of other children and the demands of the group. If, for any reason, the ego is at a level where impulses and intrapsychic conflicts are not accessible to it—such as in the psychotic, the psychopathic, in early infantile fixation or regression, or intense neuroses—the child is unsuitable for these groups. Children with *oedipal and preoedipal primary behavior disorders* with or without neurotic traits, *character disorders, confused sexual identifications* and *mild neurotic reactions* are eminently suitable for these groups. Among the latter are included children with fears emanating from an external situation and not from intrapsychic anxiety, such as castration fears, for example.

In the case of *preoedipal behavior disorders* where arrest in emotional maturity has occurred as a very early age, the ego remains n a state of arrested development and the acting out of infantile narcissism is at a high level. Groups cannot affect children with this type of personality malformation nor assimilate the intensity of the disturbances they create. The hilarity, playfulness, animation, demandingness, and provocativeness they introduce into the group, prevent the emergence of an essential *therapeutic climate*. The personality being fixed on a preoedipal level, the superego is undeveloped, as is also the ego, and the child is devoid of or is subject to minimal anxiety. This, though structurally different, is analogous to psychopathy and, since in activity groups no interpretations are given and no restraint exercised, the groups cannot assimilate such children.

It must be emphasized, however, that in the case of children with preoedipal behavior disorders the difference is a quantitative one and depends upon the age at which fixation had occurred. Children who had been traumatized at a later stage do not present so serious a picture and many of them, therefore, are accessible to Activity Group Therapy. The difference lies largely in *the age at which the reactive behavior originated* and in its intensity.

The *oedipal primary behavior disorders* are accessible to Activity Group Therapy because both the ego and superego have developed sufficiently to submit to external pressures and restraint; also because social hunger is a motivation sufficiently strong to mobilize ego strengths necessary for fitting into a group.

Among the *character disorders* that are accessible to Activity Group Therapy are the infantilized, effeminacy in boys, masculinized girls, the submissive and the aggressive, the latter within specific limits, however. Since character generally is determined by the nature of early adaptations a child had to make in relation to people in his environment, expecially parents and other effective persons, its malformations can be corrected by a new type of adaptation demanded by the therapy group. The group provides a *corrective social milieu* where a new set of responses is required and different demands are made. As the child makes an effort to adapt himself to this new culture, new behavior and response patterns arise which become incorporated in his personality. I have pointed out elsewhere that one of the major differences between children and adults is that *children incorporate experience* and make it a permanent part of themselves. Adults' rigidities and defenses do not allow such easy introjection. Their character remains unaffected by experience, which is quite different in the younger set.

Another determining element in character is *identification* with adult models and ego ideals. When these are faulty or inadequate, a character disorder results. During latency, the child's personality is at the height of flexibility and malleability and his identifications are both strong and shifting. The therapist, the peers in the group and its culture, become models of identification; consequently, in planning a group, it is essential that they be wholesome and corrective. The constitution of an activity therapy group and the personality of the therapist are therefore of extreme importance for its therapeutic effectiveness. For this, among other reasons, great emphasis is laid upon the character of the therapist rather than upon his educational qualifications and experience. He must be, unlike the children's parents and teachers, a mature, self-contained, nonperturbable person, after whom the child can model himself. To be of greatest effectiveness, there must be in the group among fellow members "supportive egos," who among other things serve as models of identification.[5]

---

5. It must be noted in passing, however, that unless the therapist and the group climate are

After a period of experimentation with aggressions and the reactions of the new environment, the infantile and the effeminate children find new alignments in relation to their hyperactivity or lack of assertiveness, as the case may be. The example of others, their reactions, and the realistic demands of the situation, bring out new patterns and alignments. The infantile finds an operational field in which his immaturity does not yield secondary gains; where more mature behavior pays off more. The emasculated boy finds in the group a life canvas in which his biologically determined trends are not blocked and frustrated as they were in the past. Through successful experimentation with his latent assertive and aggressive impulses, and the identification with desirable models, his earlier submission is transformed into more suitable adaptive patterns and manner. Similarly, girls with masculine identifications and traits have the opportunity of identifying with a woman therapist and fellow group members and alter their behavior and self-awareness, and as a result their character is changed.

The *aggressive child* is curbed by the group and, impelled by his social hunger, accepts the new demands made on him. He curbs his behavior, provided, of course, his aggressiveness does not stem from psychoneurotic drives, as already indicated.

The degree of withdrawal and self-absorption of *schizoid children* is considerably reduced through activity groups, though, for reasons described one cannot expect more than limited growth in these children. When they are able to countenance acting out and the atmosphere of hyperactivity that sometimes prevails, they are activated and new channels for outward movement are opened up to them. However, the nonthreatening permissive atmosphere and the mediated reality demands help schizoid children only when they are placed in groups of low aggressivity. What has been said of the schizoid children is equally true of the latent schizophrenic and borderline cases. We observed that these groups offer them considerable support. Only one or two schizophrenic children can be absorbed by a group, and the greatest care must be exercised not to expose them to threatening situations or to the aggressions of uncontrollable children.

---

accepting and permissive neither of the two will be accepted by the young patients as models of identification.

Children in latency with *mild neurotic constellations* and reactions, including fears, have improved in activity groups. Because of the emerging strength of their ego in a favorable group environment, the elimination of negative feelings and the corrected self-image, their inner conflicts, if they are not intensely charged with libidinal urges, become accessible to ego controls. The neurotic reactions are thus *sloughed off.* However, as already indicated, when a full-blown psychoneurosis is present, or where the superego restraints are too prohibitive, treatment other than Activity Group Therapy is indicated.

A definite counterindication for Activity Group Therapy is overt and latent *homosexuality*, in both boys and girls, and a strikingly effeminate character in boys. Boys with latent homosexuality or with strong effeminacy provoke anxiety and aggression against themselves from the other group members. Some children with these trends often act them out by playfully straddling over fellow members, or by provoking them to do so. Sometimes more overt acts occur, such as touching or caressing of the buttocks of other members, and in some rare instances a boy would grab the genitals of a play fellow. However, anxiety and rejection is activated even without such overt acts and generates hyperactivity and attack.

We have found that girls do not display similar reactions toward their mates. They do not attack or openly reject the masculine girls, though a good deal of anxiety is caused by their presence.

Other *counterindications* are active psychoses, physical handicaps, organic and mental deficiencies,[6] the spastic, bodily deformities, physical stigmatizations, abnormalities or deficiencies that make a child stand out in a group as exceptional, the unusual or grotesque, the blind, the crippled, the excessively small or large for their age, and children with any other characteristic that may set them off from the average. As in other types of nonresidential treatment, psychopaths are among those that are excluded from activity groups, as are also active delinquents and children who steal outside of the home, because the temptation they may hold out for other members of the group as well as because of their inaccessibility to situational therapy which activity groups are.

---

6. Special groups for mentally deficient children may be of great value. However, these groups cannot be considered as therapy but rather as educational, evocative, and reality expanding.

Unlike other therapies, in activity groups children are grouped together not in accordance with clinical criteria, or similarity of syndrome or pathology, but according to their *behavioral patterns*; that is, some of the patients assigned to a group are aggressive, others are shy, the behavior of still others approximates the average.[7] Because acting out is prevalent in these groups, neither continuous chaotic hyperactivity (nodal behavior) nor continuous hypoactivity (antinodal behavior) can be tolerated. These two modes of reaction must alternate and this alternation is achieved through group balance [129]. Where verbal communication and interpretation are the matrix of the therapeutic process, whether with children or adults, the interpretations serve to control and inhibit excessive behavior. In activity groups these controls must come from the patients themselves; therefore, the balancing of the group in terms of behavior of the participating members, their effect upon each other, and the total group atmosphere, are the prime consideration.

Conclusion

A study of the counterindications shows that there are two types of counterindications in all group psychotherapies. One set of the counterindications is derived from inherent problems of patients, the other from the effect they may have upon each other and the group. Both factors have to be considered in screening patients for groups. We found that some patients who might gain from group treatment had to be rejected because of the adverse effect they would have upon others in the group or upon its total climate. The consideration of all the factors involved in placing or rejecting patients and in grouping them requires great objectivity, vigilance, and prolonged training and experience with the various types of therapy groups one is employing.

Additional elements are the attitude and value system of the therapist, which can be classed as falling under the category of countertransferences [19]. Suitable selections can be made only (1) by those therapists who are acquainted with the variety of treatment methods available; (2) when they are unbiased and free of

7. The terms "instigators," "neuters," and "neutralizers," are applied to these respectively to designate their effect upon the group.

TABLE 3

*Indications and Counterindications for Activity
Therapy Groups for Children in Latency*

INDICATIONS	COUNTERINDICATIONS*
Clinical	*Clinical*
Oedipal primary behavior disorders	Severe psychoneuroses
Some preoedipal primary behavior disorders	Psychoses
Character disorders	Psychopathy
Mild neuroses	Neurotic characters
Situational anxiety (anxiety hysteria)	Severe anxiety states
Some latent schizophrenics	Latent homosexuality
Some schizoid personalities	Disturbances in libido development
Characterological	*Characterological*
Confused sexual identification	Absence of minimal ego development
Effeminacy (in boys)	Absence of minimal superego development
Masculinity (in girls)	Inadequate capacity for object relationships
Infantilization	Regressive infantilism
Overprotection	Castration anxiety
Nonpathological withdrawal	Excessive generalized aggression
Inadequate ego development	Excessive aggression toward adults
Social hunger	Physical handicaps and deformities
Only children	Stigmatizations
	Mental deficiency

* Children included in this category of counterindications cannot be placed in groups even when they receive individual treatment. They can be referred to groups only after the basic personality problems have been corrected through individual treatment and who may require a period of "socialization."

preconceived notions, rigid ideas, and prejudices; (3) when they are not motivated by financial interests; (4) when they are free of preferences for a particular technique; and (5) when they have an unreserved interest in patients and their loyalties are toward the patients rather than to a specific "school" or "master."

CHAPTER 7

PARALLELISMS IN THE DEVELOPMENT OF GROUP PSYCHOTHERAPY: A FRESH HISTORIC APPRAISAL
(1959)

There are few areas of historic recording known to the present writer in which notions of developmental events have been accepted with so little scientific evaluation as in group psychotherapy. With Giles W. Thomas's review of the literature as a frame of reference, others have followed his pioneering effort to trace the development of group psychotherapy through the chronological sequence of publications by various workers in the field.[1] Klapman, Hadden, Hulse, Bach and Illing, the present writer, and many others have followed the general plan employed by Thomas and have followed, with little change or criticism, the publication sequences as the true reflection of the historical growth of this movement.

The name of Joseph H. Pratt, whose first publication appeared in 1906, is always listed in the forefront in the writings of all but one historian of this movement. His name is usually followed by Rhoades, Buck, Snowden, Lazell, Marsh, Hadden, Wender and others of the early workers in the field, in more or less that order. Among the more recent contributors are included Schilder, Slavson, and Wolf of the American therapists; and Bion, Foulkes, and Ezriel of the English group.

---

1. Thomas, Giles W. (1943). Group psychotherapy, a review of the recent literature. *Psychosomatic Medicine* 5.

This conveys the impression that there was a unilinear development of the theory and practices of group psychotherapy, and that practitioners have derived their knowledge from and based their techniques upon their immediate predecessors. Actually, an independent and fresh study of the literature and the practices reveals no such organic or articulated sequential relation in chronology. Such a revised study reveals with impressive clarity that instead of one source of thinking and one stream of growth derived from and based upon antecedent workers, there actually have been four or five quite independent origins and developments. This new approach also shows that, dynamically and theoretically, many of them are unrelated to each other; that the practices have little or nothing in common; and, further, that some of these theories and practices stem not from any predecessors in group psychotherapy but rather from schools of thought and practices in individual psychology, psychiatry, psychotherapy, and in the case of the more farfetched theories, even from sociology and philosophy.

The accounts of the evolvement of group psychotherapy have left one who has lived through this period of psychotherapeutic expansion with a feeling of dissatisfaction. While the datelines of the lives, work, and writings have been undoubtedly chronicled correctly as to their sequence, the conceptualizations of the originators and pioneers in the field did not seem to have quite the same organic relation as did the dates. It is a far cry, for example, from the didactic, mass-inspirational method of Pratt and repressive work of A. A. Low with large groups, to our work with groups of eight or less based upon Freudian and neo-Freudian psychology with its uncovering of the unconscious urges, memories, and motivations. It would be wrong and certainly farfetched to assert that the latter has evolved from or had any connection with the former or that there was a unilinear organic relation between them.

My own dissatisfaction with this tracing of backgrounds for contemporary practices perhaps stems from another, rather personal, source. My own work in therapy with *small groups*, was begun with children in 1934. As far as I knew at that time or have been able to learn since, there was no precedent for this type of therapeutic effort with children, and especially with small groups. My first acquaintance with Dr. Pratt's name or work dates from 1943 or 1944 when I received an offset copy of Dr. Thomas' article, issued by the armed forces, sent to me by a former member of my staff who was in the psychological services of the army.

Perhaps the following historical fact would clarify some aspects in the development of this movement. My work with *small groups* of disturbed children (and later with adults) was first begun as a "recreational project" with girls in the summer of 1934. Later it was modified to include indoor arts and crafts activities as winter set in. We still considered this work as part of "socializing" recreation, since all the girls chosen were deficient in their social relations. However, the reports of the impressive improvement in the girls by their Big Sisters who had contact with them led us to conclude that the "creative achievement" was the source of this change. We therefore adopted the term "Therapeutics of Creative Activity" as a designation of our project.

However, at an exhibit of the productions of the girls of several groups, doubt arose in our mind whether results of such not-too-high craftsmanship and art creations could have such sanguine effects on them. We therefore proceeded to thoroughly study and analyze one year's record of the weekly sessions of a group with a view toward trying to discover the factors that had led to the improvement. This effort consumed approximately a thousand hours. We were able to identify twenty-six interpersonal situations in the group that may have affected the participants favorably. We came to the conclusion that it was the group, per se, that held the therapeutic potential and, suggested the term *group psychotherapy* as the appropriate designation for our work. This term was unknown to us and had not been used by any of the psychiatrists or others who had employed large groups. It was sixteen years later that it was pointed out to me that the term had appeared once in passing in a publication, without defining it or suggesting techniques for its employment.

My suggestion was not acceptable to the director of the child guidance agency where this work originated for reasons of "public relations" at that particular time, and Group Therapy was accepted as a suitable compromise cognomen.

At first the study to which we have referred above led us to the conclusion that the dynamics operating were release, acceptance, "unconditional love," relatedness, and similar operational phenomena

[53, pp. 19-25]. It was many years later, and after we worked with analytic groups, that we recognized that the operational dynamics were the same as those of Freudian analytic psychotherapy, though greatly modified. For further discussion of these and related topices to our systematic structure see [6, 9, 53].

Before we attempt to further outline the historic perspectives, it will be necessary to establish a frame of reference or references as to what the essential characteristics of a therapy group are. The first and most important is that a true therapy group is a small *structured* group, not exceeding eight persons. The smallness of the group is an essential condition so that interpersonal reactions and interactions can take place. These interactions are essential in group psychotherapy; for reasons we have described elsewhere, they cannot occur in large groups [61]. Similarly, the patients in a group that is too small, say less than five, in a prolonged therapeutic relation would tend to reinforce each other's problems and "play into" one another's neuroses, as it were, without the necessary direct interactions, neutralization, cathartic elaborations, and the other corrective dynamics in therapy groups. The intensity of mutual induction is in inverse geometric ration to the size of the group, since the neutralizing and diluting elements stem from the variation in personality and ego functioning of the members of a group. The smaller the group, the lesser is the possibility for these counter-therapeutic processes to occur.

The second characteristic of a therapy group that differentiates it from ordinary groups is the function of the therapist (leader). In the therapeutic group the therapist is not the sole focus of cathexis; he does not occupy the central position at all times, nor does he take over the functions of the ego and superego of the individual members as is the case in ordinary groups. This is the essential factor that permits these groups to become mobile rather than giving rise to group fixity (organization) characteristic of other groups.

The third consideration in a therapy group is that it must be structured, that is, its members are selected by the therapist on the basis of diagnostic criteria and are grouped according to these with a view toward therapeutic validity.

The fourth element that characterizes a therapy group is the freedom and spontaneity of action and conversation in these groups. No group, whether it operates for educational, social, special interest, recreational, political, or any other end, can withstand the degree of spontaneity and freedom in action and verbalization (catharsis) that therapy groups permit and provide.

If we examine the earlier practices that have since been included by historians in the genre of group psychotherapy, it will become clear where the source of error lies. Let us briefly examine the work of Dr. Pratt and others in the light not only of our criteria but also from the view of our understanding as to what constitutes psychotherapy.

Dr. Pratt's method with tubercular patients consisted of inspirational talks and readings from secular writers and the Bible in order to generate more wholesome attitudes and a more optimistic view of life. His groups were large, consisting of as many as eighty or a hundred patients who sat in rows in a classroom arrangement facing the speaker on the platform. Those with best attendance and progress were moved frontward so that they occupied the seats nearest the speaker. The "star" patients sat on a bench facing the audience next to him. The reproduction of the child submitting to the father and trying to please is the dominant motif in this practice. Such practices may help the ego functioning of persons while they are under the influence of the idealized person or idea, but they do not engender those changes in the personality that enable individuals to continue on their own independently. They remain forever dependent upon the person or the ritual and regress when these props are removed.

The authoritarian principle involved in Pratt's "class method" in his "Thought Control Clinics" was even more prominent and rigidly applied in the late A. A. Low's "recovery" technique. Here the participants, all former mental hospital patients, were organized in chapters with rather large memberships in different localities. These were under the direction and *discipline* of one of the patients and his lieutenants who had risen from "ranks," as it were. The rank-and-file patient was required to receive the approval of the head of his chapter before he could make any decision for his life or make a move in carrying out his desires. The chief of the chapter, as Dr. Low personally explained it to me, was not available to the ordinary member, who had to deal first with an official of lower rank. The top echelon was available to him when he wanted to appeal from the decision of that official, and so in a progressive succession he was subjected to a string of hierarchical officialdom until he was able to reach, if he so wished, Dr. Low himself. The meetings that were held by the various chapters in the different localities in four midwestern states consisted of didactic lectures and admonitions. Because of the nature of this process it occurred to me that it could best be described as inspirational-authoritarian. I have elsewhere included this term among the "directive" group therapies.

Dr. Riggs, whose name is frequently mentioned as one of the earlier adapters of work with groups, "lectured" to the patients in his sanitarium through a loudspeaker and his words were delivered to the various wards and cottages by electronic means.

The lecture was the exclusive means employed by all the workers in the field in the first two decades of this century. Lazell used the didactic technique, though he himself was dynamically oriented, and, because his work was first confined to "dementia praecox" patients, he was able to uncover much of the sexual content in the hallucinations of his psychotic patients. However, he relinquished this orientation in his later work.

Of special note to the present-day group therapist is the work of the late Trigand Burrow that was introduced in the 1920s. He named his special procedure "group analysis" which later was changed to "group psychoanalysis." His were predominantly residential groups. The patients and doctors lived together and the tensions that inevitably arose from such a living situation were reacted to and analyzed or discussed by the group. To Burrow can be traced not only the term "group analysis," which has been revived or rediscovered in our own day, but also the terms "here and now" as well as the "analysis of group tensions" which are now employed by some group therapists. Burrow's work has not survived him largely because of the obscurity of his writings and the metaphysical nature of his ideas, though one cannot fail to recognize that many of his concepts are sound and conform to the best psychological and sociological thinking of our day.

Wender's early work was also conducted with large groups chiefly on a lecture, case presentation, discussion, and question-and-answer plan. Like Lazell before him, Wender had followed a psychoanalytical orientation in the explanation of psychological phenomena, and it is reported that the patients in the hospital in which he carried on this work had gained a great deal in understanding of their difficulties and some gained some control over themselves and their behavior. This work was inaugurated in the 1930s and continued for many years. Later, as group psychotherapy became known, Dr. Wender treated smaller groups by uncovering and insight-evoking techniques.

Even Schilder, who began his work in 1936 with a small, unselected group of hospital patients, did not employ free-associative catharsis which is the chief medium in a true psychoanalysis. Rather, his focus was the analysis of "ideologies" and the socializing effect of the group upon its members. The ideologies that he sought to clarify with his patients were concerned with attitudes toward self, body, possession, expulsion, aggression, cooperation, and the like. Dream analysis, however, was part of the therapeutic process in his group as it is also in psychoanalysis. In a general way, Schilder was an early pioneer in the application of Freudian psychology to group psychotherapy not only from the point of view of utilizing theory, but also as one who applied, at least in part, the psychoanalytic process to group treatment.

Even a cursory examination of the techniques we have selected as representative of the practices and, by implication at least, the principles of the workers in the use of groups prior to 1930s reveals the unmistakable fact that they do not conform to the criteria which in our opinion constitute true group psychotherapy. Their groups were large—anywhere between thirty and two hundred patients; the therapist functioned as an active leader and teacher rather than as a catalyzer and target of transference feelings. The patients had not been selected and grouped by any criteria, and their role was that of recipients of ideas, information, control, and advice, as the case may be. In some of the later practices patients did participate in the discussions and asked questions, but even here the free-associative catharsis, childhood memories, and dreams, resistance and transference analyses were absent. Rather, all the techniques of group psychotherapy predating the 1939s were authoritarian teaching; others conformed more with the modern understanding of education, that is, active, participatory learning and conceptualization.

But psychotherapy as we understand it currently goes beyond education and conceptualization. It is a realigning and reweighing of psychic forces that lead to a more' balanced and integrated functioning, internally and in relation to outer needs and demands.

Especially in the transference neuroses, this requires affect experience, or reexperience, with substitutes for earlier important persons in the life of the individual. These experiences help dislodge the noxious unconscious memories and release anxiety bound up in them which give rise to new and healthier attitudes and serve to recondition feelings and responses. Individual psychotherapy provides this through totally working through the transference attitudes toward the individual therapist or analyst; in groups these are lived out and worked through in transference relations also with fellow patients.

In the light of the above, we can further understand why a small group is a primary requirement for therapy and is effective also in good education, counseling, and guidance (where basic changes in personality are not the aim). The small groups, as we have already pointed out, provides a narrower field for emotional operation and, therefore, greater concentration of affect. It prevents loss of self-self-identity and pits individuals one against the other more poignantly and more directly than is possible in a large group. These and other situations reactivate and reawaken the hostilities and discomforts the patient had experienced in his natural family to a degree that cannot occur in large groups. Since, aside from constitutional predispositions, distortions predominantly stem from the relations with members of one's family, the duplication of these relations in a therapeutic climate is the key to psychic reintergration. This can obviously be achieved only in a small group in a face-to-face relation and intimate and affect-laden interactions.

We can therefore say with justification that *group psychotherapy had its beginnings with the introduction of the small group*, which took place in 1934. It is only in a small group that free-associative action and reflection (catharsis) can occur, valid interpretation be given, and telling insights acquired by adult and adolescent patients.

The present writer's own introduction of therapy through the group was based on the concept of a small group of eight. The number eight has since been universally accepted by therapists everywhere. Experimental studies of communication by group dynamists conducted more than twenty years later have shown that eight is the optimum number for the spread of significant emotional induction and the deeper type of interpenetration among people. In the opinion of the present writer, eight is the *maximum* for a truly psychoanalytically oriented therapy group; five or six patients would yield better results. The number eight as a limit for the size of groups has been set by us when we introduced activity groups for children at the outset and was adhered to when analytic group psychotherapy (first known as "Interview Group Therapy" to differentiate it from "Activity Group Therapy") was added.

The "hunch" that led me to the use of small groups in therapy was derived from working since 1911 with various types and sizes of groups in and out of classrooms, in "group work," in leisure-time occupations, and in formal and informal education. Many years prior to the inauguration of therapy groups I had recognized that interpenetration of personalities cannot occur in large groups where interactions are diffuse and perfunctory.

During World War II, and following American practices, a group of English psychiatrists, among whom Drs. Bion and Foulkes are the better known, did notable work with large groups of soldiers suffering from acute "battle fatigue." Despite the fact that it was not conducted along the lines of group psychotherapy as we understand it today, they succeeded in returning to active service an impressive number of those incapacitated through "shell shock." Some of the psychiatrists and other physicians who participated in these projects have carried on this work in their private practice and in hospitals after the termination of the war. It is reported that Dr. Bion has withdrawn completely from the practice of group psychotherapy. Foulkes' more recent writings would lead one to the conclusion that his work with therapy groups is of the psychoanalytic *genre*, though he still retains the conviction that the group is the unit of treatment and is inherently a therapeutic agent by *virtue of being a group*. Ezriel, who can be considered as either a member of a progenitor of the original English "groupistic" orientation, is now the foremost exponent in that country of the "here and now" group therapists. He also promulgates, as the center of his therapy, the analysis of "group tensions."[2]

Still more recently, a new theoretic orientation has made its appearance. It has as yet a small following and is practiced only by its formulator and a few of his adherents. This is the "therapeutic group

2. Since the above was written, reports have reached me that the "here and now" approach is enjoying lesser vogue at the present time.

dynamics" faction derived from the work of Kurt Lewin. The theoretic base for the formulations here is Lewinian "field theory" of sociology and social psychology. The technique employed in this type of group therapy relies largely upon the social matrix of the group and the resultant "group dynamics" that purportedly produce changes in the personality structure of the adult patients, or at least effect desirable changes in behavior and social adjustment.

Several facts seem to stand out in our rather brief recapitulation of the events in the development of group psychotherapy. One is that there has occurred a permanent swing from the large group to the small treatment group, since all the initiators, pioneers, and modifiers of the technique now work with small groups. Second, the direction that is being taken by the overwhelming majority of practitioners is along the lines of some form of our traditional or modified analytic psychotherapy. In this there is a very great range, however. The depth of uncovering and interpretation, the role of the therapist, the adherence to schools of psychologic thought, and many other factors are at great variance. The curve swings from quasi education or guidance to "group psychoanalysis," but sound practitioners encourage free communication in their patients and try to uncover significant suppressed feelings. The greatest variance, of course, is in the type of interpretation that patients receive from the therapists and the depth of insight they generate. This is conditioned by the latters' convictions, adherences and capacities.

Another major point that emerges from this fresh look at the development of group psychotherapy is that it has not been a continuum. Rather, workers in the field have out of their training, background, experience, and personality traits independently evolved techniques that conformed with these determining factors. Also, there have been considerable coincidental discoveries as well as some imitation and elaboration of one another's work.

Another aspect of the development as we observe it today is that the educational-didactic methods are being employed generally to an increasingly lesser extent, though they are still appropriate in specific situations, and that some of them have been discarded, while the analytically oriented group therapies of various shades and schools are on the upswing [9]. These as well as other aspects of the discussion in the foregoing pages are represented graphically in Figure 1.

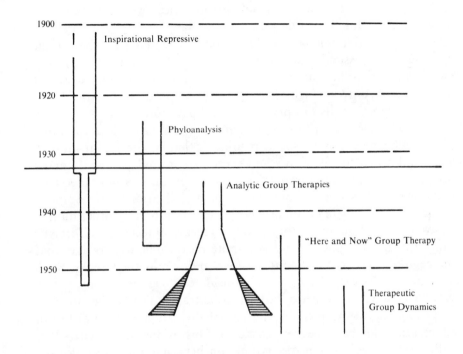

FIGURE I

In this figure we see the termination of the inspirational practices as exclusive techniques, while Burrow's "phyloanalysis" was discontinued with his death. The "here and now" technique is largely confined to a small number of practitioners. It is in vogue among a number of group therapists in European countries, in addition to England. It is, however, employed as part of analytic group psychotherapy, rather than as an exclusive method. The "group dynamic" school is in its beginnings and its future is unpredictable. The analytic groups are shown in the diagram as gaining most in therapeutic popularity, but, as already stated, the meaning of the term "analytic" is being extended considerably.

It seems to me that those who antedated the introduction of the *small*, psychoanalytically oriented groups can best be considered as *forerunners* of group psychotherapy as we know it today. I have discussed elsewhere the phenomenology of the group in modern society generally and its far-reaching influence, where it was also indicated how the group had to be assimilated into psychiatry as a result of "social homeostasis" [3]. I have attempted to show that, because of the essential democratic nature of our society, the group had to inevitably become a major and essential instrument of social function and control which, through the principle of homeostasis, had to be incorporated also in psychiatry and psychotherapy.

The fact must be kept in mind that there is always more than one person who responds to social readiness, that is, the maturation of ideas and social forces; as a result these persons independently make similar or identical discoveries, more or less simultaneously. Historically, it is idle for anyone to claim full priority or complete originality not only in group psychotherapy, but in every other human endeavor, for human history always reveals antecedent efforts or suggestions, sometimes from the remote past. Some writers aver that the beginnings of group therapy were laid down by the Greeks. Such beginnings, if they are to be considered beginnings of group psychotherapy, which is doubtful, can be traced also to the Bible.

Among the forerunners in the use of the group in mental health education, who have been neglected by historians, is Alfred Adler. Adler encouraged group discussions on personal and psychological problems, under the guidance of an adult with mental health orientation, among high school students in Vienna, as early as the second decade of this century. He did not, however, envisage these group discussions as psychotherapy as we now understand it. He recognized, and rightly so, the values for the average person of ventilating feelings in a peer group, the sharing of similar preoccupations, and the constructive values of mutual support and guidance. This work can properly be classified among those efforts which we now designate as group guidance or group counseling. Its value, if it were sufficiently widespread in schools and young people's groups, would be inestimable. Such cathartic, guidance and educational experiences could greatly enhance the mental health of the community, but it should be rigidly differentiated from psychotherapy for individuals who have already internalized noxious or pathological psychic elements as a result of a traumatic life or specific traumata.

The preceding pages are not intended to give a detailed history of group psychotherapy, which is done elsewhere [159]. They contain only its bare outlines. The intention is to indicate the error in the historic perspective into which all of us, including the present writer, have fallen by following, uncritically, Dr. Thomas's record. This is done in the hope that younger and more diligent students will undertake the task of filling in the gaps and supplying further information relative to our thesis. The brevity of this statement has made it necessary to omit the names of many "modifiers" of the technique to conform with their special bias, beliefs, loyalties, personal idiosyncrasies, and convictions—many of whom have added to the general store of our knowledge and experience, as well as to our confusion. A more complete history should include the leading names among these. It is hoped, however, that the error of considering sequences of *publication* as indicators of *initiation* of practices or identical with them will be avoided. The speed with which some practitioners burst into print varies. Some delay publication in the interest of scientific exactitude, while others are less cautious in this regard.

CHAPTER 8

FREUD'S CONTRIBUTIONS TO GROUP
PSYCHOTHERAPY
(1956)

The hundredth anniversary of Professor Sigmund Freud's birth, 1956, witnessed the appearance of countless publications in scores of languages on his life and works, on his influence upon and contributions to numerous fields in our culture and to contemporary culture itself. These have been expository, critical, and panegyric—all in praise and appreciation—most were enthusiastic, some less so, but hardly any contained the acrimonious and angry assaults that characterized many of the statements made about him during his life.

That Freud has influenced to varying degrees every area of modern culture and civilization few will gainsay. Some of the efforts and thought systems have been transformed by the insights that emanated from his writings; others have been modified as to direction and content; still others have been enriched by the addition of the new knowledges. Much confusion has been cleared up in many fields as a result of the new understandings that he contributed or which evolved on the basis of what came from his pen.

Freud's original impetus for his work came from an approach to healing mentally disturbed patients, but his observations led him to construct a new system of individual and social psychology unknown before his day. He had thrown light upon the mental constitution and dynamic processes of man's psyche which had been up to that time in the realm of speculation and conjecture, or just ignorance. His formulations of the unconscious and its operation made clear much that had been enigmatic and his theories of the libido, infantile sexuality, and the oedipal strivings clarified what had been puzzling for ages in human behavior. The patterns of functions and relations of the id, ego, and superego and the relation of instinct and social mores were now understood as a result of his pioneering and penetrating thought and prodigious work.

The arts, education, family life, the social sciences and humanities, psychology, the status of woman and her relation to life and work, the relations of men and women, parents and children, races and nationalities, the styles of dress and designing, industrial designs and merchandising, and countless other efforts, patterns, relations and institutions have been affected by his discoveries and formulations; for these have struck at the very essence and sources of life itself. Seldom does a man arise in the course of human history to enunciate a basic truth. Countless "truths" have been propounded in the past millennia; truths that dealt with specific areas or ideas. Only infrequently has mankind been the witness to the discovery of basic truths such as those of Copernicus, Galileo, Darwin, and Einstein. What these foremost scientists have done to man's understanding of his physical world, Freud has done to man's understanding of himself, a task by far more difficult and one that required greater penetration and courage.

Whether one accepts Freud's formulations *in toto* or not, whether one differs from him as to psychologic theory or therapeutic practice, no thinking person can remain unaffected by exposure to the mass of observations, information, and theory that came from this man. There are a great many derivative and modified theories and practices that have developed since Freud lived and worked in the field of psychoanalysis. These are known under many names and have special features and vocabularies of their own, but all are derived from and based upon Freud's numerous suggestions, remarks, hypotheses, discoveries, and formulations. Even those who claim different origin have been stimulated by him.

The readers of this Journal undoubtedly came upon more than one of the widespread statements on Freud in this centennial year in which multifarious aspects of the subject were presented. Of additional and perhaps special interest are Freud's views on groups and especially their relation to group psychotherapy.

Freud was aware of the difference between individual and group psychology. We find in his *Group Psychology and the Analysis of the Ego* (1921)[1] the speculation how individual psychology was transformed into group psychology. He says: "The primal father had prevented his sons from satisfying their directly sexual impulsions; he forced them into abstinence and consequently into the emotional ties with him and with one another which could arise out of those of their tendencies that were inhibited in their sexual aim. *He forced them,* so to speak, *into group psychology.* [Italics mine.] His sexual jealousy and intolerance became in the last resort the causes of group psychology."

Freud based his deductions on group psychology and group behavior upon the fundamental and quite correct studies of Le Bon and McDougall, and to a lesser extent upon those of Trotter. We find here a contradiction that led Freud to confusion as to what a group is. Although his psychological definition of a group conforms with our present-day understanding, in his treatment of the subject there is obvious confusion. Le Bon's and McDougall's studies dealt with large groups or masses rather than small groups. The latter were more the concern of Trotter, though not entirely so. While thoroughly aware of the difference in the dynamics of small groups and crowds or masses, Freud nonetheless treats these two types as one in his discussion and applies observations of one to the other. This is of course not correct, for intensification and the process of mutual induction are not only quantitatively but also qualitatively affected by numbers.

Freud's conclusion that the "group is similar to the primal horde" has to be questioned. It would be more correct if the word "group" were to be substituted by "mass." "The psychology of such a group," says Freud, ". . . the dwindling of the conscious individual personality, the focusing of thoughts in a common direction, the predominance of the affective side of the mind and of unconscious psychical life, the tendency to the immediate carrying out of intentions as they emerge— all this corresponds to a state of regression to a primitive mental activity, of just such a sort as we should be inclined to ascribe to the primal horde."

We know that masses of people and mobs in a mood of violence such as lynchings, riots, and strikes, and nations in times of strong

1. *Standard Edition* 18:65-143.

emotional disturbance such as war, behave in the manner described, but it is not in the nature of small groups to regress to such excesses or display such extreme behavior. The ego functions of each participant remain more intact in small groups than in large active masses, and the superego of each continues in its discriminative control rather than investing these functions either in the leader or suspending them altogether because of the socially sanctioned release from instinct controls that are otherwise constantly exerted by the individual.

The seeming error arises perhaps from two separate sources. Freud's era in Europe was one of individualism. Group life as we know it today in a democracy was not in the awareness even of the most enlightened in Freud's time, yet irrational behavior on the part of masses and nations was not markedly different from contemporary behavior, judging from the vast information accumulated by enthnologists and anthropologists concerning primitive society, and from historians about the less remote past. One hesitates, however, to ascribe to an intellect like Freud's a lack of comprehension of the difference between a "group" and a "crowd" or "mass." In fact in a number of passages he refers in passing to the importance of numbers in the behavior of groups. One is rather inclined to attribute this confusion to the error of the translator. In a footnote concerning this the translator explains that he had used the term "group" to substitute for the German *Masse*, and Le Bon's *foule* (the latter having been translated as "crowd" in the title of his book). In my opinion, it was to the translator's inexperience in the theory of groups that this error has to be laid. In the light of this the similarity that Freud draws between the "group" and the horde is more understandable.

Freud wrote his essay on groups in the second decade of the century, but he anticipated later theoreticians when he emphasized among many other factors the importance of the leader in group formation and group functioning. In our day the definition of a group includes leadership as one of its essential elements, for it is the centrality of the leader or a representative symbol that secures group cohesion. He was the first to call attention to the leader as a common object of libidinal cathexis and that this cathexis holds the group members together. On this point we read his cryptic sentence: "The group vanishes in dust, like a Bologna flask when its top is broken." This observation has many implications for further study and for a more conscious and more appropriate role that leaders of all types of groups and members of governmental bodies must assume to be effective.[2] His parallelisms between the group leader and the leader of the primal horde are particularly apt in this regard. However, further observation of the unconscious projections of group members upon the person of the leader also reveals their similarity to their attitudes toward a parental figure, especially the father. This fact is even more pronounced in small groups, though it is evidenced also by masses. I have elsewhere suggested that one of the mental health outlets in a democracy lies in the fact that periodically the voters can reject their father substitutes (President, governors, and other persons in authority), that is, they kill them off.

In small groups, particularly, because they are close replicas of the family, individuals are stimulated to reenact their family-conditioned attitudes and behavior. Their patterns of submission or attack upon the leader, as the case may be, and the relationships with fellow group members are determined by and stem from the earlier family climate. It has been shown that the group serves in *locus maternis*. The leader usually represents symbolically the father figure, while the group is the complementary figure of the mother. In this sense the original family constellation is reestablished in groups (and in group psychotherapy). The sternness of the leader can be tolerated with greater equanimity by a member than the chastisement, disapproval, or rejection by the group. The group is expected by each of its members to accept him and approve of him and each is more likely to adjust his behavior to the demands of the group than to the authority of the leader.[3]

The role and function of the group therapist is in a number of ways and in basic respects unlike those of the leader in ordinary small groups, but the transference projections upon him are the same in nature, though quantitatively much more intense. The therapist is the

---

2. Because of the inadequate understanding of his role, a director of a professional organization with a large personnel sought this writer's advice. When during the interview it was suggested in passing that his position places him in the role of a father substitute, he burst into involuntary laughter. His failure on his job stemmed directly from his inability to assume a parental role, having refused to have even children of his own. Successful directorship of organizations require the assumption of the good, though firm, father who loves his children.

3. I have suggested that among the transferences that appear in therapy groups, "transference toward the group" is one that has to be considered in understanding the therapeutic process and the reactions of patients [9].

target of libido cathexis to a much greater degree than is the leader of any other type of group as a result of the therapeutic process and the therapist-patient relationship. Freud also called attention to the existence of special mutual relations among members of a group that have a direct bearing upon our later understanding of interpatient transferences. He remarks that members of a group with an "outer object" have "identified themselves with one another in their ego." This identification we have found to be even more intensive in therapy groups, but it occurs on a selective basis. In these groups there are also present negative identifications or counteridentifications. This, too, Freud anticipated when after tracing identification as originating from the relation with the child's parents he remarks, "Identification . . . is ambivalent from the very first."

Freud's elaboration of the concept of identification is valuable in the understanding of this dynamic process in therapy groups. We have recognized the importance of identification as a corrective and have suggested the term "identification transference" to point out the presence of this dynamic. In *Group Psychology and the Analysis of the Ego* Freud develps this idea and puts forth three types of identification. "First . . . the original form of emotional tie with an object; secondly . . . introjection of the object into the ego; and thirdly, . . . perception of a common quality shared with some other person . . ." All of these aspects of identification are operative in group psychotherapy, as they are in other types of small groups, and must be viewed as part of the ego ideal of the individual. We are also aware that the psychotic is subject predominantly to the second type to a point of oral incorporation in fantasy so that other persons, especially the therapist, become part and parcel of his ego. The main characteristic of the psychotic is that for him the model of identification becomes also the target of intense hostility and destruction.

Many of the important features and dynamics that have been described by various writers on group psychotherapy for the most part are mentioned in passing in the essay to which reference is made here. Several references are made to the "group mind," for which term Freud gives credit to McDougall. The phenomenon of bipolarity in groups (which is present also in therapy groups) is recorded in the following terms: "it is to be noticed that in these two artificial groups each individual is bound by libidinal ties on the one hand to the leader . . .

and on the other hand to the other members of the group." And: "If each individual is bound in two directions by such an intense emotional tie, we shall find no difficulty in attributing to that circumstance the alteration and limitation which have been observed in his personality" (by virtue of his belonging to the group).

The concepts of "group mind" and "leaderless groups" to which much attention had been given by the English group psychotherapists also receive mention. The former is credited to Le Bon. The term "leaderless groups," however, is used by Freud in a different sense. By leaderless groups he means groups which do not have a personal leader, but in which his place is taken by a binding idea, ideal, or aim, such as the Church, for example. Even the term "signaling" that has been only recently introduced in the literature on group psychotherapy is mentioned in passing in Freud's essay.

Freud makes the following very significant statement in the light of group psychotherapy: "Where a powerful impetus has been given to group formation, neuroses may diminish and at all events temporarily disappear. Justifiable attempts have also been made to turn this antagonism between neuroses and group formation to therapeutic account."

This statement is of value to us in a rather negative way. The question that it suggests is whether groups per se, that is, the fact that a patient participates in a group and makes an adjustment to it, constitutes psychotherapy. Further, can the fact that some behavioral changes occur and symptoms disappear be relied on as evidence of permanent changes in the patient so that he can carry on in the future the business of living without the psychoneurotic interferences with which he had come to us? We have Freud's statement just quoted implied answers to these questions. These answers are also derived from the experience of the proponents of analytic group psychotherapy today.

The analytic group therapist found, as did others, that some patients in groups give up their symptoms rather rapidly, but they recognize that such symptom improvement can be a screen for resistance to treatment which is facilitated by identification with other group members and the group as a whole. The nature of analytic group interviews is such that direct suggestions and guidance and intellectual understanding (cognition) are unavoidable. Because of fear, discomfort and resistance, some patients readily adopt the ideas thus gained as controls for their lives and act as though basic changes had occurred in their personalities. Others are suggestible or have a need to please and be accepted by the therapist and/or the group and present similar changes.

Analytic group psychotherapy holds that such manifestations can be accepted as basic and more or less permanent only when they are worked through in transference and through the analysis of resistances. By "worked through" is meant here that the anxieties bound up in the different traumatic situations in the patient's past have been released and his feelings and current reactions made available to the examination and therefore control of the ego.

This position is supported by Freud in his statement, though indirectly. His statement has two important elements. One is a "powerful impetus to group formation" in the individual, the other is that neuroses *temporarily* disappear or *are diminished.* Such improvement can be readily observed in experience. The most common of these is the diminution of emotional disturbances reported by psychiatrists during economic depression, war, and after deeply affecting major catastrophes. The difficulties, however, reappear when the emergencies pass. His statement is also supported by the many mental healing cults that do produce desirable effects upon their adherents, though the latter are not aware of the fact that these improvements are conditioned on their continued membership and that they have grown permanently dependent upon the support of the beliefs or rituals.

As far as the statement concerns analytic group psychotherapy, it can be categorically averred that there is no "powerful impetus" in analytic groups for "group formation," nor is their aim to "diminish" the neurosis or to have it "temporarily disappear." We have pointed out on many occasions that *group mobility* as opposed to *group fixity* is one of the major foundations of analytic group psychotherapy. The group goal and unitary purpose necessary for "group formation" are absent in therapy groups; nor is the aim temporary alleviation of symptoms or decrease in the neuroses. The aim is intrapsychic reorganization of the functions and relations of the id, ego, and superego. This aim is not a *common* one; rather, there is a *similar* aim in each individual as an individual.

It is important to note in a discussion such as this that the analytically oriented group psychotherapists in the United States, who were first to introduce this technique, have not been guided by Freud's *Group Psychology and the Analysis of the Ego*. There is no evidence either in their writing or practice that they have been influenced by it. They have rather sought to apply psychoanalytic concepts and techniques to groups and in the process found the need for modifying and expanding these, though holding fast to the original course of Freudian psychology. It was also found necessary to elaborate on his concepts and dynamics to make them suitable for work with groups. The role and functions of the therapist, as well, also had to be reconsidered and redefined, though in this respect the essential orientation is in conformity with psychoanalytic tenets.

It is only upon rereading of the essay that these parallels have been drawn. The Freudian teachings that have been most valuable and without which analytic group psychotherapy could not have taken its present shape are the principles of the depth psychology he taught, the understandings he gave us of the genetics and dynamics of the human psyche, and the elements of therapy that he had established, namely, transference, catharsis, and insight, to which can be added reality testing and sublimation.

I have referred to this relation in a brief statement on the subject at the invitation of Harry Slochower, Ph.D., in *The Guide to Psychiatric and Psychological Literature*, which for the sake of brevity is reproduced here:

Everyone who is acquainted with my work and writings on group psychotherapy should have no difficulty in recognizing its genetic relation to Freud's basic formulations. Even so divergent a practice as Activity Group Therapy owes its procedures and techniques to that incomparable researcher into the human psyche. The concept of freedom of expression in psychotherapy, which is so basic, has found perhaps its fullest expression in "activity catharsis," and the behavior of the therapist, though deceptively inactive, actually is directed toward interpretation, even though this interpretation is not verbal but "action interpretation."

The activity group therapist views the child's behavior as the "overt content" and, to be effective in his role, has to perceive the "latent content" of the acts. Here are acted out inherent aggressions, basic anxiety, and infantile sexuality—all formulations of Freud's—which are treated therapeutically in consonance with sound psychoanalytic tenets. Because of the nature of children and the difference in setting, these are treated differently, the difference being operational, and not in conception or in significance. The elements of transference, catharsis, and insight are relied on in this practice as in psychoanalysis and are understood in the same light, though phenomenologically they may appear at first glance as unrelated.

In the various types of analytic group psychotherapy the similarity with Freudian theory and technique is more apparent. Free association, regression, insight, libidinal transference, and the many other dynamics characteristic of psychoanalysis are present and operative. Uncovering, exploration, revelation of the content of the unconscious, regression to infantile traumata, and the evolvement of insight and ego control are essentials in analytic group psychotherapies as they are in psychoanalysis. The difference between these practices may be described briefly as stemming from two sources. One is that patients in groups serve as *mutual catalyzers* speeding up catharsis and that the transference is *diluted*. These decrease resistance, and, therefore, render the therapy less intensive, affecting the patients' personalities less profoundly.

I came upon Activity Group Psychotherapy through pathways other than psychoanalysis, namely progressive education and social group work. However, its relation to Freudian formulations became quickly apparent to me and it was not difficult to reinterpret the dynamic phenomena in these groups in the light of Freud's basic principles. Analytic group psychotherapy followed as an almost inevitable development in which these principles are obvious [156].

Note must be taken of the fact that techniques in group therapy other than analytic are extant. These draw their *raison d'être* from other assumptions such as those of the ego therapies and group-centered dynamics. Their relation to Freudian sources has as yet not been clarified. This task still remains to be done.

Postscript: 1975

Very early in my work in 1934, I recognized the possibility of the negative effect of group cohesion on therapeutic groups. I have expressed this conviction many times before and formulated it in the following statement: "Instead of coherence essential to socio-educational groups, therapeutic groups feed upon interpersonal conflict and overt expression of hostility among the members" [16]. This conclusion was derived from my work with various types of nontherapeutic groups with children, adolescents (mostly of high school age) and adults (mostly members of labor unions). The oppositional objectives of these groups vis-à-vis the therapeutic groups make differential approaches essential in the three practices. Increase in the individual's interest and capacity for socialization, conceptual knowledge of life and the world, and discovery of latent talents are the goals in the nontherapeutic groups, and the reconstruction or correction of the personality structure and improvement in intrapersonal function in the other.

Perhaps the evaluation of these assumptions may appear simplistic when we assume that the most prevalent psychonoxious constellations—and this is certainly true of psychoneurotics—are hostility and the guilt generated by it. The obvious cure for them is to discharge the hostility without fear of retaliation or any other negative reactions: verbally for adolescents and adults and in action by children. These cathartic manifestations serve as essential bases for insight and diminution of tyrannical superego demands.

Therapists who strive for and encourage "group cohesion," which one only too frequently encounters in the literature, fail to recognize the internal processes of patients and the autonomy and stubbornness of psychoneuroses and in many instances also of character.

To test this hypothesis, Dr. Joseph J. Peters and Herman A. Rother set up a five-year rigidly executed classical research in Philadelphia of "Cohesiveness and Hostility: Their Influence and Outcome in Group Psychotherapy of Antisocial Sexual Behavior," in which six psychiatrists who conducted groups: one sociologist, two psychologists, and a probation officer participated. The data were derived from a forty-week group psychotherapy program with probationed sex offenders. Analysis shows that exposure to hostility is positively related to outcomes, whereas cohesiveness is related to outcomes with a negative tendency.

According to the authors, "The purpose of this investigation [was] to measure the relative importance of cohesiveness and hostility upon outcome . . . whether antisocial behavior continues as reported by the police . . . and after an exhaustive study found that in a one-year follow up study of the patients after termination of treatment, cohesiveness . . . tends to be negatively related to success." With respect to "contemporary detractors of long range group psychotherapy," the investigators aver that these practitioners "may be inclined to use this information as encouragement to uncork hostility upon their clients in weekend encounter, sensitivity and other instantaneous groups. . . . The attraction to such groups may in fact be a need in contemporary society to experience group cohesion. Exposure to hostility may be counterproductive if not damaging to the (non-patient) participants" (Personal Communication). These insights are very encouraging and confirm our views expressed in "Eclecticism versus Sectarianism in Group Psychotherapy" [15].

CHAPTER 9

A SYSTEMATIC THEORY
(1954)

If group psychotherapy is to take its rightful place among the healing professions, it must evolve a structural, scientific edifice in which the dynamics of the process will be made palpable to all. Agreement on some common foundations is essential to bind the practitioners in the field, even if divergencies arise in the elaboration or application of these bases. Understandably the practice of science, which then becomes an art, would differ in greater or lesser details with each group or individual practitioner. Educational, personal, and temperamental differences always influence one's choice and practice. Nevertheless, agreement is necessary as to the bases of a profession. It is these root principles and dynamics in group psychotherapy with which we aim to deal in this paper.

It is my belief that the therapeutic effects accrued are the same in groups as they are in individual psychotherapy, though they differ in some minor elements. These pertain to the therapeutic process rather than to intrapsychic dynamics which, in my opinion, are the same in all sound methods of treatment. Repair of defects can be corrected only by specific inner experiences regardless of what tools are employed. The pathology and the defective elements in the personality need specific correctives whatever the technique may be. These are libido distribution, ego strengthening, adjusting the superego, and correcting the self-image—results that are achieved through the dynamic factors of (1) transference, (2) catharsis, (3) insight, (4) reality testing, and (5) sublimation. It is in these that major operational differences in individual and group psychotherapy can be observed.

Transference

The transference in psychoanalysis is, in its purest form, unilateral; that is, it is directed from the patient toward the analyst. In other and less intensive individual psychotherapies, transference is bilateral. By this is meant that while the transference on the part of the patient is substantially the same as above, the therapist, in turn, responds to him through empathy, interest, and encouragement. This is made necessary largely by the physical face-to-face position and the greater involvement of the ego in psychotherapies other than psychoanalysis. In group psychotherapy, on the other hand, the patient-therapist transferences are modified and diluted by the presence of other persons. Early feelings and inadequately repressed memories relating to siblings as well as parents are activated. Thus, a patient who has parental transference feelings towad the therapist may at the same time react toward other members of the group as siblings. These varied affects and attitudes set up a network of emotional tensions peculiar to groups.

To differentiate these types of transferences, I have suggested the terms *libidinal transference* for that which is derived from and related to parents, and *sibling transference* where it is concerned with feelings emanating from relations with siblings. Still a third type was designated as *identification transference*. As the term implies, it is that part of the transference relation in which a patient identifies with the therapist and other members of the group and desires to be like them and to emulate them. They serve as ego ideals and models of identification. The element of identification is present in all transference attitudes, though it is not usually sufficiently recognized. The special characteristic of group therapy is that there are present a number of identification objects, instead of just one, the therapist.

The similarity in the nature of transference in individual and group psychotherapy is most recognizable in its *positive* and *negative* phases which arise in both types of treatment. In a group, just as in individual treatment, the *basic transference* toward the therapist must be positive, for without it, patients would cease coming to the group.

However, in group psychotherapy the *transference toward the group* must be positive as well. In this type of treatment favorable transference attitudes toward the therapist alone are not sufficient, for when the group attacks, threatens, or rejects a patient, he will be unable to participate in or gain from it. Patients whose basic difficulties stem from fear of, or antagonism to, groups cannot be included in group psychotherapy for they usually drop out early in treatment. Fear and antagonism stem from the pain and discomfort in one's early family. A family (group) climate in which tensions, fear-inducing interpersonal relations, rejection or neglect, threats to personal autonomy, psychologic survival, status and self-esteem predominated, conditions the individual for defensive attack on or avoidance of groups. Obviously such preconditioning is a counterindication for group psychotherapy. One of the important elements in group psychotherapy, therefore, is transference toward the group as well as individual transferences.

"Group-induced anxiety" [19] is always present and, in my opinion, stems from (1) phylogenetic engramatic (evolutionary) sources, (2) family conditioning, and (3) uncertainty of ego functioning of fellow group members. When the ego of an individual is unable to deal with these tensions and anxieties, a state of negative transference toward the group results; the patient requires a preliminary course of individual treatment to overcome his initial fears and aggressions toward groups. Sometimes, a patient is unable to participate in a group because of the presence of one or more fellow members whom he cannot countenance because they recall images of painful experiences in his past with persons whom they may resemble in some ways. The patient cannot function in their presence. The intense anger and aggression aroused overwhelm his ego controls and out of discomfort and fear he may act out or quit the group.

The usual effect of groups is that of *transference dilution*. Because of the number of objects of transference and identification and the *multiple targets of hostility,* the intensity of the transference on any one person is diminished, though the total *quantum of affect* may be multiplied many times. This quantum is particularly high in the negative transference phases and is the result of the dynamics of reinforcement, mutual support, intensification, induction, and intragroup identifications.

Still other aspects of the transference in which there is similarity in individual and group treatment are those of the *transitory* and *basic* (or permanent) phases [56]. While there is an alternation of positive and negative transferences during psychotherapy, it is essential that the basic transference should be positive. Negative transference, though essential and inevitable, must be short-lived and temporary. Pain, suffering, and discomfort bring a patient to treatment, but he continues because he has confidence in the therapist and faith in his genuine interest, though resurgence of negative and hostile feelings inevitably occurs. In fact, if improvement is to be effected, these feelings must be brought to the surface, but they cannot become dominant. Once this occurs, the treatment unavoidably breaks off. While temporary phases can be negative, the basic transference must be positive.

These rules hold for group psychotherapy as they do for individual treatment. However, in groups, the basic transference has to be positive not only toward the therapist, but also toward the group as a whole; also, negative feelings toward members in the group cannot be so intense as to be intolerable to the participant [19].

The differential nature of transference in individual and group therapy needs to be noted. Transference attitudes in the former, theoretically at least, have to flow in one direction: from the patient to the therapist. The ideal condition can be achieved, in practice only in a "couch" psychoanalysis. Detachment and absence of positive counterfeelings alienates a patient in face-to-face treatment. Thus, in the less intensive forms of treatment such as carried on by most psychotherapists, counterfeelings are present and these must of necessity be positive if the patient is to continue in treatment [19]. In groups, transference feelings are directed towad a number of persons at the same time or at different times. I have suggested the terms *unilateral, bilateral,* and *multilateral* transferences to describe these phenomena. Unilateral transferences are present only in psychoanalysis and in Activity Group Therapy. Bilateral transference is present in all other forms of individual psychotherapy and multilateral in all groups.

Schematically, therefore, we see that the nature and dynamics of transference in groups is as in Table 1.

TABLE 1

TRANSFERENCE PHENOMENA IN GROUP PSYCHOTHERAPY

Positive Negative	Transitory Permanent	Libininal Sibling* Identification Group*	Diluted* Intensified*

* *Indicates phenomena present exclusively in group psychotherapy. Others a e present in all therapies, but are modified through the group.*

Catharsis

Catharsis is the same in groups as in individual psychotherapy. It can be divided into two major divisions: *verbal catharsis* and *activity catharsis*. The former is employed with nonpsychotic adults and adolescents. The latter is essential in the treatment of children and some types of psychotic patients. Individual and Play Group Therapy, Activity Interview Group Therapy, occupational and recreational therapies in mental hospitals rely in part on activity catharsis. Activity Group Therapy employs it solely, though there is an increasing tendency to use activity catharsis in the treatment of adult psychotics. With neurotics as well, various forms of dramatics, role playing, art and music therapies and release therapy employ action as well as language. This catharsis can be characterized as *activity-verbal catharsis*. Activity catharsis, however, is the pattern in the treatment of children and is employed in its purest form in Activity Group Therapy where it is the sole method. In other therapies it can be ancillary to or coordinate with verbalization.

Both verbal and activity catharsis can occur as (1) free association, (2) associative thinking, or action, (3) directed, (4) induced, (5) forced, and (6) vicarious.

Free association is well known and most frequently used in psychotherapy and psychoanalysis. It consists of the patient's following unimpeded the articulation and sequences of thoughts, memories, and feelings as they occur. Through this maze of seemingly unrelated and confused ideas the patient recalls the traumatic occurrences in his past that have resulted in disturbing feelings concerning persons, objects, situations and events out of proportion in the economy of his psyche (cathexis) and disturb his emotional and behavioral equilibrium.

By associative thinking or *acts* [56] we designate the productions that are related to *current* experiences and concerns. The content of these we have designated as *top realities*, which are the starting point in all psychotherapies. In true psychotherapy, however, it constitutes only the starting point, for soon memories, feelings and thoughts about the past arise by the process of free association. In less intensive treatment methods, however, associative thinking and top realities may occupy a major portion of treatment and in guidance and counseling they are the sole content of the interviews.

In contrast to free association the methods of directed, induced, and forced catharsis can be employed at times in some types of psychotherapy with specially selected patients. They predominate in counseling and guidance.

Directed catharsis designates the procedure in which the therapist (or a fellow patient in a group) questions the patient in an attempt to uncover specific facts or memories that he may consider important at a given time. This practice may be necessary at certain points even where free association is the prevailing tool. Some therapists employ it as a major or exclusive technique, as in "authoritarian" and "inspirational" therapies. This method is suitable with psychotics.

Induced catharsis occurs especially in groups and sometimes also in individual treatment. In the latter it results from countertransference reactions on the part of the therapist, whose facial expression, manner, verbal and nonverbal response cause the patient to react in turn, thus setting him off on a line of communication that he would otherwise not have followed. We shall presently see how induction of catharsis occurs in other ways in group.

Forced catharsis is in a way paradoxical, for anything that is forced cannot very well be cathartic. We include it here, however, both for completeness and because it is employed to describe the situation in which the patient is *required* to give specific information as an act of submission to authority or as part of disciplinary requirements [5]. In a sense revelations by patients made under the influence of barbiturates and hypnosis can be included in this category.

As we review these methods of catharsis in group psychotherapy, we find that they vary in some respects from those in individual treatment, though similarities are equally impressive. Both associative thinking and free association are present in group psychotherapy as they are also in individual treatment. However, in groups the former may continue for a longer period. Because of fear of group reaction and the uncertainty of one's status, there are facts and feelings a patient withholds for longer periods in a group which he would more easily reveal in individual treatment. There are others, however, that are more readily uncovered in groups. There are some facts in the life of patients so deeply cathected and of which they may be so intensely ashamed that they cannot bring them into the open in the presence of others. This phenomenon explains why many psychotherapists have found the need for parallel individual and group interviews. What a patient cannot relate in a group, he does in the face-to-face sessions with the therapist. Through the process of catalysis, the group sessions serve to bring repressed feelings and thoughts to the threshold of the foreconscious and to the conscious, which are then revealed in individual interviews.

Even in activity therapy groups, children's activity catharsis is nearly always free-associative. While it may be difficult to recognize the relation of a child's act to his intrapyschic tensions and preoccupations and to discern the sequence of a series of his acts, our observation shows that such free-associative relation does exist. To be able to recognize this articulated relation requires, perhaps, special sensitivity and aptitude, but it is aided by knowledge of a case and experience with this method. For example, after a period of Activity Group Therapy, a boy of eleven who had come for treatment diffident, quiet and withdrawn, goes around the room and taps with a hammer on the walls, making a complete circle. On the face of it, this can be seen as increased security and his experimental efforts at being aggressive. However, his case history records that he was a premature baby and his act may be a prenatal memory of seeking egress from the womb. This theme frequently occurs in dreams.

Children's activity catharsis need not always be free-associative, for we know that much of it is reactive to immediate pressures, anger, and resentment. Aggressive acts or depressed behavior have often been traced to events preceding the group sessions. Failure in school, disturbance at home, defeat by peers, and similar negative experiences are discharged by aggression or are reacted to by diffidence and withdrawal. However, in most instances, such an initial act brings in its wake others in a chain of free association.

Directed catharsis is likely to appear in groups with great frequency. This is due to the fact that members of groups interrogate a patient, ask for explanations and elucidation, and otherwise offer leading questions. Since both identification and curiosity cannot be but aroused by the communications of patients, these are inevitable in group interviews. In fact, it may at times become necessary for the therapist to "rescue" a patient from the quizzing propensities of fellow group members when the exploration becomes disturbing to him. Thus, directed catharsis, while employed occasionally by all psychotherapists, and even in psychoanalysis, as a planful technique, is unavoidable in groups because of the interstimulation characteristic of groups.

As already mentioned, induced catharsis is inherent in therapy groups. One of the major dynamics of groups is mutual induction, a term that is usually applied to describe emotional contagion among humans. The inductive effect also applies to catharsis, for a statement by one sets off others to associate with that stimulus. Because of common interests, preoccupations, and difficulties, it can be expected that a statement made by one of the group would set off or stimulate associations in others. Usually, the less conflicted members of a group initiate this chain of inductive reactions which are taken up by the more conflicted and frightened patients. However, sometimes the most anxious may bring topics or reflections over which the better integrated and those whose ego controls are stronger would hesitate. Induced catharsis is a major advantage of groups over other types of treatment. Where resistances are intense, groups are very effective. The inductive effect of other patients dissolves barriers and activates each participant. Psychotherapists frequently report on patients who present difficulties in individual treatment but do well in groups. In addition to other factors involved, some being positive, others unfavorable, induced catharsis is one of the reasons for this.

Induced catharsis operates at its maximum in activity groups of children. Here the unimpeded acting out that may have been threatening to a child is encouraged by the free behavior of the other members of the group. The inductive effect both in terms of activity catharsis and emotions is a major therapeutic dynamic in these groups.

Forced catharsis is not permitted in groups, and when a patient attempts to force another to reveal himself beyond his ego readiness, it must be diverted or interpreted by the therapist. It should not be employed by the latter, though, as has been reported and probably still is done, though rarely. It must be considered as basically unsuitable and when so used is a result of fundamental misconceptions of what psychotherapy is.

The value of group psychotherapy to a certain type of patient is *vicarious catharsis*. This type of self-revelation and release is obtained when a patient identifies fully with another's communication in which the latter mirrors his problems and reactions. Where a patient, either because of neurotic anxiety or characterological impediments, finds it difficult to communicate and relieve himself of psychologic pressures, he is greatly benefited by identification with the communications of another and, as we shall presently see, may gain insight which he would not otherwise achieve. This type of covert catharsis is contingent upon a high degree of similarity of problems and capacity for identification, which are always present in group members, though to varying degrees and at different times. Thus, a specific patient may experience vicarious catharsis at one point because his problem is mirrored by another. He will not experience it when still another fellow member relates a problem quite different from his own. It does not set off an empathic response.

In addition to the mirroring quality of this process, vicarious catharsis is also conditioned by the similarity of personalities as well as by the similarity of pathology or problem. On purely theoretic grounds one can say that identification essential to this experience would be hardly possible in persons who are too divergent in their quality or make-up. Where reactions are at variance, empathy is difficult or impossible. However, in a group of patients there exist, at all times, possibilities for vicarious catharsis and the resultant release from anxiety and guilt. This is especially true of productive analytic groups.

Evidences of vicarious catharsis are replete in children's activity therapy groups. Unbridled acting out of the instigators greatly benefits the isolates and the neuters [53] who would be afraid to initiate or even participate in such activities on their own. At first such children are afraid even to observe the obstreperousness, hilarity, or destructiveness of their group mates, but in time they smile at these antics, and later participate in them, and gradually even accept them. During the initial periods there are evidences of feelings of release and inner satisfaction in the fact that they are now able to withstand aggressive acts. Of even more significance is the fact that others behave in a manner in which they would like to themselves. At first the accumulated hostility and aggression held in abeyance is discharged vicariously through the acts of others. Expression of hostile feelings which they can now accept with less conflict and guilt finally leads to self-acceptance and improved self-image.

Groups supply each patient with a number of targets for their repressed or overt hostility in the persons of fellow patients. I have bed this phenomenon as *target multiplicity,* which also has the t of weakening the libidinal transference upon the therapist. It is catharsis, since it reduces the fear of piling hostility onto one erson. Hostility can be spread around, as it were, which has the definite disadvantages as well as advantages for the therpeutic process.

When patients freely reveal themselves, they activate one another to do the same in areas that they frequently find difficult under other circumstances. In the case of induced catharsis, for example, we saw that one patient activates another to come forth and participate in the group interview or reveal some difficulty that he had held in check. This effect of one patient upon another can be described.as catalytic and the process one of *catalysis.* Catalysis is another important advantage of group psychotherapy and many patients who would otherwise be unable to break through their resistance are helped to do so. We found this to be true also of induction.

Still another aid to catharsis derived from groups is *mutual support,* especially in the area of hostility toward the therapist as a parent substitute. Some patients can express with comparative freedom their aggressive feelings toward the psychotherapist, while others, because of fear and painful memories in similar situations, are unable to bring out negative feelings. This has a deleterious effect upon the therapeutic effort. In group psychotherapy the awareness of solidarity among the patients gives each the security to express hostilities that form the foundation for psychotherapy without which no improvement can be expected.

Support can also be withdrawn from a patient by others in a group when he becomes unreasonably aggressive or is consistently negativistic toward the psychotherapist. One or more members of the group may take up the latter's cudgels because (1) of dependence upon the therapist, (2) need for ingratiation, and (3) anxiety resulting from attack upon a parental figure. However, by and large, aggressive trends are supported in groups, and this is the reason for the greater incidence of acting out in such groups than is the case in individual psychotherapy.

Mutual support is in great evidence in children's groups, whether activity or analytical, and is valuable in the treatment of the fearful and withdrawn child. Where a child had been required or forced to make adaptations of a submissive nature and was restricted and inhibited, he tends to behave similarly in other situations, including the therapeutic relation. He withholds his hostile and aggressive urges causing both subjective tension and social maladjustment. As already indicated, such patients respond to induced catharsis, but would not be able to act out without the support of fellow group members, as well as the permissive attitude of the therapist.

We have seen how *identification* aids the inductive process. It plays an equally important role in support, because the readiness for and intensity of interpersonal support is commensurate with the degree of mutual identifications. This fact has already been hinted at above when it was recorded that some patients do not enter into a supportive role in aggression toward the therapist because of dissimilarity of psychologic syndrome, attitude toward parent, or inner needs.

Another aid to catharsis in groups is the dynamic of *universalization*, which has received considerable attention in the literature largely because patients in group psychotherapy very frequently verbalize it. Awareness of intra- and interpersonal difficulties cannot but generate a feeling of stigma, difference, and inadequacy. Such feelings stem from one's own ego-ideal and self-image, which are derived from the social milieu and the cultural values and mores. Feelings about failure to live up to these culturally defined values are intensified by the communal reaction to such failure. The self-critical and self-deprecatory tendencies are greatly diminished through discovering others in the group in the same situation as themselves, with the same problems, urges, and impulsions. This discovery improves the deflated self-esteem (self-image), reduces guilt feelings and resultant anxiety which diminishes the load on the ego. As the overloaded ego is free of a part of its burden, its energy reserves can then be turned toward repair of personality, accelerated development and control of interpersonal adjustments. Defensiveness and fear of self-revelation are reduced, but the capacity for self-confrontation is increased. Memories are thus made accessible and the cathartic process facilitated. Because of this, therapy in groups is vastly accelerated. In addition to the therapeutic conditions, there is present also an educational element and the reality of the group situation. The educational factor, the reality experience, the wider operational field of function and response that groups provide, their flexibility in relations and in the interviews—all add to the acceleration of the process.

The foregoing discussion of catharsis can be summarized in the following tabular form:

TABLE 2

FORMS OF CATHARSIS IN GROUP PSYCHOTHERAPY

Verbal	Free association (vertical)
Activity	Associative thinking
Activity-verbal	(horizontal)
	Directed
	Induced
	Forced
	Vicarious

TABLE 3

CATHARSIS ACCELERATORS IN GROUP PSYCHOTHERAPY

Target multiplicity
Catalysis
Mutual induction
Mutual support
Identification
Universalization

Insight

The degree of insight derived from psychotherapy is conditioned by (1) emotional maturity, (2) elimination of ego defenses, and (3) intellectual comprehension attained during the course of treatment. To attain an appreciable degree of insight into one's own mechanisms and motivations and to understand and accept the causatives of these in one's background, experience, and constitution, one must first be freed of infantile cravings and urges and give up a considerable amount of one's narcissism. This is achieved largely through decathecting libidinal, pleasure-yielding areas of the body and by eliminating cravings and urges that have remained at levels appropriate only to earlier stages of development. The persistence of immature desires and infantile methods of gratification creates tension and conflict, prevents personality evolvement and the acquisition of insight.

As long as the ego is constrained to defend itself because the threshold of anxiety is low, or because ego boundaries have not been adequately established, the individual lacks the emotional receptivity and intellectual acceptance necessary for the acquisition of insight. In fact, the major impediments to insight stem from impelling ego defenses and character rigidities. They reject any idea, memory, or thought that assails or blemishes one's functioning or responses or deprecates in any way the idealized self. Defenses are forever vigilant to narcissistic injury and reject and act as resistances against anything that tends in that direction through blocking it, through rationalizations, or too ready admission. Intellectual comprehension and understanding, by which the last stages of incorporation of newly acquired insight are accomplished, cannot be achieved as long as one is emotionally unready and resistances to such understanding are still present. Their dissolution is a precondition that is achieved only through a sound psychotherapeutic experience in a transference relation. The type of insight acquired by patients in psychotherapy most recognized is that which is acquired through "interpretation" by the therapist.[1] In groups, however, some of the interpretation is supplied by fellow members.

Activity Group Therapy has led us to the observation that insight can also be achieved without verbalization. We found that despite their age, children in latency become aware of changes in their attitudes and values and that their frustration tolerance had increased. These changes are communicated by both verbal and nonverbal means. It seems that freedom from defensive needs, the ego reinforcement through the group, and the resulting relaxed state make it possible even for young children to become aware of intrapsychic reactions and changes. Such automatically derived awareness has been observed also in adult patients, both in individual and group treatment.[2]

To differentiate the two types of insight—that which is derived from verbal interpretation and the insight that emerges automatically as a result of emotional growth—we have suggested the terms *direct insight* and *derivative insight*. It has also been observed that patients acquire *differential levels of insight*. The depth of insight is determined by the need of a specific patient, the type of therapy employed, the circumstances under which it is carried out and, a condition that is seldom recognized, namely, the capacity of a specific patient to acquire insight.

Because of the state of transference and the variety of cathartic processes in groups, the levels of insight that a patient can attain is limited when compared with, say, psychoanalysis. However, in the hands of a skillful and well-oriented group psychotherapist, a patient

1. Interpretation must be differentiated from explanation, which is quite different in nature and therapeutic relevance. See [56, pp. 54-55].

2. In Activity Group Therapy the therapist is a neutral figure and a permissive parent surrogate. Despite the fact that he verbalizes to a minimum, his movement through the room, his differential response in action to children's acts, statements, questions and demands, constitute a form of interpretation. This *action interpretation* cannot but lead to some forms of derivative insight.

may reach deeper levels of insight (and also improvement) than in individual treatment with a comparably less skillful individual therapist. Nonetheless, the potentials of individual treatment to plumb the depths of the unconscious and the past, and to unravel the profoundly disturbing and inadequately repressed associated feelings, are much greater than in group psychotherapy. If this relation is reversed in practice, it is to be attributed to the skill or lack of it, of the therapist, and not to the therapies.

One can also expect that the interstimulation of thoughts, ideas, and understandings among a group of patients would be conducive to acquiring derivative insights to a larger degree. At the same time the level of direct insight is at a lower level due to the fact that the libidinal transference is less charged. There is an organic unity between transference, catharsis, and insight. As one is affected, the others are commensurably altered. The source of these changes, however, is the transference. Neither catharsis nor insight can be quantitatively or qualitatively affected while the transference relation remains static.

In analytic groups with young children, even of preschool age, interpretation is given by the therapist but it is leveled down to their perceptions and comprehension. In Activity Group Therapy, on the other hand, no explanations or interpretations are given. The insight is entirely derivative and, as already reported, a considerable degree of such insight is acquired through these groups.

TABLE 4

TYPES OF INSIGHT IN GROUP PSYCHOTHERAPY
Direct
Derivative

Reality Testing

A major process that contributes to the maturity of personality is reality testing. In the orderly development of the individual, he has to alter his perception and understanding of reality from the narcissistic, omnipotent level to that of reality's true nature. Reality is to the child an extension of himself and his unlimited power over it. This is modified as he grows older. External reality—actuality—may grow to represent danger or comparative security according to experience with it and the role of mediating persons, such as parents, teachers, and other adults in the enviromnent. During his life, the individual, by interacting with his animate and inanimate environment, tests its real nature as well as himself in relation to it. He may find it a source of threat or comfort, friendly or hostile, constructive or destructive. His evaluations of and his attitudes toward it are, as in the case with all other attitudes, determined by these early experiences with the significant persons in his life. It is their treatment of the infant and child that lays the basis of the *quality* of attitudes toward them as representatives of external reality and later to that reality itself.

The important process in this relation as it concerns maturity is that perception of reality has to undergo continued revision through experiencing and testing. Naturally, the response to these experiences and their meaning to an individual are conditioned by his receptivity to them and by the newly evolving powers, understandings, and comprehensions. However, in nearly all persons infantile perceptions of reality persist in varying areas and to different degrees. All persons retain vestiges of their childhood attitudes toward reality that more or less interfere with adjustment in the adult world. These are feelings of omnipotence, of magic and miracle. Few are able to deal adequately with reality in *all* areas. While one is capable of perceiving reality and handling it effectively in some matters, he tends to deal with other situations in a less mature manner. Despite this dichotomy the "average" person can function with comparative adequacy; that is, he is operationally effective in achieving physical, psychological, and social survival.

Patients who come for psychotherapy, on the other hand, are defective in these respects. Their relation to environment is a source of difficulty either in overt conflict, or because of the excessive inner strain generated by the effort to deal with it. Patients are usually either in conflict with the outer world or with the world within themselves. Because of this universal characteristic of patients, sole emphasis on interpersonal relations is sometimes laid by psychotherapists. Dynamically speaking, this approach puts the cart before the horse, for to correct interpersonal relations requires correcting first the intrapsychic states that beget the conflicts and stresses.

"Reeducation" in relationships can be effective with a limited number of persons in whom the disturbances are of a surface nature. When these difficulties are internalized and cathected and form an integral part of the personality structure, direct means cannot be effective. No real therapy can be achieved by dealing with the symptom rather than with the cause that underlies that symptom. A technique that addresses itself to and utilizes only reality factors is not true psychotherapy. It may be indicated for mildly disturbed individuals who need counseling or guidance, but not for psychoneurotic patients. They require a reweighting and reorganization of their psychic forces.

Reality testing—or better still, reality retesting—is an important element in psychotherapy because the ultimate aim is constructive and adequate adjustment of the patient to and in reality. The values of intrapsychic therapeutic experiences lie in this fact. Inner experiences make it possible for one to reevaluate conditions and reactions in a more receptive mood and diminish defensive projections of negative, hostile feelings. Psychotherapy establishes a more hospitable, more charitable, and a more objective evaluation of and response to people and events. As discontent with the self and self-hatred are reduced, there occurs a corresponding reduction also in the hostile and rejecting feelings toward others. As self-blame is diminished, the tendency toward blaming the external world is correspondingly reduced, as well as the need for hostile or defensive aggression. Thus interpersonal relations and a sanguine attitude toward the world generally are results of reconstitution of the personality rather than alteration of one's philosophy or ideas.

Reality testing is an automatic process. As one functions in the world, one registers one's reactions and difficulties. One's self-esteem or self-image is correspondingly affected by these experiences. If there is success in dealing with reality, repair to the self-image results; but when there is failure, the awareness of shortcomings and of a need for treatment become more apparent. As a patient experiences these, he brings them to the treatment interviews where he can examine them and his reactions with the aid of the psychotherapist or the group. He is supported by the therapist and/or the group which encourages him to try again. Reality testing is a major and integral part of emotional maturity and is always present in psychotherapy, whether it occurs in the therapeutic situation itself or in the operation world.

The therapy group constitutes a tangible and pressing reality to each of its members. It makes demands upon the individual which he must meet if he wishes to remain a part of it. He has to deal with the ego functioning of a number of people, react to them or withhold such reactions, restrain and compromise, attend to other contributors to the discussion and expose himself to their scrutiny. He has to learn ultimately to deal with his likes and dislikes of people, his attractions and antagonisms, absorb attacks upon himself and control his attacks upon others. Such realistic situations do not exist in individual treatment; and in fact they are not necessary. These experiences are supplied by day-to-day living and functioning in the outside world and while they may not be as concentrated and their impact less intense, nonetheless the patient is not deprived of them altogether. Interpersonal relations such as we have outlined exist and appear in the numerous contacts every individual makes in our complex world.

There is, however, some advantage in experiencing these emotions and reactions in the therapeutic setting itself where it can be analyzed, interpreted, and understood. The patient has less of a chance to misinterpret, distort, or pervert his reactions as a defensive measure. The immediacy of the events and the actualistic approach to it by the members of the group and the patient himself render the reality factor more telling and more effective. This is reality testing *in situ* and differentiated from reality testing *ex situ*, when it occurs outside the treatment setting.

This factor, reality testing *in situ*, has given rise to a group therapeutic technique described by its proponents as "the here and now" method. In this practice the sole therapeutic process consists of helping the patients to understand the inappropriate emotional reactions and responses to each other and to the psychotherapist and to analyze the "group tensions" as they appear in the interviews. This is justified by the assumption that the patient has to be viewed in the context of his present life and behavior and that when he understands these, he improves. Obviously, the basic unconscious urges and inner drives and conflicts that prompt behavior cannot be eliminated by understanding; they have to be worked through in the light of memories and earlier relationships. Only then can the noxious impulses be eliminated.

The therapist's manner of dealing with situations in the group serves as an example for the patients. His calm mien and self-confident manner are a living demonstration of ego strength and objectivity which patients emulate. We know that the ego is partially derived from identification with and emulation of parents [57]. Where parents are excitable, emotionally incontinent, afraid, panicky, and anxious, the children, too, grow up incapable of dealing with pressures and tensions. The therapist's power and calm under conditions of stress that frequently arise in therapy groups serve as models which patients first imitate and, as they find themselves adequate, incorporate into their personalities. Group members, too, serve as models for each other.

In Activity Group Therapy, as well, the situation set up for the children is one in which they repeatedly test the physical reality of that setting, the therapist's tolerance, and each other. They measure themselves against that reality, experiment with aggression and explore what reactions the total group setting offers to this behavior. Success and failure build ego strength, affect the self-image and self-esteem, and regulate the superego demands. From this network of experiences a new awareness is gained and greater powers for adequately regulated adjustment emerges.

Reality testing and acting out in the group situation itself may be compatible with or antagonistic to the progressive and therapeutic flow of the group. When catharsis, reality testing, and acting out aid the progressive flow of therapy, they are said to be "group-syntonic." When it is antagonistic or disruptive to the group process, they are considered to be "group-alien."

TABLE 5

TYPES OF REALITY TESTING IN GROUP PSYCHOTHERAPY

In situ	Group-alien
Ex situ	Group-syntonic

Sublimation

To find acceptable sublimations for instinctual urges which are inconsistent with social living is one of the aims of education and of psychotherapy. Sublimation for primitive impulses cannot be supplied to adults in the ordinary therapeutic situation itself, neither in groups nor in the individual setting, except, or course, in those instances where ancillary techniques are employed. Among these are various forms of recreational therapy, occupation therapy, drama, games, various forms of art, arts and crafts, and trades and services in institutions. Choice is made for patients or they are encouraged or steered to take part in activities and occupations that serve to discharge or redirect primitive, unacceptable urges and drives into socially approved and community-syntonic channels.

It must be recognized, however, that too ready sublimation may impede or erase psychotherapeutic effects. Psychotherapy's requirement is that the original and instinctual urges be brought into the open, worked through and understood. Sublimation is a shortcut, as it were, though a useful one. Its weakness lies in the fact that it may not hold up under the stress of living. The ego must assimilate the new modes of expression and behavior or it may not be able to maintain them. When sublimations break down under the strain of outer pressures or inner conflicts, the individual returns to primitive, direct acting out with deleterious results. Sublimations should be arrived at through a gradual elimination of the primary drives in comparative freedom and should be a part of reality testing. It is of greatest firmness and solidity when the choice conforms with some special ability, talent, or disposition an individual may possess.

The value of sublimation as part of psychotherapy is recognized by an increasing number of psychotherapists who employ social workers and specialists in the arts to work with their patients. Some equip themselves to do this as part of their practice or direct patients to suitable individual and group occupations. While sublimatory activities as such cannot be offered in therapy groups for adults, it is recognized by therapists that for some patients belonging to a group in itself serves an analogous purpose. Despite the strain of group interviews, being part of and accepted by a group has a salutary effect. Mutuality and the predominantly warm and friendly attitudes that gradually emerge and later become the dominant atmosphere in the group produce deep gratification in most patients. The group as such and the very fact of being a part of it sublimate and redirect many negative urges and habitual responses.

The need to belong and be a part of is unmistakenly evident in children, but the same craving is present also in adults. Being isolated and feeling alone leads to depression. It predisposes one to irritability and hostile reactions. In addition to other meanings, being alone means not being wanted. This feeling is characteristic of the psychoneuroses and belonging to a group that accepts and is interested in one counteracts such introversion and self-deprecation. Thus, even therapy groups whose primary aim is corrective experiences appeal also to the *social hunger* of its members. Even when the group may press a particular patient at a particular time, which may in itself be disturbing, it still yields gratification because of the evident interest the group displays in him. This reaction is similar to that of a child who feels unwanted when parents do not correct or discipline him. The absence of attention, even if it is negative and restrictive, spells lack of interest.

However, sublimations do not necessarily have to be a part of the therapeutic setting itself. We have already seen that in the case of adults the greater freedom from compulsive reactions and behavior, the increased flexibility of the personality and the emotional hospitality to the outer world, make it possible for the individual to adopt or evolve sublimations to primitive, pleasure-seeking, instinctual urges. The psychoneurotic, and especially the patient with a character disorder, is incapable of establishing sublimatory patterns and channels because of repetition compulsion, defensive patterns, and character rigidities. Psychotherapy whose effect is to diminish or eliminate these lays the basis for the evolvement of suitable sublimations.

This is not as applicable to children as to adults, however. Defenses and character rigidities characteristic of adults are not as yet present; certainly they are not as fully developed or as well entrenched. Sublimations are either nonexistent or are still rudimentary. Because of the nascent character of the child, he has to be helped to evolve sublimations for his drives and urges consistent with environmental demands. In fact, the chief test of education—home, school, and communal—viewed from biological and emotional aspects is to help the child to repress some and to sublimate other urges. When these instrumentalities fail to do so for too long a period, psychotherapy becomes necessary; but psychotherapy, too, has to help the child where the other influences failed, namely to establish sublimations. The environment—tools, objects, materials, and the attitude of the therapist—in play therapy has this effect. Particularly do the conditions that obtain in Activity Group Therapy favor sublimations. Though much of what transpires in these groups is of a displacement nature at first, gradually sublimations make their appearance. Thus children who damage walls, furniture, and tools and attack their group mates as displacement of their hostility toward family and school, soon direct themselves toward group-syntonic effort. Instead of planless cutting of wood without a recognizable aim, they now do it because they make a specific and useful object; instead of splashing paint, they now do an orderly painting job; and in place of boisterous fighting they engage in rivalrous games such as ping-pong, chess, tenpins or volley ball.

TABLE 6

TYPES OF SUBLIMATION IN GROUP PSYCHOTHERAPY	
In situ *Ex situ*	Group-syntonic

Resistance

Closely related, dynamically, to catharsis is resistance, opportunities for which are replete in group psychotherapy. We shall not trace at this point the many sources and causatives of resistance generally and in group psychotherapy, particularly. We shall confine ourselves here to outlining the types of resistance inherent in therapy groups. Groups supply opportunities for escape from participation in the interviews in ways that cannot be found in individual treatment. In both types of treatment are to be found such mechanisms as *displacement, deflection, planned communication, associative thinking,* and *irrelevancy.* Groups, however, offer additional possibilities for some and facilitate other resistances, among which are *absenteeism, lateness, distraction, abruptness, general or selective silence,* and *acting out.*

Absenteeism is comparatively easy in a group since the guilt feelings of the resistive patient are not too deeply aroused in view of the fact that he knows that the group interviews will take place without him as well. He is not as fearful of the therapist as he would be if he were the only patient and thus disappoint him by his absence. There is the element of comparative anonymity here, which is not the case in individual therapy. Similarly, lateness is not as striking in a group. A patient can come late without the same degree of fear. Lateness does not interfere as much with the progress of the interviews in groups.

In a group, a patient can distract the communication of another when it causes him discomfort or anxiety. This is in a sense analogous to deflection in individual treatment, but instead of diverting the stream of catharsis in the latter, in distraction in group interviews a patient can use a number of means, such as to change the subject, laugh, tell a story or joke.

Abruptness designates the technique patients employ when in a state of discomfort they break into the monologue of another patient that prevents him from proceeding with anxiety-inducing statements. This is done by asking a question, changing the subject, making annoying noises and similar acts. Silence is a common pattern of resistance in groups which is less endurable in individual treatment and is the most commonly employed artifice of escape in groups. Silence can be selective or general. Selective silence refers to a patient's withholding comment or participation in a specific situation or subject under discussion that has particular meaning to him, is emotionally laden, or causes anxiety. General silence is employed when a patient is resistive or fearful and keeps silent throughout one, a number of, or all interviews.

It must be noted, however, that the nature of group interviews tends to dissolve, diminish, or counteract some of these resistance patterns. Displacement of blame or aggression is readily dealt with by fellow members who seldom countenance what seems to them "unfairness." Similarly deflection, distraction, irrelevancy, and abruptness are not always successful when one or more patients in the group are interested in a topic and aim to work on it. Associative thinking that concerns itself with immediate matters (top reality) can be swept aside by exploring and by uncovering questions and communications directed by the patients against the resistive member. Of course, not infrequently such efforts may be frustrated by silence and other forms of escape available to a patient in a therapy group that buttress resistive trends. A patient is often shaken out of his silence by group mates who directly address a question to a member who persists for too long a period in a state of withdrawal.

However, resistances are overcome in groups by means other than these direct attacks. There are inherent solvents of resistances that are considerably more subtle in their operation and effect. Some of these have been described under the section dealing with catharsis. All the aids of catharsis naturally overcome resistance, for catharsis in its very nature occurs against resistance and through its dissolution. Identification, universalization, and mutual support have the effect of overcoming self-defensive resistances. Catalysis and induction produce the same result. Associative thinking, for example, yields to universalization, catalysis, and induction; while silence is overcome largely by catalysis and through mutual support. Thus every form of resistance is affected to varying degrees and in different patients to one or more of the *catharsis accelerators* listed in Table 3.

Acting out requires special 'attention in any discussion of psychotherapy, and particularly group psychotherapy. Its importance lies in the fact that it is one of the twilight areas in mental therapy. Acting out can have as profound a therapeutic value as it can be a potent resistance mechanism and a block to the therapeutic process. The dynamics and significances of acting out are complex and require an extensive discussion, which is reserved for a special paper to be written in the future. All that needs to be said of this phenomenon in connection with resistance is that acting out is one form of it in individual and group psychotherapy with adults. It is resorted to most frequently when a patient's ego is unable to tolerate the emotional content of a production or the degree of self-confrontation demanded. It is an escape from self-revelation and the resultant fear or anxiety. It serves the patient as an escape from situations that may be too painful or too disturbing and, since improvement comes only from revealing such material, acting out must be viewed as a form of resistance and deleterious to psychotherapy with adults.

This is not true of children. The most efficient and effective language the child has is action; therefore, acting out by children must be considered as the most suitable form of catharsis. Whether in individual play therapy, play therapy groups, activity interview or activity therapy groups, acting out is a normal pattern for children. Communications through action are interpreted by the therapist (except in Activity Group Therapy) in a manner which the young patient and his fellow group members can comprehend. When a child abstains from activity he can be said to be in resistance. This applies to Activity Group Therapy as it does to the other types of children's therapy groups. In activity therapy groups, acting out is the only means of communciation. In the other groups verbal catharsis and verbal interpretation are intertwined with activity catharsis. Thus, acting out is a form of resistance in the treatment of adults, but not in the treatment of children.

TABLE 7

PATTERNS OF RESISTANCE IN GROUP PSYCHOTHERAPY

Displacement	Planned communication	Absenteeism
Deflection	Associative thinking	Lateness
Distraction	Irrelevancy	Acting out
Abruptness	General silence	(by adults)
	Selective silence	

Types of Therapy Groups

In the introductory remarks to my *Analytic Group Psychotherapy* [56], I suggested that group psychotherapy be divided into two divisions, *Activity Group Therapy* and *Analytic Group Psychotherapy*. The first has been designed for a selected clinical type of children in latency and possibly for some psychotic adults and the senile; the other is applicable to children of various ages who are more seriously disturbed, adolescents and adults. I have omitted to include a rather large number of practices which do not fall within these two categories, but are widely used with various types of emotional and mental patients, especially in hospitals and other institutions. In fact, one of these practices was a forerunner of group psychotherapy introduced at the turn of the century. The omission in the statement referred to above was made intentionally, since I did not wish at that time to give these practices the status of psychotherapy, which they are not by definition. They do have the effect of temporarily releasing tensions, supplying sublimation channels, and bringing patients in greater harmony with their environment generally. They do not, however, bring about permanent intrapsychic changes, which in my opinion constitutes psychotherapy. The various group techniques in this category I have called "directive."

Before we list them, a brief statement as to the nature of each will be useful.

Activity Group Therapy is employed on a selective basis with children between the ages of seven or eight to twelve. The basic pattern is one of activity catharsis in a specially designed permissive physical environment in the presence of a *neutral* therapist and properly selected and grouped children of nearly the same age and the same sex. The environment is permissive because the children are accepted unconditionally, regardless of what they say or do. This represents to the child *unconditional love* which yields him gratification, ego strength, improves self-image, and renders him ready for a better personal and social adjustment.

The analytic group therapies for young children are divided into two types: play and activity-interview groups. The first are aimed to meet the needs of children of preschool age, the second, of those in latency. Boys and girls are included in these groups and, clinically, may be highly disturbed, neurotic children with serious symptomatology. The physical environment in these groups is substantially the same as in the activity groups, except that some limitations are imposed on the children which are interpreted or explained to them as are also some of their acts and behavior generally, that have significance in the light of their problems and difficulties. No such limitations or interpretations are employed in the activity groups. In analytic groups materials supplied and situations designed are such that they activate expression of libidinal urges and preoccupations of oral, anal, and sexual nature. This is avoided in activity groups. The children are also encouraged here to act out hostilities toward members of their families so that they may be relieved of fears and guilts. This is done by supplying them with *libido-activating* materials in which are included doll houses, bedroom and toilet furnishings and equipment and dolls representing members of the family. Other libido-activating materials are also to be found among the equipment in these groups. Catharsis here is both activity and verbal and the transference is of a libidinal nature, since the therapist is a *substitute* for parents.

Analytic groups for adolescents and adults are conducted on a verbal basis exclusively and are in every respect the same as psychoanalytically oriented individual psychotherapy. The catharsis is associative as well as of free-associative character; the transferences and resistances are as described in the sections dealing with these subjects in the foregoing pages. The various other elements and dynamics have also been described.

The *directive group therapies* present by far a greater variety than the psychoanalytically oriented groups. We find among them a number of what came to be designated as inspirational, didactic, recreational, and others. Some are derivatives from the analytic and activity groups, others are of independent origin.

The chief characteristic of the directive groups is that the leader or therapist is an active agent who either activates, directs, stimulates, or guides the patients toward certain specific discussions or activities in accordance with his judgment as to their needs. Thus, catharsis is directed, induced, and sometimes forced. Some of the techniques employed are classroom teaching, lectures, and discussions based upon verbal or visual material and free activities. In some, the therapist uses direct or subtle authority or inspires specific reactions in the patients. In one or two, definite directive or repressive measures are employed. Free association is at a minimum and when encouraged, it is focused on a topic or problem ususally suggested by the leader. In the category of directive group therapies are included also the guidance and counseling types which, as already indicated, are aimed at dealing with the top realities of the participants. None of the methods grouped in this category results in a basic intrapsychic change of a more or less permanent nature. They result rather in corrected attitudes and values, improved self-awareness, and a more wholesome view of self and the outer world. The aim of these techniques is to strengthen the participants through support, give them methods for dealing more adequately with specific personal problems, help them toward a newly developed awareness and an outlook that facilitate bearing up under stress and dealing with situations with less fear and strain.

TABLE 8

DIFFERENTIAL DYNAMICS IN GROUP THERAPIES

Type of Group	Transference	Catharsis	Insight	Reality Testing	Sublimation	Resistance
Activity	Sibling Identification Multilateral Unilateral Group	Activity Induced Vicarious	Derivative	In Situ	In Situ	Absenteeism Lateness Passivity
Play	Libidinal Sibling Identification Multilateral Group	Activity Verbal Activity-verbal Free association Induced Vicarious	Direct Derivative	In Situ	In Situ Ex Situ	Irrelevancy* Silence Passivity
Activity Interview	Libidinal Sibling Identification Multilateral Group	Associative Free association Activity Verbal Activity-verbal Induced Vicarious	Direct Derivative	In Situ	In Situ Ex Situ	Irrelevancy Silence Lateness Absenteeism Passivity
Interview	Libidinal Sibling Identification Multilateral Group	Associative Free Association Verbal Directed Induced Vicarious	Direct Derivative	Ex Situ	Ex Situ	Displacement Deflection Distraction Abruptness Planned communication Associative thinking Irrelevancy Silence Absenteeism Lateness Acting Out

*Absenteeism and lateness are omitted since parents bring children under school age for treatment.

Despite the fact that this work does not involve strictly psychiatric tools and techniques, nonetheless to be effective within their limits, it should be conducted by persons who are psychiatrically oriented. It is important that the leaders or directors of these groups be aware of the deeper implications and possible pathology in the members. This is necessary to prevent activation of tensions and anxieties beyond permissible intensity.

Table 8 is designed to show in a tabular form the operation of the various dynamics in different types of activity and analytic therapy groups. These have been selected from listings of the dynamics as they appear in Tables 1 to 7.

CHAPTER 10

WHEN IS A "THERAPY GROUP" NOT A THERAPY GROUP?
(1960)

With the growing acceptance of group psychotherapy as a method of treatment and its unprecedented spread almost throughout the civilized world, it can be expected that there would arise many misconceptions as to its nature and applicability. Some of the resulting confusions were identifiable even some years ago. These have been described in a paper published in 1953 but written some years before [5]. The aim of the present paper is to elaborate on only one source of this confusion most prevalent among practitioners in this field; this clarification is imperative for its growth and effectiveness.

In a number of my publications I have called attention to the fact that what is often passed for group psychotherapy is actually not psychotherapy in the true sense. In the paper just referred to the point was made, which I consider basic, that many of the misunderstandings in group treatment stem from the current lack of clarity as to what psychotherapy consists of, whether individual or group. In recent years, however, psychotherapists, especially case workers, have taken cognizance of differential levels in therapy. The terms "case work therapy," "supportive therapy," "insight therapy," "intermediate therapy" (in intensity between supportive and insight), and "psychoanalysis" attest to this awareness of differences in intensity and depth of treatment and the "layers" of the personality that can or should be involved in it.

In group psychotherapy as well, there is a need for a cogent differentiation of "levels" to which it addresses itself or attempts to reach in the patients' psyches. In several of my previous communications I have suggested the terms *group counseling, group guidance,* and *group psychotherapy* to emphasize the difference. The first two have not been adequately described, while the third, psychotherapy, has received extensive attention in the literature. However, the very important dynamic differences between the three types of helping people in difficulties have not been clarified—which is essential to prevent practices that are not really psychotherapy from being described and accepted as such. To do this it will be necessary that we delineate the similarities and contrasts among them.

In the upward movement from infancy to maturity, nurture, discipline, education, schooling, counseling, and guidance are the stages through which every individual in Western culture must pass at the hands of parents, teachers, ministers, peers, and the community. In primitive societies nurture and discipline were the only adaptation mechanisms employed. With the onset of civilization, schooling and education were added as essential for emerging needs of the individual to meet the new and vastly more complex demands placed upon him. As the complexities of that society had increased, counseling and guidance had to be added to help individuals, especially the young, to find their way through its labyrinths. Educational, vocational, marriage and family, and personal counseling and guidance have as a result become indispensable in the more complicated cultures of the West and more recently also of the East. Those who for a variety of reasons did not or could not benefit from these formative influences and found themselves in disharmony with themselves and, therefore, inevitably with their surroundings, became candidates for psychotherapy.

Psychotherapy in this sense can be defined as the corrective process by which an individual is rendered accessible to societal (formative) influences, who otherwise remains resistive or incapable of assimilating them. This definition implies that the patterning of the human personality is the province of education, in its widest and most inclusive sense, and that therapeutic measures are marshaled when for some reason education has not taken root. In this relation, psychotherapy alone is considered capable of changing personality; it changes its inner structure and state so that the influences of external formative demands can shape its adaptive and executive capacities in accordance with value systems of the environment and the individual's needs for self-realization.[1]

One of the points that has been pressed upon parents, educators, and therapists in recent decades is the importance of being aware of individual differences in capabilities and needs. Although socioeconomic demands are forcing more and more individuality and unique talent into the background, the mental hygienist, whatever his specific field of endeavor may be, is well aware of the pathogenic potentials in this trend toward uniformity. Both productivity and good health do not lie in this direction, for as the leveling social conditions are increased on the one hand, and integrative and controlling inner forces are decreased on the other, which is now the case, social and individual pathology must of necessity mount. It is this dichotomy in modern society that is responsible in great part for the rise in individual and social imbalance. It is also this dichotomy that forces the community to adopt alleviating measures as represented by counseling, guidance, and therapy.

In the present treatise we are concerned only with that area of counseling and guidance which is preceded by the term "personal." Educational, vocational, premarital, and family counseling are not within our purview here.

Individuals who become aware of difficulties in interpersonal relations, who suffer from some somatic symptom or emotional tensions and unhappiness may seek help for these phenomena. It is the responsibility of the therapist to determine their nature and intensity and the needs of the patient to remedy his anomaly. An examination of the history and various facts involved will lead him to determine the appropriate course to pursue in each case. This may consist of individual or group counseling, guidance, or psychotherapy.

Counseling and guidance deal specifically with ego functioning and to a lesser extent with the self-image. Psychotherapy, on the other hand, is also concerned with these, but in addition seeks to unravel the

---

1. Self-realization needs to be differentiated from self-confrontation, a confusion of terms that has appeared in psychiatric literature. Self-realization is employed here to designate the process of dynamic actualization or fruition of the potentials of an individual as a totality.

intrapsychic malformations that give rise to these and seeks to affect basic corrections in them.

Counseling

In counseling, the counselor, who may or may not be a trained psychotherapist, would lead the counselee either to arrive at or to accept from him a solution of the immediate difficulty for which help is sought. The counselor addresses himself to that difficulty, whatever it may be, and helps the counselee to resolve it, by indicating to him, and supporting him in, a line of action that would obviate the dilemma. The content of the interviews, which are usually few in number, are focused upon realities in the interpersonal or situational difficulty; the *explanations* are reality oriented; namely, only the actual events related to the felt problem and their meaning and effect are evaluated and discussed. Solutions are considered and selected to accord with the needs of the situation as seen by the participants and within the counselee's existing capacities or talents.

The counselor is an *active agent*, though he follows the precepts of all good teaching that the best solution is the one at which the learner arrives through his own effort and as far as possible by himself. Thus, while he leads the counselee on and opens doors to him, as it were, his aim is, nonetheless, to consummate a suitable resolution of the counselee's problem. For this the counselor is equipped by his superior understanding of the forces involved: the personality structure and ego functioning of the counselee to which the latter may be blind. His experience and awareness would indicate to him whether the counselee can carry out the plan. Above all, the fact that he is uninvolved and views all elements objectively places him in an advantageous position.

Counseling can be done in a *tête-à-tête* or group setting. From the examination of the process of counseling as we view it here it is obvious that group counseling is by far more difficult, if not impossible. Since there is always a *specific* aim involved of significance to a specific individual seeking practical and immediate help, the interference of other members of the group with the direct pursuit of this aim may prove a serious stumbling block. The variety of reactions and opinions may take the discussion far afield into areas and ideas not related to the immediate problem or situation with which a given individual is struggling to find a solution or a line of action.

Guidance

This is not the case in guidance. Unlike counseling, in guidance the *attitudes* and sometimes even the feelings involved in the guidee's problems are exposed to his consideration, even though the underlying unconscious motivations and their sources remain untouched. A person required guidance when the emotional significance of the problem is beyond simple ego functioning. In counseling cases it is assumed that the ego is capable to deal with the problem as a line of action is made clear. There is a minimum of blocking due to anxiety or affect in carrying it through. In guidance, on the other hand, the emotional charge such as guilt feelings, for example, is such that the ego could not function adequately before the feelings involved are brought to awareness and are understood.

In such cases support and clarification are two essential elements. Because of the accompanying affect, the patient is unable to act upon the solutions which he may have himself come upon or which he was helped to arrive at. The support of the therapist as a parent surrogate and his permissiveness release the necessary ego strengths which are otherwise blocked by fear, anxiety, guilt, superego prohibitions, and other similar intrapsychic as well as circumstantial impediments.

One of the dynamics that operate in this process is the reduction of the ego load through communication and objectification. The dilemma in which the patient finds himself is at least in part due to the strain to which the ego is subjected. This strain is the result of the unconscious urge to act and an equally unconscious and sometimes conscious fear or guilt as to the outcome of the act. This conflict not only engenders ambivalence, hesitancy, and vacillation,but consumes much of the ego energies that could otherwise be used for action. By exposing the elements involved in the conflict, a resolution can be expected which clears the decks for decisive action. The ego energies bound in the conflict are thus released to carry out the action.

In doing this several factors are involved. Clarification is the first of these. But in most instances such clarification cannot be achieved without eliminating the feelings of guilt or fear that are involved. Since these are not traced to their neurotic sources in guidance, it is accomplished by the therapist's support, that is, by his empathy, acceptance, and permissiveness. He thus assumes a superego role. It is obviously impossible to delineate with any degree of definiteness a specific role that anyone plays in life to the exclusion of all others, let alone a therapist. But it seems clear that in counseling, the counselor is predominantly an auxiliary or supportive ego to that of the counselee. In guidance he serves in that capacity as well, but his additional role is one of counteracting superego prohibitions and the so-called "pangs of conscience." The latter predominates over his ego-supportive functions.

When the patient is brought into greater harmony with himself and the conflictual syndrome is dissolved, another dynamic element is set into operation, which we have already indicated. This is the clearing of the way for action. Still another is the resulting capacity to mobilize ego energies for that action.

From the nature of the process involved in guidance it can be seen that it requires a considerably longer period than does counseling and many more interviews, the number of which is determined by the needs and capacities of a given patient and the depth and intensity of the affect involved. Even though in guidance feelings are dealt with on a superficial level, establishing the necessary transference attitudes before one can approach them takes considerable time. This varies with each individual. Also, to prevent shock or injury in the patient, it is often necessary to move slowly before he is able to confront himself with his feelings and with his own part in creating his difficulties. These and other factors delay or extend the process far beyond that of the more direct approach employed in counseling.

In most instances groups accelerate the guidance process. Group guidance, especially when the problems of the participants are of a similar nature, is not only more economical but is actually more effective. Exploration of the elements involved in the dilemmas of the participants is greatly accelerated by their interactions and by the light thrown upon them by the ensuing interchange. But of even greater help is the removal of guilt and the feeling of difference and uniqueness that results from the similarity to the others in the group. The discovery that one is not alone or peculiar in having problems and seeking help reduces stigma and guilt and raises one's self-esteem. These are extremely valuable in freeing ego energies and carrying out decisions. Universalization reduces inner constraint and corrects superego demands.

The experience of belonging to, and being accepted by, a group is by far more gratifying to the patients or clients for whom guidance is indicated than is the acceptance by an individual. Both the symbolic and biological significance of a group and the satisfaction of the instinctive social hunger enhance the individual's savoir-faire. They dispose ·him toward more socially approved reactions and relationships, in addition to the release and help that they supply.

A study of the unconscious meaning of a group shows that it represents the mother symbol in the individual's psyche. From groups he expects acceptance and protection as he had from his mother. No one can tolerate rejection and discrimination from a group. Even those who can bear up tolerably well with enmity from individuals are greatly disturbed by hostile manifestations from a group. An accepting, harmonious group helps each participant to become disposed toward feelings and behavior that not infrequently resolve environmental conflicts and difficulties automatically. This is in addition to the clarifying and supportive effect the discussions may have.

As stated, a guidance group is more effective when its members are preoccupied with the same or similar problems. The practice of forming groups for marital or premarital problems, for family problems, parents of children with problems, or special handicaps or illnesses, adolescents, delinquents, etc., is from this point of view sound. This homogeneity crystallizes the group into a unit in which each member identifies with the others and all are able to help each other because of emotional empathy and mutual understanding. Such homogeneity also favors universalization from which results reduction of feelings of guilt and uniqueness. Group "cohesiveness" of this nature is counterindicated for psychotherapeutic groups, but is essential in guidance.

Unlike counseling, guidance requires that the leader be a professionally trained person with experience in psychotherapy. Guidance borders on psychotherapy in so far as it deals with and aims at correcting feelings. These have to be understood by the therapist, even though they may not be involved deeply in the process; that is, they are not worked through in their relation to unconscious and repressed memories, associated affects, and the bound-up anxiety. If the therapist is not qualified to work on this deeper level, much harm may result to some patients from his guidance work. When the therapist's vigilance flags, the patient may be aroused to anxiety beyond the level permissible in guidance. The technique of guidance, and also its aim, is to hold anxiety within narrow boundaries, for once it reaches high intensity, its abatement can be achieved only by working it through. This leads to the need for psychotherapy and the procedure has to be altered as a result, a development that may be undesirable either for clinical or practical reasons or both. However, in some instances guidance may be a planned preliminary step as an easement to or a motivation for psychotherapy.

The therapist in individual and in group guidance must at all times be aware of the "threat areas" of patients. He has to be equipped to recognize the onset of anxiety beyond permissible levels in each and, when he works with groups, in the group as a whole. This is essential, for the forced transition into psychotherapy that would result may prove deleterious to patients who had not been selected and grouped with that intent in mind. Criteria for the two practices are in very telling respects at variance with each other. Thus the therapist needs to be able to employ skills other than those in psychotherapy. Much of his efforts have to be bent upon *avoidance instead of unrestricted exploration* involved in uncovering and free catharsis. The latter are employed only to the extent that they bring feelings and actions to awareness and place them in proper significance in the client's current life and relationships. In guidance, this is not employed in the reconstruction of his personality, however, though some changes are inevitable as in the case of every significant experience in life.

When deeper recesses of the repressed painful memories in the unconscious are activated, he must deflect the flow of communication [60, chaps. 3 and 4]. However, such stratagems have to be employed in a manner that does not appear as authoritarian, as rejection or as interference.

Psychotherapy

A distinct difference between guidance and psychotherapy lies in the fact that the communications in the latter are free associations. They are centered around a specific topic only occasionally, while in counseling and guidance the latter is the pattern of the interviews or discussions. However, it occurs not infrequently in psychotherapy as well that patients talk for a period about "top realities." But such focus is a transient one. It is rather a *part* of a larger intent; that is, intrapsychic change. Solving practical problems is not the major concern of the psychotherapist, as it is of the counselor and guidance worker.

Free association cannot but bring forth painful memories and highly charged feelings and anxiety. All of these are not permitted to make their appearance in guidance, and by its very nature cannot occur in counseling. The ego defenses are of necessity threatened in psychotherapy, which sets up resistances to communication (catharsis). The analysis of these resistances are an integral part of psychotherapy, as are also the various transference reactions. Within broad limits, no precautions are taken against arousing anxiety. "Threat areas," that is, areas within which anxiety, guilt, hostility, rationalization, and resistance are mobilized, are not respected. As these reactions make their appearance, the psychotherapist does not deflect them or retreat. Rather, since they reveal the real personality of the patient, he encourages their manifestations so that they can be used in the therapeutic grist.[2]

The aim in psychotherapy is not to resolve a single conflictual situation or an external relationship syndrome. *Its aim is to change more or less permanently the personality structure* so that it may function more adequately. This involves correction of each of the intrapsychic triad—id, ego, and superego—and their balance and relation. The aim of counseling and guidance is to help the individual to deal with *specific* situations; that of psychotherapy is to make him permanently capable of dealing with *any* situation. The ego

---

2. I have found that many psychotherapists find it difficult to adapt their techniques to guidance. Almost imperceptibly they "slip into" therapy, often with deleterious effects. They had to be constantly "pulled back" during supervision for long periods before their awareness was fixed and controls established.

weaknesses and dependency may in no way be affected through counseling; they are improved in relation to a specific problem in guidance and may even be carried over to other related functions as *secondary results*. But they are secondary results only. In psychotherapy, on the other hand, these are *primary aims* and the psychotherapist directs his effort toward achieving them.

This involves the development of insight instead of only recognition or understanding, a process that necessitates reduction or elimination of ego defenses, emotional rigidities as well as the less important intellectual comprehensions. Traumatic memories ensconced in the catacombs of the unconscious and their associated disturbing feelings are dislodged and examined in the light of their current significance and adult realities. Emotional and transference regression, an integral part of the therapeutic process, is either absent or is held within boundaries in counseling and guidance.

The well-established dynamics of psychoanalytic psychotherapy— transference, free-associative catharsis, insight, reality testing, and sublimation—are the tools in this procedure. In counseling and guidance, on the other hand, only reality testing is employed, with minimal transferences in the latter. The therapist aims to remain as passive as the patients will allow him so that the flow of verbal and emotional catharsis would not be interfered with and regression retarded. His activity is one of periodic assertion and withdrawal. The assertive role is assumed when interpretation or explanations are indicated, or when blockings of resistance set in which the patients cannot break through on their own. Through questions or appropriate statements, he helps to uncover unconscious states and to examine the nature and appropriateness of reactions, behavior, and relationships in the perspective of unconscious motivations and determinants. This is avoided in counseling, though in guidance behavior and its effect on others and as a cause of difficulties may be considered.

Obviously, the course of therapy is fraught with much ambivalence and resistance; it oscillates between positive and negative transference feelings, communication and silences, confidence and distrust, frankness, deceit, and avoidance. All these have to be worked through as products of conscious and unconscious needs and causes. The patients pass through mood swings between elation and depression, submission, hostility, and aggression, expansiveness and diffidence. These need to be observed and their meanings understood. All this takes an interminably long time, much longer than does guidance and even more so than counseling. Much of the time is consumed in evolving a positive transference so that patients will be secure enough to reveal themselves. This relation is strongly tinged with sexual libido. The therapist is invested with strong libidinal significance and may become the patient's target of sexual aim or object. While the degree of regression to the preoedipal and pregenital states is at its height in true psychoanalysis, the patient's attitudes in all real psychotherapy are colored by these irrational, infantile feelings.

In analytic group psychotherapy with nonpsychotic adolescents and adults the process is substantially as described above, though significant modifications emerge as an inevitable result of the presence of more than one patient. Transference is modified, diluted, and divided; catharsis may be vicarious as well as direct and personal; identifications can be established with fellow patients as well as with the therapist; there is a more favorable climate for acting out; and opportunities for reality testing are at hand, which is not the case in individual treatment. The catalytic effect of patients upon each other and that of the group as a whole accelerates catharsis; so do universalization, support, group consent, and target multiplicity. There are, however, also factors that retard catharsis. Among these are fear and shame, group-induced anxiety, group contagion, negative group transference phalanx, and others.

As in individual treatment, also in groups, transferences and resistances are explored and interpreted and their libidinal components uncovered; they are traced to unconscious sources, determinants, and traumata; emotional release by living through and reenactment of interpersonal and group tensions are provided and insight-understanding acquired. These developments are in a degree aided by the group. The compresence of a number of people in intimate interaction, such as a therapy group imposes, favors these dynamics. But one must be aware of the fact that while such facilities are present in groups, they also reduce the depth of treatment. Massive psychoneuroses, especially of a transference nature, require individual therapy, though groups may be used as auxiliary treatment in selected cases.

Case Illustrations

Perhaps it may be valuable, following the preceding theoretic discussion of counseling, guidance, and psychotherapy, to illustrate their application to actual situations one meets in clinical practice.

A woman is referred by her husband because of her unending conflicts with her two sons, sixteen and twelve years old respectively. Her main complaint is that they do not keep their room in proper order. The constant haggling had for years created a climate of tension in the home and the husband, being of an unassertive and passive disposition, felt disturbed but helpless in the situation. The older boy was exceptionally brilliant in his schoolwork and gave promise of becoming an outstanding scientist. His father also had a quasi-scientific occupation.

During the only interview held with this woman she elaborated and reiterated her annoyance with her boys. Her special preoccupation was the "messy" condition of the boys' dresser drawers, the disorder in which they were kept, and the difficulty in finding things in them. She spoke feelingly about the subject. It seemed to have great meaning for her.

At one point during her recital the therapist (counselor) asked: "How long have you been trying to teach your sons to be orderly with their dresser drawers?" "Oh, about seven or eight years with the older boy," was the answer. The therapist then smilingly asked: "Isn't it possible that since you did not succeed in teaching them for so long a time, you may have used a wrong method?" "What can one do then?" asked the woman. "I don't clearly know, not knowing all the facts. One way, of course, is for you to straighten up the drawers for them. Another is to let them keep their drawers in whatever shape suits them." This seemed quite unacceptable to her, though she did not respond verbally.

We were aware that this woman would not return for further interviews and that her complaints could not be worked through, and we waited for an opportunity to say something that would be of significance to her. Toward the end of the hour she said: "I can't understand it! My father who lives with us is such an immaculate and orderly person, why can't they be like him?" The therapist in a calm voice responded: "Well, then he has some other faults. No one is without faults." The woman seemed somewhat startled and for a brief moment remained silent, and then as though speaking to herself said quietly: "That's true; he had never earned a living." With this the interview ended. The therapist did not give her the opportunity to go on with this topic or to decrease the impact of her discovery.

Upon meeting the therapist informally some months later, the husband said: "We have no more trouble in my home about the boys' orderliness. What did you do to my wife? She keeps on talking about you and what a bright man you are!"

The above example of a rather simple procedure illustrates the process of counseling. Obviously there are considerable unconscious determinants in this woman's attitudes and values, chief among these in my opinion is her need to please her father or probably to show up his own failures. These remained untouched. She had the intelligence to understand the principle involved and the ego strength to bring herself under control. It is our belief that the abrupt ending of the interview which prevented diminishing the impact of her own formulation about her father was a major determinant in the changed behavior.

Another illustration of counseling that also took up only one session but was emotionally somewhat more complex is that of a woman referred by her family physician for planning for her eight-year-old daughter's schooling. She wanted her girl to attend a certain private school with a progressive educational program, but hesitated to do so. The woman was separated from her husband, a medical specialist, toward whom she entertained intense hostility and distrust.

Her communication for almost a full hour was consumed in discussing her indecision about her daughter's school plans. We were puzzled throughout as to what was actually on her mind, since it was clear that she strongly favored the school in question as against any other. We guessed that the husband had something to do with her difficulty. A few questions revealed that by court order her husband was allowed to see the girl for a half day each week at his apartment and during parts of the summer holiday. It became evident that the mother was disturbed by the relation between the father and his daughter. We then asked how the girl reacted to her visits. With considerable emotion, she said: "My daughter thinks he is a horrid man! And she is right." "By the way," we asked, "where does he live? The woman seemed to be taken aback, reddened, and in somewhat subdued voice said: "He lives right across the street from the school." "Are you afraid that your husband will see your daughter more often and will alienate her from you?" we asked rather directly. "Yes," was the answer delivered almost in a whisper.

We then explained to this worried woman the intense need of a young child for its mother, especially in a girl, and the fact that the current residence with the mother and not the father strengthened that feeling to a degree beyond any possibility for anyone to alienate the child from her. In addition, the girl's own statements concerning her father (which of course may have been a blind for the girl's strong affection for him—but this we did not touch upon) should give her no concern on that score. The woman meekly asked: "Do you really think so?" "Not only do I think so, but I would stake my professional reputation on it," was our unequivocal response. The woman visibly relaxed.

The referring family physician reported later that the girl was placed in the school in question without any unpleasant consequences and that the woman had been most pleased with the "guidance" she received.

A more complicated situation was presented by Mrs. J. who, though requiring psychotherapy to solve her problem fully, was able for practical reasons to receive only guidance.

Mrs. J. referred herself because she became concerned about her increasing need for alcohol, marital incompatibility, and general restlessness. At the very first interview she spoke of her problem with her husband who was indifferent to sexual intercourse because, she thought, of his excessive masturbation. She and the husband were of different religions and she insisted on adhering to her own, even though it was a verbal adherence rather than a ritualistic one. Mrs. J. continued coming for interviews on a weekly basis. She later revealed that she had had extramarital sexual relations and had a tendency to flirt and generally tried to attract men. She was "on the make," in her own words.

Mrs. J. was not a very attractive woman. Her dress and general personality tended to be slovenly. Despite her flirtatiousness, she obviously was not interested in making herself attractive or "playing up" her femininity. As the interviews progressed she spoke of her feelings about her father and mother. The former was a likable and kindly man whom she adored, but she did not go into her fantasies or wishes about him, nor was she encouraged to do so. Her mother she saw as a hostile, domineering woman whom she disliked. Here, too, Mrs. J. was permitted to ventilate her feelings without arousing or exploring their deeper libidinal significance.

Gradually, Mrs. J. displayed some understanding of the role of her father in her relations to men. She began to feel greater warmth toward her husband and their sexual relations improved. She no longer emphasized the religious difference between them. She stopped the intake of alcohol. Preceding these developments she began to dress more carefully; she improved her coiffure and presented a neater appearance generally. There were altogether forty-six interviews.

There was considerable unconscious material that could and actually should have been brought out in this case; due to a number of practical factors it was deemed inadvisable to launch upon a full course of psychotherapy. Individual guidance was, therefore, pursued. Cases like that of Mrs. J.'s would be unsuitable for group guidance partly because of their therapeutic needs, but more importantly because of the effect they would have upon groups.

Mrs. J. came for help because of a specific problem—heavy drinking. If this were all, she could have been placed in a group; but her sexual maladjustment, and delinquencies, the religious conflict, masculine identifications, and homosexual trends, if brought out in a group, would create more anxiety than a guidance group can tolerate. These problems can be treated in a therapy group after a course of individual psychotherapy. Individual guidance served only to pull her out of the confusion in which she had found herself at the time. How long she remained "in the clear" is not known.

The last case is that of a man who, at the age of forty-two years, found himself unable to go to his office and was generally in such a state of anxiety and restlessness that his relations with his wife and children deteriorated to a degree that alarmed him. He had suffered from this anxiety state for more than a year. At first he was able to "force" himself to go to the office a few times a week and a fast automobile drive would usually dissipate his tensions. In time, however, these remedies no longer had any effect on him. He was unable to go to his office altogether and his car jaunts only made him more tense.

When he called on the phone, an appointment was made for him for four o'clock in the afternoon. After he stated his problem, we asked him to tell us something about his current family and later about his parental home. As a young man, whose mother was dead, he had worked for his father, now also dead, in a small business. The father cooked most of the meals in a small apartment, which the patient, his father, and a brother had occupied. They ate together most of the meals and also kept house. The mother died when the patient was about sixteen years old. He spoke in glowing terms of his mother's kindliness and "goodness," her warmth and patience, and described how deeply he had mourned her death. The father never remarried. According to the patient, his own sexual adjustment was entirely adequate.

We let Mr. K. talk for an hour and a half, trying to get a clue to his hysterical behavior, but we could not identify the *nuclear problem* here. Evidently he left something out. We then told him to come on the next day at 8:30 a.m. He was instructed not to engage in any business enterprises or other matters that would divert him, but directly after breakfast to come to the office.

The next morning we asked him if he had anything to add to what he had told us the evening before. Yes, he recalled that three of his friends of about his own age had recently died in quick succession, and he described in detail how he had learned from a woman acquaintance of the death of one of them during a visit to a hospital where one of his boyhood friends was confined.

I told him quite directly: "Your present severe anxiety was brought on by the deaths of your friends and this is in some way connected with the death of your mother."

This statement seemed to open up the sluices of his locked-up memories which now came tumbling in quick succession. One of the significant facts he produced was that for some years after his mother's death, he vomited whenever he ate *between* meals. He was able to hold the three regular meals, but could not retain even slight refreshments such as ice cream between meals.

Apparently the death of his contemporaries, who obviously had strong emotional meaning to him, had reawakened his anxiety hysteria that had lain dormant for a quarter of a century.

Mr. K. was advised to submit to a thoroughgoing analysis.

Perhaps a case of the differential application of counseling, guidance, and psychotherapy in a single complaint may further make palpable the doctrine promulgated here of the differences between them.

A man comes with the problem of his reactions to his employer as a result of which he finds it difficult to adjust to his job and his fellow employees. This keeps him in a state of irritation, worry, and economic insecurity. Several interviews (sometimes only one) may reveal that his antipathy toward his boss is displaced upon fellow employees because of his general state of dissatisfaction and irritability and, what is more important in such a situation, the source of the attitude toward the employer.

This may be *(a)* characterological incompatibility, ideological conflict, or difference in opinions as to the conduct of the job; *(b)* a result of the patient's generalized rebellion against authority as a continuation of his attitude toward significant figures in his childhood; or *(c)* reaction to unconscious passive homosexual and submissive wishes toward the employer. In most instances counseling would be indicated in dealing with cases in the first category, group guidance may be sufficient for the persons in the second, and psychotherapy is essential for the third.

Dynamic Differentials

On the basis of the preceding discussion, we can now identify when a so-called "therapy group" is really not a therapy group. Briefly stated, it is a group—under whatever presentation it is offered or is thought to be—that does not follow the principles, aims, and processes of psychotherapy. These are aimed at affecting internal change of the personality, through strengthening and balancing the psychic forces, so that, ideally at least, it can function adequately under whatever stress it may find itself. Counseling and guidance are not as inclusive; they aim at solving specific problems or help one deal with a specific situation. Group psychotherapy aims at weaning the patient from past infantile dependencies and feelings of inadequacy and frustration, among other things, by more or less basic alteration *within* the psyche rather than seeking symptom or behavioral improvement. An important fact that misleads patients and the less alert therapist is that patients or clients "improve." Unless the *nature* and permanence of the improvement is assessed, it does not by itself indicate that therapy had occurred or was practiced.

Sharing, universalization, support, and the many other means by which guilt and anxiety are allayed and the load the ego carries is reduced, bring about behavioral and symptom improvement. This can be achieved through many and varying means in addition to guidance and counseling. A heart-to-heart talk with a friend, a pleasant time spent with warm friends, prayer, confession, adherence to one of the many metaphysical and mental science cults or social movements may all have salutary effects upon physical and mental health. Group participation, particularly, has a beneficial influence. It has been reported that in one experiment patients, who were led to believe, contrary to fact, that a therapist was behind a screen and directed to talk about their problems into it, showed observable improvement. This is not as implausible as it seems at first blush. The relief obtained from converting psychic pressures, anxieties, and doubts into somatic action, even though no response is given, temporarily normalizes the psychic homeostasis, but no lasting improvement can be expected from such a procedure.[3] Anxieties and tensions accumulate as the patient again faces the distressing realities of daily living, requiring a repetition of the releasing experience.

Where basic psychotherapy is indicated, a nontherapeutic group provides a new type of dependency as a substitute for the old; but the patient remains with his dependent needs and resulting confusions and stresses. In psychotherapy the aim is to reduce or eliminate the need for such external props by eliminating intrapsychic pathology.

The misunderstanding as to when a group can be considered in the category of psychotherapy stems also from the fact that guidance, particularly, should be practiced by trained psychotherapists for reasons already indicated. While the training is very useful for counseling as well, it is not essential in some instances, such as premarital counseling and general pastoral counseling with the aver-

---

3. A suitable example of this process is when people suddenly exclaim or talk to themselves as their thoughts activate anxiety.

age person without psychopathology or serious emotional distortions and involvements. The fact that understanding of psychology and pathology are required and are utilized in some of the nontherapeutic practices leads the nondiscriminating to confound them with true psychotherapy. Psychotherapy has to be identified with the *aim* and the *process* and not with the equipment of the therapist or even with results attained, for frequently even the best practice of psychotherapy fails to attain results.

If we consider work with groups on the different levels described here from the point of view of therapeutic dynamics and aims, we find that the difference is both in degree and in kind. The aims of a thoroughgoing psychotherapy are: libido redistribution, ego strengthening, correcting of the superego, and improving of the self-image. The dynamics by which these are achieved are: transference, catharsis, insight, reality testing, and acquiring sublimations.

In counseling the libido is almost not involved; in guidance it is involved only to a minimal extent; but in psychotherapy it is a major focus. In counseling the ego is strengthened only in relation to a specific situation as a result of the support it receives from the counselor; in guidance it may be strengthened in addition by the removal of the drain to which it had been subjected by conflictual emotions. Once the conflicts are eliminated, the load the ego had borne is reduced. In psychotherapy the same results are obtained but to a much greater extent and on a much deeper level. Heightened self-esteem (self-image) always results from psychotherapy; it is also partially achieved through guidance and may be effected also in counseling, but to a limited or almost negligible degree.

The therapeutic dynamics are also variously involved. We have already indicated that transference is of a superficial nature; it is fleeting and of a shallow intensity in counseling; it is considerably more intense and more prolonged in guidance and of much heightened strength with concomitant fantasies and wishes toward the therapist in psychotherapy. One attribute may be added to those already enumerated: in counseling and guidance, transference feelings are uniformly positive, while in psychotherapy they pass through positive and negative phases.

The relative content and depth of communication and catharsis in the three techniques have already been elaborated in considerable detail and will, therefore, not be repeated here. This also applies to insight. Concerning reality testing, it can be said that in counseling no reality testing is employed even though the entire action of the counselor occurs in reality. A person who is selected for counseling has the capacity for reality testing as contrasted with reality perception. If he is not adequately capable of it, counseling would not be the procedure of choice.

There is the probability that the capacity for reality testing in those patients who are selected for guidance may be of a low level, especially in the areas or relations in which they experience difficulties, and would require special attention. In psychotherapy, especially in group psychotherapy, the interpersonal impacts of the group-as-a-whole are tangible realities forcing awareness upon each participant that require of him new perceptions and new adjustments. Reality testing in groups, therefore, forms an important element in the therapeutic process.

Development of sublimations of primitive instinctual urges is not an objective in counseling or in guidance. Persons selected for these types of help usually have acquired either adequate sublimations or repressions as measured by those in the average population. The fact that they have difficulties with some specific problem does not indicate real pathology. When the latter is present, the patient is placed either in individual or group psychotherapy, or both, depending upon his needs.

Perhaps the thesis with which this paper is concerned can be briefly summarized as follows: *Through counseling and guidance we help people; through psychotherapy we change them.*

The relations of the various aims and dynamics of counseling, guidance, and psychotherapy can be summarized in tabular form (see Table 1).

Psychonursing vs. Psychotherapy

Counseling and guidance can be viewed as forms of *psychologic nursing*. Since no fundamental cure is sought or attained, the client or patient may be expected to return whenever he is presented with a difficulty in the future. In practice, this form of "nursing" is frequently all one can achieve with many patients whose resistances, intellectual or psychological limitations, or constitutional deficiencies impose limits upon therapeutic effort or serve as counterindications. One

TABLE 1

Showing the Relations of Aims and Dynamics in
Counseling, Guidance, and Psychotherapy

Aims	Counseling	Guidance	Psychotherapy
Libido redistribution	none	none	present
Regulate superego demands	none	slight	present
Strengthening of ego	none	slight	present
Improve self-image	none	slight	present
Solve immediate problem	present	present	transitory
Dynamics			
Transference	slight, positive	moderate, positive	intense, cyclical
Catharsis	none	moderate, associative	regressive, free association
Insight	none	slight	deep
Reality testing	present	present	present
Sublimation	none	possible	present

should not underestimate the value of this form of practice. In a striking number of cases it enhances the mental health of the community through preventing or diminishing conflict and tension; it helps to establish harmony in the individual with his environment and in crucial interpersonal relations such as marital and family relations, in employment, and in general social adjustment. As we have attempted to show, this can be achieved in comparatively few interviews, while in others this may be a prolonged process, even as long as that of psychotherapy. In fact, many a course in individual or group treatment is actually guidance according to our definitions.

In the treatment of borderline or latent schizophrenic patients, whose ego integration is at best tenuous, a prolonged period of counseling and guidance is essential. In the majority of cases these may be all that would be allowed so as to prevent ego fragmentation that may result from deep psychotherapy. However, in less serious cases, especially in those of pseudo schizophrenia, psychotherapy may be cautiously attempted after the ego reinforcement and strengthening of its defensive structure are achieved by the less threatening procedures of counseling and guidance.

CHAPTER 11

TYPES OF RELATIONSHIPS
(1945)

Survival in a complex and compact society implies more than its biological connotation. It means more than continuing existence as a physical being. Group living involves a sharp struggle for survival of the ego as a psychological entity, and to modern man the struggle for existence means seeking to persist as an organic unit and gaining acceptance and status within the group. Sources of subsistence are comparatively secure in modern society. One can earn his living through many occupations which are more or less obtainable. However, this is not the case with prestige and status; these come through personal effort, competition, and individual excellence. In primitive society anxiety was fixed around subsistence, food-getting, and physical survival. While these anxieties still exist in modern man, they are comparatively less intense. Modern science prevents the calamitous privation of food and has reduced the effect of catastrophes in nature. No dangerous animals lurk to destroy, and surprise attacks by head-hunting tribes are no more. Individual injuries and wars are still extant, but are the result of unexpected accident or prepared and anticipated attack. The all-pervasive expectation of danger and destruction are less pressing in present living.

While modern society has succeeded in reducing the stress accompanying physical survival, it has increased, to the same ratio, anxiety accompanying psychological survival. More secure and democratic living increases social mobility. An individual is no longer destined to remain a member of the specific economic or social group—a caste—into which he is born. There is no limit to his economic and financial expansion, excepting those set by energy, drive, and opportunity. These conditions sharpen competition and cause people to reach out beyond subsistence security; they struggle for prestige and social recognition. When possession for physical goods is a symbol of power and prestige, the struggle moves in that direction. In groups where intellectual achievement or physical prowess constitute superiority, the struggle for ego survival shifts into those areas.

We ·can suppose that one in a position of prominence achieves greater ego satisfactions than one in a lower social status unless some serious intrapsychic difficulty is present. Where the drive for status assumes neurotic proportions, is a compensation for basic deprivations, rejection, or inferiority feelings, serious personality distortions exist. The struggle for ego survival in modern man goes on in a vertical direction such as status and prestige. Almost everyone strives to secure his psychological survival in a horizontal direction: he needs response, love, emotional security, acceptance by neighbors, friends, and others.

The struggle for prestige and particularly for acceptance are attained through human relationships. The multitude of relationships to which every individual is exposed in a compact group life is more than is possible to describe in a brief treatise. The gamut runs from unbridled dictatorship to self-negation and utmost submissiveness. One difficulty in describing human relationships is that they seldom exist in pure or separate forms. Ambivalence and mixed attitudes are almost always present and an analysis of seemingly simple relations reveals many complications. Other difficulties lie in human comprehension and language limitations which make it impossible to delineate human relations adequately. Despite all this, it is essential for the growth of psychology, education, recreation, psychotherapy, the development of a sound family life and a science of sociology that we delve more deeply than has been our wont into this very complex and so far little explored dynamic of human living.

It is particularly important that psychotherapists understand and classify relationships, for the major tool in treatment is relationship, and the focal area they seek to treat is the intrapsychic malformation resulting from early traumatic relationships.

The present paper is an initial effort to present, for further thinking, investigation, and research, some of the relationships we have observed among people in everyday life, and among patients in individual and group therapy. Some of the types to be described are generally known; others are less popularly understood but are known to those occupied with any form of psychologic endeavor; a few had to be formulated to understand the interpersonal processes in group therapy. The latter have emerged as spontaneous byproducts from free interaction of children and adolescents in our groups, and discussion among adults under treatment. Therapeutic play groups and activity therapy are the more fruitful fields for these observations because of the high degree of their social mobility. The freedom with which children and young adolescents interact and choose friends permits the emergence of all types of relationships. In view of the fact that (up to the present) we have had more than 900 children and adults under observation, and because of the repeated recurrence of the forms of relationships described here, it is felt that our findings have some degree of validity. It is hoped, however, that other workers will test out, elaborate upon, confirm or disprove these findings as future experience may indicate.

Types of Relationships

Types of relationships described are domination–submission, parasitic, symbiotic, anaclitic, supportive, transference, equipodal, unilateral, bilateral, and multilateral.

Domination–Submission. This type of relationship is common and has been described by some sociologists as the basic interindividual dynamic. When one person in a relationship submits, acquiesces, looks for control to another who wields power over him, we have the most simple domination–submission complex. We are interested not only in the overt acting out of this in the actual process of submission and dominance, but also in the disposition to submit and to dominate which may not be acted out. In some instances where conditions do not favor the acting out of the dispositions, they are repressed, sublimated, or diverted, for dispositions are translated into action only when favorable conditions exist. It may be a cultural pattern where domination of men over women is socially approved, or the contrary may be true. In some cultures, economic status gives prestige and power to dominate over others in less fortunate circumstances.

A more pertinent problem to the psychotherapist is the individual's need to dominate as against the equally psychological disposition to submit. One can recognize in this complex the existence of sadism on the part of one and masochism on the part of the other. While it is possible that these elements are present, frequently the operational trends are not so intense as to justify this classification. It may be a pattern of behavior in an individual which originates in the presence or absence of some organic and constitutional elements. It may be the result of psychogenic determinants proceeding from early experiences of the child, his relations with adults who had a hand in forming his character and establishing early perceptions toward the self. When the child's drives for play, exploration, and experimentation, for example, are too violently frustrated, where his growing autonomy is too strongly and too violently counteracted, he may make adaptations of a submissive nature. On the other hand, when a child is helped to act out his native curiosity and activity drives, and his strivings for self-determination are met, he is likely to develop mechanisms of domination. Thus education, conceived in its wider meaning, determines the nature and pattern of submission and domination.

The psychopathologist, however, is not concerned so much with the domination–submission trends in individuals whose adjustments to family, vocational, and social life do not present gross problems that undermine his mental health or injure or destroy the group. The psychotherapist is concerned with those individuals whose domination drives proceed from serious emotional dislocations. Even if such domination and aggression are repressed, they still constitute a problem to the individual and to society. Repressed domination and aggressive drives may find egress through neurotic symptomatology, or the patient may take on social amenities that conceal his basic character. Whether the domination trend is converted into symptoms or is acted out, it is directed against the persons with whom the patient is most intimate, as wife, husband, parents, or siblings. Similarly, the submission trend may create many malformations in social adaptation and emotional imbalance within an individual. In extreme cases of ego neuroses there occurs what was described by Ferenczi as a "loss of ego limits." The subject loses the perception of the rights and identity of other people and uses them as though they were organs of his own body.

There is present in all relations the domination–submission factor, and as such must be accepted as normal. The congruence of ideas or opinion and agreement have elements of domination–submission. However, in an equipodal relation, which we shall describe presently, where the roles of the persons involved are nearly alike, the role of the dominant and the submissive is taken on by either of the persons. At one time he dominates, and in turn submits. It is difficult to attain what is commonly known as the "meeting of minds."

Parasitic. The relationship between the parasite and the host needs no description. However, to lay a foundation for our discussion, we may indicate that the parasite is completely dependent upon the host for his very existence. He has no means of sustenance nor has he in some instances a mechanism for digesting food. He absorbs from the host food already digested and transformed into living matter.

A parasitic relation is an example of the height of dependence. Such dependence is found in emotional relationships and can be properly described as *emotional parasitism.* Physical and emotional parasitism in man have their origin in intrauterine life of the fetus and in infancy. Parasitism is fostered in some cultures, particularly in man–woman relationships as in Oriental countries. Girls are trained from early childhood to have little status. They first depend upon the family circle. Later they join the harem of a husband. This is an extreme form of depersonalization within the limits of normality. Even in our culture, parasitic relations are fostered by parents. In the treatment of problem children we frequently find boys and girls of nine and ten who are still being spoon-fed; are attended to in the toilet; they have no friends or playmates. Dependence is nurtured by mothers whose emotional needs are such that acting as host to their children is essential to their own self-fulfillment. The result is seriously maladjusted individuals who are unable to function in any type of relationship requiring self-dependence. In extreme cases they are unable to undertake or carry through work incidental to living in a society.

College life is to a large extent a parasitic life. Young people continue in a state of economic dependence, and are dependent intellectually upon professors from whom they absorb information with very little effort or original thinking of their own. Although parasitism of women has been greatly reduced in our culture, it is still encouraged. Particularly is this true of childless women or mothers whose children are cared for by nurses and whose homes are managed by servants.

Parasitic relationships are also frequently found among children. The weak child attaches himself to a stronger one for help in manual activities and for social protection. The source of this parasitism is coddling, over-protection, domination by parents, teachers, and others responsible for the education of the child. Where education does not mobilize and strengthen native power through free and directed activity, achievement, and success, parasitism and other forms of dependence are likely to appear. However, by far the greatest source of emotional parasitism is the content in the parent–child relationship. A parent who is deprived emotionally, sexually, and socially, may fixate on the child and make him dependent. In such cases the parent becomes the host and the child is the parasite. The mother's or father's needs, on the other hand, may be such that they become emotionally, if not physically, dependent upon the child. In such instances the compelling need for giving love as a compensation for one's own love deprivations makes the parent dependent upon the object of his love, the child. Here we have a situation in which the child, through no doing of his own, is placed in a position of a host by the parent, who is the emotional parasite. Exploitative love of this nature undermines the very foundations of character and devitalizes the child.

In the therapy of such children particularly, the group is very useful. If the environment and activity do not place too many demands nor present too difficult problems, the child is gradually able to perceive himself as an autonomous entity and able to function on his own. If the parents are helped at the same time to give up their need for the child, his libidinal and other emotional distortions are greatly lessened. By examples, other children in the group give the parasitic child strength to try himself against his environment and thus overcome some of his fears and feelings of impotence. The group therapist also plays an important role. At first he permits himself to be used by the child as a host, but gradually and almost imperceptibly denies himself and places the child on his own.

The degree to which this is possible to achieve with children depends upon a number of factors: (1) the intensity of the parasitic tie, (2) resistance of the parents to the child's maturing, (3) constitutional capacity of the child for growth, (4) the age at which treatment begins. In the treatment of adults, it would seem that only a thoroughgoing psychoanalysis can be effective. A transference relation and a living out of traumatic situations which psychoanalysis supplies helps emotional maturing and throws off the dependence upon a host.[1]

Symbiotic. In biology symbiosis designates the mutual dependence of one or more organisms upon each other for subsistence and survival. What is commonly described as interdependence in modern society is a form of social and economic symbiotic existence. The nature of symbiotic relations, as contrasted to parasitism, is that all involved remain autonomous. A person depends upon members of his family and friends, and they in turn depend upon him, but at the same time have personal and independent lives.

A symbiotic relation where an uncontrollable need of two persons for one another exists, and where the fear of losing each other may be so great as to create distress, fear, and panic, is fundamentally neurotic. Suicide pacts are probably a result of such a mutual need. Emotional symbiosis is present in homosexual relations, in long-lived marriages, and where parents and offspring live together for many years.

Emotional symbiosis can best be described as a form of mutual parasitism. It is a relation in which each of the persons involved serves simultaneously as a host and parasite. Symbiosis is the foundation of social living. Group integration has its roots in symbiosis and mutual identifications. It becomes pathological when the participants lose their own identity, become de-egotized and too dependent upon one another emotionally, economically, socially, or in all three areas.

Whether individual or group treatment is employed, both persons involved in the relationship need therapy. A mother in a parasitic or

---

1. It was later found that the problem of character parasitism, i.e., when no deep neuroses are involved, is more easily reached in groups.

symbiotic relation with her offspring becomes an essential element in the treatment of her child. In some less involved cases, giving her a vital and abiding interest away from her family and her home is helpful. Group treatment for such mothers should be effective particularly if treatment is aimed to extend out into the community and to provide her with social interests that would reduce her need for the child and make her emotionally more independent. Not only would the mother herself gain greatly from such groups but the child would be freed to develop his own autonomy and to strengthen his ego. However, where the involvement of the patients is intense and is charged with unconscious libidinal tensions, deeper psychotherapy is necessary for either or both persons involved. In all such cases, however, group association is profitable as tapering off or as concomitant to individual therapy.

Anaclitic. This has been described by Freud as a relationship where one person puts forward another to handle for him the actualities of life and to protect him against them. When a person is excessively afraid to meet new situations and the pressures of external circumstances, he may seek the help of another to intercede for him. Comparatively recently, women were in an anaclitic relationship to men. It was the man who punished his children; it was he who consulted government officials when litigation was involved; who went out to battle the world for a living. This has greatly changed and the anaclitic relation between men and women has also changed, certainly in a large portion of our population. Women no longer look to a man to deal with the world for them; they do it themselves quite adequately. Sometimes economic and cultural pressures reverse roles as during the period in Eastern Europe when, due to the absence of profitable occupations prohibited to them by law, Jewish men were driven into the synagogue and the houses of learning. It devolved upon women to earn the family livelihood, deal with officials, bribe and cajole them so as to make conduct of business possible. In this case it was the men who stood in an anaclitic relation to women. They were almost completely protected by and dependent upon women for meeting the reality situations in the world, but retained the mastery in the family circle and in their restricted community.

There are individuals who function quite adequately within a limited area, in their professions, for instance, so long as their clientele continues, but they fail when forced to promote themselves. The pressure of these actualities seem too much; basic fears and insecurities are aroused which were dormant under favorable circumstances. Some are fortunate to have wives who are "good mixers" and make social contacts for their husbands, and thus lay foundations for their successful functioning. Marriages "for convenience" may also be motivated by the need for an anaclitic relation.

The overprotected child or one who has been an invalid would tend to develop anaclitic dependence. A child who has been limited and whose functions have been circumscribed may remain in anaclitic relationships to adults. Where the personality is not seriously injured, where infantilism was not unduly prolonged and libidinal distortions are not too intense, an anaclitic relationship can be counteracted by extending the reality sphere and by exposing the individual to situations of a graded complexity and difficulty. As the patient is helped to break through his basic fears and feelings of inadequacy as a result of continued success, he sheds the need for a protective person. This is accomplished through the maturing process which occurs in individual psychotherapy and, in the case of young children, in groups where reality is extended from the group into the larger community.

Supportive. One of the most common dynamics in a therapy group is the choice, by members, of a supportive ego. A child attaches himself to another member of the group for support before he can bear to face physical and emotional interactivity. It would seem as though the child feels too weak to confront this particular reality, the group. In an anaclitic dependence he would withdraw and put forward someone else to deal with group situations. In a supportive relation he deals with it himself, using others to support him in the process. To survive as a group member he needs the strength that comes from having a friend to protect and help. Frequently children bring friends who are not members of the group for such support. We encourage this in our activity therapy groups since many children would not come without such support. The use of a support is valuable for diagnosis, since we are able to observe the patient in his own setting, as it were. The type of child he choses as a friend, his domination or submission patterns, his dependence, and other mechanisms must be noted.

The nature of supportive relationships is not as yet clear. Children sometimes establish such relationships with others who are like themselves. Aggressives will become attached to other aggressive children, and a withdrawn child becomes friendly with another withdrawn child. We have, however, observed instances where opposites become attached to one another. This may have some connection with the ego-ideal situation where the aggressive child has guilt about his aggressiveness and fundamentally wishes to be different than he is. He therefore attaches himself to a more normal person as a form of living out his ego-ideal, and for identification. It may also be due to the fact that where aggressiveness is a cloak for basic fears and timidity, the child is afraid of aggression in other people.

Supportive relationships in our groups are temporary. As the child becomes more secure and more mature his need for support disappears. He stops bringing his friends, detaches himself from his supportive ego, moves out into the group and makes contact with children who earlier were a source of threat. Thus, a child who chooses a withdrawn child for his early support works out a friendship with a more aggressive child whom he formerly feared. This movement is undoubtedly an indication of improvement in the personality structure. It involves a perception of inner strength, a growing maturity, a sloughing-off of fears, diminishing anxieties, and greater self-dependence. In most cases the child develops to a state where he need not attach himself to any one or several children, but is able to react freely to all members in the group. Thus he increases his personal mobility as well as the mobility and flexibility of the group.

Supportive relations have some similarities to the parasitic and symbiotic. However, parasitic and symbiotic relations are permanent and charged with greater emotional drives and libido content than is a supportive relation. As already noted, supportive relations are temporary and transitory and are used as a tool in treatment. In individual treatment, also, patients need supportive relations. The love-starved child, the child with a weak ego, or one who is constitutionally inferior, handicapped, or stigmatized, needs support from the therapist. Big Brothers and Big Sisters are used profitably in such situations. In some cases psychiatrists and case workers also find it necessary to act as supports in individual treatment. To a considerable extent, ego therapy rests upon a supportive relationship with the therapist.

Transference. As defined by Freud, a transference relation is one in which the patient accepts the therapist emotionally in place of a parent, and transfers upon him the attitudes and feelings tied up with a parental image. This may be positive or negative. The transference relation is the pivot of psychoanalytic treatment through which the patient is helped to relive earlier experiences with his parents and others and thus resolves his nuclear traumatic and peripheral problems. The analyst helps the patient to feel and understand his early emotions in a new light and on a level of a growing emotional maturity. This complex process would not be possible without the patient accepting the analyst in *locus parentis.*

Transference relations also exist outside of psychoanalytic treatment. Frequently amity or enmity are activated unconsciously and projected onto persons who resemble one's parents. Mild transference relations, both positive and negative, are developed toward teachers, employers, physicians and others who are in the role of authority or give protection. Thus transference can occur on different levels and, while qualitatively similar, differ as to quantum. The quantum of emotion is at its highest in psychoanalytic treatment. Though in psychotherapy transference is used in a technical sense, transference relationships must be conceived as occurring among normal persons as well as among the disturbed and neurotic. However, quality, intensity, and meaning are different to the various individuals.

One of the aims of psychoanalysis is to dissolve the transference and the emotional dependence that it connotes. The patient matures to the degree that he is able to free himself emotionally, for, so long as he remains tied either to a parent or parental representative, he remains emotionally infantile. Such ties block free association with people, reduce adaptability, and hamper social development. On the other hand, working through a transference relation on deeper levels opens sluices of perception and understanding which had been closed before. Outside of these more involved levels, however, there exist many transference attitudes and relations in the life of each of us which must be considered as normal and desirable.

Equipodal. In all the types of relations discussed, elements of dependence exist. Even the dominant person in the domination-submission complex is dependent upon the person or persons whom he dominates. The need to dominate is a symptom of character disturbance. In the ideal relation, persons are on an equal footing of "give and take." Submission and domination roles are taken on at different times, but there is no drive on the part of one to subjugate or exploit the other. Such an ideal setting is not too frequently found. It is conceivable that two people who had lived under favorable conditions in childhood, or had had a thorough psychoanalysis, are capable of such a relationship. Even if we cannot attain this ideal, education and therapy must set it as their aim to help people establish such relations.

Relations and Therapy

We have discussed so far relations as they arise spontaneously and are established automatically by people who live in proximity with one another. Some of these are by their nature the concern of the therapist because they are fundamentally pathological. Others become so only because of the degree of intensity in which they exist and the undesirable effects they have upon personality.

In psychotherapy the aim is to help the individual to mature emotionally. It is not the aim of this paper to describe methods of therapy, but rather to recount the relations as they are observed among so-called normal people and among patients under treatment. In the latter we set out to produce changes within the personality which would prevent social maladaptations and so make the individual capable of establishing desirable relationships. To achieve this, psychotherapy itself uses relationships as its tool. We can identify five types of such relationships: transference, supportive, unilateral, bilateral, and multilateral. The first two have already been briefly described.

Unilateral. A unilateral relation can be discerned where emotional flow takes place in one direction, from one person to another, without reciprocal feelings. The most striking example is the relation between psychoanalyst and patient. In the transference situation the emotional flow is only from the patient to the analyst. Countertransference, reversal of this process, vitiates the therapeutic situation. This unilateral relation is also characteristic of Activity Group Therapy. The relation between the patient and the group therapist is a unilateral one, for the therapist maintains a neutral role. Because of this neutrality, each child can view the therapist as whatever symbol he may wish this adult to be. It is important also that the therapist does not give preference or sympathy to any one member of the group, but rather meets each one's needs objectively on a warm and friendly basis. He cannot develop a relationship with any one of the children without disturbing the others. The child toward whom the worker may have definite feelings becomes a preferred or rejected child, as the case may be, with a consequence activation of sibling rivalry, jealousy, and hostility among his patients.

Bilateral. Bilateral relations exist in forms of psychotherapy of less intensity than in psychoanalysis, such as in case work. The client here must feel the understanding and warmth on the part of the worker toward him if he is to overcome his resistance and blockings. The client must have friendly understanding or he is unable to break through his reservations and develop a relationship necessary in any type of treatment. It exists also, to a lesser degree, in interview group therapy where relationships must exist not only among the members of the group, but where each member must have a definite and warm relation with the group therapist. Such bilateral relations are present among friends, and in a good marriage.

Multilateral. Group therapy is founded upon the concept of multilateral relations. We have already indicated that a supportive ego which the patient chooses for himself is of a transitory nature; that individual relationships are steps in his growth to a point where he can accept a group situation. He must be able to move freely from one person to another and participate in relations where more than two persons are involved. This capacity is often referred to as a part of the "group personality." Multilateral relationships are both the tool and aim of all forms of group therapy. In fact, the paramount qualifications for assignment of clients for group treatment is their capacity, even though they may have difficulty in doing so, of facing a situation where multilateral relations exist. A patient who fears multilateral relations needs a preliminary stage of individual treatment (bilateral relation) before he can face a group situation (multilateral relation).

The withdrawn and taciturn resort to bilateral and often unilateral relations, even within the group as transitional stages. Only those individuals can be accepted for group treatment who can make this transition. If for any reasons they are unable to establish multiple relationships they will not come to a group.

Conclusion

The use of the term *dependence* in psychotherapeutic literature requires further exploration. The concept is a generic one and its operational value would be greatly enhanced if we could break it down into specific processes and relate them to specific psychological syndromes. An effort has been made in this communication to do the former, namely, to describe the various kinds of dependencies that we have observed. It would be of great value if it were possible to relate these to definite characterological constellations, and to trace psychogenic factors and educational influences that produce them. Such information would not only aid therapy, but would also supply one more directive in understanding and planning preventive education.

Much has been done in exploring the use of *relation* in psychiatry and case work. When we become aware of the existence of unilateral, bilateral, and multilateral relations we can use them with greater awareness in different situations. It also gives one more criterion for selecting types of treatment most suitable to a specific patient or client.

Finally, the material here is offered only as a first step in an investigation that we believe will prove of value if carried on further. We hope this will be done by other workers.

CHAPTER 12

RACIAL AND CULTURAL FACTORS
(1956)

Culture has been defined in many ways by technologists, sociologists, anthropologists, and ethnologists. These definitions are all good if viewed from the point of view and area of interest of these specialists. From the point of view of the psychologist, culture can be defined as the total system of mores, rules, laws, and taboos evolved by a group of people to deal with anxiety, guilt, and aggression. Religion, law, and morals, superstition, art, and folklore can be said to aim either at assuaging or activating guilt and anxiety and to regulate and control aggression. These are all aimed at assuring the survival of the individual and the group.

Because of this deeply affecting survival and security function of the cultural patterns, change in them creates anxiety and is, therefore, so stubbornly resisted. Educationists, religionists, and medical and mental health workers have found it difficult to deal with cultural rigidities among peoples, especially when they attempted changes in groups other than their own. Attitudes, value systems, superstitions, and beliefs ingrained in a culture cannot be rapidly altered or easily eliminated. It requires generations of slow, planned reeducation or life conditions to affect changes.

The difficulties that religious workers and missionaries encountered in their efforts to have the Bible accepted by primitive tribes made it necessary for them to alter some specific details in consonance with prevalent beliefs of the specific tribes before they could make the Bible acceptable to them. The changes were made to accord with those basic and cherished beliefs which when assailed activated anxiety, fear, and anger with the resulting resistance to the new ideas.

Health workers encountered beliefs and superstitions that greatly impeded, and frequently negated their efforts at introducing scientifically valid practices. The now well-known work of the Rockefeller and other foundations in introducing most elementary hygienic practices and measures in various culturally backward countries and the often insurmountable obstacles they met is an illustration near at hand of the cultural inflexibility of people. The introduction of latrines and segregation of lepers were among the most resisted measures in South American countries.[1] In other South American countries, the maternity centers are still rejected because the natives believe that fresh air is injurious for the parturients. Fear of hospitals stems from the fact that prospective mothers are required to take a bath. This is considered extremely unhealthy for a pregnant woman.

In Far Eastern nations, hospitals are shunned because appropriate rituals for dying and burial are not observed, and in countries of Chinese civilization hospitals are shunned because the dead will not be received in the nether world in the proper manner if they do not die under regulated ritualistic conditions.

Dr. Pierre Dorolle, who has studied the problem of resistance to mental health measures, reported that "in many population groups, the women are very reluctant or absolutely refuse to allow themselves to be examined by a man, even in the presence of another woman. On the other hand cases have been noted on the island of Yap in the Pacific where women refused to allow themselves to be examined by a woman or in the presence of another women."[2] In Ecuador women refused to go to a hospital to deliver the babies because the hospitals were too well aired and fresh air was considered bad for women in childbirth. Dr. Dorolle concludes the "reactions of this kind are unforeseeable unless there is a preliminary ethnological study."

The above are only a few instances to illustrate how the cultural set resists change and educative efforts, which are always a source of

1. Heiser, V. (1936). *An American Doctor's Odyssey*. New York: W. W. Norton.
2. Dorolle, P. (1954). Ethnological and health problems. *Bulletin of World Mental Health*, 6:21-30.

more or less serious cultural conflicts and will serve as a background for the topic of this paper.

It is quite understandable that prejudices and superstitions should be even more rigid and inflexible in the area of mental illnesses and nervous disorders, for in all groups, throughout the ages, these have been clothed in a supernatural cloak and have usually or nearly always been tied up with evil spirits for which various exorcising methods and rituals have been evolved. The belief in the magical and mystical sources of these disturbances and their treatment always entails thaumaturgical techniques in primitive societies. Group and individual incantations, ritual dances and sacrifices, amulets, prayers, singing, mutilations, and numerous other types of ritualistic acts that allegedly serve to exorcise evil spirits are practiced throughout Africa and Australia and the populations of Asia and some parts of Europe as well. Though in some respects different, peoples whose cultures are derived from the Chinese civilization use similar methods of expelling evil spirits in mental illnesses—illnesses that we in the Western culture understand as being real and requiring appropriate medical and psychotherapeutic measures.

During my travels in Europe and from the conversations with about three hundred visitors to my office from some fifty countries who worked in the fields of psychiatry, psychology, and social work, I have gleaned some definite differences in attitudes toward their work from those of our own—differences which are gradually diminishing since World War II. One cannot entirely overlook them, however, if we wish to understand what possibilities are offered for the spread of mental health measures in different countries and continents.

Some Belgians[3] told me, for example, that psychoanalysis, and especially group psychotherapy, cannot make rapid headway in that country because the Belgian population characteristically tends to be reticent. The pattern is restricted communication and to some extent there is a tendency toward secretiveness. When asked why this was the case, the explanation given me by a Belgian psychoanalyst and his associate (with whom I had lunched in London), was that the

---

3. It is to be noted that the characterization of different nationalities as they appear in this part of the paper are the opinion of individuals quoted and, though they have been made by natives of those countries, are to be considered as impressions rather than controlled scientific investigations.

geographic location of their country was such that in past centuries it had been in the hands of conquerors for many generations and under the control of different nations for long periods of time. As a result, the people had to exercise the greatest care not to reveal their views and feelings lest they be denounced and severely punished or put to death.

A similar observation was made about Northern countries, but the reason offered for the lack of communication and resistance to psychiatric and psychoanalytic interviews here were climatic conditions: the extreme cold, prolonged winters. The sparse population tends toward isolation and seclusiveness, which in the course of centuries became an ingrained pattern of interpersonal relations and intrapersonal adjustment. The noted Danish psychiatrist and authority on alcoholism, Dr. Oluf Martenson-Larson, has told me that the husbands of the alcoholic women whom he treated in groups regularly gathered in front of his office building seemingly waiting for their wives. He did not offer any explanation for this phenomenon, but apparently it is not customary for women in that country to go out unaccompanied by their husbands.

Some religions that employ the confessional look with disfavor upon the intimate revelations that form the psychoanalytic interview. Some years ago an analyst had become involved in a conflict with a hospital in New York on this issue which resulted in his resignation from the staff.

I became aware of these problems on purely theoretical grounds when in 1949 I prepared a questionnaire which Dr. Francine Bigwood of Brussels, Belgium, circulated at my request among psychiatrists in different European countries. In somewhat modified form her reports were published in several issues of the *International Journal of Group Psychotherapy*.[4]

The following was the questionnaire as it was prepared at that time:

(1) What is the extent and application of group psychotherapy in *(a)* Child Guidance Clinics, *(b)* Mental Hospitals, and *(c)* Private

4. Harding, G. T., Israel, J., and Bernstein, L. Group therapy in Sweden, 1:82-85. Kraemer, W. P. Group psychotherapy at the Davidson Clinic, Edinburgh, Scotland, 1:281-284. Rumke, H. C. Group psychotherapy in Utrecht, Holland 1:374-376.

Practice? (This would require a statistical analysis and a report on the number of centers employing group psychotherapy with emotionally disturbed and mental patients as well as the number receiving such treatment.)

(2) What are the training facilities? (We would like to know what training facilities for the practice of group psychotherapy now exist in your country. In this connection we would want to know *(a)* qualifications for students accepted for training, *(b)* curriculum employed, *(c)* the type of personnel and *(d)* the number of persons being so trained.)

(3) The modifications in the application of group psychotherapy that had to be made because of inherent characteristics of the culture of your country. (This would require that the following points be covered, among others: *(a)* What is the attitude of religious leaders toward group psychotherapy, *(b)* the effect of small communities in which patients know each other in everyday contacts upon revelations of their problems that of necessity must come out in group interviews, and *(c)* the attitude on the part of adults toward free acting out in Activity Group Therapy for children in the various cultures. There should be considerable difference in this respect in different countries.)

(4) List the literature dealing with group psychotherapy in your country.

We were not able to elicit answers to many of the questions, at that time, and none to item (3).

In my own work I have observed specific cultural and perhaps also racial differences that directly affect group psychotherapy. New York, having a variety of races and nationalities, favors the study of the effect of tradition, culture, and race upon practice. The differentials in response to the same therapeutic situation as we have observed them can be explained only by the variants in cultural factors. The family patterns in different groups have a specific character. The place that parents and children occupy in families, the roles that they play, and their relationships are specific to ethnic and perhaps, better still, cultural dynamics.

As an example, in the East European Jewish family the wife almost invariably assumes the dominant role with the man occupying a

recessive place. The East European Jewish family is basically matri-
archal. The control of the family stems from the mother rather than
the father. Elsewhere, I have attempted to offer a rationale for this
phenomenon [11]. Briefly, it is as follows.

After the destruction of the second temple and the dispersion of the
Jews from Palestine, an edict was promulgated that it was incumbent
upon all males to devote themselves to the study of the Torah and in
what is now considered orthodox service to God. As a result, these
two functions were the chief aim and occupation of the Jewish male
for centuries. The intent of the edict, which proved in succeeding
centuries to be effective, was to bind the nation despite its dispersal
and thus assure its survival as an ethnic unit. However, the man as a
result could not devote time and effort for the practical and material
pursuits required of a head of a family. In Eastern Europe, especially,
where the predominant majority of the world's Jewry lived, these were
shifted upon the shoulders of the women. The woman was thus placed
higher in the hegemony of the family's economic position. It was she
who came to be the chief provider through managing the business,
where there was a business to manage.

Where the husband did the actual earning of a living—and there
were a small percentage of these—his preoccupation with parochial
matters and the time consumed in the extensive daily religious rituals
left him little time for management of the practical affairs of the
family group and of social life. It was to the woman that these
responsibilities fell. She dealt with officials, bribed them, and cared
for the reality elements. This, of necessity, placed her in a dominant
role and the husband in an anaclitic relation to her.

Although, in some countries in the twentieth century, the male had
moved up to the forefront of the economic effort, the traditionally set
attitudes and roles still persist. Even in the United States, after two
and three generations, this characteristic pattern is present, though it
is gradually diminishing in intensity. It can be expected that in time
this anomalous relation between husband and wife may vanish
altogether. At the present time, however, the dominant role of the
mother gives the family a definite complexion and the children's
attitudes as well as their ego and superego development and strengths
are largely determined by this family pattern. The situation is
dramatically illustrated by the comparative infrequency of alcoholism

among Jews. Their ego and superego organization has a definite characteristic which we shall not discuss here, since it is not germane to our central theme.

While the families among Jews tend to be strongly cohesive, very little such cohesiveness is present in the Negro families that come to social service agencies and child guidance clinics in New York. In the families that are forced to seek help from social service agencies, the fathers usually carry little responsibility. In nearly all these cases the family structure is as follows: the father is out of the home, the mother is working and takes little or no responsibility for the upbringing of the children who are reared by grandparents. The children actually do not have a parental image in the ordinary sense; their parental images stem from the generation once removed. There is, therefore, less understanding, impeded communication and personal harmony between the children and the substitute parents. The ego and superego organization and the capacity for object relations, stemming as they do from grandparents, leave a definite stamp on the personality.

The defective parental responsibility and weak family cohesiveness originate, in my opinion, from the slavery under which the Negro had lived in America. Children, parents, husband and wife were usually, though not always, separated and sold as individuals rather than families. They were dispersed so that family attachments could not or were not permitted to take root and develop, an attitude that still persists despite changed social and economic conditions of the Negro in the past several generations. Similarly, the absolute ownership of the female slaves exposed them to the lusts of their masters, both owners and foremen, which jeopardized the intimate relation that should exist between husband and wife. These attitudes and weak marital ties are traditionally being carried over even into the present through the inevitable "cultural lag."

It must be noted that what has been said concerning the Negro's system of values does not apply to all Negroes. The educated and cultured Negro who was brought up and has lived as part of the nation's general culture, has in every respect the same characteristics as the general population. Family ties are strong and the family loyalties are on an even higher level than those of the average white population. We shall see presently also that while the majority of Negroes do not respond with neuroses to stress and conflict, the cultured and educated do become neurotic. Perhaps it should also be stated that what has been said here about the Negro group applies to the American Negro more than to Negroes who come from other parts of the world, particularly Jamaica.

In the Irish group, the dominant and responsible person is the man of the house, but he exercises his domination in an authoritarian manner and sometimes even with violence and frequently cruelty. In many of the cases that come for treatment of family adjustment, the father's escape from stress and strain is provided by alcohol. Again, this does not characterize the total population of Irish descent but rather those families whose stability had broken down and who seek help in agencies and clinics. The wife in these families is by and large of secondary status and in most instances seeks to adapt herself to the unfavorable situation in which she finds herself. She considers her lot as inevitable, almost as part of fate. This attitude is to a large extent conditioned by the culture in her native Ireland and by the church. The neurotic and fatalistic reactions are a result of centuries of famine, poverty, and often inhuman treatment the Irish had received at the hands of their conquerors, the English. Even the delightful humor for which the Irish are famous would seem to have an anxiety-denying aim.[5]

Family life and adaptive patterns of people reflect themselves in group therapy activities and interviews. In our work with parents' groups of mothers and fathers, we found these attitudes and values clearly reflected. The Jewish woman is characteristically assertive, dominating, and resentful, while in his communications to the group her mate reflects guilt. The women by and large are more talkative; they reveal themselves and their problems freely. The men tend to talk more about practical matters of family management and the realities of their lives and their families. In both men and women of this ethnic group, there is a remarkable freedom in communication and ease of verbalization during group interviews.

The situation is considerably different with Negroes. They communicate with great reluctance and it takes considerable time to dissolve their diffidence and apparent fear. They act as though they

---

5. Much that has been said here on the matter of roles and relations has undergone changes since this paper was written (1950). The general underlying patterns still prevail, however.

were afraid of being punished for their conduct and thoughts. A large number of the adults—and this is also true of the adolescents—are evasive and try to cover up. Group and individual therapists can eventually activate communication, but it usually takes considerable skill and time. In addition to the diffidence characteristic of the oppressed and serving classes as a result of their devaluated self-image and physical insecurity, one gets the feeling that they are apprehensive of being discovered and punished. This, too can be understood in the light of the fear of informers among their midst during slavery. This phenomenon was already touched upon in our discussion of the Belgians and was also observed in concentration camps. Preliminary individual interviews are advisable to establish some sort of relation and thus overcome distrust and shyness of the Negro patients. The security derived from individual contacts seems to have helped group communication.

We have experienced the same difficulties with adolescent Negro girls. Perhaps we did not possess the special knowledge and skill to do it, but we found it so far quite impossible to get Negro adolescent girls to talk about their intimate problems and preoccupations,[6] something which is quite easy for Jewish girls of the same age. After experimentation to establish pure analytic groups with adolescent Negro girls had failed, we introduced arts and crafts materials on which they could work while they sat around a table talking. This is a modified pattern of Activity-Interview Group Therapy for young children, without physical movement through the room and spontaneous subgroup and interactions that emerge from such free movement among young children. In these groups the patients sit and work on simple libido-fixating materials such as stringing beads, making belts, sewing, knitting, and so on.

The conversations are always perfunctory in character, dealing with superficial matters such as school, boys, parties, occurrences in the neighborhood, gang fights, and gossip about out-of-wedlock pregnancies. Only occasionally would a girl talk about her parents or grandparents. These would be mentioned fleetingly. The girls refrain from criticizing or expressing hostility toward them. Efforts at stimulating discussions of more serious personality problems and relation-

---

6. We found the same situation in groups of adolescent boys some years later.

ships have failed. There is considerable diffidence and fear about speaking negatively about parents or their substitutes. This is not the case with Jewish girls and boys who very freely criticize their parents, relate unpleasant episodes about them, including their sexual misbehavior, and narrate other uncreditable facts and fancies. The Jewish adolescent girls, but not the boys, reveal a great deal about their confusions, their feelings of inadequacy and inferiority, about their sexual practices and fantasies, and unrestrainedly reveal other intimate and anxiety-evoking material. This we were not able to elicit from our Negro girls.

In activity therapy groups as well we observed a pattern among Negro children which was absent in Jewish groups. There was a greater degree of physical contact among Negro boys and Negro girls than among Jewish children. They played together more, pushed each other around, and the girls danced together a great deal, acted out in dance and in spontaneous pantomime, and sang group songs. In the rather large number of therapy groups consisting of Jewish children which we have had, there never was an instance of dancing, singing, or dramatic acting except in one group of preadolescent girls where there was some dancing, and this we traced to a definite homosexual trend among two of the girls.

It is my opinion that the singing, dancing and dramatic acting out as observed in our Negro groups stem from the culture of the Negro. The Negroes have had to bear up under very tragic circumstances in slavery, and to bolster their spirit and relieve their anguish, group dances and singing were resorted to, as reflected in the spirituals and the abandon in some of the dances. It must be noted in this connection that while these may have been altered in form or content, they are themselves derived from, and are a continuation of ritualistic singing and dance.

The Jews, on the other hand, not having had such forms of abreaction in their background, reacted to their deprived condition neurotically. There is, therefore, a greater prevalence of functional neuroses among them, while among the Negroes we encounter character disorders and weak ego development. These disorders rather than neuroses appear because the Negroes abreacted their feelings of depression and tragedy which prevented their becoming structured in their personality, as was the case with the Jews. Because of intrapersonal tensions and conflict in the Jews, accounts for a freer flow of verbalization in their group interviews than among Negroes. The ego of the Negro is not laden with anxiety and inner conflicts to the same degree as among Jews. These differences determine the content and the nature of group therapeutic interviews.

I suspect, however, that essentially the Negro who comes for treatment or guidance is also neurotic, but his anxiety-denying defenses of evasion are so close to the surface and have been employed with such facility and frequency, that the neurotic elements are hidden from view. My guess is that behind the layers of acting out, the singing and the dancing, there is a great deal of anxiety and tension.

Another observation has recently been made relative to the differential responses of Negro and white children to Activity Group Therapy. While the effectiveness of this method of treatment is limited to white children under thirteen years of age, it was found to be effective with Negro girls up to sixteen years of age. The percentage of improvement of Negro girls treated by this method is impressively higher than that among the white patient population. In addition, a markedly larger number of referred patients of the Negro group qualified for this type of treatment than white children, especially the Jews.

This differential in both the percentage of suitability and the rate of improvement can be attributed to the higher incidence of neurosis among the white patient population as compared with that among the Negroes. The effectiveness of Activity Group Therapy for the higher age range among Negroes can be assumed to be caused by the difference in character structure in the two cultural groups, since Activity Group Therapy is designed to deal predominantly with character and ego problems rather than with psychoneuroses.

By and large the Anglo-Saxon groups tend to talk more about immediate problems and relationships in their lives. Anglo-Saxons are less introspective and are, therefore, less prone to enter into the analysis of intrapsychic states. It is quite possible that it is for this reason that in some Anglo-Saxon countries there has arisen the technique of "here and now." This approach is possibly more suitable to the Anglo-Saxon temperament and cultural conditioning which is more objective, less introspective than in the case of Jewish, Oriental, and Latin cultures. Their preoccupations would, therefore, be more centered on immediate problems. Centering upon the "here and now" and the immediate group tensions may, therefore, be a suitable method for groups of patients who traditionally and ordinarily do not tend toward introspection and self-analysis.

It would seem justified to say even from this brief discussion that the productions of patients in groups and their behavior in them have to be considered from the aspect of cultural personality patterning and the various roles in everyday life. My belief is that this awareness on the part of the therapist need not change the tested techniques of psychotherapy nor his basic functions. The awareness of cultural differences will, however, prevent his surprise and confusion when he does not obtain expected outcomes in the usual manner or in ways to which he had been accustomed. He may have to modify his methods and functions to suit conditions and be satisfied with results that may otherwise be unacceptable or disappointing.

A word about race versus culture. I could not find any special psychologic race differences. From our observation of the racial groups of patients it would seem that they are fundamentally the same as to psychologic needs, anxieties, and motivations. However, the cultural patternings did make a considerable difference in the responses of the patients.

CHAPTER 13

THE ANATOMY AND CLINICAL APPLICATIONS OF GROUP INTERACTION
(1969)

Every direct human encounter generates interaction. The interaction may be slight or intense, implicit or explicit, verbal or nonverbal; whether the results are made manifest or not, everyone involved undergoes transient internal change in though and/or feelings with concomitant somatic and psychic processes, that is, psychosomatic phenomena which, according to the nature of the protagonists or the conditions in which the confrontation occurs, may set off benign or malignant interpersonal responses. The reactions may be withheld, suppressed, or acted out in accordance with the regulative principles characteristic of each of the persons involved.

Nietzsche once remarked that when two persons meet, they at once understand one another, but later they talk each other out of it. First impressions are modified or altered for one of two reasons. One stems from social mores and the prevailing culture which extols benevolence in attitude and restraint in conduct. Harboring negative feelings is considered "bad" and "sinful." To gain acceptance and approval, one must be, or act as though one is, accepting and tolerant. Subverting the negative puts one in the company of the good and righteous. Another motive for suppressing or withholding intuitively arrived at negative feelings may be for social or material advantage. According to the nature of the motivation, alienative feelings may be an index of maturity or the road of opportunism.

The foregoing is a view of confrontation from its negative aspects. But confrontations also evoke positive and mutually beneficial responses leading to synergic thought and/or action. The point is, however, that all human contacts initially activate some degree of uncertainty and anxiety, for neither of the participants is completely at ease, nor is he certain in advance of the reactions of the other, nor does he know when and how his threat areas will be assailed. This is as true of group encounters as it is of a dyadic relationship, although degrees and intensities of the two may differ. The natural and automatic effect of a group upon its participants has been labeled by me as "group-induced anxiety" [61, p. 31]. Due to the unavoidable emotional networks that arise in small groups, they quantitatively present greater threats to their constituents than are evoked in a dyadic encounter. The heightened quantum of discomfort arises from two genetic sources. One is the variety in the styles of ego functioning of each of the participants and the unpredictability of developments. The other source is the phalanx that groups tend to form for the possible victimization of one member of the group.

The style and intensity of threat varies to a considerable degree with the cultural level of the participants. The quality of the interaction is to a telling extent determined by the level of ego functioning of the group's members. Their ego controls determine their tolerance or intolerance toward the idiosyncrasies of fellow members. A group, even one with benign social aims, may under some circumstances end in a fiasco. However, barring such an extreme, ordinary groups, that is groups with no therapeutic intent, operate under varying degrees of restraints. Ordinarily, brawls, for example, occur only in specific strata of society, and usually only when individuals are under the influence of restraint-dissolving agents such as alcohol or drugs.

Groups in which the discharging of feelings is encouraged and in which there is frank interchange of undisguised positive and negative attitudes among their members are the psychotherapy groups. Maximum latitude reigns in these, as well as in all other respects, and patients subjectively react and interpersonally interact freely, often discharging raw feelings without restraint or regard for social amenities—a situation that in any other type of group could not be tolerated.

The type and intensity of individual internal reactions are conditioned in early childhood and reflect the "culturalizing" influence of homes and neighborhoods. By culturalizing is meant the success with which sublimational channels for primitive responses and ego controls are established during the formative years of an individual. These two factors and successful repression determine the capacity for interpersonal relations and interactions. Overcathexis of feelings, opinions, and convictions—which is usually a defense against doubt and insecurity—leads to overassertiveness, stubbornness, and combativeness, which in ordinary life exist to a minimal degree in the cultivated (not necessarily schooled) person.

Despite antecedent educational and culturalizing influences, invidious mechanisms are heightened by ordinary events in emotionally disturbed individuals who constitute the membership of therapy groups. By and large, the individual reenacts in his interpersonal relationships response patterns of his formative years, and by their permissiveness and emotional intensification, therapy groups maximize individual patterns of response. The overtly aggressive person becomes more aggressive, the covertly aggressive person throws off restraints, and the frightened, timid, and diffident are abashed by the conduct of their fellow members and may (and certainly do at the outset) withdraw into silence.

In the climate of a therapy group, where regression is encouraged, disagreements, conflicts, and rivalries inevitably emerge, as do affinities, often of a pathogenic nature. These constitute important grist for the psychotherapeutic mill. The psychotherapist understands these phenomena as manifestations of the transference-countertransference dynamic stemming from earlier phases in the psychic development of the individuals involved. He also knows that they are essential to the reconstruction of the damaged personality. However, it is important to keep in mind that the ultimate therapeutic value of such phenomena does not lie in the reenactment alone or in the emotional release alone. These aberrant reactions and interactions are essential steps toward acquiring understanding and insight into the motives and needs they serve in the psychic economy of patients. Release of affect may reduce tensions, but its ultimate value lies in the insight it can give into the individual's specific psychodynamics.

In other papers [10, 16], I have attempted to identify the specific characteristics of therapy groups as opposed to those of other groups existing in a free and fluid society such as ours. By virtue of these differences, the usual controls for dealing with what is ordinarily viewed as deviant and disturbing behavior are not applicable to groups with a therapeutic aim. Neutralization, compromise, assimilation, cohesion, polarity, synergy, and the like are not available to the therapist and his group as they are to the leader of a social club, or an educational, political, or special interest group. Were they to be applied in a therapy group, the group's therapeutic objectives would be annulled. Contrariwise, other group phenomena and interactive mechanisms that do not occur at all or only minimally in other types of groups constitute the very essence of a psychotherapy group. Among the dynamics that most often occur in therapeutic groups are mutual induction, (emotional) interstimulation, and rivalry. And the greater their intensity, the better do they serve the group's objectives.

Psychological phenomena in all groups stem from three sources: reenactment, acting out, and abreaction. In nontherapeutic groups, the cohesive forces stemming from commonality of purpose, interest, or aim keep these primary trends in abeyance. When they do appear, the leader and the group members either prohibit their full exercise or they are controlled by the cohesive group forces such as the *primary group code*, social mores, and intrapsychic inhibitions, or they are resolved through the mechanism of compromise which naturally arises in ordinary groups. In contrast, in psychotherapeutic groups, where the primary group code permits and encourages freedom of action and expression, these and other disruptive eruptions are the meat of therapy. In their climb to mental health, patients in group psychotherapy must reveal to themselves and to the other group members their *real* selves; they have to throw off their facade of polish and deportment, and they must rid themselves of culturally imposed, noxious pseudo defenses and build in their stead more healthful and more appropriate defenses and controls.[1]

The group, and even more so the therapist, is thus faced with the problem of permitting the free flow of infectious negative and disruptive manifestations while still confining them within bounds consistent with therapeutic demands. The management of outbreaks in the permissive climate of psychotherapeutic groups requires, in

---

1. It is most important that the psychotherapist prevent patients from exceeding their current capacities to sustain the degree of hostility discharge. Great disturbances and suicides have been reported from so-called "encounter" groups where this was allowed to occur (1972).

addition to an unusual degree of objectivity and self-control on the part of the therapist, a thorough understanding of the latent content of the proceedings. The therapist must be able, from his knowledge of the individual operational patterns of each of his patients, to identify the sources of the outbursts, the deviant attitudes and the characteristic behavior of the instigator, as well as the others, involved in a rally or transaction. As is the case in all types of groups, the therapist must perceive from which of three possible sources behavior stems—whether the instigator's and the respondent's behavior is motivated by reenactment, acting out, or abreaction.

I have attempted on a number of occasions to stress the point that every response on the part of a therapist, verbal or nonverbal, must be therapeutically appropriate and specific to the current transaction, particularly to its latent content. The behavior of patients in the permissive setting of the therapy group may easily try the patience and psychic tolerance of the psychotherapist, generating counter-transferential, covert, and at times even overt, reactions on his part. Aside from the therapist's superior ego integration and maximal emotional noninvolvement, one of the important safeguards against the arousal of countertransferential feelings and conduct is the *understanding* by him of the compelling forces operating in the patients' psyches.[2] This is the sine qua non of therapy, for such knowledge produces suitable attitudes and leads to appropriate conduct. The therapist realizes that the patients' behavior is inevitable and, because of their condition, is beyond the scope of their responsibility at the time. This attitude of the therapist is that of the true healer, which sets him apart from most persons the patients have encountered in the past.

In line with these principles, the therapist, to be effective in dealing with difficult or disruptive behavior in individual or group therapeutic settings, must be aware of the meaning and sources of behavior. Only by acting upon such knowledge can the therapist utilize the patients' reactions for therapeutic ends. For example, seemingly infantile irascibility, uncontrollable temper, or unreasonable narcissism may need to be differentially overlooked, encouraged, restrained, or

2. It was reported to the present author by a colleague that the former "therapist" of one of her patients had in a fit of rage hurled a book at her. Another "analyst" in his anger rebuked and denigrated his patient for his inability to get along with his wife.

explored. The decision rests upon the clinical indications for a specific patient at a given time and/or the psychic tolerance of the other patients.[3] The therapist needs to draw upon knowledge of the patient's dominant current psychodynamics and his earlier formative influences and conditions to determine the most appropriate course of action or inaction. Inappropriate dealing with the behavior will not only prove to be a disservice to therapeutic outcomes but, what is even more disastrous, it may seriously vitiate or entirely destroy the positive transference toward the therapist.

Reenactment

Reenactment in human relations stems from reawakened psychic and neuronic reflex reactions established during the developmental phases of the individual. Reactivations are set off in circumstances that appear to be similar in basic respects to traumatic events of the past. The very group compresence, for example, may awaken anxieties and aggressions in individuals whose early multiple relations in the original family were a source of threat, tension, and pain.

The therapist needs to be alert to the difference between idiosyncratic character structure and behavior which can be misconstrued as reenactment. Character patterns arise from the imprinting upon the child by his environment, by identification and imitation of significant models, and by his interaction with them. The totality of demands, pressures, and influences—modified to some degree by later accommodations—together with their emotional concomitants, shape almost mechanically an individual's entity. Conduct arising from the individual's entity can be described as "characteristic." When it is socially deviant or problem-generating, the behavior is described as that of a person with a character disorder or one with general maladjustment.

The roots of reenactment under consideration here, on the other hand, lie not in habit and in conditioning but in the suppressed emotivity of earlier phases of development. The reenactment is

---

3. The other group members are inevitably drawn into such tensions and conflicts, which means that their effect on the group as a whole needs to be considered. Such tensions usually set off irritation or aggression through countertransferential reactions, interstimulation, mutual induction, and scapegoating trends.

colored by automatically arising pain, anxiety, guilt, and hostility called forth or reawakened by a current situation. In other words, it is part of the *neurotic* structure of the individual.

In view of the neurotic nature of the impulse and the pattern employed in discharging it through reenactment, the uncovering procedure is appropriate for dissolving the anxiety bound up in it. After permitting the irrational behavior to spend itself, the therapist helps the patient, at the appropriate time and by the appropriate uncovering technique, to trace the emotional relationship between his current feelings and the prototypes of his past. Reliving the antecedent situations and releasing the emotions bound up in them is the core of the treatment.

To employ such an analytic procedure would obviously be entirely counterindicated, as well as ineffective, when the behavior proceeds from primary character conditioning. In reenactment, the ego of the neurotic is overpowered by an impulse which, in a more tranquil state, would be ego-alien. In a character disorder, on the other hand, the ego is an integral part of the complex, that is, the behavior is ego-syntonic; and, therefore, the ego cannot be enlisted, as it were, in the reconstructive process. *This is the chief reason why group therapy is the treatment of choice for patients with character disorders.* The nature, setting, and interactions in groups are such that earlier psychic imprintings can be weakened and to some degree eradicated, even in adults, and new ones established, thus affecting character and behavioral changes. For the same reasons, groups are particularly suitable for child patients. Being still in the preneurotic stage in their development, children can be reshaped by a favorable active milieu [53]. This is true, too, for a large segment of disturbed adolescents [62].

Although rarely, it is occasionally necessary in clinical practice to recommend that some individuals with character disorders, such as psychopaths, hardened delinquents, and criminals, be committed to punitive institutions where their survival as social atoms is threatened and their deeply repressed anxieties aroused, thereby breaking through their narcissistic character-defense armor [56]. Perhaps this is what is meant by the euphemistic statement of turning a character disorder into a neurosis. When anxiety is aroused by the punitive regimen, the inmate tends to seek relief through communication, and when this sharing is with a trained therapist, he can be led along the path of unraveling the source of his difficulties.[4]

Acting Out

Acting out in psychotherapy is resorted to by adult and adolescent patients as an avenue of release that does not entail the risk of self-revelation to others and to oneself. Recourse to acting out is a characteristic of the regressive or infantile-fixated individual who has a need to cling to his defenses to prevent damage to his self-image and injury to his self-esteem. To achieve these ends, he resorts to withholding revelatory verbal communication. This aggressive pattern, manifested either in action or in irrelevant verbal effusiveness, serves to drown out anxiety. In the psychoneurotic, acting out is motivated by a fear of instinctual impulses and of revealing them, and for preservation of the rigidly defended self-image. Acting out can also be a symptom of an inadequate ego development which permits the ascendance of impulse. (The latter may inhere in the character organization as well as being a neurotic manifestation, and the therapist needs to be alert to this difference.) Thus, acting out can be (1) character-based, (2) defensive, or (3) a strategy of concealment.

1. An individual who has lived in a family with a prevalent culture of acting out of feelings and aggressions adopts this type of response as a matter of course by identification and imitation. The early pressures for adoption of a specific conduct shape the nature and intensity of the acting out syndrome later in life. Infantile-based syndromes can be reshaped to varying degrees by a conditioning culture or environment such as a group or any other therapeutic instrumentality in which the external situation exerts corrective pressures and demands. Therapeutically oriented interpersonal exchange in a group, reinforced by explanation and interpretation, tends to diminish this type of acting out syndrome.

4. I formulated the thesis of the unavailability of deeply repressed anxiety during the preverbal and pregenital phases in the psychopath's development during my early work with children (see "Contraindications of Group Therapy for Patients with Psychopathic Personalities," [55]). The efficacy of a conditioned environment in breaking through resistive character armor was discovered in 1935-1936 in an institution for delinquent adolescents [58], and the effect of a more punitive milieu in another project in 1957-1961 [62].

2. Defensive acting out is part of a neurotic syndrome and is strongly guarded. Assailing it directly, as is done in the case of characterological acting out, would not only further damage the patient's personality but may drive him from the therapeutic arena. Treatment of neurotic acting out is facilitated by groups, but in many instances individual psychotherapy is essential to eliminate the intrapsychic compulsions from which the neurotic acting out stems. Reactions from a group of peers are, with some exceptions, a salutary adjunct to individual psychotherapy. The group's responses and the controls it exerts as substitutes for the primary family are more likely to affect the patient's behavior than is the overt or implied criticism of the parental figure represented by the therapist. However, the group alone cannot nullify the internal conditions that begot the behavior, and the behavior will reappear after termination of group treatment.

In neurotic acting out, infantilism or arrest in development is also an ever-present element. This is attested to by impulsivity and physical or motoric reactions which are remnants of the infantile ego. Because of this infantile characteristic, the patient is susceptible to yielding to group pressure, provided it is not violent and does not attack his defense system too early. It is the therapist's function to protect him against these eventualities or to cushion their impact when they do occur. However, his main task, as well as the value of the group encounter to the therapeutic effort, is to improve the defenses in the service of which the acting out operates. The psychoneurotic patient needs to be placed in a situation in which he is sufficiently comfortable to reveal to himself and to others the hitherto guarded noxious feelings, values, and attitudes that have been inadequately held in repression or are still in concealment in his unconscious and preconscious. This requires regressive catharsis and revelations which some patients are unready to make in a group. In such instances, the basic therapy must be on an individual basis, either exclusively or paralleling the group.

Many psychotherapists find it necessary to "work through" basic problems with some of their patients as *preliminary* to their being included in groups. Some patients may require both individual and group psychotherapy from the outset. With different levels of the psyche being reached by the dual approach, eventually a degree of integration is achieved and one of the therapies, usually the individual treatment, can be terminated. A third approach is to carry the patient exclusively in individual psychotherapy until the deeply entrenched psychoneurotic syndromes have been sufficiently resolved and then to taper off therapy by placing the patient in a group so that he may test his insights in interpersonal interactions. Often, psychoneurotic patients have to be returned briefly to individual therapy for further work on specific problems which the comparatively diluted therapeutic climate of the group still cannot reach.

Neurotic defensive acting out is regarded in the same light as any other type of neurotic symptom, but with the added facilitation of a group to affect the *character element* involved. The procedures suggested are discriminately employed to supply the therapeutic needs of different types of patients; specifically, the differential quantum and character of their psychoneurotic and character components.

3. The concealment aspect of acting out usually disappears as the ego of the patient is strengthened and the need for such defenses in his psychic economy ebbs. Calling attention to a patient's evasiveness or assailing it in any other way is always risky before the ego is able to deal with such exposure. However, at times and with some patients, this may be necessary; if so, it calls for the therapist's best judgment and the exercise of great caution. When possible, it is always best to await the automatic dissolution of such noxious defenses when they no longer serve the ego and self-image needs of the patient as he emerges into health.

Abreaction

The term *abreaction* as it is used here refers specifically to verbal or motoric behavior set off by a disturbing or conflictual experience which does not serve to resolve a traumatic complex; rather, it serves to discharge heightened emotivity to reestablish emotional equilibrium. It has been pointed out by some writers that abreaction is at times in the service of resistance. I am disinclined to agree with this characterization. Abreaction is resorted to by countless people in innumerable situations in everyday living, frequently in mystifying forms and always inappropriately. The victims of abreaction are usually innocent persons who are at a loss to understand the reasons for their being harassed. A classical and commonly quoted example of abreaction is the man who is angered in the office and kicks the dog upon arriving home. Another is the man who instigates a quarrel with his wife or kicks a chair as a reaction to his suppressed rage toward his boss.

These and similar acts, unrelated as they are to the cause of the provocation, serve as conduits for discharging irritation or rage and for neutralization of the excess adrenaline that rage draws into the blood. This frees the organism of the stimulant through muscular action and reestablishes psycho-organic homeostasis. When this process involves verbal interaction, as in a therapy group, considerable violence may be set off. The fact is that the original causal disturbance may not always be generated in the group, for frequently patients appear at a session in a state of agitation generated elsewhere in their contacts and pursuits. In this state, they may explosively and unreasonably criticize or attack the therapist or fellow patients, or they may briefly withhold their irritation until some gesture or remark triggers it. The resulting tirade may be directed at those present or at some target unrelated to the group. Such a target may be a generic or special social phenomenon or a personal conflict having no identifiable bearing on the group or its proceedings.

The therapist must be vigilant against making an entirely understandable error in judgment in dealing with such a phenomenon. Its resemblance to defensive acting out is strong, for both stem from deficient ego development and inadequate controls and both have the facade of infantilism. The basic difference, which is of utmost importance in determining the course of action the therapist should take, lies in the fact that in one instance (i.e., defensive acting out) it is a persistent idiosyncratic pattern which needs to be nullified by psychotherapy, while in the other (abreaction), it is an isolated, transient outburst in which its own dissolution inheres. The former is the cumulative outcome of a long series of traumatic exposures in the patient's past, while the latter is a reaction to a specific, current happening.

Abreaction is a classic example of self-cure. It is automatic and flows from constitutional homeostatic trends. Because of these considerations, it needs to be tolerated by every culturally evolved and psychologically informed person. In everyday life, however, tolerance is not usually forthcoming in such instances. Because of the paranoid component in every human being, as slight as it may be, his implicit guilts and latent hostility reactions are mobilized. The capacity to accept or tolerate abreactive outbursts (rages) in a fellow being is an index of psychic health, and this is psychotherapy's aim for all patients.

The calm, impersonal acceptance by the therapist of abreactive acting out as a release, as nature's safety valve, places him in the role of an understanding and empathic, good parent and solidifies the patients' positive transference attitudes toward him. It also enhances his image as an object of identification, for in demonstrating strength and self-control, he sets an example for his patients. He demonstrates a tolerant and appropriate attitude for dealing helpfully with fellow humans, thereby enriching the patients' capacities for mutual acceptance and identification.

After the emotivity has spent itself and a degree of calm has returned, the therapist, addressing the patient concerned, may ask lightly and perhaps smilingly, "Do you feel better now?" And when the patient signals verbally and/or nonverbally that he is amenable to it, the therapist may further ask, "What brought all this on?" In all likelihood, the patient's answer will set off a fruitful group discussion of more valid means of dealing with feelings and maintaining mental health by discharge and sublimation.

Vectors of Interaction

Elsewhere [61, pp. 270-273], I have outlined the variety of vectors of interaction. I have listed them as occurring patient-to-patient, patient-to-group, and patient-to-therapist; to this list may be added group-to-therapist and therapist-to-group. This staggering network of emotionally charged attitudes and feelings, which are always present in overt and covert states in a freely interactive psychotherapy group, is so immensely complex that the instrumentality of an electronic computer would be required to unravel it. A glimpse of this magnitude can be gained from the mathematically possible number of interactions to *any one* stimulus or situation in a group of eight persons. On the basis of the formula suggested as applicable to this phenomenon, $S = n (n - 1) (n - 2) (n - 3) \ldots (n - n + 1)$ in which $n = 8$, the number of interactions would be 16,320. Considering the multitudinous stimuli in a group of emotionally heightened persons, the possibilities for interactions are astronomical. At times, the therapist may be hard put to steer the group's course toward therapeutically valid sequences. However, there are usually dominant "themes" and "rallies" operating in groups at any given time. These are self-selective as to the content and direction of the group's common preoccupation. It is these which the therapist utilizes in the therapeutic endeavor, and it is on the basis of these that he helps the group and its individual members arrive at therapeutically gainful understanding and insight.

CHAPTER 14

INTERACTION AND RECONSTRUCTION
(1966)

It is essential that the therapist discriminate between real change in the intrapsychic organization of his patients and apparent behavioral improvement. Conduct, even attitudes, may seemingly improve without the corresponding permanent internal alterations that would guarantee the continuance of what appears to be emotional growth and maturity wrought by the therapeutic experience. While ventilation of feelings and the experience of group approval and acceptance do reduce tensions and allay guilt, thus yielding transient improvement, such improvement may not reflect inner peace and increased happiness but only a temporarily more sanguine disposition toward, and relationship with, other persons.

The narcissistic patient who finds in the therapy group a stage for his exhibitionistic and attention-getting cravings becomes a loyal and consistent group member. Because his exploitative requirements are satisfied and his narcissism fulfilled, he keeps returning to group sessions for egocentric gratification. Despite the fact that these patients stimulate the flow of conversation and enhance group interaction, if they exploit the group for their narcissistic and exhibitionistic needs, they should be transferred to individual treatment where the sources of their disquieting behavior can be worked through. Later, if it still seems indicated, they may be reintroduced into a group. Exclusion from the group need not be followed in all instances of monopolization, however. When monopolization flows from anxiety or serves as a defense against neurotic fear or social discomfort, we can anticipate that, as these intrapsychic states are corrected through group (or with parallel individual) treatment, the symptom manifestation will automatically be sloughed off. Only when monopolization is part of the character structure is it advisable that the individual be removed from the group.

An example of a monopolizer was a woman who attended a group of married couples for four years. She employed the sessions as an arena for attacking and denigrating her husband. While she did activate considerable interaction in the group, improvement in her relationship with her husband remained imperceptible. Both were loyal attendants, though remaining untouched by the experience because the wife acted out her resentment against being a woman, on the one hand, and the husband derived masochistic gratification from the public calumny he received, on the other. (He may also have achieved a degree of infantile narcissistic satisfaction from being the center of the group's attention, humiliating though his position may have seemed to others.)

In the instance of such patients, it is mandatory to track down the psychic sources of what seems like enthusiastic volubility in the group interviews and to determine the patients' accessibility to group treatment. It is especially necessary, in addition, to determine the effect of such patients upon the therapeutic possibilities of the group for the other members. Although such patients often stimulate communication and interaction in groups, they may, at the same time, be countertherapeutic in their effect on the group. Their narcissistic manipulations and monopolization frustrate some in the group and enrage others. The characterologically more aggressive and assertive patients react with anger and recrimination; the more neurotic, in their fear, react with silence; while the schizoid and borderline or latent schizophrenic patients (if there are such in the group) withdraw into themselves. As a result, the group remains nonproductive, continuing interminably on the same level of querulousness and tension.

On the surface, there may appear to be a great deal of interaction in a group of this order. Certainly, there seems to be much going on and a great amount of heat emanating from at least some of the participants. Are, however, such frenetic group interviews of therapeutic value or effectiveness? Granted that interaction among patients is a major ingredient in the therapeutic process, it is necessary to be quite clear about why interaction is of importance and what the nature of therapeutic interaction really is.

Interaction in a strictly therapeutic (not in an educational or "existential" or developmental) sense has three characteristics which can be considered therapeutically valid. An obvious value is that it provides a tangible reality in responses and reactions; it serves as a mirror; it engenders limits to the individual's ego boundaries; it facilitates human relatedness; and it supplies an arena for testing the realities of the self and the self of others. A more specifically therapeutic value of interaction is that it stimulates reenactment of past affect-laden experiences and relations, which, with appropriate management by the therapist and through colloquy with fellow patients, leads to the unearthing of traumatic events, attitudes, and feelings which need to be corrected if therapy is to be successful. Another value of group interaction is that it is progressive, for in later stages it supplies an operational arena for emotional reevaluation of past events and memories in the light of the patient's present chronological age, psychological flexibility, and newly achieved values and feelings. In other words, interaction in a psychotherapy group is primarily and most significantly derived from transferential fantasy sources which later, as specific intrapsychic changes occur, flow into the realm of reality and constructive growth.

However, the sources in the psyche of hostility and neurotic self-destructiveness and destructiveness toward others are not dried up simply by externalization. On the contrary, the more they are acted out, the more deep-seated they become, the more deeply neuronically and endocrinologically engrammed; they grow more pervasive, more intense, and more diffuse. Anagenesis from malignancy to benevolence, from hate to love, does not take place through practice in virulence. Some outside alchemic agent is needed to transform evil into good, rage, anger, and hostility into love and kindliness, tolerance, cordiality, and graciousness.

Common observation imposes upon us the inescapable conclusion that evil feeds upon itself, that cruelty and hostility are primary and inherent in man's basic nature, and that which is human in us is given to us by other humans. As the ancients well knew, "Man is nothing without the work of man." Humanizing of the individual occurs through many social instrumentalities, but the essential mechanisms are imitation, identification, and, especially, internalization. Observations of human behavior in groups reveal that emotions are not only contagious but are vastly intensified by specific group dynamic mechanisms, for example, infection, mutual induction, and interstimulation. These mechanisms, when the tone of the group is tension and hostility, serve as quanta-heighteners raising tension and hostility to an intense, even unbearable, pitch.

Orderliness and control in social and action groups are conditioned by the ego controls implanted in each of the constituting individuals through what may be termed culture or breeding. These controls, however, can quickly evaporate when sensitive or threat areas are invaded. Then, even aim-directed groups may revert to primitive means of discharging anger and rage. The potential for regressive acting out is vastly multiplied in therapy groups, where the ego of each participant is under strain and his defenses may be either openly attacked or subtly threatened. The resulting "edginess," as it were, is intensified, and to varying degrees everyone involved is on the brink of losing control.

To be therapeutic, group interviews cannot be respecters of threat areas or individual sensitivities; self-image and ego-ideals, if they have not already been stripped of the self-deceit in which they are armored, are constantly on the verge of being exposed in their full nakedness. Added to the other strains inherent in group interviews, this heightens tension and reduces the emotional tolerance of the patients, all of which is not only beneficial but essential in true psychotherapy. Although they would prove destructive to any other type of group, such interstimulative emotional dynamics are the real source of *therapeutic* interaction in groups and, unless their intensity is counterindicated for psychological reasons, must be encouraged by the therapist.

However, the question still remains whether such interaction alone constitutes corrective psychotherapy or whether it is necessary to introduce an element that renders it therapeutic. If the latter is so, what is that element?

The therapies that emphasize, and are limited to, interaction appear to apply to adults the principle of "acting out" used in the treatment of children. That acting out can be reconstructive when employed in the treatment of selected, latency-age children in a specially designed milieu has been established by various schools and practitioners. Because of their unformed defenses, fluid identifications, general somatic incompleteness, and psychological immaturity, children are malleable; they internalize experience; and, as we justifiably said, a child becomes what he does. However, this is not so with adults. The completed neuronic engrams and syndromes in adults, having become biochemically (electrically) ingrained and being guarded by psychological and emotionally charged defenses, do not readily yield to external events and interactions. Experience, in human terms, is bipolar: it consists of an external event and an internal reaction to that event. It is the fusing of event and reaction that constitutes an experience. In adults the second element (the internal reaction) has been rendered immutable by synaptic, engrammatic, and habitually rigidified psychological patternings.

Even in children, acting out and interaction are therapeutically valid only with specific types of problems, such as mild character and behavior disorders and mild neurotic traits. They are not effective with more complicated personality disorders. For obvious reasons, because action is the natural language of the child, motility, acting out, and interaction are necessarily prevalent in the treatment of children, but they cannot be relied upon in the therapy of adults. Similarly, adolescents, although they derive therapeutic benefit from acting out and interaction, must be more restricted than are younger children. This restriction may be in the form of direct intervention by the therapist at the appropriate time, but most often it is inherent in, and flows from, reflection and verbalization.

The picture changes in the case of adults. Unrestricted hostile interaction has to be viewed as proceeding from ingrained hostility or as being a form of defensive reaction, and/or as a reenactment of antecedent (onto-archaic) patterns in human relationships. Whatever the cause, *interaction* in a group of adults, to be productive, must come under the purview of *reflection* that loosens the rigidified defensive armor and leads to inversion and introspection, retracing and recall of the past, and the uncovering of forces that operate in current feelings and conduct. The therapist, drawing upon his knowledge of each patient, must differentiate between acting out and reenactment, for the two require differential approaches.

Acting out proceeds from ego-overload and anxiety and may require intervention on the therapist's part so that traumata related to the uncontrollability can be worked through. Reenactment, on the other hand, which is culturally patterned by past life experiences and has no or only mild neurotic ingredients, can be overlooked and await the group's critical reactions and restraints. Habits, for example, are one mode of such reenactment.

It has been my uncomfortable privilege on a few occasions to be present at group sessions of adults conducted with interaction as the sole guiding principle. Much heat was generated in mutual accusations and criticisms, but little light was thrown on what was transpiring. The justification for this process was that out of the turmoil new awarenesses and new feeling relationships would emerge. This recalls to mind a visit in 1928 to a children's residential school conducted in England by Dorothy (Mrs. Bertrand) Russell where no semblance of table deportment was imposed upon the children. They ate with their fingers or lapped the food directly from the plates, and hurled victuals at one another and smeared them about. It was Mrs. Russell's conviction that the children would arrive at proper deportment on their own, a conviction her teachers did not share; they refused to partake in the meals under these conditions and ate elsewhere by themselves. A later, rather intensive, controlled study which I made proved that direct training of children in dealing with physical environment is necessary.

Interaction among group patients must be viewed as only preliminary to the essential psychotherapeutic dynamic. It is the nexus of therapy, not its essence. The essence of the therapeutic process is the *outcome of interaction*. The content of interaction must be guided toward that focus, which is insight. But insight in this connection needs to be understood, not as intellectual comprehension, but as the outcome of working through resistances and defenses and overcoming character rigidities. This alone makes it possible for the patient to view unhesitatingly the noxious components of his personality without suffering narcissistic injury; without this, emotional growth is virtually impossible. Intellectual understanding is not insight. It is the "working through" process that leads to insight and is the alchemic ingredient previously referred to.

As in all other of life's arenas, in psychotherapy as well, action must go hand in hand with reflection. The quality reflection assumes in significant psychotherapy is not that of Aristotelian logic or epistemological constructs. In its initial stages it is profoundly charged with affect, though, as the patient grows in emotional maturity and security, his reflections lose their affective components and take on a more objective character. This detachment of thought from affect is the aim and indication of psychic maturity.

The case of Mrs. S. [61, pp. 299–308], illustrates the point being made here. This highly disturbed, masochistic, thirty-eight-year-old woman with psychogenic eczema agitated her group by repeatedly interrupting the communications of her fellow patients and reiterating session after session *ad nauseam* the selfsame complaints against the conditions of her life. For forty sessions, almost a year, Mrs. S. never touched upon the internal difficulties that beset her: murderous hostility toward her mother, incestuous attachment to her long-dead father, the nursing of a fantasy that her father loved her and repression of a stealthy feeling that he really did not, the expectation that her dead father would magically rescue her from the unbearable setting of her life, masochistic submission to her husband, severe rejection of her ten-year-old son, and obsessional fear of incest between this boy and his younger sister.

It was only when the therapist, by subtle utilization of the transference, broke through to the nucleus of the problem (her escape into the father fantasy) in the forty-first session that the self-deluding inner structure that Mrs. S. had set up came tumbling down and she gradually gained strength for solving the many difficulties of her life. The lack of therapeutic advance by Mrs. S. in the first forty sessions amply demonstrates that interaction alone cannot serve the ends of psychotherapy. However, the converse is also true, for the sources of group psychotherapy *are* in interaction, and without it therapy cannot occur. Even in the comparative isolation of individual treatment, the patient's interactions with people and events outside the therapy sessions and with the therapist are the vehicle by which psychic change is effected; the total life setting is inextricably entwined in the therapeutic process.

One of the greatest values of groups is that they constitute an interactive milieu.[1] But monopolizers, hysterics, patients with intense, uncontrollable anxiety, and some types of narcissistic character disorders are unsuitable for therapy groups because they are counter-facilitants to the transition from the stage of interaction to the stage of reflection. The narcissism of some, the bid for power or the exhibitionistic needs of others, the ego-overload and self-involvement of still others continues the group on the level of acting out or reenactment. A group in which interaction runs riot can be compared to an ocean: oceans encompass a great deal of motion but little movement. Sound therapeutic interviews, on the other hand, are comparable to rivers in that movement far exceeds the water's internal motion. Obviously, emotional maturity cannot emerge from chaotic and repetitive surges of content. As the group progresses, it must flow into more orderly channels of reflection attuned to reality, calm, and self-control.

This growth in the content of interviews and the calmer mien of the protagonists is what psychotherapy aims for and is consistent with the laws of nodal and antinodal behavior in groups. [61, pp. 53–56] It must be expected that antinodal periods will occur less frequently in early sessions but that their frequency will considerably increase as the group comes to serve therapeutic ends. The growth of ego strengths and their controls are evidenced in this change of periodicity.

On the other hand, if interaction is understood to be an intellectual interchange of ideas, concepts, or philosophies, the dynamisms with which we have been dealing here do not hold or do so only to a limited extent. Rationality is not the warp and woof of psychotherapy. It is the emotionalized and conscious, preconscious, and unconscious content of the psyche to which psychotherapy addresses itself. The objectification of these contents cannot but arouse intense emotions out of which interaction in groups flows, but this flow must have boundaries, as must a river, if it is to have direction. Thus, as therapy for neurotics progresses, group interviews must focus increasingly on unraveling the internal problems of individual group members, for, if the group is permitted to remain in the amorphous state of an ocean, no constructive direction can emerge.

---

1. It should be noted, however, that patients who require the unraveling of deep intrapersonal difficulties and intrapsychic malformations cannot work them through in a group.

An illustration of emotional infectiousness in a therapy group that persisted for 135 sessions was reported by an English psychiatrist [61, p. 334]. The emotional turbulence and anxiety that one patient, a woman, generated not only prevented the other group members from working on their own difficulties but blocked them off from entering upon the reflective phase of her own problems. She kept the group on tenterhooks, as it were, and progress was impossible. It requires little insight or knowledge to appreciate how destructive such tension is for other group members with intense anxiety psychoneuroses or latent or borderline schizophrenia. . . .

There are psychotherapists who hold that "process" is more important than "content" in group psychotherapy. According to their view, interaction among patients, rather than the content of their productions, constitutes the therapeutic essence. However, it is obvious to the trained therapist conversant with the anomalies of the human personality and with the arduous task of changing it that no dichotomy exists between process and content, nor should its intrusion be permitted. Process and content, action and reflection are irrevocably intertwined, and consideration of them as separate entities in psychotherapy with adults is both unsound and unrewarding.

To varying degrees, therapies known under the cognomens of Zen, Transactional, Mimetic, Existential, Status Denial, and Non-Transferential can be classified as "interaction" techniques—some more, some less. Adherents of these methods view psychotherapy as a process in which both patients and therapists freely interact by discharging feelings. As a result, the therapy sessions are tumultuous, highly charged affairs. This may also be true of so-called "alternate sessions"; however, the stress and anxiety aroused in alternate sessions can be ventilated at the next session in which the therapist is present, which is not the case when the regular group sessions in which the therapist is present are chaotic affairs, as is true in solely interaction groups.

As has been indicated, in therapy with some children, all adolescents, and, most particularly, all adults, action must be related to reflection. The two, action and reflection, have to go hand in hand. Cognitive-interaction and affective-reflection are inseparable ingredients of both character education and psychological therapy, though on different depth levels. Therapeutic effectiveness lies in the skill of the therapist in fusing action and reflection in accordance with the canons of relevance, readiness, and relatedness.

If we were to postulate the existence of therapy groups some of which operated on interaction alone and others solely on content (or reflection), what consequences would they yield? Obviously, the solely interactive groups would mount in turmoil and tension until chaos set in. On the other hand, reflective groups would inevitably become didactic. Clearly, neither of these two eventualities meets the requirements of psychotherapy. *When action and reflection complement one another, the latter acts as a brake upon the former.* At the same time, reflection upon personality problems and noxious fantasies and acts stimulates interaction, which should be followed by uncovering exploration and, hopefully, insight.

Why do some group therapists prefer to rely exclusively on interaction in conducting of group therapy? It has been suggested that interaction *sans* interpretation can be carried on by less trained practitioners, those without special skills at conducting psychotherapeutic interviews. To let loose a group of patients at each other, to let the sparks fly where they may and trust to luck as to outcome, does not require any special knowledge, subtlety, or insight. Nor need the therapist have the exacting inner flexibility, empathy, and discipline that good psychotherapy requires. It has been suggested that the path of interactionism is chosen by those ill-equipped in the science, and those untrained in the art and skill of conducting interviews, but one is loath to accept this explanation because of its fearsome implications for the profession of psychotherapy.

Another possible explanation lies in the intrapsychic needs of the therapists themselves. Small groups of whatever nature reinvoke engrammed responses, and the behavior of each group member is characteristic of his behavior as a child in his early family circle. Both the constructive and disruptive forces that operate in all groups proceed from the corresponding patterned reactions in the members' childhoods, including the therapist. Even such a fundamental experience as is a training analysis cannot completely extirpate these responses; it can only reduce their intensity, on the one hand, and enhance ego controls, on the other. The onto-archaic mind and its urges are ever-present, and in the absence of countercontrols, they take over.

It is essential in the interests of the sound development of group psychotherapy that it be determined whether interactionism is a therapeutically valid practice based upon scientifically adequate data or a countertransferential phenomenon proceeding from the therapist's own unresolved infantile needs for conflict and interpersonal combat.

CHAPTER 15

ECLECTICISM VERSUS SECTARIANISM
(1970)

Psychotherapy, more than any other endeavor in the behavioral sciences, has passed through a period of great proliferation of procedures in the last decade. A few ' have been set forth with supportive theories of varying validity, but most are practices that stem from notions about human personality, its conditions and its corrective needs. To a large extent, they are products of individual reactions and philosophies, of temperamental dispositions and varying social orientations.

Einstein said that, "The logic of a theory must stem from an inner coherence, not because external evidence makes it the most logical over other theories." In this terse statement, he formulated a very significant neo-Aristotelian principle that governs not only theoretical formulations but is equally applicable as a criterion for social as well as clinical instrumentalism.

In view of this formulation, whatever attitudes one may have toward Freudian psychology—positive, oppositional, or revisionistic— one cannot fail to recognize the soundness of its "inner coherence." Freud's postulates of the id, ego, and superego; his assumption of the universality of oedipal ties and their consequences; his formulations of the strength and the operations of the unconscious, the residues of infantile sexuality, the presence and operations of polymorphous perversions, the basic irrationality of the human mind, and the pervasive feelings of anxiety and guilt form a coherent body upon which a theory of personality and of human conduct can be safely constructed. This coherence and its basic logic, buttressed by empirical observations, opened windows to the human soul that had been shut before, giving new direction, form, and content to the understanding of the nature of man and his behavior, and to the creative arts, philosophy, and religion.

There are, of course, other theories in all these areas. They, too, need to be considered in the psychotherapist's armamentarium, for the wider his intellectual and perceptual compass, the more effectively can he appreciate the actualities, fantasies, and problems with which he has to deal. However, it seems to this commentator, at least, that they can serve only as addenda to, or elaborations of, Freud's rich compendium on the nature and conduct of the human animal. Certainly, no one who wishes to deal with the human personality in depth can succeed without drawing upon Freudian theory for his understanding.

This assertion cannot, however, be made with respect to Freud's traditional therapeutic technique. The difficulty with the couch-based, free-association procedure seems to us to lie in the fact that it is employed in too blanket a fashion. This has led to much misunderstanding and many failures because it does not take into account varieties in the nature of personality disturbances and differences in their psychodynamics and clinical diagnoses, some of which have been formulated only in recent decades. However, the fact still remains that true classical psychoneuroses and their derivative affective disorders, by their inherent nature, do not respond to any known method of treatment except that evolved by Freud. Though effective with this category of ailments, this procedure is not applicable to the genre of disturbances characterized by Freud as "actual neuroses" and "narcissistic neuroses," which often require medical and sometimes surgical intervention. The categories of personality disturbance and social maladjustment classified as "primary or reactive behavior disorders," the group known as "character disorders," and the schizophrenias do not respond, or do so only minimally, to exclusive insight psychotherapy.

In our view, this is at least one of the reasons for the vast crop of therapies making their appearance on the psychotherapeutic horizon.

The fact that the classical technique fails to reach large numbers of patients has made it necessary to evolve more suitable procedures and has given courage to many practitioners to propound techniques upon which they have stumbled during their practice or which they have derived on some chance assumptions.

A further reason why these many innovations have arisen is the fact that , initially in the United States and later elsewhere, patients with disturbances other than the classical psychoneuroses began making their way to the clinician. In a real sense, the full-blown classical psychoneurotic is a vanishing phenomenon, if not numerically, proportionally at least. In an acting-out and increasingly permissive society, with diminishing suppressions and weakening ties in the family, new interpersonal—and hence intrapersonal—dynamics have made their appearance. As this has occurred, changes in many operational relations among individuals and groups in society have inevitably emerged. Institutions such as family, religion, education, and government, as well as others, have been modified, even transformed, by these alterations in the social arena. This in turn is reflected in the forms, qualities, and intensity of pressures and demands exerted upon the individual, thus giving rise to new types of maladjustments and character structure with which the clinician has to deal. In the social and class milieu in which psychoanalysis was formulated, the prevailing personality disturbances that patients presented required a specific type of treatment. But in a different culture in which the social and familial pressures and demands have been relaxed, personality problems have taken a different turn.

In the growth of a science or a practice, one must be prepared to travel the difficult and circuitous path of experimentation and testing, selecting and discarding. Numerous methods and hypotheses have to be tried and rejected before valid truths can be attained. Many tests and refinements are essential in such an expanding process. Such studies, however, must be pursued with utmost objectivity and by persons other than the initiators of an idea. Perhaps an illustration of this drawn from our own field of endeavor, group psychotherapy, will make this point clear.

Group psychotherapy with small groups was first initiated at the Jewish Board of Guardians in 1934. However, it was not an official tool of that agency for some years. Rather, patients of that agency were used only to test the possible effectiveness of the group approach. After the test period, Dr. Lawson Lowrey, with the assistance of a specially selected, highly competent social worker-therapist, studied the protocols of a large number of group sessions and the case records of a significant number of individual patients. It was upon the evidence adduced in this objective evaluation by two noninvolved persons that group therapy was then incorporated into the agency's practice. Perhaps it should be added that, at these initial stages, we had no inherent theoretical coherence for our work as a therapeutic procedure. Rather, it derived from creative education and the recognition of children's need for free, creative expression. This was the reason the technique was initially variously named "therapeutic recreation" and later "the therapeutics of creative activity" until we recognized the part group interactions played in the corrective process. It was then that the practice was renamed "group therapy." Perhaps it should be added that nothing was published on the project before "inner coherence" was derived, which was eight years after its inauguration.

If there are among the newer practices in group psychotherapy, and in psychotherapy generally, instances in which similar validation has been pursued with a large number of groups and patients, it is not known to the present commentator. Rather, one gains the impression that often an accidental observation, a special feeling about a specific development, or an idea derived from an isolated experience is offered in doctrinaire fashion as a valid total practice. In themselves, these formulations may have potentially great value, for they are *elements* out of which a total therapy can eventually emerge. The growth of a system (if there can be a "system" in psychotherapy) is similar to mining for gold: much valueless ore has to be discarded before a nugget of precious metal is obtained.

What is disconcerting, however, is that partial and limited observation is hastily offered and labeled as though it were a proven *total* therapeutic technique. Actually, if one examines most of the suggested "innovative" procedures, one finds that their essence has been a *part* of good eclectic practice for decades. Specific tactical strategies psychotherapists have employed to deal with specific situations are blown up, as it were, into major or exclusive therapeutic doctrines.

One illustration that comes to mind is "interaction group therapy."

Interaction is the sine qua non of the original small group therapy—
Activity Group Therapy—*with carefully selected children* in latency
in a *rigidly designed* physical environment. This method as a total or
exclusive procedure with adults still awaits validation. Similarly,
"reality group psychotherapy" is something that almost every individual and group therapist has employed for decades in specific situations
with specific patients, particularly those with behavior and character
disorders. Similarly, "behavior therapy"[1] has long been in the armamentarium of therapists dealing with especially intractable patients, as
was also that which came to be known as "paradigmatic therapy" with
very resistive patients.

Some of the "therapies" offered stem, surprisingly enough, from the
now-discarded James–Lange psychological theory that emotion arises
from behavior, that acts generate feelings, instead of the reverse. To
the psychotherapist this seems like putting the cart before the horse.
Certainly in the case of patients, incompatible behavior always
proceeds from discordant or overreactive feelings. Even "existential
analysis," as profound a philosophy and code for life and conduct as
existentialism is, has little to offer that is new to the knowledgeable
eclectic psychotherapist. The practitioner, by his own cultivation, is
cognizant of the depth and breadth of the human psyche and the
complexities faced by homo sapiens.

In dealing with the strains of adjusting to the complexities of life,
one can hardly escape touching upon the mysteries and profundities
of a human struggling with the absurdities and dilemmas of living. On
many occasions the therapist finds it necessary to shed light of a
philosophic nature upon a patient's confusions, drawing upon existential values and understandings. However, turning such abstractions
into a form of total therapy to the minimization or exclusion of other
tried and proven approaches is, in this observer's judgment, the height
of folly and destined to failure, with the possible exception of cases of
some schizophrenic and psychotic patients whose bizarre thinking
process may be affected by such philosophic constructs.

---

1. The term "behavior therapy" as employed here does not refer to the type that involves
"deep muscle relaxation," the principle of "stimulus antecedents," and progressive "desensitization." The term, rather, refers to direct dealing with a patient's conduct and reactions, involving,
when indicated, advice or instruction during interviews or groups discussions as to suitable
behavior. This strategy is effective with some patients but is counterindicated for psychoneurotics. The latter provision applies also to the use of "paradigmatic therapy."

Because of the brevity of this communication, it is necessary to omit consideration of the plethora of other therapeutic techniques. A word, however, must be said of the more extreme acting-out procedures that have recently appeared both in so-called group therapy and in a special type of therapeutic living communities. These are described variously as "basic encounters," "touching," unrestricted physical contacts, and group discussions in the nude. In view of the fact that I have not had personal experience with, or been present at, any such sessions, I would like to draw on the opinions of two impartial observers—one an American, the other English. In an extensive article that appeared in *Life* magazine, Jane Howard wrote that: "The movement methods ... vary extravagantly. Some call for groups of people to recite dreams, confess secrets, don masks, go naked or gaze with unswerving honesty into each other's eyes for a full ten minutes. The groups involved ... may celebrate their released feelings with an exuberant leap into the air."

The English commentator Nora Sayre, writing in *The New Statesman*, stated that: "Group therapy meetings, cosily called 'T-groups,' became sensitivity sessions ...; now they are 'basic encounters.' The privilege of unfurling or 'acting out' one's neurosis about earrings, hot-plates or one's job or lover to a critical cluster of co-sufferers, has charmed many away from the analyst's solitary couch.... Friends boast about the flood of tears which they released or inspired at some recent session; weeping in unison is cleansing. Eventually, some learn what all children know: that a group can make one person cry. It all sounds like a soggy, maudlin swamp, but converts assure you that it's wonderful, and clearly, they enjoy it." She further comments, "Perhaps an emotional commune is what many want."

There is much that can be said about the "therapeutics" of these groups as understood in terms of emotional psychodynamics. That they supply an arena for "release" of pent-up feelings one cannot deny. And that the participants "clearly enjoy it" may also be a fact, for is not release enjoyable and are not narcissistic and exhibitionistic indulgences a source of pleasure to those who enjoy these things?

The present commentator holds that homo sapiens is basically psychotic, that his psychosis is a rudimentary part of his personality and that it is universal. This existential or *essential psychosis* is part and parcel of his biopsychological conflictual nature and is different from *clinical* psychosis [1]. In the latter the basic psychosis is many times magnified and its resulting extent and character make it a distinguishable illness. There may be, therefore, value in "acting out" the essential psychotic needs in *some* individuals, for continuing repression of them and conformity to the "norms" can break down weak ego defenses, thus causing an onset of clinical psychosis. Hence, if such group acting out in a permissive culture is recognized only as a palliative and not as psychotherapy, and used as such with persons for whom it is suitable, one cannot quarrel with some of it.

But a serious consideration is the suitability of the participants in groups in which there is untrammeled assault on the already labile ego defenses of some individuals. Obviously, latent or borderline psychotics with tenuous ego controls and defenses may, under the stress of such groups and the complete giving up of defenses, jump the boundaries between sanity and insanity.

Perhaps the experience in an "acting-out" community of one participant known to us may throw light on the effect it can have on some individuals. This woman in her forties, a college graduate and the successful holder of an academic job, joined such a community in a western state after having read about it in the public press and magazines. She was so shocked by what was transpiring there that after two days she "ran," to use her own word, in a state of extreme panic. She averred that what she had witnessed was so "traumatic" (again her own term) that it took her weeks to overcome the disturbing effect it had had on her.

In true psychotherapy, there is room for some acting out of the essential psychosis or irrationality of patients. In a free-floating interaction and unrestrained catharsis, some patients jump the inner-restraining bounds of reality. This is permissible and even desirable, for the inner freedom that follows it propels the patient, under the skillful guidance of the therapist, toward reality and insight. Thus, true eclecticism in psychotherapeutic practice allows for multifarious manifestations during the interviews, and the therapist, individual or group, needs to possess sensitivity and understanding to make the proper choice of patients commensurate with (a) his own skill in dealing with any eventuality that may arise, (b) the suitability of the particular patient to the therapy to be administered, (c) the extent of the ego defenses of each patient, and (d) the understanding of his own limitations and countertransferential susceptibilities.

Inattention to these antecedent determinants may endanger not only the effectiveness of a group or of individual treatment but places the therapist's safety—and even his life—in jeopardy. From time to time one reads in the public press reports of lethal attacks by patients against their therapists, or members of their families, who blindly overexposed patients to the great stress of pathogenic transferential feelings.

The Essential Road to Truth

A major fallacy in proposing any *one* therapeutic procedure as applicable to all patients indiscriminately is that it seeks to eliminate contradictions. Contradictions are inherent in all human effort, especially in the intellectual domain. A tentative theory, and also a practice, approaches truth more closely than does doctrinaire positivism. In this connection, Freud stated that, "A negative judgment is the intellectual substitute for repression.... With the help of the symbol of negation, thinking frees itself from the restrictions of repression and enriches itself with material that is indispensable for its proper functioning.... The outcome of this is a kind of intellectual acceptance of the repressed, while at the same time what is essential to the repression persists" (p. 236).[2] In other words, a critical attitude toward one's own productivity by consciously recognizing actual or possible contradictions in it is the essential road to truth.

Somehow one feels that there is always present a degree of awareness of possible contradiction in every positive (especially overpositive) statement one makes even if it is not openly recognized. Only children and clinically psychotic adults are free from such latent doubt. The average person eliminates contradictions through his dreams. It is partially on the basis of this that we suggest that the function of dreams is to release the accumulation of (essential) psychotic reactions in the individual that have been denied or suppressed during a day's functioning in a so-called sane milieu.

Overlooking the extremes in current practices in what is irresponsibly characterized as group therapy, and limiting our perusal to the more rational techniques now most widely employed, the transcen-

2. Freud, S. (1925). Negation. *Standard Edition* 19:235–239.

dent general rule must prevail: namely, therapy must match the needs of the particular patient. In specific situations as they arise in the course of treatment, various devices may have to be called into action. In what is known as "insight" or "uncovering" psychotherapy, there are situations when reality and paradigmatic strategies or existential concepts and even direct advice and authoritative pronouncements become essential. On the other hand, when direct procedures are indicated, as in the treatment of character disorders and simple social maladjustments, that is, in ego therapy, exigencies may arise when deeper "working through" of feelings and attitudes may be required.

In psychotherapy, as in all situations of leadership, the leader has to follow the led. The therapist has to sense what the patient (or the group) needs and what steps will be most effective at a given juncture in the therapeutic stream. Effectiveness of treatment requires sensitive recognition of such elements on his part. This means that he draws on any artifice consistent with his understanding of the psycho- or sociodynamic situation with which he is confronted.

It was these considerations that led us to suggest gross levels in helping and changing people: counseling, guidance, and psychotherapy. The first is designed to *help* people in dealing with a specific conflict or dilemma, while the third—psychotherapy—aims at *changing,* to some extent at least, basic states in the personality. Guidance falls between these two. As already stated, in the application of all of them, however, departures are necessary when indicated in the unfolding of the therapeutic or guidance relation. It was the discovery of the inadequacies of different types of group treatment and guidance that led us to evolve changes and modifications so that we now employ eleven different types of group treatment and guidance.

The Essence of Eclecticism

The conclusion seems to press upon us that total therapy is a blending of many now discrete techniques as they best serve the needs of patients at various stages in their treatment and that sectarianism unavoidably limits effectiveness. For one thing, it is self-selective; that is, only small numbers can be reached by any one method, and even then their improvement may be only partial and temporary. To affect the total personality, or as wide an area of it as possible, a variety of approaches is necessary. This is the essence of eclecticism.

Eclecticism is more crucial to group therapy than to individual treatment. Because of the multiplicity of psychic factors in an assembly of persons, a unitary approach cannot but fail with a significant number of the participants. As a matter of fact, in an ongoing therapy group, the patients, in the course of their dynamic interactions, naturally stumble on transient procedures that parallel many of the techniques one finds described in the professional literature. The skill of the therapist in such instances is to recognize which of these spontaneously arisen dialogues and reactions are consistent with current needs of the group as a whole or of some of its members. Here the *primary group code,* as we have suggested elsewhere, automatically serves as a selective medium.

In one of our parent-guidance groups [60,61], for example, a mother introduced into the discussion a profoundly disturbing personality problem [60, 61]. Probably because of her rising anxiety, another member of the group impulsively blurted out, "Here we don't talk about our problems. We talk about us and our children." (In such instances, the group leader may deem it necessary to see a disturbed group member individually. Such a situation is a good illustration of the inherent contradictions in any one technique which we have pointed out.)

The primary group code determines—or, better still, arises from—the basic nature of the group's needs. Whether a group, or an individual for that matter, will require counseling, guidance, or psychotherapy (or intensive traditional individual psychoanalysis) must of necessity be the psychotherapist's decision, but at the same time he needs to be sensitively aware of the contradictions in the choices he makes and when indicated alter the course of the chosen treatment accordingly. This stipulation, as well, suggests a number of contradictions, for unless the therapist possesses a high degree of objectivity and emotional freedom to reflect on and face his own biases and preferences, he may be subject to many pitfalls in making judgments. Whether a therapist prefers an active or passive, a realistic or mystic technique and whether he conceives of his role in terms of involvement or detachment will be largely determined by his personality and intellectual orientation.

Few, if any, therapists can resist the temptation of choosing a milieu and a role in which they feel personally comfortable and one that is within the scope of their knowledge and capacities. Having chosen a line of action, the therapist then tends to construct corroborative rationalizations and theories to support the choice. While such an attitude is understandable in most other occupations, it is crucially detrimental in psychotherapy, for not only must patients grow in inner freedom and maturity, the therapist too has to evolve similarly by virtue of his work with other people. Rationalizations and overidentification with his own convictions and preferences must be eschewed by the psychotherapist. Effective group psychotherapy, in particular, demands the utmost in flexibility on the therapist's part, so that he may be able to meet the requirements not only of the group but also of the evolving personalities of each of its members. In group psychotherapy the flux of intrapersonal and interpersonal manifestations may at times be staggering. Under these conditions, the therapist needs to have great resources at his command and his attention needs to be facile and free-floating. Intelligent and sensitive eclecticism is the very core of his equipment.

Summary

Inner coherence proceeds from the theoretical assumptions upon which one's work is based. In psychotherapy, these assumptions relate to the nature of the human personality as a bio-socio-psychological phenomenon, or mechanism, if you will; the health needs of this mechanism; the pathogenic forces operating upon it in the course of developing and becoming; to a dynamic theoretical system for its correction and repair; and, finally, to empirical tests, experimentation and validation both of the assumptions and the corrective procedures. It is only with such a superstructure that discriminating use of the many techniques, devices, and artifices can be made. Group psychotherapy, especially, still a new practice, must be guarded against the infiltration of unproven, doctrinal pronouncements unsupported by validated results.

CHAPTER 16

ARE THERE "GROUP DYNAMICS" IN THERAPY GROUPS?
(1957)

The question whether *group dynamics* in the ordinary sense of the phrase arise in therapy groups of nonpsychotic adults is a pivotal one. Its importance lies in the fact that if such dynamics are operative, much that we understand of group psychotherapy and the intra-personal therapeutic process would have to be revised, and its practice, which is *clinical therapy* and not a sociological theory or construct, would have to be altered. The question whether we deal in group therapy with the group as a *unitary entity,* or with the individuals, that is, the patients in them, *as individuals,* may well determine the course of its development as a science and as a therapeutic tool [5, 143]. Another problem that will have to be solved is whether patients improve merely by virtue of their *adjustment to a group* or because of its "influence" on them, or because of the relationships they establish with fellow members; or whether the improvement is a result of *personality changes* that accrue from the release of anxiety previously bound up in the neurotic nucleus originating in childhood, the insight they acquire, and the new self-image that emerges. In other words, are relationships and group adaptation by themselves sufficient to serve the ends of sound psychotherapy, which is personality change? Many individuals with problems seek out groups and social movements as an escape or as a source of relief, and observation confirms that they do receive a certain degree of comfort and for a time show improvement in behavior. But these improvements are not lasting. In addition, the individual who seeks relief through these means becomes permanently dependent on one or another of these groups or movements. Freud has called attention to the fact that "where a powerful impetus has been given to group formation, neuroses may diminish and ... *temporarily* disappear." [Italics mine.][1]

In order to arrive at some clarity on these and related subjects, it will be necessary to draw upon other experiences and operational systems. To do this, let us define, on the basis of its inherences, nature and function as we know them, what a "group" is, keeping in mind that not every compresence of persons is a *group*. Because of the differences in numbers, motivation, aims and interpersonal relations, gatherings are variously designated as masses, crowds, assemblies, audiences, congregations, mobs, groups, and by still other terms, all of which imply the existence of different relationships among their constituents.

The definition that most nearly describes a "group" can be formulated as follows: A group is a voluntary gathering of three or more persons in a free face-to-face relation *under leadership*, who have a *common goal* or aim and who interact with one another relative to the common plans or goals, as a result of which personality growth may occur and latent talents and interests may be evoked. The salient features of this definition are: *(a)* a group consists of a small number of persons so that meaningful face-to-face relationships can take place; *(b)* it has leadership; *(c)* it has a purpose same for all (or for the majority) of the participants; *(d)* the participants and members are in a dynamic interaction with one another; *(e)* it fosters personality growth.

Assuming this definition as a frame of reference, a definition that is acceptable to professional group workers, let us examine therapy and social groups in the light of it. In respect to *(a)*, both groups are similar; both consist of small numbers, though therapy groups must of necessity be much smaller than social or educational groups. Regard-

---

1. Freud, S. (1921). *Group Psychology and the Analysis of the Ego.* Standard Edition 18:65–143. See discussion of this passage [8] where it is pointed out (1) that "group formation" is the pivot, and (2) that improvement is "temporary." Neither is suitable for therapeutic ends.

ing *(b)*, a therapy group does not have a leader in the usual sense of the term. A leader can be defined as the central person who personifies the conscious and the unconscious (especially the latter) needs, trends, and urges of the constituents; who initiates or sets the pace in achieving the common aim or objective of all or the majority of the membership. The ordinary group can survive only if it accepts the leader. In therapy groups, neither the therapist nor any of the patients assume such a role. The therapist does not occupy this leadership position in the group hegemony. In a therapy group, the therapist is the recipient of libidinal and other types of transference feelings and is an object of dependency. He is, therefore, the target of periodic positive, negative, and ambivalent feelings. If he functions adequately in the role that psychotherapy demands from him, he does not serve as an initiator, nor does he set the pace for the group, even though he may at times have to help a particular patient or a number of patients to focus their discussion, to garner the significance of their communications and feelings, and to acquire insight.[2]

Perhaps the most important difference between social and educational, and therapy groups, is to be found in the characteristic subsumed in section *(c)*: the same purpose or aim. Certainly members of a therapy group do not have a *common* purpose. They are not gathered to discharge a specific community function, to pioneer a cause, to find expression of a talent common to them all, or advance an interest they all share; nor do they meet for the pleasure derived from congenial social intercourse. Patients come together because each hopes to get relief from suffering and to overcome personality deficiencies that prevent or interfere with his enjoyment of life and human relationships. Each is driven most often to a resentful compresence in quest of relief from unhappiness, tensions, fears, and anxieties. By and large, the motives for attending therapy groups may be said to be the *same* in all or most of the participants, namely, to improve, but because each seeks *his own* salvation, it does not have the nature of a common motive as understood in a sociological or educational sense. Each seeks to achieve an aim *as an individual* for his own individual ends and not for the benefit or advantage of the

---

2. I have suggested four main functions for a group therapist: directional, stimulative, extensional, and interpretative [56].

group as a unit or for the sake of and in the interest of the common group aim. The patients have the *same* purpose, but it is not a *common* purpose. In my opinion which is derived from working with several hundred social, educational, business, political, and therapeutic groups, it is this factor more than any other that prevents the emergence of the usual "group dynamics."

The basic integrating force that assures the survival and achievement of ordinary groups is what has been described as *synergy*. By synergy is meant the drive, purpose, aim, and effort common to and confluent in all the individuals constituting a group or a mass of people. The cementing tie, the coherence in these groups, is the personal homogeneity of their members and/or of their interest or goal, whatever it may be, which is personified or represented by a leader, or cathected idea or ideal. This element is absent in therapy groups. In fact, as we shall show, its presence prevents therapeutic gains for the participating patients. Instead of coherence, essential to social-educational groups, therapeutic groups feed upon interpersonal conflict and overt expression of hostility among the members. They are in positive, negative, and ambivalent transference relations with each other and are mutual objects of parataxic projections and displacement. Essentially, in therapeutic groups, patients are held together by anxiety and not by pleasure-yielding occupations. The urge of each is to find relief from that personal anxiety through talk and acting out, and insight. Obviously no other type of voluntary group could survive under conditions where aggression is so rampant and anxiety so pervasive. It must be noted, however, that in both ordinary and therapy groups, the leader in one, and the therapist in the other, is the center of the emotional cluster of the constituent members. But it is equally important to observe that in order to survive, these emotions must be positive in ordinary groups, while they alternate between the extreme poles of positive and negative feelings in therapy groups.

There is distinct similarity and confluence of the two types of groups in the category *(d)*. In both types there is present "dynamic interaction" among the members, although here, too, one can readily observe differences. In the social-educational groups the interaction is largely in the realm of ideas or comraderie, even though these are not altogether free from emotional undercurrents. In the psychotherapeutic groups, on the other hand, the interactions are almost exclusively in the realm of feeling and emotions. Even ideational differences and conflicts mask feelings, especially hostility and resentment, which are always present in each participant, for it is the presence of excessive feelings of this nature that makes them "patients."

As to fostering of personality growth and uncovering latent talent, that is, category *(e)*, there is also seeming similarity, but this similarity proves illusory on closer examination. The aim and results of social-educational groups is to implant and/or activate social attitudes and values, to help acquire tools of social living. In "special interest" groups such as in art, literature, and dramatics, the effect is to activate latent talent and interest and bring them to fruition through some form of "self-expression." Under the stimulation of leaders and teachers, powers and talents are uncovered and brought to function. The latter occasionally occurs also in therapy groups as blockings and inhibitions are removed, but the aim of these groups is not uncovering talents but rather personality repair, as a result of which talent may become manifest. Analytic psychotherapy does not directly aim to achieve these; they are rather the results of personality improvement, released ego powers, better capacity for reality testing, and enhanced self-esteem that psychotherapy achieves.

In order to test the applicability of group dynamics derived from the behavior of voluntary social, educational and action groups to therapeutic groups, let us examine them now from the clinical viewpoint. The operational elements of group psychotherapy, as it is in all psychotherapy, are *(a)* transference, *(b)* catharsis, *(c)* insight, *(d)* reality testing, and *(e)* sublimation. As we compare these in the two types of group, we shall find them at even greater dissonance than in respect to the characteristics we have already examined.

We have already touched upon the element of transference and tried to show that its nature and manifestations are quite different in the two types of groups: in one it is almost always positive and largely nonsexual, in the other it is libidinized and bipolar. As to catharsis, it is obvious that no nontherapeutic group could survive long if its members are free to reveal their unmoral and immoral acts, preoccupations and urges, past and present, as they do in psychotherapy. Nor would such groups hold together if their members attacked and abused one another as they do in the latter. Under the impact of free catharsis no social-educational group could survive. The cross currents of hostility that result would easily deteriorate and disintegrate it. Nor can a social or educational aim-directed group withstand the uncovering and interpretations of hidden motives and latent meanings, which are not always the noblest or purest in nature. While interpretation (as differentiated from explanation) that leads to insight (as differentiated from understanding) alleviates anxiety in a therapy group, such interpretation would intensify anxiety were it to be offered to a social-educational group. In everyday relations, interpretation and even explanation of basic unconscious and preconscious motives and meanings generate a high degree of anxiety and resentment because they are essentially attacks on normal and necessary ego defenses.

Since reality testing and sublimation of primitive drives are carried on constantly at every point of the individual's life, they are present in all relations, group and individual, and since they are minor elements in the actual group situation of adult, nonpsychotic patients, only cursory mention of them is necessary here. One fact need be mentioned in this connection, however; namely, that the therapy group is a *conditioned* reality, planned and arranged by the therapist with a therapeutic aim in mind and an eye upon its suitability to each of the participants. This conditioning is not inherent to social-educational or action groups, in which membership is self-chosen on the basis of some element of homogeneity.

Although the term "group ego" is usually employed euphemistically, actually there is a group ego which is represented by the leader through the investment in him by the members of the group. One of the tacit demands imposed by cohesive groups upon each of its members is that he modify his ego functioning which reduces its intensity and quantum, for, obviously, were each to act out in full his own drives, plans, preferences and judgments, no group as such could come into being or exist for any appreciable time. The condition of belonging to a group is *partial de-egotizing* of the individual so that a portion of his ego is given up to the group, and especially to the leader as its representative. In other words, the individual has to submit to the group in order that he may be a part of it and groups come into being and survive because of this partial de-egotization of its members. It is out of these "discarded" portions of the individuals' egos that a "group ego" emerges. This can be represented schematically as in Figure 1.

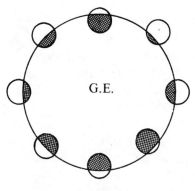

FIGURE I

A part of the ego (represented by the shaded portions of the circles) of each of the constituent members is given up to form the "group ego." This is part of the process commonly referred to as "socialization" or "assimilation"—a process essential for human survival. The more "individualistic" (neurotic) a person is, the less can he give up of his personal ego and is therefore less capable of becoming part of his social milieu. In mobs, for example, a much larger portion of each individual's ego is given up so that he is guided less by it than in democratic deliberative groups. During the periods of violent mob action, the ego of the individuals are entirely suspended, while the initiator or social reformer possesses a minimal capacity for being assimilated.

The fact must always be kept in mind that all group action, whether deliberative or uncontrolled, is a result of a group's ego (GE, Figure 1) functioning which is personified or represented by the leader who is a cathected and idealized symbol. What has been said of the ego is equally true of the superego. Superego judgments are weakened in each member by the group's primary code, its sanctions and approval. The libido thus freed is invested in the leader who becomes the representative of the "group superego." When an individual's superego functioning is at too great divergence from that of the group, he will either withdraw, or the group will reject him. An individual whose superego is either too lax or too strict, as compared with the standards of the group, generates anxiety and guilt and is rejected as a consequence.

By its very nature, psychotherapy utilizes ego and superego functioning in quite a different manner. Although it is permissive and is based on freedom of action and expression, it does not divest the patient of individual responsibility. It encourages unimpeded exercise of the id, ego, and superego, for only through free expression can they be exposed and corrected. The important tenet of psychotherapy is to give to the patient freedom to act in accordance with the dictates of his superego and the strengths of his ego, but he remains responsible for his conduct rather than having this responsibility invested in the group or the leader. The power for judging must remain with the patient. It is through the unimpeded functioning of the patient's *real* ego and his *real* superego, and not their pretend or feigned character, that the patient discovers "the reality of himself" (self-confrontation) which has to be corrected and brought in alignment with outer reality. In effect, the individual in a therapeutic setting is put on his own more severely than he has ever been before, for it is only through this testing of himself against inner and outer reality that he readjusts his psychic forces. Even in Activity Group Therapy of children, which is an extremely permissive method, the child is placed in a position where he must take the consequences of his acts. The more permissive an environment is, the more burdensome does one's task become, for freedom is the heaviest load an individual is called upon to carry.

In the differentials of the ego and superego functioning in the ordinary groups and in therapeutic groups lies one of the major contrasts of the two. As a result, the dynamics that operate in one obviously cannot operate in the other.

The factors of *group fixity* of social, educational and action groups and the corresponding *group mobility* of therapeutic groups which I have discussed elsewhere [5, 56] contribute greatly to the emergence of different types of group processes that cannot be considered in a blanket fashion. These characteristics can be represented in a graphic form as in Figure 2.

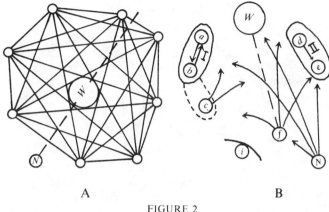

A   B

FIGURE 2

In A we see the solidity of the group formation in which the leader (W) is the center. This we designate as *group fixity*. B shows the fluidity of relations in a therapy group. There is a bilateral relation between (a) and (b) (I); a unilateral relation between (e) and (d) (II); a peripheral relation to I on the part of (c); (i) is an isolate; (f) is a floater without attachment. N in both figures represents a new member. In A he has to cut across many relationship lines to make his way into the group. In B he can try to make contact with a number of individuals. This total free and fluid characteristic of the group we designate as *group mobility*. Note that the leader(W) in A is the center, while in B the therapist (W) tends to be outside of the group context with various individuals attempting to make contact with him.

In the one the leader is the central source of security and serves as a guide; upon him are focused positive feelings of the members to varying intensities, kinds, and degrees; it is from him that stem the unified impulse of the group members to act, and it is he who in part serves as the group's ego and superego. In therapy groups, the intent is that the therapist play a functionally passive or neutral role and that the interactions occur among the members who serve as targets for each other's hostilities, as objects of identification, as catalyzers, as clarifiers, as support. The therapist who functions adequately in his role abrogates the leadership role to various members of the group at different times so as to encourage individuation and emotional maturity. This he can do only to the extent to which his patients will allow it, however, and which varies with their personality evolvement. The contrast between these two functions of the leader and their relation to the group entity is illustrated in Figure 3. The reader will

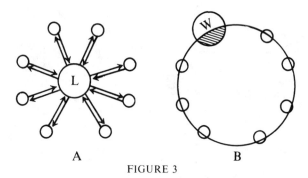

A   B

FIGURE 3

keep in mind the schematic nature of this and the other figures; also that the maximum viability can be achieved in Activity Group Therapy where the therapist assumes a "neutral" role and no interpretations are offered. In analytic groups in which he interprets, the therapist can only approach this function and relation as a limit, but not fully attain it. In A the leader (L) is in a central position, while in B, the therapist (W) functions on the periphery of the group.

One of the major characteristics of ordinary groups is that each member deals not only with every other, but also *with their relations to each other.* It is for this reason that I have suggested many years ago that a group must have at least three persons. The erroneous, though often repeated idea that two persons make up a group does not conform with the nature of groups. A definition that stipulates two as a group confuses interpersonal and group reactions as being one and the same. They are distinctly different, however. Two persons are in a direct bilateral person-to-person relation which must be differentiated from multilateral or group interactions. In a bilateral relation the individuals interact with one another without incursion or interference from others. Their relations and interactions are, therefore, comparatively simple.[3]

The dyadic relation is vastly complicated and the multiplicity of reactions and possible tensions are greatly increased by the addition of one or more persons because they impinge upon that relation in a

---

3. This is an oversimplification of the complexities of human relations. Actually, all relations, including those of two persons, are complicated by the internalized images and each one's attitudes and feelings toward them. I like to refer to these as "phantoms." Chief among the phantoms is the mother, with other important traumatogenic individuals added.

variety of ways and affect the existing and constantly arising interpersonal and group equilibria or disequilibria.

This intragroup dynamic can best be illustrated in family constellations. The interpersonal equilibrium that emerges from the relation between husband and wife is disturbed by the arrival of a child and a new group equilibrium has to be established.[4] This becomes necessary because the relation between the man and his wife is no longer a direct, simple, and linear one, as it had been. The husband no longer relates to the wife as an individual only; he also has to relate to her as mother in relation to their child. His acts and behavior, as well as his feelings, have to take into account the feelings and needs of the child and mother as individuals as well as the relation between them. At the advent of subsequent children, or the addition to the intimate family circle of a relative such as a grandparent, an aunt or an uncle, a new complex of group and interpersonal relationships emerges. Readjustments have to be made by other members of the family as well; that is, the wife and the child and the relatives deal with the relation that exists among the other members of the family group. The wife and mother, for example, adapts her reactions and responses to accord with the requirements of the father-child relation, and the child with that of the father-mother relation. These are rendered still more complex by the presence of other persons in the family.

Psychoanalytic studies have thrown light upon and adequately described the relation of the child to each parent as individuals and to them *as a couple*. This fundamental formulation has made palpable to us some of the most baffling aspects of human personality. The oedipus complex arises from the reaction of the child to the emotional and sexual relations of the two parents. Less attention has been given to the attitudes of each of the parents to the reaction of his or her mate to their child or children. That they exist and are fraught with much potential tension and pathology is evident to everyone engaged in clinical work. It is equally evident that the complexities of family processes and tensions are enhanced with each addition to the family. The addition of a child may occasionally reduce tension, but these instances are rare indeed.

The interpersonal and intragroup dynamics delineated for families

---

4. See the discussion on "equilibrium under tension" [57, pp. 68–70].

hold good for all voluntary groups whose members are in close, intimate, face-to-face relation and interaction, though their emotional significance to each other is less charged with affect than in a family group. Since the emotional investment here is quantitatively and qualitatively of lesser degree and poignancy, tensions are likely to be much less intense. However, the basic patterns are the same and are much more obvious and more intense in therapy groups than they are in ordinary groups—as evidenced in the interpatient transference reactions.[5]

Because of the nature of the group discussions in therapeutic groups, it is inevitable that feelings toward important persons in the early life of each should be aroused and acted out, verbalized, displaced, and projected upon fellow patients, especially upon those who in some way resemble the earlier prototypes, either physically, in manner, or by accomplishments. These are specially chosen as targets of affection, hostility, objects of identification or dependence, rivalry and jealousy. As in families, also in other groups, especially therapy groups, specific feelings may be mobilized toward one person. These may be positive, negative, or ambivalent; they may be transient or permanent. However, what is important is that these are not *group* reactions; rather they are *individual* reactions and assume a form, direction, and intensity that is shaped by the history and early experiences of each participant.

The pattern of acting out or withholding, the manner of behavior, and the nature of the verbalization, stem from the ontogenetic experiences of each. One may or may not arouse reactions in others or he may activate one or only a few of those present. The element of synergy is absent here. Each expresses his transference feelings in his own peculiar way. The fact that there may exist at a given time a common feeling in which all share or to which all are subject does not make it a "group feeling" or a group reaction. The intensity of this feeling, its significance, and the impulse to act upon it are different in each of those present. In fact, what seems at first a "universal" feeling or attitude in a therapy group, actually is not so, for the uncovering of

---

5. The requirement of three persons constituting a group cannot be met in therapy groups by including the therapist. Three patients are a minimum since the therapist should not be drawn into the emotional vortex of the patients.

reactions shows that there are those who are affected by it deeply, others only slightly, and still others remain indifferent. This is both inevitable and understandable in the light of the individual superego and ego differences, capacity for identification, identity in experience, and especially in the transference and projection mechanisms of each. That there should be emotional contagions is just as inevitable, but still the responses are individual, are felt by the individual and are acted upon by the individual, even though he is a member of a group. The outstanding feature of these reactions is that they are specific to, peculiar and characteristic of each member.

A group of persons in any type of active occupation sets up specific dynamics that are more or less universal. Some of them are discernible in therapy groups as well. Where there is action on the part of a group there is also some type and some degree of *interaction* among either all or some of its members. Such interaction is greater among free-acting, self-directed, voluntary groups, and is largely if not entirely determined by the type of leadership function. In groups where the leader is either authoritarian, directive or assertive, the interaction of the members will be less both in frequency and intensity than in a group in which the leader assumes a laissez-faire attitude or one approaching that character. The interaction of a number of people under the latter condition may lead to varying degrees of tension and under specific conditions, due to overstimulation, even to mob violence and disruption.

To be constructive and productive, social, educational and all other aim-directed groups have to set limits to the interaction of their members. At certain periods a common aim or agreement must emerge (group code) that holds the group to a generally accepted or agreed-upon purpose or end. If the tensions in a group prevent movement toward its aim, some means are found to resolve the tension. *Compromise* is the most common and essential mechanism in social, political and aim-directed groups and is the outcome of another process that may be termed *neutralization* [76]. When emotional drives are counteracted or the individual entertaining them is won over by placation or some other ego-gratifying strategy, neutralization of his feelings occurs. Among the chief neutralizing agents in groups is the leader who represents in the unconscious of the members the parental figure, and when he assumes the role of the good parent, the members submit to his expectations. This neutralizing effect of the leader, as we shall presently see, is exerted also in therapy groups by the therapist, though it is accomplished differently and with a different intent.

Another dynamic that is present in ordinary groups and which is an outgrowth of interaction is *interstimulation* [52]. This is the phenomenon through which persons in close proximity engaged in a common objective which can be achieved through common effort on the part of the participants, activate one another either through their attitudes, specific conduct, acts, emotions or ideas. Interstimulation in constructive effort can produce most desirable results, but when it is exercised to the ends of destruction, it can prove to be devastating in its effect, as in the case of mobs.

Of less obvious nature but equally universal and similar in process and effect is the dynamic of *mutual induction* [52]. This, however, is confined to feeling and emotion, whereas interstimulation occurs largely, though not exclusively, in the realm of action. People induce attitudes and feelings in one another without verbal or other tangible or observable forms of communication. The mutually inductive processes are enhanced and individuals grow susceptible to them with closer association and intimacy, as in the case of close friends, married couples, and other members of a family. The closer and more prolonged the emotional and physical association among persons, the more responsive they are to the inductive effect of one another, since through it empathy is heightened.

In all associations of people, positive and negative *identifications* occur according to the emotional prototypes of each participant [52]. Identifications take place as a result of constitutional similarity, background, and experience that makes people feel alike in any situation. Identification is particularly important in therapy groups for it makes possible vicarious catharsis and spectator therapy. It is for this reason that patients assigned to the same group should have, as far as possible, common central or nuclear problems even though their symptoms and clinical diagnoses may be at variance or dissimilar. Identification, however, operates differently in a nontherapeutic group.

One of the undesirable byproducts of interaction and interstimulation is the resultant *intensification* of the emotion involved and the acting out of it. Where a number of persons share a common emotion, especially that of hostility and aggression, their tonus is heightened through *(a)* removal of ego and superego restraints due to group consent, and *(b)* the need to be at one with the group, which is an outcome of "social hunger." Because of hostility or anxiety, an emotion or a drive generated or induced in a number of persons mounts in intensity. The extreme example of intensification of emotion in its negative manifestation is the behavior of mobs where id impulses are released. In a similar fashion, constructive and benevolent emotions and acts are intensified through group example, pressure and demand. Here the group superego is reinforced and the individual's need to belong to, and be a part of, his social milieu (social hunger) aids the process.

These and other dynamics described are in varying degrees present in all groups and gatherings in which interaction is present, but their utility and significance are vastly different in different types of group and the specific aims and objectives that they have. This difference is especially marked in the case of therapy groups. Whereas in all groups except the latter, the dynamics are directed toward socially approved ends by a leader, other effective members, or by the culture, in therapy groups they are permitted to run their course, their psychologic and interpersonal roots are explored and their significance to each person uncovered. The pivotal difference in the operation of psychotherapeutic and ordinary groups lies in this: *group dynamics in the latter remain the operational instruments of the synergy of a group; in therapy groups individual reactions are explored and interpreted in terms of intrapsychic determinants in each of the participating as well as the nonparticipating patients.*[6]

Thus, even the most common group dynamics described are not permitted to operate, for it is the task of the therapist, which is often discharged by fellow patients, to uncover the underlying, most often hostile, feelings, from which reactions flow. Thus, dynamics in therapy groups are "nipped in the bud," as it were, for just as soon as

---

6. There are rare exceptions to this when all the patients are involved. At any rate the intent is always to work through individual reactions.

responses are analyzed and related to their emotional sources, they no longer operate. It is this process in therapy groups that prevents the operation of the dynamics manifest in nontherapeutic groups. Therapeutically directed exploration, uncovering, and insight prevent the emergency of group synergy and the resultant intrapsychic accommodation of each participant so that unitary synergic effort cannot emerge. Thus, *the therapeutic aim in its very nature is antagonistic to group formation and group dynamics.* The reinforcement of feelings and intensification that periodically set in may result in specific dynamics if permitted to take their course. In analytic therapy groups, however, this development is prevented through the intervention of the therapist and his and other members' interpretations which tend to dissipate the building up of group patterns and group effort.

In discussing synergic or collaborative activity of a number of people, Freud says, "...experience has shown that in cases of collaboration libidinal ties are regularly formed between the fellow-workers which prolong and solidify the relation between them to a point beyond what is merely profitable... The libido props itself upon the great vital needs, and chooses as its first objects the people who have a share in that process."[7] As will be shown later, in a therapy group collaboration is not a virtue. At most times it is entirely absent, at others it is present to a minimal degree and is fleeting. Patients in groups do not collaborate, in the sense employed in the quotation, for any length of time. They *react* to each other and at times help one another, but are not engaged in a *common* (collaborative) project or process, and therefore no ties among them are, or should be, established. The libido cathexis among patients in a therapy group emanates from transference projections which have to be analyzed. When emotional ties arise among patients, that is absence of negative transference, the therapeutic effectiveness of the group is diminished and even vitiated as a result.[8]

Another dynamic manifestation of groups is *polarity* [52]. In this regard, as in others, therapy groups are vastly different from ordinary groups in the community. Polarity produces rigidity and fixity; while

---

7. *Group Psychology and the Analysis of the Ego, loc. cit.*

8. It is conceivable that a therapy group may become a cohesive, collaborative group as a result of prolonged treatment and near its termination.

therapy groups must be fluid and mobile. Interaction must be mobile and each patient's role in the group has to alter with his personality integration and emerging ego strengths. A rigidly determined, unaltered place in the group and relation to fellow patients would prevent inner change. As the individual changes, his functions and reactions also change. If this cannot occur, the corrective and reeducational process of therapy is prevented. To assure personality change, freedom and flexibility are essential in interpersonal relations for reasons already indicated, and also because it is part of self- and reality testing.[9] Polarity, as understood in sociologic and psychologic terms, would prevent this essential flexibility in the role and function of each member of the group since it generates group fixity.

There is nonetheless polarity of a sort in therapy groups. To begin with, the therapist serves as a pole on which the patients are centered. Each patient comes because of the therapist's importance to him as an object of cathexis and of dependence. But the attitudes toward him are ambivalent and because he is not a representative of an idea or aim common to all, his hold on the patients is dissimilar to that of a leader of a movement or of a special-interest group. Even though he is a cathected object, the cathexis is felt by each member separately and differently from all the others. Another emotional pole in therapy groups is each patient who serves as a special and separate pole of his own, namely, his interest in changing and improving that brings him to the group. Still a third pole of cathexis are the other members of the group.

One of the inevitable behavioral dynamics that is not preventable because of the inherent nature of human interaction (which is also observable in flocks and herds of animals) is the phenomenon of what I have described elsewhere as *nodal* and *antinodal* behavior [61, pp. 53–56]. It occurs in all gatherings of three or more persons, and the larger the number and the freer they are, the more intense is the acting out (nodal) and more prolonged the period of silence or comparative inactivity (antinodal). The periods of the nodal aspect of group behavior are characterized by mounting animation and communica-

9. This is one reason why it often becomes necessary to involve members of patient's family in treatment. Their unbending attitudes and rigid insistence on patients' roles in the family and elsewhere prevent improvement in the latter.

tion, rising noise and a general atmosphere of interaction and conviviality. When the noise and chaotic atmosphere reach a high level of intensity, sudden quiet sets in. This alternation is observable in all free gatherings, such as parties and other types of assemblies. Even mobs finally spend their energies, bring themselves under control and quiet down. In activity groups of children nodal and antinodal behavior appears in an almost steady rhythm. Although no time study has been made of the frequency and duration of the changes in the pattern, observation suggests that there may be a mathematical relation in this phenomenon.

The rise to the nodal level obviously stems from interstimulation. However, a state of tension is engendered in all the participants due to the physical and emotional exertion expended. Also organic anxiety is activated by the overstimulating and almost chaotic state into which the gathering falls and which produces a reaction in each. As a result, silence (rest) sets in. The alternation between nodal and antinodal behavior occurs also in therapy groups. There are periods of considerable interchange among the patients as well as interaction, interstimulation and intensification. There may even be present mutual induction and reinforcement of hostility and aggression toward a single target, usually one of the patients. In activity therapy groups this is allowed to run its course so that the ego and superego may become involved in the behavior and thus personality growth and integration can occur as the children bring themselves under control on their own. But in groups of adult patients, this type of acting out of feelings is checked at the appropriate time by the therapist who attempts to help the patients to recognize their behavior in the light of "therapeutic understanding." His move in this direction at once brings the nodal state of the group to a halt. As the patients investigate their actions and underlying feelings in the light of current or past emotional experiences and attitudes, the behavior is changed to that of an antinodal character.

Similarly, silence by a group (extreme antinodal behavior) is allowed to continue only to a permissible extent. One of the patients, usually the most anxious and insecure, breaks the silence. When this does not transpire, the therapist asks the group to examine the silence and helps bring into the open feelings that hold the patients in check. Here again the course of group dynamics is not allowed to run unhampered; the therapist's or a patient's intervention prevents it [18].

The nodal–antinodal group pattern can be understood in terms of *group homeostasis*. Just as an organism naturally seeks to establish equilibrium, human groups (as well as animal herds or flocks) are prone to this basic natural trend or law. Groups, as do also individual organisms in a state of tension or agitation, generate counterirritants to the excessive activation and hypertenseness which they find in the antinodal period. This process is analogous to rest and recuperation.

The following episode which is characteristic of analytic group therapy sessions with adult nonpsychotic patients illustrates some of the points made in the preceding pages.

For about the first fifteen or twenty minutes, three of the six women who had come to the session ahead of the others talked about apartments and homes, a problem that had occupied their attention for some time in the past and which was solved by two of them satisfactorily; about Open School Week and their visits to their children's classrooms; and their children's adjustment to school. Mrs. W. had arrived at about this time, wearing a scarlet sweater. Mrs. S. commented about it, asking her what color it was and saying that "it was nice." Mrs. C. said that the color was "electric red" and then added archly: "It's got its points." (This was a reference to a statement about Mrs. W.'s rather large breasts made by Mrs. C. in the preceding session, which embarrassed Mrs. W. very much.) Mrs. W. said laughingly that Mrs. C. is "starting again." All laughed briefly, Mrs. C. adding, "I have my points, too," whereupon Mrs. W. retorted rather shortly, "Yes, but they're not as pronounced." Mrs. C., again with a smile playing on her face, said, "Well, let's get back to Mrs. G.," who proceeded to talk about her moving to the new house.

A pause followed. The therapist, who was a male, referred to Mrs. W.'s remark that Mrs. C. "is starting again," and asked Mrs. W. what she thought Mrs. C. was starting. Mrs. W. replied that Mrs. C. "is starting again with her *pointed* remarks." This was an obvious play on words, referring to the nipples of her breasts. She then rather angrily criticized Mrs. C. for "always making disparaging or critical remarks about people." She thought that Mrs. C. had a need always to criticize. (Mrs. C. has a character disorder with strong masculine protest; very aggressive.)

Mrs. C. defended herself against this charge and asked rather calmly (which represented a change in this rather aggressive, short-tempered woman): "What's wrong with injecting a slight sense of humor into these sessions?" Mrs. W. protested that Mrs. C. was not humorous and referred angrily to Mrs. C.'s tendency to "always tell others what to do rather than discussing her own problems," and Mrs. C.'s seeking to "be a big shot." (Mrs. W.'s ability to permit herself to become angry was a sign of change in her. She was very insecure, docile, and placating before treatment in the group.)

Again a pause followed. The therapist asked the group what was going on between Mrs. C. and Mrs. W.

Mrs. S. recalled that "last time" Mrs. W. had realized that she had compared Mrs. C. with her brother and that Mrs. W. had at that time thought that she was less resentful toward Mrs. C. Mrs. W. commented, "Well, last week she [Mrs. C.] wasn't so bitchy; she had tapered off a little." Mrs. C. responded to this by saying that she was open to criticism. In the past no one in the group had resented her (which was not the case) and only Mrs. W. resented her now. She added that Mrs. W. must be a person who resents everyone, to which the latter reacted by sarcastically stating that Mrs. C. always had to get the last word in and that she, Mrs. W., would let her do it.

Mrs. S. who appeared to agree with Mrs. W.'s attack, though unwilling to face up to Mrs. C. in an open conflict, remarked that she would try to "criticize" Mrs. C. in "a helpful manner." With an air of sincerity Mrs. S. stated that from what Mrs. C. had described in the group, she received attention as a child only when she was "smart," but had missed out "on the other things such as love and affection." For this reason, Mrs. C. hs to keep on "using smartness." During this statement Mrs. S. pointed out several times that she thought Mrs. C. was smart but "that is not enough; something is lacking there and it alienates people." Mrs. C. seemed to accept this. (This is the first time Mrs. C. had withstood criticism without becoming hostile and vituperative.) Mrs. S. then went on to question Mrs. C. about possible envy of her siblings, but the latter denied it, saying that she was better than they in every way and that there was nothing she could be envious of in her sisters.

At this point Mrs. B. arrived. The discussion continued in the above vein for a short time when Mrs. S. in an outwardly pleasant manner and with seeming casualness remarked that Mrs. B. reminded her of someone who had been a close friend during her adolescence. (The implication was that physically Mrs. B. was like that friend.) Here Mrs. C. remarked somewhat pointedly to Mrs. B.: "See, you have your *points*, too."

The therapist, sensing that Mrs. S. had wanted to convey more to Mrs. B. by the comment she had made, said that he was interested in her reasons for saying what she did about Mrs. B. and her friend. Mrs. S. maintained that it was "just a thought," stating that by coincidence this friend had called her the other night. However, after a brief pause, she smiled and began talking about this friend, Sally, of whom Mrs. B. reminded her. She commented to the therapist with a smile: "You got me talking," and proceeded to recall that her friend had never gotten along with her mother and then said, "There is some similarity there" (to Mrs. B.). Mrs. B. emitted a sharp, hostile laugh and told Mrs. S.: "You're a character." When Mrs. S. asked why, Mrs. B. with open resentment said, "Apparently all you have to do is to go home and think about everyone else's problems." Mrs. S. commented that she must have "struck home" in her remark to Mrs. B. to set off such a strong reaction. Mrs. B. then angrily denied that she was angry.

Mrs. S. stated with evident conviction and emphasis that she wondered why Mrs. B. came at all since she apparently felt that she had no problems and denied that anything said in the group pertained to her or caused her to think about it. (Mrs. B. also has a character disorder with strong masculine identifications and strongly resisted treatment for a considerable period.) Mrs. B. pointedly remarked in response that she was too busy taking care of her home, children, and family to think about what happened in the group. She then insinuatingly asked Mrs. S. how her "home relations" had gone during the week. Mrs. S. quickly replied: "Yours should be as good, believe me!" (This interchange was significant. Mrs. S., formerly a highly neurotic, masochistic woman with psychogenic eczema of her hands, had been in the past tormented sadistically by her husband and was quite helpless and frightened in her role as a wife and mother and submissive and placating to everyone. She had made impressive improvement in all these areas and functioned very adequately as a result of exclusive group therapy. Her aggressiveness can be considered healthful. Through it she is acting out her inordinate hostility toward her mother who rejected her viciously and toward her favored brother and two sisters.)

At one point in this exchange Mrs. G., who remained quiet, laughed and said that she was going to go home, implying that she felt left out since no one was siding with her. (This gives us a further clue to the underlying meaning of the argumentativeness going on in the terms of its defense against homosexual feelings in the group, as evidenced by references to clothes and breasts.)

The therapist asked what was happening between Mrs. S. and Mrs. B. He noted that Mrs. S. had been quite open in expressing her strong resentments against her own mother in the past. She later suggested that mothers "should be forgiven," but not before Mrs. B.'s strong urging on many occasions that Mrs. S. forgive her mother.

Mrs. S. responded by saying that she thought she understood what the therapist was saying. During the preceding week she herself had noticed that she had been acting out "quite childishly" in wanting to be "first in everything." For example, in the bakery she pushed an old woman out of line. She at once tied this up with the very poor treatment she had received at the hands of her mother and with an incident several years ago where her sisters had jointly given her as a present a set of dinnerware without consulting her as to her preference. Mrs. B. interrupted Mrs. S. and argued with her to the effect that she, Mrs. S., should have taken the dinnerware set from her sisters without criticizing them. Mrs. S. with great feeling exclaimed: "Why should I kiss their asses?" Mrs. G. blushed at Mrs. S.'s remark.

Mrs. S. continued in a more subdued manner but on the same feeling level that she always was "too humble." Close to tears she described her constant attempts in the past to please people and to show her gratitude to them: for instance, her husband. She realized that as a reaction to the humility and ingratiation, she had this week gone to the other extreme.

Mrs. C., in a supportive way, told Mrs. S. that it was quite all right to go off to an extreme for a week. Mrs. C. added that she, too, would have resented the dinnerware if it were given with no regard for her own taste or the other furnishings of her home. (This conciliatory move on Mrs. C.'s part was quite surprising in the light of her usual aggressive conduct and general hostility.) Mrs. B., however, maintained that Mrs. S. was making "too much of the whole thing."

Mrs. S. again referred to her past need to humble herself because of the way her mother had treated her. Mrs. B. continued to maintain that Mrs. S. was making too much of the situation and should just have said "thank you." This prompted Mrs. W. to remark sarcastically to Mrs. B.: "You're the goodwill ambassador, aren't you?" Mrs. B. appeared to miss the sarcasm and instead took this as a compliment and described in a somewhat pleased manner that she generally was "not bothered by such things." She went on to deny envy of her sisters, referring specifically to the fact that her younger sister sometimes received better gifts from her mother than she did. She denied feeling jealous about this and proceeded to say that perhaps in some ways she had more than her sister. For instance, she had one child more than her sister had, and perhaps she was loved by her husband more than was her sister by hers. (This was a telling example of Mrs. B.'s resistance to treatment which we found to be a "character resistance." She was an inordinately hostile woman.)

The conversation lapsed and the therapist asked Mrs. S. what her current understanding was of her reactions to Mrs. B.

Mrs. S. responded with the statement that she felt she understood it more clearly now. She explained that Sally, of whom Mrs. B. reminded her, was one before whom she had always humbled herself, because she did not feel "worthwhile." In addition, Sally was small and pretty like Mrs. B., whereas Mrs. S. was tall and unattractive. (Mrs. S. was a tall, lanky, ungainly, physically unattractive woman.) Mrs. S. guessed that Mrs. B., by reminding her of Sally, had suddenly reminded her of all these feelings within herself which had made her unhappy, and that it made her angry to remember how humble she used to be toward people.

Mrs. C. left the session at this point, politely waiting for Mrs. S. to finish before saying goodbye to the group. Only the therapist and Mrs. S. responded. (Mrs. C. had to leave about twenty minutes earlier to meet her son at school.)

Mrs. B. then referred to Open School Week and remarked that according to the teachers, her son was now doing quite well, that is, aside from his reading. She stated somewhat thoughtfully that since the only place he presented a problem was at home, perhaps something was "wrong with *us*." She then added that if he ever got his reading straightened out, he would make a wonderful businessman or politician. (This was the first time in more than a year of treatment that Mrs. B. admitted the existence of a problem in her family. What was even more surprising was that she related it to herself. Of course, she at once mitigated it by saying he would make a good businessman.)

The therapist commented that Mrs. B. herself would make a good business woman or politician. She seemed highly pleased and exclaimed: "Really?" She then said that she would like to be in business but thought that she lacked the education. At one point she turned to Mrs. G. and addressed her as Mrs. C. (who was absent at the time). Both women laughed as Mrs. G. explained that she was not Mrs. C. Mrs. B. then indicated that she was probably bothered by Mrs. G.'s silence during the discussion. The therapist asked why she should be bothered by this and Mrs. B. remarked, "I don't know. I guess I just like to chatter." Mrs. G. smiled and said, "You've been doing a lot of it today."

Mrs. S. asked Mrs. B. at this point if she really wanted to know whether Mrs. G. approved of what Mrs. B. was saying. Mrs. B. was able to say quite freely and spontaneously: "I don't care if she approves or not, and you, too, for that matter!" The therapist supported Mrs. B. in this freer expression of feeling of which she was not capable in the past by telling her approvingly that she was quite spirited today. Mrs. B. laughed, seemed pleased and then described that in some earlier session she remembered the therapist having told her that she had a right to be selfish at times. She indicated that she felt she was becoming freer, describing that she had taken up oil painting and was getting a lot of enjoyment out of it.

Toward the close of the session, Mrs. W. expressed resentment against her son's continued enuresis. She seemed to seek an ally in this by attempting to involve Mrs. G. and referred to the fact that both of them had "mountains of laundry to do." Mrs. B. seemed to be thoughtful for a while and then referred to the therapist's prior remark that she, too, like her son, would probably be good in business or politics. Equally thoughtfully, she said that the therapist's remark was intended to show her that perhaps "the two of us [her son and she] must be tied up in some way and perhaps Don is patterning himself after me." She followed this up by criticizing her husband for helping Don with his homework; "practically doing all of it for him," she said.

The preceding episode illustrates the fact that there is no synergic or common effort present. Each of the participants acts out according to her own character organization, ego functioning, and transference projections. The center or focus is Mrs. S. who at the moment holds the stage, the others reacting to her as individuals, some in a positive, helpful fashion; others with hostility and attack. The reactions also vary. At times a patient is friendly, at another time she turns antagonistic. Mrs. G. remains uncommunicative throughout this episode. The topic under discussion may not have activated her either because it was alien to her own experience or because she found it necessary to remain defensive.

There are no "group dynamics" in evidence. Rather they are replete in interpersonal stimulation and activation. These are basically different in their nature. The therapist's focusing his questions upon individuals in the group, their feelings toward each other and the meaning of these feelings, prevent the emergence of common dynamics in which all participate or are involved for a common, unitary aim or purpose.

Summary

It is essential to differentiate between "group dynamics" and "interpersonal interactions." The first arises in groups with a goal common to all members who act by the consent of the majority. Synergy then arises and various activities are evolved to attain the common aim. At this point group dynamics arise, such as conflict, compromise, agreement, domination and submission. These processes are characteristic of educational, social, and action groups.

A "group ego" and "group superego" are evolved in this process of group cohesion which can come into operation only when each of the participants relegates part of the functions of his own ego and superego to the group and especially to the central person or the leader. Active leadership is essential in groups operating on the basis of synergy.

In the therapy groups, on the other hand, no common aim is in evidence, even though the aim in all is the same, namely, to overcome intrapsychic difficulties and social maladjustments. Group cohesion has to be prevented so that each can communicate his problems and work them through. This requires freedom and the retention of one's own ego and superego functioning. This process of individuation prevents synergic effort and in consequence also the dynamics that arise in ordinary groups. In therapy groups there constantly occurs verbalized and nonverbalized interpersonal action and reaction, partly as a result of transference projections and partly because of the inevitable effect persons have upon one another, such as contagion, mutual induction, interstimulation, intensification of emotions, sympathy, empathy and others. These cannot be considered, however, as "group dynamics," but rather as "interpersonal interactions."

CHAPTER 17

CATHARSIS IN GROUP PSYCHOTHERAPY
(1951)

While dreams may be the royal road to the unconscious, other types of catharsis, such as verbalization and action are secondary lanes. But these lanes must always be kept open. Since catharsis reveals the innermost feelings and attitudes of which the patient may be both afraid and ashamed, it can occur only in a positive transference relation. Through catharsis we aim to dislodge from repression and and the unconscious guilt-provoking and anxiety-inducing feelings, thoughts, and strivings and to bring them to consciousness. For obvious reasons the patient resists this and dealing with these resistances is one of the major skills of psychotherapy.

One of the sources of resistance is that the patient wards off regressing to infantile cravings, interests, and preoccupations mostly of a sexual nature that belong to an earlier stage in development. This fear of regression blocks catharsis and is one of the causes of negative transference. The patient must be assured of the acceptance and tolerance of the therapist before he can reveal himself. Only when there is the security of such a positive transference can he hazard the risk. The value of catharsis lies in the fact that it induces regression to stages in emotional development where arrest or fixation occurred. Fixations make social integration difficult or impossible and it is necessary for the patient to first free himself of these before he can make an inner and social adjustment.

Varying degrees of regression are present in all therapies: in psychoanalysis, in other types of individual psychotherapy, and in group psychotherapy. Psychotherapy that deals with the immediate problems alone has only limited values. While education, suggestion, guidance, and advice may be helpful in dealing with one's problems, they should not be confounded with psychotherapy which seeks to affect more or less permanently and to varying degrees the personality structure. In groups regression is facilitated because the members support each other, they act as catalyzers, and sanction otherwise tabooed behavior. Identification and universalization reduce guilt feelings and the total atmosphere of the group, which is friendly, aids the patient in discharging hitherto hidden feelings and breaking the dams that blocked the flow of psychic energies. Resentment and hostility that had to be held in abeyance can be discharged with impunity. Egress of emotions relieves the inner tensions that had been the root of many forms of disturbances. The removal of repressions is as important for adolescents as it is for children, even though the channels may be different. What young children gain through therapeutic play and acting out, adolescents and adults achieve through verbal communication.

At a group session of boys five to six years old, one of the boys urinated into a pan of watercolor paint, to which mixture they referred as "kacki" (feces), and other anal appellations. At their group sessions the mothers of the same children talked about frequency of urination, defecation, and sexual intercourse. As they were freed of their repressions both the mothers and the little children reacted in almost the same manner. Both regressed to the preoedipal level when they could talk and do whatever they wished. Although the form of the expression differed in the two groups, the meaning of the regression was the same for both.

A striking example of regression is exemplified in the following conversation at an analytic group psychotherapy session:

Paula said she always imagines that New York is being bombed and that people are running away from it (this was during the war). Bertha laughingly responded to this by saying that she dreams of sex. (Of special interest is Bertha's association of bombing and sex, that is, bombing is equated with a sexual attack.) Sandra also dreams of sex. Bertha looked significantly at Sandra and said that she also dreamed that she was married and had "millions of kids." Sandra interrupted her to say she dreamed her friend Anne had a baby and that Sandra was present when the baby was being born. Almost as though she tried to outdo Bertha, Sandra told of a dream in which her mother was masturbating very violently. (Sandra actually did witness her mother masturbating.) Bertha asked whether watching her mother "do it made you hot," and whether it caused her to masturbate too, and while masturbating did she think it was someone else's hand "doing it" to her. Sandra was not sure of this, her mother did masturbate, "but not all the time"; so does Sandra. Lydia said "consciously I don't," and added later that maybe unconsciously she might be doing it. Sandra wondered whether the girls felt any embarrassment at talking so openly about such things and Lydia asked why one should be embarrassed. "You talk about things with a fellow when you're in the dark, don't you?" Sandra said that was different.

Catharsis and regression in adolescents and adults occur largely, though not entirely, on a verbal level, but patients in groups reenact their attitudes toward parents, siblings, husbands, wives and others in relation to one another and to the therapist. To patients with weak egos, this is particularly valuable, since it serves in addition to overcome resistances and as a form of reality testing.

As could be expected the discussions in analytic group psychotherapy are not always friendly or placid. Members grow emotionally tense, attack one another, violently disagree, project attitudes upon other members in the group and the therapist. These are forms of acting out analogous to the cathartic physical activity of children in treatment groups.

Emotional harmony in a therapy group has to be achieved through a prolonged struggle. The parent in a family or the therapist in a group who insists on suppression of hostile impulses and maintaining a placid facade increases tensions. Catharsis is an essential part of therapy. A regimen that encourages or demands withholding hostile feelings is not therapeutic.

In one therapy group of adolescent girls, the patients repeatedly returned to the same topic of conversation. The group seemed blocked. A study of the interviews showed that the girls were unable to proceed because they repressed their hostility toward the therapist as a result of her consistent pleasantness and benign manner. Since the group had been meeting for many months, they needed to discharge their negative emotions, but could not do so because of their admiration and "love" for the therapist. She was advised to encourage expression of hostility toward herself and when she did this the therapeutic value of the group interviews were vastly enhanced. There was a dramatic change in the content and a much wider therapeutic base emerged. During this change the transitory transference became negative. The girls expressed hostility toward the therapist and dissatisfaction with the group (really the therapist).

It is for this reason also that no food is given to adolescent and adult patients as is done in activity groups and in play groups for little children. Receiving food tends to inhibit the negative impulses toward the therapist, which retards or vitiates the therapeutic process.

Expression of hostility toward the therapist is a prime requirement in psychotherapy, which should be used in the grist of the therapeutic mill. When the patients are afraid to articulate or act out such feelings, the therapist has to help them do so. Patients who withhold aggression are resisting treatment, a resistance that can be overcome much easier in a group, because of the various mechanisms present in a group for dissolving resistance, to be described presently. The therapist, through his accepting attitude, also aids this discharge of emotion because patients find, often to their amazement, that hostility does not devastate one. One need not repress it completely lest it destroy one. (It is for this reason that the nonpathologically timid and withdrawn gain more rapidly from all types of group therapy than do others. They can cast off their taciturnity, first guardedly and as they discover its safety, more boldly.) The therapist needs to be careful in dealing with negative manifestations, lest he alienate the patient by denying him the basic satisfactions he requires. The chief facility in psychotherapy lies in the fact that the patient feels free to act out or speak out infantile drives and cravings. This is tantamount to living over his preoedipal stage in life, where restraints were few and pleasure drives ran their course. Because of this feeling of unbridled freedom and unrestraint he can permit himself to throw all caution to the winds and suspends his superego. At best this is an unrealistic attitude toward the adult (parent), but it is only temporary, for once the fundamental transference has been worked through, it changes.

The change occurs through the maturity of the patients which reduces cravings for infantile indulgence and through the more realistic dealing with them by the therapist. He explains, restrains, criticizes, suggests and, when indicated, interprets.

Too intense hostility in a group is very disturbing. Each group has a limit for the density of hostility and aggression it can bear.

Elsewhere [16, 128] I have described the behavior of groups as having two phases: nodal and antinodal. The nodal phase is one during which the peak of hyperactivity is reached, which is followed by a period of equilibrium, quiet and constructive activity which is the antinodal phase. The therapeutic process occurs at the point where hyperactivity is transformed into a state of equilibrium: self-control, compromise, mutual understanding, and when neutralizing factors set in. It is at the point of transition from the nodal to the antinodal state of the group that psychologic growth, integration, and maturity occur. I have also indicated that in a group where there is constant or too frequent eruption of aggression with inadequate or infrequent transition to equilibrium, little improvement can be expected. In such circumstances the group is in constant turmoil, conflict, and anxiety, which affect every member. The neurotic grows more anxious and may stop coming in for treatment. Others either become more entrenched in their undesirable behavior or feel too threatened by it. The child whose infancy has been prolonged finds an operational field that meets his desires only too well, but his needs for growth are not met in such a group. On the other hand, in a quiet group where there is constant equilibrium, little interpersonal activity occurs. Each is preoccupied with his own interests and continues in the same state of development at which he came with little or no intrapsychic change. Therapy occurs where the group follows the pattern of alternate nodal and antinodal stages, for psychological changes usually accompany the transition from disequilibrium to equilibrium. These general principles are as applicable to interview groups as they are to activity groups.

The very fact that patients overcome hostilities and antipathies toward each other indicates emotional growth. It means their capacities for object relations have been enlarged, tendencies to project diminished, and that aggression was brought under control. These are all indications of ego strength and social adaptations.

An illustration of the value of catharsis is supplied by a very aggressive girl of five who had been very distressing to the group and the therapist because of her particularly disturbing behavior at one of the sessions. The therapist was aware that the child was to have a tonsillectomy (against the therapist's advice) the next day. During the course of the session she struck children, destroyed their projects, hit the therapist on the back with a hammer and kicked her in the abdomen while the latter was leaning over trying to pacify the child. The girl called the therapist vile names. The therapist told the girl that her behavior was probably due to the fact that she was to have an operation the next day. Was she afraid of the operation? In response the girl said: "I am frightened," then interrupting herself said: "No, I am mad. I am not mad at you, but I want to kick you and I want to spit in your face, you dumbbell, you big horse." Our little patient had become quite calm by the end of the session and on leaving she shouted to the therapist, "Goodbye liar" (the therapist's name being Lia). However, as the elevator door was about to close she jumped out quite suddenly, embraced the therapist and ran back into the elevator.

The episode would indicate that the fundamental transference toward the therapist was positive which was disturbed by the stress through which the child was passing as a result of the anticipated operation. The very fact that she felt free to act out her distress and behave in such an aggressive manner in itself would confirm this, as well as her impulsive embracing of the therapist before she left the building.

Perhaps the greatest contribution that Activity Group Therapy has made to the general field of psychotherapy is its discovery of the value of acting out in a favorable setting. *Activity catharsis*, which is its special contribution, was found to do as much for children as verbalization and free association for adults. It was found also to follow the same laws and have genetic relations as does verbalization. Activity catharsis, too, has manifest forms and latent content, which the therapist must perceive or understand. The therapist's ways of dealing with children's behavior constitutes interpretation, but instead of verbalizing it, he interprets it by acts and attitudes. This we term *action interpretation*.

In order to stimulate activity catharsis children should be supplied with appropriate materials and situations. Their play and activity materials have to be suited to their age, and designed to stimulate catharsis. Clay, water, fire, paints, brushes, dolls, mannikins, guns, soldiers, rubber darts, dollhouses with furniture that includes beds and toilet fittings, are among the equipment suitable for young children. These are among the essentials, and such peripheral tools and equipment as wood and airplane models may also be added for the older children. The equipment is used spontaneously and phantasy about the play and games is elicited by the therapist. An occasional question and interpretation is in order, but the therapist should remember that acting out through play is as valuable to the child as verbalization is to older patients.

Dollhouses that have a number of rooms with bedroom and bathroom furnishings are particularly valuable for children below school age. In his play each child reconstructs and refurnishes the "house" in a manner that reflects his particular preoccupations. One may place both parents in a bed, and the child in another room. Another beds the child and the mother together, with the father in another room or bed. The latter is often left out altogether. Still another child places the father outside of the house trying hard, but unable, to get in. Some children cause the father and the child dolls to fall out of windows. Some place the bedroom on an upper floor, while another child locates it as the first room upon entrance into the house. The bathroom receives similar diversity of treatment, with the toilet bowl being the center of attention.

Other materials provided are also used variously and the uses they are put to reflect preoccupation with some of the basic organ functions and phantasies about them. Water and fire are used to discharge urethral, sexual, and sadistic phantasies; clay and paints sublimate anal drives; and chewing, shouting, and eating assuage oral cravings. Materials supplied to children of different ages should not be too varied or too difficult for them to understand or manipulate. Materials of greatest value are those of low resistivity and complexity. For the young child they need to be soft and pliable, such as clay, plasticene, paints, and water. For older children they can be more resistive such as wood and metals. Gradation in resistivity aids in the development of power and improved self-regard, and especially in appropriate catharsis. Materials listed in the above paragraphs can be described as *libido-evoking* and the activities resulting from them as *libido-revealing* in contrast to *libido-binding* activities and materials in analytic group therapy. The former can be permitted because in analytic group therapy interpretation is employed, which is not done in activity groups.

Young children's behavior in therapy groups is very regressive. They rush about helter-skelter, fight with one another, make demands, are provocative and unreasonable. As their emotional pressures and anxieties are lessened, behavior becomes more controlled and more mature. Conversations in interview groups of adolescents and adults are also of a regressive nature. They are concerned with childhood grudges and strivings and speak of matters that are taboo under ordinary circumstances. In young children such unrestraint takes the form of hilarity and diffuse aggression; adolescents and adults resort to release through language. In both instances, there is regression to an infantile (preoedipal) level.

Explosive behavior, which may become violent at times, may also serve the same purpose. (Such behavior is anal in nature and is in fact frequently accompanied by passing of flatus. It has been shown that passing flatus and belching are used as aggression.) Such acts by one tend to stimulate others to join in hilarity and destructiveness. There is little therapeutic value in such behavior. In individual therapy, behavior is more likely to be related to the child's central problem than it is in groups. In the latter aggressiveness may be initiated by one of the children and taken on by the others through suggestion, infection, or social hunger, quite unrelated to their central problem. It, therefore, has no meaning in terms of the child's basic difficulties. Free acting out, the same as verbal free association, has value only when it is related to the patient's psychological difficulties. When it becomes diffuse, it may have opposite the desired effect, namely, it may disorganize personality, weaken the ego, and prevent general integration.

It must be expected that after the initial insecurity is overcome in the early stages of treatment, there will be considerable diffuse hilarity and "wild" behavior. This is the preliminary stage in acclimatization, testing of reality and of the therapist. In a sense, this is the most trying period for the latter for not only does he have to withstand aggression and frustration, but he also has to convince the children of his basic acceptance of them, and at the same time prevent disorganization in the group. Frequently, hilarity is suggested by activating materials [53] which should be eliminated. Shortening the treatment hour is also a good device, or introducing food at a high point in hilarity to calm the children, a walk outdoors, or storytelling can also be effective. When hyperactivity continues, it may be advisable to reexamine the personnel of the group. There may be one or more children not as yet ready for group treatment, or the grouping may be wrong.

Much has been said in favor of release in children through aggression. Without going too far afield, it needs to be stated that aggression and acting out have therapeutic value only when they are related to the basic disturbance of the patient. If no such relation exists, the resulting diffuse and uncontrolled hyperactivity reinforces his fixation on a level of immaturity. To be of therapeutic value abreaction must have a relation to the basic problem of the individual. Climbing, for example, is a healthful occupation for all small boys, but of especial value when it reflects growing masculine aggression in a castrated child or is a form of reality testing.

Acting out as such probably has several values, the understanding of which would help understanding the therapeutic process generally. Primarily it is a means by which the patient seeks mastery over his life situations, as is the case in primary behavior disorders. It also serves patients for whom other means for emotional discharge are unavailable, which is the case with children in whom impulse is greater than ego controls. Children are further handicapped by the fact that their language facilities are incommensurate with their emotions and they substitute action. Most frequently, however, acting out is a result of a weak ego development. Where the ego is unable to deal with impulse, the id takes precedence and finds egress in direct action. By these means the burden the ego has to bear is reduced. Frequently when one is unable to reveal himself to his own gaze and to that of others, he becomes defensively aggressive, or one may ward off depression through hilarity and hyperactivity.

Acting out, as a preliminary to verbalization, is of great advantage for eliciting catharsis and establishing a positive transference. Because it tends to diminish anxiety and resistance, it is valuable in the treatment of children as well as adults. As the patient succeeds in strengthening his ego and craves group acceptance, he curbs his aggression and gives up bizarre and unsocial behavior.

We found that in both activity and interview groups diffuse acting out gradually becomes canalized, more purposeful, and more self-disciplined. Children grow less aimless, begin to work on definite projects, improve in their relations with one another. Instead of continuing to be general and unfocused, the interviews of adolescents and adults as well point more to their problems and difficulties. These improvements occur through the inner integration which follows on the wake of strengthened ego, also because of improved attitudes of patients toward each other in terms of antagonisms, dependencies, ambivalences, tolerance, and cooperation, the changing role of the therapist, and the nature of the transferences.

It must be kept in mind, however, that next to fear of each other, regression is the chief source of anxiety in groups, as well as in all other types of psychotherapy. Both children and adults struggle against revealing themselves. They are afraid of punishment and stigma, associated with under-mature behavior and regressive cravings. During the oedipal conflict the child strives to please the parent of the opposite sex and replace the one of his own sex. In this striving he fancies himself strong, responsible, and worthy to be accepted by the parent. He is chagrined when he is made to feel small and weak. This feeling of stigma and smallness is associated with regression throughout life, and is resisted. To encourage regression is one of the important tasks of psychotherapy.

The group therapist needs to be constantly aware of the latent content and the direction of the group interviews. His knowledge of each patient's difficulties needs at all times be poised for action. A well placed question, well timed, opens the sluices of the unconscious and of free association, which is further aided by the catalytic effect of the other group members. The therapist needs also be aware of the periods when fear, anxiety, and resistance appear in the group. At these stages he needs to help the patients overcome their differences and fear through the appropriate use of the transference and by giving support. He may, according to indications, analyze the resistance of the group, incite or facilitate expression of hostility to himself, or reassure the members of the group of his acceptance of them. The direction to be taken is indicated by the nature of the blocking, the manifest and latent content of the discussion, and the anticipated anxiety sources inherent in the situation.

One of the dynamics that serve to block catharsis is *deflection*. One is impressed with the frequency with which the strategem of deflection is used by patients in group interviews. Various emotions a patient feels toward the therapist of which he may be afraid, are deflected on other members (who are, of course, less threatening), or upon persons who are not present. Such persons may be siblings, parents, mates, or friends. In terms of therapeutic dynamics, deflection is a form of resistance and although it serves to reduce anxiety, it may, if used too frequently, vitiate or block the therapeutic process. The therapist may have to deal directly with deflection as a form of resistance and interpret it.

With a similar objective, *escape* is employed by some patients. Escape is usually accomplished by the patient's withdrawal from participation in group interviews or by changing the subject. Young children and patients in activity groups withdraw to a corner and work by themselves. By so isolating themselves they escape the tensions of group participation. An example of this in an interview group is as follows:

Sandra was reminded of a song, "A Man Ain't Nothing but a Little Boy." Laughingly Georgia said: "My father is in his second childhood." Rose said: "That's why you go with boys younger than yourself even though you always talk about liking older boys." Reva (who was greatly involved with her father) apologetically and self-consciously changed the subject. She said she knows that she had been absent for a few weeks, but even during her absences she was still preoccupied with the question she had asked the group, which was not answered.

Still another escape for patients is provided when they focus attention on another member and thus redirect it from themselves. This has therapeutic value as well, for as the problems of another person are discussed, the patient can venture much further in the exploration than when he is the subject under consideration. He thus gains through identification and may improve sufficiently until he can mobilize power to admit the relevance of the discussion to himself. (This can be described as *identification theory*.) The value of such deflection and escape is apparent, for it diminishes fear. A group member may press an especially painful point with a fellow member because he seeks to clarify that point for himself. Thus each can use the others in the grist of his own therapy. This process is one of the major values of a group for through exploring the difficulty of another and identifying with him, he evolves insight into his own problem. Thus a patient in a group may be a spectator or a participant. The strategem of escape and deflection can also be employed by the therapist when he becomes aware of rising anxiety in the group members which may be contraindicated at a given time.

Among the dynamics that accelerate catharsis in groups is *catalysis*. Each person present activates all the others to expression and action. It would take us too far afield to discuss the psychodynamics of suggestion, induction, and interstimulation that occur in groups [see 16] beyond the point of saying that the effect of the least conflicted person has a releasing effect upon the others. Thus the least inhibited and least frightened individual opens the ground for the others, as it were. Patients who have been unable to verbalize their problems, phantasies, and preoccupations in any other relations were enabled to do so in group interviews. The catalytic effect is undoubtedly charged with sexual libido and the catalyzing influence occurs on a self-selective basis. One member of a group may activate some and have little effect on others.

Mutual support among the members in groups is another factor that aids catharsis. What the individual may be afraid to verbalize when alone with a therapist, he may easily express when in a group, for he feels at one with the other members in it. Mutual support is particularly valuable in helping patients discharge hostility and aggressive feelings toward the therapist. Mutual support is analogous to group sanction and the superego demands are to a greater or lesser degree suspended by it. The individual, therefore, feels more at liberty to reveal himself and his repressed feelings. Mutual support is a factor of group morale, although it differs from it in some specific and important respects. The element of identification that is ever-present in mutual support is of immense importance in group treatment and activation of catharsis.

Universalization is still another process that favors catharsis in groups. When patients discover that others have problems similar to their own, entertain the same forbidden thoughts, and are given to unacceptable impulses, their guilts are greatly reduced. The emotional burden of each member of the group is lightened thereby, and he is able to admit to himself and others his forbidden impulses. Because other members of the group have the same phantasies and strivings of which they are ashamed and afraid they no longer have the need to employ defensive disguises, subterfuges, amenities, and facades. They no longer need to appear as paragons of righteousness and the burden the ego carries is thus lessened. Universalization must be viewed as one of the major contributing factors in activating catharsis, relaxing the patients, and accelerating the therapeutic process.

Both verbalization and action have an organic relation to the traumatic difficulties of patients and both occur through free association. Even in activity catharsis the child's and adult's actions represent an associated chain in which each act is articulated and genetically related to the preceding act. Free association is the rule in behavior as it is in speech.

In group psychotherapy, and perhaps also in other therapies, we must differentiate between free association and *associative catharsis*. In free association the patient brings forth emotions and thoughts in a vertical direction, as it were, leading toward earlier traumata. Frequently thoughts and feelings do not take such a direction. They are likely to be more lateral, that is, deal with more immediate problems and preoccupations. This is associative catharsis in which correlative contemporaneous events come to mind because of their bearing on the event or situation with which the patients may be concerned at the time. This may or may not always lead him back to the past and he may rather deal with the situations and emotions in the present as they relate to the problem at hand.

The early interviews in therapy groups are always of the associative thinking type. They concern themselves with the immediate problems in the lives of the patients and the circumstances related to them. As transferences are established the discussions are likely to become more of the free association type, though even in the earlier phase there are frequently flashbacks, as it were, to the causes of difficulties.

The therapist who is acquainted with the *nuclear problems* of each of the group members can recognize when they use associative catharsis as an escape. While he cannot pursue a patient and press him to go beyond the limits of his readiness, this awareness alone helps catharsis. An effective method is to use the universalization technique, namely, make a statement that has universal application. The relevance of the generalization and the response from the other members of the group break down the defenses of the particular patient.

It cannot be assumed that free association and associative catharsis are entirely separate and mutually exclusive. They are genetically related and are both present in the verbal productions and actions of patients in groups and in individual treatment.

The therapist plays an important part in making the group interviews fruitful, though very little remains to be done by him after the initial or warming up period in this regard. The patients carry on the interviews largely on their own. But this is made possible because the therapist is present and gives the interviews direction and meaning at some critical points.

Group interviews may be undirected and desultory. Changes in topics may occur frequently, and conversations lag. The therapist understands this as either resistance, intellectual confusion, lack of clarity of a problem or of the therapeutic aim. He deals with the situation according to the needs of the group by supplying information, giving suggestions, or exploring latent emotional content. But before he can do this adequately he must be cler not only as to the state of the group, but also of the direction the group is ready or is attempting to take. Even though he cannot press the group into a special discussion or analysis, he can suggest a question upon which, in his judgment, either the group or some members in it are seeking clarification. The therapist's recognition of direction is of utmost importance. Such *directional orientation* is necessary for individual patients as well as for the group as a whole. It is usual for patients to be preoccupied with their attitudes toward themselves, parents, boyfriends, wives, husbands, children, siblings, school, sex, even though these discussions of topics may be veiled and intertwined with numerous others. The therapist needs to be aware of the umbral and penumbral preoccupations at a given moment and prevent the group from disgressing too far afield from the main aim. Frequently interviews may have direction and content, but the therapist may feel that the patients are ready to plumb deeper their problems than they are doing. In such instances he helps the group to extend their explorations and insights.

On occasion *stereotypy* sets in in groups as it also does in individual psychotherapy. One or more patients repeatedly return to the same topic. This can be viewed as a form of resistance—as a reaction to inadequately established transference, resistance to change or improvement, or a blocking due to emotional cathexis. By repeating the same material or returning to the same dream, the patients are attempting to convey to the therapist their concern or preoccupation with a special problem with which they need help. They also serve notice on the therapist that he has not understood them and that he has not met their needs in that regard. The therapist's perspicacity in such situations is of utmost importance, for his failure to respond to the needs of the group blocks catharsis, and hence, also, therapy.

CHAPTER 18

THE PHENOMENOLOGY AND DYNAMICS
OF SILENCE
(1966)

Silences in group psychotherapy are universally considered as resistance with which the therapist is inevitably confronted at one time or other during group interviews. These resistances may be induced by the group process itself or they may stem from various intrapsychic sources, such as the usual id, ego, and superego resistances. Impending limitations or inhibitions to the expression or fulfillment of id drives, threats to ego defenses, blemishes to the self-image, and invasions of superego demands tend to set up barriers to self-revelatory and self-incriminating communications which form the substance of resistance.

On a number of occasions we have, however, referred to the fact that silence in psychotherapy has a multitude of meanings. It is neither unicausal nor simple in its structure and manifestation. We have also suggested that, as in all other aspects of psychotherapy, in the phenomenon of silence as well, the *elementaristic* approach is necessary to understand it properly and deal with it effectually.

This complex phenomenon can be approached psychologically, metapsychologically, and operationally. In the first of these, silence can be considered from the point of view of its place in the psychic economy and as a function of the adaptive style of an individual; the second would translate it into metapsychological terms as to its sources in, and its relation to, libido and aggression, for example;

while the operational approach, with which the psychotherapist is most concerned, would view the phenomenon of silence in terms of its relation to the ongoing therapeutic process. However, as already indicated, the latter approach, as well, cannot ignore the tracing of sources and clarification of their meanings.

Because the present communication is an attempt at elucidating the phenomenon of silence as it relates to group psychotherapy, considerations will of necessity be limited to the operational area of the problem and its most frequent causes.

In the first place, it is common observation that silences occur on the part of individuals (and more on the part of some than others) and on the part of groups as a whole. Thus, we can classify silences as *(a)* individual and *(b)* group silences. Then again—and this is true more of individuals than it is of whole groups—silence makes its appearance under specific conditions: either when a specific subject is brought forth or because some person or persons are present. On the other hand, some members of a group are consistently on the silent side, while others are overcommunicative to the point of monopolizing the group discussions. These phenomena can present us with two distinct characteristics: namely, *(i)* selective and *(ii)* general silences.

In the first category fall those instances when recourse to silence is made because of a *specific,* though transient, reason stemming from the group interview; while into the second category—general group silence—fall silences to which no *specific* cause can be attributed when the group as a whole is involved.

We thus discern four types of silences during the course of group discussions: General Individual Silences, Selective Individual Silences, General Group Silences, and Selective Group Silences.

General Individual Silences

A nonpsychotic person who characteristically has recourse to silence may fall under one of two classifications: characterological or neurotic. In the first group fall persons who are so constituted temperamentally that verbal communication is a minimal necessity for them, as in the extreme cases of schizoid personalities; others whose identifications with silent parents were established at an early age; and still others are those who have assumed a pattern of catatonic defense due to early pressures and resulting fears. There are also the persons who due to unwise toilet training have assumed the displacement stance from below to upward, that is, verbal retention paralleling fecal retention; that is, silence can be a reaction to overwhelming repressed hostility; and it can be due to fixations at earlier levels of development.

However, the vast majority of the population who are given to silence resort to it for neurotic and counterphobic reasons. Among these are all-pervasive anxiety; generalized fear and timidity; early family constrictions; anticipation of rejection or punishment; threat to self-esteem; sexual insecurity; defective body image; fear of self-revelation;[1] and guilt.

Selective Individual Silences

In this category, silences appear when the topic under discussion either does not concern the individual or has no relevance to his current needs or preoccupations. Such silences may be caused by the fact that the content of the group's communication is beyond the individual's intelligence or level of emotional development, that is, the *factor of readiness* is absent. Selective silence also appears when the content of the communications touches or invades a *threat area* in an individual, that is, when anxiety is generated as a particularly sensitive subject is touched which the individual is emotionally unready to face himself or to expose to the view of others [61]. This silence can be subsumed under the category of unreadiness. It also falls in the category of *defensive silence*. Defensive silence, however, extends beyond these limits, for it is resorted to equally by persons in and out of groups, in the general population as well as by patients. Every individual resorts to it at different times as a defense against activating attack, losing face, revealing oneself, because of discomfort due to inevitable *group-induced* anxiety, and need for concealment; it occurs in a multitude of situations encountered in the complex world in which we live. Still another source of silence is the negative attitude of

1. Silence is not the only means of preventing self-revelation; loquaciousness is another defense against revealing significant and closely guarded affect-laden or guilt-provoking content. In psychotics this defense takes the form of word salads and babbling.

anger, spite, and resentment a situation induces. This silence comes under the headings of *acting out* and *passive resistance*.

General Group Silences

General group silences usually occur in therapy groups during initial stages in periods of heightened group-induced anxiety and the resulting fear and timidity of its members. These incidents grow less frequent after the period of acclimatization, as discomfort is diminished and the ego operations of the various members are made manifest. Prolonged contact diminishes threat and resulting caution, facilitating communication and reducing the occurrence of such defensive silences. General group silences may be caused by psychological illiteracy, that is, when topics or contents are beyond the patients' understanding and they are intellectually unable either to respond or inaugurate an interchange. General group silences represent at times a resistance phalanx to the ongoing therapeutic process, and are mobilized by a predominant negative transference feeling toward the therapist, or by prevalent general hostility or anger on the part of the group members at a given time. On the other hand, general silence often appears due to a common intense emotion or reflection (cogitation) upon a specially affect-laden feeling or significant thought. A group may also fall into a transient general silence in response to a particularly clumsy statement or act by the therapist impinging upon the transferential relation between him and the group. Then again, a group, as is true also of patients in individual psychotherapy, may sink into silence to activate a communication from the therapist. Silence may be used by patients as a tool to provoke the therapist into speaking, either as an act of hostility toward him, as a means of obtaining clarification of a problem, or to signal its readiness for an interpretation which the members fear to formulate for themselves and are hesitant to bring into the open.

Selective Group Silences

Because the nature and functions of groups are so vastly different from individuals, structurally and dynamically, incidences of selective silence are comparatively rare in groups. The differentials in the emotional development and in intellectual levels among the members militate against the appearance of such silence. A group does not have a unitary personality nor a definitive ego function as does an individual and therefore cannot *select,* as does an individual, what is appropriate or inappropriate. There are always individuals in a group who will react idiosyncratically even at the cost of discomfiture to the rest of the group.

It is conceivable, however, that some topics may be taboo to a group, especially in its initial stages. Topics such as race and religion, incest, oedipal feelings, suicide, homicide, and similar subjects may be met with silence if introduced prematurely. However, as defenses and inner threats are diminished in the process of psychotherapy, such evasions disappear. Nonetheless, it must be recognized that strong emotions, such as shock, pity for and sympathy with a fellow member, and intense anxiety, do bring on temporary silences which can be tenuously classified as selective silences.

Endogenic Versus Imposed Silences

The silences discussed so far stem from internal sources, either in individuals' psyches or due to internal dynamics of the group's inherent nature. In therapy groups, however, as is the case in all human relations and interactions, silencing efforts from others constantly occur. In therapy groups, these take the form of interruptions, changes of subject, quarrels, and verbal and sometimes physical conflicts. Negative transferential and countertransferential feelings make their appearance during the course of interviews as disagreements, interruptions, denigrations, irritation, and a multitude of other maneuvers having as their aim to cut off or silence a communication of the target persons.

Not infrequently, silencing onslaughts on the part of group members are defensive in their intent, as when a patient seeks to terminate or prevent a discussion that threatens his ego or awakens guilt in him before his defenses have been worked through in psychotherapy. At other times, efforts at silencing one patient by another stem from transferential memories of power members of the individual's early family who have prohibited or limited communication or have employed silencing strategies due to rivalrous feelings or characterological overassertiveness.

In modern family relations, the ancient adage that a child should be seen, not heard, has been replaced by the canon, "Listen to your child," which can be paraphrased as, "Let your child talk." The responsive, and therefore stimulating, human environment of the family which allows freedom to initiate and react on the part of children is a basic precondition for mental health. However, in most contemporary families extremes in permissiveness, on the one hand, and silencing, on the other, prevail. What is important to mental health is that a balance between the two be struck. Either may lead to self-alienation and social maladjustment. In one instance, excessive withdrawal and defective capacity for object relations occur, while, in the other, overaggression and domination of others are the results. In the one instance, excessive fear and timidity become the dominant traits of the individual; in the other, the oedipal and sibling rivalries, which are often at the root of loquacity, are carried over as character traits into adult relations.

Every group psychotherapist is faced with these problems at one time or another during group interviews and may be perplexed and frustrated either by the oversilent or overassertive patient. The unraveling of these character traits, therefore, becomes a major concern in the treatment of such patients. It is questionable whether these personality difficulties can be dealt with directly since the patients are usually unaware of their atypicality. Even if a degree of awareness is present, it is entirely intellectual. In the psychoneurotic patient, direct treatment of these conditions—silence or overloquaciousness—is also not possible. Treatment has to be directed toward uncovering the underlying memories and feelings of which the traits are a result; that is, the therapist must wait until the nuclear problems from which they stem are resolved and the anxieties that generate the silences are reduced or eliminated and the behavior pattern is automatically sloughed off.

Iatrogenic Sources of Silence

The part the therapist plays in inducing silence in a group needs special attention. Apart from the transferential resistances that are present in all types of psychotherapy, and particularly those that are directed toward the therapist as a person *in locus parentis* who appears to the patient to be responsible for his current discomfort and stress, the therapist's attitudes, manners, and style of conduct and communication contribute to silences in groups.

We have attempted to list and describe elsewhere [61] the multitude of sources of countertransfeence feelings on the part of a therapist and the forms they take. However, not all of them activate silence, for negative attitudes and inept activity on the therapist's part may also mobilize feelings of anger and hostility and provoke vociferous disagreement and other more or less violent responses from his patients. The conduct on the part of therapists that may throw a group into silence are *(a)* abruptness; *(b)* badly timed injection of a "shocking" explanation or interpretation (that is, when the patients are not emotionally and/or intellectually ready for it) of an affect-laden or threatening topic; *(c)* an attack on or criticism of a member of the group (which mobilizes solidarity among the patients and resentment against the therapist); *(d)* an irrelevant statement or explanation, and *(e)* manifestation of overt anger or irritation on his part.

We have elsewhere [61] attributed repeated reintroduction by the patients of a subject during group dicussions (stereotypy) as a means of communicating to the therapist his failure to help them to resolve a problem, work through a highly cathected feeling, or clear up a puzzlement. Silence also may be this type of stereotypy and have the same intent, namely, signaling to the therapist his failure to meet the group's needs. On the other hand, a significant statement or a profoundly affecting interpretation by the therapist properly offered and well-timed may result in a *silence of cogitation,* which should not be prematurely interrupted. Such silences must be allowed to yield the full measure of benefit to the patients, and in the hands of a sensitive and skillful group therapist can be the "kick-off" for most beneficial intrapatient communication and interpatient interchange, with very fruitful, soul-searching, and insight-generating outcomes.

Silence as Communication

In psychotherapy, and in life generally, silence can be a form of communication. The difficulty lies in the fact that the percipient cannot always be certain as to the latent meaning of a particular incident of silence: whether it represents resistance, defensiveness, anger, spite, agreement or disagreement, or one or more of the multitude of moods, feelings, and attitudes of which man is capable. The situation is similar to the age-old riddle of whether a bell ringing in a desert outside of human earshot is making a sound or not. There is much justification for taking the negative position. The air is replete with a vast variety of waves and movements, only a limited range of which are within the register of the human ear. A great many air waves are "heard" by other animals, such as dogs and insects, to take common examples, that do not constitute sounds to homo sapiens. Thus, it is reasonable to assume that air waves become sound only when they are perceived by an appropriate organic apparatus.

The term communication posits that there are involved a source—the communicant (which may be a representtion as well as a voice)—and a recipient. Silence, therefore, can be said to become communication only when its meaning is understood by a recipient. In the absence of such understanding, silence cannot serve the ends of communication.

The only saving grace of silence in humans as contrasted to the bell-in-the-desert phenomenon is that it is most often accompanied by facial, eye, or postural expressions which may reveal its meaning to a perceptive observer. The human face (especially the regions around the eyes and the mouth) is so constructed that it is affected by and reflects thought and feelings. The perceptive observer can garner the meaning of a silence through these physical manifestations, which are considered as part of *nonverbal* communication, a significant mechanism in human consort. However, it is of utmost importance that the percipient does not misinterpret the signals.

The correct understanding of the latent meaning of silence is particularly important in psychotherapy. An error in judgment, if verbalized by the therapist, may significantly affect the transference attitudes of patients. Patients feel that a therapist who does not *understand* cannot be of help. Therapists should aim to transmute silence into verbal communication by such strategies as nonresponsiveness (until such time that the patient spontaneously begins to speak), by asking an appropriate question (such as what the patient is thinking about or why the silence), or, when certain of the patient's feelings, by an appropriate explanation or interpretation.

Obviously, adult psychotherapy, whether group or individual, cannot be carried on totally through silence. Its matrix is verbal interaction with the therapist and/or fellow patients. Feelings, memories, and ideas must be canalized through language, thereby setting off reactions in others which form the warp and woof of psychotherapy.

On Dealing with Silence

Therapists need to distinguish the nature and intent of silences and deal with them sensitively, for, after all, spiritual enrichment and aesthetic and intellectual creativity take place in the unneutralized state of the libido in silence and are achieved mostly in isolation. In psychotherapy, as well, the alteration in the psychic structure of patients occurs in the periods of silence between sessions when the automatic reweighting of the inner forces occurs through realignment, introspection, and self-examination. However, these are not the exclusive services of silences, for, as already shown, they may be of *negative* intent. We underscore the word negative because it is so only in a restricted sense. When silence is a means for interruption and blocking communication, it is negative in relation to the ongoing therapeutic process. However, from the point of view of dynamic psychotherapy, such maneuvers are the warp and woof of its process and are part of the therapeutic grist. The very phenomenon of silence needs to become the subject of a group's examination. Not infrequently, the resulting discussion of the reason for a group's silence may prove to be the beginning of fruitful uncovering of unconscious and preconscious feeling-attitudes and help resolve deeply embedded early traumata.

In this, the therapist's initiative is the leverage, for he may face the group, and occasionally even an individual member, with the temporary muteness and restraint and help trace their sources and services. However, the therapist needs to exercise utmost caution here. He must be fully cognizant of the meaning of a specific silent episode and take appropriate steps in accordance with his understanding. In dealing with silence, he must be more vigilant than in responding to verbal communications, for through silence an individual often defends sensitive areas of his being which he is unready to make common property. The clumsy or rough invasion of these threat areas shocks the individual and may destroy the positive transference toward the therapist.

A therapist cannot expect patients to function outside and beyond the nature and resources of their idiosyncratic temperaments and psychic states. The naturally withdrawn or schizoid adult or the one whose diffidence stems from early identifications (and has, therefore, become a deeply ingrained life style) cannot be expected to embark on a career of loquaciousness, any more than a leopard can change his spots. Such a person may become, to a degree, more communicative as the neurotic elements are worked through or by means of the process of reidentification which occurs in groups as well as in individual psychotherapy. But we cannot expect such a person to burst forth with volubility. His characterological idiosyncrasies cannot be violated without doing damage to him and to his relationship with the therapist.[2]

Again, when the therapist perceives an episode of general silence in a group as a period of cogitation or as the effect of a deeply felt experience, event, or communication, he needs to remain passive until the silence is broken by one of the group members. In periods of such affectivity, the anxiety generated always propels some member to seek escape in verbalization or, as sometimes occurs, in counterphobic, spontaneous outbursts of laughter.

On the other hand, when the silence represents a phalanx of resistance or hostility toward the therapist (depending upon the state of the *basic* transference of the group toward him), he may find it advisable to face the group as a whole with their prevalent attitude and interpret the prevailing transference feelings. This can be done by direct confrontation or by an appropriate question as to the reason or meaning of the silence. The first strategy involves the therapist's interpretation of the underlying transferential feelings; the second would serve as a kick-off for a fruitful exploration by the patients of their own feelings. The latter usually leads to awakening significant memories of early traumata and current stresses.

A therapist needs to be vigilant to silences on the part of individuals

---

2. The numerous reports of mental breakdowns and suicides in the early stages of the so-called "encounter groups" were the result of imposition, by the leader and the group, of conduct, especially communication, beyond the patients' ego capacities and superego tolerances. See [15].

or groups that result from limited intellectual capacities, low comprehension, or çonstitutional or neurotic emotional flatness. In such instances, he needs to trim his therapeutic sails to these permanent (or transient) limitations so as not to overwhelm his patients and force them into even further withdrawal into silence as a refuge.

CHAPTER 19

SOURCES OF COUNTERTRANSFERENCE AND GROUP-INDUCED ANXIETY
(1953)

Countertransference is always one of the major concerns of the psychotherapist. Patients are ever aware of and responsible to him as a person, to his attitudes, feelings, and overt and covert reactions. This awareness delimits the effectiveness of the therapeutic effort and determines the conditions for success or failure. The patient registers the psychotherapist's emotional state, preoccupations, worries, and frustrations. His feelings of elation, pleasure, sadness, and discouragement with regard to therapeutic events, as well as matters outside the treatment room, do not pass unnoticed by the ever-vigilant and easily affected patients. Because of this effect of his thoughts, moods, and responses upon them, and upon the treatment process as a whole, the therapist must be aware of himself, his attitudes and feelings.

Ideally—and this is more of a wish than an actuality—the psychotherapist should be completely neutral and devoid of feelings about either the patient or the outcome of treatment. Actually this is impossible and its desirability doubtful. The psychotherapist, being human, cannot be completely detached and impersonal, for patients feel uncomfortable under such circumstances. The patient has to feel that the therapist is interested in him and that he is ready to help him. Without this the patient would not be able to establish positive transference feelings toward the therapist, and the treatment, as a result, would bog down.

The intensity of feelings is largely determined by the nature of the therapy. In a thoroughgoing psychoanalysis where the analyst is not within the patient's visual range, and contact between the two is almost nil, detachment can be much greater than in other types of therapy. Where psychotherapy is carried on in a face-to-face position, where the transference is not as regressive, excessive detachment on the part of the therapist may alienate the patient. He must feel the therapist's interest in him or he would become chilled into resistance, anger, and incommunicability. It is to indicate this important contrast that I have suggested the terms of unilateral, bilateral, and multi-lateral transference relations in psychotherapy [11, 57 p. 214].

The therapist is the object of the patient's libidinal strivings; he is also the target of hostile and love feelings that are associated with them. It is impossible for one, no matter how objective, to remain entirely unaffected by them. Having been born of woman, having had a father, and having passed through other innumerable experiences of human relations in and out of the home, he cannot remain completely unaffected. Like all humans, he too is subject to prejudice and preference, he responds to beauty and charm in his female patients and feels uncomfortable in the face of overt hostility and aggression. The difference is in degree only. I believe it was Freud who commented that both the patient and the analyst are neurotic; only the latter is less so.

Hence, all one can count on is that the therapist has worked through his problems, that he is aware of his condition and processes and that his impulses are under better control. We cannot assume that he is completely free of the cravings, strivings, and conflicts from which his patients suffer. We can only expect a lesser intensity. Whether he is aware of it or not, he reacts differently to the different personalities of his patients and to the same patient at different times largely because of their resemblance to people who had affected him favorably or unfavorably in the past and, therefore, arouse in him emotions associated with these memories. Such reflex emotions are not within the purview or control of the conscious. They are autonomous. Few are free of early images and inadequately repressed memories. However, the intensity of reactions in an integrated person is less than in the average and certainly should be less in the therapist than in the patient, for in him they are more accessible to the conscious. Neither is the therapist free of a desire to be successful in his efforts and to achieve therapeutic results. Even though he recognizes that he should not have such aims, he cannot fully divest himself of the understandably human frailty—the desire to achieve and to succeed.

I have elsewhere described the types of countertransference as being of three categories: *positive, negative* and *aim attachment*. A fourth type has been since suggested by Loeffler[1] which he designates as *ambivalent* or *inconsistent* countertransference.

Sources of Positive Countertransference

Positive countertransference manifests itself when the therapist has a favorable and friendly attitude toward a specific patient or when he prefers some patients in a group. Such attitudes can arise from a number of sources. One of these is the therapist's own ego-ideal that the patient may represent. Positive countertransference may arise from memories the therapist has of individuals in his past who have been particularly positive, friendly, and preferred by him. These may also be members of his family, friends, or teachers, for whom he may have had feelings of a libidinal nature.

Positive countertransference may also arise from the therapist's need to be liked by his patients and he may therefore exert himself to be accepted. Though this need usually springs from an underlying negative emotional base, it is disguised in a facade of kindness or a benevolent manner. A therapist may also fall into the trap of a positive countertransference when a patient makes gratifying progress in treatment either through the motive of submission or by actual improvement. Some patients in groups help accelerate or support the therapeutic effort which accords with the therapist's intention and aim. Thus, by playing into the therapist's need, they reduce his anxiety and he may become selectively well disposed toward such patients either out of gratefulness or because of a feeling of success or relief. A more subtle method of activating countertransference frequently is the

---

1. Solomon, A., Loeffler, F.J., and Frank, G.A. (1953). An analysis of co-therapist interaction in group psychotherapy, *International Journal of Group Psychotherapy* 3:171–180.

patient's manner. This is particularly true where the therapist is male and the patient female.

Femininity and charm may throw the therapist off balance and cause him to respond in a way that may affect the relation adversely. This is particularly deleterious in groups. One of the more obvious of the difficulties that it begets is sibling rivalry. Negative feelings on the part of other patients are activated toward the "preferred child" and toward the "partial" parent figure. Such attitudes on the part of patients toward a fellow group member and the therapist may create serious difficulties in the therapeutic climate. The climate may become more or less permanently hostile preventing adequate catharsis leading to change in the patients and to their improvement. Such hostile reactions can be used in the therapeutic grist only when the cause is fantasied. When there is the reality factor, namely, the therapist's real preference of some patient to others, interpretation cannot be effective. Interpretation of negative sibling transferences of this order (as a repetition of early childhood jealousies and hostilities) are of great value, but they must not be confirmed in reality in the therapeutic setting. The actual existence of a situation buttresses the latent hostile feelings toward the therapist, and the patients as a group may become so negativistic as to make restoration of a relaxed atmosphere (antinodal period), necessary for therapy, difficult or impossible.

This should not be taken to mean that a therapy group has to maintain a balanced and friendly atmosphere. Rather, groups, as individual patients, must become hostile, aggressive, and disturbed. Such "acting out" of infantile feelings, the replica of childhood, are activated and interpreted. It is these vestiges of the past that produce current difficulties and must be dealt with by bringing them out into the open with associated emotions which are worked through. However, such negativism and hostility (nodal periods) have to be alternated with relaxed (antinodal) periods.

Countertransferences are conveyed by the therapist also in more subtle ways, for feelings are conveyed by the slightest of gestures, facial grimace or contortion, bodily posture, changes in the expression of the eyes, and even thoughts which patients quickly and unerringly register.

Sources of Negative Countertransference

There are greater possibilities for negative countertransferences in group psychotherapy than those of a positive character. The painful memories aroused in the therapist by a variety of patients are always likely to activate in him either conscious or unconscious feelings of discomfort, fear, hostility or anger, in relation to one or more persons in a group. Some may resemble parents, siblings, teachers or others who had hurt or injured him or had in some other way made him feel unhappy in childhood. Unless he is thoroughly aware of his own feelings or has had a thoroughgoing psychoanalysis, he may react negatively to such patients.

Memories of childhood are not the sole sources of negative countertransference. Another source is the patients' resistance to treatment or their antagonism to the therapist as a person. This form of negative transference is more difficult to deal with in a group than in individual treatment. In the latter, where the relation is between the patient and the therapist, resistances can be dealt with directly through interpretation, or the therapist may remain passive until the patient himself becomes uncomfortable and breaks through it. In a group, feelings and attitudes are contagious and are intensified. Resistance on the part of one patient is usually taken on by others, thus interfering with the therapeutic process and with consequent frustration to the therapist.

Frustration inevitably produces reactions and unless the therapist is capable of a high degree of detachment, it arouses emotions which are registered by the patients. Interference with reaching a goal is always disturbing. We shall discuss this situation at greater length when we go further into the question of aim attachment. Here we can only say that the goal for the therapist is to keep the group going, as it were, so that he feels successful. When this is threatened by patients through hostility or resistance, counterfeelings toward the patients are understandably aroused. These are conveyed by subtle means already described, as well as by change of voice, cutting off a particular patient, by impatience, or manifest or repressed anger. This type of countertransference is easily observable and more obvious among teachers than among psychotherapists.

Teachers prefer bright pupils and those who fit into their need for submissiveness, passing examinations, and attaining high marks. Without realizing it they frequently become punitive and rejecting of those of their pupils who fail in these and similar respects, because they do not yield the teacher gratifications of success, achievement and goal attainment. Conversely, because the failing student represents resistance to the teacher's efforts and the frustration of his goals, his negative feelings toward such pupils are aroused. While in therapy we cannot expect such feelings to be as intense, nor their expression as obvious, the underlying emotional trends are still of the same nature. It is therefore necessary that psychotherapists be aware of such emotions and not fall prey to them.

Another danger of negative countertransference lies in the reaction of members of the group to the therapist. We have seen how the therapists's positive feelings toward a patient activate negative sibling transferences to him and toward the therapist as a parent substitute. In the case of negative feeling they, too, would be turned against him, because he then becomes the punitive, rejecting parent. This is well demonstrated by a boy aged ten years, whose younger brother, six years old, was preferred by the mother. She disliked her older son and treated him punitively. Despite his preferred state, the younger child once told her that he was afraid that some day she would turn against him as she had turned against his older brother.[2]

Similarly, in group psychotherapy, patients may feel that once a therapist is abrupt, critical, or sarcastic, or ignores one of them, he may some day treat others in a like manner. As a result they become disturbed, suspicious, uncomfortable and even hostile toward him. This occurs for a number of reasons. One is that, as in the case of the child just quoted, they feel that he may turn on them as well. Another is the discovery that the therapist is weak, has little self-control, and is a victim of prejudices and other such feelings as they are themselves. He therefore no longer represents the ego-ideal of the strong parental figure, and a model of identification so important in all types of therapy, guidance and counseling. It also buttresses their latent hostility toward him and fulfills their desire to see him as inadequate.

---

2. This confirms the validity of my insistence that no child be punished or rejected in activity therapy groups. Even justifiable and desirable restraint would stigmatize the adult as a punitive person, whose punitiveness may turn upon the others as well.

In their fear that he may attack them, just as he had attacked one of their number, they turn against him before he can reject them.

Still another reason why such negative countertransference toward a patient may arouse feelings of negativism toward the therapist on the part of the group lies in the basic identification of each member with siblings against the parent figure who is their common enemy. This is a survival of family attitudes where children identify with one another in their suffering and unite against the parents for mutual protection and support.

Countertransference feelings may also arise when the therapist feels he is being displaced by an aggressive patient who is in rivalry with him. Such patients talk out of turn, take over the management of the group, interpret impulsively the statements of others, and generally attempt to manage the group interviews. This may affect the therapist in a number of ways. He may become rivalrous of, or resentful with, the particular patient, or he may become discouraged because the patient's influence may have an unfavorable effect upon the therapeutic interviews. Such aggression on the part of a patient may result in the eventual disintegration or termination of the group. The therapist's anxiety in relation to this may make him terse or impatient with the offending group member, which too may change the image of him as a positive parental figure and a strong person.

As in individual treatment, countertransferences can also set in through the communication of patients by virtue of the therapist's own association to a specific situation in the interview. A therapist's mind may ruminate at certain points in the interview because a particular subject or situation discussed activates memories from which he has not freed himself. Frequently, in therapy, one finds oneself mulling over a statement or a description of a situation and going off into one's own reveries, as a chain reaction, losing touch with what goes on in the group interview. These thoughts are an indication of the therapist's inadequate freedom from his own past disturbing and traumatic experiences.

As in all other relations, negative countertransferences can also be a reaction to positive impulses toward a patient. Sexual attraction that a therapist may feel toward a given patient may cause him to prefer him or her, to act with special consideration, or conversely, to react by withdrawal or by ignoring that patient as a defensive measure.

Sometimes it may be expressed defensively in humorous or sarcastic remarks. Therapists must be constantly on guard against these very subtle and indirect ways of revealing themselves. Since they occur as a result of deeply unconscious strivings—both his impulsions toward, and flight from—a patient may be purely autonomous and unconscious reactions that the following illustrates.

In one of my seminars on analytic group psychotherapy, a psychiatrist reported on one of his female patients. She had had difficulty in her sexual adjustment with her husband, always remained ungratified and unable to have an orgasm in the past. As a result of treatment, she had grown able to enjoy sexual intercourse. The doctor then became aware of feelings of disappointment and resentment because of this change in his young and very attractive patient. Evidently he had unconscious urges toward her which, without realizing it, he had hoped in the deepest recesses of his unconscious to be able to consummate sometime. It is also possible that the therapist may himself have had some difficulty in his sexual adjustment with his wife and had become jealous of the patient's husband who now was being gratified. It is such subtle manifestations of countertransference for which the therapist must be constantly on the alert. He may have to seek help for himself by further psychoanalysis to overcome the conditions that bring about these feelings. It is significant that when the psychiatrist narrated the above situation to the seminar group, he suddenly stopped and asked, "Well, where do I go from here?" At this, the other members of the seminar burst into loud laughter, apparently perceiving his conflict and embarrassment.

It has been also reported to me by others that they observed definite homosexual trends on the part of psychotherapists in groups, who have behaved in the interviews in a manner that disturbed patients. This can be considered as a form of countertransference, in addition to the personality unfitness of the therapist to function in that role.

In Activity Group Therapy particularly there is an abundance of possibilities for arousing countertransference feelings. The hyperactivity of the members of the group, their unbridled aggression, lack of consideration of and destructiveness toward the environment and each other, and not infrequent manifestations of cruelty, overtaxes the tolerance of the average person. Free acting out, boisterousness and destructiveness, cannot but outrage the sensibilities of the ordinary adult and arouse anger and resentment. In the initial stages all therapists find these groups both emotionally and physically exhausting because of the self-restraint that they are called upon to exercise. It is difficult to endure the seeming insensitivity that the children in these groups frequently manifest. They present the therapist with a heavy emotional load. Therapists in activity groups require support from the supervisor. They have to be helped to understand the meaning of the manifestations in these groups and accept the fact that they are exacerbations of emotional tensions under which the children live. Aggressive behavior can be compared to temperature rise in medical patients and has to be viewed and accepted as such. This understanding and emphasis is essential as a preventive of countertransference feelings that such behavior inevitably arouses in the average individual. The therapist has to guard himself as well against overintense sympathy and compassion with victims of the group's aggressiveness.

Aim Attachment as Countertransference

The third type of countertransference I described is aim attachment. The pursuit of goals is part of the human psyche. Effort must have a goal. This is not only characteristic of man but also of all organic life, for all organisms pursue goals. The difference between the goals of other animals and those of man lies in their complexity and variety. The goals of lower animals are all directed toward physical survival as individuals and as a species. All activity is directed toward that aim.

Although one can say that in the last analysis the goals of man are very much the same, their manifestations are more complex, due to his psychic organization, his capacity to abstract, symbolize, and distort, and especially because of his need for psychological and social survival in addition to physical survival. Being a member of a group, particularly of one with moral sanctions, creates numerous responses and needs of which other animals are devoid. Man is subject to the same laws as are lower animals and more so because psychological goals are frequently more urgent and more imperative than physical survival, which is to a large extent secured by society as it is now constituted. It is therefore understandable that the therapist, whether he is aware of it or not, would be pleased when he is successful, and dissatisfied when his patients do not improve.

The need to be successful proceeds from a number of causes. One is the positive effect it has on the self-image, namely, the perception that one is adequate and potent. Another was expressed by a psychotherapist in one of my seminars when he said, "There is one aspect of success and failure in therapy that we ought to recognize and that is there are times when the patient is about to fail, not because of anything that we did or did not do, but because the nature of the patient's problem is such that he is not accessible to treatment at a given time." This he thought inevitable. "However," he continued, "our need to succeed is not a part of our relation to the patient. Nor is it tied up with the patient himself. Rather frequently it is necessary for us, for our own personal survival, to see that our patients improve. If we are in private practice we know that patients who improve will send us other patients. If we work in hospitals or institutions, we want to prove ourselves adequate to our superiors, for they have the power to pass upon our qualifications and to assure our continuance in our jobs and promotion. These external needs for success are one of the great sources of what we have been discussing here, namely aim attachment, but are important, nonetheless."

Such external sources of aim attachment must be considered very seriously in our present-day society. It is difficult to be completely detached under these circumstances, for we cannot ignore the imperatives of economic survival. Another major element that motivates human effort is the impelling need to overcome ever-present feelings of inferiority and inadequacy that are part and parcel of the human psyche. They are inescapable because the child, being small and living in a world of adults more capable of achieving things which he himself craved, develops an image of himself as weak and inadequate. This is further increased during the oedipal period that emphasizes his sexual unacceptability and impotence which grows even more acute during adolescence. These and other feelings are always present in one and cannot be entirely eradicated by any known method. Hence, the therapist who fails in improving patients cannot but suspect his own inadequacy as being the cause. This is a real problem for the psychotherapist which can be only decreased in intensity by a thoroughgoing psychoanalysis.

Aim attachment may arise through the therapist's need, for his own security, to set an aim and a direction for a patient or a group, or through his failure to perceive the needs of his patients or the meaning of the latent content of their productions. Some therapists set definite objectives to attain, either in a given interview or in the total treatment process. In some instances this may be correct. The incidence of error is increased when directing or steering the patients is planned in advance. Impressions and problems in the intervening periods between interviews may alter needs. Relevance and immediacy are equally essential for individual and for group interviews.

Another source of aim attachment is the desire to be accepted and liked by patients. This is an anomalous factor in psychotherapy. On the one hand one should be liked by his patients, especially in certain settings, or they would not come for treatment. This is particularly true in social service agencies and outpatient clinics in hospitals. Basic positive transference on the part of patients is essential for sound and promising psychotherapy, but positive transference is valuable only when it spontaneously arises from the therapeutic relation and not when the therapist makes a bid for it.

In my *Introduction to Group Therapy* [53], published in 1943, but written some four or five years before, I specified that a major qualification for an activity group therapist is that he "must not have the need to be liked by children," for such a need is a result of dependency, feelings of inadequacy and insecurity of which patients quickly take advantage. It also connotes ego weakness and therefore deprives the patients of ego support and an adequate object of identification. When patients recognize the psychotherapist's weaknesses and neurotic needs, they will attack and seek to destroy him in their effort to eliminate these weaknesses in themselves. In a group, particularly, negative urges are readily mobilized and intensified which frequently results in the dissolution of groups.

The case in point is that of a group psychotherapist who was persistently challenged by his group and questioned as to the validity of his technique. He attempted repeatedly to explain himself to the group. Apparently his insecurities had been activated by his patients' reactions to him and he proceeded to impress them with his educational background, knowledge, experience, and achievements, even listing some of his publications. One of the patients described it as follows: "I swing between loving and hating him and when I make a demand on him he 'throws the book at me.' If he could only understand what I and the others in the group are after, he would not have to impress us so much; besides it does not do any good anyway."

Apparently the therapist, instead of interpreting the negative transference of his patients and thereby helping their emotional maturity, allowed his own feelings of inadequacy to take precedence. In this state of countertransference he blindly began to boast and seek to impress his patients with his importance, so as to be accepted by them. This is one example of countertransference toward a group as a whole, its effect in blocking the therapeutic process and causing disappointment to patients.

Another type of aim attachment which I have elsewhere briefly touched upon [57] emanates from research studies of the therapeutic process while it takes place. I have indicated that when the therapist has an aim other than treating the patients, his judgments and responses must of necessity be affected. His preoccupation with the significance of communications, other than as they relate to the treatment itself, cannot but interfere with free-floating attention to the patients' verbal and nonverbal communications. It also affects his responses and interpretations. Divided interest is inevitably registered by patients; in addition, the therapist is likely to overlook or misjudge developments in the group. The attempt to study and analyze material while treatment is in progress may bias the therapist to pursue the interviews so as to obtain specific material for his research rather than follow the free association of his patients. Psychotherapists, whether individual or group, should avoid seeking specific material or study on a research basis current developments. This is better done in retrospect, after the conclusion of treatment. This leaves the therapist free to give himself to the therapeutic process itself without interference from secondary or peripheral interests. Division of aim vitiates the process and affects negatively the therapist's function. It certainly would affect the transference relation with the patients and his free-floating attention. Research in group psychotherapy, as well as in all psychotherapy for that matter, should not be carried on by the therapist simultaneously with the treatment. It should be the task of persons other than the therapist or be pursued by him after the termination of treatment.

The dramatic demonstration of divided interest has recently come to my attention, when a group therapist attempted to carry out a role assigned to her other than that of therapist. This was a group conducted in a child guidance clinic setting. The administration required that definite information be obtained concerning the individual patients in the group, in this case, adolescent girls. A combination of circumstances had arisen in which the therapist's countertransference feelings were aroused when the group became disorganized and hilarious. This was the result of both their temporary hostility toward the therapist and her failure to understand a remark made by one of the girls. In this state of disturbance the therapist proceeded to tell the girls what the agency expected from them and that they were required to submit to individual interviews to get their background histories. Not one of the patients returned and the group disbanded.

Although there are a number of other elements operating in the dissolution of this group, one of the major ones was that she stepped out of her role as therapist to represent the administration of the clinic. A divided role is always a risk to the therapeutic relation between patient and therapist, and it is particularly bad in a situation where patients perceive countertransference feelings on the part of the therapist, as was the case here.

Aim attachment in relation to patients as individuals and also to the group as a whole is, therefore, one of the very important sources of countertransference. The failure of patients to improve arouses frustration and tests the therapist's frustration tolerance. It may be expressed as a negative, hostile, orally destructive, authoritarian drive. It may also arise from positive feelings toward patients, as well as from the need of the therapist to be successful, his insecurity concerning his own skill, and the need for assuring himself of his ability as a therapist, or from some other ulterior motive.

Ambivalent Countertransference

The concept of ambivalent or inconsistent countertransference is a useful one. However, ambivalent countertransference consists of no more or less than successive alternations of positive and negative countertransferences toward a patient or a group. It arises from the therapist's own basic ambivalent attitudes and unresolved feelings. The inability to steer a consistent emotional course through one's reactions to situations, whether comforting or disappointing, is a problem in the ego organization of the therapist rather than the therapeutic situation. It is an outcome of a personal ambivalent syndrome and instability that would render the therapist unsuitable to function effectively.

Countertransference Toward Group as a Whole

The therapist's need to exert authority over a group as a result of his own earlier experiences is another source of countertransference. It is a reaction formation to dependency which usually stems from identification with an authoritarian parental figure. The therapist may insist that the group pursue a definite goal or he may set problems for the group to discuss. This procedure is characteristic of a number of "repressive," didactic, and directive techniques. As a matter of fact, techniques are preferred by psychotherapists because of the nature of their countertransferences; that is, their needs and attitudes toward patients determine the type of therapy they prefer or choose. Thus an anxious or shy person may adopt a passive role or he may be overactive as a reaction formation. When these patterns of function are a result of unconscious psychic states of the therapist rather than deliberately planned for therapeutic results, they are obviously undesirable.

Thus, an examination of the techniques employed by different psychotherapists, would reveal their origin and preferences as stemming from their peculiar countertransferences which in turn have their root in character structure, ego organization, or neurotic difficulties. Psychotherapists, no matter how well prepared for group therapy, are not free of their share of hostility, aggression, guilt, fear, insecurity, and anxiety.

Group-Induced Anxiety

Our second major interest in this communication deals with group-induced anxiety, which, in my opinion, is one of the chief sources of countertransference in group psychotherapy. All groups evoke anxiety in all people. No person can be in a group without feeling anxious, even though the group may be one to which he is accustomed. The degree of anxiety is diminished with acquaintance and length of membership in it. However, no person feels as comfortable in a group as he does with one individual. An individual is seldom as threatening as is a group, where anxiety is always present. This is caused by one of three factors or a combination of them.

Biologically, members of the same group, whether human or non-human, are a threat to one another. Though groups are a protection against danger and favor survival, they are also sources of considerable tension to the individuals constituting them. Observations on other animals show that while they tend, by the "instinct" of gregariousness and need for security, to seek the proximity of one another, periodically there arise sudden combats between individuals in a flock or herd. Although congregates yield security for physical survival and are a protection against danger for each, rivalries for food or the acquisition of a mate always arise. Antipathies arise quite spontaneously, and frequently for unexplained reasons, among other animals as well as people. Causes for some of these antipathies are sometimes apparent, such as striking differences, membership of different subspecies, organic defect or ailment. The atypical member of a flock or herd is subject to cruel attacks that frequently result in the death of the individual.

Among humans these reactions are vastly more complex, but are nonetheless present. The combative engram is present in each member of every group which is a common source of anxiety. In humans the anxiety may be even more intense since each is in rivalry with every other, overtly or covertly, for status, recognition, and acceptance. Anticipated rejection by a group is a source of fear and anxiety to everyone, and the fear of being slighted, criticized, attacked or humiliated is ever present.

Anxiety in human groups also stems from earlier family relations. Attitudes and responses toward groups are replicas of family experiences. Every group, particularly small groups, represent in the unconscious of the individual his family, and he inevitably acts out the primary relations in them. He who had to be aggressive in order to get attention and psychologically survive in his family, or had to ingratiate himself with parents and to submit, will repeat these patterns in other groups. The derivative hostilities and aggressions that accompany such adjustments are implicit in all group relations.

Groups, therefore, threaten each member because he is perennially in a state of expectation of attack, rejection, rivalry, and aggression.

Still another source of group-induced anxiety is the uncertainty of the ego functioning of the individuals in it. While one can be to some extent certain as to the ego function and reactions of an individual, one never feels as certain of him when he is a member of a group. Neither can one be as secure of a number of people in interpersonal reaction as of an individual. In a group, the people present create a factor of unpredictability as to how any one or all may act.

An element that creates uncertainty as to the ego functioning of group members proceeds from the universally observable fact that ego functioning of individuals is altered by a group. Behavior of an individual with whom one is well acquainted and whose reactions are known frequently surprises one when he is observed in groups. Many feelings and responses untouched in individual relations are set off by groups. Anxiety and insecurity are intensified, aggressions and hostilities enhanced, fear and withdrawal set in, which are either less intense or altogether unobservable in individual relations. The drives toward domination, submission trends, the bid for status and acceptance are activated by groups as substitutes for the family. Members of groups being subject to anxiety, react in an unexpected manner and in ways that threaten others. There is, therefore, set up a network of mutually induced anxieties and fears.

Some of the dynamic manifestations that occur in groups are those of induction, interstimulation, infection or contagion, mutual identification, rivalry, and neutralization. The ego controls of each member of the group are greatly reduced and partially invested in the group which takes over these controls. Superego restraints are diminished in each member, since the group is invested with the sanctions and prohibitions relative to his behavior, which is ordinarily exercised by the internalized superego. These dynamics create innumerable currents of tension and anxiety to which the therapist is subject. He, too, is caught up in this vortex of feelings.

As a matter of fact, therapists with experience in individual treatment only, where they are more or less fully in control and know the ego functioning of their individual patients, are subject to considerable fear and insecurity in groups. This fear is aroused by their own reactions to groups, by the unpredictability of the ego functioning of the patients and the group phalanx, as well as by their inexperience in dealing with a number of patients who reinforce one another. They may also feel uncomfortable as to their inadequacy for dealing with groups. It is my conviction that the use of "auxiliary therapists," "co-therapists," and "observers" stems from this insecurity. The presence of another person on whose support the therapist can count gives him greater ease and security with the group.

Group-induced anxiety produces various defensive reactions on the part of the therapist. He either withdraws and becomes "over-cautious" and thus overlooks opportunities for interpretation and appropriate direction of the group interviews, or he may become overactive and domineering as a defense against his timidity or fear. The timidity that all therapists experience at the beginning of group treatment usually wears off in time. They grow more secure through success and through discovering themselves adequate for the task. However, in many instances, timidity persists for a long time as demonstrated by the fact that some continue in their use of "auxiliary therapists" and "observers."

Thus we see that the psychotherapist is subject to id impulses, to anxiety when his ego defenses are threatened and in some instances also when his superego is strained. Feelings of inadequacy and defects in the self-image, of which no one is entirely free, are enhanced in groups, and the therapist, because of his own needs to be accepted and to rise to his proper status, is subject to varying degrees of uncertainty and anxiety which affect his functioning. Fear of losing face is increased in a group situation, because antagonism and hostility toward him as a parent figure are mobilized and intensified.

The psychotherapist is not free of personal preferences and sexual urges. Other personal responses already enumerated interfere with his free-floating and relaxed attention. The difference is only in their intensity and therefore the degree of interferences. But this difference is of utmost importance. They are present even in thoroughly analyzed therapists as they are in those who had no personal analysis. Because of the face-to-face position of the patient and therapist, interferences are more likely to arise and are stronger in other psychotherapies than in psychoanalysis.

CHAPTER 20

TRANSFERENCE PHENOMENA
(1950)

The major dynamic in all psychotherapy is the transference relation between the patient and therapist. This element in the therapeutic process has been vaguely recognized even among the ancients and more clearly so in recent years. When Socrates recognized the existence of mental disturbances apart from physical illness, he prescribed "sweet words," as a cure. We now hear about the "bedside manner" and of the "therapeutic personality." The fact is commonly recognized that some persons are more able to evoke a friendly response than do others, and that physicians and psychotherapists possess these qualities to varying degrees. In practice one finds patients with whom a particular therapist cannot establish a workable relation at all, while they are attracted almost instantaneously to another.

The initial empathy a patient feels toward the prospective therapist is as good a guarantee of success in psychotherapy as one can have. The fact that during treatment there may arise negative feelings and hostility toward him does not detract from the basic soundness of the therapeutic relation. The persisting original sympathetic attitudes of the patient will help to sustain him during these negative phases, however.

When the patient comes for treatment he tests the therapist against the unconscious and conscious attitudes he acquired before and during the oedipal confict. These can be direct reflections of the parental image, they can be a distortion of the real parent, or a negation of him. He may desire the therapist to be fully or partially like his parent, or the very opposite. This preference is determined by how successfully the patient has repressed his incestuous drives toward the father or mother, and whether he has built up supplementary, confirmatory, or negative images in later life. He may have added images to those of the real parent that he had for some reason found desirable.

These are among the reasons why some patients readily respond to one therapist and cannot accept another. Rapport is probably rooted in the resemblance of the therapist to earlier images which the patient unconsciously recognizes or, better still, perceives. The initial and automatic response is an instantaneous reliving of emotions experienced in the past through the person who evokes pleasant or painful feelings. These early experiences determine the establishment of object relations generally.

The relation described here has the quality of identification as well as of transference. This type of transference can be characterized as *identification transference* as differentiated from the *libidinal transference*. In group psychotherapy, identification transference is particularly important since it extends to the other members of the group as siblings.

A type of transference that is evident in group treatment is that which originates in sibling relations. Psychoanalysts have observed that their patients feel jealous of other patients and of the analyst's family. In addition to the fact that there is sexual libido involved in this reaction, there is also present the desire to be the only child; not to share the therapist. In individual therapy, the therapist can prevent the patient's meeting face-to-face such "rivalrous" persons. In group psychotherapy such separation is obviously impossible. The therapist, as well as the patients, have to face this situation as a result of the compresence of a number of patients.

Patients who have not adequately worked through sibling rivalries in their earlier family life reveal it unmistakenly in groups. They employ all sorts of direct and devious ways to monopolize the therapist, to hold the center of the stage, and to command the attention of the therapist and the other members. Usually the compulsive—neurotic and narcissistic individuals—"act out" in this manner. Their persistence and domination is accepted by some and resented by others. The latter respond by either challenging or cruelly pursuing the culprit through prying questions, arguments, and attack. The responses of the various members of the group are determined by their early sibling relations. Because of their narcissistic identification, the members who have themselves suffered through sibling rivalry are likely to come to the support of the "victim," while those who have had the upper hand in the past join in the torment. These attitudes, however, are influenced by a variety of other circumstances besides earlier sibling rivalries.

In groups, transference of various types may lead to mutual support, to discharge of resentment, or to evoke guilt feelings. The characteristic subgroups and clusters that develop within the larger group serve a definite purpose for each. The weak and frightened seek the support of those they feel can understand them and with whom they feel rapport. Others whose sibling attitudes are antagonistic may attach themselves to one another because of sadomasochistic cravings, while still another type of patient forces a fellow patient to admit infractions and impulses of which he himself feels guilty. This type of transference we designate as *sibling transference.*

The sibling attitudes of rivalry, jealousy, domination, submission, and deceit make their appearance. They are manifested in the patients' relation to one another, even though in most instances they are a reflection of attitudes toward the therapist as a parent substitute. Likes and dislikes of members of a group are important to each patient involved, but are even more so since they affect the group atmosphere.

We have found that in analytic group psychotherapy,[1] initial antipathy and antagonisms do not deter the final emergence of positive transferences among members to the same extent as they do in children's activity groups, where no interpretation is given or insight encouraged. The explanation of the contrasts in the two types of groups may lie in the fact that the therapist's neutrality and relative emotional inactivity in the latter leave the children more on their own and aggressions are, therefore, under control to a lesser extent. In interview groups, negative feelings may be expressed directly toward the therapist, which is not the case in activity groups since the

1. Play group therapy for preschool children, activity-interview for selected children in latency, and inteview groups for adolescents and adults.

therapist's neutrality does not activate them and substitute targets have to be found, namely, the other patients or objects in the physical environment. Proper grouping of patients, therefore, is even more important in activity groups than in the others.

The patients adopt the therapist *in loco parentis* and the therapeutic relation frees repressed libidinal and aggressive cravings toward him. The early drives toward the parents and resentment to their frustrations are naturally redirected toward the therapist. This is the inevitable outcome of the dynamics of repression and therapy. When the nucleus of a repressed constellation is affected, the associated emotional vectors in the syndrome are activated. Thus, when the therapist is accepted as the parent symbol, the related positive and negative feelings come to the fore as well as the latent covert strivings associated with the parent. The therapist, then, becomes the recipient of love and hate, and at once the libidinal object and the frustrating agent.

If the therapist is a person of the opposite sex, the neurotic patient, especially, wishes to make him or her the sexual object and have a child by him. If the latter is of the same sex and homosexual drives are not aroused, he is perceived as the impediment to fulfilling the libidinal strivings toward the parent of the opposite sex (as is the mother or father), and therefore, hostility toward him is likely to appear.

In the early stages of analytic group psychotherapy, the therapist has to play a neutral role, similar to that in Activity Group Therapy. This becomes necessary in order to allow for a period of acclimatization, or warming up. Definiteness and direction by the therapist would not only delimit and set the stage for treatment, but would also increase the members' suspiciousness of him, and reinforce their expectations to be frustrated by him. Latent hostility would then be activated.

Transference is rooted in infantile sexuality, as described by Freud. By infantile sexuality we understand the totality of the gratifications of a pleasurable nature and the strivings of the infant and child to gain all the pleasures from the mother, and to a lesser extent from the father. This may not involve genitality. These earlier strivings he has to give up during the oedipal struggle and work out more mature and more realistic attitudes toward each of the parents.

The role of the therapist is to a definite extent determined by the degree to which the oedipal struggle has been resolved. A child in the preoedipal stage of emotional development would present behavior deviations in many respects different than those originating in the oedipal phase. While overt behavior may be the same, its latent meaning is quite different: one is a narcissistic, self-indulgent, imperious demand of a young child or infant; the other has a definite neurotic coloring with attendant conflicts and anxieties, symptoms, and abreactions. Behavior disorders are accordingly classified as oedipal and preoedipal.

Before we proceed to discuss transference as it relates to group psychotherapy, two distinctions that bear directly on our topic need to be made. One of these is the difference between *fundamental transference* and *transitory transference*.[2] Another is the degree to which transference is employed by the therapist.

The fundamental transference consists of the oedipal involvements and infantile sexuality which we have described above. As already indicated it is present to a lesser or greater degree in all types of psychotherapy. It is also discernable in other types of relationships such as attitudes toward employers, policemen, and other persons in authority, and toward men or women, generally. The transitory transference is temporary and as its name suggests, appears and vanishes as the patient is pleased by the therapist or resents him for some denial or frustration. When the fundamental transference is positive, the periods of resentment and hostility are easily overcome. But when it is basically negative they are exaggerated in the patient's mind and the treatment relation may be jeoparidized or negated.

One very neurotic woman has had complicated involvements and serious difficulties in her family life. During the group interviews she talked about the husbands and children of the other members of the group and her neighbors. At one of the sessions the therapist turned to her and said: "You always talk about other people. You have troubles of your own. Why don't you talk about them?" The patient, her face

---

2. Activity Group Therapy has demonstrated that the attitudes of the patients to each other and toward the therapist may alternate between love and hate, submission and aggression, but a group can have therapeutic value only when its fundamental atmosphere is a positive one. I am indebted to Dr. J. H. W. Van Ophuijsen for the formulation of the concepts of fundamental and transitory transferences which was based upon our work in group psychotherapy.

flushed, at once stopped talking. She seemed hurt and depressed throughout the remainder of the session and spoke sparsely also at the subsequent sessions. The therapist had overestimated the intensity of the transference as well as misjudged the effect the statement would have upon the patient, whom she had unmasked too violently in the presence of the group.

The therapist, whether in individual or group treatment, has to be always on guard as to what the fundamental transference toward him is before he can use it as a tool in treatment. Patients withdraw from treatment, especially in free clinics, through the improper use of the transference or by tactless dealing with a patient during its negative phases. The early period of treatment, whether in a group or individually, has to be devoted to establishing a positive fundamental transference, after which authority, criticism, and even deprivation can be employed.

The use of the transference dynamic in psychotherapy is predicated on several factors. First, there is a difference between the *presence* of transference and its *use*. In all good psychotherapy transference is present, but the therapist does not always see fit to make use of it. By this is meant he does not utilize the opportunities offered to give interpretation or exercise authority. The use he makes of the transference depends upon the need of the moment. This is the art of therapy which cannot be described. It depends upon the state of the patient as well as the skill of the therapist. The major difference between analytic group psychotherapy and Activity Group Therapy is that in the latter the therapist does not use the transference.

One of the many complications in the transference phenomena in groups is *multipolarity*. In individual therapy the therapist is the sole center or focus of transference. In the group there are others present who also have emotional meaning to each patient. They attract or repel one another on the basis of fear, need for support, homosexual attraction, resemblance to one's parent's or siblings, similarity of problems, activation of unconscious trends. When one or more members of a group enter a phase of negative transference toward the therapist, they may redirect the positive feelings they so withdraw from him upon other members of the group. It is customary for patients to be drawn together in the face of the anxiety that such negative feelings evoke. They seek protection in one another, become friendly, agree with one another's statements, and leave the room together on the way home. Thus, hostile feelings toward a common target, in this case, the therapist, intensifies the positive relations among the group members. Therefore it can be said that negative transference toward the therapist augments the positive transference among the patients. However, frequently where a patient has strong hostilities toward the therapist and his ego is too weak to deal with them, he may displace them on his fellow patients and "act out" his hostile feelings.

These processes occur at periods of negative transitory transferences, and when the fundamental transference is positive, the group equilibrium iş soon established. When negative transference is in ascendancy, permanent discord and disorganization among the group members sets in. Multipolarity is observable in natural families as well. Where children are subjected to parental rejection, the older may take on the protective parental role toward the younger. Frequently out of hostility toward the parents these positive attitudes change into hostile ones later in life when the young are no longer helpless.

Thus we have in the group a network of libidinal, sibling, and identification transferences and attitudes in the center of which is the therapist. While he occupies the apex of this network, he is not the sole transference focus. In fact in a true therapy group, as differentiated from mass therapy,[3] the discussions among the patients most often leave out the therapist altogether. It would seem to the casual observer that his role is a minor one, but the freedom to talk and reveal repressed impulses stems from the therapist. If for any reason he fails to convey this feeling of freedom and acceptance the cathartic and catalytic processes are blocked.

The value of the therapist is illustrated in a group of neurotic adolescent girls, sixteen to seventeen years old. They have been in analytic group psychotherapy for about a year and a half during which period they have talked very freely and without stimulation from the therapist about many intimate problems and personal matters, such as hostilities toward parents and siblings, fixations on

3. Group therapy is employed here to designate the small group of five to seven patients who have an opportunity to work out direct personal relations with each other and the therapist. Mass therapy is the large tutorial or discussion group which does not allow for this intimacy and in which the therapist of necessity occupies the center of the stage. See [81].

their fathers, their bodies and genitals, sex cravings, masturbation. At one of the meetings the therapist had to absent herself for unavoidable reasons and was too late to cancel the session. The girls reported that all they did was sing, gossip, and have refreshments.

To reveal the very intimate material with which they were preoccupied required removing the censors, which they could not do by themselves. The therapist represented their permissive (preoedipal) parent. Their own superego was too strict to permit the free communication of suppressed thought and feelings. The factor of homosexuality also needs to be taken into consideration here. Without the protective presence of the therapist, they were afraid to remove the bars. Here the therapist represented the good mother in the preoedipal stage where restraints had as yet not been established. At the same time she protected them against the unbridled vagaries of the id.

Catharsis can occur only when the fundamental and the transitory transferences are both positive at a given time. Without them patients are blocked. Positive transference, however, cannot be confined to the therapist alone. The relations to one another (sibling transference) among the patients have to be also positive. A patient unsure of the reaction of the others or in doubt as to their support, would be afraid to reveal himself, that is, resistance would set it. It is only because patients have this security that they are able to talk and act freely. Sibling transference is, therefore, as important in group treatment as are transference relations with the therapist, but the former cannot arise without the latter. Here again we see how important grouping of patients is in analytic group psychotherapy.

Multipolarity gives rise to *transference dilution*. Since the therapist in a group is not the sole focus of cathexis, he occupies a lesser role in the emotional economy of his patients than he does in individual therapy. Transference dilution is particularly helpful to children and adolescents, who often feel disloyal and guilty when they redirect feelings from their parents to others. It is also less threatening to patients who are afraid of homosexual attachment to the therapist. Frequently patients cannot accept treatment because of their inability, for various reasons, to establish a transference relation. The diluted transference in a group is beneficial to them as a preliminary stage in treatment.

Many adolescent and adult patients who come to groups at first attempt to conceal the true state of affairs in their homes. One girl, for example, pictured her father as an ideal person and her family as pleasant. Later she revealed him as a narcissistic, immature, and irresponsible man and the home as poverty-stricken, conflict-ridden, and depressing. Another described her family as a devoted and loving group of people, though later in treatment she openly spoke of her impelling desire to kill her mother and one of her sisters. The need to present relatives as persons other than what they really are arises partly from a desire to make a good impression (ego defenses), also because these persons have special meaning in the libido economy of the patients. These are the most significant and important persons in their lives and they are, therefore, afraid to weaken these sources of security.

One of the values of transference is that the libido of the patient is redirected from these primary persons to the therapist and the other members of the group. Ego defenses are also diminished when the libido is detached from its earlier anchorages. These anchors may be one's own ego or persons close to one. When the earlier foci become less important, that is, less cathected, the patient grows freer, more objective, and able to rid himself of the quantum of love and, therefore, also of hostility and aggression toward them, either through decreased catharsis or through sublimation. While the libido remains anchored to earlier objects, resistances to therapy persist. When cathexis is lessened or displaced, emotional change occurs. As long as a patient clings to the original infantile love objects, there is little chance for change, but when the cathexis is dislodged from the self or another person, emotional growth can occur. We suggest that the process of substituting one emotional focus or anchor for another be termed *cathexis displacement.*

Cathexis displacement is inherent to the transference relation with individuals, but groups, too, can become a focus of cathexis since they are a source of comfort, substitute gratifications and security, and are less personal, hence less threatening.

These changes in emotional values are preceded by the changing function of the therapist to correspond with the unfolding personalities of his patients. Patients cannot at first accept the therapist for what he is, and as they grow able and their need for him decreases as therapy proceeds, that is, the transference is dissolved, they can view and accept the therapist, as well, in a more realistic light. Perhaps a very simple illustration of this is supplied by the following incident. A patient in psychoanalytic treatment who had radical convictions observed a Wall Street report on the analyst's desk. "Do you go in for that, too!" he exclaimed contemptuously. Because the situation was handled with tact, the patient was able to continue with his hour, though resentfully. Later in treatment he was able to accept "Wall Street" as one of the realities of the modern world. The patient idealized the analyst and put him above mundane interests, but as his own conflicts were resolved, he was able to accept the analyst in the realistic setting of the world. The analyst as reality has to be attenuated at first when the patient is unready to view him with attributes not acceptable to him. The personality of the therapist needs to be employed in accordance with the patient's readiness to accept it.

One of the difficult facts that patients in group treatment have to face is that they cannot possess the therapist (parent) for themselves. They must share him with others. We take the following interpretive note from a record of a group of adult women in an interview group that illustrates this point.

Mrs. E. (psychoneurotic) has used the group as a sibling rivalry situation. It is for this reason that she sought to dominate the group and to monopolize the therapist. In one sense the group has played into her pattern. It has given her a field for acting out her sibling rivalry drives. But on the other hand, it has helped her become more communicative, and her resistances had diminished. There is no doubt that Mrs. E. became more accessible to treatment because of the group, having failed in individual therapy before. She is not only willing but is now anxious to enter into individual treatment.

The rivalry situation in the group has great value to those patients whose problems arise to a large extent from sibling conflict, and for those who had been an only child. The need to share the therapist brings out a variety of reactions. The more fearful members are brought closer together as a result. Unable to bear up under the impending or ensuing rivalries they compromise with their wishes and redirect partial transference attitudes from the therapist to one another. This is the foundation of "group morale" and "group unity." But since some of the transferred attitudes are negative, as well as positive, conflict and hostility also arise in the relationships among the group members. As already indicated, negative feelings in the transference relation that are discharged in individual treatment against the therapist can find egress in the patients' treatment of one another. Thus, frequently cruelty that is intended for the therapist (the parent) is displaced on a fellow member. This phenomenon in therapy groups we designate as target multiplicity. A dramatic illustration of such displacement of aggression is supplied by the following incident taken from the record of an activity group of nine-year-old boys.

After a considerable struggle Richard took the saw away from Larry. Then Stephen (a very aggressive boy) began teasing Richard. He threw pieces of wood at him, threatened to pierce his eyes out with the pair of scissors and similar means. Richard continued working with the saw, but felt uncomfortable and looked helpless against Stephen. The teasing continued for at least ten minutes, with Stephen throwing things into Richard's face, and striking him. All this time Richard behaved in a frightened and helpless manner. Stephen suddenly threw a piece of wood at the therapist, who worked quite a distance away and in a different direction. As this piece of wood approached the therapist, he covered his face with his hand and the wood struck his hand.[4] Stephen pretended to be frightened and derisively shook as though with fear. He instantly turned to Richard, shook hands with him and said: "Now we are friends." From then on until the end of the session there was harmony between them. Richard was cheerful and happy for the rest of the time.

In analytic group psychotherapy hostility is seldom expressed so overtly, except by very young children. Adolescents and adults employ techniques of a more subtle nature that serve to disguise their feelings. An adolescent or an adult may instead shuffle his feet to the extreme annoyance of the members, sniffle in a very obvious and

4. This is a rare instance of direct aggression against a therapist activated by the fact that the latter did not restrain the boy to allay his guilt and anxiety. The act also served as discharge of the boy's hostility toward a parental figure.

disturbing manner, interrupt the speakers, suggest that the session end prematurely, complain about the usefulness of attending sessions, or make sarcastic and derogatory remarks about other members, the clinic, the caseworker, and sometimes even the group therapist who is present. One adolescent girl described the therapist as a dissolute old hag. But despite this she faithfully attended group sessions, which gave the lie to her statement and acts. It revealed the temporary negative phrases in the transference. The fundamental transference was positive.

However, the requirement of good individual and group psychotherapy is that the patients express hostility toward the therapist. This can be achieved by conveying the feeling that the therapist is not a punitive person. Often it is necessary to even directly encourage it. But rampant expression of hostility activates fear and guilt and disturbs both patient and therapist. A group cannot continue in a state of hostility and recrimination among its members. When hostility grows too intense and prolonged, the various transferences may become permanently impaired; the group grows uncontrollable and disintegrates. Members of a group reinforce and reinfect one another, emotions mount and many negative outcomes can be expected. This aberrant behavior is made possible by the fact that members of a group become *de-egotized* to various degrees. They lose part of their autonomy and self-control. As a result, the superego of each is weakened and one gives himself over to the "mob spirit." This is associated with the principle of libido economy.

Rise and continuance of hostility in a group is especially activated when the therapist is trapped into a negative countertransference. When he shows displeasure, annoyance, or anger, his position as a central person is changed. He is no longer the tolerant, accepting person; no longer the source of security; or the ego-ideal. The natural hostility toward the parent figure is at once mobilized and intensified. Hostility becomes diffuse, group disorganization sets in, and the position of the therapist grows precarious. The transference control, which is the chief tool in treatment, disappears and he, as well as others, may become the victim of the group's wrath. When the censors to behavior are removed, early oedipal hostility asserts itself and is redirected toward any one in authority or who in any way represents it. Such reactions have been experienced in hospitals for mental patients, in institutions for delinquents, and in prisons. We have also had expression of it in a number of instances in activity groups of prepubertal boys.

One such group of thirteen-year-olds made it a practice to overturn and pile up the furniture in the therapy room, throw objects around, and generally upset the room before they left. This was repeated at two or three consecutive sessions. It was obviously a prolonged period of negative transference toward the therapist who was in training and still young and inexperienced. It was observed that this rowdyism took place after the refreshment period at the termination of the session when the therapist was washing the dishes.

The method of coping with this situation was as follows: The group did not meet in the regular room for two sessions. Instead they took trips. One of these was to a movie and the other to an industrial and scientific museum. The succeeding two or three weeks, when they returned to their regular room, the therapist and the boys left immediately after eating and before the dishes were washed. The worker then returned to clean up the room. After this there was no recurrence of the disturbance in that group. The trend was broken and the interval gave the group an opportunity to establish more positive transference attitudes.

When such aggressiveness appears and bids fair to become an established trend in an activity group, the group is at once dismissed without any explanation or excuse. When the members of the group press for a reason, the therapist simply repeats: "We better go home." Particularly there is consternation among the children when they are dismissed without refreshments. They question: "What, no food?" The therapist calmly says: "We are going home." He does not allow himself to be drawn into any discussion nor does he give any explanations. The act is always adequate to convey the meaning and intent.

This procedure is one of the few in which the transference is *used* by the therapist in activity groups. Because of his permissiveness in the past the fundamental transference towards him is a positive one, and peremptory denial brings home to the members the undesirability of their behavior.

Transferences in groups are sometimes intensified, at other times diminished. Negative feelings toward the group therapist would tend to be mobilized in a group through the process of identification, infection, and intensification. It takes little to activate latent hostility and aggression toward a parental figure or anyone in authority. All that these require is group sanction and the security that it provides against punishment. It is in the negative phases of the transference that members of a group give each other the greatest support. As is well known, a common object of hostility is the greatest unifying agent among people in the ordinary community. It is so also in treatment groups. The therapist, therefore, finds himself the target of intense hostility and aggression which may be expressed directly or by veiled outlets such as humor, sarcasm, or indifference.

When the members of the group complain against persons in authority such as parents, teachers, employers, or mates, they are accusing by implication the therapist who, being in a position of authority, is also, as far as the patients are concerned, guilty of similar acts and attitudes. The therapist has to stand ready to receive these aggressions unperturbed for a number of reasons. It facilitates free associations and catharsis, which are the very foundations of therapy; also because this serves to increase identification and object relationships. Since patients in a group can discharge aggression on the therapist together, they are brought closer to one another and the positive sibling transference is intensified. Perhaps an even more valuable result is that as the patients displace hostility from their natural parents upon the therapist the building of their superego is thus facilitated.

Transference in groups is intensified not only in its negative, but also in its positive phases. The latter rise to a high pitch when there is rivalry for the affection of the therapist. Rivalrous strivings are present in adult therapy groups as they are in groups of children. The patients who happen to be in a state of rivalry at any given time, mobilize a great deal of positive feelings toward the therapist to outdo the others, but develop strong antipathy for one another which may infect the group. This situation needs direct handling, as it may lead to the deterioration of the group and cause members to drop out.

The symbolic position the therapist occupies is quite clear. It is also clear how he can establish through constructive attitudes positive fundamental transferences among the group members to each other. This has been proven time and again in activity groups for young children. The persistent tolerant and mild behavior of the therapist, his consistent acceptance of the children's personalities as they are, reduces primary cruelties to one another. Because the adult does not attempt to inhibit them and does not moralize or correct, the positive transference the children evolve toward him, diminish the negative feelings toward one another. This process is similar to one in a good family. Where parent relationships are harmonious and the children are loved and accepted, there is also basic harmony among the latter. Being little frustrated there is less hostility toward the parents to displace on each other and thus the building of the ego and superego is facilitated.

Another factor that has to be considered in the development of transference in psychotherapy with young children is that the mother still occupies an important role in their psychological economy, and that other adults are not too important. The mother is still the most significant person in their lives and no one can displace her. Dependence is still intense and "separation" (individuation) had not as yet been achieved. As the children grow older, physical and some degree of psychological separation from the mother is affected. They then can establish transference upon others. Thus we may expect greater rivalry in groups of older children and adults than in groups of very little children.

A boy of six in play group therapy was boisterous, careless, and destructive with the materials when other children were present. On occasions when he happened to be alone with the therapist he acted demure, punctilious, and subdued. He kept asking the therapist when the other children would come. He seemed uncomfortable when alone with an adult. The history of this boy is that he was the only child of a very rigid, compulsive, and tyrannical mother, who was in group therapy at the same time that the boy was being treated. It was evident that the discomfort he felt with his mother was reactivated by the woman group therapist.

This mechanism is further demonstrated in a situation when a woman therapist took a group of three boys and two girls between the ages of five and six to have refreshments at a restaurant. The moment the children entered the restaurant they began calling her names. One of them said: "You are a crook." Another added, "You stole the money," (for refreshments), and they continued baiting her along these lines. One of the boys later said to the therapist: "You are my mother." A girl then said: "You are my father," and another: "You are my father."

The act of being fed by an adult seemed to recall to them a family relation and their difficulties were reactivated. When this occurred, the person who presents the greatest problem to each child came to mind first. Thus we see that the preoccupation of the boy was with the mother and with the girls it was their fathers.

In Activity Group Therapy the therapist may not permit himself to become the emotional focus in the group, although he is inevitably the psychological center. In view of the fact that group therapy aims to provide a treatment situation through interrelationships among the members, the therapist's becoming the dynamic focus would block the therapeutic process. He can easily become the dominant symbol through asserting himself either by talking, helping children with their work unasked, and similar means of directing attention to himself. In analytic group psychotherapy, on the other hand, his role is more assertive because transference is employed directly and interpretation is given. Such assertiveness in activity groups would block free acting out.

At the fifth session, nine- and ten-year-old boys in an activity group began setting a bonfire on the floor of the room. For some of the boys this was the second or third session. At one point the therapist felt that the fire was becoming dangerous and had extinguished it. Instantly the boys ran helter-skelter up and down the stairs to the balcony in the room. They then proceeded again to start small fires until the therapist peremptorily prohibited it. The most aggressive boys took brown paint and painted the ping-pong table and also part of the wall of the room. Later the therapist found the words "you stink" painted on the wall.

Aside from the significance of much of what transpired, including the use of brown paint, this incident is illuminating from the point of view of the transference. Aggression followed closely on the heels of frustration, which is a very common reaction. A rather significant dynamic in this episode is the displacement of hostility against the adult upon the physical environment. In the child's mind the room and the objects in it are associated with the adult. Still another element is the opportunity for sublimating early infantile (regressive) interests as manifested by fire and brown paint, which is associated with feces. The most direct attack against the worker consists in the painting of the words "you stink" which also represents anal aggression. In this group the fundamental attitude was negative, hostile, and narcissistic as revealed by reading the records of earlier sessions. It is the function of the therapist to transmute this hostility to positive attitudes through acceptance and permissiveness.

The nature of the transference in activity groups [53, 128] is essentially the same as in other types of psychotherapy. The attitudes the young patients have toward parents and siblings are faithfully acted out in the group. In fact in most instances there is little need for their background history. It is revealed in behavior. Children's behavior in groups, as is well known to those who work with them, is more revealing than is language. Words may be used to veil feelings and attitudes. A patient may even be on guard in his behavior when alone with the therapist, but the catalytic effect of the group and the partial de-egotization that occurs makes him less aware and less cautious of his acts and words. The fact that the children transfer their basic feelings toward parents upon the therapist is made evident not only in behavior, but later in treatment also by their speech. Some begin the relation by being hostile, overfriendly, suspicious, or indifferent. As treatment proceeds, the integration of positive and negative feelings and the elimination of ambivalence reflect themselves in the patient's total behavior and adaptations.

Throughout the course of the patient's hostile and aggressive acts, there lurks his craving for a satisfying and positive relation with the therapist and other members of the group. It is because he is unable to enter into such relations that he first has to express negative feelings as a defense. Before he can enter upon a positive phase the patient has to break through his self-protective mantle of aggression against the therapist and others who represent parental and societal authority. By accepting the manifestations of negative feelings and hostile acts, the therapist facilitates this transition. The sustaining element in the transference relation is the patient's basic desire for acceptance and approval. His seeking it is the foundation of therapy both in groups and in individual treatment.

At the present stage of our knowledge the following points can be made concerning the nature of transference in group psychotherapy.

1. Transference in individual treatment and group treatment are essentially the same. Any differences are quantitative rather than qualitative.

2. Transference in group treatment is less charged with libido. Because of the diluting factors, it is reduced in intensity.

3. Sibling and identification transferences are present in a group which supply multipolarity and dilution to the transference.

4. Transference manifests itself in positive and negative phases as it does also in individual treatment, but in groups there is intensification and infection of feelings which makes dealing with them somewhat difficult.

5. Transferences are established incomparably quicker in groups than in individual therapy. This is facilitated by mutual support and protection that the patients give each other. For the same reason catharsis is accelerated.

6. In activity groups the therapist does not *use* the transference relation. Assuming a "neutral" role he permits the group members to act out their impulses and allows the others to react to this behavior. Because of the resulting pressure of the total situation the child modifies his behavior and attitudes to conform to the reality of the group. In later stages of treatment the adult becomes a realistic person and exerts controls and restrictions that represent reality.

7. Because in analytic group psychotherapy, interpretation and insight is given, the therapist can act in the role of a restricting and prohibitive parent earlier in treatment. He can call attention to the negative feelings which the patient—child, adolescent, or adult—has toward him and work through these attitudes. However, it is important that the therapist does not take for granted the existence of positive transferences.

8. In all types of group psychotherapy, and in this respect they are similar to individual treatment, the patient transfers his fundamental feelings upon the therapist and sees him in whatever role he needs the therapist.

9. The therapist plays out the parental role more realistically in a therapy group than he does in individual treatment. The group (family) is a realistic situation for children, especially.

CHAPTER 21

GROUP PSYCHOTHERAPY AND THE
TRANSFERENCE NEUROSIS
(1972)

The Psychiatric Dictionary, fourth edition,[1] offers the following definition of a transference neurosis: "A transference neurosis ... is the reappearance of the early infantile Oedipal situation. The analyst represents one or both parents as a love-object, as if he were really the original parent in the original infantile setting of the patient. The patient also *lives out* all his old ego attitudes and incest prohibitions." [italics mine].

Fenichel elaborates on this theme in somewhat more depth when he says:[2]

The closer the transferred feelings to the normal emotions of love and hatred and the closer the transferred aims to the normal genital aim, the easier is the analytic work. The closer the transferred emotions are to the archaic "incorporation" world of the infant, and the more pre-genital the transference aims are, the more difficult does the task become. In general, therefore, the difficulty of an analysis corresponds to the depth of the pathogenic regression [p. 541].

1. Hinsie, E., and Campbell, R.J. (1970). *Psychiatric Dictionary*, fourth ed. New York: Oxford University Press.

2. Fenichel, O. (1945). *The Psychoanalytic Theory of Neurosis*. New York: W.W. Norton.

The fact must be particularly noted that "the more pregenital the transference aims are, the more difficult does the [therapeutic] task become." This statement corresponds to this author's earlier warnings in reference to the efficacy of group psychotherapy for the neuroses. Pathogenic input in the pregenital and especially in the preverbal and preconceptual stages in the development of a child appear later in life either as neurotic traits, where the input was mild, or as a "character neurosis," where it was massive and prolonged. Not only group psychotherapy but also traditional psychoanalysis is inefficacious in such conditions, for *reconditioning* of archaic neural and glandular responses as well as emotional desensitization is needed, and this requires that the therapist take a more active role than is the case in a transference neurosis. Because these conditions have strong character components, many such patients would benefit from parallel analytic group and individual psychotherapy.

A patient does not present a transference neurosis when he first comes to the analyst's consulting room. The transference neurosis arises after the patient has been given time to establish significant positive or negative feelings, or both, toward the analyst. It is then that the therapist, by virtue of his position and role, assumes the same place in the psychic economy of the patient as did his parents during his formative years.

With establishment of the transference neurosis, work can begin on analysis of the counterinstinctual reactions in the pathogenic structure of the patient, the bound-up anxieties and guilts that need to be dislodged and purged, as it were, in order to clear the way for reconstruction of the personality. When the channels which have been blocked and/or distorted by the noxious feelings accumulated through experiences in relations are thus cleared, homeostasis is established and the patient's personality and his resultant behavior is normalized. Cognition and rationalism are made possible, which is not the case in character disorders, for example. It is the *living through* or, better still, the reliving of traumatic infantile experiences in the light of new conditions and chronological age that facilitates the resolution of the neurosis. This requires the patient's investing the analyst with the attributes of his parents, but in a climate in which he is not inhibited by fear or conformity from expressing his hostile or incestuous feelings toward the analyst as a parent substitute.

Since many neurotic and psychoneurotic patients have in the past acted in a similar manner toward their parents as toward the therapist, the question can be asked: "Why was not the expression of hostility toward them therapeutic?" The answer to this logical query is the prolonged intimacy of the background against which the overt or covert conflicts were carried on; the parent reacted disapprovingly or punitively toward the patient, provoking guilt reactions. These reactions served to convince the patient of the correctness of his feelings about his parents and about himself; they increased his self-deprecatory attitudes and guilts, and, most damaging, they raised the level of anxiety.

The patient has also encountered these psychonoxious responses from other persons when he has displayed or acted out his erratic traits. He has been rejected, disapproved of, avoided, or verbally denounced when he annoyed his fellow men and behaved over-assertively toward them.

The treatment of such psychoneuroses is not only a strenuous but also a time-consuming task. The time factor is irksome to the patient and sometimes even to the therapist, but it is essential, for attempted shortcuts only vitiate the process or result in failure in the treatment of a true psychoneurosis. The process consists mainly of devolution of accumulated tensions, projections and rationalizations the patient has defensively built up during his lifetime, and the time dimension is, therefore, pivotal in the treatment process.

The latter point may become palpable if we contrast the genesis of the transference neurosis with that of another major type of neurosis, the traumatic neurosis, which can be diminished in intensity and in some cases even resolved by less regressive therapeutic processes. A traumatic neurosis is so designated because it originated in a single or small number of specific, reinforcing events in the life of an individual which jarred his sense of security and aroused extreme fear, anxiety, and guilt. The two major elements are the *intensity* of the traumatic input and the *speed* with which is assailed the individual. An event such as the sudden death of a significant, libidinally invested person can be the source of a traumatic neurosis. Another is unexpected, sudden exposure to the primary scene or severe punishment and shame at being discovered at a highly prohibited activity such as masturbation. An airplane accident or being trapped in a fire can produce a chain of irrational fears and debilitating anxiety in one who is particularly sensitive and thus disposed to exaggerated reactions.

To summarize: a full-blown psychoneurosis differs from a traumatic neurosis in two respects: *(a)* It is the outcome of *prolonged* instinctual suppressions, especially of sex; *(b)* it originates in the oedipal conflict, which is not the case in a traumatic neurosis. Thus, it is the time factor and the intensity of the emotions involved that make necessary prolonged devolution of the neurotic constellation.

The other element that differentiates the two types of psychoneurosis is the foci that operate in their genesis. In the one, the full-blown psychoneurosis, the focus is people: one or both parents. In the traumatic neurosis the affective focus is an occurrence, even though a person or persons may be involved. For example, a male patient, who apeared otherwise to function adequately in every respect, presented the problem of sexual impotence. In exploring his background, he recalled that as a boy of about ten or eleven years of age he was surprised by his rigid, middle-class father at a window watching two dogs in the act of coitus. The outraged parent not only severely punished his son for his "shameless" act but exposed him to the derision of the rest of the family and some friends. Coitus had, therefore, become taboo to this man's superego.

The neurotic nucleus in this case was the shock he sustained during his childhood. The father was a comparatively minor element; anyone who so demeaned him in the esteem of his relatives and friends and assailed his superego would have produced the same traumatic reaction, although it probably would have been less emotionally charged and have had less meaning.

Because the libidinal content of the transference psychoneurosis attached and proceeds from a person or persons, its resolution has to involve a person who has the skill to activate the output of the noxious emotions generated by the original pathogenic individuals, usually the parents, and incorporated by the victim. The person who can achieve this has to assume a positive place in the psychic economy of the patient; that is, he must not replicate the parents' reactions, must be nonjudgmental, noncritical, and nonpunitive. The patient needs to develop a positive transference toward this person, the analyst, so that he can reveal long-guarded feelings of shame and guilt with a feeling of safety. This takes considerable time.

Further time is consumed by the unraveling of the mass of other hurtful relations and events that have been built upon the oedipal foundation, a slow process because of the nature and intensity of the resistances and defenses. Dealing with these resistances and especially with defenses, and helping the patient to break through them without threatening, antagonizing, or alienating him is a subtle skill the therapist must possess. Careless or erroneous dealing with them destroys the positive aspect of the transference. When this occurs, treatment is usually broken off.

The only course by which the analyst can avoid the many pitfalls that arise in the course of psychoanalysis is to remain overtly passive and, especially, silent. This is particularly imperative in the early stages of the analysis. The value of inactivity on the part of the analyst extends much beyond caution, however. The analyst's inactivity is essential to prevent interference with, or cause a change in the direction of, the concatenation of the traumatic experiences and bound-up anxieties and guilts during the regressive process toward the nuclear problem. For maximal results the patient needs to relive or recall in a new context and meaning the traumatic events of his past and discharge his accumulated anger, often against the analyst as a parent substitute. An uncalled-for remark during this highly charged state of the patient may cut off the flow of feelings and memories and play into the omnipresent latent resistances to self-revelation.

The analyst's passivity also serves to convey subtly to the patient that the resolution of his problems is his own responsibility and that he has to overcome his difficulties through his own efforts. In other words, he has to rely on himself and not look for support to the analyst as he did to his parents. This is a very important element in helping the patient in his movement toward maturity. However, the analyst's judgment as to when the patient's ego nears a point of being overloaded is of critical importance. In these instances the analyst may relieve the patient's turmoil by a remark or an interpretation. Nonetheless, the elements of independence and self-realization in the self-sustaining catharsis have to be carefully preserved to their maximum.

Drawing upon his own resources and finding his way through the maze of conflicted and severely cathected emotions with little help is a new experience to the severe psychoneurotic. He may be irritated and impatient with the passive role of the analyst, and he may need to be encouraged to proceed on his own by the therapist's explaining the workings of the analytic process. Here, too, keen judgment and skill is required to respond differentially to different patients. To a patient whose nuclear problem has arisen from indifference and neglect by parents, the psychotherapist's silence may represent a replica of the patient's parental neglect. It will then arouse severe negative transferential feelings and lead to the termination of the treatment or seriously retard it. In such instances, the analyst reiterates the free-associative rule and its necessity to the therapeutic procedure. He thus conveys to the patient that his seeming aloofness is an essential strategy, not a result of indifference.

The patient needs to arrive, *as far as possible by himself*, at insights into the genesis and the quality of his intrapsychic and behavioral difficulties and the nature of his problem-generating conduct. But seldom can this be achieved without the analyst's interpretation at some points in the treatment. At strategic times, the analyst needs to step in and offer explanations and interpretations to aid the patient's understanding, but the rule is that interpretations must be offered only at a point when the patient is close to understanding but is unable to verbalize it because of his resistances or lack of cognitive capacity. The analyst's intervention in interpreting resistances at the appropriate time clears the path for the patient to face unpleasant truths with a minimum of hurt or shock.

Explanations as well as explorations in a valid psychoanalysis of a full-blown (transference) neurosis may be offered earlier in the treatment with caution when the patient seems confused through affect surcharge or when he appears unable to proceed. An exploratory question may also be offered when a sudden break appears in the logical continuity of a patient's communication. This strategy is a means of indirect resistance interpretation by making the patient aware of a resistance to disclosing some particularly charged event or experience.

To further bring into relief the complex and subtle process of treatment via a transference neurosis, we shall explore the comparatively simpler procedures of dealing with a traumatic neurosis. In the case of the patient who suffered from sexual impotence, for example, the breakthrough occurred in the following sequence. He had spent some months relating his conflictual background and his many disturbing experiences with people, especially women. One day he suddenly became visibly disturbed and grew silent. When asked why he had stopped talking, he meekly, with a defensive half-smile, narrated that, as he was talking, he suddenly recalled the incident when he was surprised by his father as he was watching sexual intercourse between two dogs. From this point on therapy proceeded at a much easier pace. The patient related better to the therapist, grew more open, more understanding, and in a comparatively short time recovered from his psychogenic debility.

A colleague, an unusually perceptive and intuitive psychiatrist, related the treatment of a case of a severe neurotic allergy to dogs in a woman. This woman, in fact married to the psychiatrist's cousin, could not enter a home containing a dog without very severe symptoms arising in her even before she had laid eyes on the animal. The two cousins, both refugees from Hitler's Europe, had lived in different parts of the world and the two families had made only recent contact with each other in New York.

The psychiatrist suggested that the woman might be helped if she would come in to see him. The treatment was face-to-face psychotherapy rather than a couch analysis, since the psychiatrist wished to explore the woman's problem before deciding on the course treatment should take. During the interviews, the patient talked only about dogs. When the therapist asked why she was so interested in dogs, the woman grew rhapsodic about the wonderful life dogs lived. They are loved and taken care of, she said, but, most of all, they are free to do whatever they wish and to go wherever they wish. The perspicacity of the therapist revealed itself when he quietly said, "And they can have sexual intercourse freely and without any restraint." "Yes," explained the patient, "Yes, that's it." She was submitted to regular psychotherapy for a period of months during which her repressed incestual wishes toward her father were thoroughly explored, with the result that she was freed of allergic symptoms.

What both of these patients required was release of the repressed anxiety bound up in the traumatic events rather than unraveling of the intricate web of noxious feelings resulting from a prolonged traumatic life span. Once the unconscious anxiety was freed from repression, the sluice gates that held back the flow of the *élan vital* were opened and the personality was normalized.

The cases that seem to be "miracle" cures, in which an appropriate formulation of the cause or nucleus of a problem by a therapist has wrought dramatic improvement in a patient, are probably in the category of traumatic neuroses. While, in the hands of a highly perceptive and intuitive therapist, early formulation is a valid procedure, it should be employed with great caution, for the therapist must be certain that he is not dealing with a true psychoneurosis requiring a transference neurosis as part of the treatment. Should a mistake be made in this regard, the shock would cause the patient to withdraw and in most instances terminate treatment.

Alfred Adler's standard technique of asking patients at the very outset for their first memories appears to be valid and has excellent potential both for understanding a patient's nuclear problem as well as being a starting point in treatment. Obviously, the first memory would be concerned with, and therefore will reveal, the basic cathected event in a person's life, positive or negative. However, its meaning may not always be clear, especially to a novice in therapy and occasionally even to the more experienced. It is, therefore, advisable to delay formulation of the meaning of a first memory until a later stage when the problems involved have been revealed more clearly. Nonetheless, first memories can be useful clues to much that a patient produces later during the psychotherapeutic sessions.

It would seem that the treatment tasks in cases of transference neuroses, and certainly for character disorders, are widely at variance. The exploratory procedure is essential in the first so that the patient's psychic laminations over his infantile wishes and fantasies and the accumulated hostilities, anxieties, and guilts can be unraveled against his resistances, vertically and regressively, step by step. This is not necessary, in fact counterindicated, in traumatic neuroses in which the nuclear anxiety is focused at one point and, therefore, is reached more readily than in transference neurosis.

Thus, the conditions under which a transference neurosis can be generated and effectively employed are:

1. The analyst must become in the transference the target of the patient's initial infantile feelings of hate and love which the patient must be able to discharge freely and unreservedly without discomfort or fear. This is a precondition for the emergence of a positive transference as well as for the purging of noxious feelings that have

been held in suppression, disturbing the patient's psychic homeostasis and keeping him in perpetual inner turmoil and at odds with people and his environment.

2. The flow of free association by the patient must not be interrupted unless it becomes necessary to protect the patient against the overloading of his ego. The spontaneous sequences in the devolution during free association must be preserved for they conform with the emotional sequence of events. (The sequence of events may or may not be in chronological order, but the anxieties connected with the events always are.) Interruption of a patient's free flow of communication may also divert him from his movement toward the focus of his difficulties.

3. Because of this the analyst must remain silent and inactive so as not to interfere with free association, but the more important reason is that any reaction on his part reawakens in the patient memories of noxious treatment by parents, teachers, and other significant adults sustained in the past. These memories and his negative transferential feelings projectively arouse resentment and lead to blocking of the cathartic process. Still another negative effect is the failure by the analyst to demonstrate respect for the patient and to have patience, which to the patient are signs of maturity.

4. The core of the transference neurosis is the patient's investment in the therapist of libidinal strivings as a parent substitute. The question of the sex of the analyst has received considerable attention in the psychoanalytic literature. To discuss this moot question would take us far afield from the intent of this paper, but it can be said that many hold that in the unconscious of the patient the significance of the analyst in a transference neurosis is always that of a mother. There are ample grounds for this belief.

We can now examine to what extent, if at all, these conditions for the emergence and proper dealing with a transference neurosis are present in the group therapy process. It is obvious that the depth and intensity of transferential feelings, positive and negative, toward the therapist *in loco parentis* cannot possibly arise. In the first place, in group therapy, the group, as a unitary entity, greatly outweighs the therapist in psychic importance to its members. The erroneous use of the so-called alternate session in which the group meets without the therapist may be the result of a vague recognition of this fact.

In the second place, the therapist is not the sole object of transferential feelings. Other individual patients, for varying reasons, mostly resemblances and memories, serve as transference objects, as does the group as a whole. The transference feelings in groups, therefore, cannot be as intense as they are in individual therapy since they are diluted because of this multiplicity of relationships, attitudes, and interactions.

Thirdly, the libidinal element in the transference neurosis is weak because of the dilution of the transference, and therefore, the patient cannot work it through therapeutically in a group situation.

The essential requirement for the dissolution of a neurosis—free association—is quite impossible in a group. The members constantly interrupt each other and divert the trend of a communication as some element stirs in them relevant thoughts or feelings. This unavoidable condition in groups prevents both regression and movement toward underlying pathology and nuclear problems. The patient whose tensions and anxieties are so intense as to require the involvement of a transference neurosis as part of treatment grows frustrated by these interruptions and the level of tension in him is raised, thus intensifying his problems.

Disturbance of the tenuous emotional equilibrium of a patient can also be caused by the very presence of another member of a group. Dr. Alexander Wolf reported that when a new female patient was introduced into one of his therapy groups, another patient suddenly arose and loudly announced that, "As long as that woman is in the group, I will not come," or words to that effect. When seen individually, she revealed that the new group member reminded her of her hated sister and she could not abide her presence.

A group unavoidably abrogates the three basic requirements for "working through": the individual libidinal transference, the passivity of the recipient of the psychoneurotic's feelings and communications, and free association. In view of this, we must conclude that a transference neurosis cannot be treated solely by group psychotherapy. However, the analytic process can be greatly facilitated and accelerated if the patient, after working through the major content of his problem in individual analysis, is placed in a group. The group provides him with an experimental milieu in which he can test himself and his newly found powers for relating to others. As stresses appear as a result of the group experience, they become valid and effective grist for individual analytic sessions. This socialization phase serves as a means of reeducation in the ongoing reconstruction of the patient's psyche.

Dr. Bernard Glueck, the well known psychoanalyst and psychiatrist, told the present commentator more than thirty years ago that since group therapy had become available, he had made it a practice to refer his analytic patients to groups as a tapering off device so as to give them an opportunity to test themselves against the social reality of a group and find if they could sustain themselves in direct interaction with others.

I once found myself seated at a professional luncheon next to a psychiatric caseworker, a former supervisee of mine of some years past. She had been in group therapy with a very competent therapist, but now, she said, she was in analysis. "A couch analysis?" I asked. "Yes. My, what a difference!" the lady exclaimed. "Finally I am getting at the problems which were not touched in the therapy group. It's hard work and it is upsetting, but I feel I am getting at my basic difficulties and am beginning to understand myself, which did not happen in the seven years in group therapy." "But don't you think the group opened you up some, so that you can work better in your analysis?" I asked. "Maybe," she responded. Next to this woman sat a friend of hers. Upon hearing our conversation, the friend volunteered, "I too gave up group therapy and went into analysis. It's hard work, but I think it pays off," she said with conviction. Obviously the nature of the disturbances in these two women, who had been in different groups conducted by different therapists, required working through via a transference neurosis.

CHAPTER 22

THE NATURE AND TREATMENT OF ACTING OUT
(1956)

Attitudes Toward Acting Out

There is a tendency on the part of psychotherapists to look askance at acting out. It is justifiably considered to be disadvantageous in adult psychotherapy and a deterrent to the treatment process. The term "acting out" automatically evokes in one's mind a negativistic, resistive attitude in the patient, who may be as a result difficult or altogether inaccessible.

In ordinary life, acting out of feelings, especially among the more educated and cultured, is taboo; those who indulge in it are looked upon with suspicion and are frequently excluded from their social set. This reaction stems from the anxiety aroused in those who witness acting out, because of their own susceptibility to react to it in a similar manner that would reveal their own weakness and inadequacy in ego control. Anxiety is aroused also by the manifest irrational element of the acting-out behavior and the fear as to its direction and end product. Acting out also reactivates fears and discomfort suffered in childhood in consequence of some acting-out adults, who screamed, quarreled, or punished. Even acting out of self-pity, despair, and dramatization of suffering that should arouse sympathy causes irritability and annoyance in most spectators, since it mirrors their own weakness. There is also present here the element of guilt, because the spectator is not in the same plight as the subject; also because he feels he should help, but is either unable or unwilling to do so. Emotions are highly contagious, and the degree of the infectiousness is determined by the degree of susceptibility, empathy, and identification in the spectator, and his similarity of temperament and experience with the subject.

Acting out by adults is commonly considered an indication of inadequate personality integration and ego strength, and those who indulge in it are regarded as unreliable and untrustworthy. The intolerance toward character weakness and aggression that culture fosters is a source of much of man's mental unhealth. The disapproval of and proscriptions imposed upon the individual against them cause psycho-organic disequilibrium and neurotic tension.

Where sublimations have not been adequately established—and it would be impossible to do so completely for all aggressive impulses in man—a health-engendering society and tolerant human relations, based upon understanding and emotional flexibility, would permit a degree of acting out. Man's basic fear of others' ego functioning and his unconscious destructive urges make this permissiveness difficult to accept or tolerate. Acceptance of aggressive acting out on the part of others is conditioned by one's acceptance of one's own aggressions and by the security of one's own controls over them. An individual who is uncertain of his own capacity to deal with his aggressions, which is almost universal, fears the discharge of aggression in others. He ascribes (projects) his own incapacity and weakness to them. To remain unperturbed in the presence of anger, vituperation, and destructive acts requires a great deal of inner security and an understanding of self and of others. These are rare attributes. The condemnatory attitude toward discharge of inner stress through aggression and the ego inadequacy it reveals obviously cannot be acceptable to the psychotherapist.

The Phenomenology of Acting Out

Psychotherapy requires that the patient communicate freely his feelings, attitudes, values, memories, preoccupations, troubles, and anxieties. Without such freedom of communication, which is the essence of catharsis, no therapy can occur. Communication even by adults cannot be confined to language and verbalization alone. Patients, as do all other persons, resort to or are involuntarily involved in nonverbal forms of communication, such as grimaces, neuromuscular tensions, changes in facial color, stance and posture, expression of eyes, involuntary movement of arms, legs or torso, as well as by gross bodily movements, activity and motility. To prohibit or restrain these is to cut off significant and frequently the only channels that a patient may have for communicating at a given time, thus impeding the therapeutic process and even negating its effectiveness.

Acting out can take many and devious forms. When a patient raises his voice in anger, grows red or pale in the face, clenches his fists, tenses his body—he is, in the strict sense of the word, acting out. More commonly recognized forms of acting out, however, are the situations in which a patient threatens to or actually causes bodily harm either to a fellow patient or the therapist; when he threatens to or actually throws objects; when he screams in anger or walks up and down the room, or smokes compulsively. But acting out includes also the patient's provoking the therapist to anger or verbally attacking the therapist or another member of a group; manifestations of dependence on the group or any of its members or the therapist; or when he attaches himself either to the therapist or a fellow patient as to a parental figure, as a sexual object, as a rival or a target of hostility. Acting out also includes any form of direct physical or sexual contact or efforts at seduction. Manifest expressions of jealousy, rivalry, the effort at displacing a fellow patient or the therapist, monopolization, are also included in acting out. Evident attempts at arousing pity and sympathy, protection and help, extragroup socialization with fellow group members, also fall in the category of acting out.

In other words, acting out of adults can be considered as being all actions and behavior in a therapeutic setting other than verbal communication. But even verbalization can assume the aspect of acting out, in fact, it *is* acting out, when employed to convey anger, spite, hostility, attack, teasing and other of the multifarious nuances conveyed through language; or withholding it, as in silence.

To prohibit acting out would place the therapist in the position of authority and set up barriers between him and the patient. Instead of prohibition, the therapist must rather utilize acting out as a channel to the patient's unconscious and a link to his childhood memories, character disorder, or neurotic tensions, as the case may be. The patient is rather encouraged to reveal his feelings, thoughts, conflicts, and confusions in the present so that a link can be established between them and earlier stages in his development from which they flow. It is only through this connection, which the patient has to recognize and accept, that therapeutic insight and emotional maturity are achieved in work with adults and neurotic children.

Acting out can occur within the therapeutic setting itself or it may be resorted to by patients outside it.[1] By this strategy the patient indulges his narcissistic needs and prevents examining and "working them through"[2] with the therapist or the group. This acting out we describe as *ex situ*, as differentiated from acting out *in situ*, that is, in the group.

Acting out by adults is always a symptom of regression as well as of a weak ego. Through it, the individual reverts to an earlier pattern of response to inner tensions, a stressful situation or relation. It is, therefore, a mirror of the individual's ontogenetic experiences. For this reason it takes different forms and is resorted to under different conditions and circumstances by different people, whether in therapy or in everyday living. As he acts out, the individual reenacts past responses stored in his memory, or he reverts to the use of a tool or technique that proved either effective or satisfying in the past. Some of the responses are retained in organic conditioned reflexes as engrams, others in psychologic memory.[3] Regression as it relates to psychotherapy can be *therapeutic, pathologic, parapathologic,* and *induced.*

Therapeutic regression. Therapeutic regression is that type of returning to past feelings and behavior that includes retracing the steps in the development and organization of the individual's psyche.

---

1. This is analogous to the behavior of some child patients who are conforming in the home and family, but present problems and maladjustments out of the home—at school, with playmates, and with neighbors.

2. I have elsewhere defined "working through" as the process of eliminating resistances and defenses so that one's feelings, memories, and reactions are made available to the ego for examination and control. See footnote 8.

3. It probably would be very difficult to establish the boundaries where organic reflexes end and psychologic memory begins.

Therapeutic regression occurs in a transference relation to a therapist as a parent substitute and, in the case of group psychotherapy, to fellow patients as replicas of siblings and other important persons in the patients' lives. Through transference and gradually evolving insight, decathexis of objects, and the dissolution of defenses, the patient makes his way toward emotional maturity, personality reintegration, and more appropriate and more efficient ways of dealing with life situations. In this type of regression the ego of the patient remains structurally intact. Rather emotional elements and blockings are involved. The patient speaks about or acts out his feelings and works through his defenses and compulsions.

Pathologic regression. In pathologic regression, on the other hand, the ego goes through a process of disintegration. The patient returns to earlier phases in his development not only affectively but actually. The reality sense and reality perception (not testing) become not only *as if* but *as* that of the past. This process occurs in psychotic deterioration through which the patient returns to earlier infantile stages in his ego and libido development, that is, where the defenses and repressions are given up.

Parapathologic regression. Between these two modalities lies the parapathologic regression. This is the borderline of regressive movement in which the ego does not become fragmented or disintegrated, but where behavior and reactions exceed the limits of either normal or therapeutic regression. Encopresis, diurnal, and to some extent also nocturnal, enuresis, excessive and compulsive masturbation; stealing, sex perversions and other activities of this nature that indicate disorganization and dislocation in the instinctual life of the individual without psychoses present can be classified as parapathologic regression.

Induced regression. Induced regression is the regressive behavior that is stimulated in one person by another through the dynamics of induction, contagion, and identification. In therapy groups induced regression occurs very frequently because of the patients' weak ego development and high level of identification; also, since acting out is directed overtly and covertly against the therapist, the latent hostile feelings toward authority are easily stirred up. An elaboration of this phenomenon will be found in the section on Advantages and Disadvantages of Acting Out later in this paper.

Being one form of regression, acting out can be considered in the light of these classifications. Acting out, as well, can be therapeutic, parapathologic, pathologic, and induced. One can add also *normal acting out,* for in view of man's basic nature, acting out is an essential safety valve for his emotions and as such, has to be permitted, if not encouraged. Normality is determined by the effectiveness of ego controls, the reality of the stimulus, the appropriateness and the intensity of the response, the speed of recovery and the effect it has on other persons.

The phenomenology of acting out as a regressive process is related to three dynamic elements: (1) the ontogenetic experiences of the individual, (2) the intensity of the external stimulus, and (3) the capacity of the ego to deal with the stimulus. Ideally, an individual should have adequate ego resources to deal with any demand or stress that emerges from his life setting. In this maximal criterion everybody fails, but the well-integrated person, though he may be unable or unwilling to expose himself to noxious external demands and pressures, should be able to control his affect and impulses so as not to create undue tensions and unpleasantness. Where an individual overreacts to his detriment and that of others, he reveals inadequacies in ego development and its inhibitive powers. Acting out, therefore, can be viewed as a condition of the individual in which the id impulses overwhelm the ego and become predominant. Such impulsiveness is permissible in children in whom ego development is still incomplete. Thus, in the therapy of acting-out adult patients, two aims have to be kept in mind—the diminution of affect (decathexis) and ego strengthening.[4] These we shall discuss later in this paper.

In *therapeutic acting out,* as in therapeutic regression, the ego structure remains intact, its controls are not impaired, even though their strength is diminished temporarily, and the capacity to restore equilibrium internally and in relation to the environment is preserved. Thus, given enough time, the patient would bring himself under control without outside aid. However, what makes acting out therapeutic is the fact that through the skill of the therapist and the responsiveness of other members in a group, it is used as grist in the therapeutic mill. In *pathologic acting out,* on the other hand, restora-

---

4. For a theory of ego and its correction, see [57, pp. 16–20, 45–53].

tion of equilibrium cannot be achieved by the patient himself without the ministration of drugs, direct restraint, or some other form of therapeutic intervention. Since the ego is not intact and withdraws from reality, external measures become necessary.

In *parapathologic acting out,* external measures, though less drastic, are also necessary. The narcissistic and the usually pleasure-yielding nature of this type of indulgence frequently makes it difficult for the ego and the rational segment of the psyche to assert themselves. The odds against them are too great, as it were. The gratifications resulting from the narcissistic and biologic pleasures and the self-assertiveness involved are strong; they silence and placate them. The ego is bribed, as it were. The dynamic process is similar to that in the case of addiction, that is, where the ego is inveigled into giving way to the anticipated pleasure resulting from the diminished responsibility to control and inhibit. Because of this it is necessary to invoke external controls in parapathologic as also in pathologic acting out. Thus sexual acting out on the part of patients, for example, needs to be prohibited in therapy and the *impulse* considered therapeutically in the treatment interviews, for the impulse is more accessible to analysis when it remains ungratified than when the tensions are eliminated through fulfillment. Similarly, addicts in psychotherapy are prohibited from indulging, even though they usually transgress the instructions, but the very fact of yielding to the impulse against the therapist's or group's wishes is a more fruitful therapeutic situation than is gratification without an awareness of disapproval.

On a larger scale, war and murder are parapathologic forms of acting out of primitive, animalistic drives and are often reactions to real or fantasied danger and threat to one's biological or psychological survival. Unusual proneness to physical fights is a form of acting out of primitive emotions, where early patterning of the personality has not achieved sufficient sublimational modes of expression or adequate repression and control by the ego.

As in the case of induced regression, acting out as well can be *induced* for the reasons given for regression. Induced regression and acting out have minimal value in therapy, since they are not related to nor do they stem from the intrapsychic tensions or nuclear problems of each of the participants. Acting out, a part of the cathartic process, has value only in so far as it uncovers these problems and leads to their source.

Etiology and Treatment

Acting out is the transmutation of emotional tension into physical expression that may stem from temperamental dispositions, organic disequilibrium, or psychogenic stress characteristic of a given individual, and from inadequate ego controls of general or specific impulses. Transmutation of emotional tension into physical activity and motility involves the ego as well as the soma. We deal here with a borderline phenomenon; as we already stated, a degree of acting out may be essential to health for a given individual because of his constitutional and organic conditions which necessitate release through physical expression. When opportunity for such discharge is blocked, serious disturbances in the psycho-organic state of the individual may occur. However, when the acting out exceeds the limits of comfort to others, is uncontrollable or too violent, it has to be dealt with by persons other than the subject himself.

Acting out may occur more violently in a therapeutic situation than under ordinary circumstances, because of transference reactions, which are always charged with intense affect, since feelings toward earlier important figures in life are stirred up. Another reason is that in therapy the ego defenses are threatened and the patient's established controls undermined, which result in free-floating anxiety and hostility. During psychotherapy and because of the transference relation, the patient's libido is stirred up as well, adding to the load the ego has to bear, and unless the ego is strong enough to deal with these added demands and disturbances, it gives way to the id, and discharge of feeling takes place. The onrush of feelings can be compared to that of water when a dam gives way. In this connection, the therapist must be aware of the limitations of the ego strength of his patients, lest he overwhelm the ego, which may result either in withdrawal from treatment or excessive disturbance that in extreme cases may set off a transient psychotic break.

As we shall presently see, the need to act out stems from many sources, but the pattern it assumes is determined by the ontogenetic experiences of the individual. It is a common observation that while the number of emotions acted out is comparatively small, the variety of ways in which it is done is very extensive. One also finds that a given individual has characteristic ways of acting out. Thus, one resorts to physical attack, another to vituperation and profanity, another to threats, still others employ anger, spite, jealousy, or silence.

The choice of ways of acting out can usually be traced to earlier conditioning experiences, imitation, and identifications. A patient who has come from a family whose members acted out feelings, resentments, and hostilities and openly discharged them against one another, is likely to adopt the same direct and open methods of acting out against others later in life. Where hostility and aggression caused one to withdraw, become submissive and quiet, this pattern becomes characteristic of the individual in his general adaptations and in a therapy group as well; if fear had been the prevalent feeling of a child in his family and he withdrew, withdrawal may become the dominant pattern of behavior in a therapy group also.

Silence is one form of acting out a patient's fears and anxieties that stems from early experiences in adaptive demands imposed in the family group, though it can also serve as aggression and passive resistance. In another paper [36] I have described a form of "catatonic defense" against domination and pressure from members of one's family where ego resources are too weak to deal with the demands.

Acting out serves patients (and other persons as well) in a number of ways:

As release. We have already indicated, though briefly, that acting out serves as a release from organic tensions, pent-up emotions or a sudden upsurge of feelings that overwhelm the ego. As such, it is an important "regulator" of the organism, for it has as its .aim the establishment of a psycho-organic equilibrium. As already pointed out, its effect in ordinary life, however, may be negative in so far as the subject may react with guilt and shame, because of social disapproval of and taboo against such behavior. In psychotherapy, whether individual or group, acting out within specified limits is accepted and even encouraged.

As abreaction. Closely associated to the release function of acting out is abreaction to the productions, behavior, and personalities in the group itself. The need for release stems from internal stress and conflict with which patients come to the therapeutic sessions. However, events and personalities in the group itself frequently set off intense feelings of anxiety, anger, and resentment. Patients whose ego strengths do not measure up to these strains discharge their feelings in some form of observable behavior such as excessive and rapid verbalization, anger, attack upon one or more persons present, leaving the room, or by withdrawal and silence. These abreactions can be employed fruitfully in exploring the patients' feelings, their cause and their relation to earlier or current determinants. Recognition of the existence of motivations for an overt act, the acceptance of their existence and the willingness for self-confrontation strengthen the ego which is involved in acting out, in addition to other gains.

As resistance. The most accepted view of acting out is that it is a form of resistance to treatment. This is true, and in the case of adult patients, resistance must be viewed as its salient feature. The ego finds in acting out a shorter, easier, and more primitively direct route to discharge anxiety, guilt, and aggression than working it through by the devious, prolonged, and arduous road to verbalization and insight. Acting out is a quick way to rid oneself of the unpleasant feelings to which one is subjected at a given time and to find rapid release from anxiety and guilt. This is, however, true only to the extent to which acting out remains on that level, and is used in that manner.

As in other forms of resistance, acting out has to be understood in the context of the therapeutic syndrome. As in the case of all resistance, the patient is led to become aware of it and explore it in relation to himself and the therapeutic situation. The therapist here needs to help the patients in the group—the subject and the spectators—to recognize it as resistance and relate it to specific elements and themes of the interview in progress. It is through uncovering such self-protective subterfuges of the unconscious and exposing them to the examination of the rational part of the ego that psychic growth and emotional maturity are achieved. It is, therefore, essential that any acting-out resistance be understood whether it be absenteeism and silence or attack on the therapist and others. In this the therapist plays an important role; for though members of a group usually are alert to many of their fellow patients' strategies, resistance is less likely to be recognized by them for what it is.

Acting out as a form of resistance to treatment is employed by patients also outside the therapeutic setting. To prevent the usually painful revelations and discussion, patients take steps in their personal lives that resolve external conflicts or solve situational and relationship difficulties. This is done not as a result of emotional maturity and intellectual clarity achieved through psychotherapy, but rather as an escape from the arduous process of treatment, as a means of defeating the therapist, to exhibit superiority and capability, or as prevention of pain and discomfort. These acts, though performed outside the group sessions as well, have to be treated as resistance to treatment. The motives and intent in this seeming self-reliance and good management have to be explored. The therapist confronts the patient with his act and explores with him and the group as a whole the reasons for such seemingly expeditious behavior.

As a reaction to fear. Acting out through aggression or withdrawal and silence may be reactions to fear and discomfort in group situations. This discomfort may arise from memories of the pain experienced and threats to self-esteem in the original family of the patient; it may stem from exhibitionistic trends, from self-consciousness having a sexual source, from a distorted body image, or a fear of revealing a particularly guilt- and anxiety-evoking thought or experience. The latter may be conscious, preconscious, or unconscious. In either case the patient is wary or defensive and will abreact by aggressiveness or will be demure, cautious, quiet, or entirely silent.

Obviously a patient with the syndrome of fear cannot be dealt with directly. Directness and effort at exploration and uncovering may cause further withdrawal, adoption of different means of concealment, or the patient may decamp from treatment altogether. Such patients require security and acceptance as a first step. The support of a group through identifications and universalization and general atmosphere of tolerance, acceptance, and helpfulness dissolve diffidence and fears, making the patient accessible to other more direct treatment procedures.

However, the strategy of watchful waiting on the part of the therapist is not as easily applicable to aggressive abreacting to fear. This behavior may prove distressing to the others in the group. Overacting patients not only vitiate the therapeutic atmosphere but may actually cause the group's disruption. On the other hand, restraining such patients would only increase their panic and justify their distrust. Most patients with these syndromes are unsuitable for groups; they require a period of individual treatment to work through the intrapsychic difficulties that necessitate this particular pattern of adaptation.

As provocation. The aim of acting out in a group may be to provoke aggression against oneself. The motive for this may be the need for punishment, conditioned behavior through early family relations, psychic masochism, or latent homosexuality. Provocative members are a strain on the group as a whole and are sometimes unendurable to some neurotic and emotionally intolerant patients. However, in most instances provocativeness is accessible to group treatment. The reaction of the group members and the mirror they provide have a salutary effect upon patients who resort to it. Ordinarily the therapist finds little need to deal with it himself, since this behavior arouses other members to action.

There are occasions, however, when the therapist has to step in to allay the tension and anger engendered by a specially provocative patient. He can do so by directly attacking the act, but not the patient, explore and interpret it for what it is and what its intention is. The therapist can ask the group to explore the reasons of the behavior; he may explore with the patient in question his own motives so that he may relate his current acts to his past, or the therapist may supply the explanation himself.

Psychic masochism tends to disappear through group psychotherapy due to the inevitable ego-reinforcement that results from it and the improved self-image and self-esteem. Unless the group reacts punitively and with rejection, patients with this character disturbance gain rapidly from group treatment. Latent homosexuality, on the other hand, is not as accessible, and such acting-out patients may create considerable problems in groups. In the first place they generate a high level of anxiety by their very presence. The unconscious of the members of the group responds to the personality of such a patient and they feel threatened, partly because of everyone's susceptibility to it and partly because of the reactive cultural conditioning against it. The therapist, on the other hand, cannot bring it to the awareness of either the subject or the other members. This pathology requires a slow and careful unfolding in treatment in which oral dependencies, sexual identifications, and early fixations have to be explored, all of which can be done in groups, though individual treatment is a much more effective tool in such cases.

As striving for status. Acting out may be employed with the purpose of gaining status through self-assertiveness, submission, exhibitionism, or rivalry. A common means for attaining this end is intellectualization with display of knowledge and information on related and more often unrelated topics under consideration. By these means the individual strives to achieve status and prestige. Frequently patients given to this pattern are verbose, domineering, critical, and attempt to choke off participation by other members through dogmatism and authoritativeness. They attempt to displace the therapist by answering questions addressed to him and freely giving information.

The striving for status may be a continuation of the patient's family pattern in which rivalrous and assertive conduct was fostered; it may be a result of feelings of inferiority which he wards off through self-maximation, or a reaction formation to castration anxiety. Often exhibitionism reflects an eroticized intellect which has become the center of potency rather than the genitals. Because of early emphasis on the importance of intellectual achievement or strong physical inferiority feelings, the intellect may be invested with genital powers and significance, a clear case of displacement "from below to above." Women with masculine strivings are subject to intellect erotization, but often, though not always, they seek status through feminine attractiveness, exaggerated charm and emphasis on appearance. All of these are disguises for their masculine strivings, however.

Both the male and female syndromes in the striving for status can be corrected through group psychotherapy. The ease with which status is attained, the negative reactions to efforts at domination, the new and corrected identifications and improved self-image—all tend to counteract these and other strivings.[5] There is, therefore, no need for special measures or intervention on the part of the therapist here beyond the ordinary role he has to play in the group.

Difficult to deal with in groups are patients who make a bid for status by massive exhibitionism. Exhibitionism is closely related to and is a derivative of narcissism with strong sexual overtones. Few patients with strong exhibitionistic tendencies can be retained in groups without setting off strong hostility in the others and consequent anxiety, the intensity of which may become so high that in course of time it may disrupt the group or seriously undermine its effectiveness.

5. The exception to this rule is where strivings for status stem from narcissism. This aspect of it will be discussed presently in the section under that title.

Patients in groups can seek status by submisiveness, compliance, ingratiation, placation, and bribery. This adaptive manner has to be accepted until the underlying psychologic causes are overcome and the patient alters his behavior. Behind the external timidity there always lurks latent hostility, which should be brought out into the open. The characterological and fear elements and the possible sexual seduction that may be hidden can be left untouched in the group interviews, for unless they are severe, they automatically disappear with the intrapsychic changes that result from psychotherapy. The total atmosphere and the attitudes of the patients and therapist encourage more assertive conduct, which is later reflected in an improved total personality. However, the therapist needs to be vigilant with this type of patient, for their manner may cover serious pathology.

Emotional hypochondriasis. Though they form a small segment, some patients repeatedly dwell upon their tragic lives and backgrounds. Session after session, as in a treadmill, facts and fancies are reiterated, each narration a replica of all the preceding. They recount unhappiness, mistreatment, and "insurmountable" difficulties in the past and in their current lives. Little variation is supplied in this repetitive circle of events and tragedies, the aim of which is the yearning to be pitied and to receive sympathy. As though he entertains a belief in the magic of words, the patient has a vague expectancy that pity and understanding will remedy his difficulties and his problems will disappear as by magic. The pattern of these patients is analogous to hypochondria, but instead of organic complaints, emotional stress is their point of fixation. This can be termed *emotional hypochondriasis* which has a strong element of narcissism, in addition to affect hunger, and a hidden trend to control persons in their environment. There may also be present a strong hysterical quality and in some instances also a psychotic element. Reality distortion is one of the characteristics of emotional hypochondriasis, and considerable sado-masochistic drives are present.

This pattern is employed as resistance to personality change, and, therefore, to the therapeutic effort, which is magnified in groups by the fact that the pity-seeking patient seldom fails to involve others in his emotional machinations, since the appeal is to the tender feelings of the listeners. Their superego being involved, prevents the latter from reacting negatively or unfeelingly; they usually offer advice that is repeated session after session, with consequent impediment to the therapeutic movement for all concerned. The nefarious aspect of it is that the behavior of one patient plays into and reinforces the natural trend toward resistance in every member of the group. All readily fall in with the subject's needs and devote the sessions to talk about his problems, give advice, make suggestions, and evade their own treatment. This is especially true of women's groups.

The patient and the group feed upon each other, each encouraging the other to dwell on the nonproductive recitals. Because the pity-seeking patient is so thoroughly immersed in his sadness and tragedies that strike a responsive note in the other members of the group, the therapist has to take a hand in breaking through the vicious circle. He has to confront the group and the patient with the reality of the situation, treating it as character resistance. The group members readily perceive this significance, though the offending patient may be slower in recognizing or accepting it. If the patient is too threatened, or where the quantum of affect or pathology counterindicate direct interpretation, the therapist may help him explore his background and feelings and give them dimension. Periodically he should turn to other members of the group so as to shift the focus of centricity away from the specific patient. As these strategies are repeated frequently enough, the patient in question will perceive that his self-preoccupation is not acceptable and he may either abandon it or withdraw from the group.

As a defense. Acting out, especially of an aggressive nature, is employed as a defense against expectation of attack from others or from a feeling of being unaccepted. While it has its roots in intrapsychic deficiencies, it is activated in interpersonal situations and exacerbated by group tensions. As such it has valuable therapeutic possibilities, for it provides opportunities for analysis of the interpersonal transferences that may exist among the group members and toward the therapist.

Since the ability to accept fellow human beings for what they are is an indication of emotional maturity, working through of interpatient attitudes and feelings provides the group with valuable therapeutic possibilities. The therapist must openly and pointedly recognize the emotional tensions in the group against which the abreaction occurs and help the patients unravel their individual feelings and the group tensions current at the time. The more sibling hostility is revealed and worked through, the better for the therapeutic activity of the group. Frequently defensive acting out is a temporary and short-lived reaction because the conditioned expectation of attack from the group is not confirmed. Usually, however, defensive acting out takes the form of silence and when it is accepted or tolerated by the group, the patient in time automatically overcomes his diffidence.

As a test. Closely related to the above motive for acting out is a patient's testing of the therapist and the group. This type of behavior, as well, disappears as he is assured of its acceptance of him.

As contagion. Acting out can become widespread in a group because of the element of contagion. Latent hostility and aggression are readily activated in a group by the hostility or aggression of one of its members, who can be designated as the *instigator* [53]. Through the processes of induction and intensification it can become a serious problem in group psychotherapy, requiring skillful and secure handling on the part of the therapist. This aspect of the problem will be dealt with later in this paper, but it is necessary to state at this juncture that it differs from the other types of acting out described by the fact that here we are faced with a group phenomenon as differentiated from acting out by individuals. In such a case the therapist has to deal with mass reaction rather than with an individual, which is vastly more fraught with difficulties and danger. The ego reinforcement and superego sanctions that group unanimity furnishes may cause transgression of reasonable bounds. Since the hostility is usually directed toward the therapist, the group lacks an integrative focus which he represents, and it may be disrupted. The comparatively uncontrolled discharge of hostility generates anxiety and guilt, which cannot abate or be allayed without outside control. The therapist must ever be on the alert against *unanimity* of any sort in therapy groups, for unanimity is always derived from hostility against the therapist.

Contagion in acting out, whether through overt acts or through widespread silence, is derived from the latent, unconscious or preconscious hostility to any parent or authority figure; but it can be caused also by specific interpersonal dynamics in a group. Chief of these is homosexual anxiety, activated by one or more of the group members. Another libidinal source is heterosexual competition in mixed groups; still another is widespread sibling rivalry for the attention or affection of the therapist or the group. I have elsewhere pointed out that sexual acting out among members of heterogeneous groups is usually a displacement of libidinal strivings toward the therapist [32]. If the group therapist is a male, the women patients gratify their sexual transference urges toward him by substituting the nearest male objects, fellow patients.

Several women patients who acted out sexually, each with a number of fellow male group members and who had inevitably left the groups as a result, stated to their subsequent analysts that they thought that by gratifying themselves in this manner, they would be rid of their neuroses. Their behavior is analogous to acting out on the part of girls who have unresolved oedipal urges toward their natural fathers and who become promiscuous or prostitutes.

As neurotic symptom. (a) In evaluating the phenomenology of acting out, the therapist must always keep in mind its neurotic sources. Because the term "neurotic" has come into indiscriminate use, it would be essential that its exact meaning be ascertained as a measure against confusion.

Although the underlying causes for some of the various types of acting out may be termed "neurotic" (in so far as they are exaggerated or overintensified reactions incommensurate with the stimuli or irritants) the term is employed here in its classical sense, namely, the unresolved conflict between the superego and id with which the ego is unable to deal adequately. Another characteristic of the psychoneuroses is that the conflict originates in the sexual libido (in terms of its content) and in the oedipal conflict (in the dimension of time). The result of the unresolved conflict between the psychic forces is "the symptom," which for reasons not always clear manifests itself either in purely psychogenic behavioral reactions or in somatic disturbances.

In a comparatively small number of psychoneurotics such symptoms may not make their appearance, but instead the intrapsychic tensions propel the individual to unceasing activity, frequently of a random nature. The impulsivity that characterizes such patients serves to discharge internal conflict through action by transmutation of emotional into physical energy. This impulsivity is not accessible either to examination by the ego or to its control. The pattern becomes a part of the character organization and is structured, as it were, into the total personality. Because of this internalization and its being part and parcel of the character structure, the term "neurotic character" is employed to label it. Sometimes it is referred to as "impulse neurosis." The acting out *is* the symptom.

Stemming as it does from the structure of the personality itself and being inaccessible to the ego, the behavior of patients with neurotic character disorders is difficult, if at all possible, to reach through psychotherapy. The patients with this disturbance, therefore, have to be excluded from groups.[6] They are unable to contain the overwhelming anxiety and throw it off in incessant overt acts and speech, and infect all the members of the group. They monopolize the interviews and block the free flow of group participation, thus intensifying feelings of frustration of their fellow members, which, in turn, increases their anxiety further. Such patients have to be eliminated not only because they are inaccessible, which of itself is sufficient reason, but even more because of the deleterious effects they have upon the therapeutic process and the other members of the group.

(b) Related to the type of acting out described are the "traumatophilic" patients, patients who have a neurotic need to create difficulties for themselves and are, therefore, prone to activate rejection and attack, suffering and unhappiness. Such patients keep groups always in a stir and prevent their members from effectively participating in the therapeutic process. The effect such patients have is the same as those described under the section entitled *As provocation.* The difference, however, is that the basic neurotic conflict from which traumatophilia stems requires deeper analytic unraveling than groups can provide. In addition, traumatophilic patients do not give the group members a chance to work on their problems, and they, too, have to be eliminated from group psychotherapy.

(c) Another neurotic acting-out syndrome is compulsive talking that affects groups adversely. Compulsive talking is part of a neurotic character syndrome, but it may appear also apart from it. It is found among compulsive persons, among those with intense dependence needs, and as a part of a character neurosis. It is doubtful whether compulsive patients in whom the inner need for talking is intense

---

6. "Neurotic character" has to be differentiated from "character neurosis." The latter is accessible by analytic group psychotherapy.

could be assimilated by groups because of the inhibiting and frustrating effect they have upon fellow patients.

As narcissism. Acting out by persons who exploit the group for narcissistic ends presents a special difficulty. A striking phenomenon, as we have observed it, is that groups do not react more negatively to the acting out of narcissism than they do. Many of the mechanisms and patterns described have narcissistic coloring, but there are patients whose character disturbances stem from what is clinically considered as "primary narcissism." The manifestations of narcissism, its etiology and pathogenesis are too well known to require detailing here. These patients are assertive, exhibitionistic, and exploitive and do not fare well in therapy groups.

Groups are more helpful with narcissistic children than they are with adults, partly because of the nature of childhood narcissism as compared with that of adults and because free group life and interaction are a *growth-producing milieu,* which leads them to alter their personalities and their mode of behavior. However, where the acting out is intense and compulsive, it interferes with a group's therapeutic activity, and the patient may have to be withdrawn from the group after a period of trial to be placed in a group at a later date.

As character disorder. The syndromes of neurotic character, compulsiveness and narcissism are not the only categories of character disorders that produce acting out. Women with masculine, and some men with feminine, identifications are overbearing and dictatorial in manner and statements, and are difficult on their fellow patients because they, too, interfere with the therapeutic process through their assertiveness and domination. These women and men are not easily affected by psychotherapy, but where the character rigidities are not too inflexible, group psychotherapy is the treatment of choice for them, though the prognosis is never certain in these cases. The reactions of the group and the mirroring of their behavior by fellow patients do help to some extent in making inroads into their character. Another factor supporting their improvement are the models for corrective identification provided by the group.

The Categories of Acting Out

It is clear from the preceding that the phenomenon of acting out is not unicausal, nor are the nosology, etiology, and therapeutics uniform. It is multicausal, requiring diagnostic understanding and suitable therapeutic intervention. Such specificity is not limited to acting out, but must be applied to all aspects of therapeutic activity. It is my belief that only through such singularity will the effectiveness of therapeutic effort be assured. While they may serve as frames of reference or as conceptual orientation, blanket theories and generalizations, impressive and enticing as they may be, can help but little in the actual workaday practice of the therapist. Practice of any craft or profession requires knowledge of the phenomenology and dynamics operating in its various detailed manifestations. There are, however, some basic generalizations discernible in acting out, a brief enumeration of which follows.

Acting out as regression. As already suggested, acting out always connotes either a regression or a fixation. It is regression when an individual reverts under stress to a pattern of behavior he has outgrown and which is no longer appropriate either to his chronologic age or social role. The pattern that he reenacts and to which he reverts is one that had been employed earlier in his development, especially during childhood. This genetic regression is demonstrated most in the forms of acting out described above under the headings of *Provocation, Testing, Striving for status, Emotional hypochondriasis,* and *Abreaction.*

As fixation. Patients in psychotherapy who have not progressed from infantile levels in some aspects of their personality, but have remained *fixed* at those levels, cannot be said to *regress* to an earlier stage or pattern, because they have never grown beyond it. They therefore behave not *as though* they are children, which is the case in regression, but *as* children. These fixated feelings, attitudes and responses form part of the character of the person and present special, but not insurmountable, difficulties to all types of psychotherapy, including psychoanalysis. Acting out through fixation is demonstrated by the following forms we have described: *Narcissism, Character disorder, Defenses, Reaction to fear, Neurotic character.*

As ego asthenia. Acting out is always a symptom of ego insufficiency, attempting to deal with autogenetic (internal) stress or those external stresses that produce internal strain (exogenetic stress). The anxiety in the face of tasks too difficult for the ego powers makes it susceptible to acting out in various forms, such as excessive verbalization, heightened affect, random activity or mobility (by which means one controls the environment through infantile omnipotence) or through attack (the aim of which is destruction or elimination of the offending or invading person or situation). As the ego is threatened or assailed, it defends itself against weakness and anxiety by mobilizing primitive attack or by withdrawal. The latter is in some respects similar to the death feint of some animals in danger. Examples of this are *Reaction to fear, Striving for status* and *Contagion.*

As ontogenetic recapitulation. We have seen that the form which acting out takes is a replica of earlier life patterns that either served effectively or satisfyingly in the past or which were forced upon the individual. Thus, the statements of some writers to the effect that acting out has no genetic relation is not substantiated. Acting out has a direct relation to the individual's past and is a direct outgrowth of his adaptations and the strategies it was necessary for him to adopt in his adjustment to his environment. These are stored up in the unconscious memory and when the ego and its controls are weakened by stress, they become operative, assert themselves, and propel the individual to act out in habitual, though perhaps forgotten or latent, ways. Ontogenetic acting out is demonstrated by the forms described as *Abreaction, Resistance, Provocation, Emotional hypochondriasis, Defense, Testing, Neurotic symptom, Character disorder.*

As phylogenetic recapitulation. The emotions of anger and hostility and the patterns of aggression and withdrawal by which regression is manifested are not all ontogenetic; some are rather phylogenetic survivals of primitive stages of man's biological and social evolution. They had served as tools for survival but had become obsolete in the course of his social development. They remain as hidden reservoirs, as neuronic engrams which come forth from the racial storehouse and become operative in the life and behavior of the individual. Such primary emotions as fear, rage, love, jealousy, and hostility can only be *shaped* by experience but *not engendered* by it. Their roots are in the instinctive needs in the struggle for survival and appear in modern man in vastly modified and disguised forms that often obscure their original source. It is these phylogenetic trends and urges, among others, that patients act out during group sessions. The aims and results of psychotherapy are repression of some, the transmutation of others, and the sublimation of still other instinctive responses into suitable social forms. The phylogenetic recapitulation forms of acting out include *Release, Fear, Striving for status, Contagion,* and *Narcissism.*

Child vs. Adult Acting Out

The preceding considerations of acting out in therapy groups have been directed to adult nonpsychotic patients. Acting out can be beneficially utilized in the therapy of adults, as already pointed out, but it is neither essential nor is it a preferred method of catharsis. Acting out by children, however, is essential, whether in groups or individual therapy. Action and not words is the language of the child. The level of his conceptualization, the limited facility with words and ideas, the still incomplete controls of mobility, the need for manipulation and exploration—all impel the child to motility. He communicates his thoughts and feelings through action, which the therapist has to understand and respond to appropriately. Just as the verbal communications of adults have their manifest and latent counterparts, children's *action communication,* as well, consists of the overt (manifest) acts and behavior which have latent meaning that a trained therapist in work with children can properly discern.

Acting out is the appropriate form of catharsis in all child psychotherapy. In individual play therapy as well as in the analytic types of groups for children—Play-Group and Activity-Interview Group Psychotherapy—the acting out is controlled and directed through uncovering and interpretation, as well as by direct restraint when that is indicated. In activity groups it is allowed to take its course. The therapeutic results accrue from individual interactions in the group, the *primary group code,* as it subtly emerges and the neutrality of and *action interpretation* by the therapist.[7]

Acting out and catharsis are synonymous in child psychotherapy. However, there are degrees and areas of activity catharsis that exceed the limits of permissibility. These are the possibility of physical injury, excessive impulsivity and unpredictability of behavior, as in borderline psychotics and the brain injured (especially where other

---

7. Because of the avoidance of interpretation and the controls that accrue from it, the selection and grouping of patients is of vital importance and essential to the survival of activity therapy groups.

members of the group are involved), mounting destructibility and uncontrolled physical attack upon fellow group members or the therapist.

The Therapist's Role in Acting Out

The psychotherapist's role in acting out has been indicated in each case, though briefly, under the various phenomenological classifications. From these the reader will have deduced that in the case of acting out, as in all elements and situations in psychotherapy, no blanket technique is available to him. His response and his dealing with it have to be appropriate to the situation, the specific patient, the effect upon other members of the group, the group as an entity, the therapeutic indications at the moment, and above all, the transference relation that exists between him and his patients.

All the suggestions of dealing with acting-out patients and groups in the preceding pages have been made on the assumption that the basic transference relation is a positive one and that acting out is a transitory negative phase of it. Any move toward curbing or exploring behavior of patients without positive transference, would reinforce negative and hostile feelings in them, with deleterious if not disastrous results. All of the therapist's responses and acts must take into consideration the transference attitudes that prevail at a given time. The factor of timing, so rightly emphasized in psychotherapy, needs to be extended to include not only the readiness of patients, but also its applicability to the relation between the patient and therapist, as well as *the therapist's own readiness*. The latter is a factor that is too often overlooked, but is especially vital in dealing with acting out.

In whatever form it occurs, acting out is always felt by the therapist as a tacit attack upon himself; and in this he is right. Acting out occurs in transference, and the therapist is the sole target in individual psychotherapy and at least the major focus in a group. To accept attack with equanimity is no small task, even for objective and detached individuals, and therapists are not free of the need to be accepted, respected, and treated with consideration. Bearing up under direct or tacit attack is particularly difficult in a group because of the possibility that the hostilities of other members would be mobilized as well, thus creating a phalanx against him. This does not mean that the therapist should not face this situation and at infrequent times even encourage it. The expression of hostility in transference has valuable therapeutic potentials. What I wish to convey here is an awareness of the difficulties and strain, and the importance of the therapist's self-confrontation in this regard. He must not undertake a task that he cannot fulfill, for a display of weakness or sensitivity would affect undesirably his role as ego-ideal and object of identification. This is true of adult patients as it is of children. Any display of vulnerability intensifies and mobilizes aggression in patients and when the libidinal investment in the therapist is withdrawn, his function and value are diminished or invalidated.

An important function of the "supervisor," or one who "controls" group psychotherapists, is to prevent them, particularly those who are new to the practice, from exceeding their own tolerance, for the therapist must always retain his status as ego support and object of identification for his patients. To do this he has to remain imperturbable. As he gains confidence through experience and his security increases, he can allow greater acting out and show of hostility. The supervisor's awareness of the therapist's limitations in this regard is of utmost and even critical importance.

Some group therapists shy away from acting out and employ various strategems to prevent it. The most common of these is the assumption of a manner of extreme kindness, graciousness, and paternalism. This succeeds in holding patient's hostilities in abeyance, but the therapeutic results are greatly diminished by it. *Where there is no hostility there is no therapy.* When hostility remains unexpressed and not "worked through"[8] one can achieve at best only some degree of symptom or behavioral improvement but not psychic equilibrium (that is, an efficient relationship between the id, ego, and superego) which requires egress of hostility in a therapeutic transference relation and the insight to which it leads.

Some group therapists who placate their patients by various means rationalize it on the ground that they play out the good parental role. Other therapists devaluate their status by participating in the group interviews on the same level as the patients. They describe their preoccupations and reactions even to the extent of discussing their

8. For the dynamic meaning of this phrase see [103].

intimate relations. The equalization of status of therapist and patients prevents mobilization of hostility toward him. Since he does not function *in locus parentis* the transference reactions are not activated, but for obvious reasons psychotherapeutic objectives cannot be attained in this relation. In a sense this plan approaches the method of the "leaderless group," which, on the face of it, is therapeutically invalid.[9]

There are group therapists, on the other hand, who consciously or unconsciously encourage acting out by their groups. Although activation of hostility is necessary at specific times and when therapeutically indicated, stirring up groups (or individual patients, for that matter) as a blanket technique is counterindicated. To be therapeutic, groups have to alternate between *nodal* (highest pitch of hyperactivity) and *antinodal* (quietude) behavior; as I have already suggested, the peak therapeutic effects occur at the point of antinodality [128].[10] It is here that the emergence of ego controls and the personality integration process are at their highest. Nodal behavior among adults is naturally very much less intense and less frequent than among children, and the therapist should not maintain a group at a level of nodal acting out.

Therapists who have not undergone a thoroughgoing psychoanalysis, therefore, retain unconscious motivations, act out, at times actively but most often passively, unconscious needs. In some instances these may be the need to discharge their aggressions, or activate group antagonism and turmoil which are replicas of the behavior in their families, for some unanalyzed or improperly analyzed therapists are themselves not free of traumatophilic trends in varying degrees. The difficulties they encounter, which are of their doing, yield for them unconscious satisfactions. There are some who gain from group turmoil a sense of importance and power; while others feel they are effective and important—they earn their money, as it were—when things are difficult. As a result of these and other unconscious motivations, therapists may encourage acting out unnecessarily, as others, for equally unconscious reasons, prevent it when it should occur for therapeutic advantage.

9. By definition and by phenomenological function, there is no possibility for a group to remain leaderless. It may start as such, but soon indigenous leaders appear. No group of people can function without a leader. Without leadership, groups disintegrate.
10. This principle applies to analytic groups as well, in fact, to all groups and assemblies of every kind.

TABLE 1

The Phenomenology of Acting Out

Forms	Types	Causes	Services	Categories	*Advantages*	Disadvantages*
Verbal	Normal	Organic tension	Release	Regressive	Self-revelation	Prevention of insight
Anger	Therapeutic	Psychic tension	Abreaction	Ontogenetic	Action communication	Intensification through contagion
Spite	Parapathologic	Threat to ego defenses	Resistance	Phylogenetic	Mirror reaction	
Teasing	Pathologic	Fear	Provocation			
Screaming	Induced	Emotional hypochondriasis	Striving for status			
Threats	*Ex situ*	Contagion	Arouse pity			
Nonverbal		Neurotic symptom	Defense			
Body tension		Neurotic character	Testing			
Involuntary movements		Traumatophilia				
Grimaces		Compulsiveness				
Facial color		Narcissism				
Expression of eyes		Character disorders				
Posture		Ego asthenia				
Throwing objects						
Smoking						
Silence						
Absence						
Lateness						

*These two topics have not been discussed in the present paper.

One of the strategies that favors especially *ex situ* acting out are the so-called "alternate session" that some group therapists employ. These are meetings where the patients foregather in the absence of the therapist in addition to those at which he is present. Lacking a person who represents or symbolizes authority, a parental figure, and a central focus of object cathexis for the group members, their hostilities, counterhostilities, affections, and friendships are not canalized and employed therapeutically but run riot. The libidinal cathexis which is ordinarily fixed on the therapist is diffused and is attached to various other members which leads, in mixed groups, to sexual acting out. The abrogation of the rule of social incognito in psychotherapy also results in the patients' confusion as to their role and relationships. Even the conversations at sessions from which the therapist is absent have the characteristics of acting out because they are not directed or focused, and interpretation is lacking. Usually one of the most disturbed and narcissistic patients takes over the leadership of the group and, having no training or insight into the latent content of the productions, confuses his fellow patients.

Such free-for-all sessions, with the attendant amorous consequences, may be very pleasing to patients. They feel unhampered and uncontrolled by the therapist or by impositions inherent in therapy and in society generally. But emotional reeducation and intrapsychic changes are never pleasurable; patients must suffer; only in suffering does change lie. Persons who seek change have to bear pain, for "suffering is the crucible in which the soul is purified." Whatever pleasures, peace and "happiness" accrue are *a result of* psychotherapy. Happiness is not part of the *process* of therapy.

CHAPTER 23

STEPS IN SENSITIZING PARENTS
TOWARD SCHIZOPHRENIC CHILDREN
(1963)

As a move toward more effective results in guiding parents to understand and deal with their children in a child guidance clinic, two steps were taken. One was the separation of parents of schizoid and schizophrenic children from those with nonschizophrenic children; the other was that both parents, father and mother, were included in the same group. The latter step was a departure from our usual procedures, which have been described elsewhere [60].

Both empirically and theoretically it is ordinarily considered more efficacious to place fathers and mothers in separate groups and to form the groups on the basis of the sex and the same age range of the offspring. Since all are faced with more or less similar situations and in many instances with identical problems, the parents carry on more focused and aim-directed discussions. This favors more pertinent and relevant interchange. The common interests and preoccupations assist in clarifications and suggestions.

The separation of fathers from mothers is motivated by two considerations. One is that the role of the father in the daily life of the child is vastly different from that of the mother. Of necessity, each deals with different aspects of the offspring's life, both because of differences in the symbolic meaning of each and the difference in contact with the child in point of time and content. Also, the role of each parent is determined, in part, by the sex of the child. This bio-socio-psychological variability needs to be kept in mind in forming and conducting child-centered guidance groups for parents.

In the instance of the group under study here, however, these considerations were suspended, and both parents were included in the same group. This step was taken because we came to recognize that the parents were not cognizant of the real nature of the illness of their children; they were not aware of the children's fragility and limited capacities for school achievement and for establishing social relations. All of the parents, fathers and mothers, made demands on the children far beyond the children's capacities. This unfeeling and insensitive treatment served to increase the children's anxiety, enhancing their sense of failure, worthlessness, defeat, and doom, and intensifying their rebellion and suppressed hostility.

When the parents of schizophrenic children were members of groups that included parents of nonschizophrenic children, the decisions arrived at for dealing with the latter did not apply to their special circumstances. Indeed, plans and insights suitable to the nonpsychotic youngsters proved deleterious when applied to the youngsters under consideration here. As one mother accurately remarked, "The problem with my son seems quite different from the problems of the others."

The six couples who formed the original membership of this special group were parents of four girls and two boys of high school age. To this group were later added the parents of another boy. The problems of the children had a wide range. One girl was schizoid, withdrawn, asocial; one boy was delusional in his conversation; another boy hallucinated on occasion. The girls and boys were being treated in separate groups, except for the hallucinating boy, whom we soon transferred to individual treatment, with good symptom improvement eventuating. The following year the delusional youth was also referred to individual therapy. At the end of the year, one of the girls was removed, on our recommendation, to residential treatment in a school because of the mother's serious problems. The other three girls improved sufficiently for treatment to be terminated, although one was continued in individual guidance on an occasional basis. All four girls had two years of group treatment.

The parents were not told why their group membership was altered from separate groups of which they had been members. This presented no problem since the new grouping was inaugurated in the fall, the beginning of the clinic year. We found the parents cooperative, their attitudes ranging from intense eagerness to moderate interest. In all instances the mothers fell into the former category, as did one of the fathers, while one father was comparatively aloof although he attended all sessions. His attitude was a result of his personality; he was at least schizoid, probably schizophrenic. The father of one girl never attended the group. The group met alternate weeks for ninety minutes.

Note must be taken of the fact that all the parents had been members of "mixed" guidance groups for short periods and were acquainted with group procedure, but they had not been able to concentrate in those groups on their children's special peculiarities and special problems. In the new group the parents were able to agree, after only a brief series of discussions, that the children of all of them were shy and deficient in relation to their peers. Some, including one father, related their own shyness during adolescence, and the mother of one of the girls concluded that she had pushed her sixteen-year-old daughter too fast in arranging a birthday party for her; the celebrant "went into a panic" when the guests, all girls, sang happy birthday to her. Another mother reported that her son "burst into tears and ran out of the room" in a similar situation. Several parents disclosed that their children were diffident in their polite talk to strangers but arrogant toward their parents. This seemed a common phenomenon in the families represented in the group. Another more or less common theme among the group members was that the youngsters had achieved, as a result of attendance at the clinic, some improvements in school and in relationships; a few of the youngsters actually held simple jobs successfully during the preceding summer. Some of the daughters were very attractive but considered themselves ugly. In conversation the boys and girls always stressed their failures and inadequacies, never mentioning their assets and achievements. We called attention to this fact but refrained from explaining it beyond inquiring whether this negative image might not be the result of the parents' and schools' high expectations and demands which the boys and girls could not meet.

This rather threatening question was raised only because it was an extension of what the parents had said concerning "pushing" their children too fast. We followed the cue they gave us, and they were in a sense ready to accept, if not to respond to, this suggestion. One of the more psychologically literate fathers, a welfare worker, Mr. S., wondered if they did not "expect our children to grow up too fast? We resent it when they don't meet our standards." Mrs. C. remarked that her sixteen-year-old daughter could not even call for a taxi, adding, "I tell her she is grown up enough to do it, and if she can't (use the phone), then she does not need a taxi." Mr. and Mrs. S. reassured her that "clumsiness is part of growing up. All of us were like that at one time, and all kids are like that." Mrs. C. remained adamant, however, saying, "I can't treat her like a baby all the time." When Mr. K., the father of a boy, suggested that "too many things are turned into an issue," Mrs. T. reported that when she yells at her daughter "for three days," the girl will do what she wants her to do but "then she is back doing exactly what she used to do before."

The leader here took the first step toward sensitizing the parents to the uniqueness of their children saying: "There seem to be two trends in the discussion. One is that our children are still very dependent, very much like babies. At times we are not aware of this and make too great demands on them. They appear frightened by it and, in a sense, they say to us, 'We can do nothing, expect nothing from us.' We would not be impatient if a small child fussed and said no, but we would expect him to do things and we would help him by being kindly but firm and ignoring his fussing. On the other hand, there seems to be a tendency to treat these children as though they really cannot do anything for themselves, and we are so helpful that it reinforces their convictions of helplessness."

At the next session, two of the mothers elaborated on the defiant withdrawal of their girls during the preceding weekend. One girl had gone to her room and spent almost the entire weekend there by herself, "probably day-dreaming"; the other mother described her daughter's reluctance "to participate in the family." Mr. and Mrs. S., on the other hand, reported remarkable "reasonableness" on the part of their son in a particular circumstance, whereas they had expected great resistance. Mr. S. concluded by saying that the incident led him to believe that "We really do not know our children."

We explored with the group the manner in which the parents asked or ordered their children to do things in the home. It was obvious to us that the parents' authoritarian attitudes and impatience aroused rebellion in their hostile and angry offspring. We therefore decided to raise the question of how their mates would respond to the same tone of voice and peremptoriness. This stopped them all. As the question was bandied about by all the members present, they became aware of the inappropriateness of their approach and explored better ways of dealing with the children. However,the solutions were largely in the area of devices and artifices, rather than subjective attitudes. Suggestions such as posting notices on the family bulletin board were made. One of the fathers suggested that "perhaps because we always tell our children no, they always tell us no in return." Mrs. H., whose daughter spent the entire weekend in her room, offered an important observation at this point which we utilized later. She observed that her daughter seemed to "structure" the days for herself. Perhaps, she said, this is a key to the "management problem." This was not picked up at this point for we felt that the parents did not as yet understand their children enough to apply such an approach beneficially, for structuring may be used in the service of domination. The session ended with Mr. S.'s statement: "We have to try to understand why they (the children) don't want to do anything. If we could understand this it would be helpful."

We considered it our chief task to bring this understanding to them.

At the next session the parents talked about their children as "overreacting, repressing feelings, and having no confidence in themselves." They tried to trace the causes for this in the children's backgrounds. At this point, we pushed forward our idea by stating that while there undoubtedly were relations in the home that contributed to the children's difficulties, the fact could not be overlooked that some children are born more sensitive than others and what seems like "overreacting" is actually the nature of the child and he cannot control his behavior or do better.

One of the mothers responded to this immediately, stating that this was certainly true of her child and quoted a number of instances to confirm the leader's assertion. After considerable group discussion, Mr. K., who was not too perceptive a person, said that he felt that "it is true that our children are extremely sensitive" and proceeded to say that sometimes when he asked an entirely innocent question, his son considered it as a critical statement. Mr. C. explained this as a means of getting attention, but his wife definitely disagreed. She elaborated on this and ended by saying: "It is almost as if these children need to punish themselves." Mrs. S. jumped in and exclaimed: "This need is a tremendous one on the part of our children!"

In their own way the parents had recognized three major mechanisms of the schizophrenic; hostility to parents, their paranoid quality, and the self-destructive urge. Understanding the nature of the children was carried further by Mr. K., who, in contrast to the earlier extreme pressures he placed on his son to achieve higher school grades, now expressed his gratification with his son's being placed in a class of retarded children because "the pressure has been removed from him and he is actually showing responsiveness to other people, which he did not before." He added, but without rancor, "It is still true that he does not do anything in school."

In a later session the same father calmly stated: "He [the boy] is immature and frightened, and to remain in school for another year and a half where he does not feel stigmatized and where really nothing is expected of him might be helpful, because things are happening to B." He then narrated a "very satisfactory and helpful conversation" between the boy and his parents. Mr. K. was elated as he added, "He has never opened up, never talked to us the way he did this time. This is the first time a wedge has been established in the wall of silence between B. and me."

Mr. S. pointed out that what was important in this development was that the son had sought out the father. The leader reinforced this thought by stating that the youngsters under consideration were extremely fearful; they were afraid to come to the parents with their problems. The leader emphasized how important it was for the parents to establish themselves as "friends" in the eyes of their children.

Mr. C., who was rather punitive toward his borderline and very disturbed daughter, followed this statement up with: "Perhaps we don't give our children enough support. When they were young we acted as judges, always deciding for them what was right and what was wrong. Perhaps what these children need is our support and not our acting as judges." Several parents, in a wave of confession, then spoke of losing their tempers or showing irritation with the children because they seemed to be unable to do things on their own and constantly demanded help.

At the next session, Mr. S. suggested that they talk of other topics than kids—he was "sick of talking about kids"—but he soon turned to his wife and asked her to report on their son. M., said his mother, had extended his money-earning activities and was getting on well, but had difficulties with his Spanish teacher. The mother was called in by the school principal to discuss this. The mother had observed the Spanish teacher before and found her a woman "full of rage. She walked up and down the room like a caged lion.... For M. this must be an upsetting experience." She did not blame him for his reaction to this teacher, she said, and when the principal asked her to see her son's instructors, she refused, stating that it was up to him to coordinate their work with respect to her son. He backed down and promised to follow up on the matter. She ended her recital by saying: "This is an indication of the change in me. Ordinarily I would have gone and exposed myself to all the unpleasantness. Now I was able to let my disgust come through." Both parents agreed that they were "different people" since coming to the group. Having reduced their child's dependency on them, the parents too had become less dependent.[1]

A rather extensive discussion ensued at this point in which all the parents described their children's reactions, which led Mrs. C., the least understanding of the mothers, to conclude, "I guess our children are all alike." When the discussion veered to the children's irritability, Mr. K. described his feelings when he returned home from his office. He anticipated problems and when he saw, perhaps, a coat lying out of place, he at once lost his temper. "Maybe," he said, "B. is reacting the same way." Mrs. C. made the point that children need time when they come from school to "readjust themselves from the outside to the home" and that parents needed to give them time and not pounce on them with questions and suggestions as soon as they entered the house.

This thought was reinforced by the leader and concrete suggestions were made as to ways of receiving the children and helping them to reenter the family arena without too great strain. Suggestions of the same nature had been made before, but apparently without lasting effect. Recognizing the importance of this, we decided to take up this matter again as a planned step toward furthering understanding of the

---

1. One of the chief functions of the leader of a parents' group is to demonstrate by his conduct the attitudes he wishes the parents to adopt toward their children.

children's intrapsychic structure. The leader accordingly said at the appropriate time: "Some of these youngsters harbor a great deal of hostility toward us. This is part of the nature of their problem. When they express anger and we become upset by it, we only intensify their anxiety and thereby increase their hostility." Thus, the third characteristic of the schizophrenic syndrome of which the parents were by now aware, hostility, was brought to their overt attention [61, chapter 16].

Since they had all experienced the underlying hostility of their children, this statement evoked universal response. Mrs. K., however, was puzzled by the fact that when she called B.'s attention to his anger, he always told her that he was not angry. The leader explained that in the children they were discussing, anger was so much a part of them that they could not recognize it, which, the leader added, was true of their other feelings and reactions as well. One of the mothers concluded from these remarks that parents *"should not take these outbursts personally."*

Five sessions (ten weeks) later, the parents brought out a number of common characteristics in their children: they played with children younger than themselves on an immature level; they were unable to relate adequately to their age peers; they became compulsively absorbed in a single interest; they lacked control, etc. Here we played another trump card, as it were, a strategy of pivotal importance. The leader suggested that perhaps these children were *born with some lack* that made it impossible for them to grow the way other children did. Mr. B. reacted to this by saying it made him think of his (delusional) son. When he was a small child and was bounced up, instead of showing fear as young children usually do, he would stretch out his arms as though he were going to fly, "as though he had no reflexes, as though his wires were crossed somewhere." Mr. S. wondered whether there was "something physical lacking" in these children. Mrs. C. remarked that sometimes she felt that this was the case with her daughter.

The leader exploited this newly emerging awareness by putting forward the idea that there was a possibility of an actual physical or biochemical deficit in the children, that there was "something lacking at birth, perhaps something chemical." It was suggested that the compulsive activity to which the parents often referred was a way by which these youngsters kept themselves together and interested in at least a part of the reality around them.

At the same session, love was one of the themes, and various episodes relating to it were described by several parents. Mr. A. narrated an incident that had puzzled him. His son wanted a special object for his hobby collection that could be obtained only in Manhattan, and the father suggested that M. go along with him since he too was going to the city. M. asked his father whether he would go with him directly to the store and was told that Mr. S. would have to stop off first to see his own father, who was ill.   "Never mind," said the boy impetuously, "I'll go to New York myself. You don't really want to take me. You do it only because you think you should." Various suggestions were offered by the others in the group as to ways of dealing with this reaction, none of which seemed to be appropriate. The leader again emphasized that this response was a result of deep-rooted insecurity, a feeling of worthlessness, of being unworthy to be loved, and above all, of an inner emptiness, a longing for love. Wasn't M. saying, "You do not love me," or, "I do not feel you love me?" What helped children like M., the leader continued, was consistent acceptance and respect, along with a degree of firmness that would not outrage them but instead would support their weak egos.

Out of a clear sky, Mr. B. asked: "Is it possible that food is equated with love by these children?" When asked by the leader to explain, Mr. B. reported that for the first three months of his life, his son was starved because the doctor insisted on breast feeding. Finally, on their own, the parents put L. on a bottle, and he took two bottles at a time. When asked why this situation was permitted to go on so long, Mrs. B. said, "That was the trouble. He was a very quiet child and could not communicate like other infants by crying. I still cannot communicate with him even now. It is part of an inborn lack in him."

At the next session, Mrs. K. reported that her daughter was resisting attending her therapy group, ostensibly because she had some extracurricular activity in school "which means a great deal to her." Mrs. K. said that because of what she had learned in the group, she had decided not to make an issue of it. (The girl continued as a member of her therapy group without interruption.) At the same session, Mr. and Mrs. H. reported that their daughter was "more cooperative" at home. The mother had talked to the girl "woman to woman," admitting that she, too, had negative feelings about some of the household chores. This admission seemed to have a salutary effect on the girl. The mother recalled that her daughter had once said to her: "When you see me neglecting my room, why don't you do something drastic?" and she concluded that, "Maybe she wants me to be direct with her and ask that she participate in the family."

The leader asked the group whether they could explain why this talk with the girl had had such a good effect, but none could suggest a reason. The leader then asked: "Could it not be that it was because Mrs. H. talked with P. in a friendly though firm, manner and did not command her?" Mrs. H. at once recognized that this may have been the cause for the change in the girl, and Mr. B. added that, "Sometimes the right thing said at the right moment can do wonders."

During a discussion about the irritability often displayed by the youngsters, Mrs. K. affirmatively said that observing her daughter and the apparent unreasonableness of her reactions convinced her that it must be "physiological," and Mr. S. expanded on the subject and ended by saying, "When these children are the least lovable, they need the most love from us, because they cannot control themselves." (Later it was necessary to clarify that loving did not necessarily mean being maudlin, that these youngsters, because of their ego weakness, required firmness as part of loving.)

At another stage in the interview, when excessive eating by a few of the youngsters was discussed, Mr. S. made a statement revealing a rather deep understanding of the nature of the youngsters under consideration. He said: "These children seem to be empty and this is an emotional thing, and, in a way, when they are given food, they seem to take out of it the feeling that the parent is giving love along with the food and that is perhaps what calms them down."[2]

In a discussion of the uncontrollable temper of some of the children, Mr. B. described a scene in which his younger daughter (not a patient) in a fit of temper threw herself on the floor, screaming and kicking, Instead of becoming enraged and punishing her as he would have reacted in the past Mr. B. lay down next to her and went through the same motions. The girl at once stopped, looked at him, and said,

---

2. Here these rather ordinary people have on their own come upon one of the predominant characteristics of schizophrenic orality.

"Daddy, you look silly." "Well," said he, "that's the way you look." She had never thrown a tantrum since. The leader drew a parallel here between this episode and another with the older brother, our patient. In the latter the father had lost his temper and become punitive, while with the girl he had controlled his irritation. As a result of this comment the parents concluded that, "To help our children we must learn not to break down."

As an illustration of the parents' increased sensitivity to, and understanding of, their children, the following is taken from a discussion by the parents at the twelfth session. In previous sessions, Mrs. C. repeatedly complained of her daughter's talkativeness. At this session, she again remarked that her daughter talked a great deal. The leader now asked why the girl had a need to talk so much. Mrs. C.'s response was: "P. may be talking so much in order to avoid talking about her problems or listening to the problems of others because this may arouse her feelings of anxiety." She wondered whether it would help if she explained this to her daughter. Her husband quickly responded by saying: "I don't think it would do any good. I act in the opposite way. When I get disturbed or anxious, I withdraw into myself and keep quiet; P. chatters. I don't see any point in pointing it out to her." Mr. S. agreed that the chatter was a "defense against things that bother the girl." Mr. B. stated that he, too did not see any value in discussing it with the girl. "She would only take it as a criticism," he added, and later described that when his mother had done this to him, he had felt she was "picking on him. Mrs. C., however, continued to adhere to her conviction that talking with her daughter was the right approach. The leader asked if her admonitions to her daughter had ever been effective, and Mrs. C. admitted that they had not.

Mr. B. raised the question: "Don't we point out too much the things that are wrong and not enough the things that are right? He said he believed that the difficulty with their children was that "they are too much absorbed within themselves and take certain things for granted." The leader supported Mr. B. in his assertion and elaborated on the egocentricity of the children under consideration. Mr. S. joined in the conversation and remarked that it was really unfair to be critical of these particular youngsters because they "really cannot help it." He then narrated a rather significant episode. His son (a marked borderline case with bizarre behavior) played with very young children, and Mr. S. and his wife used to go out and chase the younger children away. However, after the discussions in the group, they decided not to interfere, and the boy continued to play with children seven and eight years his junior.

One day a woman accosted his wife and complained of their son hurting her boy. Upon returning home, Mrs. S. told her son of the incident and explained that she and his father did not object to his playing with young children if that was what he wanted to do but that it was embarrassing for her to get complaints about his conduct. M. responded that he himself did not understand why he played with younger children. "It must be an escape," he said. He then asked his mother if she did not ever want to escape. She explained to him that everybody does at one time or another and that she herself often did but that it was not usually a good idea. She gave him an example of a practical situation in their family life in which escaping from doing an unpleasant task would bring immediate relief but in the long run would entail even more difficult effort. She added that she realized that as he watched young children playing in front of their home, he must think what an easy life they had and that he would like to be like them and have it easy too. The son seemed to accept this, but asked why the children involved would have to complain to their parents. The mother explained that, being little, they could not deal with the situation and sought their parents' help. The boy thought for awhile and then said that he would not play with little children any more. In talking to Mr. S. about this incident, the boy ended by saying, "After all, there's a difference between those kids and myself." Since that time the boy had never again played with young children. "It worked like a charm," Mr. S. added.

Mr. B. attributed the outcome of this episode to "timing." "If you say it at the right time, it works," said he. The leader questioned whether it was the manner, the approach, that might not have produced this desirable effect, rather than the timing, and whether the changed attitude of the parents was not the deciding factor. There were some differences of opinion on the matter, which ended when Mr. S. said: "This is a common problem with all of us. We cannot seem to ignore (overlook) anything our children do. We have to regulate and push, and this doesn't really help them at all."

As the girls' therapy group progressed,[3] Mrs. C. noted that her daughter had become more sensitive to other people's feelings, whereas in the past she had seemed oblivious to them. Mrs. M. reacted to this by saying that, "Some of these children feel unloved even though they have been loved a great deal." Since joining the group, she remarked, she had tried to be less critical of her son, C., and found to her surprise that he began to laugh and sing, "something he had not done for a long time." Mrs. B. reported that her son had made "great improvement." When he first came to the Center, he had had no friends but now he did and he seemed to be having fun. Mr. B. added that, "L. not only has friends, but his two best friends happen to be the top students in the school." Mrs. H. described how her daughter, who had been frightened and shy, now hurried home on Fridays to do her homework and then, quite on her own, traveled to a nearby city by train to spend weekends with her aunt where she participated in group activities with other adolescents in the community. "It took P. a long time to get to this point," added Mrs. H. Mrs. C. remarked that when she told her daughter that she seemed to be "getting better" in her relations with other girls and suggested that she might like to invite some of them for a weekend, her daughter said, "I'm not ready to do that yet," indicating that as the parents had acquired insight into their daughter, the daughter as well had acquired insight into herself.

It must be especially noted that the attitude of all the parents in the group toward their children has grown more benign. The parents have made an effort to understand empathically; they have reduced their expectations for achievement, become more supportive and more sensitive to their offspring's inner weaknesses and struggles, and have conceptually recognized the basic personality difficulties and the dynamics of the schizophrenic process. All this was achieved without directly naming the malady or describing its nature. Instead, the parents were aided in arriving at conclusions based on their own observations. This was achieved with guidance from the leader and through their interactions with one another in the group.

---

3. The children of the parents in this group were treated in groups with nonschizophrenic youngsters. Boys and girls met in separate groups.

CHAPTER 24

COORDINATED FAMILY THERAPY
(1965)

The proliferation of "family therapy" in recent years necessitates an examination of its effectiveness in the light of our understanding as to what constitutes psychotherapy. We must ask whether the results that it sets out to achieve are in fact, achieved, and if not, whether it is possible to achieve them at all. We must examine family therapy in the light of the definition of psychotherapy as a process in which reconstruction of personality takes place and more or less enduring changes are effected. Reconstruction of personality is further defined as the consequence of intrapsychic changes occurring through the uncovering of inadequately repressed and unconscious determinants of conscious feelings and conduct, the result of which is that the functions and dynamic relations of the id, ego, and superego are altered to accord with the requirements of mental health.

Psychotherapists, especially those in the specific area of child guidance, have been aware for the past three decades of the importance to their work of interpersonal relations in the family. Parents and siblings have, therefore, been varyingly involved in the treatment of children as the therapeutic needs seemed to indicate. In the past the secondary family members were treated or guided *as individuals*. What is new in the current practice of "family therapy" is work with the family *as a unit*. The feelings, attitudes, and reactions of all the members of the family are brought into the open in the presence of each other. The new therapeutic "group" involves parents, siblings, grandparents, and other relatives who happen to share a common abode and as a result affect each other's lives.

The risk in such a procedure is of irrevocably disrupting the family by overloading the capacity for tolerance in some or all of its members, and the intensification of resistances to self-revelation in such a setting. It can be anticipated that therapeutic interviews with entire families may either be stormy affairs, may fall flat, or may present many other difficulties in interpersonal relations that may prove destructive or at least therapeutically unproductive. It is illusory to assume that interviews with families in a clinic faithfully reproduce the home climate or that they always favor voluntary revelation of subsurface content stressful to other members of the family group. While some young children may act out and even verbalize feelings, adolescents and adult family members can hardly be expected to reveal noxious and hostile feelings toward their blood relatives or disclose their vigilantly concealed fantasies, wishes, and transgressions (which is essential in psychotherapy). Although the family group setting may be fruitfully employed to work through some administrative and management family matters, as well as roles and procedures, affect-laden and guilt-laden feelings and intentions are either withheld or, if revealed, often create an intolerable climate in the home that may result in stress and family disruption.

Our own experience, supported by that of many other practitioners, unmistakably indicates that in groups of couples much less is disclosed than when the marital partners are seen separately. For example, during the absence of her husband in a group of couples, one wife divulged intimate family matters which neither had mentioned in the other's presence. She concluded her rather lengthy recital by the statement: "I couldn't say these things when my husband was here." In another group of couples in child-centered guidance, the husband presented himself as an ideal understanding father to his (latent schizophrenic) son. In session after session he described his sensitive and highly appropriate treatment of the boy, but when the group was separated by sexes, the mother reported numerous acts on the part of her husband that gave the lie to his claims. She detailed his impatient, repressive approach to the boy and his general authoritarianism, information she had withheld during her husband's glib recitals, afraid to arouse his enmity.

In the course of a recent investigation into the case of a seventeen-year-old boy with a serious psychoneurotic problem, who engaged in delinquent acting out and was in the early stages of drug addiction, the present writer, following his usual practice, interviewed each parent separately before meeting with them as a couple. Although the father showed himself far from reasonable in his attitude toward the boy's difficulties, he presented himself as a fairly good parent. According to him, he and his son had a tolerably good relation (though he did admit to one recent physical encounter between them), and in answering questions put to him, he claimed to have given time to his son, attending ball games with him and in other ways participating with him in free-time activities. The mother, on the other hand, described her husband as having been antagonistic to the boy (born after four miscarriages) from "the moment he was born." This antagonism persisted, the father having always been impatient with him, irascible and domineering. When the parents were seen together, the mother remained subdued throughout the interview. Only occasionally did she contribute to a statement her husband made, and once or twice meekly and cautiously disagreed on some minor point. Nothing of significance was touched upon as to their own interpersonal relation or their treatment of their son.

To circumvent the resistances we have encountered and to minimize the risk of increasing the tension in families, we have experimented in the last four years with a plan of family treatment that can best be described as *coordinated family group therapy*. The referred patients were adolescent boys and girls of junior and high school age (fourteen to seventeen years). These patients were placed in treatment in para-analytic group psychotherapy, with the groups being divided according to sex and a two-year age range. The fathers and mothers of the patients were seen in separate groups, they, too, being grouped according to the gender and age of their children [23]. Thus, fathers of girls were grouped together, while fathers of boys met in different groups, and the same principle was applied in the grouping of the mothers. The parents' groups were conducted on the principles of child-centered group guidance, with the seriously disturbed parents receiving individual psychotherapy as patients on their own account. Assignment to the parents' groups was made in accordance with the criteria developed for these groups [60], and they met fortnightly.

Each of the three sets of groups involved in treatment of a family was conducted by a different therapist (for the adolescents) and "leader" (for the parents). Girls' and boys' groups were assigned to female and male therapists respectively. Fathers' groups were led by men, while those of the mothers were in the charge of women. Although the "leaders" of these groups were experienced therapists, under this plan no one staff member was involved with a child and a parent at the same time, that is, a staff member who conducted a therapy group did not have contact with a parent or any of his patients, either in group guidance or in individual therapy. This separation of function prevented distrust of the therapist, decreased resistance, and avoided confusion in the transference.

The adjective "coordinated" is utilized because of the fact that (*a*) all three leaders and therapists involved with each family were supervised by the same person; (*b*) all three were encouraged to exchange facts and observations of members of families with each other in informal encounters at the clinic during occasional free periods and at lunch hours; and (*c*) formal "integration" (case) conferences were held at regular intervals (or called by the supervisor at any time when developments in a family made unitary, coordinated steps necessary or some critical developments were in the making that required attention from all). Also included in the regularly scheduled integration conferences were other staff members, such as the individual therapists of a child or a parent, psychologists who had tested the teenagers, personnel (usually the psychologists) from the referring schools, and at times a staff psychiatrist.

A pivotal element in the coordinating process was the extensive protocols of each session recorded by each of the therapists and leaders of the groups. These were carefully read, annotated, and cross-referenced by the supervisor in advance of his weekly sessions with the individual workers so that the interactions of the individual members of the family group, indeed its total climate, readily and unmistakably emerged.

Critically conflictual situations, malignant attitudes, and damaging acts never failed to come through in the communications of one or more of the three family members, father, mother, and child.[1] These

---

1. Sometimes the number was four when a sibling was also in treatment. In that event, the sibling's therapist was included in all formal conferences and the informal sharing of information.

revelations alerted us to the need of taking therapeutic or guidance steps to correct or diminish family-group or individual pathology as it appeared. Sometimes these steps related to one person only—father, mother, or child—and could be dealt with in his or her own group. More often, several members of the family generated the difficulty. In such instances one or both of the group conductors[2] were apprised of the facts by the supervisor so that, being aware of a situation, the therapist could take an opportunity during the discussions in his group to elaborate on the problem and its significance, without, however, directly relating it to the person involved unless the latter voluntarily applied it to himself. When the subject did not arise spontaneously, the group conductor was advised to introduce it subtly in relation to another topic at some future session.

Depending upon the time sequences of group and supervisory sessions, the information gleaned from any member of a family as recorded in the protocols was communicated to the parallel workers by the supervisor during the supervisory hours by an interoffice telephone conversation, by the marked protocols (left in their mailboxes with a note), or by a written or verbal suggestion that two or three workers exchange pertinent current information on the family.

An illustration of this complicated-sounding but simple process is the subject of money allowances. This subject is unfailingly brought forth in the adolescent groups, especially where the membership stems from middle-class homes. By virtue of its realistic and symbolic meanings, the question of an allowance is charged with rather strong feelings and is a source of considerable tension and conflict in many homes, a conflict that is carried over to other areas, causing much distress and unhappiness. In the therapy group of adolescents the subject may be approached by exploration of the feelings toward the self, as rebellion against dependency and striving toward self-reliance and independence; or the subject may be viewed in the context of the reality situation. However, it is obvious that this is not a problem that a teenager can solve by himself, especially when it is charged with strong affect and is only a part of a larger conflictual setting. The parents have to be guided to deal with it with sympathy, flexibility, and understanding. Being apprised by the therapist of the adolescent group that the subject has come up, the leaders of the fathers' and

---

2. The common term "conductors" is employed here to describe both therapists and "leaders."

mothers' groups can direct the discussion to the topic in their respective groups.

With the subject of allowance as a starting point, opportunities are offered for elaborations that can lead to increased awareness on the part of the parents of the turmoil in which adolescents live, their struggles within themselves and with their environment, their confusions, their fears and anxieties. The matter of allowance, though it may seem a minor one, is of utmost significance, especially to boys in the light of their strivings for maturity, responsibility, and a self-image. Discussion of such specific problems in child-centered guidance groups usually extends into other related areas in the psychosocial development of personality.

In one of our groups, a sixteen-year-old boy complained that he was unable to do his homework because his mother piled after-school chores on him. She made demands on him to clean his room, wash the kitchen floor, attend to the garbage, vacuum the rugs, work on the lawn, burn the leaves, etc. Neither the mother in her group, nor the father in his, had at any time given any indication of this situation. Having been apprised of these facts in the boy's group, a discussion in the parents' groups of the suitable scope and extent of an adolescent boy's participation in the home and its positive and negative effects on him were considered. The boy was supported by his group mates to assert himself against such an invasion of his autonomy, and the parents were helped by theirs to recognize the unsuitability of certain attitudes toward a growing adolescent.

A category of more difficult problems is represented by a family in which a boy was born eight months after the adoption of a baby girl by a then childless couple. The mother, who adored the girl, conceived a murderous hostility toward the boy. The boy, now fifteen years old, spoke openly in his group of the brutal treatment he was receiving at the hands of his mother and his strong resentment against his sister and his father. The mother, on the other hand, was rather uncommunicative in the discussions in her group. After many months had elapsed, the boy complained of a statement his mother had made; in the midst of a violent quarrel between the two, his mother had said: "The Center (clinic) makes me come to the meetings because they want to make me a better mother. But they can't do it! I know you and I are at war and we'll see who will win out!"

We realized from the boy's reports that a guidance group could neither mitigate nor resolve this woman's problem, and she was accordingly removed from the group and placed in individual treatment. The boy received support from his group by their empathic reactions, advice, and suggestions. This, coupled with the opportunity to ventilate feelings, diminished the emotional load forced upon him by the family. The boy later verbalized his relief in finding that the other boys were in somewhat similar straits and carried burdens much like his own. Without revealing that we had information on his wife's treatment of the boy, the father was sensitized to his son's plight and needs through the *general* concepts presented in the group. As a result, the father supplied some measure of support to the boy at home, reducing the latter's tensions, which resulted in a better adjustment on his part.

Complaints against and dissatisfactions with their children were lodged by the parents just as frequently as the other way around, if not more. The standard complaint was the offspring's attitude toward, and achievement in, school. The second most frequent concern was related to the children's disobedience and lack of responsibility and cooperation in the home. As could be expected, the third most recurring subject was antagonism among' siblings.

Following the rule of child-centered group guidance of parents, generalities occupied a secondary place in the discussions. Guided by the leaders, the parents were helped through group discussion to identify specific reasons for their children's acting out and to find ways of dealing with them. The group guidance leaders carried forward conclusions as to management and to understanding the maturation process that activated the children's behavior, so that whatever steps were taken proceeded from *awareness of needs*.

The information on the children's attitudes and conduct supplied us by the fathers and mothers was passed on to the therapists of the adolescent groups (or to the individual therapists, when they were involved), and this information was used as grist for the therapeutic mill at the appropriate time and in the appropriate context. From the inner relaxation and increased understanding which resulted, there emerged perceptually more harmonious family climates which not only made life for all concerned less strenuous but also aided in the reconstructive efforts of the children's therapists and lightened the load of teachers in the classrooms.[3]

3. For details of the improvement in the family climate of patients, see [60].

Perhaps one instance which illustrates the importance of clarity in conveying ideas to parents will add to an understanding of the nature and possible pitfalls in the practice of coordinated family group therapy. A sixteen-year-old boy complained in his group that his father "was now on a togetherness binge. Everything must be done by the whole family together." Upon the insistence of the father, the family took auto rides together, went out to dinner as a group, and visited the golf course as a unit. This irked the youngster, who was especially annoyed at the continuous presence of a much younger sister. The leader of the father's group channelled the discussion at the next session toward the need of adolescents to be independent and to seek out a life beyond the family. These ideas were discussed and elaborated by the group and the therapist leader. At the next session of the mother's group, the mother of the boy plaintively described the events of the preceding Sunday. When the family was about to go to a restaurant for dinner, the father peremptorily announced that only the parents and the girl would be going to dinner, that the boy was "old enough to find his own company and become independent." The mother was made extremely uncomfortable by her son's absence and the obvious rejection of him by the father, and during the meal she called home to find out what the boy had eaten and to ask him to join the family at the restaurant. He angrily told her that he had already eaten, having found food in the refrigerator, and added, "Anyway, I would not go out with you even if you asked me." Obviously, the father had acted upon an "idea" acquired in the group discussion without having been made aware of the subtle process involved in freeing a boy from ties to his family.

A rather difficult situation was presented by the W. family. Both parents complained of their sixteen-year-old daughter's neglectfulness, uncooperativeness, and procrastination, especially as concerned her homework. She usually delayed her studies until almost midnight, thus causing difficulty in arousing her in the morning and frequently occasioning her being late to school. The father reported that he went into his daughter's bedroom a number of times during the evening where he would find her lounging in her pajamas and reading material not related to her schoolwork. He would remonstrate with her about her lackadaisical attitude and the lateness of the hour.

The parents' bedroom was next to that of the girl's, and during the group discussion it evolved that the father would have the television set going every night until after midnight, but, he said, he would "turn it down low." In her group the girl freely talked about her "inability" to get her work done on time and the fact that she could never get to her lessons "till late at night." She volunteered that she would often become interested in works of fiction and nonfiction not related to her school assignments. The mother reported that she and her daughter would frequently get into violent arguments because the girl, arising late, demanded that the mother drive her to school. Their arguments always ended in the mother's capitulation.

Some months after the groups began meeting, the father, in puzzlement, reported that in the period intervening between the last and the current group session (which were held fortnightly), he and his wife had come home from a vacation trip early one evening to find their daughter fast asleep. Both could not understand it, they said. For years their daughter had never fallen asleep so early. To us, however, this incident made clear the girl's reluctance to retire and her father's interest in her bedroom occupations. Here were manifestations of a very subtle, oedipal, incestuous acting out on the part of both: she to provoke his frequent visits to her bedroom and his vicarious enjoyment in doing so. In the light of these dynamics, their altercations assumed symbolic sexual meaning. We also considered the father's playing the television late at night as a subtle form of communication with his daughter. This shed light also upon the intense conflict between mother and daughter.

In the parents' groups the matter was treated on an administrative basis, namely, that *(a)* the girl should be placed on her own responsibility as to her schoolwork and suffer the consequences of neglect and *(b)* the father should turn off the television set early in the evening so that the girl would not be "distracted." However, we recognized that the father required individual guidance and perhaps psychotherapy, which was instituted with the leader of the group as the therapist. The daughter and mother were continued in their respective groups.

Conclusions

As is obvious from the preceding material, an important value of coordinated family therapy, as compared with whole-family guidance, is that it makes possible flexibility and individuation in treatment. It allows differential individual or group psychotherapy or guidance or both for each member of a family according to his specific needs.

CHAPTER 25

VITA-ERG THERAPY WITH LONG-TERM, REGRESSED PSYCHOTIC WOMEN (1967)

The Psychotic Syndrome

The fundamental assumptions on which our therapeutic procedure is based are, briefly, that psychosis is a withdrawal from reality and the creation of a world of hallucination and delusions as defenses (1) against incestuous urges fed by unwise or pathogenic parents with which the ego of the potentially psychotic patient cannot deal, and (2) against murderous hostility toward parents (especially the mother) and all other persons as substitutes of same and that the psyche of these persons is in the perpetual throes of fear and overwhelming anxiety which both "impotenize" and render them periodically frightened and submissive or enraged and assaultive.

To psychologically (and biologically) survive with this vortex of conflicting emotions that perpetually assail his psyche, the victim of this turmoil denies all feelings, responsibility and relatedness by either withdrawing from the real world and creating for himself a tenuous fantasy life consistent with his ego resourses, or he takes refuge in stupor characteristic of "frozen catatonia." In both strategies the patient withdraws from the objective world into himself [61].

This project was conducted at Brooklyn State Hospital under NIMH grant No. 2M-61-64, and under the supervision of the New York State Department of Mental Hygiene.

It therefore follows that restitutive or rehabilitation efforts for psychotic patients, in addition to appropriate chemotherapy (which is still to be evolved), are directed toward (1) reversing psychic energies from inward (centripetal) flow to an outward (centrifugal) flow, and (2) increasing the patient's capacities (and tolerance) for human relationships, which are at a low ebb and often nonexistent.

In the first instance, the aim is to enhance contact and progressive interaction with outer actualities (erroneously characterized as reality) and to improve comprehension and acceptance of the outer world through expanding exposure to it by *realistic* needs and by graduated demands to engage the maximum of each patient's potentials. The second objective, increasing capacities for relatedness, is in a sense subsumed in the first, since other humans are part of external reality.

To the psychotic, however, people are an even more strenuous actuality than are inanimate things, though the impact of the latter can also be threatening to his debilitated, defenseless ego. These inner reactions vis-à-vis the outer processes must be the ever-present and painstaking concern of the therapist and all other hospital staff. The psychotic has to be helped to break through his defensive encapsulation and isolative existence, and at best his dreamlike state, by gradually building bridges between himself and the inanimate world around him. At the same time as these bridges span the chasm between him and the world, the actualities of that world must be expanded in quality and complexity to continuously challenge his gradually strengthening ego and clearer perceptions.

The ward staff must never lose sight of the cardinal fact that the psychotic patient is in perpetual dread which he perceives as anxiety and seeks relief in narcotizing drugs, only to fall prey to the same anxieties when their effect wears off. *It is this basic fear that the staff at all levels needs to be aware of* and seeks to allay by their benign attitudes and supportive mien and acts.

Therapeutic Bases

The roads to reality in the treatment of hospitalized psychotic persons lie in their relations with the staff, especially with the "attendants," who are in the most direct, intimate and extensive contact with patients, the ward nurse and the doctor, whose charismatic images hold hope and magic promise. The foundations of the bridges to reality are the feelings of security engendered in patients by these staff members. They must be kind and understanding and offer comfort and security which are essential to the patients' forming wider contacts and assuming responsibilities.

Obviously, interpersonal relations are fostered more effectively, and certainly more economically, through *voluntary* group interests in which at least two persons participate. When the conditions and necessity for relating and interacting flow from a genuine action interest that engages the individual, rather than scheduled and imposed by staff, they are *real* and motivated relationships. To achieve this, hospitalized patients should spend as much of their daily existence as possible in engaging and stimulating activities with others, and these activities should be *self-initiated.* A study of patients' reactions to the various "interests" and activities to which they are "taken" by attendants at scheduled hours showed that none participated full-heartedly. A few responded in a listless manner, but the majority remained inert and unresponsive, or fell asleep. It was therefore necessary to evolve a plan of operation which would activate *spontaneous* inner responses that would reactivate the *élan vital* of each patient on the level of, and according to, his natural idiosyncratic interests.

Activating patients toward meeting life and assuming responsibilities required (1) a fundamental reevaluation and re-planning of their physical environment, (2) supplying them with meaningful interests that could kindle whatever spark of life survived their cataclysmic psychic collapse, and (3) nurturing the spark through gradually expanding operational reality.

The Wards as They Were

The project described here was conducted at Brooklyn State Hospital and was concerned with two "disturbed" wards, each housing sixty-five of the most intractable, as well as the most inaccessible, patients in the hospital. The hospital as a whole has been conducted for more than a decade on an open-ward basis, of which hospital director Dr. Nathan Beckenstein was among the earliest advocates in the United States. In these two wards, however, the patients had to be isolated and locked in for their own safety and for the protection of other members of the hospital community. With few exceptions the women looked typically disheveled and unkempt, wearing facial expressions characteristic of deteriorated mental patients. Most had inward, withdrawn, lethargic expressions, others were wild-eyed. The majority were uncommunicative while many were to various degrees manic and assaultive.

On our first visit with Dr. Beckenstein, we found most of the women sitting about inert with vacuous expressions, seemingly resigned from life. Ten or twelve were lying on the floor, some asleep. Many others were just milling around aimlessly. Several continuously paced back and forth the full length of the ward, some barefoot, others with only stockings on, while still others had unmatching shoes. Screeching and screaming arose from time to time from different parts of the ward. Several patients were in restraint (camisoles) with a few showing physical effects of their belligerency. A frightened-looking small bearded woman with sunken cheeks and deep-set, sad eyes was tied to a bench to protect her from the aggression of her ward-mates. She was mumbling incoherently and waving one hand before her face, pendulumlike. (Later on, as an atmosphere of quiet on the ward and a degree of inner tranquility emerged among the patients, she was allowed to move about freely without untoward episodes.)

Two girls, one Negro and the other white, had their arms tightly around each other, so that their plump bodies were pressed into one another. One of the pair was bright-eyed, attractive, immaculately dressed, clean looking and highly rouged and powdered. The other was extremely fat and flabby, wore an ill-fitting dark dress, had an oily face and staring, insane eyes. The two kept marching back and forth, but stopped long enough to exchange a few words with the director and inquire as to who the visitor was and what he "wanted." This Siamese-like relation between the two girls was of long duration and continued for five or six months into the new program, when it automatically dissolved after the doors were unlocked and the first patient assayed forth into the hospital community to establish friendships and join a social group on her own.

A small number of patients on both wards were in a state of stupor and in various degrees of frozen catatonia. One girl in particular attracted attention by her foetal position. She sat from morning till night with her back against a wall, and at a particular spot, with legs folded up and face buried in her knees, dressed in her nightgown.

When her head was lifted by a staff member, it proved to be limp and her eyes unseeing and unfocused. She did not respond to her name or to any other communication. Like her neck, her body was limp and her mind blurred. She had remained in this state for years, we were told. When forced to rise and walk toward the dining room, she did so as if asleep. Often, as she sat so immobile and encapsulated, a stream of urine would be seen flowing from under her into the room. Accustomed to this phenomenon, the other patients seemed not to be concerned about it.

Understandably, the many demands on the attendants and nurses made it impossible for them to turn immediate attention to everything that was occurring on the wards and much had to be overlooked or rectification delayed. Because of all the pressures, the attitude of the attendants and other staff members seemed to imply that conditions of the wards and of the patients were the best that could be achieved; that their role and functions were to continue as they were, namely to "keep going," accept conditions and deal with whatever vicissitudes arose, resolving difficulties by medication and in some cases, discipline and even punishment. The traditional principle of discipline for infractions was the guiding assumption since staff were custodially oriented and were, in addition, too pressed to apply the protracted techniques of relationship and persuasion. They perceived their responsibilities as consisting of keeping the wards clean and the patients safe, with little regard for patient improvement and for appearances or aesthetics. The prevalent atmosphere was one of acceptance, with no hope for better things more consistent with mental health principles, and without interest in improving the life setting on the wards.

As striking as the individual patients were, what most disconcerted as well as challenged us was the climate of turmoil and tension that the wards presented. The outbursts of violence and the screaming (which on the surface seemed unprovoked and without cause), the indifference of the patients toward themselves and seemingly toward life itself (beyond the craving for cigarettes and candy on the part of a few and a professed desire to "go home" by others) at first seemed very discouraging. How to inspire hope and counteract untrammelled resignation seemed to be the main and the most difficult task that faced us.

Many conflicts arose—usually over possession of goods, also for other sometimes real but mostly imaginary provocations. These conflicts, unless aborted by attendants (at some peril to themselves), led to face-scratching, hair pulling and other minor injuries. They seemed to spring spontaneously from the seething hostility that is part of the schizophrenic syndrome. Patients who sit crowded for days in confined quarters without externalizing energies, inevitably flee into a world of private dreams, introspectively live over painful and frightening situations of their past, and must needs attack anyone who would become, in their fantasy, those threatening persons connected with the pain and frustration of the past.

The Program

Observation of the patients on these wards confirmed the validity of our assumptions as to initial therapeutic needs: warm, sympathetic treatment by staff and libido-activating interest that would be suitable to them as women and as individuals. It was clear that what they required as a first step was a quieting environment and inner motivated response to *actual needs* and necessities. Accordingly, we designed a physical setting in which the living process itself demanded that they take on responsibilities and participate in the ward life, and occupations that flowed from *realistic needs* rather than artificially created off-ward situations which did not proceed from such needs or involve inner spontaneity. The ward thus became a *life setting* from which interest and activity flowed as they do in ordinary life.

Since we were dealing with female patients, the setting had to be planned to suit members of their gender. Accordingly, we had arranged to supply sewing machines at which the attendants worked at first as a visual suggestion for the patients. We provided materials for sewing such objects as aprons, dresses, and other clothing; also knitting materials for potholders, hat sweaters, and dresses. We built an up-to-date electrical laundry with a washing machine and drier for their personal effects and irons and ironing boards; also a spic-and-span modern electrical kitchen where patients, on their own, baked and cooked for their periodic parties, and for their own dining tables.[1]

1. Later, as the patients began to improve, we introduced a midmorning "coffee break" on each of the wards, for which the patients, unsupervised by staff, baked cake and cookies, prepared the coffee, served it, and did the dishes.

We equipped a room for simple beauty culture with wall mirrors and rudimentary equipment and supplies. Tables for games and for "creative occupations" involving art materials such as crayons, water colors, drawing paper, and brushes, materials for paper cutting and and pasting, and paper folding were placed in the day rooms of the wards. Knitting, crocheting, claywork, tiling, and materials for other arts and crafts standard in occupational therapy as well as other forms of creative work, were introduced.

Music and dancing were part of our program. For this a movable piano was made available exclusively to the two wards, and when patients rose in degree of intactness, plays that included music and dancing and original writing were made available but not pushed. The patients participated in the planning, rehearsing, staging, and performing.

Small group and ward meetings, outdoor recreational activities, special interest groups were held regularly. Walks on and off the "campus" and excursions for picnics or surf bathing were added as patients became ready for these diversions and wished to participate in them. As far as possible with the types of patients involved (many of whom fell into the inert category) spectatorism was discouraged. Some of these patients had to be motivated by staff personally for they needed to be made to feel wanted and secure before they could break out of their defensive fears and withdrawal. Thus, the original thought of patients being freely involved in an *expanding reality* was quite automatically realized as an organic evolvement of activities and patients' growth. *The spontaneous arousal of wants and inner responses are of the essence for the patient's return to reality, and not merely occupations as such.* It is with this end in view that provision had been made on the wards for constructive *visual stimulation* and free choice.

To repeat, the significant feature of the activity sector of our program was that instead of *impressing* groups of patients and "taking" them to various occupational therapy shops, recreation, music, art, beauty culture, etc., which is the usual practice in hospitals, most of these interests and activities were now part of the day-to-day life on the wards and selected by patients according to their need or preference. In line with this, each of the two wards was assigned an occupational therapist and a recreation therapist, who displayed their wares to visually stimulate interest. Their example and that of the attendants, who daily took up these occupations, gradually drew many interested patients into the activities. The strategy attracted an increasing number to join them around the tables or "centers of activity." The day staff regularly took their positions *the first thing in the morning* following breakfast and were busily engaged in sewing, knitting, crocheting, making potholders, working in colored tiles, drawing and painting, playing checkers, dominoes and other table games with patients, working on geographic and other puzzles with them, as well as doing the household chores which, in the past, occupied their time exclusively.

The value of the freely chosen occupations lay beyond creativity, productivity, and even evoking interest. Even greater values than these are derived from the *manner* in which they are employed. While *vita-erg therapy* relies on spontaneity, relevance, and meaning, because such activity bring the patient closer to *actual life* and stimulate his psychologic processes in healthful channels, its effectiveness lies even more in the fact that the patient feels respected by being given freedom of choice (even freedom not to participate) and is treated by the staff as an equal rather than a small child in need of help, guidance, and direction.

The equipment and activities of vita-erg therapy are not in themselves new. What is new is that they are made an integral part of the daily living environment and what gives them further significance is that they take place in a favorable human climate created by a sympathetic and understanding, relaxed and freewheeling ward staff. By eliminating programmized submission of patients (and staff), vita-erg ward therapy encourages self-discovery and lends zest to the ward life.

The most meaningful occupations and chores for some patients were found to be household duties such as cleaning dormitories, the ward, shower rooms, and lavatories; to others it was baking cookies and cake and preparing and serving the mid-morning coffee to the ward community; still others were interested in cooking. For some, the most rewarding occupations were individual creative projects. In all cases the satisfactions which activated choice also activated the centrifugal flow of the patients' life energies and brought them closer to reality and self-realization. Whether it was sewing a dress, a slip, or an apron; knitting a hat or a sweater; drawing a picture that evoked praise; making cigarettes for one's own needs and for fellow patients; performing, singing and dancing in a play—all of these and many other activities spelled achievement and helped bring the repressed, mute, hallucinating, encapsulated patients to the world of actuality, thereby decreasing isolativeness, diffidence, and fears. These stimuli and spontaneous re-motivational experiences may or may not have had salutary effects without chemotherapy. Our guess is that there were many among our patients who would have done well without drugs, but our original plan to introduce placebos on a selective and experimental basis as patients improved, was not put to a test. Drugs continued to be dispensed routinely. This was thought to be essential, since *all* the patients had come to rely intensely on them and the effects of discontinuation were too unpredictable.

An interesting observation on the effect of the vita-erg therapy plan on the ward climate is that there has not been even one instance of frozen catatonia during the two years on which this report is based, while in the past, even with the benefit of drugs and electroshock, it was not unusual to find several patients relapse into that defensive state of immobility. Another outcome was the vastly improved comeliness and general appearance of the residents of the wards. They no longer presented so shabby an appearance. Financial limitations and other difficulties prevented elegance, but the grooming has become commensurate with the economic and cultural backgrounds from which most of the patients had come. This development has confirmed our contention at the staff seminar sessions that good grooming cannot be imposed from without. Improvement would come automatically with a more benign self-image and self-respect. Events have validated this claim.

The Seminars and Meetings

To effect the changes we sought, a new orientation and new perception in the ward staffs as to their part in the lives and improvement of patients was essential. This was achieved by a continuous weekly *practicum discussion seminar* which was, and still is being held with the attendants and supervisory staffs as auditors. Emphasis is placed on examining the problems attendants face in their daily work,that is, exploring the meaning and significance of specific developments and possible alternate means for dealing with them in the light of the *nature and problems* of the patient or patients involved. Purely theoretical presentations are eschewed. Theory grows out of, and is related to, experience on the wards and to the actual situations encountered. One session a month is devoted to a case study in depth of a patient whom the attendants find particularly difficult. A complete anamnesis including full social, medical, and mental health histories is presented, the psychodynamics and nuclear problem are identified, specific diagnoses established, and suggestions for the special social treatment of the patient are arrived at by general discussion.

During the first year of our project we held, following the attendant's seminars, weekly luncheon discussions with the supervisors, physicians, and nurses, who were responsible for the day-to-day implementation of the program, and who had been auditors at the preceding attendants' seminars. Since these more advanced sessions had followed the discussions with the attendants, the various ideas and problems from the earlier session were re-discussed and expanded. The sessions also served as forums of cross specialist communication which tended to harmonize, integrate or better still orchestrate the specialties for the benefit of patients.

We made a special point of encouraging—and planfully established—communications in every direction within and among the groups of attendants and nurses, ward staff and specialists, the different specialists, departmental heads, and between and among all these and the administration, and finally the business office. We were aware that our enterprise could succeed only when the impact and effect of the various discrete and vested interests were fused into a unitary effort, rather than impeding and sometimes even negating one another. We achieved this by numerous group meetings, individual interchanges, and informal contacts.

The seminars and meetings yielded many results. Chief among these was the growing awareness in the marginally educated and professionally untrained attendants of "patients as persons rather than just patients to care for, to train and to discipline," to use their own formulation. Focusing on patients in the discussions—rather than the habitual preoccupation with ward cleanliness, routines, keeping records and "housework" chores—engendered a degree of sensitivity toward their plight, suffering, and needs. This new attitude was formulated by the attendants themselves as a "feeling of compassion," having rejected after two intensive discussions the term "love," suggested by us.

As a result of these and similar developments, the interest in observing behavior of patients had been greatly sharpened and a curiosity to understand it emerged. Some of the attendants (unfortunately far from enough) have become to a considerable degree self-motivated to gather and report for discussion observations of, and information on, specific patients and their families who visit them. These observations proved useful in dealing with individual patients and their families, which we have attempted as far as possible with our limited social work staff. Many therapeutic measures and changes in the conduct of the wards resulted from attendants' suggestions.

A wealth of ideas had come also from the two-hour "supervisory" staff luncheon meetings (which often extended to three hours). As indicated, the content of these was drawn from the attendants' seminars, from our own observations on the wards, and from reactions and comments from various levels of supervisory personnel and staff of different specialties. Without this cross-professional communication, the project could never have even gotten off the ground.

In evaluating the procedure described, hospital director Dr. Nathan Beckenstein, an observer and occasional participant in the attendants' seminars and a guide and active leader in the more advanced luncheon discussions, stated: "These meetings are serving well and are making the staff more aware of what is going on in the wards between attendants and patients. Many ideas are being brought to the surface which were latent before and many new ideas are introduced by the seminar leader. The auditors' group has been apprised of the plan and has suggested programs. One of their functions is to teach attendants to take over activities from the specialized staff (occupational therapy, recreation, etc.) and be used by the latter mainly as resource specialists."

Dignity and Respect

Above all else we sought to raise the dignity of our patients as human beings. We sought to eradicate the feeling of worthlessness that the psychotic has of himself. One of our patients revealed this in all its tragic nakedness when in an hysteric outburst she exclaimed through her tears: "I am nothing. I am nobody. No one cares about me. I am shit." To achieve our end we had to find ways of inducing *respect* in the staff—first toward themselves, before they could in turn respect their patients as members of the human family and view them as victims of nature and nurture who deeply and poignantly feel their plight, but in their utter helplessness had abandoned all hope. The subject of respect toward patients, therefore, occupied many of our discussions and we, as well as Dr. Beckenstein, scrupulously and persistently demonstrated it in our dealings and relationships with patients and staff on the wards.

We succeeded with great effort and dogged persistence in eliminating the camisole, isolation of patients, employment of deprivations and punishments, as well as "babying" and patronizing patients. We persistently impressed our staff with the importance of treating and addressing patients as they would any other adult, including use of "thank you" and "please," of not issuing orders in a peremptory, commanding voice, and not grabbing patients by the wrists to restrain them or leading them by the wrists like prisoners.

Changes in Environment

But in addition to the new attitudes and relationships which were to varying degrees engendered in the staffs, and the improvement in the patients' appearance that led to raising their self-worth, a suitable physical setting for life on the wards was also essential.

Among the major improvements were walls painted in pastel colors, chosen by staff and discussed with patients, to replace the institutional gray; enclosing the ten toilet bowls in cubicles with swinging half-doors; providing privacy in showering by a system of curtains; opening the dining room to visitors on visiting days and enabling patients and their relatives to sit comfortably at separate family tables and in comparative privacy; removing restrictions on smoking and confinement to wards. These and similar changes fostered personal autonomy and self-regard. However, the change that had contributed most in this area and cause genuine elation, as verbalized by the patients, was the privacy provided them in the toilet setting. Our social worker reported that patients knew no end of joy in this change and that in the past many insisted on going on visits to otherwise unpleasant homes just to have such privacy even for a brief time. The music therapist had reported that patients immediately on entering his studio would repair to the toilet. The improvement second in popularity was the kitchen.

Evidences of Improvement

The improved physical and emotional climate of the wards, and particularly the altered attitudes of the attendants, had an electrifying effect upon our patients. Three days after the program's inauguration, the ward climate was transformed. A visitor upon entering, even when the doors were still locked, would have met with a scene that would have warmed the cockles of his heart. Most of the patients, who only several days before milled about, bewildered and tense, now sat at the "centers of activity" with a staff member at each, absorbed in either manual occupations or table games; some sat apart knitting or crocheting; several played at shuffleboard; still others, mostly the older long-term patients, sat quietly, but instead of the previous staring into the void, they vicariously participated by watching the activities and the unfamiliar scene, which served to draw them out of their former encapsulation and self-absorption. A few addicted strollers were still at their task, however, as yet unable to tie themselves to any interest.

In time, one found patients sitting about in groups of three or four quietly talking; another group of four busily engaged in the kitchen with the large percolating electric coffee urn, others setting out seventy cups and saucers, laying out trays of cookies which patients baked the day before, piling all this on wagons in readiness for serving mid-morning coffee; two patients on their own initiative quietly absorbed in a card game, or six to ten patients sitting together with an attendant and quietly conversing or playing and watching some table game.

As our program progressed and free mobility was made possible by the unlocked doors, patients went out of the building unsupervised and some even walked off the grounds. Groups of patients went on trips, and under the leadership of a staff member formed bathing and picnic parties at the ocean front. As many as twenty-two patients could now be managed with no control and no mishap on lengthy bus trips.

The patients took the responsibility for preparing their own lunches, each paid her own way with money supplied by the hospital, and even spontaneously sang songs during the private bus trips. During the second year of the program, Dr. Beckenstein reported that a goodly number of patients from our wards volunteered and successfully manned booths at the annual public bazaar of patients' productions, and presented colorful dances at the annual field day.

It was now not unusual to see women taking loving care of fellow patients in distress, and in one instance it was reported that several patients sang to quiet one of their disturbed mates. In the dining room, patients fed others, either disturbed or less able to handle the implements (a practice which we discouraged since it infantilized the recipients of such care and continued their dependence).

Although from time to time fights did break out among the patients, since the assaultive trend dies down very slowly, there was only one instance of assault in the two years against a staff member who tactlessly provoked the patient by ignoring the rules we suggested for treating disturbed members of our community. Assaults on attendants and even psychiatrists were not uncommon before the initiation of our program.

Reactions of Observers

The observable outcomes of eight and one-half months of ward vita-erg therapy in operation (which was preceeded by three months of orientation of staff) were formulated by the then Secretary (now Chairman) of the Board of Visitors:

"We went through the entire W——— building. It was the first time that I had seen Wards A and B in several years. What a change! On Ward B the door was open, the patients were quiet and orderly, sitting around tables and doing occupational therapy, knitting, crocheting and needle work. I also saw a room set up as a kitchen which the patients were using for making coffee, cookies, etc. Then there was a room with washers and driers for them to do their own clothes. At the far end of the ward, there was a room set aside as a beauty parlor where patients could primp up. The appearance of the patients was a good indication of how well this facility is used.

"On Ward A [the "worst" ward in the hospital] there has been considerable progress but not as good as on Ward B. The door is still locked but the patients were generally orderly and came running up to us, inquiring who I was, making all kinds of requests, such as, 'When am I going out?' *They did not seem to be so concerned about going home.*" [These doors, too, were unlocked soon after.]

The Director of Occupational Therapy for the State of New York visited the wards about three weeks before the Board of Visitors. "She was very favorably impressed with both wards. She was surprised to learn that the patients were not specially selected for the project and that these were considered the two most disturbed wards in the Institution. She felt that our patients did not seem overtranquilized, and also that the attendants handled a particular episode that occurred during her visit extremely well. She visits all of the institutions in the State and felt that this particular project was the best she had seen and would be well worth emulating in other institutions."[2]

The state medical inspector, after the first year of the project, declared at our seminar that "these were the best disturbed wards of any hospital in the state. I visited all of them."

A more detailed evaluation is contained in a report by a member of the administrative staff after conducting a federal official through our wards. The report follows:

"Mr. H. expressed a desire to photograph our most disturbed female wards as he felt that female patients act out their psychoses in a way that is more dramatic. Dr. Beckenstein and I took him to Wards A and B. He just sat on each of the wards for a while in order to 'feel the climate...'

"Mr. H. carried a camera and flash equipment with him. A number of patients asked him what he was doing there and he simply answered, 'I'm going to take pictures.' Some patients asked him to take their pictures and this he did. After spending about a half hour on each of the wards, Mr. H. asked to be taken to the wards where 'destructive patients are kept, where patients throw feces around.' Dr. Beckenstein and I assured him that he was on our most disturbed wards, and that these were the most regressed female patients in the institution. He then thought that perhaps Dr. Beckenstein's presence had an effect on the patients and that the employees

2. From a report by the hospital's supervisor of occupational therapy.

were working with the patients in the manner they did because of his presence. Dr. Beckenstein, therefore, left the wards.

I remained on the wards with Mr. H. from about 10:45 A.M. until about 12:15 P.M. We went from ward to ward and he photographed whomever and whatever he thought would be of interest. Two patients had crying spells and he followed the attendants and the patients into the Conference Room on each occasion.[3]

"He noted that there was only one patient lying on the floor and questioned this. I told him that patients were not only allowed but encouraged to lie on their beds when they wished. He was surprised to learn that the dormitory was not kept locked. I took him into the dormitory on one of the wards. Only three patients were lying on top of their beds. One patient was doing some dusting and when asked by Mr. H. why she was doing this, she answered, 'Because I live here.'

"The usual morning activities were going on. Some of the patients were working on occupational therapy projects; some were playing games and some went out on walking parties; some did not participate at all.

"Just before noon we went into the patients' dining room. Two attendants were in there with three patients and were encouraging and helping them to feed themselves.[4] About noon, patients started to come into the dining room in groups of approximately fifteen, got in line by themselves, picked up their trays and food, got seated and started to eat. He was particularly impressed by the feeling and kindness that our attendants showed to the 'slow feeders' and was pleasantly surprised that there was not a large lineup of patients waiting to receive food. There was no din, pushing or shoving and there did not seem to be any personnel overtly directing this activity.

"We left the floor at this time and while I was prepared to show him other wards of the hospital, he wanted to return to Wards A and B, after lunch. We got back there at about 1:15 p.m. On Ward B, eight patients were in the kitchen baking cup cakes, some were playing games and others were doing occupational therapy. On Ward A,

3. This was one of the smaller rooms we set aside and furnished for calming disturbed patients, thus preventing group contagion. The room was also used for small meetings of the ward staff.

4. At the initiation of the program, 28 patients were classified as problem eaters and were fed separately on the wards instead of in the dining room. Following a series of discussions at the seminar this number was reduced to three who were physically incapable of handling tableware.

pretty much the same activity was going on. Some of the patients were preparing to go to a music appreciation session, and we went over to the lounge to see this group.

"After this period he left very much impressed by the wards, but with possibly some doubt that he had really seen our most disturbed patients."

Limitations of Vita-erg Therapy

It would be a grievous error and detrimental to future generations of patients to assume that vita-erg therapy is a cure-all for hospitalized psychotics. It was first experimented with on wards of seriously deteriorated, long-term chronic and hitherto "hopeless" cases, but this was only circumstantial. Few patients of this order can be sufficiently improved by a therapy such as this to warrant their return to the "normal" community.[5] That there have been observable salutary changes in patients, that they presented a more normal facade, much more rational behavior, and an impressive increase in relatedness, was attested to by many observers involved in the process and many more staff members outside its orbit. It was commented upon by visiting relatives of the patients and transferred staff members who dropped in on their former haunts. But one would be seriously misled were one to claim that basic structural changes were affected by this method in our chronic disturbed psychotics so that they could hold up against the demands and pressures of an unfriendly world. The improvements must be considered as *functional* in response to the more benign environment and better treatment by staff.

Vita-erg therapy would be much more effective with patients whose egos are more intact than the patients we are dealing with in our limited experiment. The normalization of the environment, its stimulation and responsiveness, the human relatedness and arousal and security and self-worth characteristic of vita-erg therapy would prove more effective, and more rapidly so, where the psychic soil is more fertile than is the case of our patients. In our case we have succeeded in rendering many of our "inaccessible" patients receptive to relationships that form the basis of true psychotherapy. We have

5. Since the above was written and contrary to our caution, a number of patients have been discharged directly from the wards without the benefit of any other help. This and other matters will be reported in the future.

eliminated much of the moroseness and intransigence of, and increased the predictability in, our patients, thus rendering them better subjects to direct therapeutic intervention. Thus, we must consider these techniques at the present largely as preliminary steps for the vast majority toward direct individual and group psychotherapy, by gifted and well-trained therapists, and appropriate chemotherapy, yet to be evolved.

This initial presentation of our work would be incomplete without recording our deep appreciation to Dr. Nathan Beckenstein, the director of Brooklyn State Hospital, for his full-hearted support during many trying periods encountered in our work and his tolerant understanding of the aims of this project. It must be noted that the funds for much of our equipment, which were not inconsiderable, were not available through the regular state channels, and it was he who made them available through his efforts with private sources.

It would be impossible to convey the travail, the soul-rending disappointments, the exhausting tensions and the trying patience encountered in breaking through the ironclad, entrenched, conventional value and attitudes. Only Dr. Beckenstein's unwavering faith and steadfast support made it possible to see it through.

In the third year of our project, the two wards have been employed as an in-service training facility for attendants. Groups of four from other wards are being assigned to each of ours for a period of four months to expose them to the climate, the new attitudes toward patients, and the new techniques in relating and dealing with them. This had the effect of diluting the intensity of our work, but the humanizing effect it has upon other areas of the hospital may compensate for the loss.

CHAPTER 26

GROUP PSYCHOTHERAPY AND PSYCHODRAMA
(1955)

The origins of psychodrama[1] date to the early decades of the century, around 1915, when Dr. Karl Joergensen of Sweden had introduced his *Stegreiftheater* or the *spontaneity* theater.[2] The idea of the spontaneity theater was transplanted to the United States by Dr. Jacob L. Moreno, who had conducted such a theater in the early 1930s in one of the meeting rooms at Carnegie Hall in New York. Bach and Illing, however, have traced the origin of the *Stegreiftheater* to Georg Simmel, who in the 1890s laid the theoretical foundation for sociometry as well as psychodrama.[3]

As practiced in the American version, this method consisted of inviting two or more persons from the audience, which was entirely

---

1. On the Bulletin Board of the Wellcome Medical Museum, listing medical pioneers, the following appears: "Biagio Miraglia (1814-1885) worked at the hospital of Aversa, near Naples. He issued the first Italian Specialist Journal of Psychiatry. He pioneered the use of dramatics as a form of group therapy—'Psychodrama'—later taken up again by J.L. Moreno in Vienna and called the 'Theatre of Spontaneity.' This form of impromptu theatre has its links, of course, with the Stanislavsky movement."

In the playbill of the famous play "The Persecution and Assassination of Jean-Paul Marat as Performed by the Inmates of the Asylum of Charenton Under the Direction of the Marquis de Sade" the following is noted: "Between 1797 and 1811, the Director of the Charenton Asylum in Paris, Monsieur Columier, established regular theatrical entertainments as part of the therapeutic treatment of patients."

2. Harms, E.: Farce, fashion or sociologically sound. *Nervous Child,* April 1945, p. 186.

3. Bach, G.R., and Illing, H.A.: Eine historische Perspektive in der Gruppenpsychotherapie, *Zeitschrift fur Psychosomatische Medizin,* 1955.

composed of lay persons, to enact roles spontaneously in an interpersonal situation, selected and assigned by the director. Typical situations were the eternal triangle, the relation between husband and wife, parents and children, employers and employees, neighbors. Sometimes the entire plan of the "spontaneous" play was outlined. In other instances only roles were assigned, the specific situation briefly indicated and the invention of the dialogue and the evolution of the situations left to the participants. The "audience" or spectators remained quiescent throughout.

Both dialogue and events unfolded from the "free association" of each of the actors as stimulated by and in response to the statements of the other. With an eye on keeping the interest of the audience alive, the director of Joergensen-Moreno method intervened only when the flow of the dramatic performance bogged down, and one or more of the participants required a "booster" or special encouragement.

In its early stages these performances were attended by persons who were interested in artistic self-expression, and especially in spontaneous self-expression of which Cizek, the Viennese art teacher, was the leading, though by no means the only exponent. It must be remembered that in the 1930s "creative expression" in the theater, in literature, in education and in art, had been a dominant motif, as indeed it was in all the self-expressive fields. That was the cultural climate of the day. It was in this period that "free verse," cubism, dadaism, surrealism, e. e. cummings, originated and flourished.

In such an atmosphere spontaneity in drama could not but attract attention. In fact as part of a performance arranged by Moreno and his spontaneity group in a regular theater, a small orchestra improvised melodies and orchestration as they went along without previous planning or rehearsal. Or so it was claimed. The spontaneity theater, therefore, attracted a group of persons who were absorbed in the artistic, evocative, and self-expressive modes and few, if any, recognized in these open, public performances, any therapeutic content. That some of the "actors" may have been affected by the experience is undoubtedly true, since all spontaneity, in whatever form or medium, proceeds from and is rooted in the unconscious and the dreamlike states of the creator. No effort on the part of the director had been made to follow through on these performances psychiatrically, except in a few and rare instances and this was done largely in private.

Later the proponent of Dr. Joergensen's method in America, Dr. Moreno modified and embellished it to accord more with psychiatric concepts. These alterations emerged in a form now known as "psychodrama." The basic concepts and principles of psychodrama are the same as those of the spontaneity theater of Joergensen. However, the introduction of the professional "auxiliary ego"— namely, a person who has been trained to varying degrees in psychodrama—changed the complexion of the method.

Because of his understanding of the latent content of the production and communications of the patient, the competent "auxiliary ego" is able to *lead* the patient to evoking feelings and engendering understanding of his problems. It is then assumed that the patient can find his own solution once such an *understanding* is brought to his awareness.

Later, Dr. Moreno had devised a "three-level circular stage" where the performances were given with the audience still in a spectator role. Again, these performances were thrown open to the general public at a fixed admission charge and were given regularly. Sometimes members of the audience were drawn into a discussion by the director of the scene that had been performed. Frequently members of the staff or private patients assumed the role of either actor-patient or auxiliary ego. Dr. Moreno claimed that the spectators received therapy by virtue of witnessing the psychodramatic performance and through the discussions, a phenomenon to which he gave the name of "spectator therapy." This assumption would be extremely difficult to defend. Psychotherapy is more than that.

Psychological drama has a history as long as human culture, both in its primitive forms, in the Greek civilization, and in modern times. There is nothing new in the relation of drama and human emotions; audiences have witnessed such performances from time immemorial, but there is no record of psychological changes or cures in any substantial numbers of these audiences. Certainly Shakespeare and innumerable troubadors and actors have presented in dramatic form the problems and tensions of living, but no one has ever claimed that conflicts, anxieties, obsessions, compulsions, phobias, hysterias, or psychoses have been corrected as a result of witnessing dramatic performances.

Of noteworthy fact is that the *group* had not participated in the psychodramatic performances, nor were its members allowed spontaneous reaction to them. The spectators, of which there were numbers larger than would come under the cognomen of a "group," remained inert and inactive even though they may have had emotional reactions to the performance, as one always has also to regular theater. The setting did not allow for responding to the stimuli activated by the actors nor to participate in the cathartic activity and in acquiring insight, or at least understanding. In fact, the circular three-level stage set apart—and the brilliant and colorful overhead lighting effects in a subdued room—left the audience in the dark and prevented any form of participation. This physical distance and emotional inaccessibility between the actors and the audience have, in the opinion of those who understand the group therapeutic process, militated against any form of psychotherapy.

There is now a trend in the field of psychodrama or spontaneity theater in America away from histrionics and back to simplification of this setting and a return to Joergensen's original method without theatrical embellishments and striking effects of stage and lights. Some practitioners carry on psychodramatic scenes in simple small rooms with comparatively few patients in close proximity to one another with the opportunity for all those present to take part or respond to the dramatic situation as they are emotionally activated. This technique is closer to the analytic group psychotherapy method which is the prevalent practice with adult patients throughout the world.

Psychodrama is one of many means to activate communication and catharsis. Communication can be induced by unrestricted verbal association (or by activity in children), through various forms of art, through various types of didactic methods, through visual techniques, and so on [9]. The drama is only one of these methods but it is much more restrictive both in form of expression and in its capacity to evoke content.

In the opinion of experienced psychotherapists, psychodrama is neither necessary nor effective in work with psychoneurotics.[4] Psychodrama should prove of value, however, in the treatment of psychotics whose perceptions of self and of reality is distorted. The

4. Hadden, S.B. Historic background of group psychotherapy. *International Journal of Group Psychotherapy,* 5:162-168, 1955.

psychodrama plays into the sense of unreality of the psychotic, since it is imaginary and a form of fantasy. At the same time, it gives him a specific entity and a role which he can assume. If the role is properly chosen for him, the psychotic can live over in play form (as do children) some of the traumata or the memories of them and helped by the conductor, if he is properly and professionally trained and is skilled, to see them in the context of the current situation. This has value in strengthening the reality sense of *some psychotics*.

However, for nonpsychotic patients, role playing is artificial; it limits and prevents free association which is essential in all psychological treatment. The fixed role in a psychodramatic production militates against adequate revelation of the unconscious, since the unconscious is revealed through an unhampered chain reaction in the emotional structure of the individual (regression, free association) and it must be free to follow its own vagaries and irrationalities. It is through the free flow of the unconscious and its associated feelings, thoughts, and events, helped by the therapist, that the patient clarifies internal confusions. Through the support of the therapist against diffidence, shame, and fears, the ego defenses are diminished, with resultant emotional flexibility. By this process new insights can be acquired into one's psychic functioning.

In psychodrama it is the "auxiliary ego," whose function it is to *lead* the patient's reactions to clarification; and in this, even the most qualified and insightful may miss the point, no matter how skillful he may be. A further disadvantage of psychodrama in the therapeutic self-revelatory and freely communicative process is the fact that the other actor-patients who participate in a scene may act out their hostile aggressions against a patient with serious or deleterious consequences.[5] Thus the free association process and the regressive steps necessary for treatment are blocked or prevented, not only by the psychodramatic setting itself, but also by the ego functioning of other patients who play vis-à-vis each other.

It is the consensus of therapists of various dynamic schools of psychology that the self-exploratory procedure on the part of patients is the most effective technique, especially with psychoneurotic adults, and the less interference with it, the more effective is the therapeutic

---

5. In fact, the present writer witnessed such a scene where the director, in this case Dr. Moreno, had to step in and "rescue" the patient, who, being a borderline case, grew very disturbed.

process, for in psychotherapy with adults reflection is more important than is action.

Spontaneity theater, psychodrama, and their derivatives such as role playing, can conceivably be helpful to persons who may or may not be ill as a "rehearsal technique" and a *preparatory* step, for a situation in which they may have to find themselves and about which they feel uncomfortable or insecure. Dramatic playing out by mother or father with a child in advance of the examination by a doctor as a preparation to the actual experience takes the edge off the fear that the child may have in visiting a physician or dentist. The return of a prisoner to the community may be played out in dramatic form. An army inductee's lot would be greatly lightened if his first steps in the army camp were acted out in advance. This would diminish anxiety incident to adjustment to a new situation and new relationships. The discharge of patients from mental hospitals would be greatly facilitated were they to play out in groups the possible reactions they may expect from the community. This anticipatory, vicarious experience would mitigate their discomfiture, which would equally be true of prisoners before release so that they may dramatically play out both their intent and their fantasies.

Thus psychodrama can be usefully employed as a "catharsis inducer," a rehearsal technique, and a means of communication, but never as total therapy. The "drama element" has been, in the opinion of the present writer, vastly overplayed by the enthusiasts of this method. The dramatic situation or the performance actually takes the place of verbal communication (catharsis) in the analytic psychotherapies and is only one part of the therapeutic process. The other and the equally, if not more, important part is the face-to-face discussion with the conductor (therapist) that follows the dramatic sessions. These are usually underplayed or underestimated by the proponents of psychodrama. The objective and rational psychodramatist, however, recognizes the significance of the second step and its essentiality. Psychodrama has to be employed with discrimination and with patients for whom it is suitable. Blanket use of psychodrama is not only wasteful, but is definitely injurious and confusing.

The present writer welcomes the new trend in psychodrama wherein the action takes place in an ordinary room devoid of theatricality, where a *small group* of people are in close physical proximity and free to participate spontaneously in the dramatic situation either as actors or as commentators and discussants. This return to Joergensen's original technique will have a salutary effect on its development. It is our belief, however, that psychodrama has its greatest usefulness with the psychotic patient and is quite unnecessary and unsuitable for other types of emotionally disturbed and socially maladjusted patients.

CHAPTER 27

GROUP PSYCHOTHERAPY AND SOCIAL PSYCHIATRY
(1964)

The generic definition of social psychiatry employed as a frame of reference in this paper is threefold: *(a)* social psychiatry as envisaged here is the application of psychologic and psychiatric principles to the conduct of a community and society generally; *(b)* the recognition by mental health practitioners of the effects of social conditions upon the health and unhealth of the individual; and *(c)* the involvement of the community and its resources in the treatment of emotional disturbances, social maladjustments, and psychiatric ailments.

Because of the locus in which modern psychotherapy has been carried on, namely the privacy of the interviewing room or the now antiquated hospital, and its sole emphasis upon the patient's pathogenic primary relations, it was inevitable that both the theory and the practice of the art of psychological healing should remain individual-centered. This attitude may have been suitable for its time and its comparatively simple setting. However, as the evolving social events gave rise to infinitely more complex cultural, economic, political, and international stresses and the resulting complexities in interpersonal relations, the new strains are overwhelming the individual as well as his contemporary society. In the last few decades, the more alert, intellectually hospitable and adaptable psychotherapists have, therefore, taken cognizance of the conditions under which their patients lived and the effect of these conditions upon them. This new awareness led them to also take steps in relating their work to the life setting of their patients in addition to the human condition that solely preoccupied them heretofore. This new direction was at first taken with caution, but as the light of knowledge ws thrown upon the genesis of psychiatric disorders, bolder and more assertive movements in diagnosis and psychotherapy were introduced.

A considerable stimulus toward the recognition of the influence of life conditions upon mental health were the two world wars which had occurred in almost one generation, and their sordid aftermaths.The dislocations they caused in the lives of untold millions revealed how destructive stressful conditions can affect mental health and degrade human personality. The effects of combat, concentration camps, social isolation, persecution, forced immigration, and the like, were too obvious and too telling to be overlooked by any intelligent observer. These and similar sociopsychological phenomena have in essence alerted all the world to the destructive effects of extremes in the human condition upon the psyche. Workers in the behavioral and healing sciences have especially taken cognizance of these phenomena.

In view of the fact that the locale of the catastrophic events occurred within the social perimeter it was inevitable that the various behavioral and corrective sciences and arts should be brought into closer theoretic and operational cooperation, a cooperation that yielded a revised view of social phenomena and their influence upon the individual and his world. Out of this confluence of interest and congruence of approach to psychosocial manifestations, there emerged unique and new understandings, enriching social and individual psychology. It has also given rise to social psychiatry and community psychotherapy.

However, the point must be stressed that this integration and its variegated derivatives have only enhanced, not displaced individual psychology, clinical psychiatry, and psychotherapy. The clinician is still enthroned where the end product of emotional traumata or mental deterioration in patients are concerned. His specific knowledge and skills still are essential and it must be recognized that his community orientation and services emanate from individual-centered practices, even though these are of necessity modified and vastly enriched by the new discoveries and the newly evolved understandings. Though the reserves of the clinician's armamentaria have been reciprocally greatly enhanced by what came to be known as social psychiatry, and his field of operation immeasurably widened by it, there are still vast numbers of patients whose therapeutic needs can be met only in the cloistered interviewing room by individual and/or group psychotherapy.

A psychotherapist is in error when his social and interpersonal orientations blind him to the internal reconstructive needs of patients whose basic difficulties can be modified or nullified only by individual psychotherapy. Errors in judgment and decision in this respect always prove disturbing and even destructive to patients and frustrating to the therapist. On the other hand, the oversight of social and group needs in the treatment of certain patients also has deleterious effects upon the course of therapy. The basic training of the healer must always be individual-focused and directed toward understanding of personality, its nature and psychic deviations. Extrapersonal situations and socioeconomic conditions, important as they are, take a secondary place and serve to buttress the psychotherapist's understandings and his work.

There is no dichotomy in the above postion; there is no conflict in the clinical practice between individual psychotherapy and social psychiatry. The two are fused—or should be—in the awareness and skills of the healer. A psychotherapist who gives little or no heed to the social backgrounds and current conditions of his patients can at best be only partially effective, while another who would direct his attention toward the ethos exclusively at the neglect of intrapsychic disturbances or pathology, would find himself far afield of his patients' therapeutic needs. The reweighting of the psychic forces that constitute the essence of psychotherapy is not achieved by pointing at the mores of the world and its stresses and inequities. Understanding them does not eliminate emotivity or alter ego function. Where psychic damage has been done, repair is achieved in individuals through intrapsychic processes essential in the reconstruction of personality. These the psychotherapist must put into operation.

Social psychiatry has beneficially widened the scope of this operation by pointing up tools beyond the clinical frontiers. Recent community studies, for example, have yielded incontrovertible evidence of greater susceptibility of economically depressed sections of urban populations to mental illnesses than are the more materially advantaged. While no dynamic evidence of the *direct* relation between poverty and mental illness has as yet been adduced, the phenomenological evidence at hand points to greater incidence of emotional disturbances and mental illness among the poor. The drain upon psychic reserves by the demands upon an individual inherent in the human are further overstrained where the state of physical health is low, when living conditions are crowded, and where there is anxiety about economic insecurity. The reserves needed to withstand the ordinary stresses of life are overstrained where these are added to one's burdens. One of the responsibilities of social psychiatry is to make known these and related social facts that shape and undermine the mental health of individuals and of the community. It also behooves the social psychiatrist to exert whatever influences are at his disposal upon persons who hold economic and political power to influence them to ameliorate life conditions and lay plans for social settings more favorable to mental as well as physical health.

Social psychiatry has made significant contributions both to the clinician and to the social sciences. It has thrown light upon the pathogenic effect of social and community relations and their place in generating, correcting, and stabilizing internal personality processes and in improving interpersonal communication. A most noteworthy contribution of social psychiatry to mental health in recent decades has been in the treatment of mental patients, first in the hospital setting [25] and later to some extent *in situ*. In fact, it can be said that contemporary social psychiatry had originally derived its impetus from this work with psychotics, but, to the credit of its protagonists, the operational scope had not been confined within hospital walls, for social psychiatry has soon moved onto the broader canvas of the community.

Also, to the credit of this discipline, most significant and highly reliable studies have been made by its workers of the etiology of mental illness. The relation of incidence of mental illness to specific conditions in society and neighborhoods has been brought to light and stimulated private and, more significantly, governmental agencies to take steps to ameliorate conditions. In some of the more developed and forward-looking nations, extensive and intensive measures have been taken and research projects instituted aimed at prevention of excessive psychological stress and reducing the plethora of psychic breakdowns. Social-psychologic studies have uncovered endemic conditions as well as pathogenic epidemics that arise from social stress and, particularly, those from social emergencies and catastrophies.

The most palpable and rewarding single contribution of social psychiatry at the moment is in the treatment of the end product of mental deterioration, the psychoses. It has succeeded in taking the understanding and treatment of the psychoses from the realm of mystery and has given it meanings that are instrumentally usable both in therapy and in prevention. Whether it is the therapeutic community,[1] the open-door hospital, the day hospital, the night hospital, foster home residence, the halfway house or the special type of "social club"— they all flow from the concepts inherent in social psychiatry. Credit for this development must be given to the British group of psychiatrists who have been in the forefront of these developments, particularly Drs. George Bell, Joshua Bierer, Maxwell Jones and T. P. Rees.

The ultimate cure for psychoses still lies in the realm of biochemistry and in the future, but the current alleviation of the consequences of this group of conditions is constantly being improved, thanks to the efforts and insights of these pioneers and by other workers and researchers. They are bringing expanding professional insights into the importance of human relations in the genesis, perpetuation, and "cure" of the psychoses. They have annulled the "self-fulfilling prophecy" that psychoses are irreversible, which dominated psychiatry until recent years, and have demonstrated that corrective interpersonal relations and favorable family and community life conditions can ameliorate symptoms and arrest the process. Even greater social and personal gains lie in the fact that the world has come to recognize that in a great number of instances the stresses that bring on psychic breaks can be avoided by favorable human relations and circumstances.[2]

In addition to these monumental contributions to the healing arts, the socially oriented psychiatrists and other psychotherapists are on the threshold of making inestimable contributions to the mental health of society, as a whole, as they are slowly turning their attention to such areas as the family, the school, management and labor

1. An early experiment in the application of the principles of a therapeutic community was the work in an institution for delinquent boys and girls in 1935, described in [58].

2. This principle has been confirmed by the author [63].

relations, the community and the like. These developments are reflected in a symposium [145] held at one of the conferences of the American Group Psychotherapy Association as early as 1953 on the "Application of Group Psychotherapy Techniques in Nonclinical Settings" which dealt with executives in the United States Government (Laughlin); in industry (Blum); with teachers and other school personnel (Herrold); in counseling mothers in dealing with children (Grunwald); in training staff in correctional schools for delinquents (Kotkov); in work with social offenders (McCorkle); in radio broadcasting as a means of spreading information on mental health (Steiner); and in the community generally (Slavson).

In a volume published in 1956 [59] chapters are included on work with mothers and fathers, personnel in industry, alcoholics, drug addicts, unmarried mothers, delinquents, premarital guidance, sex and marriage problems, mental hospitals, and general consideration of community mental health—all aiming at raising the level of the mental health in the community by prevention and treatment.

Group psychotherapy antedated social psychiatry and there is evidence that it has been a precursor as well as a stimulant to the latter. Social and community psychiatry and psychotherapy lean heavily on group psychotherapy as well as on other types of interacting and functional groups. One leading practitioner of the "Open Door" plan in a mental hospital, for example, emphasizes such a generic relation. Dr. Nathan Beckenstein, Director of Brooklyn State Hospital, believes [personal communication] that "the essence of the 'open door hospital' is group therapy," and Dr. Maxwell Jones was generous enough to volunteer the information during a conversation with the present author at Atlantic City that he had drawn upon the present writer's *An Introduction to Group Therapy* [53] in his pioneering work with the therapeutic community in a hospital setting.

The important fact must be noted that the social psychiatrist differs from the individual and group psychotherapist by the fact that he does not aim to unravel psychoneurotic difficulties in patients. He rather deals with ego functioning which places him beyond the clinical frontiers. This development has proven of immense value to the *general field of community mental health*. In the extraclinical areas enumerated such as parenthood, marital adjustment, educations, industry, mental hospitals and the like, the involvement of ego function is the mainstay of therapy, which is not the case in full-blown psychoneuroses (stemming from significant traumata and/or sexuality). This is particularly important in view of the increase in the number of current patients with character disorders as compared with some decades ago when persons with neuroses formed the bulk of the patient populations. In the United States, at least, where this phenomenon now seems to predominate, it can be attributed in great part to family disruption, relaxed social and moral controls, pleasure-centered values and profit-motivated mass communication and amusements.

It was group psychotherapy that has demonstrated the applicability of "ego therapy" to specific patients. Beginning with *selected* groups of children in latency, with whom group ego therapy is eminently successful, the idea was extended to include adolescents [6] and adults with character and conduct disorders and with social maladjustments (where no deep neuroses are present). We can assume with justification that these demonstrations of the effectiveness of ego therapy through groups formed the foundation of social psychiatry, later greatly extended and implemented on a broader scale.

One of the areas that should properly be the concern of the social psychiatrist, in addition to the others suggested, is that of the leadership in society. Persons entrusted with power and leadership should be subject to clinical scrutiny by clinicians and others as to their physical health, stability, emotional flexibility and social values and attitudes to insure equitable and objective treatment of those who are in any way dependent on or subordinate to them. This would not only enhance their own inner values, their productivity and their peace of mind, but would also have like effects upon dependents, subordinates and co-workers, and thus upon the community generally. Some such scrutiny should apply to parents, teachers, recreationists, foremen, employers, policemen, judges, businessmen, heads of industrial and governmental departments, and all others who exert authority over people. Awareness of personal drives and malefic motivations, suitable values and attitudes and the resulting conduct in consonance with well-being and mental health in persons with authority would diminish stress in the population and its destructive consequences to the community.[3]

---

3. "Group dynamic" seminars and, lately, "encounter groups," serve these personality-expanding purposes.

Experience shows that improvement in function and communication in many persons with adjustment problems does not always require prolonged or intensive psychotherapy. In the case of such individuals, freely interacting groups of peers with common needs, aims, and preoccupations, meeting in a group climate of mutuality and conducted by leaders with integrity and perceptive nonjudgmental attitudes can overcome many of their difficulties. Unless individuals are neurotically driven to harsh treatment of others and to commit destructive acts, such paratherapeutic guidance and counseling groups can adequately improve conduct, relations, and communication. Child-centered guidance groups for parents, for example, and other types of family group treatment [24, 60] are derivatives from the original intensive group psychotherapy and have proven valuable armamentaria in social psychiatry and community mental health. In these areas group psychotherapy and its derivative techniques can serve social psychiatry significantly.

However, recent developments marked by the justified acclaim (but unjustified blanket application) of the tenets and practices of social psychiatry are showing signs of overshadowing essential strictly clinical services that many patients and situations require. We are witnessing developments similar to those of group psychotherapy itself. Psychotherapists increasingly employ groups with patients in a blanket situation. They randomly assign patients to groups which cannot but result in indifferent and not infrequently even in disastrous results. Even the most tried and widely validated psychotherapeutic procedures, when applied indiscriminately, prove inefficacious and in some cases deleterious to patients whose problems are not accessible to these procedures. Discriminative diagnosis and the suitable application of the proper remedies are the sine qua non of successful psychotherapy, as they are to all human endeavor. Thus, placing individual therapy patients in groups, especially adults, may be as wasteful as it is to expose others to dyadic therapy who require the reality of human interactions and direct confrontation.

There are evidences of rather widespread similar practices on the part of medically and nonmedically trained workers in social and community psychiatry who attempt to resolve even deeply entrenched and psychoneurotic disturbances and behavior mechanisms by operational means characteristic of their specialties, neglecting to employ with such persons the available, more deeply affecting analytical procedures.

CHAPTER 28

BOUNDARIES OF GROUP PSYCHOTHERAPY
(1974)

Among the many reasons for current discontent among the more psychologically mature and aware students in high schools and universities is their conviction that curricula imposed upon them are what they term "irrelevant." By this is meant that the content of the courses do not grow out of the pragmatic necessities and bewildering demands of their complex lives, nor do they throw light upon the newly emerging society which is unmistakably in the making.

The antiquated bodies of facts and information (as differentiated from real knowledge that begets wisdom) accumulated in past eras of academe no longer seem pertinent or helpful to one learning to understand the world around him or charting a course in life in our progressively fragmented and alienated society.

Unfortunately, unlike former generations, the past can teach us little in this regard. This is well demonstrated by the bewildering nature of the so-called "generation gap," a phenomenon inherent to human society since its origin. Generation gaps have in the past risen automatically as the young moved toward maturity and found themselves in the grip of pressing realities and responsibilities toward

Appeared as Introduction in *The Fields of Group Psychotherapy*, paperback, New York, Schocken Books, 1971.

which they needed time to grow. At present, the unmistakable rebelliousness of youth, their massive dislocation, and their widespread violence as manifested in riots, arson, and bombings are not mere differences in *modus operandi* of life or of values and aims. There has always been the conflict that arose from the fact that the young have always lived more or less hedonistically in the present, while their elders were preoccupied with their future and viewed youth only as a stepping stone to that future. The difference was in the *mode*, not in the *aim*.

In contemporary society, what is described euphemistically as the gap between the generations is in reality a basic, irreconcilable rift. The generations differ radically as to the fundamentals of their aims and values in modern industrial-commercial society. In other words, the youth look to a completely altered order—in all major respects quite unlike that created and nurtured by generations of their forebears.

If we were to succumb to the temptation to elaborate upon these brief remarks we would have to stray far afield from the needs of the student and the intent of this volume. The relevance of these remarks to the subject matter of the book lies in their application to the as yet not fully perceived, though latent, "student revolt" against the attitude toward knowledge, its values, and especially the process of acquiring it.

"Knowledge" attained by prevailing traditional methods of being taught—studying texts, memorizing their content, and regurgitating it through examinations—can be rightfully described as *twilight knowledge*, or perhaps as just information. A person can be well informed, but little knowledgeable. Unlike information, which can be passed on from one to another verbally or through print, *real knowledge* must be acquired through one's own effort, mostly through self-initiated research or even more so through his own thinking. Everyone knows from experience that an accumulation of clouds brings on rain. But how does it occur; what is the process that transforms clouds into raindrops? Or, "plants need water for their growth." But why? How does the water promote that growth?

That clouds turn into rain and that water promotes growth of flora are facts of information. But seeking out the causes and explanations of how these phenomena occur—what are the dynamics, the forces—

constitutes a process of acquiring true knowledge and reflects the difference between a generation *gap* and a *rift*. The intellectually passive acceptance of *a priori* statements and assumptions—without questioning and curiosity and the active pursuit after understanding of their dynamisms, inherences, and possibilities, whether in nature or society—underlies the rift in generations.

But how does the mature and evolved student proceed on the path of real (not twilight) knowledge? The true student driven by an inner curiosity seeks out on his own information beyond what is presented to him by teacher and textbook. But he goes even further; he does not accept the information at its face value without understanding sources, meanings, and relations of facts. He eschews ideas without their context or origins, to achieve total understanding of their relation to life and its processes. He also investigates, largely through his own mediation, relationships of ideas to each other and to the totality of personal and social dynamics.

An example of blatant (and possibly also tragic) twilight knowledge is demonstrated by a psychiatrist who reports on "an unsuccessful group psychotherapy experience . . . from private practice. Eighteen patients with characterological and psychoneurotic disorders were unable to maintain group cohesiveness, nor did they benefit greatly from one year of weekly group psychotherapy. Factors involved in the failure of their experience," opines the psychotherapist, "include: (1) the group therapist's negative counter-transference feelings; (2) the types of socially withdrawn individuals selected for the group; (3) the failure to form a 'core group' to maintain continuity."

The reasons given by the writer reveal the lack of true knowledge of several key elements in the formation of therapy groups and in the practice of group psychotherapy. He seems to have been guided by general concepts without understanding their nature and applicability, that is, by twilight knowledge.

In the first place, a psychotherapy group cannot exceed eight patients; fewer are even better. Eighteen persons form a *mass* and not a group. Psychologically, the value of a group—as differentiated from a mass, a crowd, a congregation, a mob, or any other gathering of people—lies in the fact that, by its small number, interpersonal interactions can be generated and relations among individuals involved and invaded by other members of the group; that is, psychological *interpenetration* occurs. At first, the number eight was set by the present writer at the initiation of small group therapy (based on his experience with informal education groups and social group work). Later the limit (eight) of interpenetration was established by controlled experimentation: The psychological diffusion in large groups makes activation of rigidly guarded revelations and psychic interaction impossible. Discussions tend to assume an intellectual rather than an emotionally charged character.

The second mistake (and this is a major breach of practice) is to have placed in the same group psychoneurotics and character disorder patients. Unless carefully selected, such individuals operate from completely different psychic sources and irreconcilable frames of reference. How one can expect to achieve "group cohesion" (even if this were desirable, which it is not) among patients some of whom operate from deeply affecting *inner* conflicts and intense guilts, while the others have no such conflicts and whose guilts, if they arise at all, are quickly sloughed of by a joke or as promptly dismissed? In such a group climate, the psychoneurotics suffer greatly as they are unable to ventilate their feelings and thus diminish their suffering.

In addition, these patients become victims of the derision of others who cannot empathize with such suffering and offer such frustrating advice as to "forget about it; what was in the past is gone." They are concerned with the here-and-now, and relationships with people have little meaning to them. Nor are they sensitive to negative reactions to their lack of understanding and their callousness. Obviously, group interviews in such a setting do not provide a fertile ground for corrective transferential relations, catalytic influences, and the generation of insight.

The impediments to therapeutic effectiveness through improper grouping are greatly multiplied when some of the character disorders stem from psychopathic (not psychotic) sources. The narcissism of the psychopath, his incapacity to feel guilt, and his indifference and lack of empathy toward the feelings of others cause great distress to the psychoneurotic, who cries out for understanding and help.

The expectation on the part of the psychotherapist for group "cohesiveness" is another evidence of the absence of true knowledge. It is rather an uncritical recourse to the common usage of the term in the everyday language of the ordinary person. Cohesiveness is contraindicated for a true psychotherapy group. It is useful in counseling or guidance (to be described presently), but must be avoided in true psychotherapy. Group cohesiveness results from the individuals constituting it giving up parts of their individuality and at least partially subordinating their egos to the will or interest of the group. This condition is essential in all "action groups," for no achievement of aims is possible in a divisive group.

In a psychotherapeutic group, on the other hand, each member must retain and exercise his idiosyncrasies, individuality, and ego functions so that they may come under the scrutiny and analysis of group members, the therapist, and the patient himself. Such helpful insights would be denied in a cohesive group. In fact, as divisions, differences, and conflicts come to the fore, each patient's awareness is aroused as to his noxious, antisocial, and transferential reactions—that is, projecting onto others his feelings toward members of his family or other important persons in his life. It is this awareness and the helpful reactions and explanations by fellow members and the therapist that are at the core of therapy through and by the group. Obviously these cannot be manifested in a cohesive group.

The appearance of negative countertransferences on the part of the therapist was quite inevitable in these circumstances, for his therapeutic aims for the group were completely frustrated. The fact that he was able to endure these frustrations for an entire year attests to his psychic strengths, or possibly his callousness or even masochism. But he has no one to blame but himself, for it was all of his doing. There is the feeling abroad that in group psychotherapy, all one needs to do is to gather up a number of persons who seek help and bring them together, and one is in business. It is true that group treatment can be considerably easier than individual psychotherapy for the therapist, since the groups carry on most of the continuity of the interviews. However, this can occur only in a properly constituted group. Because this group was initially ill-conceived, it could not "maintain continuity," as the therapist complains.

The chief skill a group therapist must possess, and which can be acquired only by prolonged training and experience, is the ability to recognize the suitability of patients for group treatment, and—what is even more difficult—to combine them so that they may be mutually helpful to each other therapeutically. The very fact that no "core group to maintain continuity" arose should have signalled the therapist of his errors. It meant that the element of *commonality* was lacking, which is a prime requirement for a good working group.

The therapist's plaint that there were among the patients "the type of socially [sic] withdrawn individual selected for the group" is another symptom—and a very serious one—of his twilight knowledge which erroneously holds that groups unfailingly activate the withdrawn and silent ones. This is true only of comparatively rare persons, who because of early traumata are afraid of individuals and feel more secure in the protection of the compresence of others and their own anonymity.

The silent patient in a therapy group (as well as the diffident participant in other groups) presents a serious challenge to the therapist or leader. The causes for volubility readily reveal themselves to the discerning eye of a therapist: the participants may be temperamentally hypomanic; they may be reacting to feelings of inferiority or anxiety that groups as replicas of early families generate in them; their verbal assertiveness or aggressiveness is a habit-pattern acquired during sibling rivalry. Loquacity may disguise hostility and a castration (impotentization) drive originating in one's family relationships; it can be a challenge made to the therapist as a substitute for a tyrannical parent; it may be a symptom of a feeling of panic in the presence of a group or a displacement "from below to above" of compulsive urination.   .

The dynamics of diffidence and withdrawal, on the other hand, cannot be as easily discernible, though nonverbal facial and postural reactions may offer keys to the subsurface turmoil that paralyzes the silent one into his silence. Some of the reasons may be repressive training by parents and teachers; fear of the reaction of the group members to assertion; neurotic fear of self-revelation and resulting punishment or loss of status. However, the most ominous dynamic in the therapeutic situation is that consistent withdrawal may mask a psychotic process. Silence, in such instances, serves as a defense against a psychotic break. In this case the therapist must be vigilant not only while trying to activate the patient into articulateness: he must rather protect him against the onslaughts of fellow group members. A strenuous role thus devolves upon a therapist. While his role must characteristically be as passive as conditions indicate, and he must avoid displaying preference to any one of his patients, the schizophrenic's pseudopsychoneurotic defense, nevertheless, must be protected.

The therapist can prevent this impasse and many others that inevitably arise as a result of indiscriminately accepting patients into a psychotherapy group without adequate assessment of their character and pathology. When there is any doubt about any group candidate, psychological testing, including a Rorschach, should be a prerequisite. Having made an error in placing a patient, especially one who remains silent, the therapist needs to see him individually in a series of sessions to assess the situation and decide whether the patient should be continued in the group.

Note must be taken of the importance of the size of the group, to which reference has already been made. Even a normally shy individual—and many are so temperamentally—would be overwhelmed when faced with seventeen strangers, exposed to abhorrent intimacies by fellow group members, and required to reveal one's own. It is quite possible that, were the group upon which the comments had been made not of such impermissible size, some of its silent members would have eventually found their voices and participated, at least marginally. Quite often one finds in practice that silent or sparingly communicative patients derive deeper insights than the verbose. Being basically introspective, they more readily and more deeply apply the insights formulated in the group than do their extroverted mates.

We have given over a considerable portion of the preceding discussion to psychotherapy groups, which form the majority of groups in the so-called "helping professions." However, considerable numbers of persons who seek relief from their psychological discomforts and help in dealing with interpersonal conflicts in their lives may not need to enter into deeply affecting areas of their psyches. These "patients" or clients can be helped by groups where the interviews do not plumb deeply repressed feelings and hurtful early memories; they rather concentrate on current situations that puzzle or disturb them and for which they seek resolutions. Their difficulties may stem from conflicts on the job, mild marital stresses, confusions in the parental roles, or maladjustments in social relations generally.

Of course, all of these *may* also be symptoms of deep-rooted neurotic or character syndromes that cannot be resolved by superficial means. Nonetheless, in considerable numbers of persons, feelings of discomfort and deviant conduct do not necessarily stem from neurotic states; they are rather the results of habit, early conditioning, imitation, or identifications. They should not be unnecessarily submitted to disturbing analytic procedures. There are greatly less strenuous and briefer methods available for them, both in individual and in group approaches. Such therapy is usually described as counseling, guidance, or psychonursing.

In both individual and group counseling, the interviews or discussions are narrowly limited to specific problems that confront individuals in personal relations and to conflicts in making decisions in some significant area of their lives. Whatever explorations are made, they bear entirely on the external facts and not on feelings or attitudes. Exploration of the individual's subsurface feelings and their generic backgrounds or sources is scrupulously avoided, to prevent arousing strong emotions that may confuse the counselee and divert him from directly dealing with the problem with which he is confronted at the moment. Counseling of this order is best done on an individual basis, since members of a group would unfailingly complicate the situation through the inevitable diversions and variety of ideas and suggestions.

The skillful counselor, who need not necessarily be a trained psychotherapist, leads the counselee to arrive at his own solutions through appropriate questioning and, when necessary, through suggesting a variety of possibilities for the counselee's consideration from which he can choose a course of action most suitable to his understanding and capacities. This procedure conforms with the best educational practices, wherein learning takes precedence over teaching.

However, there are prospective "patients" who, though not requiring deep analytical uncovering of unconscious and repressed feelings to solve the problems they are faced with, are nonetheless so involved emotionally that they could not follow up on pragmatic or instrumental devices as suggested in counseling. A procedure of "guidance" was found to be effective with such persons. Examples of such situations are parents who experience difficulties in their relationships with their children or incompatible married couples. Mere instruction helping to formulate modi operandi would in most instances prove ineffective. The emotional content in these relations would militate against effective application of "techniques."

The attitude of the parents toward their children and married partners toward each other would abort impersonal, exterior manipulative devices. The parents (and in some instances the children) need to become aware of their own attitudes operating at the root of the difficulties, as does the marital couple. If the guidees are not driven by inexorable intense emotions and seem to be "reasonable" individuals, bringing to awareness their own part in creating their difficulties quite frequently brings harmony into the hitherto disturbed relations. Obviously this cannot be achieved in one interview, which is often the situation in counseling.

The process of "bringing to awareness" does not mean abrupt or concise direct statement of facts by the guidance worker or therapist. It rather means a slow development of facts, attitudes, and situations as the guidee presents his problems either in individual or group sessions, led on by questions from the leader toward the nuclear focus. The leader, however, must be alert against activating in the guidee deeply affecting emotions and memories that would lead him into psychotherapy.

In the event that the guidee brings forth such matters, the leader or therapist must ignore them and bring back the guidee or the group to the original topic at hand. This and other procedures are amply illustrated in the body of this volume by the various contributors. In fact, the strategy of deflection is very frequently employed in psychotherapy as well, when a patient plunges into an emotionally highly charged topic or area in his life before, in the opinion of the psychotherapist, he is ready—that is, emotionally strong enough—to deal with it. Unresponsiveness on the part of the therapist is usually sufficient to block progress in the undesirable direction.

The greatest concern to the psychotherapist, the counselor, and the guidance worker are the patients who, though on the surface they appear to be only moderately disturbed, are actually latent or borderline schizophrenics. Particular attention must be given to patients and others seeking help who present symptoms of a compulsive neurosis or display "ideas of reference." Though it is not very frequent, somatic (medical) symptoms may screen an underlying schizophrenic process which can break out in full severity when the symptom is removed and the psychic energies that had been bound up in the preoccupation with the pseudo-illness are loosed uncontrollably.

The function of the compulsion in the psychic economy of the potential schizophrenic is generally to hold impulses in control, or to restrain the psyche from entering into areas with which the individual's ego is unable to deal. It is a form of built-in self-cure, so to speak, or is at least a prevention against psychic disintegration. An idea of reference serves a similar purpose.

The singular idea to which the potential schizophrenic repeatedly refers as the cause of any difficulty he experiences frees him from entering introspectively into himself for an explanation. Such attempts at insight would disturb his tenuous psychic equilibrium and bring on a transient or permanent psychotic break, depending upon the intensity of cathexis (feeling) that may be involved and the strength of the individual's ego. The practiced eye or keen intuitive capacities of a therapist or trained guidance worker can frequently discern underlying pathology in otherwise seemingly innocent deviant conduct or symptom of a patient or guidee. However, it is not only advisable but imperative that even the slightest suspicion of such pathology be referred to a clinical psychologist for an appropriate series of testing, Rorschach included. In fact, probably as a result of unfortunate experiences, the late Dr. Wilfred C. Hulse required such tests from *all* candidates for his therapy groups.

The case of a young married woman in her thirties well illustrates the importance of vigilance with regard to this matter. The woman suffered from a severe case of asthma and was under treatment by a physician. The patient's husband, being a member of one of the "healing professions," suggested that his wife undergo analysis. After a short period of treatment, the analyst recognized the gravity of the patient's condition and telephoned the physician to suggest to him that he avoid curing her of her physical malady, which was the woman's defense against a psychotic break.

The physician understandably could not accept such an extreme prognosis and proceeded with his medical treatment to a successful conclusion. A short period after the termination of treatment, the patient became psychotic and was placed in a sanitarium for mental patients. One night she suffered an attack of asthma and, since no one was nearby to help her, she suffocated to death. The striking element of this incident to the present writer is that he had once met the woman at a small dinner. There had been not the slightest indication of her psychic malady in her manner or appearance.

A potential schizophrenic is more readily detected in individual psychotherapy than in a group, though many errors are made by inexperienced and unintuitive practitioners. In a group, the latent or borderline schizophrenic can escape into silence from intolerable anxiety, which stratagem is rarely available to him in a person-to-person confrontation in which one of them, the therapist, is studiously nonparticipating. One instance of such escape known to the present writer was a young woman in psychoanalysis who communicated very sparingly while on the couch, but when an especially sensitive subject came to her mind she would simply fall asleep.

This was in the early days of psychoanalysis, more than fifty years ago, when everyone was considered a suitable candidate for psychoanalysis. In this instance the analysis continued for several years with no discernible effects upon the patient. While ordinarily the patient's behavior would be considered as "resistance" to therapy, in our view this was a case of what we term a *defense against therapy* [60. chap. 10]. Schizophrenics are highly sensitive: they seem to have almost an instinctive discernment of their ego limits and react with defensive anxiety to invasions of these limits. In some cases they escape into full-blown psychosis, which may be episodic.

The occasional reports of the homicide of a psychotherapist by a patient occur when the former callously pursues the uncovering of the patient's unconscious beyond the latter's capacity to endure the ego strain. Frequently attacks of lesser violence result from the awkward dealing with homosexual transferential feelings on the part of the patient toward the therapist which remain unperceived by the latter. This is hardly likely to occur in a group because, the transferences in a group being multiple, that is, divided among many people, their intensity seldom rises to a degree where physical attack becomes the sole outlet.

Two occasions of homosexually-based violence and one murder of a psychiatrist (and wounding of his wife) occurred during training by the present writer. In one instance, a patient in his late thirties, who had shared an apartment for many years with his father, called the psychiatrist on a Sunday morning insisting that he must see his mentor forthwith. The latter gave him an appointment that very morning at his office, but upon arrival the patient attacked him physically (with no weapon). Fortunately the psychiatrist was a tall, heavy-set young man, and the patient was easily subdued and dispatched by the police to a mental hospital. The fact that the patient had lived alone with another male, especially his father, and the probability of his being in a subordinate relationship to his male parent, should have served the therapist as a warning of the hazards in the transference relationship.

In the second instance, the indication of the homosexual component in the doctor-patient relationship was more clearly indicated. Involved in this was a brilliant physician with an extensive Viennese psychoanalysis, who wished to enter the profession of therapy. One morning it was necessary for me to confer with the doctor at his own office. As I was in the waiting room, a young man passed me on his way from the consultation room to the hallway of the second floor of the apartment house where the office was situated. Some fifty minutes later when, at the conclusion of our conference, the trainee and I emerged into the hallway on our way to lunch, the patient was still standing at the door. As we came out, he surveyed us suspiciously and joined us in our descent of the flight of stairs to the street level. I warned the comparative novice in psychotherapy of the seriousness of this event. However, he had apparently taken little heed of my warning and was attacked by the patient at his next session a few days later. This patient too found his way to a mental hospital via police intervention.

A third instance with other connotations that ended in a fatality involved a professor of psychiatry who was a member of a training seminar in group psychotherapy in 1950. He had attended only two sessions when I saw a newspaper report of his being shot to death and his wife injured by one of his former patients.

The circumstances that led up to this tragedy were as follows: The psychiatrist was instrumental in committing the patient, whom he had been treating as an outpatient, to a mental hospital. One evening, upon being released, the patient went to the doctor's residence and rang the bell at the entrance door. Upon opening the door and seeing the patient, the doctor spontaneously said, "Oh, it's you!" Whereupon the patient pulled a revolver out of his pocket and shot him dead. The noise brought the doctor's wife running downstairs. The patient fired at her also, wounding her but not fatally.

There are a number of psychic dynamics that may have operated in this tragedy. Of course, one can assume that the doctor's committing the patient to a hospital represented rejection or frustration of homosexual strivings on the part of the patient. But the element of revenge against what seemed to the patient unwarranted treatment of him may also have played a part. Then again, the doctor's dealing with him may have been a reactivation of the patient's hatred of his father, against whom he entertained homicidal impulses. This would then be a purely "transferential murder," as most murders are. It is quite possible that, had the doctor welcomed the returned patient as a friend, the tragedy may have been averted altogether.

We have concentrated attention on latent and borderline schizophrenic patients because of the risks involved both to the patients and to the therapists. Uncovering rigidly defended unconscious content and motivations constitutes a serious threat to the psychic, and frequently also somatic, integrity of the personality, causing disastrous ego fragmentation and consequent violent acts and reactions. Particular violators in this area are the practitioners of the new groups of various types known under the generic term "encounter groups," whose specialties are massive regressive games and rather callous dealing with feelings in the name of catharsis, openness, and uninhibited relatedness. Disastrous outcomes and incidents of suicide are reported from all sides. One cannot expose highly cathected feelings in persons too fragile to withstand the insult without paying the price.

As we have indicated, patients in analytic groups can protect their fragile psyches by consistent or selective silence [18], or by absence from sessions for a period of recuperation from the stress to which they have been subjected. These escapess are not available to patients where the stage is set for action and *all* are expected, and even instructed, to participate. Confrontation of patients in analytic psychotherapy, which is customarily and effectively employed in treating

other types of character disorders, is contraindicated for schizophrenia (which falls psychodynamically in the category of character
disorders). As in the case of children's therapy, the schizophrenic's
therapy also has to rely mostly on ego support and wholesome
relationships with the therapist and others.

Until such patients are strengthened by these largely humane
measures—when they are able to view rationally *some* of their
judgements, impulses, and acts—they often require extensive periods
of what we term *psychonursing*. "In practice, this form of [psy-
chologic] 'nursing' is frequently all one can achieve with many very
disturbed and also psychotic patients, and with patients whose
resistances, intellectual and psychological limitations, or constitutional deficiencies impose limits on therapeutic effort... In the treatment of borderline or latent schizophrenic patients... [psychonursing]
is all that would be allowed so as to prevent ego fragmentation that
could result from deep psychotherapy.... Psychonursing is [also]
employed with senile patients, with persons with physical or mental
deficiencies, the intellectually retarded, and with dying individuals,"
i.e., terminal cases [61, pp. 126—127; chapter 16].

Schizophrenia occurs in a great variety of intensities and forms (in
terms of content and symptoms). However, knowledge of two major
classifications is essential to the general practitioner of psychotherapy.
These are *real* schizophrenia and *induced* schizophrenia. After
decades of oscillation and controversy as to the causes of the malady,
the accumulation of clinical and experimental evidence points to the
biochemical, metabolic sources in the body, particularly to the
function of the adrenal glands. There is almost feverish research being
conducted in many centers and by many individuals along these lines.
Certainly the successful remission of symptomatology and induction
of symptoms through chemicals already available give ample support
to the constitutional theories. However, it is also known that some
patients who present schizophrenic-like behavior are (or may be)
biochemically intact, but their deviances from the norm are due to
conditioned responses to continuous and prolonged strong traumata
during the most vulnerable period of an individual's life—his
childhood—and extended beyond those years.

A child who is subjected during his formative years to extreme
stresses, especially stresses that confuse him about what is real and

important—as in the case of the "double bind"—will automatically adopt patterns of reactions (such as excessive fears or noncausal apprehensions) and perceive reality (or rather *actuality*) in distortions characteristic of schizophrenia. We term this state *induced schizophrenia*, which is small by percentage but numerically considerable. The bewildering complexities of the current civilization and culture, which also intimately and profoundly affect family constellations, are fertile ground for the spread of induced schizophrenic-like characters and conduct. Among the patients who recover are the induced schizophrenics. As to the real (organic) schizophrenic—once a schizophrenic always a schizophrenic.

CHAPTER 29

ARE SENSITIVITY GROUPS VALID SUPPLEMENTS IN AN EMOTIONALLY DEHUMANIZED SOCIETY?

(1971)

The comparative popularity of the new genre of groups such as T-groups, sensitivity, transactional, interactional, encounter, nude, gestalt, existential, etc., labelled as therapy groups, is a phenomenon in American culture that merits the attention of anyone concerned with human welfare and mental health.

While techniques employed in these groups and by various practitioners differ vastly, there seems to be among them a common underlying thread, namely, the pursuit of a mode for relatedness which the participants seem to want. They are aware, each in his own way, of a lack in their abilities and skills to relate to others satisfyingly and healthfully, a lack attributed by their leaders, conductors, therapists (whatever the organizers of these groups are designated) to a basic inability to feel free with each other or, as is currently designated, "open." They seek means for facilitating human relations and acquiring a capacity for communicating with ease and enjoying human contacts.

The groups operate on the assumption that once the participants have found the courage to react to one another forthrightly, without restraint or consideration for each other's feelings, the emotional dams that blocked interpersonal relatedness will automatically evanesce for good and all, and each will then be made ready to navigate as a more contented atom in the sea of humanity.

No heed is given to the underlying conditions that cause the self-imposed isolation, to the sources of the discomfort in the presence of others, to the uncontrolled feelings of unrational and unprovoked hostility, or to the aggressive, hostile reactions of the individuals involved. The putative remedial structure is built upon the foundation that once one is helped or permitted to freely act out one's destructive feelings toward others in the group, "honestly" and unreservedly, he is freed of his malignancies and morbidity and is rendered capable of establishing benign human relations and of functioning adequately forever more.

There is no rationale or coherent theory given as to the process by which these phenomenal alterations within the personality occur. Persons who seek help in such groups have been divesting themselves of noxious feelings and hostile attitudes throughout most of their lives. This cathartic discharge of aggression may have served to relieve them of emotional pressures in the past, but it had no permanent corrective effect upon them. They have continued in their self-defeating campaign to emotionally isolate themselves from their fellowmen with resulting discomfort, suffering and depressions. Why one episode (as in the case of a twenty-four or forty-eight hour marathon) or a limited number of such episodes of unrestrained discharge of feelings would create such fundamental changes in adult humans remains unexplained.

The possible reply to this may be that in the T-group or sensitivity group, the streams of abuse from others and frank, unrestrained self-exposure do not evoke guilt and feelings of self-abasement. This sanguine condition is attained through the attitude of the leader and the other members of the group and is unquestionably a very important factor, and should be a vastly significant element in giving temporary relief to those participants who do not crumble under the impact. The claim that it also alters permanently their personalities and behavior and is carried over to other relations beyond the group awaits to be established. Another valid rationalization for the permitted unrestraint in discharge of hostility and the resulting confrontations is the elements which are characterized as *universalization* and *commonality*. That others, as well, may be victims of the same or similar difficulties does decrease feelings of uniqueness and it does minimize guilt and feelings of worthlessness. The discovery that one is not alone in having objectionable traits and disturbing problems is a source of considerable consolation. The Talmud avers, "The suffering of others is half of our consolation." The mechanisms of universalization and commonality are primary also in analytic group psychotherapy and in psychoanalytically oriented group guidance. The crucial differences between "traditional" techniques and the "innovative" practices under discussion here, however, lie in the fact that in the former, the emotional growth is derived from the continuing process of insight acquisition and emotional reeducation. This does not appear to be the case in the latter groups which, theoretically at least, rely upon the magic of behaviorism. A valid illustration of the ineffectualness of behaviorism in altering life patterns is that of the speech of adult foreigners. Belief that pronunciation will improve with continued use of the new language proves chimerical. Persons, who after many decades have acquired rich vocabularies and understanding of the nuances of words, retain their original mispronounciations without direct speech correction. This is not the case with immigrant children. Even older children who begin their speaking careers with the same foreignisms as their elders, when exposed to school and street experiences with indigents, completely lose their foreignisms and their speech soon grows indistinguishable from the latter. This analogy may at first appear as inapplicable, but closer analysis will make clear its relevance to some of the queries raised here.

Activity Group Therapy with latency children relies entirely on free, unrestrained interaction buttressed by creative activity and automatic ego support with hardly any verbalization from the therapist. This method was pragmatically found to be almost unfailingly effective with children presenting specific problems. This specificity eliminates psychoneurotics, psychotics, and the brain damaged, but has proved to be eminently successful with various character and behavior disorders and some types of mild affective difficulties.

At first, changes in the young children—eight to twelve years of age—were considered by many as "miraculous," since no standard play or interview techniques were employed. Actually, the source of the changes lay in a characteristic of childhood which one loses as he grows older and is not found in adults altogether. We are referring to the malleability of the child's personality due to the absence of deeply established neuronic engrams and rigid defenses which arise later in life. We have referred elsewhere to this phenomenon as the child's capacity to *incorporate experience*. The child may intellectually *learn* some behaviors and responses from experience, but his personality is not changed by such learning. Once character is wrought through the maturational process and experiences with the environment, and when defenses are fully established, it grows inflexible.

One recalls a pertinent question raised by the late Dr. Wilfred C. Hulse about twenty-five years ago during a seminar session in which some who are now luminaries in the group therapy movement participated. This occurred at the time when the only established technique was Activity Group Therapy. We were still groping for procedures suitable for adults. The query Dr. Hulse, who was then a newcomer to the field, propounded was: "If children can improve by unrestricted acting out, why can't adults improve by the same method?" The question went unanswered, but some of us in our own minds knew intuitively that it couldn't work. It was decades later, as work with adults was extended and deepened, that it became clear that experience alone cannot modify adult character. Adults may in some instances evolve ideas and comprehensions, but their character structures cannot be permanently affected. Many years later we condensed our findings in an aphorism: "In therapy of adults action and reflection must go hand in hand." Ego defenses and character armor do not yield to either one of these. Both are essential in a dynamic implementation.

Perhaps an abstract from an unsolicited communication from a concerned practitioner to us illustrates this point. The rather worried lady said in part:

"I feel great concern for...I am seeing more and more naive individuals being drawn into these groups. Several of my clients have had very bad experiences with encounter groups and the marathons. Couples who attend these groups are often pressed to express the most intense kind of hostile feelings towards one another and with absolutely no follow-up. One client called me at 7:00 a.m. in a semi-hysterical state after a five hour session at an encounter group which she and her husband attended weekly. She had since left her husband and is living with a male member of the group.

"In ——— we have an organization which...specializes in

marathons which have earned the title of 'psycho-karate'. Reports are drifting in of people leaving there with bruises, black eyes, and even broken bones, yet apparently those groups are flourishing and their leaders are waxing financially fat."

What made possible such extreme consequences in the encounter (acting out) groups is the inflexibility of character traits of adults vis-à-vis children: the proneness to substitute displacement targets is much greater in adults and adolescents than in children. One always encounters in groups the enraged remarks in which fellow patients are likened to hated parents, siblings, or other persons. Merely acting out or even verbalizing these feelings with no self-generated insight does not divest one of such suppressed feelings.

Perhaps another tangible illustration of the ineffectualness of thera-peutic techniques without "working through" basic sources of the mal-adjustment of adults is contained in Kenneth Lamott's very detailed report (in the New York Times Magazine) of a twenty-four-hour interaction marathon session.[1] Following the code of these groups, a male patient objected to what he thought was the leader's mauling a young female patient in the group. "Well," said the leader-therapist, "That's just the way I am. I like touching people, I like girls." "I still don't like it," retorted the patient. "There's something about the spectacle of a middle-aged man like you laying hands on a young woman that makes me uncomfortable." "A palace revolution!" whooped the leader joyfully. "Always we have a palace revolution."

Another male patient joined in by saying in part, "I'm talking about all the other people you're always laying your hands on." "Perhaps," responded the leader, "the trouble isn't me. Perhaps the trouble is you." The patient suggested that the reaction of the leader's wife (who served as co-leader) be explored. The leader enthusiastically acqui-esced. "Let us ask the beautiful and intelligent P———." The author of the article (who was a participant in the group) says, "He turned grandly to his wife of 28 years, with whom he boasts to have carried on several thousand constructive domestic fights, and asked: "What do you have to say about this grave accusation?"

"I don't mind seeing you kiss other women, but when you put your hands on their breasts or their bottoms, I think it's disgusting," the

1. Lamott, Kenneth, "Marathon Therapy in a Psychological Pressure Cooker," *New York Times Magazine*, July 13, 1969.

wife said crisply. "A real palace revolution!" exclaimed the leader with combative pleasure. "Everybody is against me! Even my beautiful, loving wife! What are we to do about it?" He then folded his arms, looked penitent and continued, obviously addressing the group: "I'm sorry. I'm not sorry for myself, I can't help that. But I'm sorry to be a dirty old man. Is that all right with everybody?" Then, "Now that we settled this extremely important matter, what are we going to do next?"

Apparently the numerous encounters with this problem in the fifteen years of this type of group practice has not affected the leader's unseemly character component. Aren't, therefore, the outsiders, those who are not professionally and financially involved, justified in casting some doubt on the efficacy of the technique? One is also somewhat taken aback that the professionally trained leader characterizes his conduct as part of his "nature," rather than recognize that it stems from psychogenic sources and therefore should be amenable to change through suitable psychotherapy.

The doubts concerning the practices under consideration here are buttressed by some findings and reactions that have come to me unsolicited as a result of the nationwide publicity given my paper delivered at the 1969 conference of the American Group Psychotherapy Association.

The executive director of the American branch of the international association of college faculties wrote in part: "I have been much concerned about the dangerous potential of the techniques used in some sensitivity training sessions.... Participation in an Esalen seminar and in one offered by Carl Rogers' Institute has reinforced this fear, particularly because I know of first-time participants who tried using the techniques they had just observed on their own campuses. This is at least a national-wide tendency." The writer asked for and received a copy of the paper for distribution among his widespread membership.

The effect on a female participant in a weekend marathon encounter group, in which nudity and some water therapy was included, was described to her former psychotherapist in an hysterical early morning telephone outburst. The patient, obviously in great distress, said among other things: "I was stirred up, shattered at the brink of such fatigue. I couldn't stand it. I could have died ... I feel it in me like I could drop dead ... I'm worn. He [the leader] makes one have love feelings over and beyond the point of comfort. He has men and women facing each other naked, staring into each other's eyes. They put each other's arms around their necks and are told to respond any way they want. It's too erotic, too sexual. Then he stops it short of a sex orgy." A year later when she again talked about this obviously traumatic experience, she said, "This is a very dangerous thing. It's like LSD. I'm experiencing moments of complete panic and euphoric highs. I feel like I want to die." Concerning the leader as a person, she stated that he is "crafty, mercantile, diabolical, fantastically penurious, one who is going beyond madness of ———. (Here she mentioned a prominent leader in this type of practice.)[2] She then reported that "a young married woman who took part with her husband in the nude marathon was taken to a hospital where she screamed in her sleep that she was 'being attacked, devoured and raped'."

In describing the effects of "sensitivity training" groups under church auspices, a psychiatrist from a midwestern state wrote to a colleague, "Clearly there have been two suicides, seven divorces and two defrocked priests resulting in the parish in the last three years through ignorance and over-zealousness. And these groups did nothing more stimulating in group sessions than chuckle belly, Hero sandwiches, back rubs and the like. It was the discussions and acting out far into the night immediately following the group sessions that seemed to do the damage." Elsewhere in the letter the writer makes the point, however, that "education for human relations can, with all the good will in the world, wind up to be therapy, or its opposite."

The effect of a T-group upon two highly-placed professionals of the present author's acquaintance also points up the risks of this instrumentality. The two men had been members of such a group with professional colleagues in one of the important mental health projects in the U.S. The group consisted of the top echelon professionals:

2. It is noteworth that the reporter in the *New York Times* article characterizes the group leader in somewhat similar terms during the evaluations (judgment by a jury) of each participant at the termination of the marathon. He told the leader that "in spite of the skill with which he had led us through the marathon, I thought he was at least half charlatan, with a vast talent for exhibitionism and showmanship. The other half, I conceded, probably contained some genius." The leader "responded with good humor and irony, declaring with a flourish that a bent for showmanship was part of himself and that he couldn't act otherwise...."

psychiatrists, psychologists, and social workers, some of national prominence. Frank, uncensored confrontations of each other's attitudes and conduct on the job and off was the rule. The two men endured the massive psychic disturbances for about a score of sessions until the onset of the summer, when the sessions were suspended, but the experience left them so unhinged that they refused to continue. We have not been apprised of the reaction of the other six or seven participants, but the group was not reconvened after the vacation period.

The psychotic break of a member in a T-group at Bethel, the fountainhead of group dynamics, T-, and the various other derivative groups during the summer of 1969 is another warning of the risks these groups present to certain individuals who should not be exposed to the strain and the inevitable emotional chaos that they generate. In an announcement of training and educational courses of an institute in California, where various types of "innovative" groups are employed, including naked group sessions in and out of water, the following frank statement appears: "Many marathon, basic encounter and sensitivity groups are designed to open people up and enable them for perhaps the first time, to express their feelings and engage in risk-taking and creativity-enhancing experiences. *However, they often do not significantly help the participant to adequately 'close up again'*" [sic]. The announcement proceeds to say that on a particular weekend a specialist in rational psychotherapy has been called in from the East to teach how the closing up process can be set afoot.

The question then arises: Why the relative popularity and survival of this movement?

A clue to the answer to this question may lie in an article entitled "The Tranquil Society... or Why LSD?" by Robert M. Schweider and Richard G. Kohlan of California State Polytechnic College, a brief summary of which appeared in 1969 in the Weekly Newsletter of Teachers College, Columbia University. The two authors report on the results of interviews with fifty dropouts, users of LSD, mostly males eighteen to twenty-five. The summary reports that:

All the subjects interviewed repeatedly emphasized that they viewed LSD, not as an *escape* from anything, but as an aid in a search for something. What they were searching for primarily was relevance in their everyday lives.

The authors state that many of their subjects were drawn from suburban backgrounds and viewed suburbia as a "consistent producer of conformity." They report that suburban children complain there are too little variety and too few opportunities for meaningful experiences and relationships in their lives. They found that if the causes of LSD use were to be understood, the conformity pressures of suburban life had to be explored first.

The authors also cite the growing "dehumanization" of higher education as an important cause of LSD use among youth today. The college degree may now function as a rite of passage, replacing physical tests of manhood customary in the preliterate tribes. It is the degree which abruptly entitles the individual to the rights, privileges and responsibilities of the adult world, they contend, without giving him a real opportunity to develop as an individual.

The authors attribute the growing use of LSD to a society which "inhibits the development and expression of feeling." As a result of their lack of meaningful experiences in everyday life, students turn, in consequence, to folk-rock songs, eardrum-damaging music, blinding light shows—anything that will permit them to FEEL. They do not necessarily demand feelings of pleasure; even feelings of pain are considered valuable— they overcome numbness and tranquility. Often their need to feel finds an outlet in drug—induced highs through marijuana, barbiturates, amphetamines and LSD.

Combination of drugs are used in the effort to experience diverse sensations. A majority say they discover, through the use of these drugs (especially LSD) that they can finally begin to relate to other human beings in a meaningful way.

The authors write: "The discovery most frequently expressed is that much is to be gained by the use of that which causes one to feel and enables one to talk about one's feelings. Suddenly one feels rapport with humanity, a new synthesis of intellect and emotion. Those interviewed reported that LSD had enabled them to overcome emotional inhibitions and to break down their ego defenses; and many said that they had discovered for the first time intense feelings about themselves, others and the world."

It can be said in brief that the young people interviewed lived in a climate of emotional depletion and isolation. They felt lonely, on the one hand, and were enduring an identity crisis due to inappropriate stimulus deprivation, on the other. The drugs served to narcotize them, thus dulling senses and substituting transient escape from the miasma of depression. By their own assertions they reveal having been cut off from any deep, meaningful relations in their families and, as is usually the case in such circumstances, were unable to find a satisfying place in the world around them. Differently stated, they were deprived of the sustaining love, or what Dr. John Bowlby calls "affectional ties," prime preconditions for adequate inner and interpersonal adjustments.

The fifty individuals studied are fairly typical of the population in all technological-commercial, dehumanized societies where every man is an island by himself. In these cultures, family climates and relations alienate their members from each other and, therefore, also each from himself. This results in emotionally vacuous, socially unoriented and, in many instances, disoriented individuals. Under these conditions the instinctual allotropism—a primary survival urge even in most elementary organisms in nature—is shrivelled. But since one must live in inescapable interdependence, later in life he feels isolated and lost.

In order to adequately understand those conditions and find possible remedies for them, it would not be amiss to draw a parallel between physical and spiritual nutriments in the development of the personality. Children deprived of essential food vitamins for long periods of time grow up physically and intellectually defective. Deprivation of essential spiritual nutrients—we shall call them *spiritual vitamins*—also results in physical and psychic defects but weighted in the direction of the emotions. The primary spiritual vitamins are (a) sustaining love, (b) uninterference with the orderly unfoldment of the body-mind, (c) evocative interests, and (d) healthful interpersonal and social relations.

One deprived of one or all of these to any great degree remains throughout life in a state of spiritual hunger, just as one's body craves for basic nutritional constituents which it lacks. Unlike other animals, man is subject to a multitude of hungers and most of them are not physical. According to the young people interviewed in the study, LSD released their dormant allotropic urges, rendering them capable to relate to others and experience the pleasures of camaraderie. The innovative groups, which inappropriately operate under the banner of "group therapy," offer the setting for "relatedness" by planfully and volitionally overcoming *in situ* fears and inhibitions. This process is analogous to the commercial "enrichment" of foods by replenishing nutritives lost in manufacture or preparation. In a real sense, the tacit intent of "sensitivity training" by the various techniques and titles is to replenish missing elements in the emotional constitution of their participants.

The element of such emotional reconstitution is present in all types of sound psychotherapy, since it is an essential condition for its effectiveness. No results can be achieved where the basic transference-countertransference attitudes between patient and therapist, whether in group or in individual treatment, is basically negative. It is hoped that through psychotherapy or guidance positive feelings emerge toward family, friends, neighbors, and people generally, in which the therapist is the transitional prototype. But here, these benign feelings are an intrapersonal outgrowth from prolonged relations in which the sharp edges of feelings are dulled and the ego is strengthened to take over where impulse and instinct operated before. In this prolonged cathartic and interactive process the patient's total personality is involved as he relives early traumatic feelings but in a new perspective and in a corrective human climate of the therapeutic setting.

Behavioristic actions and specific motions or postures vis-à-vis persons, as directed by a leader or a tape recorder, do not contain elements of the living or living over process. They are mechanistic and stripped of life—qualities that had created the difficulties in the first place. Strangers facing each other, looking into each other's eyes and touching one another "in anyway you feel" may be good as games and perhaps for "loosening" up the strangeness and self-consciousness that always exist in any new encounter, but how is all this carried over into life generally? How are the security and confidence structurally imbedded in character so that they operate in the wide and complex canvas of life? What are the inherent psychological or logical processes that facilitate such transformation? It did not seem to work even in a specific situation as reported in the article in the *New York Times Magazine* quoted above. After a couple, twenty years married and now on the verge of separation, have finally come to an understanding on a seriously conflictual matter, the leader directed the husband to kiss his wife. The husband "stood up, bent down. . . . and kissed her lightly and rather formally." Obviously the "brutal frankness" by which the compromise was arrived at, did not awaken affectional ties on his part. The quality of his act revealed that he still harbored resentment against his wife's demand for independence and self-determination.

The same questions can be directed to the practitioners of groups where the *modus operandi* is uninhibited mutual evaluations of each other with "brutal frankness" and complete freedom to discharge hostility and affection, as the case may be. Such actions without the element of reflection as part of the therapeutic medium would be difficult to defend. There is little doubt that these effulgences supply relief through discharge of hostile feelings and make one feel temporarily better, but how about the victims of these attacks for one thing?

In the *New York Times Magazine* report the least attractive woman in the group, living in perpetual anger due to the fact that she had been deprived of men's attention throughout her life, was neglected also by the group due to her abrasive manner. When finally given a chance to talk, she bitterly complained of being ignored by men. Even though she was unattractive, she said she had "much love to give." The group's response to her was that she was "a bitch" and proceeded to demean and upbraid her. The recipient of this brutal frankness "began to cry noisily. She went all in a heap in her chair," sobbing. Though calmer and better controlled after this outburst and seemingly able to hold up better under the not too flattering comments about her for a while, she later in the session once more "reverted to bitchiness." When the group again resented her, she took up her coat and purse and left, returning a half hour later (probably to get her $95 worth which was the fee for the twenty-four hour session each of the eight women and seven men had paid. One of the men had also left the group during the session, but was brought back by the leader). At the buffet dinner which was served at the end of the marathon session, the recalcitrant lady sat by herself in a corner away from "most of the rest who sat on the floor around the coffee table." She confided to the writer of the report, who joined her, that "the marathon had been a waste of time." Her unaltered behavior and reactions buttress our doubts of the effectiveness of "brutal directness" to generate sanguine feelings and kindliness. At one point one of the men told her "Damn it,...if you went out and cut your throat, I don't think anybody here would waste a tear on you," a most untherapeutic assertion to a woman who had been rejected all her life.

To the present commentator, the unvalidated claims that frank confrontation and what appear to be interrelational games and "brutal frankness" reduce abrasiveness, alter character, or aid lasting improvement in interpersonal and social relationsions are not justified. Nor do they engender general adaptability and self-control. It seems reasonable that one may be made more aware of oneself and one's reactions by these strategies, but everyone knows that awareness alone does not guarantee judgment and control, either in the psychoneurotics or in character disorders. People are perennially made aware by others of malignancies in their daily contacts; but instead of sloughing them off, they most often become even more embittered, pugnacious, and disturbed. *There is no therapy without the element of mature affectional attitudes and acquisition of insight.* Bitterness generates more bitterness.

Unquestionably, in continuous groups, friendships and intimacies will inevitably arise and many will grow more comfortable and, therefore, more relaxed and less abrasive. But what are the dynamics by which these new feelings in adults will be carried over to other relations in their lives? That this can occur in certain children has been proven beyond doubt for reasons partially advanced here. But from our existing knowledge of the nature of adult habits, defenses, and the deep-rooted mechanisms of displacement and projection, the processes by which changes through mere action and interaction can occur, need further evidence. Even the depth psychotherapies do not speak of "cures." The term they employ is "improved." This caution is based upon the honest recognition of the rigidity of the adult personality structure and the persistence of early imprints deepened by prolonged repetition. Thus, unlike food additives, our hypothetical emotional vitamins are not assimilated; they do not become part of the adult character and personality. Behavioristic and mechanical movements or declarations are not assimilable by adults and do not become operable in their lives.

We have already suggested that the proliferation of group techniques and their popularity lie in the predominance in the current commercial-technological society of character disorders. Groups *are* more suitable for persons in this category. But in our view, groups that encourage regression to the point of infantile indulgence of nakedness have minimal or no therapeutic potentials and prove harmful to many. "That they supply an arena for 'release' of pent-up feelings one cannot deny. And that the participants 'clearly enjoy it' may also be a fact, for is not release enjoyable and are not narcissistic and exhibitionistic indulgences a source of pleasure to those who enjoy these things?" [15]. The intent of psychologic therapy is to overcome infantile, narcissistic elements, not to nurture them. This is not meant to mean that psychotherapy seeks to squelch spontaneity. Spontaneity is at the very core of psychic life, but it needs to be differentiated from untrammeled impulsivity. Only infants and very young children can afford such luxury. Luckily, life itself imposes limitations upon such "self-expression," and in the integrated human adult spontaneity is controlled. In fact, an important distinguishing feature between the child and the adult is selective capacity and controlled spontaneity.

Another source of the responsiveness to these groups in certain areas of the U.S. which has been hitherto overlooked is that patients who seek out the type of relations the innovative groups offer are profoundly lonely and frustrated, either realistically or neurotically, beyond a normative degree. They are unable for psychological reasons to seek out and sustain satisfying human relations and the short-cut directness is eminently suitable for such individuals since it gives them immediate feelings of closeness, friendship, and intimacy, as spurious as they really may be. It is incumbent on the leaders of such groups to prove that they are also therapeutic if they persist in characterizing their work as group therapy or even guidance. The fact that some individuals feel better after sessions and perhaps for a brief time after, is no proof that they are therapeutically beneficial beyond supplying short-lived relief from tensions.

In fact, patients and therapists who seek pleasure are in a state of resistance. Inner change, as all readaption, is willy-nilly accompanied by discomfort and often by much suffering. Schopenhauer's apothegm comes to mind in this connection: "Suffering is the crucible in which the human soul is purified." Where the aim is internal change rather than psychic nursing, the aftermath of interviews is seldom exhilarating. To be fully effective, therapeutic sessions should engender introspection and self-analysis. Unlike somatic treatment, where the therapeutic agents are medication, in psychotherapy the patient is at once a patient and his own medicine. He has to work on himself; a therapist or a group can only set him off upon the road to self-cure. But he must cure himself. It is because of their dilution of the effect of interviews that we held out against after-session snacks and gatherings by patients. In a real sense, the innovative groups under consideration here, and ever more true of weekend sessions with their nude sun and water bathing, jogging, and discussions, are recreational in nature. Admittedly, it is recreation of a special kind, but they bear all the hallmarks of recreation. In fact, there is already on the market a rather elaborate parlor game called "Sensitivity," which replicates the process and much of the content of T-groups.

Finally, the association of this work with group therapy or group psychotherapy is entirely gratuitous. The variety of T-groups now extant stem from the late Dr. Kurt Lewin's original "Social Field Theory" and laterally from his "Group Dynamics," designed to employ free group interaction with members of executive staffs of corporations to improve their attitudes toward each other and thus render them more productive on the job. Bethel free-interacting summer seminars in Maine, with so-called "leaderless" groups, have been carried on for several decades by his pupils and followers before this operation was taken up by others with the intent, or perhaps the claim, to help individuals in their adjustment to life generally.

It may be appropriate to conclude this communication with a statement by a dedicated psychotherapist, who has had an extensive opportunity to observe a variety of groups under consideration here and is highly involved in the welfare of patients. It may be somewhat overreactive and emotional, but essentially represents the feelings of many others, both participants in and students of this new phenomenon, when she said in part: "They [the leaders and participants of these groups] are struggling with oedipal conflicts, conflicts of identity, and many wind up embittered, vengeful and acting out homosexuals. There is a direct connection between unresolved oedipal conflicts and the rise of Hitlers in the world and the concomitant decay and corruption of people and governments."

An anonymous writer on failures of psychology demonstrates how far afield one can venture, how one can lose his bearings when he completely abandons the securities of tried basic assumptions in the bewildering expanse of the human psyche. Despite the fact that these groups aim at breaking down the defensive and isolative features among individuals in our dehumanized, individualistic society, the author concludes: "As to the relations between the psychological studies and the humanities, it should be more like an identity than any other type of connection. The central psychological task is to disembed subtle rational unities within the flux of experience. That, too is the central task of the humanist. *Let each humanist construct his own psychology. Let each psychologist reconstruct his own humanity"* (italics ours). But then, to quote a sentence from the same disquisition, "*they* who know not what they do, cannot tell us what to do." Agreed.

CHAPTER 30

CONCERNING GROUP PSYCHOTHERAPY
(1974)

Psychotherapists as pragmatic, clinical practitioners ought to eschew sociophilosophical entanglements as part of their professional clinical practice. By the very nature, these two systems cannot but create confusion and diminish clarity and effectiveness of *practice*. The more practitioners stray from directly relevant content of their theoretic orientation, the proven therapeutic armamentaria and the tested knowledge of the structure and functions of the human personality and its vast potentials for deviations, the more likely are they to diminish their proficiency.

The global task of psychotherapy, especially with adults and adolescents, is to correct those states of patients' beings that render them impervious to the ordinary constructive influences of everyday living in the society in which they find themselves. It is largely this incapacity for interpersonal adjustment and the absence of adequate flexibility present in the complex conditions of an ever growing technological commercial society which are the root causes of the emotional disturbances that turn people into "patients."

Part of symposium of thirty-four contributors on "My Philosophy of Psychotherapy."

Believers in "free will" take the position that one is completely responsible for being what he is and how he behaves. But we know quite well that no one is self-created or self-conditioned: everyone is a product of specific hereditary dispositions and of the totality of *educational* influences that shape his psychic (as well as his physical) personality. A common error is made even in professional thinking that "schooling" is education. In fact, traditional schools have been and still are *counter-educational* in their repressive climates and barren, irrelevant curricula. The mass of parents and pedagogues, and the total cultural climate will, and must, become aware that at best even the most suitable schooling can be only a minimal part of total "education" of the individual. Only then will their roles in the shaping of human character and personality be altered, with more sanguine outcomes.

The Task of Psychotherapy

A patient is a person whose adverse conditioning pressures and overt and covert demands on him during his formative years did not favor emotional wholeness and spiritual and intellectual expansion. It is, therefore, the task of psychotherapy—and all other corrective and rehabilitative social instrumentalities—to alter or eliminate to whatever degree possible the rigidified deleterious responses and behavior patterns of patients, pupils, and clients. In other words, the aims of these corrective agencies, such as private practice, clinics, and institutions, need to be directed toward reconditioning emotional responses and other neurotic constellations of their charges. The specific aim of these efforts, and especially of psychotherapy are *(a)* strengthening the ego, *(b)* correcting the superego, and *(c)* improving the self-image of patients. The problem then arises as to what are the means and procedures by which these aims can be achieved?

It is in this area that the greatest proliferation of methods and, therefore, confusion exists. A detailed discussion, even a mere listing of them, would be impermissible here. We shall, therefore, have to content ourselves with a very brief delineation of a few major techniques: the analytic and the great variety, which we shall lump under the generic category of "behavioral therapies." Among the latter are such treatment practices as Zen, existential, transaction,

Gestalt, sensitivity training, reality, paradigmatic, and a host of others to which a large group have been added known as "encounter therapy," especially in the area of group psychotherapy. Many of these vanish into limbo as quickly as they appear; others after a brief, ephemeral existence. Actually, most of these "innovative techniques" are overexpanded and overemphasized parts of the well-established psychotherapy that experienced practitioners have employed in the course of their daily work as conditions indicated. These stray minutiae are offered as total therapies.

My own orientation is derived from Freud's basic and monumental psycho-topological formulations: id, ego, and superego, the primacy of the oedipal complex and infantile sexuality. Human psychopathology stems from the distorted strengths and dynamic interrelations of the first three and from the parental treatment of the other two during the periods of infancy and childhood of the individual. Experience, however, has taught me that the application of these phenomenological units in growth and in therapy presents us with far larger variations and complexities than their original applications in traditional psychoanalytic treatment of psychoneurotics and hysterics. This divergence from tradition made it possible for me to conceive treatment in and through groups with their later developments and wide applications by me [53, 56, 61] and a host of other psychotherapists throughout the world, including a few "emerging" nations of Africa.

Fitting Treatment to Personality Needs

It would not be permissible to elaborate on these rather interesting developments and the colossal amount of work, experimentation, and research this consumed during many decades. We found that of central importance is the principle of fitting treatment modalities to the needs of specific personality and clinical entities. This in turn led to the sharp differentiation and definition of *levels* in dealing with patients: counseling, guidance, and psychotherapy, and the importance of emphasis on categories and diagnoses. Clarification of these at a time when patients were cast under a blanket grouping has greatly enhanced the effectiveness of therapy and the evolvement of differential treatment methods. There are evidences that blanket treatment of patients is still in vogue in some quarters.

In a week-long program on psychotherapy on one of the national television networks recently, four "leading psychotherapists," some medically and others psychologically trained, representing three treatment approaches, did not once mention the application of different modalities for different clinical entities. Patients were discussed in a blanket fashion as though all of them are identical, requiring identical treatment approaches. "The Screaming Technique," for example, was presented as an exclusive, total procedure seemingly applicable to all categories of patients. One wondered how screaming could be therapeutic to a psychopath or nonanxiety character disorder. All the other participants were guilty of the same omission.

During my work of four decades with a very large number of patients, especially in a training and supervisory capacity in a variety of neighborhood clinics that included patients of different racial, ethnic, and socioeconomic strata, it became clear that this blanket approach was not only ineffective, but proved actually harmful to many. I found that thorough knowledge of the anamnesis and etiology of each patient's disturbance, leading to a diagnostic and psychodynamic understanding of him, is the sine qua non of successful practice. The determination whether a patient is neurotic, a psychoneurotic, a behavior disorder, a simple maladjustment, a character disorder or character neurotic, a borderline or full-blown schizophrenic or psychotic of varying degrees and subclassifications, gives the therapist the tools for determining the generally appropriate treatment modality for a specific patient.

The dynamic processes of analytically based individual and group psychotherapy are: transference, catharsis, insight, reality testing, and sublimation. The major requirement of character disorders, for example, is direct confrontation (best achieved in a group); the psychopath needs restraint and inhibition (preferably in a therapeutic residential setting); the psychoneurotic's treatment consists of regressive uncovering of internal conflicts in a libidinal transference relation, while the bases for the schizophrenic's therapy are ego support and identification with the therapist, and the psychotic's therapy ought to be a carefully blended combination of the treatments of the schizophrenic and the character disorder, namely, a tender relation blended with direct control of behavior and life pattern sensitively and selectively applied [63].

The above therapeutic strategies are not exclusive to each category of patients. They are the *major approaches* and, when indicated, others are brought into play. Thus, at certain stages, psychoanalytic insights may be employed with a psychopath and restraint exerted upon a psychoneurotic, especially when a patient is blatantly about to commit an act or carry out a plan that would prove destructive to himself or others. The treatment of schizophrenics, while basically permissive, has to be tempered by good-natured advice or control so that his ego may be strengthened and able to function more appropriately. The intuitive and sensitive therapist judges when divergence from the prescribed treatment is indicated.

These understandings led to the principle of *nuclear problem,* that is, the central traumatic event or formative pressures from which the disturbing emotions and anxieties stem in the psychoneurotic, or the conditions and experiences that shaped the character of the individual with a character disorder. In the case of a traumatic psychoneurosis, it is essential that the specific event which gave rise to it be eventually recalled by the patient. The recognition by the therapist of the background roots of problems has two basic values. One is that the behavior and communications of each patient assume specific meaning, usually hidden from him; its other value lies in that, by having in mind the nuclear problem, the psychotherapist can direct the patient by leading questions or statements at the *appropriate time,* bringing it to consciousness where it can then be dealt with during the treatment interviews. The revelation of nuclear problems is especially important during the intervals between treatment sessions when the patient consciously cogitates, but even most importantly unconsciously works on it. For I hold that treatment interviews play a comparatively minor role in the improvement of psychologic patients. Improvement and recovery occur mainly during intersessions when patients test themselves against the realities of their world and the unconscious processes set in motion by the impact of the interviews—individual or group—and in fact in their sleep and in their dreams.

In traditional psychoanalysis and psychoanalytically oriented therapies, patients fall silent, precipitously change the subject or reveal increased anxiety as the critical events of their problem areas are touched or begin to rise from the unconscious. The therapist needs to exercise sensitive judgment in dealing with these phenomena, especially in work with psychoneurotics and schizophrenics. Being cognizant of the nuclear problem, he may inquire why the changed attitude of the patient, thus helping him to break through to the core of his emotional complex against resistances. On the other hand, he must ignore it if the patient is unready for the revelation and thus prevent depression.

The critical event may reveal itself in an act, or a conceptual formulation that touches or reveals a patient's nuclear problem. When a psychoneurotic comes to the point when he suddenly bursts forth with a statement that he hated a parent and entertained wishes for his death or entertained a compelling impulse to murder him, this would constitute a critical event on which the therapist needs to build the next steps in treatment. In the case of a character disorder, however, when a patient at some point comes to the recognition that his conduct which he adopted from his father is unacceptable, or when a boy suddenly bursts out "I really want to be a girl!" (which not infrequently occurs in therapy groups), we have the manifestations of a critical event. When a meek, submissive patient challenges for the *first time* a bully, or conversely, a bully submits to a less aggressive sibling or fellow group member, a critical event in the therapy of each has been reached.

Many other therapeutic dynamics are operative which have been described by this author in other publications, but the above several should suffice to illustrate the gradual unfolding of my work through reflective and self-critical experience. One of these developments, of course, was group psychotherapy, the roots of which were psychoanalysis (in a modified form), progressive education (of a sound quality) and observations of the reeducational effect on children and adolescents of creative recreation [51, 52, 54]. In fact, the serendipitous origin of group therapy in 1934 was a project in creative recreation with young girls which, at its inception, was known as "The Therapeutics of Creative Activity." We soon discovered, however, that this original pattern—later to become known as Activity Group Therapy, for latency children—had to be modified to meet the needs of different ages and types of problems, and came to be known as "play groups" for preschool children; "activity-interview groups" for latency children with more complex personality difficulties than could be reached by the nonverbal activity therapy groups; and para-analytic groups for adolescents (that include guidance and education, in addition to uncovering therapy). For adults we have developed counseling, guidance, and analytic groups to suit their intellectual and emotional capacities and the clinical nature of their difficulties and needs [60]. However, we still hold that full-blown psychoneurotics can be helped *only* by traditional Freudian psychoanalysis.

Psychotherapists need frankly recognize that no complete "cure" is possible for adults in any type of psychologic therapy. One may hope for improvement in reactions and behavior in adults, that is, reducing emotional intensity, the degree of irrationality in reactions, and the clinging to rigid ego and superego defenses that blemish enjoyment of life and hinder satisfying human relations. Only preadolescent children can be basically changed through appropriate psychotherapy skillfully applied—and the younger they are, the more gratifying the results. The constitutional immaturity of children, their unfirm identifications and weak, easily yielding rudimentary defenses render them malleable by *corrective experiences* and restitutive relations [64]. This capacity is is greatly diminished in postpubertal stages and is almost nonexistent in the predominant majority of adults, in whom habits and defenses are rigidified, rendering radical changes most difficult and most often impossible. It is for this reason that I have given significantly more time and attention to child patients who *internalize experiences*, in contrast to adults whose unyielding personalities remain impervious to the ordinary external events in their lives and only partially accessible to therapeutic effort.

Much to one's disappointment, one finds that even in the most "successful" psychoanalytic patients only the sharp edges of feelings and reactions are blunted, which *does* make them more amenable to life, but *characterological residues* still persist. In the various character disorders this process is reversed: the character may be altered to a degree, but *neurotic* residues remain. This is the rationale for parallel individual and group treatment for some patients and the use of groups for "tapering off." In these instances, the neurotic elements are reduced by individual treatment, and character is corrected by group pressure.

A word should be said about the numerous so-called "innovative" groups of recent genre. As already indicated, most of these are merely exaggerations of minor transient devices or techniques employed in what is now labelled in some quarters as "traditional" psychotherapy.

Most "new techniques" are the fruits of idiosyncratic hunches of not always responsible or knowledgeable individuals blown up to "systems." The severity of their deleterious effects recently led law enforcement government agencies to investigate their practitioners, an unprecedented development in the professional world. Unfortunately, group psychotherapy, the youngest branch in the healing sciences carries the brunt of this humiliation. The reasons for this are too obvious to require elaboration. These groups with their interactional techniques are dubious responses to the new type of patient that rampant technology and criminotic commercialism have given us.

Freud's work was triggered, and his therapeutic theories evolved, in a repressive cultural climate that bred psychoneuroses, mostly hysteria, which was especially malignant in the rearing of children. Rooted as it was in guilt and instinctual suppression, it could not but generate subjective conflicts between the life force (id) and the social controls and values (superego). With the increasing "permissiveness" of "self-expression and self-fulfillment" in more recent generations, conflictual forces in the individual have been greatly diminished and are reaching a point of untrammeled libertarianism and anarchy. The weakened external controls of the family, the vanishing power of religion, and the resultant changing social mores have produced generations of character disorders and psychopaths of varying degrees of intensity, which are not accessible to uncovering psychotherapy. Patients of this order must be reached by confrontation therapies rather than exploration, requiring a lower level of expertness in practitioners. This tends to quackery and charlatanism.

Responsibility for Improvement of Society

Caught up by the climate of political and social activism and rebellion, psychotherapists of recent genesis have become laden by feelings of responsibility for political and economic improvement of society as a whole. This holistic urge misleads many to include social revisionism into the very body of the clinical practice. They emphasize to patients in their therapeutic interviews the degenerative effects of our current criminotic and disordered society, often to the neglect of patients' unconscious problems. One case that came to our attention, for example, was a very seriously disturbed and maladjusted young woman who had been in treatment with no relief for many years by a therapist, a devotee to the sociological theory of psychopathology. The nuclear problem of this patient turned out to be a severe homosexual tie to a married younger sister that deeply disturbed her and which was not touched in the course of the years of treatment. "Whenever I raised a problem of my feelings," she later complained, "my therapist would try to show me how the world conditions were responsible for them." This is perhaps, an extreme case, but it indicates a not uncommon trend.

As in other trades and occupations, it is incumbent upon psychotherapists *as citizens* to participate actively in their communities and in the affairs of the world, *but only as citizens*. Psychotherapy, by virtue of the resultant improvement in the mental health of individuals, contributes willy-nilly to the welfare of society. Any additional efforts, especially of a political nature, toward correcting its ills beyond that must be kept from the clinical arena. In line with their expertise, psychotherapists can, however, make significant contributions to the increase in awareness of the general populace for the need of enlightened dealing with children in families and schools. They can help to promote and found treatment facilities for disturbed children and guidance to parents, but unless patients raise these questions, they should scrupulously avoid bringing them into the treatment situation.

Of crying need is guidance and therapy for pupils with problems in public education, and it is incumbent on the healing and helping professions to exert influence toward installation and development of these services for such children and all parents. The prophylactic effect of integrating mental health beyond psychologic testing, diagnosing, and making referrals, as is at present the case—and even that inadequately and perfunctorily done—would be a blessing. It should be the duty of schools to extend training, which should be compulsory by law, to all current and prospective parents, who should be licensed to bear and especially, to "bring up" children.

The currently widespread concern in all social strata with the results (of which the worst is yet to come) of the vanishing social order cannot but affect and involve everyone. But only the few evolved individuals who can discern in it the indisputable fact that these grievous developments are clarions of a new social order in the making can view them with some degree of equanimity; the degeneration of moral and economic values, which served so well in the past, but are no longer serviceable, is evident to any open-minded person. In a real sense, the world is currently passing through the birthpains of a new society built on new values and human relations. But this is not a nine-month gestation period, however; it is a protracted process that will bring increasing suffering to mankind for a great many decades before the new era will fully emerge, being the twenty-first civilization in human history.

But homo sapiens would do well to take some preparatory steps toward the new world that's a comin'. And the most important of these in the view of the present commentator, is bringing up mentally healthier generations of children and youth with new values and strivings, who would be able to constructively utilize the opportunities for building the more salutary world. In a real sense, this is what the small militant *avant-garde* among them tell us. And in this, psychotherapy and all the other mental health efforts can contribute greatly while still keeping, for the present, their clinical work unadulterated. However, we must ever keep in mind that man's redemption can come only through fundamental politico-economic reconstruction. Patchwork reform will no longer do, for every social "reform and economic improvement" generates new problems in a world whose foundations are no longer tenable. "Nothing is as powerful as an idea whose time has come." But *the* time comes on the wings of economics which determine human values and relations.

Our venerable editor has asked, "Would you attempt a prediction of the future role of psychotherapy as a profession and in the life of the nation? A popular Yiddish apothegm goes something like this, "Only a fool takes on the role of a prophet." However, fool or not, one can hazard some judgments and in some of the preceding pages such judgments are implicit. One can say that, as the ineffectiveness of many of the numerous so-called "innovative" theories and techniques becomes more apparent and increasingly less financially profitable, enthusiasm for them will decrease and they will then be evaluated more soberly and disappear into limbo. The confusion and turmoil that they caused in the United States in the last few years, and in Europe, already reveal signs of abating. The test of time is the best test of all for history reveals that masses are slow in discerning, but in the long run their instinctive reactions are unfailing. For how else could homo sapiens, confused and frightened as he is, have survived?

We must also take cognizance of the future results of the medico-physiological researchers, who are opening new vistas in understanding the causes of human behavior and their chemical and metabolic origins. The results of their work may displace much, if not all, of psychotherapy, especially when they succeed in evolving chemotherapeutic procedures to establish psychophysiological homeostasis in the human organism. The full impact of these developments is as yet not in the offing, but impressive steps in that direction have already been made.

PART TWO

Group Psychotherapy:
Children and Adolescents

CHAPTER 31

FOUNDATIONS OF GROUP THERAPY
WITH CHILDREN
(1940)

Workers in the field of psychotherapy and case work have greatly expanded their methods in the last two decades. They have come to recognize that since the causes of mental disturbances are many, treatment must be correspondingly varied. They realize that not all the causes of behavior disorders, inner stresses, and tensions can be relieved by any one method. Since psychopathic and neurotic states have many causes, therapy must vary in accordance with the needs of the specific situation.

In an article dealing with psychotherapy, Dr. David Levy lists the following as methods of treatment now employed: insight therapy, suggestion therapy, training therapy, affect therapy, educational therapy, psychoanalytic therapy. Other types that one comes across in reading contemporary psychiatric literature are impromptu therapy, attitude therapy, relational therapy, authority therapy, tutorial therapy, interpersonal therapy, interpretative therapy, habit therapy, release therapy, and so on. In our own work we have found that satisfying experiences and relationships that either compensate or substitute for disturbing or traumatic situations have definite treatment

When first published in 1940, this paper was entitled "Group Therapy." The method presented here was later designated *Activity Group Therapy*, as differentiated from *Activity-interview Group Psychotherapy*, introduced later.

values. We have, therefore, designated these measures as *compensatory therapy* or *substitutive therapy*, as the case may be.

Among the newer methods now employed with success in a number of mental disturbances and social maladjustments is *group therapy*, with which the present paper deals specifically. It may be helpful to distinguish at this point between "group therapy" [therapy "by the group"—ed.] and "therapy in a group."

In the January, 1939, issue of the *American Journal of Orthopsychiatry*, Betty Gabriel, a case worker, described her treatment of very young children in a group. Therapy in a group is practiced through discussion of the individual's problems in the presence of other persons besides the therapist and the patient. It was found that some patients get more release and gain deeper insight when people with similar difficulties are involved in treatment. The group also has the effect of stimulating the formulation of problems and thoughts that can be used with profit in the treatment situation. Some patients feel more secure when others besides the therapist are present.

Group therapy, as we employ the term, is treatment in which no discussion is initiated by the therapist; interpretation is given only in very rare instances under specific conditions.

The beneficial effects and emotional reorientation in this type of therapy arise from the very fact that individuals live and work together, come into direct and meaningful interaction with one another, and as a result modify their feeling tones and habitual responses. In this connection, we conceive a group as *an aggregation of three or more persons in an informal face-to-face relation, in direct and dynamic interaction with one another*, influencing each other deeply and fundamentally, each one's personality being permanently modified as a result. This definition implies small number, age and sex, homogeneity, social similarity, and in some cases educational parity as well.

Group basis of personality. Psychology and psychiatry are recognizing more and more that man is essentially a group animal and must be viewed as such, whether in therapy, in education, or in life generally. The destiny of man, savage or civilized, is irrevocably tied with the group. His growth and development are conditioned by the group's values and attitudes. In the healthy personality the group urges expand to include ever wider areas and ever larger numbers of persons.[1] Where social interests and participation do not expand, the personality is a defective one. Even the normally introverted person makes contacts with the world to a widening degree, though the pace may be slower and the social area smaller than in the case of the extrovert.

Despite these awarenesses, however, little is known as yet of the function and mechanics of group life in development and therapy.[2] This is due to the fact that until recently studies were confined to the effects and influences of individuals upon one another. The change of attitudes and behavior in problem children—not to speak of normal boys and girls in free-activity day or boarding schools—indicates, however, that group life is a potent force in personality organization. Similar observations have been made of delinquents in institutions and in mental hospitals where adequate group life is permitted and encouraged. From these observations the conclusion is justifiably drawn that group interaction has a therapeutic effect as well as being essential in personality growth generally.

Foundations of group therapy. The Jewish Board of Guardians has, since 1934, carried on an experiment in group therapy, as differentiated from therapy in a group. In its present stage, it is based upon four major concepts:

1. Every child needs the security of unconditioned love from his parents and other adults who play a significant role in his life. If they do not provide this love, substitutes for them must be supplied. The psychiatrist, the case worker, the Big Brother or Big Sister, or the group therapist are such substitutes.

2. The ego and sense of self-worth, which are frequently crushed in problem children, must be built up. This is done in group therapy through recognition, by praise and encouragement of all constructive effort on the part of the child. Destructive behavior, on the other hand, is ignored by the adult; its correction comes from the group itself.

3. Every child needs some genuine interest to occupy his leisure time. In group therapy we provide activities in the constructive,

1. *The Group in Development and in Therapy* [74] describes eight distinct types of group to which one adjusts in the course of normal development.

2. I have described the following group mechanics: interstimulation, interaction, induction, neutralization, intensification, identification, assimilation, polarity, rivalry, projection, and integration [52].

plastic, graphic, and other arts and occupations. There are various tools and materials at hand which the children use freely, creating in whatever medium appeals to them. The amount of latent talent that has been uncovered amongst these children is astonishing. If it is true, as many observers believe, that the incidence of artistic talent is greater among problem than among "normal" children, then supplying the opportunity for creative self-expression in a group environment looms as an important tool in the prevention of delinquency.[3]

4. The fourth value of group therapy in rebuilding distorted personalities lies in the opportunity it presents for a significant experience in group relations. Of primary importance is the generous praise that members of these groups spontaneously offer one another. But the opportunities for personality interaction are much more numerous. The members of the group work together; they quarrel, fight—and sometimes strike one another; they argue and haggle, but finally come to some working understanding with one another. Sometimes this process takes six months or more, but once it has been established, it becomes a permanent attitude on the part of the individuals involved. We have evidence that these are carried over to other group relationships in the home, at school, and in play.

These are only the cardinal principles out of more than a score of minor ones that have been formulated and that we hope to present in a forthcoming publication.

The process of group therapy. As group therapy is constituted at present, it operates in more or less the following manner:

Each group meets in the neighborhood in which its members live. It is supervised by persons carefully selected on the basis of their educational background and personality attributes, who have completed a course of specialized training in group therapy leadership. The first part of the meeting is spent in free activity, free play, or idling if the member so chooses. The latter part is devoted to a social period; refreshments are served, and the group sits about a table, eating and talking in family fashion. These meetings are varied by trips to places of interest in New York City and its environs, as well as by visits to gymnasia, picnics, and outdoor play in the parks.

3. In a recent unpublished study of post-institutional careers of delinquent boys, we find the following significant statement: "Of boys having an interest in athletics, music, animals, reading, stamp collecting, and so on, 60 per cent adjusted as compared with 25 per cent of those who had no interests at all."

As soon as the members have achieved sufficient maturity, they are referred, according to their needs, either as groups or individually, to existing "Y's" or settlements. A report recently received on a group of girls who had been transferred to a neighborhood center reads: "While your girls are handicapped both intellectually and economically, compared with other members of the 'Y,' they seem to display an inordinate interest in and understanding of music compared to our own members. They are also interested in other arts." We attribute this to their frequent visits to museums, concerts, and the opera, and to the victrola music played and discussed at group therapy meetings for a period of two years.[4]

We have had a similar experience with another group in a settlement house. Here also the girls participated in all the activities, sent representatives to the house council, paid their own dues, elected officers, and generally functio:.ed as an ordinary constructive club. In all of these activities, the girls were able to participate effectively. Because of various conditions, the majority of these girls were transferred from the case work department for treatment by the group process alone. Others were supervised by Big Sisters in cooperation with the group therapy department.

The early beginnings of our groups may be very disturbing to the children and to the worker in charge, as well as to the building in which the group is housed. Behavior is not only boisterous, but in some cases even destructive. The children's pent-up hostility is permitted to find adequate discharge. Clay is used for missiles instead of for its legitimate purposes; it is aimed at bull's-eyes on walls and ceiling and used in other destructive and symbolic ways. Paints and milk are spilled on floors. The furniture may on occasion suffer at the hands of our boys. Our clients engage in fist fights, quarrels, abuse, recriminations, and other methods of discharging hostility. Throughout, the worker remains neutral, and if others do not volunteer, sets out to clean up the mess at the end of the meeting.

Because the adult remains indifferent to the rowdyism and is engaged, during these periods when he is being tested by the patients, in some constructive occupation, the children gradually calm down and begin to display more controlled behavior. One of the groups that

4. Some years later we designated such groups as *transitional groups*, that is, for the transition from clinical to community milieu.

had upset and littered its meeting room regularly was moved to other quarters. The members, on their own, decided to be more careful about their new room because this was "our home." Gradually growth in responsibility takes on more mature forms. It is evidenced by the fact that the members put away materials unasked, take proper care of the dishes, economize on the cost of trips and food, and so on. Only recently, a group of thirteen-year-old boys would not let the worker buy them the customary refreshments because he had hired bicycles, and they felt that the cost of renting them was enough money spent for that day.

Why we permit rowdy and destructive behavior in the early life of a group becomes clear if we analyze the situation in terms of interview psychotherapy. Just as in the latter the client is allowed to express verbally all his resentments and hostilities, so in group therapy we allow him to do it in action. To many children, release through action—especially if it takes place in a group—is more significant than through speech. The *permissive attitude* of the group worker is exactly the same as that of the case worker and the psychiatrist. Here also, however, to have one's hostility accepted by an adult in the presence of others is a convincing sign of *unconditional love* and is a source of great security to the child. Authority and restraint come from the group itself and only infrequently from the adult in charge.

To illustrate the effect of this work, we shall present several concise case histories. Two of these are intended to indicate the response of clients in the initial stages of group treatment, which is usually the period of greatest progress. The other material presented deals with clients after prolonged membership in therapy groups.

Case 1. Paula, aged twelve, was a shy, withdrawn child, whose mother was dead and whose father was going blind. There were four other girls in the family. Two were married, but the married children showed no interest in Paula. After her mother died, Paula had been taken by a Mrs. W. to look after the house. Paula did all the housework and helped in Mr. W.'s cigar store. When referred to the agency she was, however, living at home, neglected and used as a drudge by her sisters, doing most of the heavy cleaning and making of beds, but getting no pocket money. She went to Mrs. W.'s apartment every day after school to earn small sums. She had no friends and no contact with girls or boys of her own age.

At the first meeting Paula gave the impression of being on the defensive. When playing word games, she would try to show off. When the other girls could not give the correct answer, she immediately answered, "I know," and ridiculed the others. She never looked the other girls in the face; she looked "very sly." She did not help with the dishes at the close of the meeting when the other girls washed them.

Paula seemed very resentful of what other girls had. One of the girls wore a wrist watch. Paula wanted to know what she was doing in the "club." She thought it was only for poor girls! Because of her work at Mrs. W's, Paula came to the group whenever she could. She usually came late. She told the worker that she "got the devil for not coming home right after school."

After seven weeks, the report on Paula was as follows:

"Paula seems to have lost her resentfulness and has made two friends. She insists on helping them and is always the first to offer to put away the materials. The girls are very helpful to her, as they realize that she has a hard time of it. They don't show it in any way except by being friendly toward her. She enjoys working on materials, and hates to lose one minute. At first she would not try anything unless she was sure she could do as well as the others. Last meeting she started to paint, first telling the worker that she was very poor at it.

"Her whole make-up seems to have changed. She is always very pleasant to every one, admires the clothes the other girls wear, and takes suggestions from them."

We may add that Paula is now, at nineteen, earning her own living, is a member of a settlement club, has a boyfriend, and is quite a happy, though a very limited, person.

Case 2. Another member of the same group was Joan, aged thirteen, who was referred to the agency because of poor attendance at school, though her scholastic standing was good, and because she was said to be "running wild." She masturbated in school. Her mother worked. Her father was a drug addict and never worked. A sister, eight years older than Joan, lived at home with her common-law husband and a son. The husband had a wife from whom he was not divorced. This sister was in the habit of discussing her marital problems in Joan's presence. Joan ate at drugstores and restaurants with her sister. She was sullen, oversure of herself, aggressive, and disagreeable. There was no home life and no control whatever was exerted upon the girl.

Joan was sophisticated, better dressed than the other girls, used quite a bit of make-up,and in the group demanded the public eye. From the very first, she discussed only her boy friends and the clothes she desired for spring. During the first few meetings she sat around and worked a little on embroidery, but would not enter into general conversation, except where it pertained to her directly. She had no interest in the other girls unless they went out a lot socially. She would come in every other week or so, always late.

This attitude gradually changed, and after she had been two months in the group, we read in the report:

"The last two meetings, she came in promptly at 3:30 p.m. and stayed to the end. She greeted all the girls cordially and entered into conversation with them. When a discussion of modern art arose (because of a painting one of the girls had done), she listened and admitted that she knew nothing about it, but it sounded interesting, she said, and she would like to see some modern art. She made a very nice clay basket at the last meeting, whereas before she had scoffed at the painting and clay work the other girls were doing. At the last meeting she asked Jean to walk home with her. Jean was the most backward girl in the group, whom the other girls asked to do odds and ends for them, such as turning on the radio, getting pencils, and so on. When a trip was being discussed, Jean was the only girl who could not go on a Saturday, which seemed the best day for the others. It was Joan who suggested that they might go on some other day, so that Jean would not miss the trip."

The results of about twenty months of treatment are more tellingly evidenced by the following two cases:

Case 3. When referred to the agency by the school, Paul, aged fourteen, was a seriously upset child. He was maladjusted at school, played truant, and disturbed the classes by his strange behavior. He frequently had very serious attacks of temper. During these he became quite violent, and on one occasion threw a knife at his father and almost injured him seriously. Paul was brought to court twice and was committed to the psychiatric ward of a city hospital for observation. He had a particularly intense hatred for his twin sister and a strong resentment against his mother. These arose from the fact that the sister had been a cardiac case from infancy and required special attention. Paul felt that he had been neglected and discriminated against since childhood. This feeling of resentment he extended to include all women, whom he hated intensely. When he was transferred to a woman case worker, he used the opportunity to verbalize the hatred in no uncertain terms and heaped abuse and epithets on her. He was very contemptuous of his father. The latter was unattractive and ineffectual, never having earned a living for the family. Paul was ashamed of him. The family was poverty-stricken. The boy went about shining shoes and turned all his earnings over to his mother, as if desiring to accentuate his father's worthlessness. Paul was always unkempt and dirty-looking; his clothes were too small for him and lacked buttons, and generally he presented a sad and sorry picture.

There seemed to be little movement in this case, especially when Paul was treated by a man. The woman case worker, too, despaired of helping him and planned to institutionalize the boy. In the course of the case work treatment, however, the boy was referred for group therapy. Here he showed considerable progress, and the evidence was presented to the psychiatrist during a treatment conference. In view of the boy's evident improvement under this type of treatment, the psychiatrist advised that it be continued.

When Paul came to the group, he was at first inordinately withdrawn. For months he had no contact with the other boys, working by himself in a corner. At the refreshment periods he sat apart from the others. He spent much time lying on the floor on his abdomen reading "funnies." He often acted like a little baby—would shut himself up in the lavatory and scream that he was unable to get out. He liked to pretend that he was a monkey.

The group worker ignored this behavior, and after many weeks, Paul began to play with materials, and soon discovered that he could do things that pleased him and the others about him. The praise from the other boys in the group seemed to mean a great deal to him. He later became attached to the two brightest boys in the group, twin brothers, and they became fast friends. He worked with them and began to see them outside the group.

The improvement in this boy is described both by the case worker and by the group worker as "quite remarkable." He is now, after two years, poised and self-confident, behaving like a mature, responsible person.

The gradual change in Paul's personality can perhaps, best be illustrated by the following abstract from the camp report, after the first year of the group treatment:

"Paul's relationship to both the staff and co-campers this year was excellent. He was well accepted by his immediate group and became the leader of the bunk. He showed a deep sense of loyalty and cooperation and asked to be appointed a junior counselor. Although this request was not granted, he was made an unofficial junior counselor within the bunk group, and reacted splendidly without resorting to domination of his mates. On several occasions he defended younger boys against the onslaughts of bullies. No negative opinion was to be had on him from any member of the staff. All found him to be respectful, friendly, and warm.

"If we are to judge by last year's report, Paul's improvement in his ability to make friendships was indeed remarkable. He seemed free and at ease in the group.

"In general this boy seemed to have made a phenomenal adjustment."

A year after his discharge from treatment by the agency, we had the opportunity to talk to the director of the settlement to which Paul had been referred by us. He was exceptionally able in many arts, and had built a closet for the settlement house with the help of some friends. His social adjustment was excellent. He dressed well, was neat in appearance and well-mannered. "He is all that could be desired of a boy his age," the director said. This is an encouraging picture of a boy who was twice hauled into court as a delinquent and once committed for psychiatric observation.

Fundamentally, Paul did not want to be a boy. To his childish mind, to be a girl meant to be loved. Was not his little sister, who was born with him, loved, while he was neglected? The only explanation his immature mind could supply was that he suffered from his maleness. He, therefore, did not want to be a boy. Also, to get attention, one had to be babylike, like his sister. Hence his inordinately infantile behavior. But the group accepted his maleness. He could be a boy among boys, and to be a boy did not mean to be rejected and frustrated. One could be a boy and still be accepted like everybody else. He no longer feared to grow up., and so he did grow up. The case worker helped him through insight therapy, but she states that without the group, little or no progress might have been made with this client. In this case, the interview method in itself was not sufficient. Paul needed a masculine environment and a cultural matrix that would help him accept his masculinity and his own maturity. Because of his limited intellectual capacity and emotional disorganization, he was very poor at school; he had no friends at all— a lone wolf. In the group he found his niche. His manual work attracted attention and praise. He was finally and unconditionally accepted both by the case worker, a substitute for his mother, and by the group worker, who served as a father surrogate. He gained a positive relation with sibling substitutes. He evolved a feeling of self-worth, a feeling that he later verbalized in his interviews with the case worker and in his conversations with the group worker.

Case 4.[5] Ray, aged fifteen, came from a family of five illegitimate daughters, whose father had deserted the family when they were very young, and whose mother eked out a miserable living as a janitress in a tenement in a very poor section of the city. In addition, the mother was ill, depressed, and constantly complaining. She traveled from one social agency to another, seeking aid.

Ray was particularly disliked by her two older sisters and her mother, so that she was isolated within the family group. She was entirely friendless in the neighborhood as well. At the time she was referred to the agency, Ray was associating with older boys and men, black and Puerto Rican, who constituted the population of the neighborhood. She had no friends except these men, and was entirely on her own. At school, she was making a very poor adjustment.

Neither intensive case work treatment nor Big Sister guidance was possible in this situation for various reasons, chiefly because of the mother's and the girl's attitude. She was, therefore, referred to a therapy group. Group treatment lasted from August 1934, to September 1936.

Although seriously withdrawn and frightened at first, the easy, permissive, and quieting atmosphere of the group and the kindly, though reserved, attitude of the worker gave Ray courage. She spoke

5. The author is indebted to Mrs. Mary Froelich for her aid in compiling the material in this case.

in monosyllables at first; later she was able to participate in general conversations and discussion. She was very backward in manual dexterity and had no interest in arts and crafts. But she became the leader in a play that the group wrote and prepared for production. With two other girls, she wrote the dialogue.

On Ray's birthday, the girls of their own accord gave her a party. Ray, very happy, sat at the head of the table. The girls sang songs to her and insisted that she make a speech. Ray stood up, and said: "Thank you, my friends. I don't know what else to say except to tell you what a nice party this is." This was undoubtedly the first birthday party Ray had ever had, and it was the first step in her being accepted by the group as a whole. From then on, Ray really became a part of the group.

On her own initiative, Ray started a library with the magazines and books that the girls and the worker had brought. She made a file and an index card for each book and magazine. She took great pride in the library. At one meeting Ray was absent and a new girl substituted. When Ray returned, one of the girls asked for a magazine. Both Ray and Josette, the new girl, walked over to get it.

Said Ray: "Who is librarian here?"

Said Josette: "I am."

Said Ray: "I thought I was."

"That's all right," said Josette. "You can be it."

"No," said Ray, "if you want to be librarian, I don't care. I'm the bookkeeper and that's enough for me."

She later explained to the worker that she understood what it meant for a new girl to have something to do. She, too, had felt shy and uncomfortable when she first came to the club, she said, and she could appreciate how Josette felt on joining. For that reason she was glad that Josette had taken on the job of librarian. Josette, who was infantile in appearance and manner, was never accepted by the girls, but during the two years the group met, Ray always displayed a protective attitude towards her.

We read in the record: "Ray graduated from school and a stenography course. She obtained a job in the fall of 1936 in an office."

The value of the group experience to Ray was manifold. She was a deprived and rejected child; the group accepted her. She was hostile and aggressive; in the group she was able to express these emotions without fear and without increased anxiety. She was unloved; the worker, and later the other members of the group, gave her adequate substitutes for the love that she lacked. She was insecure and frightened; the worker at first, and later the entire group, provided an environment and relationships that reassured her. Her friendship with two of the other girls gave her an opportunity to pass wholesomely through the homosexual phase in her development, and the group helped her to pass on to the heterosexual stage (through periodic parties with a boys' club). The group removed her, sporadically at least, from the social pathology in her home, giving her a glimpse of another way of living. Faith in herself was built up through her activities and through her social success as a member of a group. The worker saw to it that she never failed in her work or with the group. Although she was not creative with materials, Ray participated in group life. She was bookkeeper and librarian, and took part in writing a play. This adjustment would have been possible in a small group only. The worker gave her security in contrast to the instability of her family. Such experiences as the birthday party given for her by the girls gave her the feeling of being wanted by the group. Her fear of people was gone, as was evidenced by her reaction at the "Y." There the group grew much larger as new girls were added and the group became a part of the whole organization. We see that she can face realities and even accept some leadership.

At regular intervals joint conferences are held between the case worker and the group worker to discuss the clients that are carried cooperatively by the two departments.[6] These meetings are designated as "integration conferences." We take the following abstracts from one of these discussions, the case being that of James, who had been a member of a group one year:

"Case worker feels that James' development, in the light of his background, is startling. Two years ago, at the age of twelve, he was brought to the agency by his mother, so cowed and frightened, withdrawn and introverted that, by contrast, the boy is a different child altogether. Even the receptionist at the office noticed the transformation. While in the past he would not even answer a

---

6. About 30 percent of the cases received group treatment only. Later, all cases accepted for groups were treated by group therapy exclusively.

greeting, now he smiles to people, says 'hello' to them, talks as he sits in the waiting room, is able to travel alone. This was not possible for him in the past.

"Even though he is not fully accepted by the group, the fact that the group did not reject James means a positive acceptance to this boy, because of the contrast to the treatment he was receiving outside. Case worker feels that the center of the boy's treatment was the group and not the individual therapy. Because of his innate limitations, interviews with him were not effective. Case worker, therefore, feels that James' case should be transferred entirely to the Group Therapy Department."

Values of group therapy. —Group therapy seems to be of help in the following situations:

1. For clients of specific individual characteristics, such as extreme hyperactivity or withdrawal, originative and imaginative children, children with rich phantasies, and the egoistic who cannot develop a transference for the worker.

2. For dull children who are unable to participate in interview therapy; also children so repressed as to be unable to communicate their problems and difficulties.

3. For definite individual therapy needs that make group supplementation necessary; in our analyses we have found eleven such values of the group for the case work process.

4. For five types of social maladjustment.

Group therapy is employed (1) as supplementary to case work treatment; (2) as a tapering-off of individual treatment; (3) as a continuation of individual treatment for the purpose of socialization after the case is closed; and (4) as exclusive therapy.

Among clients unsuitable for our groups are (1) children who steal habitually outside of the home;[7] (2) boys who are active homosexuals; (3) neurotic delinquents; (4) certain types of oral aggressives; and (5) the compulsive homicidal.

Very little can be said in a brief paper such as this concerning the discharge of unconscious material by our clients in the type of group we have described. We have not discussed boys who make clay figurines and jab them with knives. We have not made a special point,

---

7. Most children who steal from their homes, and who seek to satisfy love and attention cravings through it, find in our groups these satisfactions and stop stealing. On the other hand, we have failed with nearly all children who steal outside the home if they seek punishment. Our groups cannot restrain, restrict, or punish.

for example, of younger boys who played with clay and murmured under his breath: "Mummy, mummy, what would you like to have? Jewels, castles, pretty things—what would you like? I'll get them for you! I'll get anything you want for you! I'm the leader of a gang of robbers!" Thus did the boy play out this phantasy in the group.

The use of material for sex phantasy is of extreme importance. We have also omitted the boy who made a coffin out of red plasticene and a mummy of green clay, with arms crossed on its breast. He placed the lid on the coffin and talked about his brother. His case history reveals the significance of this free association. The set-up of the home was one in which the brother was a preferred child. Nor have we quoted the instance of derivative insight: the child who drew a picture of a fat woman and said, "I don't like fat women. My mother is fat." We have not touched upon the number of children whose sex conflicts are so intense that they set things on fire. In the group, we provide materials to satisfy the fire-setting drives. We were able to discover many types of homicidal and suicidal personalities among our members by the kinds of activity in which they engaged in the group. We have also no opportunity here to describe inordinately repressed children, such as the extremely submissive boy who could not speak above a whisper because of his intense hidden hostility. In this particular case, the group, without the supplementary aid of case work, was able to release the pent-up hostility. Then the case worker was able to step in and by insight therapy redirect his energies.

Quite evidently, in a brief discussion such as this, it is not possible even to indicate, let alone describe, the many avenues of service to our clients that these groups offer, and less possible to point out the numerous lines for exploration, study, and analysis of this work and its usefulness, not only in therapy, but in school and group living generally.

CHAPTER 32

THE NATURE OF GROUP THERAPY
(1943)

This paper is based on the experience of about nine years in group therapy with approximately 800 children, 63 distinct groups, and 96 group years. It deals with a type of interpersonal therapy for young children first developed at the Jewish Board of Guardians and which has since been tried in many centers in the United States.

The idea of treatment of adults in groups is not altogether new. It has for some years since been employed by Drs. Trigant Burrow, Paul Schilder, Louis Wender, James Sennett Greene, and others.[1] Treatment is carried on through interviews in groups in which the patients' problems are ventilated, inner pressures and anxieties released, and guidance given by the therapist as well as the patient participants.

We, on the other hand, deal with children of the ages from 8 to 15,[2] through activity (rather than interview), and with the resultant interpersonal interactions and their therapeutic effect. It must be made

1. See: *A Brief History of the American Group Psychotherapy Association, 1943-1968. International Journal of Group Psychotherapy*, 1971, Vol. 21, No. 4.

2. The age limit for entry into groups is twelve.

Originally entitled "Group Therapy with Children," this paper was the first public presentation and part of the first symposium on group psychotherapy held at the 1943 Conference of the American Orthopsychiatric Association, nine years after inauguration of what later became Activity Group Therapy, and is thus of historic as well as scientific intererest.

clear that activity therapy which is emphasized here is not the only type of group therapy being employed either at our agency or in similar efforts at other agencies. Because of different treatment needs of clients,[3] we later introduced "group interview treatment" or *collective psychotherapy* for adolescents, a combination of activity and interview for younger children, group treatment with mothers, and *transitional* groups for children.

Activity Group Therapy here described is a type of noninterpretive therapy in which no interview is held. If interview therapy is required, it is given by a case worker or psychiatrist at another time. Thus, among our patients are children who receive individual treatment concurrently with group treatment, (cooperative cases), and children who are treated in groups only (exclusive cases).

The general setting for Activity Group Therapy is work in simple arts and crafts for an hour or an hour and a half. This is followed by a period during which the patients and the group therapist cook, serve, and eat together. They then clean up the room. The meetings are varied by occasional trips, picnics, and excursions, in accordance with the needs and readiness of the members and the seasonal opportunities offered. It will be readily seen that the group is a substitute family with the positive elements a family should have, and that the worker is a substitute parent. In fact, many of our children refer to the workers as mama, pop, and "unk."

The patients accepted for treatment have all experienced destructive or undesirable relations with people. We therefore aim to correct attitudes and perceptions through a new type of experience, so that the children can enter into constructive personal relations. In addition to the total friendly and permissive atmosphere of the group, the materials and tools serve to prevent mutual invasion on the part of the members before they are ready to accept one another. They work on materials rather than on each other. This is a rather important phase in the treatment, for it serves to redirect aggression and, in some instances, is also a means of sublimating it.

Group therapy is *situational therapy* as differentiated from interview and treatment by interpretation. We have evidence, however, that insight is acquired by our young patients as a result of their own thinking, and comparing their abilities and attitudes with each other and their own in the past. "I used to fight all the time," says

3. Originally "client" throughout.

a boy. "Now I work and am too busy to fight." Another addresses one of his fellow members thus: "You remember when we were enemies? Now we are friends." And still another: "I used to think my little sister was a pest. Now I think she is kind of cute."[4] With security and self-acceptance comes also acceptance of others and a more friendly and relaxed attitude toward the world.

To young children, experience, as understood in terms of subjective response and adjustment to an external occurrence, is often more telling than verbal formulations. In face, even in individual treatment, skill is most manifest where the interview is made an emotional experience. This inevitably proceeds from a well-adjusted relation between therapist and client.

The *situational configuration* of a therapy group can be said to consist of (1) the client, (2) the therapist, (3) the situation, and (4) the activities. We shall discuss these elements at different points, but it will be necessary to keep in mind that they are functionally one and inseparable.

What type of problem child can best be served by group therapy? What is it that a child with personality difficulties and social maladjustments needs to get from such a group? By and large, we can say that in order to gain from any group experience, it is necessary that the individual have some initial capacity to relate himself to others; he must have a desire to be with other people, to belong, to be a part of. This we designate as *social hunger*. Whatever the psychologic syndrome or personality problem, clients assigned to groups have some measure of social hunger, latent or overt, for without it no contact with them is possible.

Since eventually satisfactions must come from constructive activity rather than from destruction, and people must become sources of gratification rather than of pain and threat, the child must give up his need to resent or fight the world. Instead, he needs to develop a desire to be a part of it. Psychotherapy can help in this, but it can be successful only when there is a foundation for it within the personality of the client. We found that only children who have this initial capacity and some degree of social hunger respond to our treatment. Thus, intensely psychopathic clients and those with some form of behavior disorders are not suitable for group therapy. Social hunger in group therapy corresponds to the transference relation in individual

---

4. These spontaneous reflections we have since identified as "derivative insight."

therapy. Just as a patient who is unable to establish a transference with the therapist is not accessible in individual treatment, so is a client with no social hunger inaccessible in group treatment.

We have found that even narcissistic children gain from a non-repressive group. They take, however, a very long time and improvement is first observable in other relations—the home, the school, the play group—even though their behavior is not affected in the group itself.

We are dealing with the child whose ego structure is defective. Our clients are those who were directly infantilized by anxious or overprotective mothers or whose infancy was prolonged by rejecting, rigid, hard, unloving parents. They are also children whose identifications had been established with wrong models or images in the persons of the parents or parent surrogates. It is therefore necessary to supply them with opportunities for corrective identifications. This is done through the group therapist and the other children in the group. It becomes clear even from this brief statement how important is the personality of the therapist as well as the choice and grouping of clients.

In many of our clients the superego is either overintense and tyrannical, as in the neurotic child, or it exerts inadequate control over impulses and primary narcissism, as in the child with a behavior disorder and in prolonged infancy. In the one case, the child must find release from the emotional pressure under which he lives; in the other, he must internalize restraints and controls. The authority, restraint, and controls that arise spontaneously and naturally from the group relationships and working conditions are, in most instances, acceptable to the client. He submits because he derives basic satisfactions from the situation. Here we rely on the child's social hunger, and the *supportive ego*. This supportive person may be the therapist or a co-member whom the client naturally likes or who meets his emotional needs at a given period in his growth.

In the initial stages of our treatment, and as a result of the permissive atmosphere of the group, group therapy temporarily suspends the child's superego. He can act out his problems and difficulties; he can reveal his true nature and his hidden impulses without fear of retaliation, criticism, or punishment. This may create considerable confusion, aggression, and turmoil at the sessions, but *activity catharsis* is essential to equilibrate the personality of each of the participants. The withdrawn child remains quietly at his task; the assertive and aggressive gains release through action, until balance is attained.

We see how important is the choice and grouping of patients. If grouping is incorrect, the anxious and neurotic child grows too frightened to come to the sessions, or when he comes, his anxieties are further increased. He is thus traumatized. The overaggressive provokes and instigates aggression to a point where no group equilibrium is possible and therefore no therapy can occur.

Because the child is plastic, and because he absorbs from experience at a greater rate than do adults, his total personality is affected through the release, control, and relationships in the group. One of the results (and we consider this a major outcome of group treatment) is that his superego is extended and, to a varying degree, also transformed. The early superego is derived from the fear and anxiety of being abandoned, punished, or maltreated. As he matures, the average person learns restraint, not because of fear of punishment, but because of identification with the desires and needs of other people. This growing awareness of others engenders a superego which can be designated the *group superego*, as differentiated from the *infantile superego*. It proceeds from satisfying group experience, growing identifications and associations with individuals, and finally leads to integration into groups. Thus, the child no longer perceives other people as a danger and a threat, and can therefore establish relationships without fear.

In the disturbed and maladjusted child, identifications and strivings toward the group have not supplanted, as it were, the fear-laden, infantile superego. A therapy group, such as we have described, helps in the process of extending the early fears of mature self-restraint. Hyperactive children have gained greatly through the free, unimpeded release in our groups. Some attach themselves to a satisfying interest such as carpentry, and canalize their energies in a sublimatory, *libido-binding activity*. Children who are too inhibited to communicate their problems to a case worker are freed from their inhibitions and, as a result, there is greater movement in individual therapy as well.

Then there is the child who is nonverbal—with language limitations, either constitutional or cultural. He may be inhibited, distrustful, frightened, of low intelligence. These conditions would impede communication and understanding in individual treatment. Group therapy is evidently indicated in these cases.

Through the work in arts and crafts, eating together, trips and excursions, and the accepting and permissive atmosphere in the group, the schizoid child is activated. He need not use his self-protective withdrawal in an environment that is friendly and non-threatening. The mildly schizophrenic child, too, has here a con-ditioned and attenuated situation of things, occupations, an adult, and the other children to lead him back to reality. Children whose compensatory phantasies interfere with their social adjustment and with the development of an inadequate sense of reality, have actualized some of these flights into unreality through their free, undirected work with art and other materials. The recognition they receive from the group therapist, fellow members, at home and at school reduces their need for self-maximation and grandeur. Many children in this category have entirely given up this mechanism. As they gained status, they substituted achievement for phantasy. Children with prolonged infancy and the overprotected child gain much from the experience provided by a free group life with the emergent restraints and graded group pressures. The most perfect attendance is found in this group of patients. The neurotic child can act out his anxieties without fear of retaliation or threat. With security gained through this, he is able to talk out his problems with his case worker or psychiatrist.

Perhaps the group of boys with whom we were most successful are the emasculated boys who had overdominating mothers, who grew up in an exclusively or predominantly feminine environment, or have been in competition with sisters. Such boys acquire feminine charac-teristics, become submissive or ingratiating, and are commonly known as "sissies." They build up phantasies about the danger and destructiveness of masculinity and some express a wish to be girls and actually imagine themselves as girls. The improvement in these children as a result of a nonthreatening masculine group environment and relations is really quite remarkable.[5]

The primary and most essential element in a therapy group is that it must be a carefully planned and a consciously organized body. A therapy group stands or falls on the insight and skill in grouping. Essentially, the group must consist of children who potentially have

5. This is tangibly illustrated on film [187].

therapeutic value to one another. Obviously, a beaten down and reject-ed child would only be more traumatized if he were to be assigned to a group where he would continue to be beaten and persecuted. A fright-ened, withdrawn, and sensitive child becomes only more frightened and withdrawn in a tumultuous and aggressive environment. If these children are each to be helped to make better social adaptations and overcome their personality problems, they must have an environment in which their particular difficulties are counteracted and their needs are met [i.e., they must have corrective experiences in the group—ed]. This is accomplished through a planned group in which the inter-personal relations have, in the long run, positive values for every participant.

The difficulties that arise in fitting together seven or eight children who would be useful to each other in treatment are apparent. Luckily, there is no need to fit in all of the children in this manner. In a group of eight, there emerge a number of subgroups of two and three who are suited to each other. A weak and dependent child will attach himself to another member who gives him security, or he may lean upon the group therapist for such transitory support. In either case, this supportive ego functions only for a brief period. The friendly and comforting environment and relations soon make the child secure enough to go on his own and to interact freely with others in the group.

The aggressive child whose aggressiveness does not proceed from serious pathology, and whose social hunger is adequately strong, soon curbs himself because of group pressure. Children gang up on him, demand that he conform and not interfere with their comfort and activities. If this restraint does not arise from the group spon-taneously, which is usually the case, we place in the group an equally aggressive or an older child. The conflict for power is then confined to these two and is usually resolved as they become fast friends. The danger here lies in that these two together may tyrannize the group. If this occurs, a third aggressive child is added. Three children do not act in unison because rivalry is set up among them. Sometimes nothing can be done to check such hostility, and in our experience so far, thirteen children have had to be removed from groups as inoperable despite all our strategies, and re-referred for individual therapy.[6]

6. This was made unnecessary as experience extended and judgment improved in accepting or rejecting referred patients.

Restraint may come from the group therapist as well as from the group.

We are able to identify, so far, four types of patients as related to their function in the group: *instigators, neutralizers, social neuters,* and *isolates.* Children of various clinical syndromes and diagnostic categories are found in each of these classifications. Hyperactivity and withdrawal may be neurotic symptoms; they may also be character manifestations more or less normal to the particular individual temperament, or they may be behavior disorders. In assigning patients for interpersonal therapy, the child's function picture rather than the clinical diagnosis is important. However, one must be aware of the latter in order to anticipate future developments. Free expression of hostility may be in some cases not only bad for the group, but destructive to the patient as well. One must at all times know the meaning of each child's behavior, as well as understand the effect of that behavior upon the child himself, other children, and the total group atmosphere.

Another major element of the group setting is that it is a *permissive environment.* In the early stages, the child can use the environment in whatever way he wishes. He can make friends or withdraw, work or idle, construct or break, quarrel, fight or fraternize. This free use of the environment by the patient in accordance with his own particular needs is of utmost importance. The child is convinced that he is loved, since he is allowed to do whatever he wishes. He discovers that the world is not necessarily frustrating, denying, and punitive. The patient gains in his feeling of autonomy, and because of the friendly and accepting attitude of the adult, he relates himself to people. Inability to relate is the predominant cause of our patients' maladjustments, and when they can find their own way into a group at their own pace in their own particular manner, we have a truly therapeutic medium.

The neurotic patient finds in this permissiveness relief from his feelings of guilt concerning his behavior and impulses. He discovers that hilarity, aggressiveness, and destructiveness do not destroy one. He feels reassured. For a long time he watches from a distance the play and aggressiveness of his fellow members, but cannot bring himself to take part. Gradually he begins to participate vicariously by looking, laughing, turning lights on and off, or tripping another child. After some months, he takes part furtively at first, and quite freely later, in all the activities of the other children. Display of hostility makes these children very anxious, and some may not return for a number of weeks. In some cases release through individual treatment must precede group treatment. Almost all of the neurotic patients overcome the fear of their impulses, with constructive effects upon their total adjustment. In fact, one study of our work indicates that neurosis is one of the four characteristics of our successful cases. The others are: aggressiveness at home, having no friends, and the child must be under thirteen years of age.

The opportunity we offer to each child to use environment in accordance with his particular needs is of immense importance. We believe that psychotherapy consists of removing the patient's resistance to the world, his self-encapsulation, as it were. Once this is done, living in a social environment is itself a therapeutic situation. As long as the patient isolates himself either through resistance, active aggression, or withdrawal, the world cannot get at him. He remains in a state of isolation and develops or continues with antisocial attitudes. When we make it possible for our patients to go out into their environment to a degree to which they are ready and in a manner suitable to them, we not only give them release and comfort, but their perception of the world as a hostile, destructive force to be feared or attacked changes. It is in this changed attitude that our therapy largely lies.

The therapeutic processes in individual treatment and group therapy parallel each other in many respects. Transference, catharsis, insight, relationship, attitude formation, authority, and limitations that are present in individual treatment have their counterparts in a therapy group. Group therapy, in fact, can be effective only when this similarity exists. The therapeutic process is the same whether it is in individual treatment or in the group. The difference is that the elements are derived largely from different sources and in different ways.

In some respects the group situation is more realistic to the young child: he is with other children; is active—which is a basic need of the young organism; he interacts with numerous facets of a realistic situation; he gains status, evolves interests, and relates to his contemporaries. Throughout, he tests this reality. He seeks to discover its nature and response. Will it hurt or reject him? Is it in any degree dangerous? Is it friendly and accepting? As he acts out his impulses and problems, the group reacts to him, and if he desires to be a part of the group, he curbs or modifies his behavior. As the withdrawn child gains strength and assurance, he tests himself against the group situation and the activities to gain further reassurance. He does this time and again, each time growing in strength, self-reliance, and self-acceptance.

The reality which we set for our patients extends beyond the group and its permissiveness. Eating in restaurants, trips, and excursions serve to take the children beyond the comforting confines and relations of the treatment setting. Some children cannot face this challenge and stay away, but they gradually gain in power and take part in these extramural activities. Reality is further extended and each patient is tested against it through the addition of new members, being assigned to a new group, changing of the therapist, and similar devices and strategies. Nurturing and feeding are also gradually reduced, materials become unavailable and their use restricted, food is no longer supplied, the therapist exerts mild pressure and constraint, and other methods are employed to dissolve dependence and aid the maturing process.

Such a group as described is one in which there is considerable *social mobility*. Our patients cannot fit into organized and stratified groups. They either cannot or are only too willing, as an escape, to submit to rules, regulations, group purposes and aims. Such groups of *social fixity* threaten some; others find their regimen and rules a comfort and escape through submission and ingratiation. To belong to a group of social fixity requires a certain amount of depersonalization, and many of our children are not capable of it. Others are depersonalized and need to build up confidence, self-assertiveness, and aggression. The value of a neutral environment from which each can draw according to his needs is obvious. Personal balance is achieved in a therapy group, however, not through habit formation or "learning," but rather by correcting intrapsychic disturbances, acquiring substitute mechanisms, and sublimations.

We have stated that the first condition in our work is proper grouping. The second major factor is the personality of the group therapist. From what we have already said, it would seem that he is required to be all things to all children. Some may project upon him their hostilities toward parents and teachers; some become dependent upon him, some monopolize him, and others may seem indifferent. It would appear that the adult must meet the needs of all the children, which is, as can be readily seen, not a very simple matter. Should he attempt to do this actively, he would set up much confusion, emotional chaos, and hostility of the members toward one another. He can meet the requirements of the children by being a neutral person and as passive as one can be in a group. It is rather important that he does not activate a strong transference relation. Transference upon the adult is established to varying degrees by the clients themselves. This is almost inevitable, but what is important is that transferences be established toward fellow members, for it is because of their inability to do this that we accept children for group treatment. In this particular type of therapy, the focus of treatment is the relations among the members, and the adult should play a recessive role. This he can achieve by not obtruding himself, by not becoming the center of activity or the sole source of information, by abstaining from actions that stimulate and feed dependence.

Such neutrality on the part of an adult means to children that he is a kind, accepting, and approving person. Coupled with the facts that the therapist supplies and gives food, furnishes tools and materials, is helpful in case of need, and is kind and responsive, the adult emerges in the role of the all-sanctioning and comforting principle in life. In the child's mind this role is translated in terms of *unconditional love*. The child tests the genuineness of this love by exaggerated, aggressive, and irrational acts to see whether the therapist is really what he appears to be, and he must pass this test. He cannot become anxious, express disapproval, or display irritability by facial expression, muscular tension, or verbally, This requires a personality structure in the therapist capable of withstanding, without a feeling of discomfort, the turmoil, cruelty, and aggressiveness of the members toward each other. The fact that aggressiveness is accepted by an adult in the presence of others convinces the child he is being accepted and loved. Whether he intends it or not, the adult is a restraining agent by the very fact of his being an adult. When the child comes to us, he has already built up attitudes toward adults. To him, they have a definite prestige. He expects prohibition. Try as we may, we cannot entirely divest ourselves of the symbolic authoritarian role the child projects upon us. However, by accepting the child and by not frustrating him actively, the therapist does not arouse resentment, aggression, or defiance toward himself. Restraint continues the child in his state of dependence, and the fact that he is thrown upon his own resources helps the maturing process, even though it may temporarily increase anxiety.

A child of prolonged infancy, if not charged with too intense emotions, needs restraint. The child who is loved but overindulged, tends to persist in his infantile pattern. This may be manifested by annoying and interfering with others, by wheedling and whining, and dependence. The group therapist restrains and guides such a child even in the early period of treatment. However, even in these cases, restraint cannot take the form of disapproval or rejection.[7] It must be given with a kindly mien, though firmly, with no emotion and on a realistic basis. It should never take on the form of repression or nagging. Usually, infantile behavior continues in a group when there is more than one such immature child present, for they tend to reinforce each other, and reassignment of one of these into different groups according to individual therapeutic needs has proved effective.

Control and setting of limitations by the therapist is not confined to such children alone. At appropriate times in treatment, some limitations and denials are imposed upon all patients, but they are never arbitrary or unkind. The timing of limitation and denial and their discriminative use with specific patients are of utmost importance. Bad use of these may undo many months and even years of treatment. When denial occurs before *frustration tolerance* is established in the members of the group, the consequent feeling of rejection only reinforces the child's conviction of the cruelty and unfairness of the adult world. It intensifies his hostility and defiance, activates retribution on his part, which may take subtle and indirect forms.

Rebuke and restraint if applied prematurely often bring on the defeat of the adult. Children have numerous ways in which they can defeat us. They can challenge or disobey, they build up patterns of passive resistance, they steal materials and tools, they incite the hostility of other children. Authority, therefore, must be used with caution and adapted to the total group and the individuals in it. It should be employed at stages of treatment when it can be effective. When this is not done, it may destroy the treatment situation. It must

7. This subject is discussed extensively and illustrated in [64].

be kept in mind that attendance in groups is entirely voluntary, and when we fail to satisfy the children's cravings or hurt them, they drop out. This is another way in which they defeat us.

Since our project in group therapy was set up in 1934, there have been a large number of similar experiments in group treatment in different parts of the country. There is some disagreement on the part of other workers in this field as to the function of the therapist. We feel that there is unanimity in the basic concepts. The differences proceed from the fact that work was carried on in different settings, with different age groups, different types of workers, and probably different groups of children in regard to problems, age, and cultural backgrounds. Variation in any of these and other factors require adaptations of techniques. Since group therapy is situational therapy, any changes in the elements of the situation must of necessity require appropriate readjustments.

An important fact must be recognized in group therapy which does not exist to the same degree in individual treatment. A number of sources of restraining authority besides the adult are present here. These arise from the group situation. Interest in a project, for example, restrains the child's impulses for immediate and easy results. Eating together makes it necessary to evolve some order at the table. Among the other restraining relations and situations are those which arise from the need to share and take turns with tools and materials from other children and the building superintendent.

In conclusion, a word of caution is perhaps necessary. Group therapy, in any of its forms, is no substitute for other types of psychotherapy. It is effective only with clients whose treatment needs are specifically met by it. It must be related to age, the nature of the difficulty, the readiness of the client to enter into a group relation and numerous other factors. Under no circumstances must it be viewed as anything approaching universal application.

In our experience we have found that group therapy is entirely adequate in the treatment of some children, for some it is only of partial value, it is of no value to others, and may be injurious to clients whose problems and personalities are such that they are traumatized by permissiveness. It can be employed only in agencies where there is psychiatrically trained personnel and where psychiatric consultative service is available.

Postscript

Dr. Nathan Ackerman, one of the presenters at the symposium, raised a number of questions relative to its topic to which the present author was asked by the Chairman, Dr. Lawson Lowrey, to respond. The following are several brief abstracts of my remarks.

Dr. Ackerman's analysis of group therapy suggests many lines of study and exploration. The questions he raises concerning the nature of the therapeutic process in a group and the permanence of its effects are challenging to the group therapist. Answers to many of these will be derived empirically through further testing and study. Enough has been done, however, to give some indications of the values of this type of treatment, some already described in this symposium. What is said here about group therapy is equally true of any type of psychotherapy.

Two points stand out in Dr. Ackerman's discussion. One is epitomized in the sentence where he says, "A systematic growth of insight is not afforded by group therapy, but is by psychoanalysis." This is quite true. Group therapy [Activity Group Therapy—ed.] is not intended to develop "insight" in a client concerning his intrapsychic dynamics and unconscious strivings. Dr. Ackerman is right that in our groups "certain levels of insight can ... develop spontaneously" and our experience certainly confirms this. In our records we find many spontaneous statements by our clients definitely indicating evolving insight. When a child begins to compare his current relations with his siblings with those of the past, we may assume that insight is developing. When a client can talk of his personal deficiencies or strengths, without boastfulness, or when he compares his early reactions to the group with later ones, there is reason to believe that the child is acquiring insight. It is true that this insight is on a different level than that achieved through psychoanalysis.

However, in this symposium we are dealing with a special type of group therapy—*Activity Group Therapy*. We have other types of group treatment where development of insight is the chief aim, such as *play-interview* groups for young children. In *group-interview* therapy for adolescents and mothers, problems that concern the clients are discussed by the members of the group with some stimulation, elaboration and insight-provoking explanations by the group worker.

Here insight can be developed as in psychoanalysis. The only limiting factors are the equipment and qualifications of the group case worker as compared with those of a trained and qualified psychoanalyst.

Dr. Ackerman rightly points out that an evaluation of any type of psychotherapy must be related to its special field and its defined objectives. We cannot expect from Activity Group Therapy for children under fourteen the same type of results as from insight therapy or a thoroughgoing psychoanalysis. Group therapy cannot claim to reach deeply distorted personalities, although our experience might lead us to think otherwise. We have had isolated cases that responded to neither case work treatment nor to psychiatry, but did respond to group therapy.

Another point stressed by Dr. Ackerman is the matter of transference. He quite rightly states that "in a group the leader can be all things to one child, or one thing to all children, but cannot be all things to all children at the same time." Our thinking is that the leader is anything the child wishes him to be. This is the beginning relationship and the worker must receive projections of the child's fantasies concerning adults and reality. The child may see the worker as his enemy or persecutor or view him as the universal breast from which he can assuage his love hunger. However, as the child lives in the graduated and constantly expanding realities of group relationships, his perceptions of reality are enhanced. The relation between worker and client is not static. It changes as the client's personality changes or matures. Nor is it always the same; it fluctuates and varies with the client's needs and perceptions.

We can not confirm Dr. Ackerman's statement that "dynamic factors within the group would tend within certain broad limits to restrict the potential psychological expansiveness of the individual." If Dr. Ackerman has in mind adults, we would be inclined to agree with him. But to the child before adolescence, group living and group identifications hold limitless growth potentials. In fact, the young child grows largely through association, and to a lesser extent through learning, insight, or ideas. The young child is not ideational or introspective; he is a function-mechanism and his psychological expansion is a result of function and not thought. Activity Group Therapy is acting out and experiencing impediments, controls, and guidance from the total setting. Whatever "thinking out" occurs is secondary, and improvement in the child may come entirely without insight.

The careful choice of clients for this type of psychotherapy is of utmost importance, since it is not a blanket universally applicable treatment method. (Nor is there any one of which we know!) If we select clients with perspicacity, treatment results are gratifying and extensive. However, when an error is made in submitting an unsuitable patient to this type of treatment, we not only have indifferent results, but the patient may be harmed. The only type of patient who can be placed in Activity Group Therapy is one who has what we term *social hunger*. Such a condition is also a delimiting factor. Unless group therapy is employed within its own limitations, it holds no promise as a therapeutic agent.

The reduction of ambivalence is a prime essential in any type of psychotherapy. As a child accepts himself and his own impulses, then modifies his behavior to meet the demands of reality in a group; as he learns to accept authority, personal or impersonal, and submits to its demands, much of the ambivalance must of necessity disappear.

One general point should be made. There is a certain amount of danger in applying criteria of individual therapy to group therapy. The methods employed, the age and type of clientele are so different that differential criteria are needed. Dr. Ackerman is not unaware of it when he says, "In applying such psychological constructs to group phenomena we must keep in mind that their operational significance in this field is different from what it is in individual psychology." Certainly the dynamics of group therapy, though analogous, are vastly different from those in individual therapy.

It is noteworthy that whenever group therapy has been attempted along the lines of permissive environment, acceptance of the child, and free activity in arts and crafts, the results have been startlingly the same. Dr. Peck's paper further confirms this finding. Many of the developments of sibling rivalry, of release from hostility, and confession of deep-seated problems which he reports have occurred in our as well as in other groups. Our experience confirms the point that there is a value in having "a few better adjusted children . . . who might supply the group with additional leadership."

Dr. Peck's findings reinforce our contention, doubted by some therapists, that the group is definitely a substitute family. We see from

Dr. Peck's paper how the children act out family attitudes, sibling rivalries, jealousies, needs for domination, deceit, and submission. One of the important departures of his particular experiment lies in the fact that Dr. Peck combined an individual relationship with the impersonal neutral role of the group therapist. The technique of combining interview and individual relationship with leadership of a group is worth further exploration.

CHAPTER 33

MATURATIONAL AND PSYCHODYNAMIC FACTORS
(1968)

The growth of the theoretical sciences most often occurs via a two-directional process: from the general to the specific and concomitantly from the specific to the general. This is not the case with the applied sciences and their derivative practices. The effectiveness and vigor of the latter are rather derived from starting with theoretical bases, but identifying specific areas of applicability, on the one hand, and from devising and applying techniques uniquely suitable to these areas on the other. This epistemonic law applies to psychotherapy. The time has long passed when blanket psychotherapeutic practices and generally accepted and highly respected theories and techniques can be applied universally. They have all been found wanting when so applied. Just as the mathematical, the physical, and medical scientists, psychotherapists, too, have reached a level in their professional competence to recognize and identify on clinical and psychodynamic bases the need for specificity. Further, unlike other applied sciences, psychotherapy requires that it be practiced with flexibility. Variability is the essence for attaining success.

Dealing as psychotherapists do with nascent psychic forces in a multiplicity of combinations and interactions, to be effective they have to resort to variegated approaches within a specific area. Whatever understandings are formulated for a clinical diagnostic category or age and sex segment, each patient's individual uniqueness as a person requires modifications in applying the standard procedures. There are too many forces, too great a variety of influences, attitudes, cultural conditions, and value judgments involved in the formation of personality for it to be susceptible to any one blanket procedure.

The growth of psychotherapy as a science and the increase in its effectiveness will, therefore, depend upon refinements of techniques properly employed. But one will always have to keep in mind the fact that even when the height of refinements is reached, there are always the intangible and undefinable elements in the art of therapy which, as in all art, will defy formulation.

The present paper addresses itself only to one of the variables in psychotherapy, namely, the variable of age. The concept of age as employed here includes not only the individual in the dimension of time, but also in the dimension and quality of events and response, that is, experiences that have been absorbed and assimilated by him to form what is referred to as personality. Thus the values of the micro- and macrocultures have to be considered as well as the concept of chronological age. A dramatic illustration of this phenomenon is, perhaps, the character of contemporary adolescents in the United States as compared with those of past generations and the current youth in countries of other cultures.

There are definite biologic and concomitant psychologic characteristics of the human personality that can be related to the life span of the individual, which can serve as guides to the nature and process of the therapeutic intervention. For example, experience confirms the theoretically sound expectation that psychotherapy with children is less difficult, less protracted, and that the outcomes are more basic and more lasting than with adults. This can be explained in terms of Freudian topology—id, ego, and superego—during the child's formative stages and the malleability of the young organism as compared with older persons. The dependencies of the child, his ego formation and fluid identifications, his unformed superego and uncrystallized ego defenses—all render him pliable and subject to change through situations and relationships, for "ego defenses" can be shown to be a type of psycho-organic engrams. This conviction is borne out by the efficacy of good education with the ordinary child and by Activity

Group Therapy with children with problems. Because the neuronic engrams had not been as yet crystallized, they can be altered more easily. In adults the engrams are rigidified, especially where they are overcathected. The persistence of images and their cathexes form part of the resistance to therapy, for it is by this internalized "reality" that the adult patient lives and which has become part of him. Giving up these images creates a void with nothing to take their place for the adult to live by, and the source of security upon which he can draw in the interim is the positive transference upon the therapist. This is not the situation in child psychotherapy for the child still has his parents upon whom he can fall back.

Communication between the therapist and his child patient is of a vastly more primitive and instinctual nature than is that between the therapist and the adult patient. The child is much less verbal and responds more with feeling than the adult. The significant communications of the child are predominantly nonverbal. They contain more feeling and action than is the case with the adult, who inhibits and/or transforms them into concepts and language. The child's preoccupations are more autistic or at least more self-centered than those of the adult. The adult who is a patient is of necessity preoccupied with allotropic concerns, since the setting of his life imposes them upon him. The child, too, is concerned with others, but he is preoccupied with the few persons who are close to him and perceives them as extensions of himself, as entities belonging to him, who exist to meet his needs. These perceptions, of course, vary in degree in children of different ages, and in adolescents, but of whatever intensity, it is much greater than in any nonpsychotic adult.

When we speak of communication in the therapeutic setting we are actually dealing with the part of therapy that is identified as catharsis. The catharsis patterns of preadolescent children are vastly and most importantly different from those of adolescents and adults. However, a systematic discussion of the subject under consideration requires that first the transference phenomenon be elucidated. This is advisable since transference precedes significant catharsis, as catharsis precedes insight. The dynamics of psychotherapy which we shall consider in their order of importance and perhaps also in their sequential appearance are *(a)* transference, *(b)* catharsis, *(c)* insight, *(d)* reality testing, and *(e)* sublimation.

There is considerable doubt whether transference in the strict Freudian sense is present in children of preschool age. Observation of young children is individual and group treatment seems to indicate that they do not develop transference attitudes of the same nature as do older children and adults. The adult patient redirects emotions to the therapist *as though* he were the parent. He is fully aware, however, that the therapist is not his parent, and that he is not actually like him. The phases of positive and negative feelings are attached to an *image* of the parent in effigy, as it were. There is always the awareness of the difference in identity of the two persons. In cathexis displacement which occurs in transference, the two foci are not confused. The individual is clearly aware of both of them: it is rather a *transfer of emotions* from one to the other that occurs, but the different entities persist in the patient's awareness.

This ablity to detach and transfer emotions (cathexis) is still not a part of the equipment of the young child. Because of his narcissistic state, objects and his feelings about them form a unitary complex: he perceives them as one, much as primitive man does. Objects—things, toys, and people—are not entities, they are rather a part and extension of himself.

He is still in the stage of oral incorporation. Individuation or autonomy has not begun or is only partially achieved. This narcissistic identification eliminates, or certainly limits, object relations and conditions the transference. Another reason for the young child's inability to develop transference relations is that he still has the original love object, the parent. This and the child's less verbal state and his still undeveloped ideation make interview therapy unsuitable to his needs. The small child has means of communication other than language, that is, action.

When the young child acts out his love or hate toward the therapist, he does not do so as though the therapist were the parent, but rather that the therapist *is the parent*. What the child would like to do to the parent, he does to objects and pets, and to persons in his environment, such as siblings, nurses, relatives, and the therapist. If he is restrained from such action, or when these targets are not accessible, he creates others as objects of love or hate, in phantasy. Whatever these manifest substitutes may be, the real targets are the parents, but because the child fears losing them or being punished, he either represses his aggressions or displaces them.

This egotropic perception of the therapist changes with the advancing age of the child. As the child increasingly detaches himself from his oedipal involvement with the parents (which occurs between about four and eight years of age) and enters the period of latency, the substitutional fantasy slowly dissolves and he now perceives other adults as separate from his parents and reacts to them in a manner more suitable to reality.[1] The transference of adolescents again assumes a stereotype character as it did in early childhood. In the earlier phase, however, the transference reflected the feelings toward parents, positive or negative as the case may be. In adolescence, on the other hand,˙ the transference is initially intensely negative, which the therapist can, with effort and subtle skill, transform into a positive one. For several reasons, the enumeration of which has to be omitted here, the suppressed antagonisms in children to all adults (as displacement objects for parents), break through in adolescents to the full extent of their latent violence, a violence that is now directed toward the therapist. Thus, antagonism is expressed as resistance, in disguised sarcasm, open defiance, silence, or withdrawal from treatment. These reactions are frequently intensified by therapists' incapacity to empathize and identify with adolescents.

In the case of adults, no stereotypes, such as in the young child and adolescent, exist. The transference attitudes are individual and selective. Each patient perceives the therapist in the light of his conditioned attitudes toward his parents or other important persons in the past who may have affected him in the course of his life. Each can be considered as having a psychological template (emotional or conceptual outline) in his psyche into which he fits all adults who assume a role in his life. He then displaces upon the persons who assume these roles the accompanying or associative feelings (engrams) lodged in his memories and fantasies. One of the tasks of the psychotherapist is to draw out hostile feelings toward himself which a patient has repressed, thus regularizing such feelings in the context of reality.

Communication, too, varies in character according to age. Communication in therapy becomes catharsis when its content and form are emotionally significant in the context of reorganization of personality. Feelings can be expressed through play, as in the case of the

---

1. From this aspect, the transference is part of reality testing in the treatment of children.

very small child, through constructive and destructive activity in children in latency, or through language in older children, adolescents, and adults. It must be noted, however, that language can, and frequently does, accompany also nonverbal cathartic forms in children. However, language usually *accompanies* action, the latter being the *sine qua non* of children's catharsis.

Action is the language of the child and a child therapist, therefore, has to be attuned to that language and understand it. Practice indicates that perceiving the latent meaning of an act is usually more difficult than of an utterance.

The therapeutic setting for the various age levels, as well, greatly differ. The most complicated setting is in the therapy of small children. Their need to express their fantasies requires tangible objects that can serve this need. They need materials of low resistivity and objects to project their fantasies such as water and plasticine, sand, dolls of various characters, animals, masks and movable toys of a nature that will at once make the therapy room attractive, arrest interest, stimulate communication, and serve as targets toward which feelings can be projected.

For older children whose ego development has reached a level of individuation, the materials in the room should be of higher resistivity and tools and games of a nature that suggest more practical outcomes. In fact, the difference between play and activity, as we employ these terms, lies in the fact that play action is an end in itself; in activity, as we employ the term, action is to varying degrees aim-directed. The setting and the equipment recommended for Activity Group Therapy is suitable also for individual treatment, but it needs to be amplified and extended.The equipment for activity groups remains almost completely static throughout the course for treatment, since the primary aim is to generate interaction among the young patients. In individual and group analytically oriented treatment, materials and games are added that may serve to stimulate the unconscious and the child's libidinal strivings that need resolution. Patients with such needs are unsuitable for purely activity therapy and we have devised what we term "activity-interview" groups for such more neurotic children in the latency years.

The equipment for child action psychotherapy falls into two categories: *libido-binding* and *libido-activating*. The former is only employed in Activity Group Therapy, since the patients accepted for it have predominantly character and conduct disorders, though they may also have mild neurotic traits. Children in the years described as latency who suffer from more severe neurotic disorders require an active transference relation to acquire insight (on their own level) to resolve their difficulties.

In the case of adolescents, no special equipment is necessary beyond a table, preferably a round one, and suitable plain straight chairs. The procedure employed is direct interview, though we found that concomitant quiet activity such as sewing and knitting and jewelry making for dull girls of very deprived homes aid verbal communication. Adults, too, require a simple setting as described, though too often more comfortable lounging chairs scattered in a room are mistakenly used by group therapists, thus eliminating physical proximity and a work atmosphere.

The degree of insight that a therapist can evoke in a small child is limited. Interpretation, if given at all, needs to be factual and direct and should be resorted to sparingly, or the child may become confused, threatened, and wary. In the psychological treatment of the very young child (and even those in a higher age bracket) we need to rely upon the living and relational situation, rather than on mentation and concepts. Interpretation is inherent in the physical setting and the attitudes and conduct of the therapist. We first exploit the dependency strivings and insecurities. The therapist satisfies these at the start and gradually aids the emergence of individuation and independence. However, dependence is part and parcel of childhood and when dealt with appropriately forms the foundation of human relationships and sociality later in life. The child should not be shocked out of his dependencies; rather, we must follow maturational readiness and ego strengths before he can assume a role of self-dependence.

The child perceives the environment created for him by the therapist and the therapist's response to him as interpretation. The setting and responses have to the child the same meanings as words and concepts do to the adult. We have labeled this type of interpretation as "action interpretation." However, as already indicated, verbal interpretations may be also employed, but sparingly and in words that the child can understand and which have meaning to him. Of greater effectiveness, especially with younger children, is the medium of reflecting the wishes, thoughts, demands, and feelings the child expresses or conveys. By reflecting them in words, the therapist conveys the fact that he understands and empathizes, thus making the child feel secure and loved. Verbal reflection also serves as a means of reality testing for the young patient.

While subtlety and sensitivity are essential also in verbal or direct interpretation, such strategies as reflection are seldom necessary in analytically oriented psychotherapy of adolescents and adults.

The importance of the therapeutic settings suggested here for reality testing are quite obvious. The disturbed child always comes to the therapy situation with a defective sense of reality. Partially because of his short span of life, his immaturity and limited experience, his narcissistic and animistic perception of actuality dominate his feelings and thoughts. These inadequacies, and frequently distortions, are unintentionally fostered by all parents. Few, if any, parents are equipped to help a child make the needed transition from fantasy to reality in accordance with the laws of mental health. In the case of the young patient it is essential that we employ the therapeutic living situation to make this transition healthily. Here, more than in any aspect of the treatment the therapist plays a pivotal role. Not only does he create a stable environment, but he also makes it accessible by providing the freedom to test it out, to experiment with it, to use it in a creative or destructive manner. Actually, this does not constitute the essence of reality testing to a child. Its essence is the therapist, his acceptance of the percipient (the child), his kindliness, and his interest.

There is some misunderstanding of the term "permissiveness." It is not, as some aver, synonymous with unbridled liberty and unlimited acting out. It is trite to say that such lack of outer controls inevitably begets ego weakness later in life. The absence of controls overloads the child's current ego strengths and makes him feel both anxious and unwanted. This is true not only of children of all ages, but also of adolescents as well as of some adults.

In a recent publication some confusion was reflected in the area of application of controls in child psychotherapy. This confusion arose from the fact that Activity Group Therapy was designed for non-neurotic children in latency with basic ego strengths, defenses, and superego formation who can gain from group pressures and demands. The clientele for such groups is highly selected and most carefully grouped. The controls emanate from the individual children or the group both through passive and active disapproval and restraint. The therapist, as well, exercises controls in Activity Group Therapy, but he does it by creating a human as well as a physical milieu that inhibits exessive acting out. However, as described in the literature, under special circumstances the therapist may exercise direct control either verbally or by removing a youngster from the room. However, this he does very, very rarely and only when all other restraining influences in the group fail and the therapist becomes convinced that the child cannot bring himself under control on his own. Usually such children are referred for individual treatment.

For the sake of brevity we shall only enumerate the main characteristics or dynamics in the treatment of adolescents.

In interview psychotherapy with adolescents, especially of the psychoanalytically oriented type, it is essential that certain rules be observed: (1) The therapist must not press for revelation of deep layers of the unconscious; (2) the interviews need to deal with *top realities*, namely, with current interests and preoccupations of patients; (3) only a minimal anxiety necessary for involvement can be permitted; beyond that point anxiety has to be prevented, allayed, or diverted; (4) introspective or uncovering therapy has to be preceded by "psychological literacy" involving a conceptual (as differentiated from emotional) understanding of some basic psychological processes; (5) completely "free association" is not as suitable a method in the therapy of adolescents as it is for adults; *associative thinking* is more frequent, namely, horizontal association of ideas, thoughts or events (as differentiated from vertical, emotionally regressive free association); (6) in treatment of adolescents the therapist needs to be much more active than in the treatment of children and adults and may assume a didactic and an information giving role; and (7) while there are "budding" psychoneurotics among his patients, by and large the therapist addresses himself to the character and ego functioning phases at this stage.

Needless to say, the therapist and his educational and personality equipment are the pivots of psychotherapy. It is equally obvious that emotional resonance, empathy, intuition, perceptiveness and understanding are seldom the possession of one person in all areas of the psychotherapeutic spectrum. The personality of the therapist that may be most effective with children may not be as effective with adults, and one equipped to treat psychoneurotic adults may be a complete failure with psychotics and other character disorders, and one successful with adults may fail dismally with adolescents and children.

It is obviously impossible to delineate here in detail the characteristics of therapists in these various areas and settings. Under the circumstances, one can only resort to generalities. Empathy and understanding exist where there is a factor of commonality and emotional contiguity. Thus, a person who has completely left his childhood behind, that is, whose childhood has been too deeply repressed and is rigid and humorless, will obviously not be able to establish emotional contact with and evoke response from children. Similarly, a therapist who is unable to identify with the adolescent's inner struggles and understand and sympathize with his conflicts and hostilities will be greatly handicapped in reaching his patients at that stage of their development. And the therapist who is unable to maintain an attitude of empathic objectivity and sympathetic detachment and insightful response will be of little help to his adult patients.

CHAPTER 34

DIFFERENTIAL METHODS IN RELATION TO AGE LEVELS
(1945)

When there are no organic foundations for them, psychologic problems stem from interference with the child's normal growth, from blockings of the natural trends to autonomy and self-reliance, or can be traced to emotional insecurity in the home and maladjustment in group living. The orderly growth of a child requires biologic and psychologic security. He must feel adequately protected from danger and certain of physical survival. But such security is not enough. His strivings to become independent as his powers evolve, and as he grows stronger, must be met as well. This involves sloughing off the authority and protection of parents and other adults who are ordinarily responsible for the child and who now must gradually transfer this responsibility to the child himself. If the child is to grow into a balanced adult, the natural movement from dependence needs to be encouraged and so canalized as to strengthen his ego and fashion his character.

Either denial of the trend to self-reliance and autonomy, or its acceleration, increases the child's anxiety and rebelliousness against those who frustrate him. In either case—retardation or acceleration—there is covert rejection of personality as such. When he is unnecessarily inhibited, the child translates this as a rejection of himself.

Restraint, while necessary in training, should be employed as a tool for helping growth rather than to arrest development. Anyone who still cannot view relationships in a rational and objective manner, interprets prohibition to mean rejection.

On the other hand, where the child's growth is accelerated in any direction through the zeal of parents and teachers, his psychomotor organization is strained and the development of the personality is unbalanced. Exaggerated strivings of this kind on the part of parents, teachers, and other adults set up psychologic concomitants. When adults desire a child to be different from what he really is, they reject him as he is. The child is fully aware of it, even if he cannot formulate his awareness cognitively. He feels undesirable and inadequate. Such feelings of inadequacy become fixed and cause many psychologic dislocations and compensatory character traits and behavior.

Needs of growth and security are many and are expressed in numerous ways at various stages in the individual's growth. They also differ for different individuals. The basic and most universal of these are full acceptance by parents; security in their love, and a harmonious relationship between them. These foundational requirements are too commonly known to all who deal with children to require elaboration. Progressive educators and other enlightened persons are also fully aware of the value of appropriate creative activity and psychomotor expression in the development of an integrated and balanced personality. Less common is a recognition of the importance of the *family as a group* in this connection; nor are other, extrafamilial groups stressed in discussions on education and therapy.

Overlooking the group as it affects psychosocial and psychosexual development in our culture is a serious defect in schools and in therapy. It is at the root of many personality maladjustments and of much social pathology and it is growing increasingly apparent that the individual cannot be understood or treated apart from his culture. The totality of the conditions of his life, the biosphere, affects and molds him: in a broad analysis, it is part and parcel of his personality. Even infants and young children are influenced by it via parents and nurses, as the latter are in turn affected by the socioeconomic and psychologic conditions of their lives. Just as a plant cannot escape the effects of sun rays and weather, man cannot escape the pressures and tensions of his social environment. The kernel of a democratic society is the group. The capacity for group action and the individual's adaptation to group living are the foundation of the democratic life pattern.

Association with groups must be recognized as a prime experience for life in our culture. The capacity to work with and become a part of a group is an indication of a well balanced person. One who isolates himself is as disturbed as one who pursues association too vehemently or one who consistently gets into difficulties with people. The values of groups to the individual are many. Clusters, colonies, schools, flocks, herds, and groups are universal in nature. They are essential means for biologic survival in lower animals and in man; it has its roots in nature. Man, however, *consciously* uses groups for enhancement of personality and for psychologic survival. Every healthy person in our culture strives to be well thought of, respected, and wanted. Perhaps these cravings have their origin in the family through dependence on parents and their surrogates, through sibling relations and rivalries. They are further enhanced through cultural values, such as school grades and scores in recreation, and through community approval. Despite the many conscious and tacit artifices for promoting social values, group life must be recognized as an extension of biologic life and as an integral part of nature.

Whatever the raison d'être, an important fact to be recognized in dealing with people in education and therapy is that the craving for acceptance by and association with other persons is a primary one. One of the universal complaints of a neurotic is that people do not like him, and one of his common fears is the fear of group association, which, according to him, must result in failure. Though the neurotic's disturbance is intrapsychic, it manifests itself as a social maladjustment and his most ardent striving is to overcome this handicap. But social maladaptation is not confined to the neurotic alone. Patients with other difficulties are similarly afflicted. Whether an individual falls within the clinical category of neurosis, psychosis, behavior or character disorder, or psychopathic personality, his difficulties are in relation to people. It is therefore understandable why an effort should be made to explore the possibilities of employing the group as a corrective tool. In the orderly growth of an individual in our culture, he comes in contact with eight types of groups. While all of them contribute to ego building and social adaptation in similar ways, each makes, in addition, specific contributions to the formation of character. The groups, in the order in which they become important to the individual in our culture, are listed in table 1 [see also 74]. It should not be assumed that these groups are disparate. Most of them are coextensive, and the individual comes under the simultaneous influence of several of them at any given time.

It may be helpful at this point to establish some orientation for the concept of orderly development and the various phases of growth as they relate to our topic. It will also be helpful at this time to define the role of the adult during the different phases of the child's development, as a reference for the various functions that the therapist has to assume in the treatment of children at different age levels.

TABLE 1

Group	Major contributions
Family	Acceptance and conditioned love
Nursery or play group	Social experimentation (socialization)
School	Creative–dynamic expression
Unisex groups	Identification (socialization); sexual reassurance
Heterosexual groups	Heterosexual adjustment
Occupational groups	Social adequacy; economic security
Adult voluntary groups	Social acceptance (socialization)
Family	Mating; parenthood; self-perpetuation

Different phases in child development, as is well known, have been categorized by many students and writers. These classifications deal variously with biologic and organic growth, psychologic development, learning stages, and social development. Since at present we are concerned with psychological dynamics, interference with which creates problems in personality, we shall classify the several phases as those of *nurture, discipline,* and *education* [140].

During the developmental period of the child when he is disciplined in his nurturing phase and/or nurtured in his disciplining phase, personality problems are generated requiring correction later in life. Frequently children come for treatment manifesting also intense anxieties of a neurotic nature resulting from such pathological situations as sleeping in the parental bedroom, being frightened by the dark, or having developed a tyrannical superego or obsessive fears and anxieties. Treatment, therefore, must be suited to the particular presenting problem, in which the age factor is of major importance.

A child can be so deeply rejected in the family that he cannot satisfactorily relate to others. The anxiety aroused by human associations is so great that his behavior presents a serious problem to groups and individuals; he disturbs the home atmosphere, the school class, and the play group. On the other hand, the child's aggressions may become inverted and result in withdrawal behavior, or schizoid, or may form a basis for a neurosis later in life. Still another type of child is the one with a character disorder as differentiated from a mere behavior problem. Here we are confronted with personality qualities that proceed from the adaptations that the child has had to make in order to survive and be accepted. A child who has not had the comfort and security of love and satisfying relations acts out his early infantile demands, satisfaction of which may cause general improvement. But when, let us say, a child submits to the frustrations and denials of his early life, or when he is forced to make adaptations to pressures from parents and others at an early age, these patterns of behavior and feeling tones become characteristic of his personality as such, and they present themselves as character malformations.

Although we can assume that the sources of maladjustment reside within the personality itself, that is, that they are intrapsychic, the contributory factors are outside of the individual and can be described as extraindividual. This is particularly true where the child's personality has suffered injury. Common to our culture are suppression of spontaneity, inhibition of autonomous trends, and faulty feeling relationships with the supportive individuals, such as parents, nurses, siblings and teachers. Where tensions have been intense, the organizations of the libido and the ego become to varying degrees pathologic. The correction of the states that interfere with the individual's satisfactory functioning in his social milieu is the natural concern of psychotherapy.

Until comparatively recently, psychotherapy was confined to the individual interview (with or without derivation of insight) on the basis of a transference relation of varying degrees of intensity. However, it has been found that in specific disturbances, *experience* and *group situations* can correct behavior, overcome fixed early impressions of people, and, where the patient is helped to perceive himself and others in a less lugubrious light, remove psychologic distortions and blockings. In some instances, especially in young children, fundamental changes in the psychic structure can be effected by this method. A child who can be assured of his own worth may overcome the blockings of spontaneity and self-expression that have resulted from early repressive, frustrating, and fear-producing experiences and helped to overcome his repressed aggression. When children are helped to discharge hostility without fear of being destroyed, their natural impulses and drives are released. As a result, inner tensions are reduced or removed and behavior grows more normal and acceptable. They become able to accept the normal regulations and restraints of reality.

It is understandable that a full-blown psychoneurosis requires individual therapy, since the center of the malady lies in the early relations to the parents, which are tinged with sexuality. The transference relation with the therapist is central in the treatment here. The confusion of libidinal cravings in a psychoneurotic can be corrected through a true transference only. Such a transference in not necessarily indicated in other types of problems; in such cases the relationship can be on a less deep level. In the treatment of a disorder of behavior or character we deal with peripheral personality, while in a psychoneurosis we deal with its core. We have also found that, at least as far as children are concerned, actual supportive experience in realistic situations can correct character malformations and behavior in which no deep neuroses are involved. Since the characteristic patterns of reaction are acquired through early adaptation to situations, they can be corrected by reliving different and corrective experences. This is specially true where the neurotic anxieties are not very intense and the child is still young and in a formative state.

What has been said does not mean that transference to the therapist can be eliminated in any type of psychotherapy. The difference lies rather in the depth of the transference and the use that the therapist makes of it. Of necessity, the transference is less intense in group treatment than in individual psychotherapy, both because the types of patients that can be treated in groups require a less intense relation, and because it is greatly modified through the multilateral relations that exist among the members of the group, a transference toward the group [33].

The values of the group lie in the fact that it accelerates the initial steps in treatment, that transference to the therapist is facilitated, and that intermember transferences are established. Members of a group give one another support and each feels less threatened by the therapist and by the material produced. It is a matter of common observation that productivitiy is incomparably facilitated in groups than in individual treatment, and that patients reveal problems at a considerably greater rate. This is true of adults as well as children, in neuroses as well as in other types of personality problems. The fact that other persons have similar difficulties makes each one feel less unique and less stigmatized than he otherwise would. The group members act as emotional catalyzers and activate one another to discussion of their difficulties. We designate this as *universalization.*

Group psychotherapy is practiced on different levels, and in discussing its functions in therapy it is necessary that these levels be kept in mind. While the objective in all psychotherapy is the same, namely correction and improvement of personality and social adjustment, it should be recognized that the processes by which these corrections can be achieved vary in different treatment situations. For the very young child, for example, prolonged experiencing of relationships and a favorable environment are adequate. An inhibited child whose growth has been blocked develops patterns of withdrawal and a general quality of unsatisfyingness in mood and character which eventually will stamp his personality. When such a child is provided, while he is still young, with opportunities for releasing spontaneous drives, and is encouraged to act out or play out his emotional preoccupations, he can be started well on the way to psychologic balance. This is especially so when the mother (and sometimes the father) can be treated as well. A therapeutic setting that provides the materials and opportunities for acting out feelings and impulses will tend to change the basic moroseness and withdrawal. There are, however, many instances in which deeply disturbed children may need individual therapy solely or in combination with the influence of a group or a therapeutic nursery class.

For a child who has been abused, frustrated, or punished, or whose parents and nurses have been cold, restricting persons, therapeutic groups provide the possibility of experiencing human relationships anew. Groups are especially valuable for children who have for various reasons withdrawn from contact with adults. Such children have the opportunity to relate themselves to persons of their own age and within range of their own emotional and social capacities. Through appropriate physical activity and creative work, it is possible for the child to discharge feelings and thus break the dams that block the flow of energy. Repressed resentment and hostility can be discharged with impunity. Such egress removes inner tensions that have caused many forms of disturbances, such as fears, nightmares, and restlessness. The removal, in the group, of inhibition of self-expression, is equally important to older children, adolescents, and even adults. However, the methods of achieving this vary of necessity in accordance with age. What little children can gain through play and acting out, young children in their latency period and early puberty achieve through manual activity, creative expression, play, and free interaction with one another. Older adolescents and adults require verbal expression and insight to gain the same benefits.

Children's early behavior in groups is very infantile. They rush about helter-skelter at times; they fight with one another, make demands, are provocative and unreasonable. As their basic problems are resolved, their behavior becomes controlled and mature. We have observed that the conversation in interview (analytic) group therapy with adolescents and adults is also at first of a very infantile nature. They seem to throw off the customary restraints and freely speak of matters that are taboo in ordinary circumstances. While in young children unrestraint takes the form of hilarity and diffuse aggression, in adolescents and adults the same impulses are expressed in language. In both instances there is, however, a return to the infantile (preoedipal) level, where the individual was free to act out and do whatever he wished. This is made possible by the accepting and tolerant attitude of the therapist (the good mother) and the assurance that each member receives from the others in the group.

In both activity and interview group therapy, however, the flow of energy gradually becomes canalized: more purposeful and more disciplined behavior emerges. Children begin to work on definite projects and their relations with one another show growth. The conversations of adolescents and adults point to their problems and difficulties. This is made possible by the changing attitudes of the patients toward one another, by the changing role of the therapist, and by the development of the transference dynamic. As the life of the group progresses, early antagonisms, dependencies, and ambivalence among the members of the group are transformed into more definite feelings of tolerance, acceptance and cooperation. The therapist's role gradually changes from that of a neutral, passive, and accepting person. At different stages he becomes an active participant, an image of authority and restraint, and one who understands and interprets problems. The change in functions is determined by the growing maturity of the patients and their increased capacity to accept and cope with reality.

The very important differences in the ego structures of children of different ages make differential treatment imperative. The very young child, of prenursery or nursery age, has not yet fully repressed primitive impulses and strivings. The taboos and social amenities that come later in life are as yet either nonexistent or rudimentary. The child is still able to act out his primitive nature and when he is made afraid to do so, resorts to fantasy and substitute gratifications, usually of a pathologic nature.

We are agreed that problems in young children arise from lack of security and interference with primary functions. It is, therefore, necessary in the therapy of very young children to supply them with materials through which they can act out problems around these functions and by means of which at the same time spontaneous drives to activity and association can be fulfilled. Water, clay and plasticine, water colors and finger paints, are primary requisites. Dollhouses, and dolls that represent mother, father, and babies are used in working through fantasies associated with persons in the family, and toy bathroom fixtures help to discharge repressions and fears established in toilet training and to overcome rebellion against the parents associated with evacuation and voiding. Sometimes the child's association in relation to his play is elicited, and simple "interpretations" are given by the therapist. But when the disturbances relating to these areas have not assumed too great proportion, living over in play of the traumatic situations, under the guidance of a friendly and comforting adult, is sufficient in itself.

The infant or young child is very much a part of the mother, both from the point of view of his own feelings toward her and from those of the mother's feelings toward him. This relationship can be described as symbiotic, and whenever it is in any way pathogenic, treatment of both the child and the mother is essential. Since the child's personality is still weak, he cannot retain improvement against the pressures of his relationship with the mother. *Treatment of mothers of young children is nearly always indicated,* and in many instances treatment of the mother alone is adequate to correct whatever problems the infant may have. This is true in the treatment of children at all ages, but is especially so where infants and young children are concerned.

The use of messy and plastic materials like clay, plasticine, and water has an effect of regulating the child's behavior because of anal satisfactions that he may receive from such play. It is therefore more valuable to set the stage so that he can redirect or sublimate his interests through creative effort. Sometimes direct suggestion for work with suitable materials is indicated.

Little is known as to what the value of a group to a child or three or four may be. The ordinary processes that one observes in groups of children of ten and eleven, for example, do not seem to operate. Very young children appear to act very much like isolates, but the tendency to isolation must be assumed as normal for babies and very young children. Organic immaturity, intensity of emotional dependence on the mother, and the natural fear of the unfamiliar cause the child to isolate himself in his own preoccupations and fantasies. Only occasionally does he break through the walls of his ivory tower of imagination to observe or speak to another child. We can assume, however, that these stray and occasional contacts have great value to the developing child, in normal growth and in therapy.

As the infant grows into childhood he has to give up his autism and narcissism, and his natural egocentricity must be transformed into the ability to make contact with other persons and later to share with them (allotropy). Though we usually find little actual contact or cooperation among nursery children there is great awareness of one another among them. This awareness is revealed by imitation, manifest suggestibility, occasional struggles for possession of tools and materials, rivalry for favor with the teacher or therapist. It is this awareness that is important, for through it the growing child breaks the confines of his encapsulation. This process can be characterized as *psycho-osmosis,* that is, interpenetration of personalities without overt or observable action.

The skillful therapist is able to contrive situations in which association can take place. The most common of these occasions are the eating and cleaning-up periods and the outdoor playtime. But one cannot expect too much sociability from children at this age, though more of it appears at mealtime than at any other period. Contacts among such very young children are at best fleeting and perfunctory, for the egocentric (autistic) trends are predominant.

The therapist's role here is not as permissive as it is in dealing with older children. We have seen that freedom is the primary condition for therapy, especially freedom to express aggression and hostility. But freedom and restraint have to be balanced in education and in therapy. The younger the child, the more restraint he needs. Self-restraint is learned when the child incorporates the restraints of adults whom he accepts and trusts. The young child emerging from the period of nurture (when all his wants and whims were unconditionally satisfied) needs time, strength, and maturity to incorporate restraints. Discipline and authority acceptable to him, and *graded in intensity,* are necessary for the child's personality integration, but they have to be applied with discrimination and care. The frightened and withdrawn do not need such control; rather, they need release. The overactive and aggressive need restraint. Their diffuse aggressiveness and pugnacious trends have to be impeded. Since the child has not as yet established inner controls, these controls must come from without, namely, from the adult. It is to a kind and acceptable, but firm adult that the child will give up his egoistic and narcissistic characteristics [38].

In therapy groups, children between the ages of five and seven have a tendency to explosive behavior that may become at times violent. They tend to stimulate and reinforce one another and join together in rather extreme hilarity and destructiveness. There is little value, therapeutically speaking, in this explosive behavior.[1] In individual therapy the therapist can treat the causes of the aggression through release, play therapy, and interpretation, for behavior here is more often related to the central problem of the child than it is in groups. In groups, aggressiveness is suggested by one of the children and taken on by the others without its having special meaning to them, except

---

1. Such behavior is anal in nature and is in fact frequently accompanied by passing of flatus. It has been shown that passing of flatus and belching are used as aggression.

that they "let off steam." In groups, therefore, explosive activity is not always related to the central problem of *each* member, and has no particular meaning in terms of therapy of basic difficulties. Release through aggression and hostility has its greatest value when it is related to the problem. When it becomes diffuse, it may have the opposite of therapeutic effect, namely, it may disorganize personality, thus preventing personality integration.

It must be expected that in the early stages of treatment, after the initial insecurity is thrown off, there will be considerable diffuse hilarity and "wild" behavior. This should be viewed, however, as a preliminary stage in acclimatization and testing of reality, especially testing of the therapist. This is the most trying period for the latter. He must convince the children of his basic acceptance of them and at the same time prevent too great disorganization of the group and of the children. Most often hilarity is suggested by activating materials which should be removed before the next session [53, pp. 191ff.]. Shortening the treatment hour is a good device. Introducing food at a high point in hilarity, a walk outdoors, or a story can also be effective. When hyperactivity persists, it may be advisable to reexamine the personnel of the group. There may be one or more children not as yet ready for group treatment.

An example of the effect of activating material in group disorganization is offered in the following situation. Water in pails was made accessible to chidren from four and a half to five and a half years old. Because this gave them an opportunity to splash, pour the water back and forth, and throw it at one another, the group was soon in a state almost of panic. They threw paints, water colors, clay, and other materials into the water and onto the floor and trampled on the resulting mess, screaming at the tops of their voices and pushing one another around. This was the result of the therapist's unwise procedure in encouraging these very young children to carry water in pails and pour it into basins. Because the children were physically not ready to do this satisfactorily, some water was spilled on the floor; this provoked the extreme behavior. The group became quite uncontrolled and the therapist was unable to check it except by extreme and arbitrary means, thus jeopardizing her role as therapist. It was, therefore, necessary to remove temporarily the opportunity of using water, and only a small pitcher of water for drinking purposes was placed in the room.

Had the group therapist planned the setting better and not encouraged the children to undertake a task beyond their strength and powers of coordination, she would not have generated disorganization in the group. It was discovered that the therapist had to help the children a great deal with their other work because the tools she had supplied were too advanced for them. Drills and saws were too difficult to manage and therefore the therapist had to become involved, which increased dependence upon the adult. It also kept her very busy which, in turn, made her tired and unconsciously irritable. As a result she was at times peremptory with her young patients as shouts for help came from all sides. Removal of these overdifficult materials and tools helped greatly in stabilizing the group. It was also found that a period of an hour and a half indoors was too long for children so young, and brief walks around the block or along the nearby river after about fifty minutes or an hour of activity reduced much of the tension. When the children became too hilarious, the therapist read to them, which served to quiet them down. Picture books that the children themselves could read were also helpful.

One therapist directed the children's activities into overmature channels. For example, she supplied jigsaw puzzles, with the intention of interesting children of four and five in the activity. This was evidently an overmature and overdifficult task. The adult should work with materials that are within the children's capacity and interest range rather than initiate occupations that will require help and direction. It was easier for the children to take up the same activity as the adult when the worker played with blocks. Her supervisor also suggested that materials and tools be laid out on a table, instead of being left in a closet too high for the children to reach; this would also utilize *visual suggestion*. Among the materials were plasticine, blocks, a few simple tools, male and female dolls, a monkey marionette, crayons, and large sheets of paper. Because of the children's hyperactivity, paints were temporarily eliminated and large crayons easy for children to hold were provided instead.

Much has been said regarding the value of release of aggressive drives in children. Without going too far afield, it must be said that the release of aggression (abreaction) has therapeutic value when it is an extension of basic emotional and character disturbances. If there is no such relation, diffuse and uncontrolled hyperactivity extends the child's immaturity. Physical combat among preschool children is infrequent. It occurs most often among children between seven and twelve and is accompanied by intense anger, redness of the face, screaming, and tears. There is probably less fear than anger in the fights of very young children; this seems to be reversed in the case of older children. In the latter, an element of fear also accompanies fighting. It is of comparatively little value for the ordinary child of four or five either to win in combat or be vanquished, and the therapist should not permit continuance of the situation. It is advisable to stop fights between young children as soon as the conflict arises. This does not apply as much in the case of the frightened and inhibited child who through the treatment situation has reached a stage at which he can mobilize power to fight. He should be allowed to win a fight or two. Older children need be allowed to bring a struggle to a conclusion through their own or group efforts.

Restraint in therapy may be either active or passive. *Passive restraint* is derived from a situation or from behavior of the therapist as a result of which the child controls his own acts. In Activity Group Therapy [53, 129] for children between the ages of nine and twelve or fifteen, restraint is almost entirely of a passive nature as far as the role of the therapist is concerned. The situation is so arranged that the materials and tools, as well as the group relations, exert a limiting influence upon the child. Only in rare situations does the therapist use direct control or restraint. In the case of particularly aggressive children with psychopathic trends, or of infantile, overpampered children, direct restraint may be employed. However, in the case of children with behavior disorders or neuroses, direct restraint is not used until the treatment has gone on for a long time, in fact, not until nearly the end of treatment. In the case of very young children, however, the restraint must be direct and early, because situational or passive restraint is not apparent to them [37, pp. 599].

As we move on in terms of age, we find that we must vary the materials, the equipment, and the role of the therapist. For some older children in latency, playing with fire is essential. With adequate precautions in setting and equipment, it is possible to supply them with this activity. The less hazardous fire equipment consists of electrical pyro pens with which the child can burn wood and paper and thus work through sexual aggressive trends. An electric stove should be part of the equipment, or cans of sterno placed on asbestos pads are very helpful. The *resistivity of materials* is also adjusted to suit age levels [53, 128].

With the older children, the therapist is more permissive than with little ones. Much freedom must be given to children between the ages of seven and twelve, so that they can find their own way in establishing relationships and evolving self-controls. We have found this procedure suitable because at this age there already exists a degree of awareness of good and bad behavior, of right and wrong. Having passed through the oedipal stage and having identified to a degree with parents, the child can take on some of their mannerisms, values, and attitudes. We must therefore utilize for further growth whatever values the child has already incorporated by experiment and experience reactions. He can register the reactions of the other children and of the therapist, build restraints, and pattern his conduct so as to become acceptable to the group. At some time during these years there appears in a child a need for association and play with other children and it is intensified in a free group. The road inward to the child's personality in patients who are selected for group therapy is the exploitation of this trend, which we describe as *social hunger*. During the years between the ages of seven and twelve, the egocentric trends are normally transformed into social trends. However, some of the group control at these ages, especially in the younger age range, must proceed from the therapist. Though the children are more ready to evolve group controls than they were in prenursery and nursery years, they cannot achieve this entirely on their own. The function of the therapist, therefore, must be graded to the evolving personalities of the children and their readiness to form a group amalgam, as a result of which they develop controls for behavior. The younger the child, the greater the activity of the therapist [64].

Because the present paper is devoted to group therapy for children up to the age of twelve, variations in treatment of children beyond this age are omitted. However, for the sake of completeness, it must be said that children chosen for group therapy at the ages of ten years and up must be those who are capable of adapting themselves to a group situation and ready to give up egocentricity and undesirable behavior in return for the acceptance of the group. If for any reason such social hunger is nonexistent, as is the case in psychopathic personalities, extreme neurotics, and psychotics, treatment in groups is counterindicated. When the appropriate choice of clientele is made, and the group is balanced in terms of aggressive, normal, and withdrawn children, therapy through the group can be effective. When, however, the combination of the group clientele is faulty, very little can be done for them either through manual activities or the activity of the therapist. The therapeutic medium lies within the group itself and not in extraneous appurtenances. A therapist in charge of an imbalanced group will be compelled to act in the role of the adults who originally contributed to the genesis of the children's problems. He will be compelled to act as a repressive force and authority, instead of as the symbol of tolerance, acceptance, and kindness that the patients require.

In summary, the function of the group in the treatment of young children lies in three areas: (1) play and activity; (2) association with other children of the same age; (3) the role of the therapist.

Materials must be planned to provide displacement of aggression and hostility upon objects as substitutes for parents, siblings, nurses, and teachers. The materials in the case of very young children, especially, should afford substitution for inhibited activity on the biologic plane, such as oral, anal, and urethral functions. They should supply gratifications of the polymorphous trends of the child and give satisfaction to both his sexual and nonsexual cravings. Playing with fire has sexual meaning in the child's fantasy, while playing with clay and water satisfies anal and oral cravings. Shouting and receiving food from the therapist also assuage oral cravings. Materials should not be too varied or too difficult to understand or manipulate at a given age. The child has to see results of his efforts within a short period of time and should not be expected to postpone gratifications unduly. Materials of greatest value are those of *graded resistivity and complexity*. Materials for young children must be soft and pliable, such as clay, plasticine, paints and water; but as the child grows older more resistive materials, such as wood and metals should be introduced. This gradation aids in the development of power and self-regard.

The values of a group to children of different ages, as already indicated, vary greatly. In all instances, however, its major significance for therapy lies in the fact that it supplies a field in which the child may relate himself to others, thus helping him to break through isolation, withdrawal, and rejection of people. The natural craving for others causes the individual to go out of himself, as it were, into the human environment, thus leading from egocentricity and narcissism to object relationships. There is also opportunity for the child to test himself against others and to discover the boundaries of his ego. The presence of other children also offers the possibility of developing patterns of relationship with human beings of the same intellectual, emotional, and social development, in which the feeling of sameness and, therefore, of comfort and security exists. This is particularly of value to only children or to children with intense sibling rivalries. Each child utilizes the group in accordance with his needs and capacities, especially as they relate to age. Very young children's groups are less mobile than are groups of older children and require a more carefully set environment. The activities are less varied, repetition of occupations is not as irksome to very young children as it is to older ones, and relationships are on a less personal basis.

As the children grow older, their autonomous trends find expression in the pattern of the group. They control the situation more, formulate codes, or develop tacit controls for behavior. Definite friendships make their appearance and generally there is greater interaction among the members. At this stage, therefore, the group can be used consciously as a tool in treatment, since the older child needs group association and acceptance more than the preschool child does.

The function of the therapist also varies with the age of his young patients. His participation must of necessity be greater in the group of younger children, who are still dependent upon support from an adult. Much of the necessary authority must come from the therapist. The therapist here has to act as authority more frequently and in a more direct manner than where older children are concerned. Where authority can evolve from the group itself, the therapist need not, in most cases, exercise it. His role is constantly changing, both in relation to the ages and to the evolving personalities of the children. While he functions *at first* as a source of security and support, his role changes to one of guidance and mild authority.

CHAPTER 35

TREATMENT OF AGGRESSION THROUGH ACTIVITY GROUP THERAPY
(1943)

Before elaborating on the treatment of aggression through group therapy, it may be helpful to clear up several basic points. First, we need to come to some understanding concerning the meaning of the term *aggression* as I think of it. Numerous acts leading to survival by man and animals—and to some extent also by plants—involve aggression against the environment. The needs of life make it necessary that we manipulate, control, direct, and subject things and people to our will. The intensity of these mechanisms varies with the character of the individual, the type of relations he has with people, the special setting in which he operates, as well as the total cultural atmosphere. The hunter, for example, in the act of hunting is constantly aggressive against shrubs and bushes, as well as animals. By comparison the laboratory scientist may seem to be less aggressive, but actually he is equally so intellectually. Each of us functions aggressively as we sell and buy, make our way socially, seek status, and in other such everyday activities. The therapist, however, is not concerned with these manifestations of aggression. Rather he is preoccupied with aggression that is excessive for meeting the needs of a given situation, when it is diffuse and uncanalized, and when it is hostile.

Aggression as differentiated from other activity, is directed activity, having definite *purposes, direction and object*. The object (or recipient) may in some cases be the aggressor himself, characteristic of some neuroses and psychoses. In abnormal or pathological aggression the factor of hostility enters in a purely unconscious form, but its presence is recognized by the fact that the aggressor aims to provoke, injure, or destroy the object or recipient. It seems to me that there is an error involved when we say that frustration leads to aggression. Frustration *may* lead to aggression, but more often frustration begets hostility. The fact remains, however, that within limits and to the extent to which it serves the ends of survival and creative effort, aggression is a normal form of behavior. Only when it is excessive, uncontrolled, hostile, destructive, does it come within the purview of the therapist.

A second point to clear up is the difference between aggression and hostility, which will be only briefly mentioned here. Strictly speaking there is no such entity as aggression. There are aggressive acts and it is through such acts that we observe aggression. Hostility, on the other hand, is an *emotional state* which may or may not manifest itself in overt behavior. It is rather a motivation and an emotional quality that begets or accompanies behavior. It may, however, remain unexpressed as in passive resistance, pathological withdrawal, excessive passivity, noncooperation. In the neurotic it is often manifested as symptom.

Third, in judging aggressiveness in patients, it is necessary that we evaluate behavior in terms of the specific culture in which the individual has his roots and by which his character has been shaped. What may be considered excessive aggressiveness in a person in one cultural group may be quite acceptable in his own milieu. Unacceptable table manners in one group or neighborhood are quite acceptable and normal in another. Personal manners of children who come to us for treatment, their food anxieties and similar behavior patterns may shock us, but they become quite acceptable if considered in relation to their background. This principle must also be applied to their attitudes and behavior toward each other and toward adults. The patients' directness, indiscretion, "disrespect," and boisterousness may not be at all pathological viewed in terms of the total cultural environment and early background. Everyone around them, including parents, behave in a similar way. They have been "brought up" to such behavior. In fact, were these youngsters different, they would not be acceptable to their neighborhood peers. They would be stigmatized as weak and sissy, become scapegoats and generally be socially maladjusted in their surroundings. Thus, the needs of survival in certain sections of a large city require a degree of aggressiveness which may be considered undesirable elsewhere.

Another point requiring clarification as preparation to the main thesis of this paper is the nature and practices of group therapy. The group therapy to which we specifically refer consists of treatment of socially maladjusted and personally disturbed children in which the therapeutic agents are the group situations, the interaction of the personnel of the group, the activities that grow out of the setting, the expanding reality to which they are exposed, the complete freedom of expression, and the growing restraints emanating from the situation.

A therapy group consists of a maximum of eight children within a two-year age range and having fairly equated social maturation, psychosocial developments, physical size and other similar factors. The group is provided with arts and crafts materials, toys and games to which there is free access for use at will by the members. They also have free access to each other, and there is communication interchange, combat, quarrels, friendships and whatever else spontaneously arises. The children eat together at the end of each session and frequently go out on trips, excursions, to the theatre and restaurants. The adult is a neutral person, and strives to remain passive.

Because children in these groups are permitted to act out their difficulties freely and unrestrainedly, their latent problems, anxieties, and preoccupations—their true characters—are revealed. In fact, in a group under the stimulation of other children, these are brought out vividly even in those cases where they are withheld or disguised in individual treatment. As a result of observation of some 800 children (at the time of this writing), we were able to relate types of aggression (and their treatment) to specific characteristics. A full discussion of our findings in the area of character formation is reserved for future publication. I shall confine this discussion to the treatment of aggression as such, omitting etiology, manifestations and other elements. Group treatment of nine types of aggression which we have been able to identify is briefly outlined in what follows.

1. *Aggression emanating from prolonged infancy.* A child who has been overprotected and pampered at home tends to continue his infantile behavior in other relations as well. He is playful, provocative, annoying; he demands attention, cajoles, begs, wheedles, and demands. The other members of the group usually reject this behavior and the infantile child finds himself excluded or harassed by his contemporaries. The social maladjustment of such children is quite intense even though in some instances they get along well at home. However, in most cases, the parents who are largely responsible for this state of their child, become impatient, annoyed, and rejecting. A therapy group offers to these children many possibilities for maturing. First the therapist (the substitute parent), while accepting the behavior, is at the same time objective and restraining in his manner. At first he does not react to the childish cajoling, wheedling, and annoyance; neither does he seek to exploit the child for his emotional needs, as is the case with the parent. He does not feed the child's craving to continue in a state of infancy by telling him he is "cute," or by being amused. He rather lets the child navigate on his own and make the necessary adaptations acceptable to the group. If the child wishes to be accepted, which is the basic assumption in group therapy, he will make these adaptations. He will check himself and behave in a way that would cause the group to accept him.

The group therapist does not always remain neutral and inactive in the case of the infantile child. As the child becomes secure, the therapist restrains him in kindly but firm fashion, and encourages constructive activity whenever he shows any inclination for it. In almost all instances these children initiate projects largely because the other children are actively occupied. Another therapeutic element in a group is the presence of other children (substitute siblings) with whom the adult, the tools, materials, food, and privileges must be shared. If he wishes to survive in the group, he cannot be the preferred or only child. This is a disturbing reality which he must accept and grow up to. In a group such as we have described, the patient has the incentive to change, and models after whom he can pattern himself. The more mature and more constructive members are busily occupied and make things that are freely praised. They become objects of identifications and sources of ego-ideals.

The group is exposed as a part of the treatment procedure to progressively extended reality and through trips, excursions, limitations, and constantly changing situations planned by the therapist. As the child adapts to these and becomes more self-reliant and better self-controlled, his reactions become more mature and more realistic. Our observations show that the nonthreatening but constructive atmosphere of the therapy group and the restrictions that grow out of group living in the presence of an accepting but nonseductive and nonexploiting adult, help the child mature and his uncontrolled aggression gradually disappears. This is especially true if treatment is undertaken early in the child's life.

2. *Aggression as a means of attention-getting.* This type of behavior is a manifestation of complex intrapsychic mechanisms. For the sake of brevity this discussion is confined to children who feel inferior and as a result seek attention from people around them, the objective of their aggression. A child who feels inadequate may either completely withdraw or develop patterns of self-maximization and impose himself upon others, since he needs to feel important, strong and powerful. To overcome a basic feeling of weakness, helplessness, and impotence, he feels the need to be the center of things and claim the attention of everyone around him. Ordinarily, children with these feelings start projects but do not finish them. They flit from one activity to another and need help in this area from the adult. To finish a job may mean to the child that he will be judged. This he seeks to prevent, since *he expects an unfavorable response.* Some children in this category do not finish jobs also because of early experiences in the home, school and other relationships in which they were made to feel weak and helpless. They therefore expect failure and are afraid to finish a job lest their expectation of failure be confirmed.

For children with attention-getting aggression because of inferiority feelings, the group is an exceedingly effective method of treatment. Particularly is this true of those children who happen to have some special talent. They work in clay, paints, and other media. They make plaques, pieces of furniture and similar objects that bring praise from the therapist, from the other members of the group, and later from teachers and parents as well. They are encouraged to participate with the others in games in which they are helped to succeed. Unless the attention-getting mechanism is complicated by serious personality malformations, it yields to group treatment. We must always keep in mind, however, that in attention-getting there may be the element of infantilism, neurosis, psychopathy, and even psychosis. At this point we are discussing the common variety of attention-getting aggression resulting from a feeling of inferiority or inadequacy.

With such children, the group therapist is actively encouraging. He helps the child over difficult places in his work and protects him against the impact of the group. This is done subtly, for obvious protection and helpfulness by the adult would not only create tension in the group, but would also emphasize the child's inadequacy and confirm his feelings of worthlessness abut himself. Group therapy has evolved strategies and techniques by which the therapist can meet the child's needs without aggravating the problems.

3. *Aggression as a release of organic tension.* This form of behavior is often described as hyperkinetic and may be caused by one or a combination of several conditions. It may originate in organic tensions; it may be a symptom of neurotic disorder; it may also result from energies. Where constitutional factors are present, medical treatment may be indicated. We are concerned here with aggressive acts that emanate from suppressed physical and mental drives. The reaction to frustration may have the appearance, of neurotic behavior, but actually is a result of suppressed drives for normal, wholesome activity. We have found, for example, that talented "problem" children become normalized when they have the opportunity to work in fields that fit their special talents. Because they find fulfillment through expression and gain social recognition and status through achievement, they grow poised and happy. They no longer need to express their cravings through substitutive and divertive aggression. Suitable activity for these children is libido-binding.

Children and young people who are repressed physically may act as though they are neurotic or emotionally disturbed but, as the suppressions are removed, they behave quite normally. The neuro-muscular craving for function and activity must be satisfied, thereby establishing equilibrium essential to poise and social adjustment. Canalization of energy is important for humans, and group therapy is valuable here. It not only supplies opportunities for free, unimpeded activity, but helps the child discover latent abilities and directs him toward constructive occupations and interests.

Regulating and sublimating aggression of this type should be the concern of education in the home and in the school. One gains the impression that homes and schools rather activate aggression through their rigidity, discipline, frustrations, and suppression of normal activity drives. Substituting with young children cognitive learning for muscular and esthetic experiences and motility is undoubtedly a major cause for the persistence of this type of aggression. Anxiety about success and failure in school further contributes to emotional tension relieved by hyperactivity and aggression. Frustration of essential motor activity, however, begins long before school age. Very young children are inhibited by their parents and nurses for their own comfort and as protection for the furniture. Congestion in the home and street, the absence of play space, and unsympathetic supervision are among the many elements that serve to inhibit the young child. These result in cumulative tensions, relieved through hyperactivity.

We omit for the present a discussion of the concomitant emotional tensions which build up attitudes and feeling tones in the growing child. Prohibitions and limitations that counter the natural development of powers and expressive drives constitute to the child rejection and hatred. As the adult applies restrictions and metes out punishments which seem "reasonable" enough to him, the child perceives them as hostile acts. In psychotherapy we must deal with these attitudes and they form the basic reasons that the group therapist is permissive and neutral, and the children are permittd to release tension through free unimpeded activity.

4. *Aggression as acting out of "neuroses."* The anxieties characterizing neuroses are so varied and so deeply laden with unconscious meaning and latent content that the therapist must proceed cautiously. To begin with, children with neuroses are unable to enter into a relation with other children, cannot share the therapist, and are frightened by the manifestation of aggression and hostility on the part of the other members in the group. In fact, many of these cannot bear the compresence of others. They can face life only in isolation or under conditions which they set. Some are unable to accept love and kindness and are frightened by attention and praise. Such patients require individual treatment to a point where they can participate in a group of low pressure and permissive environment.

Children who act out their hostilities in the group must be permitted to do so without restraint or control. In fact, it is of the utmost importance that they be placed in a "mild" group, that is, a group where the other members will not be rejecting or punitive toward them. The largest number of children, especially in the younger age groups, are not definitely neurotic. They may have neurotic trends or neurotic traits, yet can participate in group activity such as we supply for them. However, our present view is that in all children with neurotic constellations, group therapy can serve only as supplementary to individual psychotherapy.

The value of a free group experience lies in the fact that the child can act out his problems without fear of retaliation, punishment, or criticism. He can behave as he wishes and reveal himself as he really is without incurring the disfavor of the adult or children. As a result, his guilt is allayed and his conflicts are reduced. He discovers that other children, too, have problems similar to his own and that he is not as different as he had felt. Feelings of loneliness, guilt, and worthlessness are thus supplanted by a more hopeful outlook. Through free activity in a group the child is released, and group therapy under these conditions serves as *release therapy*. Our observations prove that such children become more productive in individual treatment through this release. They become more communicative and improvement is not ony accelerated by group therapy but is also more thorough.

5. *Aggression resulting from maturity phantasies.* Although most infantile children have a fundamental fear of growing up, we have observed a number who, although they possess this fear, have phantasies and exaggerated strivings to be grown up. Their early identifications with parents of the opposite sex are faulty. A boy whose father is weak, altogether absent, or rejects his wife intensely, may phantasy himself the protector of his mother and assume (or act as though he assumes) responsibility for her. The normal striving to be worthy of the mother is intensified and prolonged in these cases. Such attitudes are especially intense where the mother is seductive, dependent, and exploits the child for her emotional needs or as a weapon against the father. In many instances the boy is sexually overstimulated and is disoriented in this area as well.

The form of aggression in such children is both interesting and difficult to deal with in a group. It is interesting because these children act as adults, quite the opposite of what one usually finds in the treatment of children. The disharmony lies in the fact that the child is socially maladjusted because he cannot function on the level of other children of his own age—he is *too old* for them. This disharmony also expresses itself in relations with other members of the family, especially the father, in school, and with playmates. The difficulty in group therapy lies in the fact that the aggression is directed toward the other children in a form that would generally meet with the approval of society. They dominate the group, but along lines of maturity, responsibility, and economy. They insist on good behavior and self-control by the others. They are inhibitors, miniature "witch hunters," tyrants and, as we term them, the "group's superego." As a result, the accepting, releasing and permissive atmosphere and relations upon which we rely for therapy are blocked or vitiated.

The tyrannical and self-righteous attitudes toward group mates is supplemented by a subtle and indirect aggression against the therapist. Such children render him psychologically impotent by taking over responsibilities for, and the administration of the group. They check on materials and tools, buy and prepare food, and settle conflicts in the group. They not only seek to possess the adult but also *strive to be* the adult. In one instance a boy of fifteen whom we classified in this category actually asked the therapist to leave the room, so that he could handle a conflict between two other boys.

A major treatment need of such a child is to redirect identifications from adults to his peers. This is accomplished in most instances by careful and well-planned group placement. Boys and girls who manifest strivings to be prematurely grownup are detrimental to the others whom they dominate and frustrate, while they are themselves unable to submit to the will of others. Group placement must be with the view of making it possible for the child to make friends with at least one child through whom he can make his way into the group. In this we apply the principle of the *supportive ego*. The group therapist cannot deny himself, use authority, or in any way frustrate them without the risk of losing them.

6. *Aggression resulting from effeminacy.* When early identifications are not in accord with the requirements of "normal" development in our particular culture, or where either one of the parents, especially the mother is overdominant, boys may develop a character aptly described as the effeminate (castrated) character. Such a character is also found among only boys in families of many sisters, where the

total atmosphere is feminine and the boy must fit himself into it. Many become submissive and compliant, lack initiative and are unassertive. However, considerable hostility may underlie this facade. Many who fall within this classification become actively aggressive, with marked arrogance and provocativeness. They behave as though they seek to activate the aggression of the other members of the group. With weaker children they can be quite hostile and even sadistic. This is considered a character disturbance which can be treated successfully by exposing such a child to a living situation in which he can take on masculine charateristics. Intimate relations with boys and a nonexploiting adult is very effective in the treatment of effeminate boys and are among our most successful cases. Aggression disappears because there is general improvement in character structure. Due to past effeminizing influence, they had built up phantasies of the danger and evil of masculinity, and some responded with exaggerated reactive behavior. That boys act as boys in the group, play boys' games, wrestle and fight, and engage in manual activity characteristic of boys in our culture, gives such patients security with regard to their own masculinity. Forming friendships in a group extends their identifications with male images. The fact that the therapist, despite his masculinity, is nonthreatening and nondestructive, also helps develop security in relation to the child's masculinity. As his behavior gradually becomes normal and he is accepted by other boys and plays with them, the need for the compensatory arrogance and provocativeness disappear.

7. *"Deflective aggression"* is an interesting phenomenon. This type of behavior is found in a great many groups of children and adults, as well as among larger groups, even nations. When a child is afraid of possible attack from a very aggressive boy in a group, he becomes anxious and uses the following strategy, both to resolve his anxiety, and to redirect the possible attack. He attacks a third child, one probably weaker than himself, and through various strategies involves the potential aggressor with him in the attack. The two combine to torment their victim whom they persecute, beat, and otherwise make uncomfortable. Thus, the child, fearing possible aggressiveness against himself, saves himself from his peril. This may become a permanent relation of the three boys. Frequently the third boy chosen as a protective object of attack also becomes a scapegoat for other members of the group.

The aim of treatment is to build security and self-reliance, so the fearful child may have courage to face the possible attack. This is difficult to do in a group situation where alignments have already been created. Subgroups tend to become strongly entrenched and are difficult to deal with after they have been formed. They result from an erroneous original grouping and once such a mistake has been made in the group personnel, it may not be possible to work out the problem. It is therefore necessary to withdraw either the child who is a menace or the one who is menaced and place him in a group offering more suitable therapeutic relations.

8. *Oral aggression*, we have found, is the most difficult type of all to deal with in groups. This is found in individuals whose relationships with other people seem to consist of incessant verbal attack, screaming, and cursing. They almost constantly quarrel with other members of the group; criticize, order their group mates about, find fault with them, and generally make their presence known through screaming and verbal attack against those around them. Most behavior of this nature is not associated with sadism; indeed, it is not even hostile. It is rather a form of social contact which seems to proceed from early fixation on an oral level. It can be described as the lowest primitivism of social behavior and, so far as we can see at present, is probably untreatable; certainly it does not respond to group therapy. The giving and nurturing atmosphere of a therapy group does not quench the psychological insatiability of these children. To permit the acting out of oral aggression in no way alters the need for imposing upon people and dominating them; these individuals continue in their imperious, querulous, gossipy practice.

Oral aggression, as here described, is seldom found in boys, and when it is, exists only in a very slight degree. Aggressiveness in boys has other outlets in our culture; they can fight, physically attack the environment, and sublimate through various types of physical activity. Our oral aggressive girls have special physical characteristics; they are plump, of good complexion, good-natured, and voracious eaters. We have found it necessary to eliminate all such cases from our groups.

9. *Aggression that proceeds from hostility.* Aggressive acts which serve to act out a client's crystallized hostile drives for destructiveness and sadism obviously cannot be tolerated in a group. We may be

dealing with very intense behavior disorders, psychopaths, neurotic personalities, or a combination of these and other trends. When sadism motivates aggressiveness, we face the problem of protecting others of the group against the onslaughts of the sadistic individual. When hostility has already become very deeply entrenched in character and the youngster's drives are dominated by destructiveness, a free group environment is obviously unsuitable and such children must be removed. Treatment would have to be suited to the particular problem and intrapsychic condition.

It is to be noted that accepted psychiatric categories were not employed in this discussion. It is useful to classify patients in such clinical categories as primary behavior disorders, character disorders, neurotics, and psychopaths, but for the purpose of group treatment of children it is necessary to consider the nature of the nuclear problem of the client, his intrapsychic dynamics, and the goals which he aims to achieve through his behavior. Some of the groupings used in this paper fall into these categories. However, the nature of the child's goals and the propelling forces within his personality may be different from others in the same diagnostic category. We can state with some degree of certainty that psychopaths cannot be treated by our type of group therapy. They need groups of high pressure with considerable discipline and authority to restrain their behavior as well as develop relationships. Neurotic personalities also cannot be included in our groups. We feel, however, that accessibility of patients is rather a matter of degree and intensity of the problem than the nature of the problem itself. We have therefore found it of greater value to describe our clients along the lines used in this paper. This approach helps us in prognosis as to the outcome of treatment, determining the suitability of the client for group therapy, and grouping children in such a way that they would have therapeutic effect upon each other.

Since the group is our treatment instrument, it must be constructed such that it will have therapeutic value for all the members. We must have a group constellation in which the problems will not be intensified. Improper grouping may traumatize some children. A classification such as we employ helps greatly in preventing mistakes in constructing the therapeutic groups.

Finally, the point must be briefly made that aggression as such cannot be treated either through groups or individually. In psychotherapy we are concerned with correcting the character malformations and neurotic drives—of which aggression is a symptom. When we speak of the treatment of aggression, we really have in mind the total psychological syndrome of the client and his characterological states producing the aggressive manifestations. The aim of therapy is not to treat a symptom, but rather to correct personality defects which produce pathological and diffuse behavior. It seems to this writer that we cannot rightly discuss treatment of aggression apart from the total personality of the patient.[1]

---

1. An extended discussion of aggression with respect to character, neurosis and psychosis, and from anthropological points of view may be found in [112; also 61, chaps. 10, 12].

CHAPTER 36

TREATMENT OF WITHDRAWAL THROUGH
GROUP THERAPY
(1945)

The present paper is complementary to one on "aggression." In that paper aggression was described as a normal manifestation of living organisms which becomes pathological only when it assumes forms or intensity that interfere with constructive adaptations. The normal functioning of the human psyche is expression and aggressiveness. All living organisms survive by virtue of their aggression, whether they are autonomous entities or parasitic. Aggression toward environment is the means through which they can live, nurture themselves and their offspring, and assure conditions necessary for survival.

The point was made that in psychotherapy aggressive behavior, as such, does not form the focus of treatment; rather, treatment is directed toward the total psychological syndrome of the patient and his characterological states which produce such acts. It was also stated that "the aim of therapy is not to treat a symptom, but rather to correct personality defects which produce pathological and diffuse behavior." This is equally true of withdrawal as an adaptive mechanism to life and to social situations.

As a balance to the aggressive pattern, survival needs require avoidance and flight. It is therefore necessary to view avoidance and withdrawal as a normal mechanism of life. Only where withdrawal of energy (libido) is to a degree where the organism's effectivenesss or his persistence as an entity is threatened, is there indication of pathology. Withdrawal is accepted as normal in cases of danger or illness, but when adopted as a characteristic pattern, there is an indication of personality malformation. If one is unable to make easy contact with his environment, to exert the necessary effort in performing the duties incidental to living in a specific culture, or to play out one's expected role in life, he is subject to psychological blockings that are in many respects similar to the physically handicapped. He is unable to participate fully in the life around him and derive the pleasures and satisfactions it offers.

The psychotherapist is concerned with the restrictions of the personality and their consequences, while the teacher and sociologist are more interested in their effects upon personal efficiency and compensatory behavior, especially of a hostile and criminal nature. To help overcome blockings to expression, and correct the conditions within the psyche that employ withdrawal as an adaptive mechanism, it is necessary to understand its causes. As is the case in most psychological phenomena, withdrawal is multicausal. It serves different ends to different persons and may have a variety of meanings to the same individual. An effort will be made in the present brief study, which is based upon our observation of children in groups, to describe some of the causes we were able to identify.

For the purpose of our present study the concept of withdrawal is expanded to include mechanisms other than the actual removal of one's self from a given situation, either physically or psychologically, characterized by withholding of response, not participating, inability to communicate, and manifestations generally described as "isolationism." Our concept of withdrawal includes whatever diminishes or blocks expression of energy.

Withdrawal in any of its forms, such as mutism, stuttering, compliance, indecisiveness, lethargy, apathy, taciturnity, docility, submissiveness, and ingratiation, is derived from two causes: fear and disguised hostility. In psychotherapy it is necessary to explore further some of their manifestations and nature. The most common among the latter are various forms of submission, compliance, ingratiation, placating, and bribing, which serve to reduce anxiety and fear, but at the cost of expansion and development of personality.

Inhibition of Spontaneity

The infant and child are activated by energies accompanying organic and psychological maturation. These are at first unorganized and diffuse and are characterized by a lack of restraint. Restraints and the organization of impulse occur later in life through the educational process, identification with adults, and pressures from individuals and groups. The manner in which impulses are organized and employed depends upon the treatment they receive during the formative years of the child. If impulse is violently and harshly repressed with actual or seeming rejection, the child may as a result become either violently aggressive or excessively withdrawn. In the first instance it is rebellion against adults and is a form of counter-rejection. This is most likely to occur when the child is very young and has not as yet established the necessary identifications with adults and a willingness to give up gratifications for them. In later stages of development the child is likely to inhibit his impulses so as to avoid punishment, prevent guilt feelings, or to overcome the fear of losing the love of the parent or nurse. The child senses what the adults wish from him, and he takes on patterns of behavior to please them. Usually withdrawal is accompanied by considerable anxiety and may be laden with neurotic fears and tensions. It produces a personality that can variously be described as inhibited, restricted, or constricted.

Inhibition of the child's spontaneity is the inevitable and automatic result from association with unhappy, limited, restricted, or hostile parents or nurses. The spontaneous outcropping of activation is either checked by the adult directly, or is withheld by the child, since he feels disapproval when he becomes active. Accompanying such physical inhibition there is also emotional constriction, and in many also a diminuation there is also emotional constriction, and in many instances also a diminution of intellectual growth. Where the outer pressures are less great the final personality may not be inhibited, but instead restricted; that is, the individual functions acceptably but his field of operation is more limited than it might have been if he had been given freedom of action. Constriction results when the impulse for expression and activity has not been too deeply repressed but the expression of it is limited. Frequently there is present in withdrawn individuals a conflict between the impulse to expression and a fear of it which gives rise to inner conflict resembling a neurosis. Persons so limited have an overwhelming feeling of inadequacy and inferiority.

It must be kept in mind that a degree of restriction is essential to normal development, though much of it is unnecessary and even harmful. It is caused by adults' impatience, hostility, and rejection, and stems from our current philosophy of education. In patients who come for treatment, the withdrawal pattern has deeper emotional roots, some of which are outlined below.

Where the child's natural spontaneity has been excessively inhibited, the psychotherapist seeks to release repressions and supply channels for the newly acquired powers of self-expression. The permissive atmosphere, the opportunities to work with various types of materials in activity therapy groups, to communicate freely one's feelings in interview groups, the accepting and nonthreatening therapist, and the example set by less conflicted fellow members, are particularly suitable for inhibited, restricted, and constricted persons.

The younger the child is at the onset of treatment, the more rapid the improvement and more thorough the recovery. A child who has not acquired the tools for self-expression, or is afraid to employ his natural aggressions because of early threatening conditions in the home, finds in a group both encouragement to make contact with reality and the avenues to do so. Such releasing experiences are offered by group therapy and in those schools where free activity and easy relations are encouraged, improvement is rapid. One must be aware, however, of the possible presence of neurotic difficulties that may make necessary deeper individual psychotherapy.

Failure in Sibling Rivalry

Many of the inhibited or restricted children come from families where sibling rivalry and antagonisms are very intense, and the less successful of the siblings in the struggles finally gives up. Having consistently failed in either outdoing or becoming equal to the more successful sibling, a child may become resigned to inevitable failure. In doing so he also gives up other aggressive efforts, as though his energies are paralyzed. Indecisiveness sets in, fear of competition becomes predominant, and the individual evades situations in which effort or aggressiveness is involved. This type of withdrawal does not necessarily result in a schizoid personality: rather, it is an adaptation in which a devaluated self-esteem predominates. The individual perceives himself as unable to achieve, and supports his conviction by a nihilistic philosophy. He sees no value in achievement, for things do not really have too great a value. Thus he becomes a school failure, has few or no friends, is lackadaisical and slow, and dawdles. The fact that he attracts attention through such negative means has some value to him. It is one way in which he can outdo his preferred and more successful sibling. This type of behavior falls in the category of passive resistance, and is characterized by evading exertion because the child is convinced that he cannot succeed. He thinks in effect, "I don't want to succeed because to succeed would mean to be destroyed by the other sibling and the parent, or to destroy them."

In addition to the fact that there exists in such children real emotional debility, there are also the elements of rebelliousness, resentment and repressed hostility toward parents and siblings. In some instances passive resistance is accompanied by violent hostility; in others, hostility is covered over by exaggerated affection, submissiveness, and even protectiveness of the successful rival. Frequently there are present disguised or direct death wishes against parents and siblings, as well as fears of being killed by them.

To a child who has failed in sibling rivalry, substitutive relationships and ego gratifications are of the utmost value. The group gives him opportunities to work through any type of relationship—positive or negative—and to gain acceptance and recognition through work and creative effort. At first his attitude toward members in the group are similar to his attitudes at home. Hostility, aggression, fear, jealousy, spite, and resentment are directed toward the members (siblings) and therapist (parent). However, as a result of the new perceptions he gains of himself, and a growing recognition of the positive characteristics of the other members of the group and the therapist, more positive attitudes arise; these in turn are carried over to the home and family, and to the school.

One of the chief aims of group therapy is to strengthen the ego; when this occurs, fear of people is reduced, facilities to relate to others are improved, the protective withdrawal is sloughed off, and the child becomes more spontaneous and outgoing.

Guilt

Withdrawal can also emanate from a deep-rooted feeling of guilt and the fear of being unmasked; such individuals keep to themselves. Guilt may arise from hostile feelings and even homicidal drives toward members of the family, from incestuous desires, masturbation, forbidden thoughts, disapproved activities, or impulses. To relax the bars may mean to "let the cat out of the bag" as it were; to prevent any untoward act or utterance that may do so, one must inhibit expression or risk being punished. An individual laboring under such apprehensions is in constant fear that his motivations and impulses might come through if he lets himself go.

Unless the basic difficulties surrounding such withdrawal are overcome through psychotherapy or psychoanalysis, it persists into adulthood and becomes the permanent organization of the personality or the basic character structure.

In a treatment group for adults an unmarried young woman of about thirty-two, who was greatly inhibited and participated little in the discussions, did a great deal of painting. Her drawings were rather colorful and had distinct character and to the discerning eye revealed considerable repressed sexuality. They were predominantly red. However, she invariably blotted out her drawings with black paint after they were finished. This continued for some months before she was able to leave her paintings unblotted, and then participation in the group discussions greatly increased. She was able to speak more freely, and general improvement in her adaptations was reported by her friends and relatives. The blotting out of the drawings which revealed her unconscious, is a physical counterpart of what occurs in the psychic processes of withholding expression. It is a form of blotting out (or preventing from appearing) repressed guilt evoking material. This pattern is laden with a neurotic conflict frequently requiring deep individual psychotherapy.

It is universally recognized by all who work with therapy groups that anxiety and guilt are diluted by the group situation. The fact that other members in the group are similarly afflicted reduces feelings of guilt; the awareness that one is not unique diminishes anxiety. As a direct result of this discovery, the individual becomes less fearful of his own impulses. As others freely speak about or act out their hostilities and aggressions, each gains the courage through identification and support to accept his own forbidden feelings.

At a group interview of adolescent girls, one girl (Pearl) said: "From this group I learned how to talk properly. I feel that I have gotten a kind of 'lady poise.' " The girls helped her achieve this, she said, because they did not make fun of her, even though they called attention to her many mistakes. From listening to the girls, she better understands others now because they did not make fun of her, even though they called attention to her mistakes. From listening to the girls, she better understands others now because she better understands herself. She used to think that she had a "strange character." Here she found that other girls did the same things she did. Mrs. K. (case worker) used to tell her things and often gave her examples of how other people act and behave, but she never believed this. In the group she saw and heard the kind of things Mrs. K. had been talking about. What did she mean by a "strange character?" She was a little bit like R., she said (another member of the group). She used to stay at home and indulge in fantasies and daydreams. Now she knew that the other girls did the same things. Yes, she belonged to another club once, but there she used to talk nonsense, because down deep she was afraid that she was different. "Here I became serious, I didn't act nonsensical after the first meeting, when I felt more accepted by the girls." The girls helped her to a better vocabulary. She improved it by "thinking before I speak." L. recalled that Pearl used to laugh about nothing at all, just kind of giggle. Pearl explained that it was because she did not feel secure. She did not know how she would be accepted because she thought herself strange.

In interview groups, adolescents reveal their masturbatory activity, and repressed negative feelings to parents and siblings. They confess to stealing and other infractions against family, school, and society. Such catharsis has important therapeutic value as a release of tensions and renders the patient accessible. He need not hide in silence and withdraw from participation.

One means of mastering anxiety is to withdraw from the zone of danger and to renounce the activities which activate anxiety. The group helps greatly in diminishing those tensions. Perhaps this is why success in treatment is more rapid in groups, and transference relationships are established much faster than in individual treatment.

Play Therapy and Activity Group Therapy are valuable in treatment of young children because they give them the opportunity to discharge anxiety through play and sublimation. Aggression, hostility, and guilt-evoking feelings are redirected toward objects and acted out in fantasy. All of this tends to make the child less cautious and less withdrawn. Discussion, elaboration, and gaining insight serve the same ends for adolescents and adults.

Narcissism

As a source of withdrawal narcissism is more or less a common occurrence. Where inadequate and unsatisfactory relationships in the home exist, there is arrest in development of the child in his transition from autoeroticism to a socialized personality. The individual does not acquire the normal craving for association with people and draws upon himself for the satisfactions that are ordinarily derived from friendships. Inadequate indentification with adults in the family may cause the child to grow incapable of object relationships and he withdraws from people. Actually it is not really withdrawal; it is rather the absence of centrifugal emotions or what Dr. Adolph Meyer described as allotropy. This is not necessarily accompanied by a neurosis. It is rather a defective character formation which can be overcome, especially by the young child, through friendly, non-threatening relations with individuals and groups.

Groups are particularly helpful here. Such children need a setting in which they can start at the point of their developmental arrest and at first give of themselves as little as possible in return for satisfactions they receive. They can then move further in relationships as they become capable of it and at their own pace. Persons who are intensely egocentric or narcissistic are not accessible to group treatment, however, for response to such treatment is conditioned on a minimal need for relationships or "social hunger." When preoccupation with self approaches the point of an ego neurosis, group treatment is entirely unsuitable and the effectiveness of individual therapy is also questionable, for libido can become so inverted as to make it impossible for the individual to establish a reference. This would make him inaccessible to any type of psychotherapy.

The narcissistic young child, however, can gain a great deal from group relations. The emotional activation in groups is considerably more effective and more rapid than in a relationship with an adult. Blockings are removed more rapidly because identification is facilitated in a group of even-aged children, and the child is thus more easily enticed into relationships.

Catatonic Defense

A person who feels the environmental pressures as too great a threat and perceives himself unable to cope with them may adopt an attitude of impenetrability and aloofness that often baffles the ordinary observer. Such individuals seem as though they are entirely unaffected or little affected by what goes on around them. They discharge their major responsibilities, such as earning a living or caring for the home, but are emotionally frigid, speak little or not at all, and leave the management of most affairs to others. Such persons have been characterized as "living corpses," but the appellation of "catatonic defense" is perhaps more suitable.

Persons who seem to function in an acceptable manner in business may become extremely withdrawn when they come home, or in any other threatening or distressing environment. They maintain what seems a studied quiet and remove themselves psychologically and sometimes even physically from the situation. This is a form of catatonic defense against being hurt or expressing resentment and hostility. Feeling unable to deal openly with a marriage partner, for example, may cause one to adopt such a defense.

A case of catatonic defense in a father of one of our boy patients was described to the writer. Whenever a home visit was made, the mother managed all interviews. She was a power-driven, aggressive, managerial person, and the husband sat by quietly at the interviews, either averting his eyes or reading a newspaper. On some of these occasions he moved away and looked out of the window. This was his defense against his overpowering wife.

This condition is sometimes found among children where fears as to what they might do, or what may be done to them, are great enough. In groups, they concentrate on working with tools and materials. They do not as much as turn their heads even in periods of extreme hilarity and playfulness by the other members, and spend hours on end for many weeks in such a state of withdrawal. There comes a time, however, when they do take cognizance of their surroundings by first turning their gaze toward the disturbance and later smiling in amusement. This is followed by furtive and subsequently bolder participation. The unrestrained expression by other children seems to give them the courage to overcome the overpowering fear of being hurt or destroyed.

The situation just described demonstrates the importance of at least two elements in group therapy. One is the necessity of group balance; that is, the need to have active (instigators) as well as passive (neutralizers) members; the other is the need for a permissive environment. Members of therapy groups serve as "balancing wheels" to each other when grouped in this manner. When groups consist of one type only—passive or aggressive—they become either quiescent and unstimulating or overactive and disturbing. In either case the group is devoid of therapeutic value.

The value of a group to children who have developed such a defensive mechanism of nonparticipation and withdrawal is quite clear. The permissiveness of a therapy group and the nonthreatening attitude of the therapist makes it unnecessary for the child to continue in his withdrawal. After a period of observation and testing, he grows secure in the nonpunitive and the secure environment and gathers courage to give it up. He participates first cautiously and later more confidently. As a result of this experience and the positive relationships in the group, he can muster power to deal with persons in it and with the expanding and dynamic reality provided through changes in personnel and therapists, and through trips and excursions. As he becomes more a part of the interpersonal situation in the group and social relations outside, the self-corrective process within the ego structure continues.

We have had no experience with adults in the treatment of catatonic defense. It is understandable, however, that interpersonal and group activation should be of great value in psychotherapy of adults either as exclusive treatment or supplementary to individual therapy. In some instances patients might give up their defenses more easily in a group than in individual contacts.

Withdrawal as Retaliation

Children frequently use withdrawal as a weapon against adults when they perceive that it is irritating to the adults whom they dislike or to whom they are antagonistic. In some instances they develop mutism or stuttering. In less extreme cases the child refuses to carry out routines of everyday life, does badly in school, dawdles, is late and generally acts irresponsibly. The more the adults display anxiety or worry, the more the child is likely to use these means of annoyance and irritation; the more they press him, the more he withdraws from participation.

Occasionally this pattern of behavior is adopted where the child is emotionally too involved with one of the parents and withdraws the libido from the other to spite him. Another motive for spiteful withdrawal is when a child against his will is made to take charge of younger siblings. This imposition may engender in the child a dislike of all children as he projects his hostility. A boy of ten once vividly described his feelings of paralyzing fear as he sat alone at home watching over his sleeping younger brothers and sisters while his parents were preoccupied with their own interests out of the home. This boy suffered from extreme withdrawal at home and at school; he had no friends and was not able to play any of the children's games or participate in their interests. Through group therapy alone he was helped to overcome his basic dislike for children and acquire facilities for working and playing with them. He made a satisfactory social recovery.

Neurotic Withdrawal

In extreme cases of withdrawal there may be present an intense drive to return to the ease of the intrauterine state, where no effort or adjustment need be made. Catatonia is such a state, and so, to a lesser degree, is schizophrenia. In still less intense disturbances, withdrawal can be a result of neurosis, as already indicated. The blocking of energy is often accompanied by deep neurotic fears of being attacked or destroyed, fear of achievement and of the responsibility it entails. Achievement and aggression may symbolize incestuous coitus, and to prevent anxiety the individual withdraws from activity. The neurotic state manifested in inverted love causes withdrawal.

Such and similar problems may or may not come within the purview of group therapy. Deep neurotic involvements of this nature require individual psychotherapy or psychoanalysis. However, even such patients may be accessible to treatment in groups and nearly all can be helped through a supplementary experience in multiple relations. Young children whose neurotic states are incipient or who display neurotic traits slough them off as their egos are strengthened and their social adaptation improved through group therapy.

Value of Group to Withdrawn Patients

Group therapy helps an inhibited individual mobilize by activation. The patient overcomes basic fears and anxieties and finds an outlet for expression of reactivated libido. Group therapy supplies him with (1) a friendly and releasing environment, (2) suitable materials, (3) children or adults to whom he can relate or imitate, (4) supportive relations with co-members and the therapist, (5) ego strengthening, and (6) derivative or direct insight. The young child mobilizes power more easily because his inhibitions are not as deeply rooted. As he becomes older the inhibitive pattern is transformed into character traits, and is then less accessible to treatment, if at all. In the group the child discovers that to get what he wants he need not wheedle, placate, or bribe; neither is it necessary to withhold his impulses as an escape from tension and effort. Growing strengths increase self-esteem, and is in turn followed by acceptance in the home and elsewhere. This newly-gained strength and the discovery that one need not fear one's wishes and powers lift the bars to self-expression.

An important element in group therapy is its uniform, changeless environment. The members of the group know the room and its furnishings, the type of relations, general content of interviews, and the tools and materials [128]. Changes make disturbed children and adults even more insecure. In this constant environment they need not make new adjustments or meet new challenges.

Another major element that helps overcome withdrawal is the "supportive ego" [53]. Because of his fear to face the realities of the situation, a member of the group chooses one of the others as support through which he overcomes his fears and misgivings. Usually there are a series of supportive egos chosen in accordance with the growing and evolving personality of the patient before he becomes a part of the setting.

It has been observed by all who employ the group as a treatment tool that withdrawn patients overcome this trait much more rapidly than do the hyperactive. Groups—especially activity therapy groups—have a releasing effect. The first stage in developing attitudes in the group, beyond the acclimatization or warming up period, is activation. The setting encourages acting out repressed impulses, fantasy and infantilism, and each member has a catalytic effect upon every other. Thus it can be expected that a group is indicated for the shy and withdrawn, unless the neurotic syndrome is such that association with others in an intimate relation is undesirable, as in cases of anxiety hysteria, obsessional neuroses, paranoia, or homosexuality.

CHAPTER 37

AUTHORITY, RESTRAINT AND DISCIPLINE
(1950)

The discussion in this paper will be limited to children under twelve years of age, since attitudes, relations, and needs undergo a change at this period in an individual's life. Another factor that requires some clarification at the outset is the concept of discipline as it is employed here.

Discipline is usually associated with restraint and punishment inflicted by one person upon another. It is most often associated with the authoritarian imposition by an adult of his will upon a child, although the term is sometimes employed in other relations as well such as those of employer and employee and army officers and enlisted men. The more enlightened understanding of the dynamics of discipline, however, is that it is an internalized system of selective responses to external stimuli and demands that involve self-restraint or self-control.

Liberalized education aims to develop a selective capacity or judgment in individuals as to appropriate responses, qualitatively and quantitatively. We know that in a state of insanity the individual is incapable of such appropriate responses; his responses are either overcontrolled or are devoid almost entirely of the inhibitive restraints of the ego. While the selective capacity, one of the characteristics of a balanced personality, is minimal in the psychotic, it is also defective or inadequate in personality disorders of a less pathological nature such as psychoneuroses and character disorders. As can be expected, it is almost absent in the young child, since it is an outcome of guided interaction with reality, a process that takes a considerable period of time in the human offspring.

The second requirement of the integrated person is appropriate inhibitory and regulatory mechanisms to hold in check instinctive (id) impulses that may interfere with individual survival, with social orientation and group acceptance.

The third is acquisition of permissible gratifications of pleasure cravings and channels for effective and purposeful activity. These are the aims of a sound home, school, and social education and in psychotherapy we are dealing with individuals who though circumstances have not evolved intrapsychic mechanisms necessary for an effective and satisfying social adaptation and inner peace.

The original capacities for selective, inhibitive, and directive mechanisms are of course determined by dynamic relations in the family. It is generally accepted that superego development occurs through the influence of parents or their surrogates. But the selective, inhibitive and directive, that is, executive, powers of the individual that make up his ego are also derived from the same source. The relationships with, and the examples set by, parents and other important persons in the family have a permanent influence upon the future of the child's emotional development, the quality of his responsiveness and his self-discipline. Adults, themselves incapable of dealing with situations adequately, condition their children by example to respond in like patterns. Anger, irritation, violence and similar reactions induce disposition to the same type of behavior in children who repeatedly witness them. In a like manner, calm, capable, and self-controlled adults engender in children the disposition for effective regulative powers. Example, however, is not alone in the wholesome development of the human personality. Direct impediment, prohibition and encouragement, and even infrequent mild punishment help the child internalize the regulative powers of his elders. It also involves the setting of the stage in the home and school and dealing with situations by approval and disapproval. The child's inner authority is a derivative of acceptable (to him) outer authority which he internalizes. But to do this, discipline must be applied without violence or evoking resentment and defiance.

Social interaction is inherently disciplining. The average individual, not blocked by neurotic or compulsive displacement and projections, soon discovers the conditions under which he can experience most satisfying social contacts. As he becomes aware of these conditions, impulses, as well as behavior, come under control as an adaptive necessity for survival as a social entity. This regulation of behavior in response to needs and convenience, approval and disapproval of others, subjugates inappropriate instinctive drives, infantile phantasies, and self-centeredness. All of these are modified and to a considerable extent eliminated as one reaches maturity through the imposition of social demands. Social acceptance, being a primary and urgent need, favors development of inhibitory forces in order not to impair one's standing as a social entity (social hunger).

The regulative mechanisms of the psyche constitute a complex phenomenon which cannot be discussed here without going too far afield. Briefly it consists of a number of elements such as superego restraints, need for approbation, fear of punishment and rejection, esthetic strivings, material advantage, desire to please others, and narcissistic interests. This complex of ego formation and its executive powers are a result of the total educational process which in many instances is faulty and, therefore, produces persons incapable of dealing with inner impulses and with the demands of the outside world.

It becomes clear that the ego strengths cannot be evoked through verbal communication or by the teaching of principles. Power is engendered through active, dynamic interaction and through actual experience with the world and people. Effective human environment includes the emotions, ideas and principles of people as well as objects and materials. The "psychological disposition to inhibit instinctive impulses" is derived from a totality of experiences in the home and at school, with playmates as well as the larger world and through contacts with persons who for one reason or another influence the growing personality of the child and adult. The regulative principle, therefore, emerges from the summation of the planned and incidental influences to which the individual is subjected throughout his life.

Psychotherapy seeks, among other things, to correct the errors of the adult world that overemphasizes external or direct discipline at the expense of helping evolve self-restraint by slow stages through identifications and ego development. Repressive methods weaken the ego. They also induce resentment, retard emotional growth and establish types of suppressions that may later prove troublesome to the individual and to society.

Following the mental hygiene concepts of growth briefly indicated, it becomes clear how important in psychotherapy are authority, restraint, discipline, and experience. Particularly are they imperative during latency when the libido is directed centrifugally, namely, away from the family and toward the external world. It is at this period that identifications are most easily and most fruitfully established and relationships with persons other than members of one's family grow in psychological significance. The role of the adult in psychotherapy, however, has to vary in accordance with the chronological or mental age of the child. I have already indicated on a number of occasions that a group therapist functions differently with children of preschool years than he does with older children. It is also recognized that in selecting children for group therapy, it is necessary that they are activated by a desire to be accepted by others, which we designate as *social hunger*. This desire in itself is a motive for self-discipline.

In very young children social hunger is either rudimentary or nonexistent, since their central libidinal preoccupations are still with their parents and object relationships outside the home are of no great consequence. Their ego is still unformed, their inhibitive and selective capacities in a nascent state, and sublimation channels practically nonexistent. The therapist must, therefore, function *in loco parentis* and directly restrain or use valid educational means for controlling objectionable activity that disturbs others or proves injurious to the child himself.

Of more therapeutic value than is restraint, however, is the interpretation he gives the child as to the intent and significance of his behavior. Appropriate interpretations lead the child to perceive the projective and displacement nature of his behavior. Because of this understanding and especially because he accepts the therapist by virtue of the transference (or substitution) relation, the child inhibits behavior unacceptable to the group or the therapist. In this manner and by the mechanism of repetition the child incorporates the will and the power to inhibit himself. It must be noted, however, that this occurs only when the transference relation with the therapist is of a positive nature and the child wishes to please the therapist as a parent substitute or to be like him.

In a group of six-year-old boys conflict arose between two boys as to who asked the therapist for help with their planes first. Each insisted that he was first and when they could not come to an understanding for some time, the therapist said that she thought that John was the first one to ask her for help. Morris' reaction to this was to say that the therapist was "a dope." The therapist countered by saying: "You're angry because I am helping John first. I do this because he asked me first, but I really like you both the same." As soon as she had finished with John's project she turned to Morris' and helped him with it.

This is an example of a discipline situation in play (analytic) group psychotherapy for very young children. Without admonishing or punishment the therapist had demonstrated to Morris the need for self-control and to relinquish his unfounded claim to another child because he thought it was due him. The feeling of satisfaction Morris gained from this experience was revealed later when he went over to look at John's project and said that the latter's plane was "gorgeous."

At another point Morris wanted to use up the materials belonging to a boy who was absent at the session. When the therapist called it to his attention Morris stated that because Charlie was not there he had a right to use his materials. The therapist said to Morris: "Morris, you want to have more than the others. You think that if you don't have more I don't like you as much. I like you as much as the others even though I cannot let you have more things than the others have."

Charles started to put paint into the pan of water and said: "I am going to squirt it at Fanny (the therapist)." Morris became interested and Rhoda said: "That's a good idea." The therapist said: "I don't want the paint on me." Charles started throwing things around and hurled some water against the wall. He then took a saw and Morris a hammer and said: "We are going to hit you, Fanny." Morris said: "I am hitting you on the ash can (buttocks)." Both attempted to strike the therapist who said: "Wait a minute, boys," and removed the saw from Charles' hands saying: "Charles, see the saw? There are these edges on it that we have to keep in good order to use it." She then replaced the saw. Charles said: "I am going to find another one." Morris dropped the hammer and said: "We aren't crazy here," and went back to work on his clock. Charles said: "Oh, our paint, where is the paint?" The therapist pointed them out to Charles. Charles took a bottle of red paint and began to pour it into a pan. He said: "I will throw this around." Morris said, "Don't throw it around." Charles said, "I will be careful. I will get it just in the pan."

Here the authority exerted by the therapist was taken over by one of the children and he assumes the role of the restraining person.

At another session Charles and John began setting bits of paper on fire on the electric grill, which the therapist considered to be dangerous. (This is not prohibited for older children in Activity Group Therapy where a special setting is provided for fire making.) The therapist, therefore, decided to restrict this activity and told them they could experiment with other objects but not setting paper on fire. The boys gladly fell in with this idea and attempted to set fire to various types of nonflammable objects such as crayons, pieces of metals, bits of clay. Although this involved a considerable amount of movement, going back and forth for things to heat, there was less distractibility than in the earlier sessions of this group indicating increased self-control and purposiveness.

Allan challenged Charles by saying that Ed had said he cold beat up Charles, concluding: "Let's see, why don't you fight him now?" The therapist asked Charles what he would be fighting for. Charles lunged quickly, full of rage, and had Ed on the floor. Ed and Charles kicked each other. Ed began to cry. He rolled up in the shape of a fetus. Charles said he didn't mean to hurt Ed. He really did not know why he was fighting in the first place. Ed, however, remained in the fetal position for about six minutes. Charles then tried to fix the plane on which Ed was working and made other efforts at appeasement. Finally Ed got up and went back to his work on his plane.

Here a child's own guilt serves as a disciplining and restraining force.

At one of the sessions, Rhoda, four years eleven months old, became very aggressive, almost frantic. She danced and screamed, made rotating movement with her hands, sometimes with her arms raised. She stamped on the block game with which Lewis was playing on the floor, and kicked the blocks. She then rushed up to the small table, grabbed the puppets from the children and threw them around in the room, breaking them. She grabbed a hammer and hit the therapist with it on the back, then took a box with parts of a puzzle and threw them into the air. She then rushed to the large table, where

Lewis had worked with the watercolor paints before, and had just grabbed one container of paint when the therapist restrained her, holding Rhoda's hands and telling her that she knew Rhoda was frightened. Was she upset because she was going to have a tonsil operation the next day? While the therapist spoke she guided the child to a vacant corner, taking a chair with her. She sat Rhoda in the chair and kneeled down beside her so that both were about on the same level. The child stopped struggling and smiled for a moment, then kicked the therapist in the stomach. Having done this, she looked timid and said: "I am frightened," but abruptly stopped and said: "No, I am mad. I am not mad at you but I want to kick you. I want to spit in your face, you dumbbell, you big horse."By this time the children had gathered around. The therapist then asked Rhoda again whether she was frightened because she was going to have her tonsils taken out. Rhoda nodded her head and became subdued.

The therapist's direct impediment of the child's violence and uncontrollability had diminished her anxiety and supplied the inhibitive controls that the child had not had within herself. In addition, the therapist's display of *understanding* the cause of her fear gave Rhoda security as to the therapist's love as well as strength. It is by this and similar processes that ego controls are internalized by children.[1]

When the children in a five- to six-year-old group were told by the therapist that she was going to be married and would stay away for four weeks, one of the boys at once called her by her official name rather than the first name which he had used before. The children asked a number of questions concerning her marriage. One of the boys then became very aggressive toward her and tried to jump down from a table onto her back. Distractability in the group was noticeably increased. With the exception of one, they were unable to concentrate on their work. The others ran about the room, starting one occupation after another. A boy who had been particularly fond of the therapist, withdrew from her and did not address her for some time.

The therapist sensed the disturbance in the children and pointed out to them that their distractability and hyperactivity had something to do with her telling them that she would be married. They must have

1. For further discussion of treatment of children by this method see [56].

some feelings about it. What is it that they don't like about her getting married? The children did not respond to this.

At the subsequent two sessions the boy who had withdrawn from the therapist again attempted to get close to her physically. There was an increased attempt on the part of one or two of the children to get up on tables and jump on the therapist's back. One continued to avoid the therapist, but displaced his mounting hostility on another member of the group. The therapist again attempted to elicit the children's feelings about her being married and the fact that she would not meet with them for four weeks. She stated that she understood their being angry about this. A few of the children said it was quite true that they did not like her being married and going away from them. The boy who was particularly fond of the therapist began to build a fire on one of the tables.

Even though only little response was elicited, the therapist's verbalizing the children's feelings markedly reduced their anxiety.

In Activity Group Therapy with children in latency direct impediment of behavior is used only rarely and interpretation is never given. Restraint is employed only on a diagnostic basis and after a thorough understanding of the child's mechanisms, the meaning of an act, and his capacity to accept frustration and authority. Infantile children, that is, children who had been overindulged, overprotected or over-restricted, particularly only children, require judicious control of objectionable behavior. In such children, ego development has been limited by virtue of the fact that they have not been allowed to deal with reality at their own level during their growth, leaving them weak and unwilling to restrain their impulses and unreasonable demands. Children who had been overcontrolled, who as a result feel insecure in human relationships, need to act out their impulses in a regressive manner before further growth can occur. *Activity catharsis* is very desirable for them as preliminary to establishing subjective restraints which arise from inner growth. To be permitted to act out means to be accepted and loved by the therapist, as a parent substitute. The controls that arise either from the group as a whole, from individual relations, or through direct interactions of one or more children in the group serve further to buttress the maturing process.

Restraint in group therapy can be *passive* or *active*. Active restraint is direct prohibition of acts by the therapist, which, as already indicated, is used very infrequently and on a carefully planned diagnostic basis. Passive restraint, on the other hand, is constantly employed in groups. In fact, the setting of a therapy room must be based upon the principle of passive restraint. By passive restraint we mean the setting of a situational configuration that includes elements in the environment which in themselves condition children's behavior This applies especially to situations that may be dangerous or emotionally disturbing. Thus, a therapy room should have no doors beyond one for entrance to and exit from the room. If there are doors to closets or other rooms, they must be accessible to the children so that phantasies and curiosities, which are chiefly sexual, would not be aroused to disturb them. All cupboards should be outside of the walls.

Windows should be so protected that there is no danger of the children's falling against or through them. Thus, if windows extend low and near the floor, guards must be placed to prevent stooping over. If in playing table tennis or ball window panes might be broken, they should be protected with wire mesh. In one of our rooms the staircase from an upper floor led directly to a door opening onto the street. The door had a large glass panel. Children are prone to run downstairs and push a door impulsively and cut their wrists if they should break the glass panel. To prevent this, we placed a stout, framed wire mesh against the glass pane. These precautions obviate the necessity on the part of the therapist to caution the children against danger or to restrain them in their activities. The therapist has to prevent confirming the phantasy children have that adults are negativistic, dictatorial, rejecting.

Another example of passive restraint is the following. In one of our nine- to ten-year-old boys' groups, the bottom of the work table which we found in the room had a tool cupboard underneath which could hold two children in cramped and close position. Crawling into this enclosure and closing themselves in had become a regular activity of the group. This was repeatedly instigated by a boy who, though young, had feminine identifications and homosexual tendencies. As this game was repeated a number of times, we tore out the cupboard, but the boys began running into a large built-in closet where the materials and tools were stored. The shelves ran lengthwise along the wall providing a large space for playing in this dark enclosure. The boys preferred playing with the door closed, as other members of the group would lock the door on those inside. It was evident that this game was far from being beneficial because of its phantasy provoking nature and other implications. We, therefore, rebuilt the shelves crosswise in the front of the cupboard with a back behind them so that the boys could not go into the closet. These are but a few illustrations of passive restraint that is constantly employed in group therapy.

Another example relates to food, a most important item in the sessions. In one instance the early arrivals in a group of eleven-year-old boys had taken to consuming the food as soon as they came to the sessions, which aroused considerable consternation in those who came later. In phantasy this meant that they were being punished by the therapist who rejected them or preferred the others. Considerable conflict, strife, and retaliation resulted. It was then decided that food be sent into the session room about an hour after the time set for the meeting, when all the children were usually present. Thus, this particular difficulty was eliminated.

Another occurrence was with a group of ten-year-old girls who adopted the pattern of going to a nearby park weekly instead of holding sessions indoors. We felt that the therapeutic gains from these trips were minimal. They lacked the direct face-to-face interreactions characteristic of indoor sessions which were at this stage more desirable for the girls under treatment. After three or four such excursions, we sent a letter to the therapist indicating that there was a limit of thirty cents per person set to their expenditures. We said in the letter that in view of the fact that these trips had proven rather costly it was necessary to limit the expense. Since the fare to the park and back was twenty cents, and only ten cents were left for refreshments, the girls had given up the idea of going to the park. Excursions were later arranged at appropriate times.

A group of twelve-year-old girls took to painting pictures on the walls of the treatment room. In view of the fact that this room was used by other groups, as well as for other clinical purposes, the paintings on the wall proved to be distracting and annoying. It was also felt that this was an act of aggression against the therapist and the clinic. Instead of directly prohibiting this activity, the pictures were painted over the color of the walls before the next session. When the girls came in the following week, they said: "I guess they don't want us to paint on walls," which they never did again.

The therapists were in no way involved in any of the restraining acts. If restraint or discipline was necessary, it was done by the "office," an impersonal authority which did not impinge upon the children's relation with the therapist.

Another type of passive restraint that the therapist employs in Activity Group Therapy we designate as *action interpretation*. The therapist's response or reactions to a child's behavior assume special significance which may have inhibitive and other effects upon his actions and upon his general development. When children indulge in destructiveness, the neutral role of the therapist requires that he does not look directly at what is going on. Watching without comment implies approval. It is essential that the therapist be aware of the course such activity takes so as to prevent heightening of destructiveness and possible physical injury, but he must do this without direct observation. Aggression may take the form of hammering on a wall or table, attempts at breaking a chair, setting pieces of wood or paper on fire, painting on walls and furniture, throwing objects through windows at passers-by, and similar acts.

Because members of a group are accustomed to having their activities accepted and achievements recognized in a positive manner, denial of attention or approbation constitutes interpretation. It reflects the therapist's attitude and constitutes interpretation of a passive nature. When a child verbalizes hostility against or disapproval of another, the therapist does not react to it in any way. He is impassive and unresponsive. This conveys to the child that the therapist does not wish to be involved; also that he does not accept negative feelings on the part of one child toward another. Occasionally children attempt to draw the therapist into a discussion of their relations to members of their families to which the therapist against does not respond, an indication that this is an area in the child's life into which he does not wish to enter. When children at the "refreshment" table conduct themselves in a disorderly, rowdy manner and eat sloppily, the therapist does not correct or admonish them. Rather, his own deportment must in such instances be unimpeachable. He continues eating in a way that sets off by contrast their own, thus conveying that the prevailing behavior is not acceptable to him.

When a habitually dependent, though actually capable, child seeks help with projects which it is felt the child can very well do by himself, the therapist pretends that he does not hear the request. Usually when the child repeats the query once or twice without eliciting a response, he proceeds on his own. Unless the request for help is insistent, the therapist remains impassive. This unresponsiveness serves to convey to the child the therapist's attitude toward his feigned helplessness. It is, of course, important that no error is made in judgment where the child is genuinely unable to proceed either through lack of skill, feeling of inadequacy, or general anxiety.

When a member of a group seeks the therapist's approval of an act in which the other members are involved, he refers the child to the group. This is done in the advanced stages of treatment. When a child, for example, asks permission to take some essential tools or materials home at the early stages in treatment, the therapist is always permissive and giving. However, as the child's frustration tolerance is increased, he refers him to the group, who may either allow or refuse the request.

These and similar strategies are employed to invoke the children's own growing powers to restrain impulses, regulate oral wishes, and accept outer authority, as well as build inner mastery. Throughout, the therapist does not deviate from his neutral role, for it is obvious that he cannot discipline children. They can act on and discuss it together. Due to the fact that children's phantasies about adults are that they are unfriendly, negativistic and rejecting persons, the therapist, who cannot work these feelings through with them in interviews, must assume a *neutral* role. Because of his permissiveness, the image of all adults changes in the unconscious of the children. When they accept him as a suitable love object and a model for identification, their attitudes grow more wholesome toward all adults and the world generally. When this occurs, they automatically take on self-restraints from him. For these and other reasons the therapist must be a calm person, never ruffled, constantly under control, displaying no irritation or displeasure and remain throughout unpunitive. It is in identifying with these positive characteristics of the therapist that foundations for the ego strengths and superego development in children are laid. Emotional growth occurs indirectly, automatically, as a response to a satisfying relation with an adult rather than in direct prohibition and restraint that tend to arouse hostility and regression.

CHAPTER 38

PLAY GROUP THERAPY
(1948)

In the application of group therapy to various personality problems we have found that the accepted techniques of either activity or interview therapy (or group analysis) are not suitable for very young children. In the case of activity groups, unrestrained acting out without the necessary inner controls that are ordinarily present in the more mature person, leads to chaos beyond the group's tolerance. The ability of any given group, as well as individuals, to withstand or absorb hostility and aggression has definite limits. Each individual and each aggregate of people has its own capacity to tolerate aggression or hostility density. When these limits are exceeded in groups, tension and anxiety set in which are expressed in hyperactivity, rowdyism, or wanton destructiveness. Unless restraints are applied by some outer agency such as parent, teacher, leader or therapist, the group becomes severely disorganized and uncontrollable. This is true of all groups whether children, adolescents, or adults and is the primary reason why grouping is so important and the choice of children suitable for group therapy has been repeatedly emphasized by us.

It has also been observed that different members of groups are affected differently by overt boisterous behavior or by repressed hostility. The endurance for these emotions varies in individuals and is conditioned by character structure and early experiences with aggression and hostility in the family. The superego in the young child is still unformed and the executive functions of the ego are less effectual during the preoedipal and early latency stages than during later development. The young child is, therefore, still devoid of the controls that emanate from the repressions and inhibitions which have been only partially evolved or not at all. In view of these circumstances the function of the therapist (parent and teacher, as well) is in fundamental respects unlike that with older children. He needs to be more active and more fully in control of the group's activities as well as of the behavior of each member in it.

In group play, patterns of behavior and problems emerge that are not present in the play of one child. Interstimulation and the various types of interaction inevitably arise from the concurrent activity of several children, which is referred to as the catalytic effect—positive and negative—they have on one another. The anxiety stimulated by the presence of other children and the support they give one another in their hostility toward the adult induce hyperactivity and destructiveness seldom encountered in the play of one child. It is, therefore, necessary for the therapist to be more vigilant as to the trends and possible developments in a group than in the treatment of one child, and employ strategies and techniques to prevent disorganization, emotional tension and anxiety. Since the young child's unconscious is near the surface, it is not difficult to stimulate its flow in play activity, which may have no meaning to him in terms of his specific personality problems and needs, or may be even detrimental to him at a given stage in treatment.

Acting out has value only when it is an outcome of, and related to, the unconscious of the child and his emotional conflicts. Diffuse hyperactivity which may express hostility toward the environment, including the therapist, is in itself not therapeutic. The value of acting out lies in the relation that it has to the conflicts of the patient. Acting out of hostility by an older child, an adolescent or adult, makes him aware of the true intent and significance of his actions. This is shown in various forms of guilt manifestations such as confession, placation, submission, and restitution—all of which indicate the presence of superego formation which is still not present in the very young child.

insight into the meaning of behavior. It, therefore, has little or no therapeutic value beyond release. Because of this absence of superego formation, low degree of guilt, weak ego structure, and basic narcissism, acting out alone does not meet the treatment conditions of group psychotherapy.

For this reason, acting out has to be limited, restrained, and directed with young children. At the same time it is necessary that the therapist call attention to the latent meaning of behavior. This form of interpretation has several therapeutic values. In the first place, a relationship is established akin to transference, because the child feels he is understood by the therapist. Secondly, it makes him aware of his real problems and the meaning of hostile intent of his behavior. He becomes vaguely aware of the fact that his aggressive behavior in the group is only a substitute for aggressions he feels toward other persons. In a more neurotic child, interpretation serves to bring forward repressed impulses, conflicts, and anxieties, and makes the young patient aware of his real difficulties.

When using play therapy, whether in group or in individual psychotherapy, the therapist must be aware of the significance and meaning of play in its many facets. He must recognize that play to a child is what serious, productive work is to an older person. Through play the child carries out the tasks of his life, and he uses play for many other ends as well. To review the many theories of play, such as experimentation with reality, discharge of excess energy, recapitulation of the phylogenetic experience of the race, a form of mastery, an effort to attenuate reality, would take us far afield.

Play in education and in child development has been evaluated and described in an extensive and rich literature and need not be repeated here. It is necessary to call attention to the fact, however, that to the therapist play has additional meaning, as well as the developmental. He is interested in the fact that through play the child expresses traumatic fixations, conflicts, and hostilities and that he employs it as a means of communication and abreaction. The child also uses play to disguise genuine conflicts and difficulties, or he may use play to relax tension and anxiety. Of greatest importance, particularly to the group therapist, is the fact that as the young patient discharges aggression and seeks to overcome traumatic anxieties through play, it serves as a regulative mechanism. The therapist also sees group play as a possibility for overcoming narcissistic and autistic fixations and for discharging libido centrifugally through relationships with others in the group. The child discovers the advantages of such relationships, and his ego-libido drives are redirected outwardly toward his playmates and the objects he uses in his play, which are usually cathected.

The play therapist is also aware of the importance of play as a sublimation of primary instinctual drives which in their primitive form are socially not acceptable. The service of play in finding permissible and acceptable outlets for primary impulses is of considerable value with which one must reckon. The catalytic effect of the others in a group greatly helps in this.

The specific advantage of the group in play therapy lies in the catalytic effect that each patient has upon the other, which makes it easier for them to act out and to bring forth in behavior phantasies and ideas. Another value of the group is that it reduces the tendency to repetition. The young child, particularly, tends to repeat the same activity. This is largely due to the limited scope of his capacities and experiences and the security that a known situation gives him. He is either afraid or unable to evolve variety in the use of play materials. While he is full of phantasy his imagination is comparatively limited. When several children play together, their interaction and mutual support help to employ the materials progressively, rather than to become fixed at one level of self-expression. This has been observed in educational and in therapy groups and constitutes what is often referred to as a "growth-producing environment."

In play groups—and this is to a great extent also true of other groups—children assign to themselves roles which are reflections or extensions of their basic problems. In such roles one either plays out the awareness of what he is or a hopeful phantasy of what he would like to be. Thus a child playing the role of a dog may feel himself being treated with the same indifference and impersonality as is the dog; he may seek to get the loving acceptance and protection which a pet receives in the home, or he may attribute to himself the oral strength that is usually associated with dogs. In a group such phantasies are reinforced and find easy and natural means of coming through in a variety of play forms and activity channels.

As in all psychotherapy, the fundamental dynamics are present in such groups. These are (1) relationship, (2) catharsis, (3) insight and/or ego strengthening, (4) reality testing, and (5) sublimation. Acting out by the young child does not bring about awareness of or

In group psychotherapy there are multilateral relations among the members, in addition to the attitudes they may have toward the therapist. These relationships serve to neutralize the transference toward the therapist and aid the cathartic process. The anxiety created by hitherto unacceptable behavior is lessened by the acceptance and support the children give one another. Under these circumstances it is easy for them to express hostility toward the therapist and reveal themselves in the light of their difficulties.

In Activity Group Therapy, as in psychoanalysis, the relation between therapist and patients is unilateral. Feelings are directed from the patient to the therapist, the therapist remaining neutral and to a large extent also passive. In play therapy for young children, however, the therapist reacts to the behavior and feelings of the children, in a manner similar to case work [11]. In the latter, as in group play therapy, the relationship is bilateral. Thus group play therapy, in its essentials, resembles individual psychotherapy, though largely modified in some secondary aspects. In both the transference is a bilateral one and the role the therapist plays in other respects is also similar.

The functions and equipment of an activity group therapist with children in latency are in many essentials different from those of a group play therapist. Though the activity group therapist must understand the hidden meanings in behavior (as does also the group play therapist) he remains largely passive and overtly unresponsive. The group play therapist, on the other hand, responds to the acts and utterances of the patients to help them acquire insight. The element of insight is the essential difference between activity groups for children in latency and play groups for younger children.

Catharsis is an essential factor in all psychotherapy. Through it the patient is able to divest himself of conflicts and emotions fixed through traumatic experiences in early childhood that form the root of personality disturbances. Thus, through play and language layers of repressed feelings are unfolded. Play is only one means, and the most suitable means for children, for communicating the content of the unconscious and the distress that pressures of environment create, that is, catharsis. Play under specially set conditions and in the presence of a permissive, understanding adult, is a form of commmunication as well as catharsis.

Concerning the factor of reality testing, tangible objects, relationships with others and actual situations constitute true reality to the child. They are more real to him than are ideas and words. Here he has an opportunity not only to experience, but also to test himself as to his powers and mastery. He has things and materials with which to work and play. He either fails or succeeds, and as a result evolves perceptions concerning his own powers and abilities. He tests himself against others in submission-domination, anaclitic or symbiotic relationships. Through the new relationships he evolves new patterns and new attitudes. During this period he begins to realize himself as a person; evaluates his powers; measures them against the realities of his environment, and eventually adjusts his behavior in accordance with his feelings of weakness or strength, as the case may be . Play activity becomes a measure of the self in relation to reality. This is the element of ego strengthening as well as reality testing.

Ego strengthening, which is so important in the psychotherapy of children, occurs in play groups through the same dynamic situations as in activity therapy groups and in all psychotherapy, for that matter. The acceptance of the child by the other children and the therapist begets the conviction that he is loved, and—what is more important— that he is worthy of love. The result of this new awareness is a more wholesome self-image and perception of his worth which in turn help integrate powers and bring impulse under control. Thus the executive function of the ego as a control of impulses and the mediator between the self and outer realities is strengthened.

In psychotherapy of older persons, especially in psychoanalysis, the factor of insight is of paramount importance in this connection. Insight acquired through release of emotional tensions and over-coming resistances to unlocking the gates of the unconscious further strengthens the ego, as well as being a source of new values and more wholesome understanding. The degrees and levels of insight that a small child can acquire, however, are subject to speculation. Through our own observation in this regard, we are inclined to believe that children are capable of high degree of insight, though it may manifest itself in forms other than those to which we are accustomed in adolescents and adults. Theirs is a more perceptive type and less verbalized or cognitive, but frequently one is impressed with the uncannily penetrating remarks children make about situations, themselves and others.

One of the important values of all play therapy, especially in a group, is the fact that sublimations are ready at hand. Whatever the stage of the child's libido organization may be, as he finds sublimation for it in group situations, his primitive drives are transformed into controlled socially-approved patterns of behavior and more adequate adaptations to reality. Anal-urethral cravings, for example, are expressed in play with water, paints and clay. Genital interests are worked through symbolically in occupations such as drawing and painting, fire-setting (which should be permitted), pyrography with an electrically-heated stylus, squirting of water, shooting of guns, rubber-cupped darts, play with family dolls, toy furniture and doll house—especially toilet equipment. Some of these toys also serve to discharge as well as sublimate aggressive drives, sibling rivalry and hostile feelings. In the group each member works out attitudes toward siblings and other members of the family. Thus catharsis, reality testing, and sublimation—though each having a distinct function—fuse in the play of very young children in groups, and perhaps also in all therapy groups.

Anger and aggression find numerous means for sublimation and displacement in play groups. A child may bang against things in the room or he may hammer a toy. To redirect hostile feelings he may destroy toys, tools, and materials or he may hammer boards together with a view of making some useful object. Instead of directly attacking the therapist, as a substitute for a parent, he may paint or deface the walls and furniture. In the young child displacement and sublimation often go hand in hand as do transference and substitutions. They may often be confused.

To illustrate some of the general principles in the preceding pages, we submit an abstract of a record of a group play session with three boys, five to six years old. Brief comments on some of the major dynamics of the events that took place in the group are also included.

John is the first to arrive and seems a little more friendly than during the past few weeks.

John: Where's everybody?

Therapist: They'll be along soon. (John seems to have considerable hesitation in coming to the play room where the group meets, but he finally does when the therapist says that the others are coming soon.)

John (immediately going over to get paper): I want a lot of colored paper. Who was here last week?

Therapist: Judah and Mike.

John (angrily): My mother said that nobody was here last week. Where is Mike?

Therapist: Mike will be coming.

John (He seems very restless): I am going to my mother. Mike isn't here.

Therapist: Why are you going to your mother, John?

John: I am going to get a nickel. My mother said nobody was here last week and now she has to give me a nickel.

Therapist: John, you can go to your mother after our meeting but I think you should stay here now.

John seems to hesitate and wanders around the room. He looks at the paper. He comes over to the therapist and puts his paper down.

John: I'm not going to stay because Mike isn't here.

Therapist: John, are you afraid to be here in the meeting room alone with me? (He does not answer but seems to get relief from the therapist's saying this. He relaxes immediately.)

John: I am going to work on my plane. (He begins to saw which he does very well. Speaking proudly and boastfully): Look at the thirty cents that I got from my grandfather. My girlfriend, Janet, also gives me money. (He shows the therapist the thirty cents.)

John feels uncomfortable being alone with the therapist. This discomfort is partly due to his displaced hostility from his mother on the therapist and partly because of his sexual preoccupations in regard to the former. He substitutes the therapist for his mother and the same anxieties that are associated with her come to the surface now.

John is disappointed that the therapist, like his own mother, has not given him siblings (playmates). She disappoints him and he is angry at her; he wants to punish her by leaving her and going to his mother, whom he plans to victimize for lying to him, which is probably his phantasy.

When the therapist interprets to John his feelings toward her, he at once relaxes and settles down to work. The therapist understood him and since she understands him she is less of a threat. To be understood also means to be accepted, and his negative transference is at once changed into positive feelings. As a result of this rapport, John feels secure and boasts: he is liked by others as well. Even his girlfriend gives him money. In this is implied a defense against his sexual impulses as well as hostile feelings toward the therapist: she is not the only one in his affections, there are others, i.e., the basic transference is a negative one.

Mike is the strongest member of the group on whom John relies and whom he fears.

Mike arrives and appears to be angry.

Mike (to the therapist): I was waiting for you downstairs.

Judah arrives wearing a mask.

Judah: We put paint all around your office because you weren't there.

Therapist: I waited until our time to go upstairs. If you were angry, you boys could have told me rather than painted my office.

Judah (enthusiastically): My uncle gave me this mask. He just got back from overseas and, boy, you should see the souvenirs he brought for me.

Mike finds some candy that was left from the last session and grabs it.

John (trying to grab the candy from Mike): That candy belongs to me. Give it to me.

Mike and John start running around the room while John keeps trying to get the candy from Mike.

Mike: It does not belong to you and you can't have any candy.

John: The candy is so mine.

Mike (throws a piece of candy across the room): There you are. Run and get it.

John (picks up the candy): Come on, give me some more. The rest is really mine.

Mike (throws another piece which John runs after): And you're not getting any more.

John: I'm going to run out and tell my mother.

Therapist: Why are you going to tell your mother?

John: I'll tell Mike's mother.

Therapist: Why don't you tell Mike?

John ignores the suggestion of the therapist. Mike stops fighting him.

Mike (to Judah): Why don't we go out and get water for the painting.

Mike and Judah go out to get water for the finger painting. John begins to work with the paper, cutting out a design on orange paper which he had crayoned black. Judah and Mike come running back into the room.

Judah: I am going to make a witch picture.

Mike: I am making a Halloween picture, too.

The boys work for a while. Then Mike tries to put paint from his hand on John. Judah follows and tries to do this also.

Therapist (to Judah and Mike): Why are you boys angry at John?

Mike: Because John got here early.

Therapist: But John got here at the time he was brought. Mike, maybe you just don't like the idea that someone else is here alone with me.

Mike: You're right.

Mike then pretends to dab paint in John's direction without really doing so.

Therapist: Mike, you just feel like acting silly now.

Mike: Gee, you're right again. You're becoming a mind reader!

Both Mike and Judah are angry. It is easy to guess the cause of their anger. They act out their anger against the therapist by messing up her office, which is in another part of the building, and by depriving John of candy. Later Mike, the most disturbed of the three boys, reveals the reason for his hostility toward John. He acts out his sibling rivalry and as the therapist helps him to understand that he is jealous of John for being alone with her, his anger abates. He pretends to throw paint at John, but does not actually do it. The therapist is somewhat defensive about John: she seems to justify, or at least explain, his being alone with her. This can be interpreted that she prefers John, which is both bad and untrue. The interpretation of Mike's feelings alone would have been sufficient. When the therapist says that Mike is just being silly, she expresses her disapproval and exercises control over him which is necessary with very young children.

All three boys go on working. Judah finishes his painting.

Judah: Well that's done. I guess I'll work on an airplane now. (To the therapist): Would you help me?

Mike had started several "war paintings," all at the same time. He finishes them all at the same time after working diligently. The therapist sees no design in them, although she believes that Mike is using his hands more freely and is actually finger painting rather than working the way he did last week, which was just piling paint.

Judah draws an airplane on wood and comes over to the therapist:

Will you saw this for me? Gee, I'm glad you got the saw you promised me.

John (Moving closer to the therapist): Would you make me something, too?

Therapist: Of course I would. (John seems very pleased at this.)

Judah: Gee, I have an idea. Let's all make pumpkins out of wood. This is how we could do it. All we have to do is to nail pieces of wood together into a square.

John (to the therapist): Could you help me saw this piece of heavy wood?

Judah then starts to nail the two pieces together but has to hunt for the nails. John goes over to him and hands him a nail that he has found.

Judah: Thanks a lot. (John seems pleased by this.) John, come on and help me with this work. You could even start one for yourself.

The hostility felt by Mike and Judah is now sublimated in activity: aeroplanes and war paintings. The therapist, however, notes that Mike is much freer in his work which is very important for this boy. Judah is pleased that the therapist got the saw he wanted and because of this warm feeling toward her wants her to work with him. This in turn makes John jealous and he, too, wants her help—an expression of sibling rivalry. When John gives Judah the nails and Judah in turn invites him to work with him, there is personality growth beyond narcissistic preoccupations and an expanded capacity for object relationships. John's act can be seen, however, as a placation because of his own fear of the hostile feelings he harbors toward Judah, but as Judah acceps him, i.e., forgives him, he feels relieved.

Mike: Let's all go now.

Judah: I want to finish. (He leaves his wood and takes some of the paint with which he starts to paint a picture on the wall.)

Therapist (to Judah): You know we are not allowed to paint on the walls of the room.

Judah: Oh don't worry. It will be okay because no one will know I did it.

Therapist: That doesn't matter. We are still not permitted to paint the walls.

Judah (continuing to paint): I think it will be all right. Look at the paint that other people put on the wall.

Therapist: Maybe you are angry because other people use this room.

Judah: That's right.

Mike (Chiming in): You're right.

Therapist: You see, the toy cars are ours and so is the bulletin board.... If you want to leave, I think we should go now. (They all wanted to go.) I think you should all go outside and wash.

They follow the suggestion. This is the first time that any of them have gone to wash their hands before going to eat. Because someone is in the wash room there is some delay. Mike starts banging on the door. Judah runs for a hammer and starts banging. John also participates: he kicks the door and bangs on it. They are finally able to get inside.

Judah (to the therapist): Would you get paper for me? I want you to lift me up so that I can get the paper for myself.

Mike: I want paper, too.

John: Me, too.

Judah and John are with the therapist. This disturbs Mike and he suggests terminating the session. Judah does not want to go, and because the therapist did not counter Mike's suggestion, he attacks her by painting the wall. When she remonstrates with him he finds every plausible means for justifying his act and finally he and Mike admit that they are angry because others, as well, use the room, i.e., the therapist loves other children as well as them. Judah's choice to paint a house and an owl is in itself significant.

The fact that John, a frightened and withdrawn boy, can participate in an act of such direct aggression as banging and kicking the door is very valuable to him. He could not possibly have done it when alone. The example (catalysis) of the others gave him the courage to do it.

Judah: Let's go down through the back stairway.

The group follows Judah's suggestion. There is no running ahead. All three walk alongside the therapist. Judah and Mike take her hand and John takes Judah's hand.

Judah: Let's stop at the stationery store.

Mike: Yes. I see something I want.

John: That's a good idea. I see something, too.

Judah: I want a collection of books but all the things cost too much. I only have a dime. (He gives up the idea with some difficulty.)

Mike: Let's go now. I think we should stop and eat first, though.

Judah and John agree and they all choose vanilla ice cream sodas and eat without playing with the ice cream the way they formerly did.

Therapist (while the boys are eating): What would you like to eat next week?

Judah: Frankfurters.

Mike: Yes, frankfurters.

John: That's right, frankfurters.

Judah: And please have plates, and forks and knives and mustard and flowers—daffodils—and then we'll all sing: "Here comes the bride."

Therapist: Who is going to be the bride?

Judah does not answer.

The back stairway is dark and has special significance for these boys as it also had for the children in other groups. They are afraid and keep together and cling to the therapist. Note that John, because of his timidity and fear of contact with the therapist, holds another boy's hand both in this instance and later on. In the discussion of refreshments, Judah brings forth the idea of a bride. Did he see himself marryng the therapist (his mother)? One can only speculate on this. When asked by the therapist who the bride would be he does not answer; he represses it.

On the way to the five-and-ten cent store, John tries to put chalk on the therapist and Mike sort of hits her with a gun. This really takes the form of pushing the therapist from the back. Mike and Judah then take the therapist's hand and John takes Judah's hand again. John keeps taking out his thirty cents to show how much money he has. In the store they hesitate a great deal about choosing what to buy. They look at all the various objects and Mike finally decides.

Mike: I'm going to buy stickers and tags for Christmas packages.

Judah: I want tags and stickers, too. (He decides this although he had been handling something else.)

John: I'm getting them, too. (John also buys crayons that Judah had picked up but didn't have the money to pay for.)

The group walks back to the office.

Judah: I would like to have a hundred thousand dollars and buy a big store.

Mike: I would, too.

John: So would I.

CHAPTER 39

DIFFERENTIAL DYNAMICS OF ACTIVITY AND INTERVIEW (ANALYTIC) GROUP THERAPY[1]
(1947)

The increased interest in group psychotherapy and its growing acceptance as a treatment technique for psychological malformations, emotional disturbances, and social maladjustments makes it imperative that we continue to clarify its nature and scope, and evaluate the results. Only such constant vigilance will assure vital growth of our field and help practitioners toward greater effectiveness. The importance of differential diagnoses and treatment has been amply demonstrated in psychiatry and psychotherapy. This is equally necessary in group therapy. Differential therapy and individualization increase the pertinence of the treatment plan and enhance its effectiveness and efficiency. The more appropriately the tools of any craft are employed, the more is effectiveness assured. As the therapist is able to fit the method of treatment to the particular patient, the more likely is he to obtain desirable results.

An effort has been made by the present writer to develop criteria for choosing patients for group therapy. However, these criteria are as yet in the beginning stage. Much more research will be necessary before fully reliable standards will be evolved for choosing and assigning clients to suitable types of group therapy. We know that when an

1. We employed the term *interview*, as opposed to *activity*, until 1945, when we substituted *analytic* [56].

individual is unable, for some reason, to establish a positive transference with the therapist, a diluted relationship such as a group
supplies is indicated. Where verbal communication is blocked, acting
out in a favorable social environment is frequently the only road to
therapeutic success either as a beginning stage in therapy or as a sole
treatment method. This method is particularly valuable to young
children, to whom relationships with peers are especially important.

Observation shows that even children with neurotic traits slough off
symptomatic behavior through Activity Group Therapy, and character
is affected and corrected by it. Further investigation as to the value
of groups as sole treatment in the therapy of neuroses, or as an
adjuvant to individual therapy, is an imperative need at the present
juncture in the development of our work.

In Activity Group Therapy, spontaneous discharge of drives,
diminution of tension and reduction of anxiety are achieved through
physical and emotional activity in a group setting. This setting permits
unimpeded acting out within the boundaries of safety and through
free interaction with fellow members. Interpersonal and social
situations constantly arise through which each discharges tensions,
expresses emotions, discovers limitations, builds ego strengths, finds
self-status, and develops relationships. A limited degree of insight also
evolves. The total situation is designed to supply substitute gratifications; to give vent to aggression; reinforce the ego, particularly in
regard to feelings of failure and inadequacy; counteract deflated self-
evaluation; release blockings to expression in some patients, and build
self-restraint in others. To accomplish all this, the child or adolescent
is provided with a tangible social reality with which he deals in
accordance with his existing and expanding abilities and powers.
Through the experiences in this *conditioned* environment, modifications occur in his personality by which he acquires strengths and
facilities for dealing with the outer world and with his own impulses.

In *interview groups* with young children, manual activity may be
utilized as a starting point, but the activity itself is not the sole
treatment tool. The child's or the group's behavior is interpreted with
regard to the motives of such behavior. By these means each is helped
to understand the problem, and with the understanding, insight
gradually develops. Interpretation and insight may come from other
members of the group or from the therapist. The more patients help
one another in this respect, the better.

Adolescents and adults do not ordinarily need the medium of work materials except at periods of extreme anxiety; the presence of activity materials may interfere with the therapeutic process. Drawing, clay modelling, or doodling help diminish the anxiety created by treatment interviews. Because all have common problems and a natural need for one another, group treatment has proved to be a comparatively easy and natural procedure. Adolescents, especially, make ready contact with one another. They are able to share their difficulties with ease, and activate one another in expression of feelings and attitudes. Once ego defenses are down and self-protective reserves are removed, they readily reveal their most intimate problems and seem to be almost entirely free of what is commonly referred to as "self-consciousness." They talk easily about prohibited subjects, reveal hidden feelings about themselves, and express attitudes toward parents, siblings, teachers, and others in their environment.

Adults take somewhat longer to overcome their protective mantle, but soon also communicate freely with one another. In a group, narcissistic barriers and ego defenses are reduced and each can venture further here than in the presence of the therapist in individual therapy. The less conflicted and less frightened group members dissolve the fears, defenses, and resistances in the more neurotic and inhibited members. This is often referred to as the *catalytic effect* persons have upon one another.

To evaluate the similarities and contrasts of these two types of treatment, it may be helpful to establish basic therapeutic references for such comparison.

The four pillars of therapy which seem to be present in whatever method of psychotherapy is employed are: *relationship, catharsis, insight,* (or *ego strengthening*), and *reality testing.*[2] It is conceded that successful therapy is based on a fundamentally positive relationship of the patient and therapist; in the case of group therapy, also with the members of the group. The foundation of all psychotherapy is relationship [11].

Of the types described, those which relate to our present discussion are the transference, the unilateral, bilateral, multilateral, and to lesser extent, the anaclitic and submission-domination relationships. When the basic transference is positive, catharsis can take place; that is, the patient can regress to the level of fixation in his emotional develop-

2. "Sublimation" has been since added to these four basic dynamics.

ment. He can then either discuss his infantile wishes, or act them out. Being sure of the accepting attitude of the therapist, the patient is not afraid either to communicate or act out his feelings and strivings which are not ordinarily approved or accepted. This provides the therapist in interview groups with an opportunity to interpret and activate insight in the patient toward his own mechanisms, as a result of which he can deal with his impulses more adequately.

The counterpart in activity groups to gaining insight is ego strengthening. Unconditional acceptance by an adult, and by the group, satisfactions, successful achievement, gaining status, wholesome identifications, and the many other dynamics operating in these groups change the patient's attitude toward the self and enhance self-valuation.

Thus, it is quite clear that while we deal predominantly with the sexual libido in interview groups, in activity groups the patient's ego is more involved, and desexualized libido is more prominent. Both the ego and the libido are involved in both types of group; the difference being the predominance of one or the other, which is readily understandable in the light of the difference in the quality of the transference relationship, the age of the patients, and the nature of the therapeutic process. Activity Group Therapy is, therefore, predominantly an ego therapy, while interview groups deal more with the patient's libidinal fixations and difficulties.

Transference is present in both types of group, and in both the basic transference must be positive. Temporary transference can be negative; that is, the patient can display or verbalize temporary hostility, dislike, or fear of the therapist and the members of the group. But basically, there must be a foundation of positive feelings and trust, as true of individual psychotherapy and psychoanalysis as it is of group therapy. Lacking this, the patient will resist or terminate treatment. Patients who are unable to establish such positive feelings or who feel too threatened by any one in the group, do not return after one or two sessions.

In Activity Group Therapy, negative phases of the transference cannot be acted out directly against the person of the therapist. For obvious reasons the therapist cannot permit being attacked physically. In our rather extensive experience with such groups there were only one or two instances of such aggression. The reason such hostile acts do not occur is that each member is afraid of retaliation from other members should be attack the therapist, toward whom they are well disposed. Because the therapist is a *neutral* person, he does not provoke active aggression, though there is considerable latent hostility toward him. There is a great deal of projected and diverted antagonism, but because he is friendly, generous, quiet, tolerant, and accepts language and behavior that are punished by other adults, he does not provide an opening for direct resentment. Hostility is instead redirected toward other members of the group. We know that when a child abuses furniture, walls, and tools, or steals, he really acts out his hostility toward the therapist.

The dominant group climate in an activity group is positive, friendly, and constructive. The fact that some of the children deviate does not destroy its basic positive atmosphere. The group gives comfort, warmth, friendship, and is tolerant and hospitable.[3]

In interview group therapy, verbal attacks may be expressed directly against the therapist. Patients resent him as a parent substitute. They criticize his coming late, question or reject interpretations, openly disagree, and in other ways reinforce one another in their negative feelings against the therapist. Therapeutically such expression of negative feelings is of great value, for egress of hostility is one of the main requirements for emotional recovery.

Aggressiveness and hostility are easily mobilized in groups. At times it is blatantly directed against the therapist, but more often it comes through in disguised forms, is deflected, or substitute targets are found. Young children of preschool age in play groups may at times strike the therapist and throw objects at him. Direct expression of feelings is normal for children so young. They still have to evolve restraints, find sublimations, and build up disguises. While hostile feelings toward the therapist are evident in interview groups of adolescents and adults, they are largely confined to individuals and only rarely mobilized into a group phalanx. Fear and guilt serve as deterrents, since the therapist represents the parental figure. While it is essential that hostility and negative feelings are discharged, it is rather important that they are not reinforced, for negative transferences are very difficult to deal with in a group. It is easier, and probably also

---

3. When a question arose as to availability of food to a visitor, a friend of a member of the group said affirmatively, "In this family there is food for everybody."

more therapeutic, if dealt with as it arises in each individual, rather than permitting the entire group to be infected with hostility.

The factor of anxiety, present in all groups, is rather important. Since members of therapy groups are preoccupied with unresolved oedipal conflicts, infantile sexuality, regressive behavior, and destructive drives, there is a great deal of anxiety present especially in these groups. Anxiety, however, is more intense in individual therapy where its mobilization is permitted as an essential process in treatment. While anxiety is also present in group therapy, it does not reach the same degree of intensity. The presence of others in the environment dilutes it, becoming partially dissolved or diffuse. Awareness that others have the same feelings allays guilt and serves to reduce anxiety, for emotional and muscular activity helps drain it off. The security of mutual support is another preventive for mobilization of intensity of anxiety.

Though considerably less than in individual treatment, anxiety in interview groups is much greater than in activity groups. In the latter each member feels threatened in varying degrees, as his unconscious strivings are manifested in behavior, but it seldom reaches deep layers of the personality. Since activity (activity catharsis) is the pattern of the group's life, the patient is not prone to mobilize psychological tensions to the same extent as in interview groups where he cannot discharge them as easily. Because repressed and prohibited impulses and wishes are not verbalized, the unconscious is not exposed to view of oneself and that of others, as is the case in interview groups.

Because anxiety is allayed through the group and transference is diluted and modified by intermember transference and mutual identification, group therapy cannot reach some of the unconscious levels that psychoanalysis does. In the latter, there is no escape from anxiety. It must be resolved through transference and insight. In a group, escapes are ready to hand.

A fuller report on the transference phenomena in group therapy will be made at a later date. Our present concern is the transference attitude as manifested in the two different therapy groups. Libidinal involvements, the oedipal struggle, and the therapist's interpretations and insight-giving, create problems that rarely exist in activity groups, and if they do, are of vastly lesser intensity. Jealousies and hostilities are more intense than they are likely to be in activity groups. The interview group therapist is an object of the patient's libidinal preoccupations to a greater degree. The patient involves him in his oedipal conflict; he therefore becomes the object of the patient's ambivalent feelings and genital strivings. This does not occur in activity groups, where the therapist is a *neutral* person, and the members are in the latency period and not as neurotic as those in interview groups.

In the interview group the therapist is more the center of the emotional network, and is also more real as a person. He participates in the discussions, receives and reacts to the attitudes of the members, and generally represents the reality with which the patients are familiar. The neutral role which the therapist plays in activity groups is more unreal. This is not the way the youngsters are accustomed to being treated and they are puzzled. It has the effect of a shock and the group members need to become accustomed to this new type of adult. While at the beginning stages of treatment anxiety may be increased in some members they are selected because they possess the capacity for developing multilateral relations in a group. As they learn to function without the supervision and support of an adult, they grow in maturity and autonomy.

Because relationship, catharsis, and anxiety are so closely related, they have been grouped together in the preceding pages. We now turn our attention to an element of group therapy where the greatest diversity exists. This is the element of *insight*. It is an accepted fact that patients improve when they understand their mechanisms and become aware of the early causes of their current problems. This principle was derived from psychoanalysis and is undoubtedly true where intense neuroses are present. We have already reported our observation that some neurotic symptoms and traits disappear in children as their ego is strengthened. In interview groups, as in individual therapy, adolescents and adults are helped in dealing with their anxieties and social maladjustments in which insight is one of the major factors.

This is not the case in Activity Group Therapy. The therapeutic process here is based upon acting out, experiencing reactions of other members to behavior, and a changed attitude toward the self. The newly acquired attitudes toward the self and others as a result of the satisfactions of being accepted, loved, and permitted to behave as one wishes, are part of the process. The youngster tests himself against tangible reality. As he finds himself not wanting, his ego is strengthened. Increased strengths change his feelings of weakness, ineffectualness, and unworthiness. The unthreatening environment makes self-protective aggression superfluous and unnecessary. The result of these and the many other intrapsychic and exterior dynamics is a stronger character, a more effective ego, and improved self-evaluation.

Our observations indicate that a considerable amount of spontaneous insight occurs, which proceeds from the patient's awareness of the change within himself and his improved facilities to deal with his impulses and the outer world. We frequently find a child or adolescent comparing himself as he is now with how he had been in the past. He verbalizes his awareness of his greater powers for dealing with situations, his changed attitudes, and improvement. This is *derivative insight;* namely, insight derived from the patient's own growth rather than from interpretation by other members of the group or the therapist.

In interview groups, on the other hand, insight is a major therapeutic tool. The therapist helps each member of the group to understand his reactions and some of the causes of his psychological stress and social maladjustments. The degree of insight is limited by each member's capacity to accept and deal with it. The therapist needs to have a thorough knowledge of each group member's problem and of his capacity to withstand stress. He must be aware of the nuclear or central difficulty of each member and know where caution is necessary. A patient may well be able to accept and use insight into one problem and still be injuriously disturbed by an interpretation of another. Thus, the therapist must always address himself to the lowest denominator in the group in each situation and in relation to every problem that is brought forth.

One of the major values of group therapy for many patients is that anxiety provoked by self-confrontation and self-analysis is greatly lessened as compared with individual treatment. If he feels anxiety coming on, he may withdraw from the group discussion. He becomes a spectator but the therapeutic process within him continues. This is "spectator therapy." The patient can identify with others in the group who express ideas and difficulties akin to his own, and applies the statements made by him and others to himself. However, the free association, self-revelatory statements by some of the members may create intense anxiety and even panic in others. Interpretation by the therapist, though directed toward one member, may also create anxiety in some others. No matter how skillful and cautious a therapist is, he cannot avoid it. Individual interviews following group sessions to allay anxiety in a particularly disturbed group member are indicated in such instances.

Just as dissipation of anxiety limits the intensity of treatment in a group, the limit imposed on insight-giving has the same effect. Although catharsis is greatly facilitated and accelerated in groups; that is, group members reveal themselves and speak freely about their impulses, strivings, and even perversions, interpretation of these presents a greater risk than in individual treatment. Even where the patient fully trusts the therapist, fear of individual members and the reaction of the group as a whole still remain sources of anxiety and apprehension. One cannot be unmasked, stripped naked as it were, before a group of people. The therapist needs to exercise every caution to avoid this error. Whenever possible, insight-giving and interpretation should come from the patients themselves. They seem to display what appears an "uncanny" understanding of each others' mechanisms and underlying problems and motivations. Even very young children display keen insight into others' motives and difficulties.

At all times the therapist should be aware of where the group is heading. His knowledge of each patient's difficulties and the principles of psychopathology and psychotherapy must at all times be poised for action. A well-placed question, well-timed, opens the sluices of the unconscious and free association. This is aided by the catalytic influence of the therapist and the group members. Points of fear and resistance that periodically appear in groups must be recognized. At these stages patients must be helped to overcome their differences and fears through appropriate use of the transference relation. The therapist may, as indicated by the situation, either analyze the resistance of the group, incite or facilitate expression of hostility to himself, or reassure the group of his acceptance and permissiveness. The line to be taken is usually indicated by the nature of the blocking, the manifest and latent content of the discussion, and the anxiety sources inherent in the treatment situation.

We have already referred to the fact that ego strengthening can take the place of insight in the therapeutic process. Both the concept and its dynamics deserve a more extensive discussion than is possible in this paper. All that can be said here in this connection is that a very large number who come for help are persons whose self-esteem had been greatly deflated. Many are unable to mobilize power to deal with inner impulses and outer stresses. They are either withdrawn or have adopted defensive aggression as a pattern of life. Briefly, it can be said that the ego is weak and character is defective.

The experience of group relations, especially in activity groups, has been found to have salutary effects on such patients. This is even more universally true of young children whose personalities are still in a formative stage and who respond to experience on more basic psycho-organic levels. Changes in the character of children have impressed all who have had the opportunity to observe this type of group therapy. It must be kept in mind, however, that ego strengthening is no cure for a true full-blown neurosis. It is helpful in other personality disturbances and clinical entities, but young patients with neurotic traits have in many instances overcome their difficulties by the fact that they had learned to deal with their impulses and instinctual drives.

Similarities and differences are also found in the fourth element of our therapeutic scheme, reality testing. A group represents an important realistic situation in therapy. This writer does not hold that social reality is essential to the treatment process itself; rather treatment is a preparation for dealing with social reality. There are patients who cannot possibly face group pressures, no matter how slight. They are not ready to utilize a group situation or act constructively in it. Though patients with serious neuroses may be unable to deal with a group situation, there are patients with behavior and character disorders and minor neurotic disturbances where social relations are not only important, but essential for successful treatment.

Reality testing is an essential part of psychologic treatment, but this does not mean that reality must be always supplied in the treatment situation itself. Patients in individual treatment and institutions test themselves constantly against the realities of everyday life and find themselves either adequate or wanting, placid or distressed. Living and therapy go hand in hand. In group therapy, however, we supply a *flexible reality,* graded in complexity so that the patient can deal with it as a part of the therapeutic situation. This fact is both an advantage and a limiting factor in therapy. It is an advantage because the pressures and complexities of reality can be graded and controlled. The environment is conditioned in accordance with needs and capacities, but the reality of human relationships inherent in group therapy excludes many patients who are not ready for them. Thus, we can place in groups only persons who are able to utilize multiple relationships.

Young children, especially, require experience with reality as a part of treatment. Action is the living medium of child expression; language is not. Ideation is of small importance to the young child, but action is primary. In many instances, even with adults, direct action is more significant than explanation. The child, for example, understands impediment to his aggressiveness, when he may not accept reasoning or explanation. It is particularly telling when controls come from others his own age. There is less resentment and hostility than if imposed by adults. An activity group therapy setting is so arranged that reality is graded in intensity and complexity. Each is free to utilize it in whatever way he wishes. He can participate with or shun the others; he can work or play or idle. In this way, the child has an opportunity to test himself in the therapeutic setting, and as he finds himself not wanting in dealing with it, he is strengthened.

The reality of the interview group is a rather intensive emotional reality. Reactions to the emotions of the individuals constituting the group are more difficult to escape. Here, too, one can act out and react to others, but in a more restricted manner. Only rarely is this acting out of a physical nature; feelings are expressed through language. One can express anger, love, resentment, hatred, dependence through verbal formulation rather than actual physical acts. These emotions are utilized by the therapist in his interpretation and insight-giving, or analyzed and elaborated by other members of the group.

In both types of group, the therapist acts as support to his patients. He allies himself with their impulses as against their weak restraints. By allying himself with their instinctive drives as against their superego, he encourages catharsis, reduces guilt and anxiety. But the important realistic factors are the reactions of the members of the group, their encouragement or displeasure, their approval or disapproval, and the interpretations they give of actions and statements. Groups are a significant reality in the lives of people, in treatment and elsewhere. Group therapy, whether in interview or activity groups, provides a similar kind of reality.

CHAPTER 40

ACTIVITY GROUP THERAPY WITH A
DELINQUENT DULL BOY
(1945)

Simon, an eleven year-old boy, was referred for treatment in September 1934 because of disturbing behavior in school, striking younger children, constant fighting with a younger brother, being noisy and quarrelsome in the home, stealing, and enuresis. In school, he talked out loud, whispered, scraped his feet on the floor to annoy the class and teacher, and truanted frequently. He ran away from home and once stayed away for two days. On several occasions the intercession of the police was sought by the parents. During one of these escapades Simon was found the day after he disappeared in a cheap movie theater, miles away from his home, where derelicts congregate. He said that he had fallen asleep in the theater on the previous afternoon, and when the theater was locked for the night he was still asleep. The police handled the case briefly but closed it after a few weeks. In intelligence tests Simon received IQ ratings of 73 and 82.

Simon was the second of five children. The eldest was a dull girl, five years older than our client. She was also a client in the agency, presenting behavior difficulties, including stealing. The father had been a weak, ineffectual man, sickly and a poor provider; he had died at about the time when the boy was referred for treatment. Simon was very much attached to his father and was greatly upset over his death.

Written in collaboration with Henry Wiener and Saul Scheidlinger.

A number of social service agencies were interested in the family, which subsisted on an allowance from the city welfare department.

Mrs. H. was the tenth child in a family of thirteen. She did not finish public school because she had to go to work. After the birth of her first child she began to gain and her weight went up from 140 to 290 pounds. She was described as appearing neatly dressed, in spite of her bulk, and as trying to give an impression of refinement. She always seemed weary. Though a cold and hard person, she was protective of her children, minimized their problems, and did not volunteer any information. She had a fatalistic attitude. Her marriage to Mr. H. was a loveless one and occurred as a result of circumstances rather than attraction. The husband deserted soon after the marriage, but a reconciliation was effected four years later when they met in court. When interviewed she requested service for a third child, who also presented behavior difficulties.

Simon was a premature baby. He weighed about five pounds at birth. Delivery was normal but very difficult, accompanied by hemorrhages and numerous fainting spells. The child was breastfed for three months and then had to be spoon fed because he refused to take nourishment. He walked at eighteen months. He was sickly up to the age of three and was thought to have jaundice. He was found to be anemic and treatment proved effective. At one month of age, he was operated on for a fatty tumor behind his ear. When he was six years old, he had an operation for a double hernia.

According to Mrs. H., Simon's difficult behavior began at the age of six. At that time, while he was recovering from measles at a convalescent home, he was frightened by a nurse dressed as a ghost at a Halloweeen party. He became ill and had convulsions. After the father's death, when Simon was nearly ten, his difficulties increased.

In school Simon was described as a "little untrained animal"; at one period he was transferred to a probationary school. He was retarded in most subjects, repeating some grades. He seemed sensitive about this, crying whenever his classmates taunted him with his failures. The school felt that Mrs. H. did not know how to manage her children and expected others to train them for her. She was in the habit of punishing Simon severely. When a Big Brother was assigned to Simon immediately after his referral, Mrs. H. used the Big Brother as a punitive agent, by threatening to tell him when the boy committed some act that she did not deem proper.

We have here a dull boy whose primary capacities are so limited that he is unable to deal with the demands of our culture. His intelligence being low, he is incapable of functioning adequately in school and of gaining a place for himself. He has been thoroughly rejected at home and this rejection continues in school, where he is treated harshly and punitively. Punitive treatment has been his lot also in the family, at the hands of his mother, sister, and almost everyone else there. The child's reaction to this has been compliance toward the parents, quarreling with siblings, and rebellion in school. His deflated self-esteem has made it necessary for him to become cautious, suspicious, and submissive. His running away from home can be interpreted as a desire to find a more hospitable and friendly environment, as seeking of his father, or as retaliation against his mother, who was worried and upset by it.

Escape from unpleasantness by going to dark movie houses, where he could be alone and sleep, can be interpreted as a desire to withdraw from reality and return to the mother's uterus. Having been made to feel weak, a failure, and unable to take his place in his world, he could do little else but withdraw from reality, which could have resulted in a schizoid personality, or, if the pressures were great enough, in schizophrenia. As another factor, the many illnesses and operations that the boy incurred during his early life were traumatic. Such experiences tend to produce an infantile character; also, because by remaining a baby he could expect kindlier treatment, he persisted in acting as a child, and helpless.

Simon also lacked male identifications. The father being weak, nonparticipating in the family setup, and unable to provide for the family, did not supply the ego-ideal necessary to a boy. But Simon was strongly attached to the father, because he was the least threatening person in the family constellation. Thus the boy identified with the father's weaknesses. The available history does not indicate that Simon identified with the mother and thus acquired feminine characteristics. However, his approach to people in general was one of submissiveness and placation. What he could not do at home, namely, rebel against the mother, because of fear of being destroyed, he acted out in school and with children. This rebelliousness, however, must be considered as a positive element in treatment, for Simon has retained enough autonomy and strength to assert himself even if it is in an antisocial manner.

There is definite indication that this boy is moving in the direction of delinquency. His truancy, stealing, running away, and staying away from home at such an early age certainly would assure us that delinquency trends are present.

The Big Brother saw Simon several times. In his report dated January 1935 he stated that he and Simon had gone on trips to places of interest, to a restaurant, and also to visit the Big Brother's friends. In all these experiences the boy seemed well behaved, impressing others as being intelligent. While evading questions put to him by the Big Brother about his adjustment in school, Simon admitted having quarrels with other boys. As time went on, the Big Brother found Simon to be somewhat friendlier and more inclined to confide in him than earlier in the contact. However, the boy continued to present serious difficulties in school and in the home.

In February 1935, after a reconsideration of the case, it was decided that Simon needed deep psychotherapy and he was placed in charge of a staff psychiatrist instead of the Big Brother. The psychiatrist found the boy "jumpy, distractible, though fairly cooperative and pleasant." He felt that the basis for mental retardation might be local hypoplasia, or some birth injury resulting from a hydrocephalus. Subsequent neurologic and medical examinations yielded negative results. The psychiatrist felt that it would be hard to get at the boy's emotional conflict because he was mentally handicapped. With such a child, psychotherapy could at best help in working out aggressive drives in an atmosphere of tolerance and acceptance. Because he was attached to his Big Brother, it was felt that the latter should be used in the plan of treatment. At the second interview with the psychiatrist, Simon was uninhibited; he sang, laughed, and recited into the dictaphone. Following this interview, Simon displayed hostility and aggression, and the psychiatrist recommended that the Big Brother give the boy "much affection, only curbing him when his hostility seems to run beyond the bounds of permissibility and reality." At a later interview with the psychiatrist, Simon again talked into the dictaphone, expressing great hostility toward his younger brother and the smallest boys in his class. There was also much fantasy. As he dictated, he made violent and aggressive gestures.

However, after five or six interviews, the psychiatrist felt that nothing could be accomplished by psychotherapy because of the boy's dullness. Simon needed outlets for his emotions and a recommendation was made that the boy be reassigned to a Big Brother. The Big Brother was to help the boy to release his excessive energy and freely display his aggressiveness through suitable outlets. This would aid in giving Simon the security he lacks. Several months later Simon was reassigned to his former Big Brother.

The camp report for the summer of 1935 described Simon as "pugnacious and ready to hit the boys at the slightest provocation, even when he was accidentally touched." When the boy came back from camp he continued seeing his Big Brother infrequently, and no substantial change in his behavior was observed. In November 1935, Simon was referred for treatment to the group therapy department, but he was not placed in a group until September 1936. The Big Brother was not active at the time of the placement in the therapy group.

Out of twenty-nine meetings in the first year of group therapy, Simon attended seventeen. Simon's behavior at the meetings was very infantile. He was usually late. His clothes were very shabby, old, and tattered. He did very little work with materials and never finished anything he started. He played hide-and-seek with the boys, ran up and down a ladder, played cops and robbers and other such games, and occasionally checkers. He preferred playing with soldiers and guns, and once made a cannon out of clay. Because of the type of activity he engaged in, the other boys dubbed him "baby," which he didn't seem to mind. He objected to the other boys' bringing friends to the meetings. He complained that he had to take care of his younger brothers and sisters, since he is the eldest, and said that he had tried to find work to earn some money. His only fun was the group; he waited anxiously for Sundays, to be able to go to meetings.

After twenty-one meetings, it was necessary to transfer Simon to another group. In the new group he resumed a previously established pattern of staying by himself and reading magazines. At the second meeting of the new group, he sat outside of the meeting room and read picture magazines. He played with blocks, but occasionally participated in games with the other boys in which they pretended that they were holdup men attacking officers with armored cars. Simon made a leather mask out of black leather, which he said was a "Legion of Terror" mask. When in February 1937 a jig saw was added to the group's equipment, the boy was unable to use it. He was frightened by the noise of the saw and the sudden scraping sound that occurs when the wood is pressed too hard. The boys laughed at Simon's inability to use the jig saw; however, he was not affected by their ridicule.

The worker noted at that time that Simon's attendance was irregular. When present at a meeting, he either read by himself or played games whenever boys would play with him. He was described as quite infantile. He tried to get closer to the boys in the group but they paid very little attention to him. His efforts at working with wood were futile. He said: "What's the matter with this crazy thing? It don't want to stick together."

He then threw the wood away. He was annoyed. When Simon returned to the group in May after an absence of four weeks, he got a cool reception. No one asked him why he had stayed away. The only comment came from one boy, who said: "Whenever we go on a trip, he comes down. Otherwise he never comes to meetings."

After a year's group treatment, Simon continued in his infantile play and in his isolation from the group. He usually came only for trips. He expressed a great liking for the group therapist, however.

The Big Brother who had had infrequent and superficial contact with Simon since June 1935, saw the boy early in 1937 after six months of group therapy treatment. He was not hopeful about the boy and suggested that Simon needed intensive treatment. The Big Brother was quite disturbed once when he caught Simon looking very intently at the tip he had left for a waiter in a restaurant. He felt that Simon had repressed a desire to take the money. In addition, the Big Brother was unable to continue activity with the boy because he had become too busy with his own affairs and could not find time to attend even one conference held on the case. Mrs. H. did not cooperate with the case worker who attempted to see her on a regular basis.

However, the school and home reported some improvement at this time (1937). Simon's behavior was less provocative. An integration conference of the case worker from the Big Brother department, the director of the group therapy department, and the group therapist, was held in May 1937. The case worker felt that Simon's explosive and unreasonable behavior might be the result of a psychosis, but the director of group therapy indicated that the boy was displaying some improvement, despite its slow rate, and recommended continuing with the case. It was felt, however, that although Simon had improved somewhat, he still presented many problems that could not be reached through the superficial contacts with the Big Brother. Among the boy's chief difficulties at school were his constant restlessness and his attempt to dominate younger boys. He was unwilling to do the school work, although he seemed capable of doing it, having displayed such ability on several occasions. Despite suspicion of neurologic difficulties, the boy had made progress and it was decided to continue treatment. It was also recommended that presentable clothing should be supplied to the boy by the Big Brother department, to decrease his feelings of inferiority because of his shabby appearance, and a case worker was to be assigned to see the boy.

The latter found it hard to reach Simon. He talked about his activities at school, at home, and in the neighborhood, and impressed one as a boy very much isolated who had difficulty in getting along with children. He blamed others for most of his problems. He brought comic papers to the interviews and sat reading them, paying no attention to the case worker. Occasionally he wold tell the worker that he was lonely and at a loss to find things to do after school and on Saturdays. Most of his spare time was spent playing with his younger brother.

In June 1937 a thorough neurologic, medical, and X-ray study was made of Simon. No defects were found. Routine blood, urine, and nose and throat examination, and a spinal fluid test, were recommended. Simon's peculiar attitude at the time of the examination, his seeming indifference and lack of affect, impressed the examining physician as pointing to the possibility of incipient schizophrenia.

The mother was having much trouble with Simon at this time. He had found a check and cashed it. As a result, Mrs. H. kept him, as she put it, "a virtual prisoner" in the house, for fear that he would involve himself further because of his bad friends and his impulsiveness. During interviews, when he did talk, he expressed great hostility toward his schoolteacher. Nonetheless, he passed in his subjects in school and was promoted to the 5B grade. This made him very happy.

Mrs. H. reported that Simon was much happier and more content at home, although he was still restless at night and went to the bathroom very frequently. He was spending most of his time at home and no longer went out with undesirable companions. Before he went to camp the case worker discussed the subject of sex with Simon. The boy denied any sex activity or masturbation either at home or in school. During one interview, he expressed the conviction that masturbation could lead to insanity. In general, Simon did not respond to the case worker's attempts at individual treatment. When the mother continued to complain abut Simon's associations with delinquent boys, placement was considered by the worker.

The camp report, dated September 8, 1937 shows that Simon did not make a very good adjustment there. It was necessary to encourage him to enter into activities, to which he responded with only mild enthusiasm. He had food fads and bad table manners. He got into difficulties with his counselor and was deprived of some food at one meal. Simon left the camp grounds and stayed away for several hours. He was apparently very deeply hurt and seriously disturbed about this. The boy seemed dull and unable to grasp directions.

Upon returning from camp, Simon was again placed in a therapy group. During this period, he had no contact with a case worker or a Big Brother. His attendance now was excellent. He was present at all meetings in the first six months—up to March 1938. He struck up a friendship with another boy, Leon, who was as inadequate and dull as he. Leon felt keenly his intellectual inferiority because of which he was placed in an ungraded class at school. He was lonely and was given to boasting about an imaginary prowess and to ingratiating himself with others by offering them gifts, money, etc.

Simon now did more work with materials. Some of his hostility began to come through in a play form, and he was somewhat freer in his relationship to the group. At the first meeting after camp, he worked by himself outside of the meeting room. He came back after fifteen minutes to finish the picture on which he was working. The new group therapist found him "dull, childish, simple, appealing, and pathetic." He spent most of the time during the early part of these six months watching, coaching, and acting as a referee in fights. In fights, he sided with the vanquished. He displayed particular antipathy to Harry, an aggressive boy in whose presence he felt very tense. In referring to this relation, the group worker said: "Harry is an enigma of the unexpected to Simon, which makes him uncomfortable. When Harry leaves, Simon seems to relax suddenly as if some threat has been removed."

Simon continued to employ his device of separating himself from the group occasionally by reading or working in the anteroom. Leon, who favored Simon above the others, continued to be his only friend. They frequently sat together quietly and talked. They seemed happy to spend the entire time of the meetings in each other's company, just talking. Simon's play was still infantile. One one occasion he made a sword of a dowel stick, with which he fenced with the other boys; he was "mad with joy" and stabbed imaginary objects around the room. But because of Leon he did do more work in arts and crafts. At one meeting, when he saw Leon working with copper, Simon started working with the same material, and though he was far from finishing at the close of the meeting, he was thrilled with his progress. He showed the worker his project, repeatedly asking him for an opinion. The worker consistently praised him.

The group therapist describes Simon's relationship with Leon as one of the most interesting aspects of his adjustment to the group at that time. Leon stimulated Simon to work with materials. Once when Leon was absent, Simon continued to work on his project. This was an improvement, because previously he would have withdrawn to the anteroom. The two friends, however, continued their frequent tête-à-têtes outside the meeting room. Sometimes they would run around playing violently. The therapist felt that both boys gained greatly from their friendship. Nowhere else did they find such compatibility. Each felt unreserved acceptance by the other, which negated the feelings of inferiority they may have had in relation to the more capable members.

In September 1938, when Leon arrived at a meeting, Simon stood up to greet him. He put the magazine down on the couch where he was reading, and with Leon went immediately to the hall, where they sat and chatted. The group therapist writes: "It is strange that they had selected the cold radiator just outside the washroom to sit on when they could have used the more comfortable ante-room, but in all probability this spot was selected for its remoteness from the center of activity in their desire to avoid any interference with their interest in each other. They spent the entire morning chatting quietly. The other boys and the worker respect their privacy and except for going to the washroom, they do not go near them."

Simon began helping with cleaning up and setting the table for refreshments. He was becoming more social, talked more frequently, took a more active interest in the group arguments, and evidenced a desire to prepare refreshments. This was probably stimulated by the fact that Leon used to help in cleaning up. At first Simon worked with Leon, but later he did it "on his own."

There had been no case work with Simon since September 1937. It was his worker's feeling that it would be of little value without a preceding thorough neurologic examination to determine whether there was an organic basis for his difficulties, but this could not be arranged at that time.

Another integration conference was held in March 1938. Simon's slow growth was again noted. He was relating himself to reality more than he had before. This was quite a change from the integration conference a year earlier, when the case worker thought that Simon was "psychotic." In view of the boy's deficiencies and environmental handicaps, he was doing well. He behaved more maturely and responsibly. He now willingly took care of his younger brother and had saved money for a Christmas present for his mother. It was decided that the boy should be continued in the group and that an effort should be made to help him to acquire more friends, which seemed to be a basic need of his. During this period (September 1937-October 1938), no Big Brother was assigned to the boy and the case worker did not see him.

In the following six months, Simon was absent from the meetings once. The summary report for this period, dated June 5, 1938, shows much progress. It says in part: "Simon recognizes his limitations and attempts to compensate for them through activities in which he can achieve. He was thrilled when he learned to ride a bicycle and be like the other boys in this respect. Simon now speaks more freely and is not as withdrawn as he was at the beginning of the season. He carries on conversations more frequently and for a greater length of time with all the boys in the group and the worker. Simon has even become a little inclined to argue with the boys. His cooperativeness relative to group chores continues. Simon's care of his clothing and general personal appearance has further improved. He told the worker that he was a member of a neighborhood baseball team. It is quite likely that his experience in the group has enabled him to participate more freely with neighborhood boys and groups."

The boy felt less insecurity in the group, owing to his friendship with Leon, and because of this was able to participate much more than he had done previously. He was able to relate the group to his home situation. For example, he made a case for the stamps that his younger brother collected. He was so engrossed in this occupation that he neglected his good friend, Leon. This was the beginning of his breaking away from Leon and a sign of progress.

At a conference in September 1938 it was decided that Simon should be continued in the therapy group. Although it was thought that a supportive relation with a Big Brother would be helpful to the boy, no arrangement could be made for it. Mrs. H. was fearful of Simon's going to the hospital for a further medical examination and refused to take him there. She agreed to take him to an outpatient clinic, but though arrangements were made, she did not follow through. Partly because of a teacher's sympathetic attitude and understanding of his problem to some extent, Simon's behavior in school improved greatly. He was promoted to the 6A grade and became a monitor. He responded well to this recognition.

The camp report confirmed the fact of his improvement as observed in the therapy group, at school, and at home. The report said that "Simon had made remarkable progress during the last year." At first, his pattern at camp was similar to that of the previous summer. He was restless, annoying, uncooperative, and absorbed for long periods in comic books. However, when he expressed an interest in dramatics, and was given a part in a play, it was noticed that he needed help in reading, and he accepted remedial reading lessons. He responded well to the interest shown him by the remedial reading teacher. After a success in the play, his general behavior seemed to change. He became more outgoing and friendly. He asked to take part in still another play, with even greater success. His general improvement was so noticeable that the other campers stopped ridiculing and annoying him and became more friendly toward him. Because his relationship to adults was good, the case worker at the camp suggested that individual treatment be tried again.

Continued improvement in all of the boy's relations was observed in the six months beginning September 1938. In the group a "startling change" was recorded. A month in a hospital with a broken arm at this time had a salutary effect on Simon. The attention and service given him in the hospital ward served further to convince him that he was accepted and loved, a feeling that was established in the group, in camp, and in the neighborhood.

The boy had now been two years under group therapy. At the first meeting he attended in the third year, in October 1938, Simon was struck by a burly boy, Joseph, while the worker was out of the room. There is no record of Simon's reaction to this, but when Joseph attacked Simon again at the following meeting he said: "You bully, one of these days I'll bring in a guy twice your size that will wipe up the floor with you!"

At the same meeting he invited the boys to a Halloween party at his home. He continued his friendship with Leon. He again cooperated in cleaning up the room and went out to buy food. When the worker arrived at the third meeting late, he found the boys playing a game. Simon said to him: "You saved my life, you came just in time." He had lost this game and would have had to go "under the mill."

Simon continued helping to arrange the chairs without being asked and brought a friend to one of the meetings. He was very hospitable and provided his friend with materials and food. His dependence on Leon, however, continued. When at the meeting of December 22, 1938, Leon was absent, Simon spent his time sitting in the anteroom looking through the magazines and wandering aimlessly around the meeting room.

After an absence of three weeks because of school graduation, Simon returned, on January 26, 1939. He brought his autograph album along and the group therapist's was the first name in it. Evidently he was now beginning to attach himself to the therapist. At this meeting Simon worked industriously and completed a purse for his sister. He said that she had helped him with his school work and he was rewarding her with this gift. Simon soon struck up a friendship with Jack, another boy in the group. Jack was not a client of the agency but came to the group meetings because he was a friend of one of the members. Jack was described as a dull, sensible, good-natured boy with a cheerful disposition, who presented few behavior difficulties. He had many friends outside and was well liked by all the members of the group. Now Jack joined Leon and Simon to form a small, compact subgroup within the larger group. Jack and Simon went together to buy food for the group's refreshments.

When earlier, in October 1938 a new Big Brother was offered him, after an interval of fourteen months in which there was no such relation, Simon found it difficult to accept him. He apparently had not got over his feeling of hurt following the neglect by and separation from his first Big Brother. It took several months before he was able to establish a relationship with the new Big Brother.

He did not confide in his Big Brother. He had to be questioned and prodded. In a report of October 27, 1938, the Big Brother stated: "Simon seems to be a responsive youngster. He is somewhat withdrawn but I feel that through proper attention and stimulation, he can be made to come out of his shell. The boy needs friendship and attention and I shall try my best to supply these needs, to accept him as he is, and to act toward him at a level which will be easy for him to understand."

Simon had difficulty again in his new school, but this was largely due to the principal's attitude. Limited in his capacity and still quite disturbed, Simon was unable to accept this hard, aggressive, and dominating woman. She refused to keep the boy in her school and without the mother's consent transferred him to another school in November 1938. He in turn refused to go, but did so after considerable suasion on the part of the Big Brother, to whom Simon now became attached. The Big Brother, who saw Simon about once a week between October 1938 and June 1939, encouraged the boy and helped him through a number of difficulties at school. Simon in addition attended the group regularly, seldom missing a meeting.

The home situation did not seem to improve much. The mother and sister nagged the boy and he felt a lack of regard for him in the other children in the family. His mother still hit him. The family forcibly broke up a friendship that he had established with a boy of another nationality who lived in the neighborhood. Outside of the home, however, Simon responded well to people. He expressed himself better, and now spoke at length to the Big Brother about himself, his feelings, and his attitude toward the various members of the family. He said that he did not allow himself to be affected by their criticism. The Big Brother took Simon on trips to parks, museums, and other places of interest. The boy visited occasionally in the Big Brother's home and the two played games together, listened to the radio, went to the movies, etc. At times Simon talked to his Big Brother about the activities in his group and once he gave the latter's mother a gift of a leather wallet that he had made in the group.

A neurologic examination at this time definitely established a negative finding, and Simon was described by the physician as a borderline feebleminded boy. Though his work in school was not satisfactory and he was not promoted in February 1939, the principal did not find him to be a behavior problem. He was a sympathetic person and interested Simon in the school newspaper, to which the boy responded with enthusiasm. The principal felt that Simon's poor schoolwork was due to faulty early training, and thought it inadvisable to push him ahead in a junior high school. Another term in the 6B grade was indicated. Simon accepted this failure and displayed renewed interest in schoolwork.

During the ensuing six months Simon's attendance at the group meetings dropped off considerably. While he had attended nearly all meetings in the past, he now came to sixteen out of thirty-seven meetings, but the June 1939 progress report gives conclusive evidence of growth in him. Because of his absences Leon had made other friends in the group, and when Simon returned he found Leon a little distant. He for his part made friends with other boys, especially with Jack. He did incomparably more work with materials and, most important of all, displayed more aggression than he ever had before. On March 16, 1939, he resisted another boy's attempt to dominate him. Simon had a fight at that meeting and his friend Leon said he was sure that the therapist would help Simon with his airplane even if he had had a fight; the therapist would not be "sore" at him for fighting. At another meeting another boy made an unfriendly remark to Simon, and the latter said, "I'll sock you right between where you won't like it!"

While this was meant seriously, the remark was so unusual that all the boys burst into laughter. This angered Simon further, and he challenged the whole group to a fight. Because Leon's friendship with him had diminished, he was thrown more on his own resources and as a result he concentrated more on handicraft work. Simon made such things as little leather purses for his friends, for his sister, and for the Big Brother. He even attempted a complicated airplane model. He became involved in a violent fight with another boy, Bernard, one of the most aggressive boys in the group. The quarrel was a carry-over from an incident earlier in that meeting, when Bernard had snatched a newspaper from Simon's hand. This was the first time that he had had a real fight in the group, and the fracas, according to the report, was quite vicious. In describing it the group therapist said: "Despite the excitement, Simon was sufficiently integrated to maintain his equilibrium throughout the fight."

It was noted that the boy's general appearance and personal habits improved further. He looked more robust, was more outgoing, and displayed an increasing interest in what was going on about him. He no longer withdrew to the anteroom to read magazines by himself. He continued to be extremely cooperative in the group. He had now definitely attached himself to the group therapist and seemed anxious to please him by offering to go down to get food. This cooperativeness extended to other members of the group, who in turn were friendly and accepting of him. He confided to the worker that he had a job in a drugstore, running errands. He frankly announced to the group that he was in an ungraded class, and displayed no shame about this whatever, saying: "Well, I can't help it, and anyhow an ungraded class doesn't mean that you are stupid."

It seemed that Simon accepted the situation.

The Big Brother also reported improvement in the boy. In April 1939, he took Simon to see some warships anchored in the Hudson River. While waiting to be admitted on board the cruiser, the boy conversed with the children and adults in the waiting line. He told stories and jokes and seemed to have a delightful time. After his last contact with Simon in June 1939, the Big Brother said in his report: "I feel that Simon has improved greatly since I have known him. When I met him he seemed to be a serious, withdrawn, and unhappy youngster. Gradually he improved and in the last few months he has seemed more talkative, friendlier and happier." Contact with the Big Brother terminated at this time.

The case worker visited the boy at camp, where Simon was participating in activities and did not seem as lost as in previous years. He was very active in a dramatic group. When he came in conflict with the authorities because of a tiff with another camper, he did not leave the grounds. The camp report dated August 1939 described him as "eager for responsibility, and he liked to work. He worked well on the camp newspaper. He accepted help from the remedial reading teacher and worked very hard in dramatics. A number of members of the staff felt that the boy spent a great deal less time reading this year than he did last year."

Simon was transferred in September 1939, after three years in therapy groups and at the age of fifteen, to a transitional group, in which a transition is made from group therapy to regular club activity. The members of such groups are the more adjusted and socially mature boys and meet in a settlement house or neighborhood center. In this group Simon made progress. At the very first meeting, we find Simon acting in a mature manner and interested in activities involving the opposite sex. In October, girls were present at the meeting, and he talked to them freely. Simon was elected vice president of the club and carried out his functions well. On a trip, when the leader hesitated to permit the boys to ride alone, Simon offered to sign a paper accepting full responsibility for the group. Leon could not help but notice the improvement in Simon and once said: "It's not the Simon I knew."

When at another meeting girls came into the room, the leader noted that "Simon was charming, obliging and solicitous of the girls' comfort. He suggested that they take their coats off if they were warm, and he took it upon himself to act as guide. Simon's pleasing manner seemed attractive to the girls." He showed concern about Leon, who remained distant and sulky, standing close to the leader when the girls were in the room. Simon, on the other hand, proceeded to make a purse for one of the girls, who offered him some candy. Later on, Simon invited Leon to participate in the club work. The girls, before leaving, invited Simon to visit their club. Simon expressed regret that they had to leave and tempted them to remain with the promise of refreshments, but the other boys drove them off. In November, Simon finished an airplane. When there was a general fight, he was the calmest of all the boys. Once when the group was short of food, he offered to go without. He continued to be attentive to the leader, warmly welcomed new members, and freely took part in discussions of the group. Simon invited his brother to a Christmas party at the club in December of that year.

The progress report dated January 3, 1940, comments: "Simon is accepted by the boys but holds no strong position in the club. While he is by and large still on the timid side, he threatened to slap down Irving, a larger boy than himself." On January 5, 1940, a final treatment conference was held. Simon was found to be making a fine adjustment. At school, Simon was in the slow class in the 7A grade, and doing well. He was receiving a great deal of individual attention from the teacher and the class was coeducational. His writing and spelling had improved and he seemed to be participating in the work much better. On Simon's birthday, the boys and girls in his class gave him a surprise party. This pleased him very much.

Simon was concerned about earning money on his own initiative and put up a sign at school announcing that he would clean teachers' cars for fifteen cents a week. He was accepted by the boys in the group, although he seemed no longer to have any close friends. Simon was encouraged to complete a shoeshine box with which he was going into the bootblack business.

At the meeting of April 3, 1940, a suggestion was made by one of the boys that the club should leave the settlement house and meet at its old quarters again. We find Simon strongly defending the idea of remaining at the settlement house, in opposition to some other members, who found it difficult to be weaned from the more secure atmosphere of the former meeting room. A month later Simon, in addition to being vice president of the club, was chosen to represent the group in the house council, which comprises representatives from each club of the settlement house. In September of the same year, the boy was found ready to be transferred to a regular club in a settlement house in his own neighborhood, and the case was closed in the group therapy department.

The case worker, to whom Simon returned for some help with vocational plans, found the boy sufficiently improved to get along without further help from the agency. Simon stated that he was getting along very well; he had found a job as an usher in a movie house, and agreed that he no longer needed the worker's services.

During a follow-up visit to the home in February 1945, both Mrs. H. and a married cousin living with the family spoke about the remarkable improvement that Simon has shown. The boy had been called into the armed services two years before and was then overseas, serving in England and with the Quartermaster Corps. Prior to his induction, Simon had been attending a trade high school, where he had difficulties in grasping the subject matter, in view of his low intelligence. He soon left school and worked as a delivery boy. The employer liked Simon a great deal and the boy kept this job until he was called into the army. He was also getting along well with his mother and siblings. Two of Simon's younger brothers are at present under treatment in the agency and one of them is attending a therapy group. Simon has many friends, some of whom come to visit the family while the boy is overseas. The boy's cousin visited Simon while he was getting training at an army camp and she found him to be more mature, "very much of a man." He liked army life and had many friends among the servicemen. Simon writes home frequently, showing interest in what is happening there. Very recently he spoke in one of his letters of a nice family with whom he has made friends. He mentioned that his mother "might be in for a surprise"—meaning that he may soon get married.

The plans for treatment on an individual basis for this client did not work out because he did not feel the presence of a problem beyond the fact that he did not get along with his family. It was also unsuccessful owing to his low intelligence, his inability to formulate his thinking or understand interpretations. What this client needed was the nurture of love (which was supplied by the second Big Brother, the group therapist, and Leon and Jack) and a growth-producing environment (which he found in the group). This environment would have to permit him to be himself but at the same time provide situations, experiences, and relationships that would help to integrate his emotions and mobilize his powers. Because of the basic rejection in the family, he acted out an infant role and built up grandeur fantasies concerning his father and probably also his mother. This is sometimes described as a preoedipal stage in development. To make a transition from the state of infantile wish fulfillment to a more mature level, he had to relive some of his early relationships on a different plane—a plane that would encourage his being a mature person.

In the group he begins by acting out his infantile patterns. He plays such games as hide-and-seek, runs about aimlessly, reads joke books, and climbs up and down ladders. Thus he becomes the baby of this new family as well, which at the beginning probably pleases him. Indeed, he is referred to by the others as "the baby." However, the attitudes and behavior of other children impress him and he has a desire to become one of them, but they do not accept him, as he is too infantile. He therefore needs to grow up in order to be accepted.

Here we have in operation the principle of "social hunger," namely, the individual's desire to become part of a group and to be accepted by others [53]. Since the nonacceptance is not accompanied by hostile, retaliatory, punitive acts, he can not justify his behavior as retaliation and perceives that he needs to make a change in himself in order to become acceptable. In this, Leon becomes of greatest importance. Leon, though dull and unable to keep up in school, is a more integrated, calmer, and more mature person than Simon. The latter therefore attaches himself to Leon and finds support in him. If Simon is not accepted by the entire group, he is at least accepted by one boy. We also observe that Simon does not attach himself to the therapist until much later in the course of the treatment. Because of his history, it is impossible for him to give up entirely his defenses against adults, especially in a group (family) situation, and it takes a few years before he is able to achieve this. As far as the group is concerned, Leon is the instrument through which Simon can overcome his fear and suspicion of people. Here also the Big Brother is very valuable, but we must note that the basic distrust of adults is abated in Simon through his group experience. He does not relate to his first Big Brother as well as he does to the second. Thus the group experience and his relation with Leon help him to become more accessible to people, and he is able to identify with an adequate male image in the Big Brother and the group therapist. Leon is the "supportive ego" [53]—a factor essential in Activity Group Therapy and probably also in other types of group therapy.

Hostility that becomes diffuse and takes on such form as being annoying at school and quarreling, is acted out in the group. Simon plays cops and robbers and soldiers with guns, and later stabs imaginary persons with spears. The opportunity of finding egress for his hostility, because of the accepting and nonpunitive environment of the group, has great value to this boy. He feels guilt about some of his behavior and fears punishment. When he is able to act out his hostility and aggressions without risking punishment, anxieties diminish. He is now more accessible to positive relationships: the first of these is with Leon, later there are those with Jack, the therapist, and the Big Brother. It is interesting to note in this connection—and this fits in with the principles of Activity Group Therapy—that the supportive ego is a temporary and transitory instrumentality. The child chooses a succession of persons to support him, and usually these are progressively more mature and more integrated individuals. Thus Jack is superior to Leon; though of low intelligence, he is in every respect an average child. Jack therefore serves Simon not only in a supportive capacity but also as a model for himself or as ego-ideal. Later the therapist serves the same ends.

It is toward the end of the second year that Simon displays attachment to the worker. Later he seems to get along with all the children in the group. This movement from individual persons to the group is common in Activity Group Therapy. Each child gradually becomes a part of the group [128]. This is the case with Simon. In the third year he sets the chairs, cleans the room, purchases and prepares food, and in other respects becomes an integral part of the group. He no longer has to draw strength from others; he now has enough strength in himself to navigate in a social milieu that is still friendly and coddling. Such movement indicates inner growth and security and development toward maturity.

We note earlier that Harry, an aggressive boy, frightens Simon. At that time he is still not ready to withstand hostility, but later he not only witnesses aggression with equanimity but fights boys who are more aggressive than he. The boy has now overcome his all-pervasive feeling of weakness and sees himself capable of dealing with reality— an attenuated reality that of course has to be expanded and intensified. This is done through a transitional group [53], and later through his joining the settlement house group. Throughout the group experience, and in his relation to his Big Brother and the school, Simon is testing himself against the outer world. This is epitomized in his learning to ride a bicycle and in his challenging and fighting with fellow members. Bicycle riding is a real achievement to a weak boy with feelings of impotence. We find it an important therapeutic activity. But before this he tests himself against the materials. At first his interests are diffuse and he is unable to make any definite thing. However, he starts work in crafts, likes leather, and, finding himself successful, proceeds to do other things. All of this helps to change his image of himself from that of a helpless, weak person to that of a capable and strong personality.

The changing of the image of the self is perhaps the greatest value in group treatment and probably also in all psychotherapy. Simon has ample opportunity in the group to mobilize strengths. As his image of his own self changes he becomes more aware of his total personality and his looks, so that we find him cleaner, better groomed, and more aware of the appearance he makes. He now has courage, at the age of fifteen, to approach girls. Because of the satisfactions that he has received, he appears more robust and healthier. He makes a better impression and is more accepted by people, which makes it unnecessary for him to attract attention through bizarre and antisocial behavior.

Simon has also shown evidence of increasing insight into his own problem. On a number of occasions he has verbalized his own reactions and compared his state with his previous condition and attitudes. The group therapist makes mention of this when he says: "Simon recognizes his limitations and attempts to compensate for them." The boy speaks freely of his school retardation and admits that he "can't help it." It has been observed in many clients in activity groups in which no discussions of problems are held, that such insight makes its appearance as a concomitant of frustration tolerance and inner strength. Because the individual is now able to face himself as he is, he is also able to view himself as he was, and to see his own motivations. The term *derivative insight* is used to describe this process. Derivative insight connotes an understanding of one's problems arrived at without direct discussion with or interpretation by a therapist.

Capacity to mobilize power, and changing attitudes toward the self, are further tested when Simon begins to earn money by running errands and doing odd jobs in the neighborhood, and later sets himself up in business by making a shoeshine box. He now acts as well as feels mature. His growth is further tested in a club, in which he becomes the leading though not the strongest member, and finally as he participates in the later environment of the settlement house, where he becomes a delegate to the general council.

After treatment is terminated, Simon is able to deal with the reality of school. He faces the fact that he is unequal to the school studies. Acceptance of his limitations was begun in the group when he resigned himself to placement in an ungraded class. Increased frustration tolerance is one of the major criteria of growth [53]. Simon demonstrates growth in accepting his status in school, the lowly occupation of errand boy, and the treatment he receives at the hands of his family.

We cannot underestimate the value of a Big Brother in a case of this nature. A child so deprived of love as our patient was, will gain a great deal from any friendly relation, and after his initial distrust is overcome, he will readily attach himself to people who are kind. The first relationship was not as consistent and meaningful as it might have been. Simon was disappointed by his first Big Brother and when a change was made the emotional rift was painful and distressing. It may have reminded him of his father's death (being abandoned), as well as of the repeated rejections that he had sustained in his relationships with adults, namely, his mother, older sister, principals, and teachers. Thus he finds it difficult to accept his second Big Brother and turns to him only when in serious difficulties at school.

We must note a further factor in the improvement of this client. Even though the family remains still negative, it would seem as though the degree of rejection has been greatly diminished. We find him making a purse for his sister, who has helped him with some school work. He also makes presents for other members of the family. Thus the transition from the good family (the group) to the real family is made.

The mother still remains a rigid, rejecting, hostile person, who is not well disposed toward her son, but it appears that the boy is able to deal with this circumstance much better because of his inner strength. This is observed functionally, but he also verbalizes it to the Big Brother when he says that he does not allow it to affect him too much. Thus we see that the growing strength of a child makes it possible for him to carry pressures much better.

This case demonstrates how trends to serious pathology in a young child, both in personality structure and social adaptation, can be prevented, and existing defects corrected, through strengthening the ego without dealing directly with inner mechanisms. Our present thinking is that this can be achieved only when treatment begins before the onset of adolescence, when the child's character is in the formative stages, his adaptations flexible, and his identifications not as yet too rigidly fixed. Our group treatment was focused on strengthening the child's ego, eliminating perception of weakness or a need to fail, overcoming distrust and suspicion of people, supplying male identification and a growth-inducing environment in which growth could take place in accordance with his evolving personality. On elimination of his basic distrust of and feeling of disappointment in adults, this boy was able to build up ideals through identification with the group therapists and the Big Brother. Thus he acquired a more acceptable individual and group superego.

It is definitely felt that this boy would have become a serious delinquent if he had been permitted to continue as he was at the time of referral, and would possibly have developed more serious pathology.

CHAPTER 41

INDIVIDUAL AND GROUP TREATMENT
OF A PROBLEM BOY
(1939)

This paper[1] describes the nature and results of an experiment in which case and group work techniques were integrated in a treatment plan of a ten-year-old boy. It attempts to show how group experience can complement case work treatment, and how both can be dynamically interrelated in the treatment of behavior problems.

Marvin, age ten, was referred to the clinic by a summer play school, where it was noted that he day dreamed a great deal, was "very absent minded," and did not play with other children. At home the boy was unmanageable, demanding, and constantly behaved in a way calculated to exasperate his mother. There were tantrums of an extreme nature and constant quarrels with a sister two years younger, but physically larger than Marvin. He had no friends and spent almost all of his time at home. At school he did average work, but was unpopular with the other children because of his tendency to annoy and quarrel with them. The case worker found Marvin to be very insecure, with marked feelings of inferiority and unable to relate himself wholesomely either to children or to adults.

---

1. The significance of this paper lies in the fact that it was the first timid effort to present to a professional group the fledgling method of group therapy. The paper was written in cooperation with Mr. Charles Miller, the psychiatric case worker who treated this boy.

The home situation was a destructive one for Marvin. There was a long history of domestic friction. When he was referred for treatment, the parents had been separated for some time and the father came to see the children infrequently. The mother, a tense, neurotic woman, identified the boy with the father and definitely favored the other child. There were indications that Marvin was an unwanted child and had been rejected from the time of birth. The mother's guilt accompanying this rejection had prompted her to greatly overprotect him during his earlier years. He had never played with boys of his own age, and was quite a "sissy." As a result of the many deprivations, his ego structure was very poorly developed.

Through the case work experience, Marvin was able to achieve some measure of security. After a short period of uncertainty, during which he was fearful and strained, he threw himself into the relationship with warmth and affection. He exhibited an intense need for the worker, whom he substituted for his father. Beginning with the infantile patterns which characterized his personality, he was demanding, jealous, and lapsed into fits of anger when frustrated. He would make a scene when he had to go home. He didn't see why the worker ought to give other boys time too. If he lost a checker game he would angrily accuse the worker of cheating and sometimes leave the office. When Marvin did not go into a tantrum, refusal to meet his demands for gifts, movies, or more time, resulted in a babylike whining, crying, and pleading.

As Marvin became aware of the worker's acceptance and slowly became more secure, his need for extreme forms of behavior decreased. The strong attachment to the worker was used to have him give up his infantile patterns, and treatment became a process in which Marvin found it possible to accept increasing limitations and having fewer demands met. There was a gradual diminution of his demands, he would leave the office without complaining, and tantrums were entirely absent.

At the same time that Marvin was being treated, his mother was seen by a worker from a family agency which also handled the general family situation. Financial help and other case work services were rendered. As the mother was able to achieve some insight into her own needs and became aware of her influence upon Marvin's behavior, her criticism and nagging lessened and she was able to give the boy a greater measure of attention and affection. Thus, the improvement in mother and boy operated dynamically to lessen the destructive attitudes toward each other.

Throughout the period of case work treatment, however, Marvin continued to be unable to make friends or to enter into any kind of group situation. After eight months of treatment, he made a poor adjustment at camp. His lack of group experience, his inferiorities, both real and imagined and his insecurity in any relationship in which he was not *completely* accpeted, made any group or competitive situation intolerable. An experimental tour of a settlement house precipitated marked regression. He became depressed, and appeared physically ill, turned pale, seemed unable to walk, and had to sit down to rest. Although Marvin had been able to give up his more extreme symptoms because of the security he felt with the worker, he was as yet unable to test out this new security in any kind of social situation.

While it was felt that case work treatment over an extended period would benefit the boy, the availability of a therapy group prompted the decision to refer him there. Such a group provided a social situation in which there was a minimum of control and flexibility. It was thought that Marvin might be able to utilize and develop the security he had achieved with the case worker, and that the group was so organized as to make it possible for him to test out his insecurities without too great fear of rejection.

After ten months of treatment, Marvin began to express his unhappiness about lack of friends and the subject of the group was then brought up. At first he refused to entertain the idea, but after a period of indecision and fear, he agreed to make the effort to please the worker.

The Department of Group Therapy was added to the clinical facilities of the Jewish Board of Guardians to meet a need long felt by case workers. It is based upon four fundamental principles, and organized to meet four corresponding needs in children. These are: (1) the need for acceptance (love); (2) the need for ego satisfaction; (3) the need for creative activity; (4) the need for social reeducation. The "meetings" consist of work with various materials through which the creative interests of the individual child can be satisfied. He is entirely free to do whatever he likes. If he does not desire to work, he can be idle, observe others at work, play, or he may be destructive. As a result, many small subgroups spring up where boys (or girls) work together on a common project; help one another out with jobs; instruct each other; or converse about school, teachers, movies and other subjects of common interest. Gradually, though this takes a long time, the members learn that they must clean up the mess they have created in the room, set the table for refreshments, cook and serve the food—for every session ends with a light repast—and wash and put away the dishes. For a time the "group worker" does this, until the members of the group realize they can be helpful. Frequent trips to places of interest, picnics and outings form a part of the activities of therapy groups. After an evaluation of this work over a five year period, it was found that these simple, informal relationships, resembling those of a good family, make for changes in the children's attitudes toward the group and later toward the world generally.

The groups serve those children who are difficult to reach in the interview situation and who primarily require an attenuated socializing experience. It also provides this experience for children who cannot be absorbed into ordinary groups because of their personality difficulties, ranging from extreme withdrawal to overaggressiveness. Groups are limited to eight members and are organized on the basis of treatment needs, personality, age, and place of residence. Referral is made from the intake desk or by the agency's case workers. In addition to the detailed summary which is sent at time of referral, conferences are held by the case worker with the director of the department. The child may be invited directly through the group, or may be taken by the case worker. The trained group therapist, who supervises each group, is aware of each child's history and difficulties. Control and direction in the group are motivated entirely by case work considerations. Both group and individual records are kept, the latter being sent to the case worker and filed in the case record. The group therapist and the director of the department hold regular conferences with the case workers and supervisors for the purpose of evaluation and further planning. When necessary, a staff psychiatrist is called in to these conferences. Conferences may be called either by the case worker or the director of group therapy, depending upon the situation.

In the case under discussion, it was decided to hold regular and frequent conferences at which were present the case worker, the group therapist, and the director of group therapy.[2] Developments in both the case and group situations were followed closely and discussed in detail; the case and group work thinking was integrated and used as the basis for further planning. A detailed summary of each integration conference was filed in both records.

Marvin's group was composed of seven boys of approximately the same age. At first Marvin was very withdrawn, particularly in the presence of a large number of boys. He looked sad and forlorn and did not participate in conversations or activities. He was fearful of the group, and was less tense only when fewer boys were present. As he slowly learned that no pressure was to be put upon him and there was no threat of competitive activity, his withdrawal after a few weeks turned into very aggressive and overboisterous behavior. His favorite occupation was to stride over a boy and pretend to be riding him. He screamed and shouted, ran wildly around the building, chasing other children, or activating them to chase him.

Marvin attempted to monopolize the group worker as he did the case worker. When trips were taken, he would stay near the worker and try to keep the other boys away. At the indoor "meetings" he would constantly draw attention to himself and block, often through violence, other boys from getting close to the worker. Careful but firm attempts were made to prevent too close an attachment, both because of the boy's own need for independence and because of the negative effect upon the other members of the group.

As Marvin slowly became more secure and found that his aggressions were being accepted, he became the most aggressive individual in the group. If all the others decided on one place to go he would insist upon another. Group pressure, however, frequently compelled him to compromise or to give way to the wishes of the majority. An important factor in this progressive development was a rather strong attachment which Marvin formed with another boy, who was usually able to overcome his stubbornness by putting an arm around his shoulder and pleading with him on the basis of friendship and group spirit.[3] Marvin would melt under such demonstrations.

2. The director also supervised the group therapists weekly on the basis of extensive protocol reports of the group's and therapists' conduct and activities.

3. I later identified this as "supportive ego."

The following is abstracted from the record of the integration conference held two months after Marvin joined the group:

> Group worker reports that Marvin tried to monopolize him. Resents attention to other boys. Always opposes group decisions, accepting them finally with poor grace. Always tries to gain attention of boys and worker by unusual behavior. He is a poor sport. However, he is friendly with one boy, and shows good sportsmanship in relations with him. Still very insecure. Unable to join in any activity. Sometimes aggressively challenges boys to fight, but retreats when challenge is accepted. On the whole, he is a disruptive element. At first very withdrawn, he is now a boisterous obstructionist and other boys dislike him.
>
> Case worker feels Marvin is repeating pattern seen in case work situation. Makes efforts only on basis of security with father person. Group worker will have to meet boys' need as far as possible for time being. Competitive situations to be avoided. M. is enthusiastic about group worker, feels disloyal, becomes guilty, and protests greater affection for case worker. Note that Marvin can establish relationship with another adult and with one boy. Director points out that Marvin's extreme behavior is result of complete freedom in group. It is a testing period. He cannot believe that anything but infantile behavior will get him attention he needs. Only on basis of actual experience will he learn otherwise.

To a considerable extent Marvin was able to compensate for his feelings of inferiority and rejection by taking a leading part in the preparation and serving of refreshments at each meeting. He would cook, set the table and serve the food, ordering the others around as they helped him. The time came when he was able to go out with another boy and buy food, something which he had been afraid to do before.

A pivotal treatment situation in the group was a party which Marvin arranged for his sister, who represented an important aspect of the boy's difficulties. Although younger than Marvin, she was physically larger, tyrannized him, and took advantage of her superior position in the home. When her birthday came, he decided to give her a party at *his* "club." The party was given with a great deal of ceremony and preparation, and for once Marvin was complete master of the situation. Although his sister attempted to make fun of him and correct his behavior, he paid little attention to her and derived a tremendous amount of satisfaction from being in the superior position.

In the early period of his membership in the group, Marvin was unable to lose a game or accept any defeat without becoming terribly upset and uncontrollably hostile. He would not only scream that he had been cheated, but actually attack his opponent physically. As time went on, however, he noticed that other boys accepted defeat without much ado, that nobody seemed to feel it was a loss of prestige and, he too, began to accept defeat with more equanimity.

After Marvin had been in treatment for twenty-one months, the latter nine months of which he had been a member of the group, changes began to be evident in the boy's personality. He was no longer apprehensive, did not have alternate periods of hostility and fright, was able to play with other boys, had made friends and did not have an outstanding need to make bids for special attention. He no longer attached himself exclusively to the group worker and was able to go home alone or with other members of the group. The mother reported his considerable improvement at home, with complete disappearance of the more extreme forms of behavior. At school it was learned that Marvin was a likeable, helpful youngster with lots of class spirit and with no indications of withdrawal or unpopularity. Perhaps the most interesting indication of growth was the camp report made by a case worker. This reported stated that, while Marvin continued to have a need for special attention and was called a "sissy" by some boys, he finally won the respect of the group by his efforts, made friends, was accepted as an integral part of his bungalow group, entered into activities and generally enjoyed his vacation. It was also found that the boy's bids for special attention, which were consistently rejected, did not result in any kind of negative behavior. When he returned from camp in the fall of 1938, he registered by himself at a neighborhood house and began to question the necessity for his continuance with the case worker and in the group. He was much freer in asserting himself; was able to greet and speak with people spontaneously, and even went out of his way to meet some people whom he wanted to know. All these changes were evident in the case work relationship, where they were recognized and fostered.

After Marvin had gone to camp, and had been in the therapy group for one year, the integration conference brought out the following material:

> Group worker reports that Marvin is now able to participate in various creative activities. He was thrilled when he finished a key case, the first thing he had ever made. He is much better integrated into the group. He enters competitive situations with fair success. Although never on a bicycle, he insisted on learning when this was the day's activity. The other boys rode well, Marvin was very happy and boastful about his progress. Worker never saw a boy so genuinely happy. Marvin accepts group decisions, and has given up his more extreme behavior. He seems more secure, and has less need to gain attention in an infantile way. He is quite friendly with some of the boys.
>
> Case worker suggests that Marvin be encouraged to try as many activities as possible. Boy is completely inexperienced in masculine activities. It was decided to have athletic activities when it becomes warmer.
>
> Case worker says Marvin is beginning to question necessity for regular interviews, but becomes very guilty. Although beginning to assert himself, he still fears his drive to be outgoing and aggressive. He is beginning to separate from worker. He is much more able to accept frustrations and limitations. He joined settlement house on own initiative. General improvement in school and home is noted by the case worker.

Throughout the time that Marvin attended the group, he was seen regularly by the case worker. He was given the opportunity to express his doubts, fears and insecurity regarding the group, and on the basis of the encouragement and support which he received, was able to continue to make further effort. Many of the patterns he developed in the group situation were carried over into the case work relationship and were accepted and handled there. Each successful effort was met with praise and encouragement, and failures with noncritical acceptance.

When Marvin was going through a period of extreme aggressiveness in the group, his manner in the interviews was that of a "tough guy." For the first time he used profane language, tried to bully the case worker with threats and attempted to impress him with a hard-boiled exterior. He would furtively watch how this was being received and learned that he could test his attempts at aggressiveness without fear of rejection.

After much indecision, Marvin finally was able to make a key case in the group. Characteristically, he belittled his effort and expressed dissatisfaction with it. He felt he could never make anything worth-while. The case worker praised the key case, said he wished he had one like it and Marvin surprised the worker by making one for him. In the boy's presence it was shown to several people, all of whom expressed admiration. Marvin was quite overcome; he felt that perhaps he did have some ability and, in a few weeks, had made a number of other objects. It was no longer necessary for him to feel inferior to the other boys in this respect, and he gained the feeling of adequacy and achievement on the basis of actual experience. In this and other ways were his efforts crystallized and furthered in the case work situation.

Marvin was able to achieve initial growth in the case work situation and to develop enough strength to make further effort, as evidenced by his ability to join a group. The group provided a nonthreatening, accepting environment in which the boy could test out his new-found strength and his repressed drive for aggressiveness and independence. Contrasted with the home situation where the boy was rejected, inferior, threatened, and wanting to be a baby and a girl, the group situation provided a masculine environment in which growing up did not represent rejection and loss of love. At the same time, the case work relationship provided the necessary stabilizing and supporting influence which the boy used as a basis for growth.

CHAPTER 42

JEAN CASE: A CASE HISTORY
(1951)

Miss Headley: Jean Case was the ninth child in a family of ten. She was referred to Community Service Society when she was thirteen years old, because she was a school behavior problem. Jean cut classes, was rude to teachers, and seemed lacking in respect for school discipline and authority. She made herself conspicuous in the classroom by her behavior, was defiant, fought in class with other children and with teachers. When given the starring role in an operetta, Jean was exhibitionistic, behaved like a prima donna, and was quite uncontrollable. The school felt Jean had a good intellect, but was not functioning up to capacity.

Jean was a large, well-built girl. She was conscious of her height, as she stands five feet, seven inches, in her stocking feet. The rest of her family was comparatively short. Jean had an attractive smile and a nice personality. She was not neat, and because of family finances her clothing was generally shabby and worn. She was quite verbal and read a great deal. She had an excellent singing voice.

Study conducted at the Community Service Society of New York, and in collaboration with Hanna Grunwald, Ph.D., group therapist; Dorothy Headley, case worker; Rutherford B. Stevens, M.D., staff psychiatrist. S. R. Slavson, supervisor and consultant in group therapy. For case studies in other settings, see [48, 49, 53, 55, 57, 59, 64].

The Case family came to New York from the South. The Community Service Society knew this family intermittently for about fifteen years because of grave financial and management problems, the illegitimate pregnancy of May, one of Jean's older sisters. James, thirty-five, Helen, thirty-three, and Edith, thirty-one, the oldest of the Case children, have been out of the home for some time. May, twenty-seven, and the oldest girl living with the family, had two out-of-wedlock children by two diferent men and was married just before Jean's coming for treatment. Tony, twenty-five, served in the CCC and the U.S. Army. He worked irregularly since his discharge and appeared to be an emotionally unstable, irresponsible person. Fred, twenty-one, lived in the South with his maternal grandparents until the age of sixteen and a half, when he insisted on coming to New York. He appeared much more stable and responsible in relation to employment. Henry, twenty, served a prison sentence of two and a half years for a gang involvement. Since that time, he has been in and out of the home, and has worked irregularly. Margaret, nineteen, suffered from tuberculosis and was hospitalized for over a year and recently had a relapse. Peter, fourteen, the youngest, had an enlarged heart and club feet and spent much of his time attending different clinics. He was the only one of the children Mrs. Case seems concerned about.

Mr. Case was a laborer, earning very little. Shortly before Jean's coming for treatment he had obtained a job through the Department of Welfare as a watchman. The children and Mrs. Case seemed to have little respect for him and he was described as an inadequate, ailing, prematurely senile person. At one time, Jean had been his favorite but now he considered her "too fresh." Jean believed her father favored May while he was hard on Jean for fear that she too might get into the same kind of difficulty as did May. Mrs. Case, on the other hand, felt that her husband was not at all strict, and was completely ignored as a father by all the children, especially Jean. Mrs. Case, too, actually gave him little consideration.

Mrs. Case is an unemotional, martyrlike woman. She is an only child and speaks of her mother with great admiration. While Jean was in camp, Mrs. Case went to visit her family in the South, where she remained for three months. At this time, Mrs. Case was seriously contemplating not returning to New York. This was an extremely difficult and frightening experience for Jean, who had been in conflict with her father. She resented his excessive drinking and felt he should be able to provide more adequately for his family. She felt quite unprotected by him when the mother was out of the home. During that period, Mr. Case was depressed about being unemployed and drank heavily. According to Jean, Mr. Case would sit all day at the window, weeping and waiting for his unemployment check, while Tony, the twenty-six-year-old, sat at another window reading "True Story Magazines." Neither attempted to find work. Margaret, the tubercular girl, returned home from the hospital and tried to dominate Jean. She said that May's children were driving her mad. Jean had no privacy as she shared a room, first with Peter and then with Margaret.

The individual case work contact with Jean did not go well. She came to the office infrequently. Her technique was to run to meet trouble. For example, when Mrs. Case had threatened her with placement because of her poor adjustment in school, Jean went looking for the Children's Court in order to tell her story. In protest to school discipline, she sent the principal a strongly worded letter, stating that the teachers were more interested in their pay checks than in the children. In interviews with the case worker, Jean employed a similar technique, warding off any real discussion and examination of her feelings.

Jean seemed lost in the bigness of the family. She craved love and affection but used unsuitable methods of securing these. Her aggressiveness and pugnacity were self-defeating. Suspicious of adults, Jean was resistive to individual treatment. Because she was verbal and we felt that she would be able to make ready contacts with other adolescents, she was referred to an activity therapy group. When this was done, she immediately broke off contact with the caseworker.

Dr. Stevens: From the psychiatric viewpoint, the information we have so far about Jean is inadequate for making a structural and dynamic evaluation of her personality. We have a general description of Jean, of her family setting, and of her present behavior. We have no data concerning Jean's adjustment to the requirements of infancy and childhood. From what we know of her family, we can assume that she was deprived of the affection and feeling of security which is necessary for normal development. Her detached, rejecting mother, weak alcoholic father, and maladjusted older siblings did not provide her with a good example in reacting to the environment. It would be most surprising, if with this background Jean had developed good ego strength and satisfactory defenses against the stresses she encountered in growing up.

Although we have no clear picture of the specific emotional stresses suffered by Jean, we do know something of how she reacted to them. Her personality is characterized by aggressiveness, with her behavior at times being uncontrollable. She is defiant and rude to teachers, distrusts adults, truants from school and shows a lack of respect for authority and lacks discipline. She also behaves aggressively toward other children.

There is little evidence that she has ever learned to form lasting positive relationships. She was once her father's favorite, but he rejected her when he felt she had become fresh and forward. She believes he is harsh with her because he fears she will become pregnant like her sister, and seems to feel unprotected from him when her mother is away. She feels closest to her mother, but senses her mother's immaturity and is protective of her. She is resentful of the time and attention her mother gives to her sickly younger brother.

Summarizing, we have an intelligent and verbal adolescent girl who had suffered throughout life from emotional and socioeconomic deprivation while lost in a large maladjusted family. She has responded to a chronic state of emotional deprivation with a chronic aggressive reaction. She is emotionally disturbed, functions below her intellectual capacity, does not form positive relationships with others, and behaves aggressively to all about her.

Mr. Slavson: In accepting Jean for group treatment we have taken some risks. At the stage at which she was referred to us she appeared to be a primary behavior disorder, preoedipal, conduct type, which is characterized by inadequate superego formation and weak ego development. It also appeared that she was functioning on a pregenital level. Such characteristics permit the individual to act out with no or little restraint, which may prove detrimental to other persons involved. If such a patient continues to act out with the same violence that Jean had displayed at home and in school, the group would not be able to absorb her, for as I have pointed out elsewhere, the intensity of aggression and hostility density that a group can absorb is limited, and a girl like Jean may raise these to a level higher than the group could tolerate.

There were, however, some positive indications as well for placing her in a group. She was a member of a large family and of necessity had to adjust herself to other persons and function under some sort of limitations. She had social hunger: she craved affection though she employed self-defeating means of obtaining it.

Another positive indication was the satisfactory primary relation with her father who she felt had liked her in the past. It was disappointment in this relation as well as an inadequate mother and hostile older siblings that made her distrustful of people. The disappointment in her father had a neurotic quality which indicated some degree of a superego formation which would make her aware of the unacceptability and inappropriateness of her behavior in a group.

A consistent relationship with a warm, understanding individual is the focus of treatment in a case like Jean's, but because of her distrust of, and antagonism to, adults she was unable to establish such a relation with an individual therapist. Because of this inability to develop a transference, a group was indicated, for in groups the transference is diluted. Patients can establish varying kinds of relationships with persons other than the therapist, namely, the other members of the group. These multiple transferences decrease the fear of a close personal relation.

If we can create a setting where Jean can abreact to her frustrations without activating guilt and fear, Jean's ego would be strengthened and her self-image improved. These developments would, in turn, help her bring her impulsive actions under control and establish abilities to relate to others constructively. She would grow less dependent and could then give up her self-defeating pattern.

Mrs. Grunwald: Jean was referred for group therapy and joined the group at its fifth session. She was introduced to the girls along with another new member. During the first session she was quite shy, did not talk to anyone, and only toward the end of the session did she display an interest in the way the other girls discussed camp problems. She was afraid that having become a member of the group might mean she would have to go to a camp and was relieved to learn from the other girls that this was not the case.

At her second session, Jean raised her hand and said: "Teacher, may I go to the bathroom?" The girls laughed and told her she was not in school and if she had to go to the bathroom she could do so without asking permission. Jean left the room with another girl and returned after some time, giggling. She was enthusiastic during refreshment period because there was cake which the therapist had baked for the girls. She grabbed the leftovers. All of a sudden she became serious and told a fantasy story about her sister having died, leaving two little children for whom she, Jean, had the total responsibility. She stood up, picked up a plate and smashed it on the floor. She then looked for a broom, but gave this up and rushed to the window. Seeing some passengers standing on the railroad station nearby, she shouted to them. She abruptly stopped when she noticed the doll house and eagerly started to play with it.

When I told the girls, during this session, that because of the holiday, there would be no meeting for two weeks, Jean pounded the therapist's desk with her fist yelling: "We will meet next week; we will meet next week!" The time was changed to another day of the following week. When leaving Jean said: "Oh, if it was only next week!"

During her third session, Jean behaved in quite an uncontrolled way. She played with the doll house for quite a long time. She again opened the window and shouted at passers-by. After the refreshments she took the leftover milk home with her. The elevator man complained about her disturbing behavior in the halls.

When Jean came to the next session, she said to me, in a friendly way: "My mother thanks you for the milk." Some of the girls were painting. Jean took a brush and painted a girl's arm with bright colors and when this girl reproached her, she started to sing in a loud voice as though to drown out the complaint: "You hurt my feelings." During this and the three following sessions, Jean constantly disrupted the games of the other children. She was quiet only when she was playing with the doll house. It was during her seventh session that two of the girls who went out to buy refreshments refused to take Jean along. They said they did not mind Jean's giggling so much in the "club," but they would feel embarrassed to go to the store with her. "All right," said Jean, "next time I'll be quieter and then you'll take me." It was during this refreshment period that Jen was yelling for the biggest piece of cake, but did not take the biggest one. During this session Jean talked about her birthday wishes. She wanted a beautiful, wonderful spring outfit, directly from Paris, and champagne. When the girls asked her if she were only joking or if she was crazy, she added in a warm voice, "Mrs. Grunwald, I would like to have eight quarts of milk." Toward the end of this session, when Jean had emptied her ice cream container, a little boy opened our door by mistake. Jean showed the empty container to him and said: "Come here, you'll have some ice cream." The boy ran away and Jean again sang: "You hurt my feelings."

Jean's behavior worsened until at the seventh session, when she was singing and shouting at the window, one of the girls said to her: "Jean, stop this, CSS will get in trouble." From this time on, Jean did not shout or sing through the open window. She rather busied herself with the doll house. She smashed the father doll on the floor. She then asked help with her problems. They did not have a sufficient number of rooms. "You know why mother didn't want to change to another house? Because she didn't want to have more children." Once Jean was looking for the father figure and found him under the bed. She pretended she was reviving him and said that she is an artist in reviving. When another girl attempted to touch the doll house, Jean slapped her.

At the tenth session the girls discussed part-time jobs. Jean hoped to get a part-time job in a store and the girls wondered if she was interested in stealing. Jean said: "No, I do not feature stealing," and told a story about two girls in the neighborhood who went shoplifting and how severely they were punished. She seemed to be horrified by this incident. The girls started to discuss stealing, but Jean made it impossible for them to talk. She was jumping around the small room, banging with her fists against the door. Suddenly she turned around, cleared the table, cleaned the dishes, swept the floor and said: "Never say that I did not do anything for you, Mrs. Grunwald. Or how would you feel if I would say 'Baby' to you?"

Up to this point the sessions were held in the therapist's small office. At the tenth session we discussed moving into a larger room. Jean's immediate reaction to it was that she did not mind if we would go to another room if she could take the doll house with her. She did not, however, ask for the doll house during the early sessions in the new room. Jean was pleased with the materials. Until then, we had worked in an office that was too small and not really equipped to meet the needs of an activity group. Jean was the first to introduce the monopoly game in the group. She took over the bank, but often disobeyed the rules of the game. When the girls resented it, she tied this up with her school difficulties by saying: "Well, I will need your help also in school. I have troubles in school. It runs ahead of me." When playing ping-pong, one of the balls struck the therapist. Jean apologized and said again: "Mrs. Grunwald, I'll need your help in school." When she came to her eleventh session, Jean with pride in her voice announced that "this week everything was fine in school." The girls shouted "congratulations!" At the end of this session, Jean smashed a jar of paint. The whole place was in a mess. She made some vague effort to clean up, but did not finish. The therapist cleaned up the mess and then continued cleaning the dishes. Jean, when leaving said: "Mrs. Grunwald, you are never angry when you are washing dishes."

At the next session Jean sought the group's advice in connection with a school collection for needy children in Europe. When one of the girls said she planned to work as a junior counselor in a camp, Jean said she too would like to have a similar job. She certainly would have to behave differently than the way she does now, but, looking around said: "Here I just love it!"

Jean continued to play monopoly, pickup sticks, jackass, and ping-pong with the other girls. Once a girl offered to play Chinese checkers with her. When she had some difficulty in learning the rules, she gave up immediately and said she swears she will never touch such a game again where she has to think and is also not too sure of winning. She became extremely restless and chased up and down the room.

During this period Jean developed a friendship with Winnie. When Winnie asked me to teach her how to knit, Jean did the same. She learned very fast and was pleased with her work. While knitting she was sitting near Winnie and they discussed their parents. Winnie lived in the home of her grandmother. She complained that she is not permitted to listen to the radio. When she turns on some blues or some other songs her grandmother turns off the radio. Jean said that her mother does the same thing. She can only listen to the radio when her mother goes to the bathroom. "Thank God, she goes to the bathroom often." And when father is back, he listens to his favorite, and his favorite is the Lone Ranger. Winnie was humming the melody from the Lone Ranger and thought it was silly that a grown-up man likes to listen to such silly boy stuff. "Oh these fathers," Jean said. Both girls repeated these words for a rather long time, banging with their fists on the table and working out a kind of rhythm in which they repeated "Oh, these fathers, oh, these fathers." Winnie was very musical and later studied music.

During the fourteenth session Jean mentioned that she had started music lessons in her church; she likes the music teacher, because his eighteen-year-old son was "very beautiful."

After this session Jean was considerably more restrained during the refreshment period. It was during her sixteenth session that she addressed the therapist thus: "Mrs. Grunwald, I do not want to spoil your appetite, but it is true. I have a boyfriend, and the boyfriend went out with me last Saturday and bought me franks, popcorn and soda and pickles, and when I came home, I had the feeling as if the pickle was in my nose and I threw it all up." The girls got angry and complained that she really would spoil their appetites. "Well," said Jean, "I will stop talking about it, but, Mrs. Grunwald," she repeated, "it is true, I have a boyfriend." I told her that I had understood so. "But my mother," Jean said, "she had the nerve to wake me up this morning and guess at what time, at 6:30 in the morning. She woke me up, because I was so noisy in my sleep. I had a funny kind of a dream." Jean dramatized the dream. It went approximately like this. "There was a big wedding going on in our house. I married my sister's boyfriend. My sister married my boyfriend and my other sister got married again to her husband. Now, mother was at a loss where we could sleep with our husbands. She divided my room into a room for me and my husband, and into a library, and she put my other sister with her husband into my brother's room; but my brother came, he looked around the house and said there was only room for him to sleep in the library. He said something funny to me, which I do not remember about his having no space to sleep. And I laughed and laughed so loud, that my mother got upset and woke me up. She asked what happened in my sleep but I didn't tell her."

During the nineteenth session the girls discussed the bad housing conditions in Harlem. When Jean made a silly remark and one of the girls laughed about it, Jean said, "Why are you laughing? This is not only serious but it is tragic." The girls laughed, saying Jean seemed to mean it is tragic, but the way she was talking, it sounded funny. Jean said with tears in her eyes, that it is awful, that really very often, when she means to say something seriously, she talks in a funny way, and then people just do not believe her that it is serious. "But we know it," the girls reassured her, "although we were laughing." "That's how God made me," Jean said. The girls told her that certainly God did not make her that way, and that she could certainly change. Jean said she really tries very hard. The girls told her that they can see it, and Jean seemed very relieved.

During the next session, Jean told the girls, full of pride, that she had been admitted to high school. That day she had received her report card. Last time she got "C" in conduct and effort, and she really should have had an "F." This time, what did she get? "B plus" for conduct and effort. The girls said that was fine, but she does not earn a "B plus" at the "meetings here." Jean laughed, lifted a chair and asked whom should she beat with the chair. She was approaching a very fearful and withdrawn girl who became very scared. The therapist walked over and sat down at her side. "Mrs. Grunwald, you don't want me to hit you?" Jean said laughingly and pushed the chair aside.

At one of the sessions the girls found in the office a pad with the agency's intake forms. They had a heated discussion about the column "color." I discussed this problem quite directly with them. They then sat down and filled out the forms. Jean was quite eager to do so and told me that CSS should get new forms with much more space in the column "children" so that they could have more children. "And, do not forget, they really should leave out the column for 'color,'" she added.

During one of the last sessions before summer vacation, it was very warm, and Jean became extremely restless. I suggested that we go out for a walk and have a snack in the luncheonette. This was the first time that we went out and Jean seemed to enjoy it, but she was anxious to know before she left that next time we would be back in our room.

During the next session, the twentieth, we discussed an outing to Coney Island. While discussing it, Jean shouted: "Mrs. Grunwald, will you be so mean as not to allow me to bring my sister with me?" The other girls worked this problem out with Jean. One girl asked: "How would you like it, if I brought my brother?" Another said: How would you like it, if I brought my three sisters?" Jean said: "All right, I will not bring my sister; but, Mrs. Grunwald, it's mean anyhow." The day of the outing to Coney Island, Jean had a high temperature and had to stay in bed for four days. This was the only time she missed a group session.

When she came next time she was still quite weak and her sister came to look for her. They were worried about Jean at home. Although she had not yet been allowed to leave the house, she had run away in order not to miss her "club." She was unhappy when she learned that the club would be closed during vacation.

Miss Headley: After entering the group, Jean's contact with the caseworker lessened even more. For several months she was seen only three times and then around specific requests for concrete matters such as buying clothes and other financial problems. It was clear that the group was important to her and even the requests she brought to the individual contact emerged from discussion with other girls in the group. On the afternood when the group met, Jean could be seen walking up and down the halls. She seemed happier, would briefly greet the case worker and generally remark about how much she loved the "club."

Mrs. Case was somewhat puzzled about not receiving negative reports from school on Jean; so she visited the school. She learned that Jean was improving in her attitude toward teachers as well as toward her fellow students. The school report during this period from the vocational counselor was almost ecstatic. She felt that of all the girls in the school who had case workers, Jean's behavior and attitudes had altered most markedly. Before Jean attended the group, she used to go around the school building looking sullen and sour, but now appeared much happier and more relaxed. Jean had participated in a talent scout show at school where she won second prize for her singing. To the teacher's amazement, Jean admitted that the first prize winner had a better voice than herself. While Jean did not react as immaturely to this failure as she had in similar situations in the past, she could not quite sustain this frustration, for on returning to her classroom she reverted to insulting her teacher. However, she soon recovered from this setback and seemed to have developed a new pride in her good singing voice and was now accepted as a full member of the glee club at school from which she was excluded before because of misbehavior and general disobedience. The school reported that she now cooperated with the other members of the glee club and was a member in regular attendance.

Another report from school requested by the caseworker revealed again that Jean's conduct had continued to improve; Jean was now displaying an interest in attending a high school that specializes in music. Because of her general improvement and on recommendation of the elementary school, she was accepted in this special high school. Acceptance in such a school connotes special recognition and superior ability.

Mrs. Case was seen regularly to discuss the financial and health problems of the family. She reported that Jean constantly talked of her "club" and frequently stated that she would "die" if she had to miss a meeting of the "club." Mrs. Case in her characteristic manner was indifferent concerning Jean's attendance in the therapy group and had neither encouraged nor interfered with her attendance.

Mr. Slavson: As expected, Jean at first acted out with little restraint her infantile impulsiveness and abreacted to pressures in her life. She was aggressive toward the girls as individuals, challenged the group as a whole and occasionally verbally attacked the therapist. In time, we see her gradually bringing herself under control.

The first step in this direction was when the girls brought home to her the undesirability of her behavior and refused to take her along to buy food. Jean promised that she would be quiet in the future so that she could join them in this activity. When disapproval by her peers came to grips with her social hunger, she backed down. This was the first important step in strengthening her ego and self-control.

Of further significance is Jean's bringing to the surface her hostility toward her father and mother in the play with the doll house. Especially important is her unrestrained destruction of the father figure. Guilt is allayed in this homicidal intent by the support of

Winnie, who, too, was abandoned by her father. Both girls speak of fathers derogatorily, discharge their aggressions by banging on the table with their fists and chanting: "Oh, those fathers, oh those fathers."

When such feelings can be revealed without fear of punishment or disapproval, the ego energies that hold the hostile impulses in repression are freed and utilized for dealing with inner impulses and outer reality. The fact that the therapist and the other members of the group consistently accepted her and were happy about her success in school changed Jean's image of herself and gave her self-confidence in the possibilities of her own growth. This is well illustrated by her deciding to work as a junior counselor in the summer. A change in self-image also results in a strengthened ego.

The factor of libido recanalization also occurred here. Jean's libido attachment to her father was freed when she transferred it to the group and to the therapist in a normal homoerotic fashion. This freed libido is utilized as well by the psyche for integration and growth.

The therapist notes that after the session when hostility toward her father was freely expressed, Jean's behavior had become more restrained. She was now able to mobilize her energies to make use of her special talent, her singing voice. She also became interested in a boy. This process is one of libido displacement from her father to another male—another step in maturity. Having been freed from her infantile tie to her father, she is now able to transfer her interest to a boy but the neurotic conflict now makes its first overt appearance when after eating, she feels the pickle in her nose and vomits as a result. The sexual confusion from which Jean suffers is dramatized in her dream. It is interesting that her father does not appear in the dream but other men in a confusing kaleidoscope now take his place. She is still unclear about, or is afraid of, her own role in relation to a specific man. But she later accepts more her role as a woman when she suggests that the agency provide more space for names so that "we can have more children."

Jean's growing insight is demonstrated when she speaks at the nineteenth session of being unable to convey the seriousness of her intention. The principle of *derivative insight* operates here. Despite the fact that no interpretation was given, she becomes aware of her behavior and its effects and displays objectivity toward herself. This is another step in the direction of emotional maturity.

Jean's social awareness is also increasing. She confesses her horror at the idea of stealing which indicates a degree of superego development. She is concerned with the effects of inadequate housing in her neighborhood. Later she accepts the group's point that it would be unfair for her to bring her sister on an outing. These are only three nodal points in this development. Interspersed between these are many more evidences of her growing social awareness.

Of no small value which, of necessity cannot be brought out in a brief summary such as this, is Jean's relation with Winnie. Winnie, who was, but is not now, in every respect a mature, more wholesome and better integrated girl, served as Jean's *supportive ego*. Winnie was probably the first person, except for her father, to whom Jean had become strongly attached. We can speculate that the bond between these two girls was their disappointment in their fathers and the fact that both had unusually good singing voices. Winnie helps diminish Jean's guilt and anxiety. At the same time she serves as a pattern for identification and helps Jean gradually to bring herself under control. One of the concrete evidences of this was Jean's undertaking to study music which was Winnie's central interest.

Throughout we see the unmistakable integration of the psychic forces in our patient. Her impulses are now under greater control of the ego. Her libido is detached from the infantile object, her father, to boys in her own group. Her ego is also able to mobilize energies to pursue a special interest and to attempt to get a job. Her self-centeredness is unmistakably transformed to object relations and social interests in the therapy group and in the community.

Mr. Slavson: The observed changes in Jean's personality have continued during this period. Despite occasional regression there is growth evident in her character integration. She is more self-controlled, has a better grasp of reality and is emotionally more mature. The change is observed even by the elevator man who, as we recall, complained in the beginning about her boisterous and disruptive behavior.

As Jean's psychic energies become less preoccupied with herself, they move out in a centrifugal direction. This is demonstrated by her awareness of the conditions of the neighborhood in which she lives when she describes them to the therapist on their trip, and the reactions to her teacher whom she sees as having little awareness of the economic and social factors operating in the neighborhood.

Jean's oedipal involvement with her father has now been reactivated as is to be expected in normal adolescent development, and this is expressed in a dramatic dance and in rhythmic choral singing. Perhaps it is worthwhile to underscore this phenomenon, that is, dramatic acting out. This form of expression has never occurred in any other group in our experience, and can be attributed here to cultural and, perhaps, racial factors.

Of extreme interest is the girls' own inauguration of a discussion of their problems after they had acted them out. Acting out served to reduce the censors and ego defenses that held their feelings in repression. Now they were able to share with each other their difficulties, a development that is also noteworthy. This is the first time in our experience that a spontaneous transition from an activity to an interview group has been affected by the patients themselves, and can be attributed to the fact that the girls were thirteen years of age, and older, when first placed in a group. This is an age beyond the limits of an activity therapy group and the spontaneous change confirms the notion that analytic therapy groups are more suitable for patients after puberty.

Miss Headley: During this period the family's financial situation worsened. Mr. Case and Tony remained unemployed. May, who had contributed regularly to the family's income, fell ill and had not worked for six weeks; neither did her husband work regularly. Henry was looking for work and when finally hired as an attendant at a mental hospital never had enough of his salary left over to contribute to the family. Fred continued working on a small salary and shared his earnings with the family. Mr. Case, when urged to go to the Department of Welfare for help, was reluctant to do this because he claimed an earlier, unpleasant experience there.

The boys and their father quarreled constantly. They strongly resented his inadequacy while he felt that he had worked long enough and that they should now assume the responsibility for his support. To add to the stress of the home, May and her husband were in constant friction because of his infidelities and May's two youngsters were openly resenting his intrusion into the family.

Confusion, dissension and unhappiness were the immediate background for Jean's first year in high school. As a result she appeared at times sad and depressed and she once truanted from school for three days. By and large, however, Jean continued to show progress.

Mrs. Case did not interfere with Jean's attendance at the group. She was relieved that the school authorities ceased to call her about Jean's misbehavior as in the past, but she expressed annoyance because Jean was still careless about her clothing, went to bed late and was "lazy." Mrs. Case felt that progress had been made at school, but not in the home.

Mrs. Grunwald: Jean was in high spirits when she came to the twenty-second session after the summer vacation. She wore a pin on her jacket with the inscription, "No man is good three times." When the girls laughed about it, she took it off and replaced it by the pin of her new high school. She announced with great pride that it is a good school, but she doesn't like some of the lessons and the teachers don't like her much either. The girls discussed some of the happenings during the vacation period and then centered around a discussion of pregnancy because one of the young girls in the neighborhood had given birth to a baby. Jean took up this discussion quite seriously, saying how important it is that a girl watch herself and doesn't go around with boys whom she doesn't know too well. It would be too bad if she were to become pregnant at a time when she doesn't want a baby.

During the refreshment period, one of the girls was behaving in a silly manner, putting ice cream on the frankfurters. Jean took it off and told the girl she "should be ashamed of herself." Toward the end of the session, Jean was lying on the floor playing her favorite game, jacks. She repeated several times: "Oh, it's comfortable; oh, is it comfortable." When it was time to end the session, Jean said: "Mrs. Grunwald, did you forget that we weren't here for such a long time? Please let us stay longer today." The session ended at the regular time and Jean was singing nicely when she left. The elevator man volunteered to the therapist: "That girl changed!"

During the following session, Jean discussed with the other girls some of her school problems in more detail. She had difficulty with piano lessons and French. She asked the therapist to help her with her homework and said she had difficulty because she was often loud in school.

During her twenty-fourth session, Jean became quite jealous because of the attention the therapist gave one of the girls. She began by telling sexual jokes to the other girls. Jean said: "Do you know how an olive grew green for the first time? An old maid with a cherry grew green with envy." The therapist was sitting behind Jean. Jean turned around and she and another girl asked the therapist to go out. "We'll whistle for you," said Jean, "when you can come back." In a short time, Jean and the other girl rushed out of the room pacing up and down the hall, laughing loudly. They soon returned to the room and after two minutes Jean pointed to the therapist with a wide gesture of her arm and said: "Mrs. Grunwald, you are paged." She later explained that she paged as it is done at the Waldorf Astoria, where a page boy calls that way for "a very dignified person."

When there was some ice cream left over during one session, Jean suggested that we take it to two case workers who were still in the office.

It was also Jean who suggested that we take the birthday cake to the home of a member of the group who had missed the party arranged for her. Jean, another girl, and the therapist went to that girl's house. It was dark in the streets and Jean was very helpful in finding the girl's address. She urged us to use the crosstown bus because we were in a "bad section." She pointed out some billiard halls, with smoke-filled rooms, crowded with men. She said: "Here they are spending the money they should give their wives and children." When the bus came, Jean said goodbye, and added in a thoughtful way: "It would be good, Mrs. Grunwald, if you could change Harlem, but you surely never will be able to do it."

It was during the following session, her twenty-fifth, that Jean started a discussion around problems of the neighborhood. She tied these up with experiences in school. Her civics teacher is a prejudiced man, she said. She cannot stand the way he talks about juvenile delinquency in Harlem. "He always talks about Negroes, Negroes; and then I get mad. The other day he said that it was just awful that there was such a high delinquency rate in Harlem." The teacher cannot undestand why there are so many gangs and why boys from

Harlem turn even to killing members of another gang. Jean said that she got quite angry and said in class that she is living in the neighborhood of these boys and that she's proud of them. Some of them live under very hard conditions and often have neither father nor mother to take care of them., When they turn to killing, it's not because they are bad. They are so alone in the world and nobody loves them. "By the way," she asked her teacher, "did you know that there were also gangs in white neighborhoods?"

Jean had a dressing on her hand when she came to the twenty-seventh session. She told the other girls that her brother had hurt her with a kitchen knife. She had to go to the hospital where they put on a dressing. She was supposed to stay at home but she ran away to come to the "club." During this meeting, Jean again sat down on the floor and played jacks, which she often did in order to withdraw from a situation that was threatening. She told the other girls that Saturday evening she went with her brother to an interpretive dance and she imitated some of the dances. The girls were laughing. Another girl took this up by saying that perhaps one might interpret many things in a dance. She went out of the room, knocked on the door, entered the room with slow and awkward movements. "This is the way my father walks," she said in a half-singing tone.

Jean rose slowly, left the room, knocked on the door and also came in with bizarre movements, saying this was the way *her* father walked. Finally both girls fell into each other's arms and fell to dancing a kind of waltz. Some of the other girls clapped with their hands, to the rhythm of the dance. They participated eagerly in the dance in which the two girls were obviously acting out their resentment against the weakness of their fathers. As they danced, the girl repeatedly said to Jean: "You should see my father. He is just like yours." The girl who had initiated the dance now imitated the way her father's "girl friend" entered the apartment, and with very slow movements spread out her legs and arms and then finally lay down on the floor. Jean got quite excited.

When toward the end of this session the girls discussed plans for their Thanksgiving party, it was Jean who imposed on the other girls her wish that they wouldn't do anything during Thanksgiving week; that they would just stay in "our club."

At the twenty-ninth session, Jean was fumbling around with a Pepsi-Cola bottle and suddenly took a position behind another girl and dropped some Pepsi-cola on her head. The girl shrieked loudly. Jean looked at her, laughed and said: "Now I will do this to Mrs. Grunwald and you will see that she will not scream." She slipped behind the therapist's seat and waved the Pepsi-cola bottle. She laughed and said: "You see. She doesn't scream." She didn't, however, spill any Pepsi-Cola. She proceeded to drink the contents of the bottle with great satisfaction.

During the next session, Jean was dancing with another girl. She danced either the way she saw her father behave at home or the way she saw people moving around in the movie *The Snake Pit*. The girls started to invent text and melodies with which they accompanied these dances. One girl chanted: "Don't take my father from me. He's the only man I have." Jean responded: "I can take him away, he's no good." The other girls chanted: "At least he brings home dimes and nickels, Jean. That's something." The girls continued this dance, one girl saying: "Don't take my father away," Jean saying: "Her father's no good"; another girl defending the father saying, "At least he brings home money," and Jean responding, "The father is crying."

After this dance Jean and three older girls in the group went out of the room. When I went to the washroom to pick up a broom, the four girls were sitting on garbage cans. They had their hands folded and were talking seriously. Jean said: "Mrs. Grunwald, can't you stay here with us? It is so very hard for us. I talk with the girls about my sister. Her husband makes life very miserable for her and we are all very much afraid because men are not true. They just run away and leave you with your children and then you have to take care of your children yourself." It was the first time Jean discussed her home problems in a serious and realistic way. Until now, when referring to these problems, she had told fantasy stories, but now she showed, for the first time, great concern. The other girls also talked very seriously and then all agreed that they would like to talk about these problems, but not in the presence of the other younger girls. During the following session, the four girls again left the room for long periods and had their own "club" in the washroom.

It was felt that the wish of these four girls to discuss their problems should be met by organizing for them another group where they might talk about their problems. At Mr. Slavson's suggestion, after the thirty-ninth session (Jean had joined the group at the fifth), the activity group was terminated. The younger and some new girls were formed into a new activity group, and the four older girls constituted an interview group. Of the thirty-four sessions during which Jean had been a member of the group, she had missed only one when she was very ill. In the interview group which consisted of four girls who had previously been in the activity group, two of the girls were fourteen years of age, another, fifteen, and the fourth, sixteen years old. Altogether twenty-five sessions were held after a pause of four or five months caused by the therapist's unavoidable absence. During these twenty-five sessions one of the girls was absent once. Otherwise the attendance was perfect.

Before starting the interview group the therapist saw each girl separately and explained to her the difference between the two groups. She told them that in view of the fact that they had been interested in discussing problems and had suggested the idea, they would have an opportunity now to get together and talk about matters that concerned them. They were also told that there would be no more materials to work with, nor would there be any refreshments. It was suggested to each girl that she talk about everything that came to her mind quite freely and consider the conversations in the group confidential.

At the very first session the girls reflected this new image of themselves by smoking, something they had never attempted in the activity therapy group. As usual in these groups the first conversations of the girls concerned themselves with the immediate problems of the girls to which we refer as "top reality." These included matters concerning school, but soon the girls began to talk about boyfriends, marriage and being mothers, about their mothers and fathers, and their wishes concerning husbands and children. The discussions were sometimes followed by some activity or play, which we consider as part of resistance and which was dealt with as such.

In order to avoid some of the conversations at the early part of the treatment sessions some of the girls would occasionally bring in knitting or play jacks for short periods. On rare occasions the girls would sing together. As already stated, this acting out we consider as being manifestations of resistance to the catharsis and communication. However, an interesting reaction was observed in the fact that at each session they would pick up some discussion of the preceding session, a fact that indicated that they had thought or cogitated about the questions and discussions in the group.

Jean had continued making progress and frequently had mentioned that she was doing well at school. Her general progress as well seemed to be continuing. Soon she began to talk about being married, which would prevent her from either working or going to school. She saw marriage as an escape from reality, but the other girls did not accept this. They questioned her as to what she would do in case her husband left her. She then stated that she would go on relief. At one of the sessions Jean had reported that she now had a boyfriend and she liked him because he was from the country. She thought city boys were no good. She would rather live in the country with her boyfriend because she liked to pick flowers, plant seeds and do odd jobs around the house. One of the other girls pointed out to her that despite what she said Jean was actually planning to do some work while married.

When asked why she preferred boys from the country to those of the city, Jean said that city boys ran away from their wives after they got married and took up residences at other addresses in the city and one could not find them. Neither do they have conflicts about running away because they know that their wives and children can go on relief. In the country "people live together. When you live together," she continued, "you do not get like ..." At this Jean got up from her seat and began to act out. This time she went through the dance of the insane women which she had seen in the film, *The Snake Pit*.

At this session the girls were greatly absorbed in the discussion and when the time came for ending the session, they complained that the period passed too fast and wanted to stay longer.

At the next session when the girls talked about boys again and one of the other girls in the group complained of getting headaches when she was out with her boyfriend, Jean repeated the snake-pit dance, but suddenly stopped and told the therapist that she had seen something that day which made her hate the therapist and repeated, "I hate you, Mrs. Grunwald, I hate you." She then proceeded to tell of her needs for sneakers, of a new zipper book and a lock for school and that her mother could not give her these things since they lived on relief. In describing these deprivations further Jean again told the therapist that she hated her. The girls expressed their disturbance at the direct attack upon the therapist and suggested that Jean talk it over with the case worker who treated her mother. Jean said "no." She wanted these things immediately from the present therapist and repeated her attack on the therapist. As a result of the girls' reaction to her attack upon the therapist, Jean related this to her home where, she said, "there is always a fight going on, a fight between me and my brothers and my little nephews." She proceeded to describe how her sister had beaten the children in a rage of temper and explained that her brother-in-law had abandoned her sister, treated her badly and visited her only once or twice a week. Her sister turns over the money she earns to her husband.

Describing later the very unsuitable sleeping quarters that she occupied, Jean burst out screaming: "I just hate it at home and I fight in school, I fight everywhere." The girls pointed out to her that she is actually fighting people who are in no way to be blamed for the conditions in her home. When this was told her, Jean exclaimed, "Shut up," but she seemed quite relieved when the therapist suggested that they talk about some of her clothing needs after the session.

At the next session again the discussion was around boyfriends and Jean stated that she was very careful about the choosing of boyfriends because she did not want to have the same experience as her sister has had and tied this up with her father who was very ill, suffering from a heart condition and rheumatic fever. During the course of the conversation Jean said: "My poor father is sick, my mother has diabetes in her blood, my sister has tuberculosis and one of my brothers has a very bad nervous condition because of the war." When Winnie said that in her home there was always constant fighting going on, but that she herself had given up fighting and pretended not to see or hear what was going on, Jean replied that she was too impatient to be as tolerant as Winnie. She even struck her boyfriend the other day. She really didn't want to do it and as though justifying herself she said: "After all, girls, I did not fight in school."

At the session after the one just described a rather interesting and perhaps important conversation occurred. When the girls were drinking Pepsi-cola from the bottles, Jean said, "It is funny. Now we have a bottle to drink from instead of a cup. I got a cup instead of a bottle as a baby." The girls then attempted to recall how they were fed as babies. They could not remember. Jean complained of the fact that her nephew, who is two years old, still gets a bottle. This statement led on to a detailed discussion of weaning during which Jean stated that she was sure she did not get enough of her mother's breast. Her mother had to bring up too many children anyhow. She ended off by saying: "It's good that I now have a bottle."

In the succeeding session Jean complained about being self-conscious during the school lunch because she felt that the boys who were sitting opposite or next to her at the counter were looking into her mouth. The free association with this is rather significant, for Winnie said she too felt self-conscious the other day when she came out of her house and her boyfriend said: "Here comes my wife." Winnie said she went back into her house. Jean added: "You are really looking at your belly. I think we are self-conscious when with boys because we think they will give us a baby." This statement seemed to be too threatening to the girls because they began at once to tell fantastic stories about babies.

When at the next session the therapist would not permit the girls to stay longer than the allotted time for the interview, Jean said to the therapist: "Shame on you, Mrs. Grunwald, you don't want us to have fun." For two sessions after this Jean did not participate in the discussions, but sat quietly. However, at the third session, she had displayed her report card from school where for the first time she was not absent one day and was late only once. Her marks in her studies were also above average. At this session she again attacked the therapist and when the girls expressed shock, Jean stood up, walked up and down the room for a while, sat down next to the therapist and said: "You don't know what I am going through." The therapist said: "I can see that you are upset about something." Jean then complained about her mother's inconsistency and changeability. "I am afraid that I don't know what to do. I am like my mother. I am so changeable. I cannot help it. My mother's and my birthdays are in March and persons born in March are changeable." When the therapist said she was born in March, Jean wondered why the therapist was not changeable.

For some time after these developments Jean participated eagerly in the discussions. She appeared to be much more mature and her perception of reality and other problems was on a considerably more mature level. At the thirteenth session, when the girls talked about the gang fights in the neighborhood, Jean and Winnie interpreted these fights through the dance. Then they discussed seriously the influence of the poor environment of the boys, the crowding of their homes and the absence of even one single person to whom they feel they really belong. Not having these satisfactions, Jean said the boys feel close to their friends in the street and this leads them into difficulties. When the therapist asked Jean to elaborate on what they meant by this, Jean said, "Don't ask me. I am not a child psychiatrist," but continued to discuss all these problems seriously.

The fourteenth session occurred during the Easter vacation from school and the girls stated that they did not want to talk seriously because talking in the group was just like working. They would rather discuss something frivolous like movies.

At the fifteenth session the girls talked of the need of being loved by someone in the home before they are able to trust themselves with loving a man; Winnie, Jean, and Beatrice spoke simultaneously. They all stated that nobody loved them at home. This is why they feel that nobody else could love them outside of the home and they are afraid of being loved, and that "makes you so afraid at night."

At the subsequent session, Jean was very concerned when Winnie did not turn up. At the time she said that she had visited the clinic and had found Winnie, heartbroken and crying copiously because her grandmother was so cruel to her. Jean said that Winnie's grandmother was a religious fanatic and suggested that Winnie be taken out of the home and sent to a "home for girls." When Winnie came to the session later on and mentioned that her father had visited her, which is a rare occurrence, Jean said: "Remember I told you that my father had changed so much when he became so sick. He even gave up drinking. . . . He was a terrible drunk and even made me drunk." She then put her head on the table and described how when she was a little baby, the father would hide his whiskey bottle in her carriage and sometimes instead of getting her bottle of milk, she would get a bottle of whiskey and become drunk. "A short time ago," she continued, "when he stopped drinking, my father suddenly realized he had a family but now he doesn't know what to do with his family." Jean was very upset because her father told her that her feet were too large and she looked like a stringbean. She hates stringbeans. She hates carrots. She hates cream cheese and "that is all we had for lunch in school today." The latter she added laughingly.

The girls here pointed out to Jean how much she had improved. She no longer gets mad as frequently as she used to and now that she understands what she is mad about, it has helped her a great deal. The other members of the group stated at this point that they were proud of her.

At the following session, the seventeenth, the girls again discussed boyfriends and Jean announced that her boyfriend looked very neat and now she too was taking better care of herself. She used to be called "shrubby." She used to pretend taking a bath to fool her mother but actually never washed herself. She recalls how her mother on one Sunday braided her hair with white ribbons and put white shoes and a white dress on her. In a few minutes she was back with her dress practically black with dirt and her ribbon lost. Her mother said that "she would cut up her behind." Jean now felt that she was taking good care of herself. She particularly needed to keep herself clean and washed because she was the darkest in her family and then described the quality of hair each of the members had. Some of them had hair like the mother's and some like father's.

During the discussion of neatness that followed, Jean said: "Perhaps I am neat now because I finally got a room of my own." She now slept in a real bed which was depressed in the middle and the other day when she came home from school who was lying on her bed except her mother! Jean became angry and called to her father: "Take that old lady off my bed." She then said that she did not like to talk that way to her father because he can "see." This "seeing" was referred to as having second sight and being capable of performing voodoo. She described how her father was able to see the background of a strange woman who happened to visit their home. She then went on to say that one should never take Coca-Cola because some persons with "power" might put a white stuff into it which kills one. The girls laughed at this and wondered if she remembered how often she had drunk Coca-Cola in the group. Jean replied: "I know this is not true, but often I feel that way." She is especially afraid because her father has "a look." The important thing Jean feels is that one must do things "so that nobody would hate you." The girls discussed her ideas of voodoo and stated that it was impossible for anyone to live that way and if Jean really tried to be so perfect she would be very miserable. Winnie felt that when a person threatened you with just a look it was not so bad. It is when people withhold their anger. She recalled a boy in her class who even held his head in his hands and stared into space. He never talked. All of a sudden on the Monday of that week, he waved to her twice and she got scared. Winnie got up and imitated the waving of the boy and Jean played the part of the boy. She came closer and closer to Winnie in a threatening posture and the girls repeated this byplay several times. Winnie then talked about her nightmares and Jean mentioned that since she had a room of her own she was often afraid at night because she felt that a man might enter her room through the fire escape but she did not feel like Winnie. It was not that this man would choke her and she did not scream out in her sleep.

In the subsequent session, the girls talked about love and Jean gave a long dissertation on the difference between love and infatuation. She thought that girls in their teens were seldom in love and when asked what she felt love was, she said that when one was older and felt she wanted to make a life together with a boy, then marriage could be good. Then she went off into fantasy that she wanted to marry a husband with a lot of money who could give her a nurse to watch the children. However, she burst out laughing at this and returned to a serious discussion of marriage. The girls were impressed with Jean's remarks and said: "Today it is like we have a roundtable conference."

At the twenty-fifth session the girls again discussed their fathers as well as their efforts to find part-time jobs for the summer. At this Jean began to giggle when she described how her father watched her sister's boyfriends. One of the girls then said: "Jean, now you look like the old Jean. No, you look like Jean imitating the old Jean." Jean at once stopped her giggling. Later in the discussion she stated: "I shall be different from my parents. I want to have two boys and be a good mother but, girls, first of all we have to finish school, look for a job because it will take some time before we really can get married."

By this time Jean's appearance had changed completely. She really took good care of herself, her teachers commented on her improved appearance and other members of the staff who had seen Jean in the waiting room also remarked what a beautiful and neat girl she was. She now impressed people not only by her good looks, but also by her poise which was in striking contrast to the wild, unkempt little girl she had been two years previously. The school also reported improvement and Jean herself expressed pleasure with the work there. Despite the improvement in all the other girls, as well as Jean, they have all stated that they realize that they still had a long way to go and that adjusting to life would not be easy for them.

After an absence of four months the therapist had recalled Jean to see her on an individual basis and attempted to focus treatment on the reality problems since the family setting was very disturbing and very pressing. It was found that Jean was frequently hungry because there was no food at home. The fighting at home grew worse, partly because of the congestion. Finally, when the family settled in a housing project several months later and the older sister moved out with her two children, Jean felt greatly relieved.

We recognized that the "neurotic residue" in Jean required working on an individual basis. We were aware throughout of specific fears she had been subject to, which were tied up with her sexual conflicts and feelings of guilt in regard to members of her family. This formed the content of the individual interviews for some months. During this period the girl displayed constant improvement, although occasionally she would go into a state that resembled mild depression.

She continued her interest in music and took singing lessons regularly. During the same year the therapist was able to attend one of the solo recitals Jean gave in her church. She, as well as everyone else in the congregation, were greatly impressed with Jean's performance, charm, and poise. The opinion of persons competent to judge is that Jean has an "outstanding voice with excellent potentialities."

Evidence of Jean's emotional maturity and growth was revealed by her in an individual interview. On Thanksgiving eve, her sister's husband attempted suicide by gas but was discovered in time to be taken to the hospital and revived. When talking about this to Miss Headley, Mrs. Case was completely unsympathetic toward him and felt that "he had done a lousy job. He should have been a man and jumped off the roof if he wanted to complete the job," she stated and expressed her regret that he was still alive. She described her son-in-law as worthless and irresponsible. Mrs. Case was angry with Jean for visiting her brother-in-law in the hospital and said that had she known this beforehand, she would not have permitted Jean to make the visit.

Jean, on the other hand, in outlining the story to the caseworker, had difficulty in suppressing tears when she described her two little nephews. She described how disturbed they were when they saw their father lying on the floor in the kitchen unconscious. She then proceeded to describe how her brother-in-law was fond of Jason, the younger nephew, while he was antagonistic to Albert, the older one, who is now six years old. Jean felt that Jason was her brother-in-law's child while Albert was not. She had no evidence to that effect but she could feel it in the relationship that existed between him and the two children. She complained about her sister's whipping Albert and being horrible to him "when he does some small foolish things. He doesn't do many foolish things. He is always so scared and behaves mostly like a girl." Jean stated she tried to be good to him and encouraged him to "act like a boy." "I tell him," Jean stated, "not to be afraid of me and I am patient with him but he is so sad. He really needs help. I know that my sister is avoiding thinking about her troubles and will not come to you for help but my little nephew needs this help or he may go crazy."

The worker recalled how antagonistic and hostile Jean used to be to her little nephews and how brutally she used to beat Albert even when he vomited when he had whooping cough. "Yes," she said, "I know I used to do it but I never knew then I could have such patience as I have now and feel like a mother to him."

Mr. Slavson: The center of these adolescent girls' discussion in the interview group was, as could be expected, their urge to be mothers, which Dr. Spotnitz[1] characterized as the "reproductive constellation." All reveal their desire to have children. Jean criticizes her sister as being inadequate as a mother. Later she is concerned with the fact that she resembles her mother, being changeable like her mother. Still later she speaks of not wanting to be like her parents. These remarks uncover her doubts concerning her adequacy as a parent. When she repeatedly brings the question to the group, she wishes to clarify in her mind the doubt relative to her adequacy as a parent, which Dr. Spotnitz described as the "inadequacy constellation." The conflict between the reproduction constellation and the inadequacy constel-

---

1. Spotnitz, H. (1947). Observations of emotional currents in interview group therapy with adolescent girls. *Journal of Nervous and Mental Disease,* December.

lation, which all adolescent girls have and particularly those who are socially and personally maladjusted, is clearly revealed here. The security she received from the group seems to have diminished her doubts concerning these and other matters.

There are evidences of growing insight in the patient. Unfortunately so much of the material had to be condensed which made omission of important developments necessary. One of these is an instance when Jean verbalizes the fact that she hates things at home so much that she "has to fight in school and fight everywhere." She became aware of her projections and displacement. At other times she had stated in group discussions: "I am more quiet, I am not as jumpy and I am beginning to like work." At the same time she recognized her restlessness and feared that she may not be able to master her impulses to scream and laugh.

Such improvement is made possible through regression which in turn is a result of catharsis. We see manifested the striking contrast between activity and analytic group psychotherapy. In the first, the catharsis and regression were to a predominant degree in action. Now the regression is verbalized as seen by the girls' discussion of bottle feeding; Jean's statement that she did not have enough of her mother's breast; and her memory as a little girl when she refused to bathe and got herself dirty to the annoyance of her mother.

Jean's capacity for identification with other persons is increased, which is another sign of maturity. This is demonstrated clearly when Jean is concerned about Winnie who did not come to the session and when Winnie mentions her father, Jean is now able to talk in a more kindly fashion concerning her own father. She now has found something positive about him, namely, that he gave up drinking and has changed so much for the better. Almost pathetically she states that a short time ago when her father stopped drinking he realized he had a family but now he does not know what to do with it. Her realistic and more tolerant conception of her father is a striking demonstration of her growing objectivity and capacity to detach herself from him, which we term cathexis displacement [56, pp. 75 *et. seq.*]. By this we mean that the libido that had been attached to the father was freed and is now available for other object relations. This process we clearly saw in the interests the girls displayed in one another and the homoerotic dances and dramatizations. Later these were redirected toward heterosexual interests in boys and to becoming mothers.

Jean's improvement was so striking that the girls as well as others could not help but make note of it, all of which helped Jean's self-evaluation. When Jean reverts to her old patterns, the girls refuse to accept it as part of herself and state that "Jean imitates the old Jean."

The neurotic residue to which reference has already been made is that part of the neurotic conflict in the libido constellation of the individual which frequently cannot be reached through group therapy. In Jean's case it seems to be constellated around her mouth: the confusion between sexuality and orality when she speaks of being self-conscious when eating because boys look into her mouth. We have no evidence that such difficulties can be worked through in group treatment and our practice, therefore, has been to refer such patients to individual treatment.

The complete acceptance and the kindly understanding Jean received from the therapist strengthened her ego which was at a rather low level when she first came to us. In the past she acted out her aggressions because of her disappointment with her parents, especially the father. Her behavior served to punish frustrating adults and to attract attention, that is, attaining love. She now no longer needed these vicarious gratifications. She was more stable and, therefore, able to control her behavior.

While Jean's ego was strengthened (which made it possible for her to inhibit her narcissistic acting out) her superego and her awareness of right and wrong had also been gradually evolving. This is a direct outcome of her relation with the therapist as a good mother and served the ends of maturing her personality.

CHAPTER 43

PARA-ANALYTIC GROUP PSYCHOTHERAPY
FOR ADOLESCENTS
(1965)

The sine qua non for success in psychotherapy is the proper matching of the patient and the type of treatment to be employed. This requires a thorough understanding on the part of the therapist of the patient's personality and his problems, a knowledge of a variety of techniques of psychotherapy, and a flexibility to apply them. The most suitable "therapy" may, in some instances, be no more than advice, counseling or guidance, or a friendly interest such as a Big Brother or a guidance counselor can provide. It is from this discriminative choice of suitable procedures made on the basis of clinical considerations, character structure, the nature, causes, and sources of the patient's disturbances and maladjustments, his life setting and his life aims, that therapeutic effectiveness flows. It is essential for the therapist to familiarize himself in advance or as early as possible in the course of therapy of the pathogenic forces in the patient's life and to determine his central (nuclear) and peripheral problems. It is only then that suitable therapeutic steps can be taken with a degree of assurance of success.

The reliability of these studies and the emerging plans flow from recognizing individual needs of patients, rather than from employing blanket practices derived from oceanic principles. In both group psychotherapy and in individual treatment individuation of approach and process is essential. The plan and type of treatment are determined on this basis in both individual and group psychotherapy, but in the latter the structuring of the group is also derived from the knowledge of individuals and their therapeutic needs. A degree of homogeneity is essential in grouping of patients, and there are two of these areas in which all patients are homogeneous; these are feelings about parents and confusions and reactions in the area of sex. However, in planning treatment for preadult patients, specific developmental phases have to be considered. The most important of these is age.

It is commonly recognized that the nature of psychotherapy of children, adolescents, and adults is vastly different, both in content and procedures. One factor that determines these differences is psycho-organic development; another is their varying social facilities and intellectual comprehensions. Thus, at the two extremes of the therapeutic spectrum—children and adults—communication in one is achieved by predominantly motoric activity, while in the other it is verbal. Similarly, the insight a child can gain from treatment is vastly more limited than is that of an adult and is different also qualitatively. In one case it is almost entirely *derivative* from actions and interaction, while adults' insight is gained from cogitation and *direct* verbal interpretations by the therapist. The language of the child is action, while in the adult it consists of words. In one case the therapist has to be able to discern meaning in behavior, while in the other the content consists of ideas and open communication of feelings and stress.

Between these two modalities is the adolescent, admittedly the segment most difficult to reach by psychotherapy, the sources of which difficulties need to be understood if means are to be found for overcoming them.

Enlightened parents, teachers, and certainly psychotherapists are aware of the fact that organic growth consumes inorganically derived energies (from food) and generates psychomotoric potential (electrical) energy which propels physical, intellectual, and emotional activity. This dynamism of children and adolescents disturbs the orderliness and wishes for placidity in the adults' world. The inhibitions with which the physical and psychic dynamism of the young are met seriously interfere with the orderly development of the individual's personality. At the same time, the arrested energies and the frustration to autonomic drives that accompany it are transformed (in conformity with the law of mutual transmutability of physical and psychological tensions) into hostility against the frustrating agents, the adults.

Psychotherapists, particularly, take cognizance of the fact that tensions which originate in the soma find expression via the psyche and vice versa; libido travels a two-way path, from the soma to the psyche and from the psyche to the soma, which is the source of somatopsychological and psychosomatic symptomatology. In the adolescent, somatopsychological tensions against which all the suppressive forces of society and its taboos are mobilized are sexual urges. The taboos against them produce not only severe tensions and neurotic formations, but as is the case with all social taboos, they activate guilt. It is guilt (the special endowment of man, the only species in nature capable of it), among other operations, that is responsible for the tensions between the adolescent and his parents and pari passu, the adult world which they represent.

The human individual sustains in the course of his evolvement a number of inescapable developmental and relationship traumata, among which are: the birth trauma, the eighth-month anxiety, the two-year negativism period, the primary oedipal conflict, the pubertal oedipal wishes, and many other which are outside the scope of this paper. The second phase of the oedipal urges comes to a climax in early adolescence [148]. The health or unhealth of the evolving and growing individual is entirely determined by the treatment the various crises receive from the significant adults in the child's and adolescent's life, the two-year negativism being of most importance.

As far as adolescents are concerned, a critical phase in their development is the manner in which parents deal with their offspring's incestuous wishes, which are usually strongly suppressed and disguised. These wishes are more or less universally reacted to by open antagonism and rebellion, which require sympathetic understanding on the part of parents. The adolescent's incestuous urges do not remain entirely unrequited, for in the unconscious of parents, as well, sexual urges toward their grown-up children are present. These are thoroughly suppressed in the vast majority, but their presence is evidenced indirectly in humor, "innocent" jokes and in "teasing." In a large number of parents these feelings are closer to the surface and are manifested by freedom in undress in the home (justified by various rationalizations), by unwarranted interest in the amatory affairs of their teenage children, and unmistakable provocative maneuvers such as tickling, playfulness, and teasing. In rare and extreme instances incestuous urges are (criminally) acted out. Irritation with and punitiveness against children in adults stem, in large part, from the defensive reaction formations against prohibited sexual urges.

This complex of mutual negative feelings is a basic cause of the difficulties teachers and pyschotherapists, in fact, all adults, experience with adolescents. The difficulties that adolescents present in relation to adults and society have also a social base in Western cultures where the adolescents are denied status. Adults enjoy *power status,* and small children *protected status*, while the adolescents, who are in a process of transition, are denied any position as social atoms which leaves them without function or anchorage. To this irritating situation are added the many taboos against impelling instinctual urges and the resulting accumulated hostilities toward parents and, by displacment, toward all adults. This complex of disapproved attitudes and vortex of prohibited feelings cannot but generate a reservoir of anxiety and guilt adding fuel to the adolescents' aggressions which further confuse and frighten him.

The unavoidable fear and insecurity of the adolescent is also enhanced by the uncertainties of his future and the confusions as well in relation to his identity. Being in a state of transition from childhood to adulthood, at which period the variety of trends are in hopeless confusion, his identity is fluid; he oscillates between dependence and independence, between self-overconfidence and self-doubt, between primary reality perceptions and secondary reality elaborations, between doubts as to his sexual adequacy and inadequacy and groping for values and for a stable identification.

This is a more or less valid picture of what is euphemistically described as the "adolescent turmoil," a turmoil that is many times multiplied in intensity and quantum in those youths who become candidates for psychotherapy.

But the fears and anxieties are not limited to endogenous sources alone. Technological civilization imposes upon youth also anxieties as to their place in the future: in sexual acceptability, in occupations, as heads of families, as to their status in the community. These are a source of particular and great apprehension, since here biologic as well as social survival is involved. The feelings, projected as they are into a vague and hazy future of intangible phantasmagoria, cannot but frighten and disturb the psyche and the soma of a personality in its still nascent state.

There is a mass of other tensions to which youth are subjected in the complex civilizations and cultures of the modern world, but these must be omitted for economy of space; only those forces that bear upon the central theme of this paper have been touched on here. In the interest of clarity, we shall briefly recapitulate them as they operate in teenagers generally. The psychotherapist who works with adolescents is confronted *(a)* with facile identities and fluid identifications, *(b)* with conflicts between trends for independence and dependence, *(c)* with oscillation between the "reproductive and adequacy constellations,[1] *(d)* with transitions from homoerotic to heterosexual relations, *(e)* with increase in incestuous urges and the pursuit after non-incestuous sexual objects, and *(f)* with accumulated feelings of reactive omnipotence, guilt, anxiety, hostility, and aggression toward adults and their world.

Where is there escape from this seething cauldron of conflicting trends, fears, and doubts? Observations in all cultures with social mobility (in which freedom of association is permitted), leave no doubt as to the answer. It is groups of peers who supply the haven for the adolescent, for it is to groups of his peers that he instinctively and automatically gravitates. It is in the commonality of doubts, anxieties and fears that the insecure, groping adolescents find comfort. The mutual support and the universality of aims and preoccupations cement them into cohesive social atoms. They instinctively feel that escape and salvation lie in this mutuality and compresence.

At the outset of this paper we suggested a basic rule of psychotherapy, the matching of patient and the therapeutic procedure. Another rule can be usefully suggested at this juncture; this is the principle that at the start psychotherapy with a given patient has to address itself to the state and condition in which we find him and gradually engender in him intrapsychic states and interpersonal attitudes essential to emotional maturity and personality integration.

---

1. Spotnitz, H. (1947). Observation of emotional currents in interview group therapy with adolescent girls. *Journal of Nervous and Mental Disease* 106: 565-582.

In applying this rule to adolescents, the therapist (and in their work, the educator and recreationist, as well) has to turn to the group in his efforts at engaging the individual in a therapeutic (and the educator in a truly educational) relation. He can affect best results, and with an economy of time, if he utilizes the natural need and facilities for peer association, which aid catharsis and the emergence of insight and understanding through sharing and interaction with persons on his level of maturity and with similar comprehensions and preoccupations. This stratagem is particularly appropriate in the light of the basic antagonism toward, and distrust of, adults inherent in adolescence, which often create insurmountable blockings to the establishment of a positive transference toward the therapist. Therapists who worked with adolescents individually have experienced a block to real communication and mutual understanding and an almost impenetrable wall of resistance in most of their patients. These blockings are particularly difficult to work through because they are predominantly character and id resistances (which have always baffled the psychotherapist) that militate against establishing a positive therapeutic transference.

Another source of resistance is the adolescent's extreme sensitivity to criticism, his defensiveness and easily threatened self-image. By passing through the estate of childhood—with its characteristic feelings of helplessness and dependency and the inevitable criticisms, discipline and punishment from adults—each carries over to varying degrees a paranoidlike quality in his reactions. These reactions are naturally intensified during the period of adolescence when weakness and uncertainties become more tangibly clear, self-doubt sets in, and the individual, as a result, desperately clings to a fantasy of adequacy which he violently defends. In this condition, the best intentioned advice, suggestion, or correction is perceived as criticism, denigration, and invasion of autonomy.

But when in discussions with peers disagreements, conflicts and criticism arise, the force of the negative impact is appreciably diminished and in most instances does not appear altogether. The latent resentments against "interference" and real or fancied "persecution" attributed to adults are not triggered when reactions originate with peers. In this climate, the participation of a therapist, if sensitively and tactfully exercised, is not only acceptable but may actually be welcomed. The unrestricted freedom to act out feelings and to speak one's mind (which is another prime rule governing psychotherapy), gives the adolescent status in this (group) microcosm ordinarily denied him in the social macrocosm of the world. But what is even more important is that the group's permissiveness engenders a new image in the adolescent of himself and of adults, as a result of which the wall of separation is gradually worn away and positive transference toward the therapist emerges, setting into action the therapeutic process.

However, despite the potentials for such benign developments in psychotherapy (or counseling or guidance), the therapist has to exercise *utmost caution* not to overstep the boundaries of adolescents' psychologic tolerance, which is indeed limited. Their personalities still remain in a flux; their psychic anchorages are weak; self-identity is tenuous and fragile; realistic conceptualization is still in its beginnings, emerging from the confusions of latency and puberty; strivings are still ambivalent and unclear and, what is even more important, the relation between the id (instincts), ego (controls), and the superego (conscience) has not as yet fallen into place. Assailment of the ego and the self-image must, therefore, by all means be prevented, for the psychic forces have not been integrated and the ego's powers are still inadequately mobilized to withstand the stress. Hence, group interviews *cannot be psychoanalytically as searching* as with adults, but neither can the same degree of motoric acting out be permitted as in the therapy of small children.

We have so far concentrated largely upon some of the impediments to and the areas requiring caution in the psychotherapeutic effort. There are, however, inherent assets present as well. One of these is the natural gravitational force toward group association and cohesion which we have already considered; the other is intense native curiosity characteristic of the adolescent phase of development. Both constitutionally and psychologically, the adolescent whose orderly development has not been perverted is eager to understand his environment and beyond. From these understandings flow security, a sense of direction, purpose and controls, and, finally, a self-identity. Curiosity is a characteristic of great importance to a therapist who does counseling, guidance, or psychotherapy with adolescents, and he should have at his disposal the necessary skills, knowledge and information to engage and utilize it [61].

Thus, not all group interviews need be psychoanalytically significant or so oriented. Following the unfoldment of the patients' personalities, they may be interspersed with information, either didactically presented or Socratically deduced, or the interviews may from time to time be given over to chit-chat and trivia. Experience teaches that, when the therapist can accept these youthful vagaries unreservedly, out of such trivia and divergencies matters of therapeutic significance emerge either through the patients' own spontaneous processes and free associations or, when indicated, by the therapist's appropriate intervention. Feelings toward members of families and toward themselves, questions as to the need and value of social regulation of conduct and sexual expression, the origin of guilt and the reasons for the appearance of anxiety, the relations between boys and girls and petting, the symbolism and use of money, and similar questions through which the patients seek to attain mastery of their lives and their environment invariably arise and run parallel to ventilation of feelings toward parents, siblings, teachers, and other affective persons in the youngsters' lives.

It is also essential that in work with adolescents the therapist (or leader) give them what may be called "tools for living." Once a predominantly positive transference toward the therapist and implicit trust in him have been established, young people eagerly turn to him for guidance in living and for life's certainties essential to security. The therapist can point out—but only when it is psychologically appropriate and when the group members evince an interest or a need for them—the modus operandi for dealing with inner impulses and external situations [62]. In this genre are included elucidation of the difference in response (ego functioning) of a child and a mature person; the conscious handling of anger; responding to challenge; invalidity of pugnaciousness and its aftermath; management of conflicts with members of one's family; utilization of time, and similar practical matters. All conclusions as to techniques of dealing with life situations *must* be derived through discussion by the group on their level and through the examination of choices. Only that in which the learner participates in deriving, becomes significant and is retained and integrated into his thinking (if not always into his conduct). Active participation is a form of vicarious experience, a quality that didactic teaching lacks. Nor is discussion of much avail if it is carried on against emotional resistances and character rigidities, which should be of prime consideration in psychotherapy and must be first diminished or eliminated. It is only on the base of inner flexibility and emotional receptivity in the adolescent's psyche that the information from the store of the adults' wisdom, knowledge, and experience becomes acceptable and significant.

It is, therefore, hoped that the suggestions for "giving information" and the derivation of tools or guides for living will not be taken to mean that therapeutic group sessions have any similarity to the traditional classroom with its didactic pouring of information. Even guidance and counseling, let alone psychotherapy, cannot be essayed before some degree of release from pressing emotional problems and the diminution of conflictual relations and anxieties have been achieved, with resulting inner relaxation and the acquisition of some capacity for insight. Without such tilling of the psychological soil, planting of information and suggestions would be barren. A degree of inner freedom is a prerequisite, which is initially supplied by the attitudes of the therapist, the climate of the group, and later by proceedings at the group sessions.

The fusing of analytic group psychotherapy with guidance, counseling, advice and "teaching," as indicated, is the cardinal principle of *para-analytic group psychotherapy.'*

Because of the level of maturity and heuristic capacities, traditional psychoanalysis in its pure form and precise analytic psychotherapy as practiced with adults are unsuitable for all but the seriously disturbed and fully psychoneurotic youngster. The vast majority of the disturbed and socially maladjusted adolescents require (as do also younger children) the growth-producing medium of groups that afford them an arena for acquiring corrective identifications and new sets of values and insights in a climate of acceptance, sharing, and helpfulness and never before experienced type of relatedness. The essentiality of groups in the psychologic treatment of the young lies more than it does with adults in corrective relationships in the living situation, and all that it implies, in addition to reweighing of psychic forces, essential in the therapy of the young.

The basic guide rules in the practice of para-analytic group psychotherapy are: (1) the interviews have to be an admixture of uncovering, exploration, evaluation, discussion and a modicum of didacticism; (2) the pressing actualities (top realities) as well as unconscious and preconscious ones form the content of the group interviews; (3) the therapist must not press for uncovering the unconscious and should utilize every opportunity to impart information that adds to the patients' "psychologic literacy"; (4) the evocation of only minimal anxiety essential for involvement in treatment is permitted, beyond which point it has to be avoided, allayed, or diverted; (5) a degree of introspection and uncovering therapy has to be preceded or run parallel with the acquisition of psychologic literacy; (6) regressive "free association" alone is not suitable in work with adolescents (as it is with adults), for it may overload their, as yet, not fully integrated ego; it must be diluted by associative ideas stemming from realities and current lives and needs; (7) the therapist's role is considerably a more active one than in strictly analytic psychotherapy; (8) para-analytic group psychotherapy addresses itself more to the integration and support of the ego than is the case in analytic psychotherapy, where the center of treatment is more the libido; (9) para-analytic psychotherapy is a combination of psychoanalytic psychotherapy, counseling, guidance, and orthopedagogy.

Summary

The success of psychotherapy requires that the type of therapy be matched to the nuclear and peripheral problems of each patient. Beginning with the birth trauma, each individual passes through a series of developmental and relationship crises that are potentially pathoplastic. The most serious and most tumultuous of these is adolescence.

Because of the transitional personality organization of the adolescent, his statusless position in adult society, his fluid identifications, sexual tensions and anxieties, and his rebelliousness, the adolescent patient cannot develop adequate positive transference to an adult, thus making him difficult to reach by individual psychotherapy.

The group of peers is the haven of security for all adolescents and should be utilized in the treatment of disturbed and wayward youths. However, in these groups strictly psychoanalytical procedures are strongly resisted by the adolescent because of his emotional fragility and psychosexual immaturity. The interviews, therefore, have to be reality oriented and diluted by orthopedagogical, guidance, and counseling procedures, but these need to be based on the fundamental concepts and assumptions of psychoanalytic theory.

CHAPTER 44

AN ELEMENTARISTIC APPROACH TO DELINQUENCY
(1947)

Delinquency can be, and often is, used as a generic term and as such it should not be confused with the specific clinical categories employed in understanding patients and in planning treatment. In the opinion of the present writer, the mistake is frequently made in the use of the term as a designation of a psychological structure, rather than a behavioral pattern. It is also our opinion that "delinquency" as a term should be reserved to legalistic and possibly also to moralistic terminology. It is not suitable as a clinical designation. We cannot assume, for example, that individuals who commit antisocial acts and are therefore morally and legally "delinquent" can all be treated alike. The fact that they all commit *delinquent acts* may place them in the delinquent category legally. The clinician and psychotherapist, however, is interested in the psychological causes behind the individual acts and what they represent as manifestations of psychopathology. Rather than speak of delinquency as a category, it would be more exact to say that there are persons who commit delinquent acts. "Delinquency" has to be broken down to its specific components which the blanket use of the term obscures. This we term an *elementaristic* approach to the problem.

Persons who commit delinquent acts do so for a variety of reasons. Crime can serve to express hostile, retaliatory feelings against society as a substitute for a hated parent or other persons in authority. It is also employed to resolve inner conflicts; it serves the neurotic needs for punishment, and releases tensions resulting from the conflict between aggressive hostility and the prohibitions of the superego. Delinquent acts can satisfy strivings for status and serve as a means for establishing deflated self-esteem. When authority is challenged successfully by a weak person, it helps to build up his phantasies of power; it serves to counteract his feelings of weakness and inadequacy. A basically feminine and impotent boy may indulge in delinquent acts because he wishes to convince himself, and probably also others, of his power and strength; and a girl who feels herself undesirable and unattractive may become sexually promiscuous to prove herself worthy of attention. An emotionally deprived girl may become a sex delinquent because of the affectional satisfaction she gains from being wanted and because her needs for tenderness and friendly association are satisfied. Sex delinquency may be a form of ingratiation and submission or a masochistic, self-punishing pattern. Masculine strivings, penis envy, and castration feelings, a sense of worthlessness are among some of the other reasons that induce a girl to adopt a path of sex delinquency.

Under specific circumstances acts of aggression and destructiveness may be used to obtain status in a group. In neighborhoods where gang rule is a tradition, status is achieved by alliance with a gang, which may be to varying degrees, socially undesirable and even morally depraved. The need to belong to and be a part of a group, however, is so strong that a youngster may go along even with destructive activities in return for group acceptance and approbation. Delinquent acts may also be a result of organic inferiorities. A boy of small size or one suffering from some other physical stigma may be tempted to commit delinquent acts with others, usually older and larger in size. By doing so he gains status and feels compensated for his physical inadequacies and inferiority.

Hubert, twelve years old, an adopted son and the only child in the family, whose foster father was a prominent professional man in a small town, was referred for psychotherapy because of habitual stealing both at home and outside. He was adopted as a small child. The parents were indulgent and, being financially well off, gave him many educational and social advantages. He came to the attention of a social service agency because he had been systematically stealing for some years from the small department store in the town where the family lived. Because of the father's social position, no one suspected the boy of stealing for a long time. When he was finally discovered, it was found that he usually returned the objects he had purloined a day or two later. Again, because of the position of the family in the community, the police were not called in, and instead, the parents were told the facts. They attempted to deal with Hubert in a kindly manner, but one day, when they were away from the home, the boy stole a sum of money and some of the mother's valuables and disappeared. He was later apprehended in another city and returned to his foster family.

A study of the boy's problem revealed that his relation with the foster mother was not an entirely wholesome one. Due to her own emotional need for a child, and her guilt because she was unable to have one of her own, she provoked and acted seductively with the boy. Her overprotection and infantilization of him were a defense against a deep-rooted hostility toward him. He emphasized her failure as a woman. On the other hand, Hubert had developed a strong sexual attachment toward her. His phantasies in relation to his foster mother aroused guilt feelings in him and fear and jealousy of his foster father. The stealing episodes were aimed to provoke punishment, which he felt he deserved. Since he was not caught in the act of stealing, he returned the objects, thereby doubling the chances of being discovered and punished. Failing to accomplish this end, and in a state of intense anxiety, he decided to run away from the relationships that caused him so much distress. The boy also resented his foster parents, whom he saw as the cause of his separation from his real parents. Thus running away was an attempt at finding the latter.

Intensive individual psychotherapy was indicated here for both the boy and the mother. The mother needed to be helped to overcome her feelings of guilt, especially toward her husband, and to understand her provocative and seductive behavior that retarded the boy's psychosexual development. For Hubert treatment was directed toward helping him reveal and recognize some of the early memories and phantasies around his biologic mother, and to help him recognize his feelings toward his foster parents.

Dennis, living in a congested slum area of a large city, presented another type of problem in delinquent behavior. Dennis was ten years old when he was apprehended by the police in the company of several boys of fifteen to seventeen who regularly committed minor thefts in the neighborhood. Dennis' special function in this gang was to climb through transoms and other small openings to unbolt doors and let the larger boys in. In some instances he handed out the stolen goods through these openings. When the gang was rounded up by the police, Dennis was also caught.

Dennis was one of a large family. Both the father and the mother were unsympathetic and cruel. In addition Dennis was the target of much hostility by other siblings. He grew up to be tough, hostile, and aggressive. He was a serious problem in school, bullied children on the street, and was generally rowdy in the neighborhood. One of the chief complaints by his parents was that Dennis gave them trouble because of his school difficulties and the frequent conflicts with teachers and school authorities.

After an investigation of the home and neighborhood, and a study of the boy's character, it became evident that it would be difficult, if not impossible, to correct his social maladjustments in the environment in which he lived. The parents were ignorant, elderly, and too set in their ways to be able to change their treatment of Dennis. It was also found impossible, for practical reasons, to effect the family's removal from the undesirable neighborhood and the companions to whom Dennis had become attached.

The child's removal from the undesirable home and neighborhood was indicated and he was sent to an institution in which wholesome relationships and adaptations would be encouraged. Since the boy's behavior was largely of a hostile and retaliatory nature, he needed to be treated with consideration by the institution's staff. They could not be too repressive and frustrating and thus confirm further his conviction that people are cruel and hostile. Individual psychotherapy was not essential in this case. What Dennis really needed was the opportunity to develop friendly and warm relations with individuals and be accepted by a constructive group. These should be supplied in the setting of a good institution, since they form the core of treatment there.

Paul's case was similar in some respects to that of Dennis, but it had some elements that required modification in the treatment plan. Paul, an only boy with two older sisters, had been physically inept since early childhood. His coordination was poor and his intelligence low. He failed in school, in individual relationships, in the neighborhood, and in the family. He had been treated unsympathetically by his parents, particularly by his strong, dominating, power-driven mother and equally strong sisters. All three constantly reemphasized his worthlessness, failure, and inadequacy as a person. He was used as a drudge, ran errands, did housework, and was in other ways humiliated.

The father was a weak man, under the domination of his wife and, to some extent, his daughters. He was not as negative toward the boy; he was rather indifferent. The father's adaptation to this trying situation was to leave well enough alone and he did not protect his son against onslaughts. Paul had no friends in the neighborhood or school. He occasionally played with children, usually being on the periphery. When he was accepted by a group of rowdy boys who were committing acts of minor violence in the neighborhood, he responded to this acceptance and became part of the gang, playing a subsidiary role.

At first Paul was passively defiant and latently hostile toward the psychiatric social worker but gradually established a positive relation with her since she was kind, accepting, and encouraging. Behind a facade of submissiveness and gentle manner, he soon revealed intensely hostile feelings toward his mother, and particularly toward the sisters. He felt weak and inadequate. Having had no support even from his father and few male identifications, he allied himself with any group that would give him some degree of acceptance. This was the rowdy gang in the neighborhood. Though this gang had not been committing serious crimes, they were nevertheless destructive and so annoying that on occasion police had to be called to disperse them.

After he had established a relationship with the case worker, Paul spoke very freely and was soon able to give up the gang. However, the case worker felt that he needed more positive and constructive relationships with children of his own age and identification with boys of less destructive habits than his former gang. He was therefore referred to Activity Group Therapy where, in addition to the boys, the therapist as well served as a constructive object of male identification. Despite Paul's constitutional limitations, treatment strengthened his ego, increased his self-esteem and he made an entirely satisfactory adjustment both in school and out. After two years of treatment he presented no difficulties.

A more serious problem was presented by *Charlotte,* who was committed to a correctional institution at the age of sixteen. She was the younger of two daughters. There was continuous marital discord in the family with occasional desertions by the father. The family atmosphere was full of quarrels and recriminations and considerable hostility existed between Charlotte and her older sister, who was found to have a schizoid personality. Charlotte had slept with her father during her early teens. Once, when she teased him, he grew angry and ran after her to punish her. Being diabetic and a partial invalid, he fell and broke a leg. Gangrene set in as a result, and he died. Soon after the father's death, Charlotte, at the age of fifteen became sexually promiscuous, including commerical prostitution. She finally ran away from home, was arrested and committed to a correctional institution. When her problems were further explored, it was found that she was very hostile toward her mother and sister and entertained death wishes toward them. She also felt responsible for her father's death, having been the immediate cause of the accident that brought on his final illness. She missed her father very much since he was basically a kind person in contrast to her mother and sister. Charlotte had sexual phantasies in relation to her father. Having slept in one bed with him, she had actually lived out, partially at least, her incestuous cravings. Her earlier death wishes toward him were fulfilled by his demise. All these conflicting emotions threw the girl into a neurotic panic, and she acted out her conflicts as she did to escape tension. Whether her sexual promiscuity was an act of expiation and self-punishment, or an effort to replace her father was not clear.

Intensive psychotherapy was necessary, but it would not have been effective in the setting in which she lived. It would have been impossible to work through with her the conflicting drives and the many difficulties while she remained at home and free to roam the streets again. A period of segregation was indicated during which the therapeutic efforts could take root and she was therefore committed to an institution.

The four cases briefly outlined were chosen as samples of the variety of psychodynamics in delinquent behavior, and the need for planning treatment to suit the special situation. While all the children had committed delinquent acts, the motivations and the dynamics operating within each were quite different, requiring different approaches in treatment. It is such recognition that holds promise for success in dealing with and correcting the character in the individual "delinquent." This is an elementaristic approach that views delinquency as a symptom of emotional malformation needing correction. If we view "delinquency" in a blanket fashion we may misdirect our therapeutic efforts as well as our understanding of it. Each individual needs special study and treatment.

Hubert and Charlotte, for example, acted out psychoneurotic conflicts, one through stealing, the other through sexual promiscuity. Both had run away as a solution to the inner conflicts that their life settings had perpetuated. Both needed direct psychotherapy. In Hubert's case this could be given in the environment in which he lived. Charlotte, on the other hand, had to be removed from her environment because of its unfavorable nature and because she had come in conflict with the law. Institutional commitment was especially indicated in her case, because she had reached an age when she could be brought into an adult instead of an adolescent court on a morals charge. If she had been arrested again, she would have been committed to a prison for adults. Sometimes an adolescent "delinquent" can be treated *in situ*, if there is no risk of being arrested under existing laws and sent to jail. His age makes it necessary to remove him from the environment, for a time at least, as a preventive measure against it.

Dennis, who was a primary behavior disorder, reacting to his hostile family, had to be placed in an institution in order to affect treatment. On the other hand, Paul, though also a primary behavior disorder, could be treated while at home. Thus Charlotte, a psychoneurotic, and Dennis a reactive behavior disorder, both needed institutional treatment, while Hubert and Paul, one a psychoneurotic, the other a primary behavior disorder, could remain at home.

"Delinquents" with psychopathic personality structure require institutional treatment where rigid restrictions can be applied to their narcissistic behavior. Because psychopaths cannot establish transference relations, a group is more effective in such cases, but the group cannot be permissive or voluntary. In institutional treatment of these patients, restrictions and punishments must be inexorable.

Some delinquent behavior is a result of constitutional or organic defects and pathologic conditions such as epilepsy, schizophrenia and other psychotic states. Appropriate medical treatment or confinement in a hospital are indicated for these patients. Here, too, it is important to first ascertain the dynamics and pathology of each so-called "delinquent" before appropriate treatment can be initiated.

In view of the fact that one of the common treatment tools for delinquent children and adolescents is a corrective institution, it is rather essential that a clearer understanding of its function and plan of operation be evolved. The chief values of an institution are *(a)* the removal of the individual from the pressing or pathogenic environment in which he lives, *(b)* the conditioned environment through which corrective identifications and constructive experiences are supplied, and *(c)* the reeducative efforts of the institutional staff [58, 62].

The removal of the youngster from his environment diminishes his need to pursue his customary behavior. The overtly aggressive or covertly retaliatory acts that served him so well in his adaptations to the old setting are no longer as essential in the new. Here the relationships are different and the earlier targets of hostility are absent. It is true that he can, and often does, displace emotions upon his fellow residents and the staff. However, he can be made aware that they are only substitutes for his real hostile aims. The real objects of his hostility when present serve as irritants to set off his destructive impulses, while their absence renders him more accessible to the reeducational atmosphere of the institution. Direct psychotherapy by the clinical staff is also more effective under such circumstances. The protective toughness and deceptive mildness of the "delinquent" can be relaxed at least to some extent where they no longer serve any special purpose. Thus the resistances to, and defenses against, relationships are diminished and he becomes more amenable and accessible to external influences of his new environment.[1]

The proper utilization of this new set of attitudes, which may or may not be apparent, and the exploitation of the increased pliability of the youngster, are the main tasks of the institution. Conditioning of environment means that it is organized with the purpose of including the elements and relations that would prove salutary to the psychologic needs of the residents. It is conditioned in the same sense that a

---

1. We assume that the corrective institution is set up and functions as a reeducational, not a punitive, instrumentality.

good hospital for medical patients is: the total environment—and not only the medication—is designed to help the patient to overcome his malady.

The basic therapeutic element in the setting of a correctional institution is the attitude of the staff. Their interest in children and young people and their sympathy for persons in difficulty is so essential that whatever else is done is futile if these be lacking. It is recognized that the pivotal and the most effective reeducative situation lies in free and friendly relations between adults and children. No program of activities is itself sufficient to effect emotional reorientation of the dissocial personality. The feelings of satisfaction and the release of tension that arise from adequate creative and group functioning must be backed by satisfying parent-child relations, even if these come from parent surrogates. It is well known that the destructive impulses toward society of the delinquent youth are an extension of his hostility toward adults who figured in his early life. This hostility can be lessened and, in many cases, even eradicated through feelings of trust and affection which adults must inspire in youth. Staff and child relations are therefore a special concern of the reeducational as well as the clinical work of an institution.

Another factor is the unity and harmony among the staff, their loyalty to one another and the institution. Hostility, dissatisfaction, indifference, gossip—any such manifestations—serve to confirm and justify the child's own hostile acts and attitudes by identification and implied sanction. Tensions and disharmony among the staff create the same anxiety as that set up through the child's intrafamilial conflicts. He should not be transplanted into an environment which contains the very elements that caused his difficulties. It should rather have a corrective effect.

The institution, and especially the cottage unit, is in a real sense the substitute for a family, and even for the total community. This particular factor must be stressed. Usually an institution is viewed as a specially designed community, but to the disturbed individual who had been denied adequate primary relations in infancy and childhood the close relations of the small group are particularly important. Our studies of the attitudes of adolescent girls in a corrective institution indicate that they transferred their feelings toward their mothers to the institution as a whole. Both are restraining and prohibitive; they both deny pleasures, especially sexual gratifications, and the girls' hostilities and resentments were therefore in many respects similar to those they had had toward their mothers. On the other hand, their attitudes toward the male director of the institution were similar to those they entertained toward their fathers. They had the same ambivalent feelings toward him and acted as seductively [58].

As in a good family, the institution needs to exert restraint on undesirable behavior and to offer guidance. While the basic atmosphere is one of understanding and tolerance, restrictions are necessary. The youngster must first acquire, in some instances, self-control and social responsibility. This he can achieve only through friendly restraint by individuals whom he accepts and trusts, and with whom he can identify.

In this respect also the treatment plan should be varied for each individual. The neurotic child who has to live in a congregate community such as an institution, is subject to many pressures and anxieties that ensue from intimate group living. He may, therefore, grow anxious and disturbed; clinical service is essential for him. Psychotherapy provides the support he needs as well as the corrections for his intrapsychic difficulties. On the other hand, for a child with a primary behavior disorder, a constructive group life where he can develop relationships with his equals, attach himself to one or more adults and gain other satisfactions that help redirect his aggressions and change his attitude may be adequate.

Charlotte, for example, needed to work through in psychotherapy her basic neurotic conflicts in relation to her father, while at the same time the institution served her as a protection against coming into serious conflict with the law. Dennis, on the other hand, developed feelings of acceptance, belonging, warmth and sympathy with staff members and other children. He was able to establish a sense of his own worth and overcome his need for retaliatory, delinquent behavior. Clinical treatment for Dennis is not important, though it is not contraindicated.

In the cases of psychopathic personalities the institution provides the direct pressures that these individuals have attempted to escape all their lives more or less successfully. Authority creates anxieties in them and they seek the help of some staff member. It is necessary to bring home to them the fact that they cannot without compunction continue to exploit the world for their personal narcissistic needs. Pressure must be sufficiently great to arouse anxiety. Such pressures can be supplied only by a restraining institution, for such individuals evade all situations that impede or limit their narcissistic self-indulgence. The intense anxiety at the root of the psychopath's personality structure is so deeply repressed and overlaid by suavity and evasiveness that it can be reached only by an equally intense threat to his social survival. He must discover through inexorable and uncompromising inevitability that his antisocial or unsocial adaptive patterns are of no avail and that his security is seriously threatened. Only under these circumstances would he seek help from another person. This initial relationship, if dealt with skillfully, may be the beginning of reconstruction of the patient's character.

It should always be kept in mind that while pressures are applied routinely, the psychopath should have the opportunity to relate to at least one individual as a means for allaying his anxieties. This person becomes the substitute parent toward whom the patient can develop the type of relationship that he missed during childhood. Treatment consists in shocking the "delinquent" from his narcissistic self indulgence, at the same time supplying the support and the solace that he may get from such a relationship. The institution functions here in a double role.

Frequently the person to whom such a resident will turn is not a professionally trained psychotherapist, but it is advisable and effective that he be skilled in dealing with this type of problem, for the psychopath is not above deceiving even those who try to help him. A skilled psychotherapist is therefore most suitable.

Another aim of the institution is to create a reeducative setting. It is commonly accepted that psychotherapy is a form of reeducation. This, however, is emotional reeducation; that is, regression is permitted without fear of retaliation, and at the same time growth-producing relations and experiences are provided. A good correctional program must seek to reeducate the youngsters on the motor, intellectual, and social levels, as well as in the area of emotions. It must conform to the social realities of the culture in which the institution exists. In our culture the chief educative foci are *(a)* the family, *(b)* the school, *(c)* individual leisure-time interests or hobbies. and *(d)* recreation in groups. The institution, also should supply these.

The cottage or dormitory unit and other intimate small group loyalties conform in many respects to the family pattern. There is also academic education, but here schools ought to divest themselves of the rigid practices so common in the ordinary classroom. The teacher here must recognize that the brevity of attention span, difficulty in concentrating, restlessness and hypermotility are uncontrollable symptoms of inner tensions and may even denote serious mental disturbance. Divergencies in behavior that are annoying in the average child have to be tolerated and accepted as manifestations of the deep-rooted problems of the pupils who need correction. All the members of the institutional staff must understand and accept their part in creating a therapeutic atmosphere. This refers to the teachers as well.

Academic requirements must by all means be subordinated to permanent or temporary interests, and achievement measured by each individual's intellectual and emotional capacities. Standardized levels, marks and grades only increase anxiety in already anxious youngsters. Low marks or failure serve to further deepen insecurity and further deflate already low self-esteem. This plan does not ignore the need for *tool* subjects: reading, writing, and the elements of arithmetic, but it emphasizes individualization and genuine interests as better motives for learning than authoritarian didacticism. Nor does it counsel indulgence. In a plan of reeducation, requirements must be met, but the requirements should not be such as to intensify the youngster's difficulties.

Sufficient opportunities should also be provided for genuine recreational interests to meet individual predilections, both solitary and in groups. It is recognized that "problem children" are frequently more talented than are the average. The present writer's experience with children and young people in correctional institutions points to the fact that there are more children with superior artistic inclinations than in the general community. Recreation in an institution therefore must provide for the expression of talents as well as of phantasies. It should be varied and offer opportunities for work in the graphic and plastic arts, in music, dramatics, dancing, creative writing, as well as in physical activities, sports and games.

Our observation showed that in one such school at least, as many of the residents spent their leisure time in the library, when made available to them, as in the gymnasium, and that the chess and checker clubs were as popular as the basketball team. Such a variety of educational and recreational clubs and groups are found in the larger communities of cities and towns and they are important in the institution's reeducational program as well. Scout troops and similar organizations are very much in order here, since some of the children had already had experience with such groups; also because they serve as a preparation for fitting the children into the community when they are returned to their homes. Dances, hikes, and picnics, and other mass activities in which young people participate in the ordinary community are also necessary, as well as are interests in larger community concerns such as the Red Cross and other charitable and philanthropic enterprises. The aim should be to model the institution to accord with the total culture from which the residents come and to which they are to be returned, and to keep as much contact and continuity with it as possible. The total program should also aim to provide stimulating as well as sublimatory activities and thus normalize and balance the lives of the young people.

A girl of eighteen who had been committed on a morals charge to a reeducational institution had consistently chosen to do the most menial work, such as cleaning the toilets, the slop pails and mops, and insisted on doing this for a long period of time. She frequently got into fights with other girls who spitefully attempted to replace her. She was particularly unattractive, she had buck teeth, a protruding jaw, a long face and nose; in fact, a "horse face." Her mother was very destructive in her attitude toward this girl, repeatedly calling attention to her unattractiveness. She was the only girl in the family of four or five boys. The mother resented the fact that the only girl turned out to be a "monkey face," as she put it. She had been a sexual delinquent from her early teens, having resided in the amusement section of the town near the seashore.

Through the reeducational program instituted in the school, it was discovered that she had rather unique ability in arts, particularly in designing women's clothes. It was evident from the study of her case that her interest in dress designing was a sublimation of her homosexual interests, which she also expressed in heterosexual promiscuity. Her interests and talents were encouraged by the staff and she became one of the leaders in the graphic arts in the school. The girl was much pleased with her achievement and often spoke of her special capacities. She also began to act more maturely and in a more dignified manner. While in the past she had been submissive and ingratiating to the other girls in her cottage, she now refused to play a secondary role. She dressed better, began to use rouge and lipstick, and generally made a much more mature and suitable appearance. She also participated in many activities and played an adequate role in all of them. Her rather high intelligence helped her in this, and she soon became one of the more influential members of the group.

At one time she conveyed to the present writer the following rather significant thought. She said: "I know that I am not attractive, but I am bright. There are men who like bright women even though they are not good looking." This improvement in her self-esteem and the realistic acceptance of her inadequacies had proved of great value in her social recovery. After she was discharged from the institution she made an adequate adjustment in the community.

The value of manual activities as sublimation was demonstrated by another girl of about fifteen, who had been unable to sleep for many nights. In fact, she was so tense that she refused to go to her bedroom, and spent several nights lying on a tiny bench in the hallway of the cottage reading the telephone directory by a dim light. The arts and crafts instructor was asked to take her into the workshop and get her interested in woodwork. It was felt that through this aggressive occupation the girl would redirect her hostile feelings. After she had worked a few days in the shop she seemed to quiet down. Once, about midnight, she took a large board and hacked away at it violently until she cut the figure of a man out of it. Having done this, she went upstairs and to sleep.

It is difficult to interpret the exact meaning of this. We know that rechanneling hostile emotions through manual expression has helped other patients. The satisfaction that the girl obtained from cutting a man out of the board remains unexplained. However, a number of explanations can be imagined.

An elementaristic approach to "delinquents" which involves a diagnostic and psychodynamic understanding of the individual precludes blanket assignment to therapy groups. Some children who commit delinquent acts may be accessible to group treatment, while others are not. The "delinquent" who acts out intrapsychic conflicts which are not too great in intensity may be treated in a group. A child with deflated self esteem who reacts to it with asocial behavior, as in the case of Paul, can be built up through permissive group relationships and an encouraging group therapist. It should always be kept in mind, however, that hostile and antisocial behavior is contagious, and that other members of the group may fall into this pattern. In many cases, particularly with younger boys and girls, the risk may be quite small.

An example of the suitability for group treatment of children who commit delinquent acts can be gleaned from stealing. When a child steals only from members of his family and from relatives, he may be suitable for group therapy; but when he has a prolonged history of stealing from others in the community, placement in a group has to be considered very carefully. In the first instance, stealing may represent taking love of which the child was deprived and when love is given to him in the group the motivation for stealing is eliminated. When, on the other hand, stealing is an organized retaliatory act, the child will not give it up through group treatment and the possibility that it may become general practice in the group is considerable.

Following the example of her mother and sister, an adolescent girl had been shoplifting for mány years. As a result of discussions in an interview therapy group, she had given up this practice. Her identifications with the girls and the therapist and the activation of her superego by the group caused her to repress the impulse to steal. Similarly a group of eight-year-old boys and girls reported to the therapist on the stealing activities of one of the boys. The matter was discussed by all the children who confessed to having stolen themselves on different occasions. The boy in question gave up the stealing because, he said some months later, "we not only talked about it, but we thought about it."

In discussing the treatment of delinquents in groups, Dr. Fritz Redl had the following to say in a paper presented at the 1946 conference of the American Group Therapy Association. "Personally, I haven't seen a single real delinquent yet cured by just 'group therapy.' Whenever I thought I had such a case, it soon turned out that he wasn't a real delinquent to begin with, but only a neurotic under 'tough guy' disguise. So what we cured him of was his delinquent disguise. After we were through with that, we had a nice neurosis on our hands, or prepsychotic traits which do not react kindly to what we are trying to do, and somebody has to start treating that phase now."

Dr. Redl's conclusion can be justified on theoretic grounds, but it also was confirmed by experience. We found that "delinquents" with psychopathic personality structure do not respond to group treatment [93]. Group therapy, whether activity or interview, is based upon the patient's need to be accepted, his desire to belong to a group and his striving to be well thought of by others. This we describe as *social hunger*. In extreme behavior disorders, psychopathic personalities, and in the psychotic states, this social hunger is either very weak or nonexistent. There is, therefore, no foundation on which to base group treatment. Dr. Redl's statement also warns us of the importance of a thorough study and diagnostic understanding of each patient before he is placed in a group. It is essential that we thoroughly understand the prospective candidate for group treatment. Whether his delinquent behavior is a result of neurotic conflict, reactive behavior disorder, psychotic or organic sources can, and should be, ascertained in advance. It is undesirable, and even dangerous, from the point of view of the patient—and certainly from the point of view of the group—to assign members to it without a thorough consideration of the psychodynamic and psychopathologic factors operating in the individual.

Experience shows that the use of the descriptive and generic terms "delinquent" and "delinquency" in a blanket fashion is misleading. Only an elementaristic approach can produce therapeutic results. Both the interests of the individual and society are best safeguarded when we deal with these phenomena in the light of each individual and when treatment is planned in accordance with the clinical facts established in advance.

DELINQUENCY PREVENTION
(1950)

A group of ten-year-old boys and girls discussed stealing.[1] The problem reached a culmination when they had seen one of their number attempting to steal from a store and he was nearly caught They came with their difficulty to the therapist in whom they had full faith and who they knew could help them. Although only one of their number was accused, it transpired during the discussion that all the children had stolen at one time or another. Some continued the practice on an occasional basis, others had given it up. When the therapist asked why they stole, a number of answers were put forward. One of the children said that she stole because she wanted things she could not otherwise have, but the majority said they stole because they were angry with their parents and wanted to punish them. With the help of the therapist the effectiveness of this retaliatory behavior was further explored by the children. No definite conclusions had been reached, but some weeks later the boy who was first brought before the group as the culprit confided to the therapist that he no longer stole. When the therapist asked: "Is it because we talked about it?" one of the little girls who was within earshot of this conversation (though it was carried on in an almost whispering tone) said: "We

---

1. This was an interview (talking) group because these children were too disturbed for Activity Group Therapy. See [44].

have not only talked about it, but we have thought about it." Perhaps the above is one of the keys to the use of group psychotherapy in the prevention of delinquency.

Too many children and adolescents bear the burdens of emotional stress in helpless loneliness. The tensions created by resentment and often justifiable hostility, and the natural need for retaliation and revenge, often prove too much for an individual to bear. Sharing with others who are similarly situated lightens the psychological burden, decreases tensions, and strengthens each to bear up under outer pressures and inner stress. It is not always *therapy* that we achieve by these means.

Therapy, as we understand, is a fundamental reorganization of psychic forces in the personality, resulting in a greater harmony between impulse and act. This cannot always be achieved through the group process, nor is it necessary for the purpose we have in mind. Of great value is the strength that each induces in the other and the comfort that sharing yields. These relax the individual, making it unnecessary for him to act out his conflicts and vengeful feelings. Young children, whose personalities are still in the process of formation and whose feelings and thoughts still yield to outside influences may permanently improve as a result of interpersonal and group experiences. With appropriate help from the therapist, teachers and parents, children change much more readily than do adults and adolescents.

To adolescents particularly, group belonging and sharing of feelings is of utmost importance. The need to belong (what we designate as *social hunger*) is a primary and instinctive craving in the individual. Especially is it valuable to be part of a group where one's deepest feelings can be revealed without fear of punishment or criticism, where acts and attitudes are accepted and understood by an understanding and sympathetic adult.

I have suggested elsewhere [44] that delinquency is not a unitary and definitive concept. It is my belief that the term has only legal and moral meaning. Psychologically it would be difficult to prove that there is such a thing as a "delinquent personality." Persons in various categories and with various types of problems commit delinquent acts but in each case the act serves different needs in different individuals depending upon his nuclear problem. Antisocial acts may express hostile, retaliatory feelings against society as a displacement of hostile and aggressive feelings toward parents and other persons in the family or school. Strong inner conflicts which an individual is unable to bear with equanimity may be acted out as a resolution of that conflict, and the neurotic need for punishment because of strong guilt feelings may result in "delinquent" behavior. The unconscious seeks to purge itself of the burden of guilt by provoking punishment. Grandiosity of a delinquent nature is frequently a way through which a youngster, whose feelings of self-esteem and power had been undermined in the home and school, builds up his self-esteem. For the weak such acts serve to countermand feelings of weakness and inadequacy.

Sexual delinquency in boys may have very deep significance in their psychic organization. But it may also be a result of misguided overstimulation in the family and outside. A girl deprived emotionally, rejected in her home, where the foundations of strength and power should be laid, becomes delinquent because of her need for affection and love. The very fact that she is accepted by someone, even on such a basis, fills a void in her emotional life.

Such feelings of weakness, inadequacy, and hostility are brought to the surface in group discussions. The introspective preoccupations, fears, anxiety and tensions are dissipated in the group. Belonging to a group also reduces guilt and strengthens inner resources for dealing with difficulties and anxieties. An individual "acts out" when he is unable to deal with impulses and drives intelligently and understandingly. Acting out is a symptom of a weak ego organization, whose function is to properly control impulses and tensions. Group belonging and sharing changes the individual's concept of himself or self-image so that he sees himself in a less lugubrious light and a happier, more constructive outlook results.

Group psychotherapy for delinquency prevention can be employed in several forms. Activity Group Therapy, by means of free acting out in the presence of other children and an accepting, permissive adult, helps in all the directions enumerated. It resolves inner tensions, meets affectional cravings, yields feelings of acceptance and self-worth, supplies a field for testing out growing powers and a place for learning to relate to others with all that it involves. As a result of this experience the individual accepts himself with less guilt and tension and when this occurs he can better accept others and give up his destructive impulses for the relationships that accrue. The therapist, who is permissive, tolerant, and accepting gives the child a new concept and feeling concerning adults and, therefore, the adult world. The latter becomes a less hostile, less punitive, less frightening place, populated by "enemies" whom one has to fight in defense. Improvement in children and their more acceptable behavior in turn diminishes the punitive and rejecting attitudes of the adults around them and the vicious circle is thus broken. We have found that parents, siblings, and teachers have all modified their treatment of children because of the latter's improvement. This more constructive attitude of adults helps the potential delinquent to fit better in his social environment. It must be kept in mind, however, that this method is applicable only to children between the ages of seven and twelve and membership in these groups must be carefully selected and properly grouped [53].

Because of the brevity of this paper it is not possible to present supportive case material to show how Activity Group Therapy has helped prevent delinquent trends in preadolescent children. It will be necessary to refer the reader to some case material already published. Among these are Ray Rosen, a white girl of fourteen who was going out with neighborhood Puerto Rican and black adult men and boys older than herself. Another girl, Tess, who planned to run away from home, brought her problem to the other members of the group to settle her dilemma. Another such case was John Sloan, referred for treatment by the Crime Prevention Bureau of the Police Department, who since the age of nine participated with a gang of older boys in purloining goods from freight terminals and local markets.

The case of Paul Schwartz is also interesting in this connection. The particular difficulty he presented was his intensely disturbing behavior in any group whether at school or outside. When he entered a room in the middle of a meeting or a class he would disrupt all of the proceedings and put the group into a turmoil.

In the analytic group psychotherapy technique no arts and crafts materials are used. The entire treatment process is carried on through free-associative conversation among the members of the group in which they help each other bring out their repressed feelings and early traumatic experiences. The release gained from such group interviews, the insight attained, and the transference relationships established among the group members with each other and with the therapist, produce a general improvement in the participants. The technique stems from individual psychotherapy of the psychoanalytic type. This technique has been described in a rich literature and is modified by various psychotherapists to suit their own particular predilections and convictions. The present writer has recently published a book on this type of therapy [56]. The reader's attention is particularly called to those parts of this volume where adolescent girls discuss techniques of dealing with their sexual drives and help each other in understanding this baffling conflict characteristic of that age. Discussions of young girls who seek the guidance and advice of the group in relation to their desires to run away from home or quit school also appear in the book. Special attention is called to chapter 13 in which analytic group psychotherapy in an institution for "delinquent" girls is presented with a transcript of a group interview. Here we have clearly illustrated how young people baffled by their conflicting impulses and their inability to bear the pressures of an unfriendly adult environment strengthen one another in dealing with their problems in a socially acceptable manner. In this, of course, the therapist plays an important role.

Among the modifications of analytic group psychotherapy recently employed is one by Lloyd W. McCorkle, which he describes as "guided group interaction."[2] McCorkle had employed this technique. with adult prisoners, but it would seem to be one that should be tried out at the point of early manifestations of delinquency with adolescents and young adults. Guided group interaction is also based on free discussion, by groups, of material derived from the members' pre-institutional and institutional experiences. The talks are carried on in an easy, informal, and permissive atmosphere. The function of the leader is to encourage the members by his attitude of acceptance to verbalize their resentment and bring to the surface feelings that they otherwise tend to conceal from others, and sometimes even from themselves. It is understandable that when one becomes aware of reasons for his unsocial behavior and sees it in the light of a more mature understanding, he would not need to continue in his re-

2. Bixby, F., and McCorkle,L. (1950). Applying the principles of group therapy in correctional institutions. *Federal Probation,* March, pp. 36-40.

taliatory or self-destructive paths that he had adopted for himself. The authors of the paper make somewhat more modest claims for their technique which is as follows:

(1) Making people—personnel as well as inmates—aware of one another as personalities; (2) reducing tensions, although initially the introduction of the program may increase tension; (3) bringing greater insight on the part of some of the inmates, as measured by psychiatric and psychological examinations; (4) opening channels of communication between the "world of inmates and the world of administrators" (the number of "gripes" about the institution and its personnel decreased); and (5) providing meaningful social experiences for a greater number of inmates.

However, group psychotherapy, or any of its derivatives, cannot possibly be a total cure or preventive of delinquent behavior. Some individuals are so deeply disturbed and psychologically malformed that such techniques cannot reconstruct their deep-rooted destructive drives. Chief among those who are unsuitable for group psychotherapy are the much debated and little understood "psychopathic personalities" in [55]. However, within certain limits, and these limits will probably be widened in the future, group psychotherapy and its various derivative techniques will become a very important method in the prevention of delinquent behavior and in curing it in early and incipient states. It is particularly suitable as a prophylactic measure.

CHAPTER 46

MILIEU AND GROUP THERAPY FOR DELINQUENTS
(1948)

In a discussion of delinquency it is necessary to define the meaning in which the term is employed. The term is frequently used in its genetic sense to describe deviant behavior of an antisocial or asocial nature. It connotes the aggressive, destructive, or hostile acts which create difficulties in the community and counter legal statutes. This is the legal, perhaps moralistic, meaning of the term. More frequently, and probably more erroneously, the term is intended to describe the psychological organization of personality as differentiated from the behavioral pattern.

Experience shows that "delinquency" or "delinquent" cannot be used as an all-inclusive clinical entity. In the past we have fallen into the error of treating all "delinquents" alike. Actually delinquent behavior may be a symptom of widely diverse psychological causative, and to the clinically oriented person this is of utmost importance. It would be more correct to say that people commit delinquent acts rather than to describe them as "delinquents." This is at the present time the growing practice of psychotherapists, caseworkers, and psychiatrists. They are beginning to recognize that delinquency has to be broken down to its psychodynamic components in order to make treatment effective.

Delinquent acts are committed for many reasons and one cannot attribute them to any single cause. A delinquent act may be a convenient way to retaliate for the wrong that parents, teachers and society have done to an individual. An act which may of itself incur punishment may be attractive to a person who is so guilt-laden that he neurotically invites such punishment. Crime also serves to resolve neurotic conflicts between aggressive hostility and prohibitions of the superego. We have found that some boys who feel themselves inferior and inadequate, especially if they are unacceptable to aggressive groups in their neighborhoods, are likely to commit delinquent acts because they wish to convince themselves and others of their strength and power. Girls, too, who feel themselves undesirable and unattractive, may become what is frequently referred to as sexual delinquents. Emotional deprivations from which such girls suffer cause them to enter such relations because of the status it gives them and because of their need for affection.

One of the important dynamics of delinquency and crime is the factor of masochistic and self-punishing satisfactions that punishment yields. I have elsewhere reported a case of a twelve-year-old adopted boy, who despite financial affluence of the foster parents, habitually stole and employed the unique pattern of returning stolen goods to the stores. In doing this he wished to make certain of being caught and punished. When he was not successful in this, he stole valuables from his home and ran away. An investigation of the psychodynamics of this case revealed that the boy strove to invoke punishment for his incestuous impulses toward his foster mother and destructive drives toward her husband [44].

An example of the cause of sexual delinquency is supplied by a girl who was particularly unattractive, a fact that was only too frequently emphasized by her mother who was much disappointed by the girl's appearance. At a very early age she succumbed to the friendly attentions of men in her neighborhood to assuage her cravings for warmth and affection that were denied her in her family circle. The fact that she was an only girl in a family with many brothers may have added to her problem. She felt herself different from all the other siblings and perhaps also that she was physically atypical. She may have had also masculine strivings as an imitation of her brothers and combined with it feelings of worthlessness. All of these factors, especially when they appear in combination, would find adequate resolution in her delinquent acts.

Another contributing factor frequently encountered among delinquent boys especially, is such a common somatic deviation as small size and unusual or grotesque appearance. A boy of small stature or with some such stigma is tempted to commit delinquent acts especially with others usually older and larger in size. In doing so he grows in stature in his own eyes and those of his peers and is thus compensated for his physical inadequacies and inferiorities. The frequency with which one finds such children among those who get into difficulties with the community is especially impressive and points to very definite aims that institutional treatment has to set for itself.

At eleven years of age Peter was arrested with a gang of older boys who were involved in stealing and other destructive acts in the neighborhood. The boy was one in a large family of rejecting and unsympathetic parents and siblings. He was of very small stature and when he attached himself to the gang they found many uses for him. One was to act as a lookout; another was to climb through transoms. The status and acceptance he earned from his gang mates compensated him both for the neglect in the home and being a misfit among his peers because of his size.

More serious constitutional and organic defects that manifest themselves in behavioral symptoms must be clinically established before placement in an institution. Such conditions as epilepsy, epileptic equivalents, schizophrenia and other psychotic states require appropriate medical and psychiatric hospital treatment. Placement in a reeducational institution or correctional school may be entirely counterindicated. It is of utmost importance to first establish the dynamics and pathology, medically and psychologically, of each so-called "delinquent" before appropriate treatment can be planned.

Where delinquent behavior is prompted by a youngster's psychopathic personality structure, placement in an institution is indicated. Because the psychopath is unable to establish the type of relation with an individual therapist necessary in psychotherapy, restraints such as one finds in an institution are likely to be more effective. Control here must be consistent. It is necessary to bring home to such youngsters the fact that they cannot continue in their exploitive, narcissistic way of life. Pressures and limitations must be great enough to arouse the latent anxiety which is at the bottom of the psychopath's character even though he represses it so thoroughly and successfully [93]. They should not be given a chance to evade these or to get out from under them. The psychopath's basic anxiety, deeply repressed and overlaid as it is by suavity and evasiveness, can be reached only by equally strict pressures and threats to his security. The aim here is to force the resident of the institution to seek help from some one, preferable an adequately trained and understanding staff member. Such a relation should be utilized to help the youngster to evolve a new conception of people and of his need of them. If he can attach himself to someone who would become the substitute parent, as it were, toward whom he can *de novo* establish a relationship that he had missed out on during his childhood, he is well on the road to changing his character structure. As I have already indicated elsewhere, the person to whom such a child or adolescent turns for support should be a psychotherapist skilled in dealing with this type of problem. For the psychopath is not above hoodwinking the one who attempts to help him.

Having outlined rather sketchily, to be sure, some of the basic considerations in the psychodynamics of delinquency, we can turn now to the main topics of this paper, namely a consideration of the environmental setting and the direct use of groups in the treatment of so-called delinquents. Before we turn to these subjects, however, it is necessary to make clear the aims and objectives of placing children in institutions, or better still, removing them from their homes and community.

The factor of retribution and punishment no longer motivates us here. We also have found, by bitter experience—and at great cost to communities—that brutalizing and mistreating the delinquent and criminal are entirely ineffective in rehabilitation efforts. Our aims are rather therapeutic and reeducational. What are the means that we can employ here?

First is the removal of the child from the influences of his environment such as the home, the school, and the social group; *secondly,* exposing him to a more wholesome environment of corrective relations and experiences; and *thirdly,* planful reeducative and clinical work in a conditioned environment. To do this, our institutional community must be so planned that aggressive and retaliatory acts would no longer serve the individual's needs for recognition and acceptance. While the resident may still tend to displace his feelings upon the people in the new environment, which he at first often does, if he is treated with sympathy and understanding he soon realizes the ineffectiveness of this procedure. Especially is this easily accomplished where individual case work is part of the treatment. The child becomes aware of the difference between the real objects of his hostility and the displacement pattern he employs. Because of this realization he gives up his conviction that all people are hostile. He grows more accessible to the influences of the reeducational atmosphere of the institution and can accept with more profit direct psychotherapy from the clinical staff. The resistances and defenses he had built up toward people and the world are as a result relaxed and he becomes accessible to the effects of his new milieu.

To help the "delinquent" become thus more pliable is one of the main tasks of institutional treatment. An institution is primarily a conditioned environment, not a controlled environment. The contrast of these two concepts seems evident on the surface. Control is only a part of the picture here, and at best must be used with discrimination. "Conditioning of an environment means that it is organized and set so as to include the elements and relations that would prove salutary to the needs of residents or inmates. It is conditioned in the same sense that a hospital for medical patients is: the total environment—and not only the medication—is designed to help the patient to conquer his malady [44].

The Staff

I come now to factors in the setting of a corrective atmosphere which I have emphasized many times in many connections in the past. These are the basic attitudes and personalities of the staff. Genuine interest in and sympathy for young people is most essential. Training, intellectual comprehension, and academic knowledge are futile without them. The love and understanding that was denied to the dissocial child, which is the cause of his dissociality, must be supplied him in the new milieu. Another important element is the harmony and cooperation among the staff, their respect for one another and loyalty to the institution. These elements in human relations have always been lacking in the lives of these children and this they must find in the new environment. In discussing this subject elsewhere, I have said the following, which bears repeating: "Hostility, dissatisfaction, indifference, gossip—any such manifestations—serve to confirm and justify the child's own hostile acts and attitudes by identification and implied sanction. Tensions and disharmony among the staff create the same anxiety as that set up through the child's intrafamilial conflicts. He should not be transplanted into an environment which contains the very elements that caused his difficulties. It should rather have a corrective effect. The institution, and especially the cottage unit, is in a real sense the substitute for a family" [44].

A child whose primary relations in infancy and childhood have been defective must find corrective relations in treatment, that is, positive transference and constructive identifications. We found in group treatment that adolescent girls in an institution transfer the feelings which they have toward their mothers to the institution. Both restrain and prohibit; both deny pleasures, especially sexual gratifications. Hostilities toward both, therefore, are in many ways similar. On the other hand, their attitudes toward the male director were similar to those toward their fathers.

Despite our emphasis upon understanding, sympathy and permissiveness, restraint and control, as well as guidance, are the functions of the institutional milieu. It must serve as a training group for self-control and social responsibility. This can be accomplished best through group action when possible, through identification with staff members, and to a lesser extent, by means of rules and direct control.

A reeducative milieu must primarily create an emotional setting that will undo the destructive feelings and attitudes engendered by an unsatisfactory childhood. But reeducation as a technique needs to turn attention to desirable changes in motor, intellectual, and social functions of the individual as well. Its social realities must as far as possible parallel those of the outside world and its culture. The chief educative instrumentalities in our culture are the home, the school, individual hobbies, group recreation, and religion. The institution, too, needs to be planned to supply these.

The intimate relations that arise in the cottage unit have many elements of the family pattern, and the relations here should be patterned after a good family. The proper choice of cottage parents or supervisors is at once a most important and a most difficult task. Academic schooling is a requisite, but schools in institutions must be tolerant, flexible, and free of the sadistic drives that characterize the ordinary classroom. Teachers must accept hyperactivity, distractability, and low achievement as symptoms of emotional illness rather than challenges to their authority. Nearly all children committed to institutions are school problems and it would not do to reemphasize here their failures and shortcomings. Teachers in schools of dissocial children must accept their part in the total therapeutic setting of the institution, for they can, through their dictatorial attitude, undo the good accomplished by clinical treatment and by other members of the staff.

School requirements must be subordinated to the real interests of the residents. Academic achievement under these circumstances is secondary to the changes in emotional and social attitudes. This does not mean that children and young people should be permitted to vegetate or live an effortless life. They can be activated and this can be done without arousing hostility and resentment. We should not hold over their heads the fear of failure by applying standardized marks and grades. The aim should rather be the building of self-confidence and self-esteem. Individualization and true interests are better by far to motivate learning than fear and pressure.

Recreational Outlets

Solitary and group recreation are to be considered an integral part of milieu therapy. My own experience with young people in correctional institutions has convinced me that the incidence of talented and superior children is much greater among them than in the general community. They are gifted in graphic and plastic arts, in music, drama, dancing, creative writing. Physical recreation such as sports and games is, of course, important [125].

The larger community in our culture provides many outlets in group association which should be also the case in institutional living. Boy and Girl Scout troops, Junior Achievement, Youth Builders, free association and special interest groups need to be incorporated into the institutional culture. Experience in these groups helps prepare the youngsters for the time when they will return to the normal community . Mass activities such as dances, outings, picnics, and theatricals are also essential, and interest in larger community concerns such as the Red Cross, charitable, church, and philanthropic enterprises, should be a part of leisure time activities. Through these means continuity is maintained between the life in the institution and the larger culture to which the residents will return.

This should be one of the chief aims in conditioning the institutional environment, namely, its continuity and relatedness to the best in the culture from which the young people have been removed and to which they will eventually return. Too great a break with the culture and home environment, which is characteristic of prisons, is not only punitive in its intent, but destructive of those elements in the human personality which we attempt to encourage and develop in order to make the residents suitable members of society.

Direct Group Treatment

Turning attention from the milieu and considering direct group treatment for delinquents in institutions we are confronted with some real problems. To begin with it is axiomatic that Activity Group Therapy, where "acting out" is the sole method of treatment is, on theoretical grounds at least, unsuitable for institutions. This technique has never been tried in an institutional setting, but one can envisage the disadvantages in its use.[1] Free, unimpeded acting out among children is contagious and tends to become intensified. When it becomes widespread it may well prove disastrous. The minimal controls essential to group living and restraint cannot be relaxed without the risk of serious disorganization in the school's community. In addition there is the factor of choice that would present difficulties. Some who are chosen for such "free" groups would consider themselves stigmatized, others would view themselves as privileged. All who are eliminated would be resentful. There would arise the problem of social castes, and unequalitarian treatment—a situation that would intensify hostility and resentment.

---

1. This theoretical assumption was subsequently shown to be invalid after successful experimentation in an institutional milieu. See [64].

In only one instance was interview group psychotherapy employed in an institution with adolescent girls. This was in the Hawthorne-Cedar Knolls School of the Jewish Board of Guardians.

In an institution for "delinquent" girls, group therapy presents problems that are not ordinarily encountered in an outpatient clinic of a city, where the patients are not acquainted with and have no contact with one another except at group sessions. Catharsis was blocked in the institutional groups because the girls were afraid to make their problems known to the community. The fact that the girls lived on the same campus created difficulties. The presence of adolescent boys on the same or a nearby campus and the free social contact with them intensified the girls' fears in this regard since their past "reputations" may have defeated their natural need to be accepted and to have boyfriends. Such difficulties are not encountered in a large city clinic or hospital, but it may be expected that similar difficulties will arise in small towns where patients know each other in the community. Therapy groups need to be kept quite apart from the ordinary social groupings.

Members of therapy groups in an institution display a remarkable unanimity in their common hostility toward the school, the staff, and especially the director. This facilitates conversation, since all have the same target of hostility and the same reasons for discontent which accelerates identification, though it is only in a limited area. Hostility is freely expressed and its expression is initiated much earlier than in city groups. This is due to the fact that all have a common hostility target and can easily identify with one another on this score. Because of this the girls were, according to the group therapist, who had treated some of the girls also individually, much more productive in the group than in individual treatment.

The early interviews consisted almost entirely of complaints and charges against the staff and the institution. Involuntary sequestration from natural communities and from one's family mobilizes hostility and aggression toward the environment. The difficulty is that there are always realistic grounds for dissatisfaction which give validity to the feeling of wrongs and discrimination. Patients vent these dissatisfactions upon the group therapist, and since negative transference tends to be intensified because of the high degree of identification, the therapist may at times be hard put to it. It requires greater skill and experience to conduct interview groups in a "restraining" institution than in an outpatient clinic in a city.

Among difficulties one encounters in the practice of interview group therapy in institutions are the inevitable contacts that the patients and the therapist have with each other at times other than the regularly set sessions. The patients find it difficult to disassociate the therapist from the restraining and sometimes punitive role of the other members of the staff. This situation greatly complicates the transference relation, mobilizes its negative aspects, intensifies and prolongs resistance. Still another difficulty is attached in the school community to one who belongs to a special group from which others are barred. Sometimes being included in these groups is considered a special privilege. These difficulties, however, are encountered only early in treatment, and soon disappear as the patients become accustomed to the groups.

In the beginning suspiciousness makes the residents resistive to attending group sessions and considerable seduction has to be used here which is unnecessary in outpatient treatment in a city. If the therapist were to remain passive and impersonal, few if any of the residents would avail themselves of these groups. The therapist has to overcome the initial resistance by convincing the group members of his interest in them. Since attendance in these groups must be voluntary, one cannot exert administrative pressures to make children come to them. However, after the initial resistances are overcome, there is universal enthusiasm for these groups and there is no problem with regard to attendance.

Experience shows that group psychotherapy on an interview basis, or group analysis, is most beneficial in institutions for adolescents. Many who are unable to participate in or benefit from individual psychotherapy have made striking progress through the group sessions. Stubbornly resistive and especially hostile and recalcitrant youngers grew more reasonable and communicative, and were able to recognize and accept their part in the plight in which they found themselves. For some of the adolescent girls exclusive group treatment was sufficient to meet their needs, others continued with individual interviews, while a number who steadfastly refused to accept individual therapy have changed in this regard and fully participated in it, in addition to group discussions.

CHAPTER 47

"BREAKTHROUGH" IN GROUP TREATMENT OF DELINQUENT ADOLESCENTS
(1962)

In this paper an attempt will be made to describe a procedure for reaching fairly hardened, delinquent adolescent boys in a residential treatment program through a modified form of analytic group psychotherapy.[1] The modifications were made necessary because of the nature of the patients both in terms of chronological age and psychological predisposition and were arrived at after several years of experimentation with a number of approaches.

The group to be described consisted of eight boys between the ages of fourteen and a half and sixteen years. In contrast to our other experimental groups, in this instance, no special criteria were applied in the selection of the group except that boys who were doing particularly well in individual case work were excluded. The boys chosen for this group had not responded to individual treatment by case workers and displayed marked resistance to establishing individual relationships. Each of the boys had been seen previously by a case worker at varying intervals over a period of at least one year.

Preliminary information concerning these eight boys was gathered from the referring agencies, the courts, the schools, the parents, and the boys themselves before they arrived at the institution, and from

---

1. The therapist in this instance was Norman Epstein, who was coauthor of this paper. The "Village" was "Children's Village," a progressive institution in which the residents enjoyed much freedom.

the milieu and school during their stay. This information was later compared periodically with current reactions to determine behavioral and personality changes as group treatment proceeded. Initial reports from the cottage parents and education and clinic personnel showed that the boys selected for this group were making a marginal adjustment to the program of the institution and that attempts at reaching the boys in therapy were meeting with little, and in most instances no success.

Diagnostically, seven of the eight boys had rather severe character disorders; the eighth was a psychoneurotic boy with some schizoid features.

The development of the group during the course of fifty-two sessions will be highlighted here and the therapeutic phases traced, but the emphasis will be placed upon what we term the "breakthrough," which was brought about by a special approach to which I have given the name of "inversion," that is, the reversal from projection of blame upon the environment to self-understanding and self-confrontation.

The first thirteen sessions of the group were characterized by the boys' extreme resistance to disclosure of anything of significance in their lives and personalities. They spent most of the time in complaining about the institution (which we shall henceforth refer to as the Village) and its staff, relating numerous lurid details of injustices and cruel treatment, and reemphasizing their distrust and suspicion of all adults. The sessions were characterized by general disorder, shuffling of feet, aimless moving around the room, leaving the meeting room presumably to go to the lavatory nearby, playing a portable radio which one of the boys regularly brought, bringing comic books which they read lying on the small couch in the room or sprawling on chairs, and similar resistive and distracting conduct. Any attempt on the part of the therapist to explore the reality of their complaints and their feelings, or any mention of their families, increased physical movement and transilience in speech and action. Since there was no possibility of stimulating therapeutic productivity, we decided to bide our time until the boys themselves tired of their behavior and there would be an opening when the therapist could appropriately step in and redirect to productive ends the boys' conduct and aimless talk.[2]

2. The therapist on many occasions displayed discouragement in the weekly supervision conferences based on his protocol reports with the development in the group. He was assured by the supervisor that a breakthrough would come as he demonstrated his strength and acceptance.

Resistance was directed not only toward the therapist; the slightest effort on the part of any boy to speak of something significant proved unacceptable. This was shown by some boys walking out of the room, while others would move about refilling their cups of coffee, and still others would noisily shuffle their feet and display their distraction by similar means.

Each session of the group was recorded in great detail and was discussed by the therapist and the supervisor. Analysis of the meaning of both group and individual behavior was made during these discussions, but what was more important was that we anticipated behavior and often even verbalization in advance and the therapist was thus prepared to deal with them when they made their appearance. We consider this the major feature in the success achieved in this project. We predicted that the objectionable conduct would disappear and the boys would continue coming and that it could be dealt with later at the appropriate time. We assumed the freedom the boys found in the group, in contrast to their experiences in home, school, community, and with some of the less humanistic teachers and other staff members in the Village, would make them accessible to change.

After a period of desultory talk about leaving the group and their inability to talk about their problems in the presence of others, some of the boys began to boast of their delinquent activities, which they described in the most lurid detail. But when a boy would occasionally mention parents during this phase, at once two or three would rise and either stalk out of the room or help themselves to more coffee, while others would start their accustomed shuffling of feet—this, despite the mention of parents in these conversations being perfunctory and casual.

The twelfth session inaugurated increased boasting about drunkenness, sexual activities, delinquent conduct and violent acts on the part of the boys before they came to the Village. Richard, for example, described numerous involvements in gang activities, in stealing, breaking into stores, and of having friends in various fighting and street gangs. His narrations stimulated Wally to describe his many drinking bouts. (We knew from his case history that these had actually taken place. We also knew that his parents encouraged and supported his delinquency because of their own seriously delinquent behavior, as well as their unconscious wishes for their son's delinquencies.) When the therapist attempted, tentatively and cautiously, to help the boys recognize the meaning of their behavior, it served only to intensify their bragging, and Wally and a few of the others proceeded to describe sexual orgies in which they had participated. These included intercourse with girls in the dark galleries of movie theatres. Much of the bragging seemed so bizarre that it was difficult for us to differentiate between reality and fantasy. It must be noted in this connection and in terms of future developments that the language that the boys used in describing these events was graphically lewd, offensive to the therapist, and incomprehensible to the supervisor.

Louis, our toughest, most hardened delinquent, got into the act at this point and described his almost superhuman potency in having sex relations with so many girls that it seemed quite fantastic. For example, in the fifteenth session, he recounted how many virgins and nonvirgins he had known and described how he got them to submit to him by introducing "Spanish Fly" into their soda or coffee. He vividly described how, when they got very passionate, he would say to them, "Take it easy, baby, take it easy. I'll fuck you when I'm ready. Then I pull their pants down and put my dick in them and I screw them all around and they start jumping. They can't stand it."

The boys also bragged abut acts of violence. The peak of this was again achieved by Louis, who remarked: "Man, you ought to see what goes on around my fucking block. You park a car around there, you come back and that car ain't going to be there." For the next fifteen to twenty minutes there ensued a long dissertation about the gangs in his neighborhood, their fights, rumbles, and attacks. He recounted how he used to move with bricks in his pockets against other boys in the company of his gang and how they jumped a boy and stomped him until he bled. Louis said, "That boy was lucky there was a hospital nearby, otherwise he would have been dead." At points in his recitation, he became absolutely manic with elation. His eyes blazed and he literally foamed at the mouth as, now standing up, he described riding on a subway in company with his gang and how a member of a rival gang was stabbed with a bayonet by one of Louis's gang until blood spurted out of his back.

Although there was a realistic basis to the boys' bragging, we felt that much of it was exaggerated and had unconscious meanings. One of these was to test the therapist's reactions, his attitudes, and his acceptance of them on this score. We therefore decided to refrain from responding to any of these productions, avoiding both verbal comment and nonverbal reactions. We were aware of the place of violence in the fantasies of adolescents generally and assumed it would be particularly evident in the boys with whom we were dealing. We were also convinced that these bizarre expressions would ultimately lead us to other, more therapeutically valid feelings.

At the sixteenth session, the boys came in with strips of paper in which they had cut slits and began blowing through them, each making a noise of different pitch and loudness. Our plan had been to introduce at some point a discussion of a subject which would break through their acting out but would in no way involve them, and this proved to be such an opportunity. The therapist turned to Macy and said, "That's a very interesting noise. It sounds like the noise of an airplane breaking the sound barrier." Macy responded, "I heard of planes that break the sound barrier; how does it happen?"

Richard at once stopped his noise-making and proceeded to explain to Macy what happens when the sound barrier is exceeded. The therapist, too, became involved in this explanation, while the others continued to create a rumpus. As the therapist proceeded to enlarge on the physical laws of speed and sound, all the boys stopped their noise-making and listened to the explanation. All became involved; some spoke of the heat generated by friction that can melt metal; others compared the planes with shooting stars; our ruffian, Louis, of all people, wanted to know what "makes a shooting star." This question was addressed directly to the therapist, who gave him the pertinent facts about meteors. Louis wanted to know how long it would take to fly to a star, This gave the therapist an opportunity to elaborate on stars, distances, speed of light, and similar facts.

Questions of physical phenomena came thick and fast from all the boys. One introduced the idea of using airplanes in war and the imminence and danger of war. Wally remarked that if war broke out, he would leave the Village and return to his family. Macy then asked questions about atoms and atom bombs. From this ensued a discussion about the possibility of war with Russia, bombing, hydrogen bombs, and where could one hide from them. Various opinions were expressed. Wally said, "Maybe we ought to bomb the hell out of Russia so they can't get us." Macy turned to him and said, "I'm glad you're not the leader of this country. If you was, there wouldn't be anybody alive," to which Wally reacted by saying: "Let's stop this stupid discussion. I don't like the idea of dying." The therapist remarked that the fear of dying is a very real one in people. William associated this by stating: "Many times when I lie in bed at night after I had a date and I had a good time on the date, I lie in bed and think about what a good time I had. *All of a sudden I get kind of worried.* I begin to worry about if I will always have a good time or if I'm going to die before I can have any more good times." He then recounted a recurring dream of falling through space.

Louis, who had been sprawling in his chair, suddenly sat up and spontaneously blurted out: "I get those dreams all the time. I dream I'm running and that I fall over a cliff and keep falling, falling, falling, and boom, I wake up. Boy, they are scarey!"

Four or five of the others questioned the therapist as to where dreams come from. In response, the therapist stated the theory of dreams in simple, concrete terms. He was careful to introduce the terms, "conscious mind" and "unconscious mind," explaining how memories, experiences, and feelings are stored up in the unconscious mind and "come out at night when you can't control your feelings because you are asleep." He avoided the concept of the "ego," which was reserved for a future date, but he did introduce the concept of "symbols" and how they are sometimes used to represent something about which people do not want to think when they are awake. Richard broke in by saying, "I once heard of a book called *The Interpretation of Dreams.*" This conversation apparently grew too threatening to Wally and he attempted to break it up by initiating a private talk across the room with James.

The therapist, sensing the intense interest of the other boys in the discussion and feeling secure in the boys' attitude toward him for the first time, turned to the group and, in an attempt to interpret Wally's act as resistance, said: "What do you think Wally is trying to do?" This was not picked up by the boys, however, and the therapist said to Wally directly, "Maybe there is something that is bothering you?" This was the first time that the therapist had attempted to interpret resistance and it was without success. Maurice came to the therapist's rescue, as it were, by narrating a recurring dream about riding a bicycle. He said, "I actually never had a bicycle as a child," and proceeded to interpret the meaning of the dream by referring to what the therapist had previously said, stating, "I'll bet I dreamt it because I always wanted a bicycle."

As this session was breaking up, Richard waited for the therapist, and when they were alone, he said: "I wanted to tell you something I can't remember." He continued, *"I'll bet there is a reason for not remembering."* When the therapist agreed with this, Richard proceeded to narrate an experience on a weekend trip home from the Village. When he got off the train at Grand Central Terminal, he felt a pain in one of his legs as he was walking toward a telephone booth to call his mother. He added: "After I called my mother and left the telephone booth, the funny thing was that there was no more pain in my leg. Isn't that funny? *I'll bet my leg hurt because I was so worried about coming home."*

We consider the sixteenth session as the *breakthrough session,* from which flowed the remarkable progress in the therapy of this group.

In the twenty-second session, Wally was attempting to fix the hot plate which the boys used for heating water for coffee. He had taken it apart but could not put it together again, and he became very upset. He guiltily said, "I feel terrible about breaking the hot plate." Recalling Wally's complete indifference toward the episodes of sexual and delinquent acting out he had described in preceding sessions, the therapist remarked: "I can appreciate how you feel, Wally. As you grow up, you will find that you will have all kinds of feelings about the things you do." Apparently recognizing the therapist's intent in this remark, Wally abruptly looked up at the therapist and said, "I never thought it was so fucking hard to grow up."

The discussion of dreams became a regular part of the group's sessions. At one of the sessions, Richard brought in a dream which had occurred before he came to the Village, on a night after he had stolen something. In this dream he was being pursued by snakes. Quite on their own, the boys came to the conslusion that, *"Sometimes in the unconscious mind there is a need to get punished."* Richard could not accept this explanation, raising the question as to how this could be possible, since nobody consciously wants to get hurt. Sensing that this confusion might be present in the minds of the other boys as well, the therapist again made the differentiation between conscious awareness and unconscious wishes. It is interesting that Richard himself reformulated this statement in the following manner: "You mean in your subconscious mind maybe you do things bad just to get caught, but you don't really want to admit it to yourself. You do admit it to yourself when you fall asleep and you can't control what you dream."

At the next session, the boys were discussing girls, sex, and masturbation. The following interchange took place between Wally and the therapist. Wally, who was sitting at the other end of the room, got up, took the seat next to the therapist, and in a low voice said:

> I got a real problem, Mr. Epstein. I don't know what to do. I don't know why after I have sex with a girl I feel so rotten. I hate myself for having sex. Before I have sex, I don't give a shit. I'm real hot and I don't care what I do. I go to a dance; I dance with a girl; I rub up against her tit; I feel her ass, but then when I get her good and hot and I cream inside her, I don't know what to say to her. Sometimes I feel like saying I love you, but I can't say it. What is it, Mr. Epstein? Tell me. I want to ask you something, Mr. Epstein, maybe you know the answer. Why is it when I go to sleep I can't think of sex any more. I used to go to bed at night and if some of the boys would tell a dirty joke I would begin to get a hard on and I would start thinking of a naked girl and putting my prick into a naked girl. I can't think of that any more. When I start getting a hard on, *I think like I'm putting my prick in my mother and my hard on goes down.*

Wally seemed to be completely oblivious of the significance of what he had said. At this point, another boy attempted to involve the therapist in discussion, but Wally cut him short, and asked, "Why have I got this problem?"

Since the whole situation of sex, incest, and guilt seemed so close to the boy's conscious, the therapist ventured to say, "You just told me, Wally." Wally asked the therapist, "What do you mean?" "You know, maybe you feel that way because after you've had sex it feels to you almost like you had sex with your mother." Wally looked up at the therapist in surprise and said, "How did you know that?" The therapist reminded him of having just narrated his imagery when he was masturbating. His response was: "Yes, I did." He then went on to recount that once when his mother had caught him with pornographic pictures, she beat him.

On many occasions, the boys referred to being guilty and questioned the therapist as to the origin of guilt. The group reached a point in their "psychologic literacy" when this as well as the role of guilt in the human psyche and in society was within their grasp. In the twenty-sixth session, Wally again brought up his inability "to be nice" to the girls with whom he had intercourse and tied it up with his vision of his mother when he masturbated. He reiterated how he felt "dirty" after intercourse. This worried him, he said, because this attitude *might lead him to become homosexual.* Many distortions on the subject now made their appearance among the boys. One asked: "Is it true if you are fed by your mother's chest you are liable to become a queer?" Maurice asked whether masturbation led to homosexuality. Another boy wondered why guilt was associated with sex; this was explained by the therapist in terms of internalized social mores and superego. Almost interrupting the therapist's statement and finishing it for him, Richard interpolated: "When you break a rule you feel crummy inside." Louis remained the most unbending, as revealed by his statement: "Yeah, I feel guilty, but that don't stop me from screwing. But I still feel guilty."

Seemingly by the process of free association, Richard introduced the question of being punished by parents and stated that: "Parents always think that by beating their kids they are helping them, but they ain't helping them. They just make them sore." All the boys joined in the discussion and nearly all insisted that parents were justified in beating their children. Maurice said, "Even if your mother beats you, she is still your mother." Two of the boys suggested that had their fathers not beaten them, they would have gotten "into trouble."

James, an adopted child, said, "Let me tell you fellows a dream I once had and maybe we can all figure out what this dream is all about. One night I dreamt my father was coming after me with a big stick. Just as he was about to hit me, I woke up. What does that mean?" None of the boys were able to explain the dream. Evading the latent meaning of the dream, the therapist asked James whether his father had ever hit him. James said: "No, my father never laid a hand on me;

that's the reason the dream sounded so nutty. The night before I had the dream was the first time I ever stole anything. Do you think it's possible that the reason I used to steal was a way of *getting to see if my parents were going to do anything about it?* Ever since I was a little boy I remember the one thing that always bothered me, that was the feeling that my parents didn't care what I did, that they didn't care for me. I think maybe I stole just to find out if they cared enough to stop me." He then proceeded to tell the group that he had been adopted as a small child and he had always wondered what his real mother was like. (It should be noted in this connection that, prior to joining the group, James had frequently run away from the Village. The staff speculated that his running away was an unconscious attempt to find his biological mother. James had not run away while he was in the group or thereafter. It is significant that he was now able to reveal his origin to the group, which he had not done before.)

A notable development at this point was that coffee and cookies were no longer employed as an escape from the anxiety generated in discussions. They were now taken in a quiet, orderly fashion at the beginning of the sessions, which were held in the evening.

When, in the twenty-ninth session, Wally sparked the discussion by revealing himself as "being bad" and "being punished for it," Macy described how as a little boy, no matter what he did, his parents always thought him wrong. "When my mother would ask me to do something," he said, "sure enough my mother would tell me, 'You didn't do it right.' " He then recalled that, when he was five years old, his mother told him to move some furniture. It was too heavy for him but he tried his best. When his mother came into the room she criticized him severely. Now our silent boy, Litt, stepped in and summed up the conversation in the following manner: "In other words, what happens to you when you are small kind of sticks with you." Richard's comment was: "You take on what people think of you and *you begin to think of yourself the way other people say you are.*"

At a later session, prisons were mentioned, and Richard associated to this with a dream. He said, "In the dream I went home and while there met another boy and we stole together. We were caught by a policeman and sent to prison." He turned to the therapist and said, "What does the dream mean?" The therapist in turn referred it to the group and in a questioning manner stated, "Maybe we can figure this one out?" Before any headway could be made, however, Richard confessed that he was really worried about going home, that being at home might present him with temptations to steal again, but what frightened him most was that, should this occur, he would not be sent to Children's Village but to a prison, he would be put "behind bars." This assertion on Richard's part sparked a discussion as to how one prevents oneself from carrying out impulsive behavior, such as getting into fights or truanting. Several of the boys expressed feelings that they were doomed to spend the rest of their lives in prison since they did not feel that they had the ability to lead a life free of involvement with the law. They expressed deep concern as to what difficulties their impulses would get them into. Macy made the following significant statement: "My mother always told me that when I grew up I wouldn't be much. She always told me when I was a kid that I couldn't do anything right. How do I know it will be any different when I grow up?" Much later, the expectation of "doom" and "self-fulfilling prophecy" were discussed with the boys.

In connection with avoiding misfortune, the boys questioned how one could save face when challenged by other boys in the neighborhood to steal, lie, and play hookey, especially when one is called "chicken" if one does not participate in these activities. This discussion allowed the therapist to elaborate on the nature and control of impulses and the relation of the "self-image" and the "social image" of an individual. Before the end of the session, Richard turned philosophical and fatalistic: "Sometimes I think to myself, 'What's the point of life? You're born; you live about sixty years; you never get to eternity; there is no such thing if you know you are going to die. What's the point of all this living?" Litt chimed in: "That's not the way to look at it. You can't help dying, but while you are alive you just got to live and make the best of things. If I thought only about dying I couldn't even enjoy anything. So I don't think about it."

From this point on a number of sessions were devoted to the problems the boys would face upon discharge from the Village. Also, on their own, the boys brought to the fore repeatedly the importance of controlling impulses and not getting into difficulties again. The therapist was able to explore with them the relation of impulse control to maturity, but not before the boys themselves had tilled the soil for planting this very important seed.

During the summer, the therapist and the boys went to the city to see a movie and have lunch. The trip was initiated by several of the boys, with Macy saying, "We'd like to all go out together." Money for the trip was provided by the institution. The boys had a most enjoyable time and their behavior was exemplary. Following lunch, several of the boys asked if they could go shopping for phonograph records. The therapist agreed, indicating, however, that they would have to return to the Village by four o'clock and that they should meet in front of the restaurant at three o'clock. At the appointed hour, every boy was there. On the drive back, the boys confided to the therapist that they had had an impulse to go to their homes, that is, to run away but had decided against it. Had they been with someone else, they said, they might have run, but because they were "trusted" they could not bring themselves to do it.

After six weeks' vacation, when the group reconvened in the fall, the boys reverted to some of the topics discussed at the early group sessions. They talked about playing "hookey" and stealing, but referred to these activities in the past tense. Richard capped it by the laconic statement: "We are talking about fond memories of the past."

In the forty-second session, Wally, who was in the process of being discharged from the Village, openly described his mother's drunkenness and his anxiety about it. James, the adopted boy, also spoke about his mother, and as he did so, all the boys in the group lit cigarettes. This gave the therapist an opportunity to explain to the boys the dynamics of regression to an oral state when discomfort and anxiety set in. Wally returned in several subsequent sessions to his mother's drunkenness and his extreme anxiety and worry about the many problems which he would have to face upon returning home. At the last session he attended, he said to the group: "I'll never forget any of you. The only thing I hate about leaving is not coming here Thursday nights."

Louis, the boy who had gloried in describing gang fights, now talked about how he did not wish to return to his old neighborhood. He wished to have nothing to do with his former friends "because they are only headed for trouble." In fact, he had tried to talk one boy out of getting involved in a stealing episode when he was home on a visit, and added: "I guess my problem is I'm trying to be this guy's social worker and I can't. I had enough of robbing and stealing." He then went on to say, "I don't know, I just don't know. I want to get out of the Village, but I don't want any more trouble. What happened in the past is over. I want to go to school. I know I got a good mind. I know I can get me an education. I can amount to something." He then described how in his neighborhood gangs constantly try to enroll one and involve one in further difficulties. He said, "How can you win? You got to move out of the city to get away from this." He said he had discussed the problem with his mother and an aunt and that perhaps he would go to live with his aunt and go to one of the better schools in the city where he would not be bothered by gangs. He added, "If I can get away from my neighborhood, if the Board of Education will let me go to school outside my turf, maybe then I can get me an education, get a job and grow up in the right way." He leaned back and there was a pensive, sad look on his face as he mumbled under his breath, but loud enough for the therapist to hear, "I guess it just can't happen."

Let us look again at Louis, a boy who moved from preoccupation with sexual orgies, gang fights, brutal beatings, and most objectionable language, to one who could verbalize the following, when another boy was discussing the possibility of leaving the village:

> My father is a Filipino and his people are Filipinos. When I'm with them I don't quite feel right. I don't look like them. They are light-skinned; I am dark. My mother is dark and I feel at home with my mother's people. I don't quite know how I can say this, but I don't feel like seeing my father's people even though my mother tries to make me. It's like being outside. For instance, if I went to the Philippines, I wonder how I would feel. I'd probably not be taken for a Filipino. I'd rather always stay with my mother's people because they never ask me what I am. They just take me for a Negro.

He then turned his gaze directly upon the therapist and asked: "Do you know what I mean?" The therapist was deeply moved, not only by what Louis said, but by the depth of his feelings. The only thing he could contribute was: "I think so, Lou. You are not quite sure who you are." The thoughtful response was: "Right, that's about it. I'm half and half but I feel happier when I'm with my mother and her people, but I don't want to make my father mad by not going to his relatives. It's a pretty rough one to figure out." He stared pensively at the floor and quietly said, "I got to think some more about this."

In the fifty-second session, the boys presented the therapist with a Christmas card which read: "Thanks, Mr. Epstein, and we appreciate all you have done for us this past year. God Bless You." Every boy's signature was on the card. The therapist was quite touched, and he thanked the boys. Richard said, "That's funny, you thanking us. We're the ones who should be thanking you," and Louis added: "That's right, we should thank you. Thank you for all the good advice you gave us during the year and thank you for letting us come together every Thursday night." This was followed by a short period of touching silence.

A few of the boys described having overheard a maintenance man using profanity with sexual connotations. The boys were taken aback by this, and one of the boys epitomized their reaction by the remark: "A long time ago, when we came to the Village, we used to talk like that, but we don't talk that way any more, and the Village hires somebody who talks worse than the kids."

This session also illustrated the boys' becoming aware of internal controls, the final stage in the therapy. A boy described an incident that involved a teacher at the Village. The teacher was walking with his girl friend when he was accosted by a ruffian who accused him of stealing his girl. The teacher did not allow himself to become provoked in spite of the menacing threats made to him. The boy finished narrating the incident by saying, "What the teacher told us was that one of the last things you have to learn as you become a man is control, how to control yourself. When you learn this, that's when you're a man. I guess he's got something there because you once told us the same thing, Mr. Epstein."

Limitations of space do not permit discussion of the dynamic processes reflected in the preceding summary of the group sessions. Sequential unfolding of the latent content in terms of the nine steps leading from resistance to internalization of controls will have to await a more extensive publication which is contemplated for the future [62].

CHAPTER 48

GROUP TREATMENT OF A BOY WITH
SUICIDAL PREOCCUPATION
(1968)

Martin, age fifteen, was referred to the Youth Counseling Service by the high school psychologist who described the boy as of average intelligence who had been consistently failing his subjects for the past two years which was not in keeping with his intellectual and academic potential. Martin expressed awareness of the fact that he had been failing and was unable to concentrate on his schoolwork. The psychologist also reported that Martin had assumed a role of class clown. Martin showed some recognition that this may be a way of getting attention in the classroom; however, he found himself powerless to stop.

During the intake interview, the mother did not report any serious problem with Martin at home. However, she felt that Martin was generally quite docile in accepting restrictions and punishments. He tended to be laconic and reserved with the parents, but seemed to get along with his two younger siblings, a sister age eleven and a half, and a brother age seven.

The mother, Mrs. R., was described in the intake report as a short, pleasant-featured woman, who presented herself in a very tense but

Norman Epstein was coauthor of this paper. S. R. Slavson was the supervising consultant. Presented at an Annual Conference of the American Group Psychotherapy Association; 1968 unpublished.

reserved manner. She felt very helpless and inadequate in dealing with Martin's academic failure. Mrs. R.'s memories of her own childhood included a puritanical, undemonstrative mother and a father who was described as a rather warm, outgoing person. She commented that she had never kissed her mother until she was thirty years of age.

The father, Mr. R., was quite resistant to becoming involved in obtaining help for Martin. The intake worker described him as a rather cold, domineering, reserved person, who exuded an air of ultracorrectness in manner, dress, and speech. A prominent physical feature was his mane of wavy white hair. The mother described the father as being rarely at home. His business trips took him about three times a year far from home for ten to twelve weeks at a time. The mother felt herself very much put upon with responsibility for the care of the family, but found it extremely difficult to discuss it with Mr. R. She seemed to live in fear of her husband's temper and devoted her energies to removing any inconveniences that might upset him. The mother described the father as reacting with hurt and withdrawal when contradicted. Mr. R. had stated that it was his job to make a living for the family. All other family matters were considered to be the mother's responsibilities.

Martin's developmental history included a breech birth and near strangulation in delivery. One leg was weak and had to be massaged for a period of one year. Delivery was with forceps. Martin was colicky during the first two months. Walking, talking, and toilet training appeared to have presented little problem. When Martin was four years old, his sister was born. The mother became quite ill and this resulted in Martin's living with his maternal grandparents for approximately a year. Following this period, the mother found Martin obstreperous and mischievous and her temper was generally quite short with him.

The father verbalized feeling excited about Martin's birth; nonetheless, he rarely held the child in his arms and grew very tense when Martin cried and looked to the mother to quiet the infant. Martin was described as "a delicate child" who was considered to be "very pretty" and resembled a girl. He would regularly kiss his mother goodnight, but at the age of fourteen the father asked, "How long is this business going to continue?" Martin became very self-conscious and withdrew from any overt display of affection towards the mother.

Mr. R. often severely reprimanded Martin for failing in school and threatened him with dire punishment such as removal from school, placement in a vocational school, etc. The father often berated Martin just prior to leaving for a business trip, leaving the boy to cope with his reactions during the father's lengthy absences. Martin was unable to communicate with his mother whom he saw as a weak person unable to protect him from the father's demands and wrath.

During the intake interview, Martin recalled that, when he was four and his sister was born, his mother was always cross with him. He remembered a great deal of crying and described this period as one of turmoil. It appeared quite significant that Martin was able to recall this period in his life in such detail.

Martin was initially placed on an experimental basis in Activity Group Therapy which he attended fifteen out of eighteen sessions. The therapist noted that when Martin entered the group, he appeared reserved, stiff in bearing, and isolated from the others. He gradually began to create competitive situations with other boys and appeared unable to rest until he proved himself athletically. At times he was verbally sadistic toward his fellow group members and was constantly alert to any evidence that another boy may displace him as leader of the group. By this time he had through verbal aggression raised himself into a position of leadership. Once he felt secure in this position, he was able to become friendly toward his group peers. With the group therapist, Martin presented himself as a relatively self-reliant, self-assured youngster who kept the therapist at a distance. The therapist noted that Martin needed to appear a "superman," strong and competent, and relaxed only when he was sure of the acceptance of his peers and the therapist.

Despite Martin's seeming progress and his growing ability to relax and relate to the other children, we considered the nature of his problem would require therapy where he could verbalize some of his anxiety about himself and his situation. As a result, he was invited to join a newly formed analytic group with a different therapist. Martin resisted the change and was seen individually by the consultant of the group therapy department. Martin stated that he felt that "just playing around is not going to help me." This was recognized with him and he was advised then of the different nature of the group and the fact that there would be a new therapist. Martin agreed to give the group "a try" and joined the analytic group at its third session. He was described now as an average sized "well-built youngster, with rather soft, delicate features and ingratiating smile." His hair was blond and wavy. In spite of the somewhat feminine quality of his facial features, he carried himself with something of a rugged deportment.

During his first session, Martin indicated that he had some questions about coming to the group, feeling that just running around in the previous group had not helped him with his problems. He indicated, however, that a part of him "did enjoy the activity," because it was a way of avoiding talking about the things that bothered him. Louis, a seriously disturbed prepsychotic youngster, attempted to break up the session, feeling threatened any time a boy began to raise a problem. Martin became quite annoyed with him and said, "Why don't you cut it out, you are not in school now."

During the fifth group session (Martin's second), Seymour, a severely disturbed boy who often attempted to monopolize discussions, began to describe his recent hospitalization episode for suspected appendicitis. Seymour expounded on how it was discovered that he was not suffering from appendicitis and probably was reacting to emotional tension with physical pain. In the hospital, Seymour said, he thought of committing suicide. At this, Martin grew quite agitated, moving about in his chair and staring at the walls. He said, "I once wanted to kill myself." He abruptly stopped talking and continued to stare ahead. The therapist gently encouraged him to talk about it. Martin said, "Once I was failing and my mother threatened to put me in a vocational school, so I thought maybe the easiest way out was just to do away with myself." He went on to describe how he had often thought of using a sword; placing the sword on the ground and then throwing himself upon it. Seymour encouraged Martin to talk more about this, but it seemed to be difficult for Martin to continue. The therapist suggested that one of the reasons for thoughts of suicide was that, when a situation feels hopeless, a person can still exercise control by thinking about suicide. This helped Martin to move on by saying, "I am not sure that I always know what bothers me and that is what bothers me the most, not knowing what is bothering me." He went on to describe his school problem saying that he found himself failing and yet felt powerless to change this course. He added that he felt "stupid and inferior to other boys." When the therapist suggested that he try to recall other times when he felt this way, Martin described how often he had been compared to a cousin who is "the genius of the family." When he procrastinated with his homework, he was told by the mother, "Why aren't you like your cousin who studies all the time?" In a voice of desperation, Martin said, "I can't be like him." The therapist asked, "What does it feel like when your parents say this to you?" His response was, "I feel dumb, I feel inferior. That's right, that's the right word, I feel inferior."

Saul, a quiet, withdrawn, shy youngster, spoke up, saying that the same thing happened to him. There were times when he felt inferior, too. Martin and Saul began to trade feelings, describing under what conditions they felt "inferior." Martin summed it up by saying that one thing he did excel in was athletics, but his father always reminded him that "you cannot go to college purely on your athletic ability."

During the sixth session, Seymour described how, when he spoke to a girl, he was extremely sensitive as to the impression he was making. He stated that he acted like "a big shot" and tried to impress the girl with his savoir-faire, but trembled inwardly. Martin, recognizing it in himself, said, "I'm like that with a girl, too. When I'm with a girl I always wonder what she is thinking about me and what I am going to do is going to come out all right." He described how he tried to tune in to the tone of the girl's voice. If she spoke in a somewhat cold manner, Martin would begin to feel many doubts about himself. Martin thus revealed to the group his doubts about himself and his overconcern with the kind of impression he makes.

Seymour talked of the violent verbal fights between himself and his stepfather. Martin commented that he was glad his parents were away on vacation. When the therapist asked about this, Martin, in a very matter of fact tone, said that his parents often went off on trips and he stayed home with his younger sister and brother and was cared for by a maid. He denied any feelings of resentment about this and, pointing to Seymour, felt that this was better than being subjected to verbal abuse by parents.

During the seventh session, Seymour became aware of the fact that other boys in the group were annoyed with his monopolizing the group's attention and he threatened to leave. Martin's response to him was, "It won't do you any good to leave the group, you are running away and that is like committing suicide." Martin returned to revealing his feelings and said that he often had thoughts of being a very stupid person, intellectually inferior to other people, and for this reason met with failure in school. The therapist carefully pointed out that Martin's school problems were not due to a lack of intellect, but many feelings inside of him left him upset and unable to concentrate. Martin picked this up and went on to describe how he often thought of killing himself. He turned to the therapist and said, "Remember I told you about that, didn't I?" Saul spoke up. Addressing the therapist he said, "You told us that a lot of people sometimes think of killing themselves." The therapist agreed and again went over the explanation of suicide as a means of control over one's pain and upset and added, "You know that sometimes boys get very worried about thoughts that come into their heads. You sometimes think of hurting yourself, or somebody else, but that doesn't mean that you are going to go out and do it." At this point, Morris, a youngster who was delinquency-prone and often spoke in a tough unconcerned manner, said in a very touching way, "Sometimes when you talk you find that you are not the only one who has all these thoughts in your head."

During the eighth session, several of the boys began to talk about behavior which was directed toward getting even with parents. For the first time, Martin was able to reveal performing a hostile act against a parent. He described how his mother had gotten him angry. He could not recall the exact incident, but remembered becoming extremely angry, picking up her favorite lamp and throwing it out a window, indicating that destroying the lamp and breaking the window was his way of getting back at his mother for something she had done to him.

During the thirteenth session, Seymour, in a very provocative, testing manner, described a classmate who was reported to have had intercourse with his sister. The other boys responded with nervous laughter and darting glances at the therapist. Martin's reaction was intellectual and he offered statistical information on the number of illegitimate children born in Brazil. (Martin's father often went to Brazil on business trips.) Martin described having seen a film in school on the birth process. His most vivid memory was the woman's groans. This was followed by an intellectual discussion by Seymour and Martin concerning the advisability of reserving sexual intercourse for marriage. The boys discussed their desire to experience sexual intercourse and reassured one another that the proper time would be when they marry. The group tested out the therapist's willingness to discuss with them their sexual anxieties and fears.

Martin missed the next three sessions. He returned in session number seventeen, coming into the room looking quite guilty and dejected. Approaching the therapist, he said, "I am sorry that I didn't come for the past couple of weeks. I just didn't feel like coming. I was thinking of quitting the group, but decided not to." The therapist expressed interest at what had happened and Martin said that he felt disgusted with himself. "I'm failing pretty badly in school," he said, "and everybody seems to be pretty disgusted with me, too, especially my mother and father. They have gotten me a tutor. Now I am doing a little better because the tutor is helping me and I like working with him." Martin explained that his parents had again threatened to send him to a vocational school. The school principal had intervened by advising the parents that Martin did have good ability and his talents would be wasted in a vocational school.

The therapist picked up Martin's tone of voice and said, "You are feeling pretty hopeless." The boy smiled very warmly and said, "Yes, I am. I decided to come to the group rather than to commit suicide. I would like your help. I think maybe you can help me. Do you think that you can help me find out what is wrong?" The therapist said, "I certainly would like to try." Martin said, "Well, I don't know what it is that is bothering me. I wish I knew and this is what bothers me most, the fact that I don't know. That is why I had questions about coming to the group, whether I could ever find out what it is that is bothering me." The therapist responded, "It is like a picture puzzle; piece by piece we will find the things that fit." Martin smiled and said, "I like that idea, like we are working on a puzzle together and maybe when all the pieces are put together they will show me what is eating me." Encouraged by Paul, a neurotic youngster with a long standing history of school failure, Martin began to talk loudly but in a pensive manner. He felt that his academic failures had commenced in the eighth grade, but could not recall the circumstances. Paul pressed him, saying, "You have to remember."

Martin recalled that in the eighth grade he was told that he was a superior student and could do superior work. He didn't remember who had said this to him and went on to the following association: "My father isn't a professional man and he always said to me that is why he wants me to be a professional man." The therapist asked, "What do you think he is saying?" Martin said, "He is saying that I should be what he wasn't able to be. Maybe what he is also saying is that I should live his life over for him." (Martin's father had not graduated high school.)

Martin then revealed that when he is praised for his work he seems to lose interest. He commented that *he had just now become aware of this phenomenon.* He felt that he had always had all the physical comforts he could possible ask for. "I am always getting something I don't need. When I want something I always get it and yet I feel it's too expensive for me. I remember asking my dad for a pair of ice skates. He went out and bought me a $40 pair. He could have bought me a pair for $10 and I would have been just as happy. My parents know that I am easily distracted, and yet, they are always buying me things. Like they bought a color T.V. set, so now I sit up all night watching the color set instead of doing homework. I *let* everything distract me, but if I wanted to work I could work in a house full of noise." This prompted Paul to share with the group his daydreaming in the classroom. Martin responded by describing his own day-dreaming in class. He added that he felt that he was the only boy who did this but was careful not to reveal the contents of his daydreams.

During the eighteenth session, Seymour reported a very upsetting incident between himself and his parents, acknowledging that he had some responsibility for the turmoil that resulted. However, Seymour felt that it was quite impossible for him to extricate himself from the situation. Martin became quite interested in this and asked many questions as to why it was so important for Seymour to constantly be embroiled in fights with his parents. Seymour said, "I am sick and tired of people pushing me around and if I walk away from the fight I know that I am going to get back." Martin immediately said, "You mean you want revenge." Seymour was somewhat taken aback, but then agreed that he did think of getting revenge. Martin said, in a very low but firm tone, "I'll tell you something. If you don't change, things are going to get worse." He then added that he was thinking about his own situation and realized that he had better do some changing; if he made no effort to change, he would always fail in school. Martin indicated that he felt somewhat more hopeful about his grades. Paul agreed with Martin by adding, "There must be something, no matter how small, that you can do sometimes to get away from trouble if you want to."

During the twentieth session, Martin talked about his concern with his distractability while he was doing homework. He described how he often heard his mother and father in the other room fighting about him and blaming one another for his failure at school. Martin said that when his father was at home he had "a queer feeling inside," he grew tense, unsure of himself, and actually many times looked forward to his father's leaving on a business trip. He added that he often lied to his father about school grades. He wondered why boys lied to their fathers and, as if to answer himself, said, "Maybe they are afraid of telling the truth."

Martin spoke of his mother telling him that he was trying to kill his father through his academic failures. She had asked him, "What are you trying to do to the man?" Thinking about this, Martin murmured maybe there was an element of truth in it. Perhaps he was attempting to get revenge on his father. Martin clenched his fists and said in a voice filled with rage, "I got to get even with him somehow, he makes me feel like a baby inside." Martin, asked whether the therapist thought that he was trying to get revenge. The therapist said, "What do you think about it?" Martin said, "Maybe my mother has got something there. Funny, I never before remembered her saying it, but now, all of a sudden, I remember." As Martin was leaving that evening, he said, "I got a lot off my chest tonight. It is funny though, this business of not remembering things. I don't remember a lot of things that happened to me."

In the following session Martin told how his father, prior to leaving on business trips, would warn him about getting good marks. Martin denied any feelings of anger, feeling his father was within his rights. The therapist asked, "How would you have like to hear your father say, 'I hope you do better next time?'" Martin, halfway out of his chair, responded, "I would have given my life if I ever could have heard that from him. Do you hear me? I would have given my life." Martin then spoke of his disappointment in not receiving a warm good-bye from his father rather than being admonished.

At the twenty-second session, the therapist discussed with the group the addition of a new member. Martin responded, "You know what the group did for me? It made me feel like I was somebody. I used to feel that I was the only boy in the world who had any problem in school. I don't feel like an outcast anymore. If I hadn't been in the group, I would be in a mess now. I think I found a way out. There is something about sitting and talking here about your problems that makes you feel better. For instance, if I hadn't come to the group, I would be failing twice as badly as I am now. I think there is hope for me. This is one of the few times in my life I ever felt any hope, at least about getting out of school maybe and not making such a mess of my life." Martin suggested that the group might have similar value for the other boy.

During the following session, Paul was discussing the fact that he often procrastinated when he had to write a paper for school. Martin walked in during the middle of this and asked Paul what he was talking about. When Paul repeated what he had been telling the group, Martin said, "That happens to me all the time. When I get an "A" in a subject, I always think it is time to start goofing off." He added that he hoped that this time it would be different, although when he found himself doing well he was tempted to "mess up." Martin felt that although this might be true, there might be other reasons, too. Pondering the problem, he described how, when he received good marks, he began to feel uncomfortable. "It is like sometimes I don't want to get good marks, but I can't figure out why." The therapist tentatively suggested that this might be related to the concept of himself as a failure that he developed in early childhood. Martin tentatively agreed.

During the twenty-third session, Martin recalled a dream wherein he saw himself walking to school, carrying books. The books slipped from his hand and fell under the wheels of a huge truck. He attempted to retrieve them by getting under the truck. Suddenly, the wheels began to move, and just as they were about to roll over his body, he awakened. The therapist encouraged Martin to talk about the dream. Martin felt that the dream was trying to tell him something. However, he couldn't figure it out. He added, "The first idea that came to me was about suicide." Martin asked for help with the dream. The therapist tried to maintain this on a relatively simple level, saying, "In the dream there seems to be the theme that in going to school something overwhelming is going to happen."[1] Martin responded

---

1. This was handled rather badly by the therapist.

with, "It seems like by going to school, I am going to be destroyed."

Paul interrupted to describe an incident in which he became angry with his mother for waking him and asking him to fix a faucet. No sooner had Paul finished talking of this than Martin related a recent dream in which an airplane bound for St. Louis crashed at Idlewild airport. He said, "My father took the flight to St. Louis just before that one. I dreamed that my father was killed in the airplane. That was a heck of a dream to have, wasn't it?" He asked, "Do you think it is possible that I might have been thinking about wanting my father to die?" The therapist recognized the dire possibilities of continuing along this line and instead related it to the wish in all children to be left alone by their parents.

Paul related his concern about his father dying and that he would then have to live with a mother whom he strongly disliked. While talking, he lit a match and ignited some paper that was lying in an ashtray. When the therapist inquired about this, Martin remarked that Paul was doing it as a diversion because, "We are finding out too much about ourselves."

During the twenty-fifth session, Martin revealed that, though his parents said they would like him to get just average grades, he wasn't sure that was what they felt. The therapist suggested that perhaps he himself was expecting more from himself, in response to which he revealed his unrealistic expectations. He felt that to get a "C" in any subject was proof that "you are a very stupid, untalented person." The therapist remarked, "You have taken in and believed about yourself what you have always been told; namely, that you always have to be above average. Anything below that makes you dislike yourself." Paul spoke up, saying, "That happens to me a lot of time. I feel that I should always be doing more than I am doing. I am never satisfied with whatever I do." Martin, with a note of surprise in his eyes, added, "I spend a lot of time thinking about myself and how disappointed I am with myself. I never feel happy with myself. I don't ever look at anything and think that 'this I am kind of proud of.'" Martin questioned whether this defeated him before he even got started. "I feel that I am too stupid, that I will never do well, and so I get the attitude, what is the point of even trying?" It is too hard to be above average and yet when I am not above average I don't like myself."

In the next session, a discussion arose concerning attitudes toward teachers. Martin said that he had been thinking about his reactions to teachers and wondered why he was quick to be angered by them, but added, "They remind you of things your own parents make you do. You don't like getting mad at your parents, so you take it out on your teachers. We are so pissed off at what is happening in our lives that we just have to get even with somebody; but what happened has happened, and now you have to start thinking of yourself."

Martin was in a depressed mood, during the twenty-seventh session. The therapist commented on this. Martin said, "I kind of realize something about myself." He stopped and, staring into space, went on. "I was once a good piano player. I was told by my teacher that I had real professional abilities. A week later, I lost interest in the piano. What do you make of it?" The therapist asked, "What do *you* make of it?" Martin said, "I don't know, but if I am good in an activity I lose interest in it. Isn't that funny?" The therapist said: "It doesn't strike me as being funny. It strikes me almost like you have a built-in defeat system working. For some reason you have to find a way of defeating yourself." Martin's comment was, "That's right. All somebody has to do is tell me I am doing good and I will try to prove that I don't want to do good, or I can't do good."

Martin reported in the thirtieth session that something different was happening at home. He and his family had taken a trip the preceding week. Martin's younger brother and sister were rather obstreperous in the car. He became very upset with them and expressed his annoyance to his mother. She said to Martin, "I don't blame you for being annoyed. I can understand how a brother and sister at times will annoy you." Martin considered this a crucial indication of a difference in his mother's attitude. He also reported that his father had expressed a mild degree of satisfaction with the improvement in his grades.

In the thirty-second session, Martin appeared quite relaxed. He commented, "I am going to make it in school. I finally feel like a student." He said that the group had done a great deal for him. "A year ago I didn't know that other boys had problems, and now I know I am not alone. I find myself working like I never worked before." Rather realistically, he felt that he might meet with extreme difficulties in improving his grades at such a late point in the semester, adding that he had handed in a composition which was graded "B" by the teacher. "I didn't think it was worth a "B." I really didn't know what I was writing about, but she gave me a "B" and I figured that maybe she didn't know what I was saying either and she didn't want to admit it, so she took the easy way out." The therapist asked, "Did you reread the composition after you received the "B"? He said, "Yes." "What did you think of it?" He smiled and said, "I thought it was pretty good. It read better than I thought when I was writing it. Not only that, but the other day I wrote some poetry and I thought it was kind of silly. I showed it to my mother and she thought it was the most marvelous thing she had ever read and she was really surprised that I could write good poetry. I didn't think it was that good."

The therapist suggested to Martin that maybe he was his own severest critic. Martin answered with, "It wasn't perfect," and here he revealed again his need for perfection and the hatred of self when he found himself doing work which he considered to be less than perfect. "But isn't there such a thing as perfection?" Martin asked. When the therapist pointed out the nonexistence of perfection and the futility of chasing it, Martin said, "That reminds me of my father. He always finds something to criticize about other people. You know, some people can look at other people and say, 'well they are good, they are good at this, good at that, or at so and so.' Not my father. He always knows that people are bad in, rather than good in. Maybe I am taking after him in that way."

A report submitted by Martin's school confirmed that he was making impressive efforts to achieve higher grades. In spite of Martin's diligence in doing assignments, it was felt that he had started too late in the semester to materially affect his grades.

The mother, who was being seen concurrently by a case worker, reported that Martin seemed more relaxed and comfortable in his relationships with the family members. Mrs. R felt that this constituted a genuine change in the boy. Martin was able to discuss his feelings concerning what happened in school and at home. He was no longer remote and detached from his parents.

Martin's attendance at group sessions became rather sporadic during the next month. He claimed to be studying for final examinations. It was felt that he was portraying his conflict as he began to feel some success in understanding himself and was reverting momentarily to his pattern of self-defeat. At the end of the month, the group ended for the summer recess.

In reviewing Martin's course in group therapy, it was felt that he had made as much movement as possible within a group setting and that he was now in need of intensive individual psychotherapy. Thus, following the summer vacation, the therapist contacted Martin in the hope of discussing with him the possibility of referral for individual treatment. Martin told the therapist that he was now doing quite well in school. He had just taken a chemistry exam and had received an excellent grade. He spoke of the good study habits he had developed and the consequent improvement in all of his grades. Martin said, "I feel very differently now. I really got something from that group. I don't know if I will ever be able to put it into words, but it is like I found myself. When you find that you are not the only one in the world who has problems, that helps a great deal. I also learned that maybe my parents aren't the worst in the world. I like them a little better." He went on to describe a better relationship with his father. "He doesn't push me around anymore," Martin explained. He connected this with his own change in attitude towards his parents and schoolwork.

The therapist accepted this evaluation that things had improved. However, he commented that every person has something he carries around with him that tends to trip him up in life. "We both know that when you find things going well, something happens and you have a tendency to defeat yourself." Martin agreed with this. The therapist then moved into a discussion of his possibly going on with individual treatment. Martin decided to reserve decision, adding that he had been through a great deal and had tried to work out many things that were bothering him and reminded the therapist that his parents had never fully supported him during group therapy. He had accurately detected the parents' shame in having a child who needed treatment. Neither his mother or father had encouraged him to go for group therapy. In fact, they often passed depreciating remarks about his need for help. Martin indicated that his parents still at times make remarks about the fact that they have problems, but they never felt the need to go for help. This seemed to support Martin's resistance to further treatment.

The therapist indicated his availability to talk with him at any future date that he felt a need for going on with treatment. Martin expressed his gratitude for being permitted to join the group, and again said in a warm, sincere manner that perhaps he could continue to make progress at school and in his relationships with his parents.

CHAPTER 49

PATTERNS OF ACTING OUT OF
A TRANSFERENCE NEUROSIS
(1962)

Frank, a fourteen-and-a-half-year-old boy, was committed to residential treatment because of neglect, continued truancy, petty larceny both in and outside his home, and unmanageable, disruptive behavior at school. He had received brief treatment in a community clinic, which seemed to quiet him down to some degree, but the recurrence of his behavior and its violence made it necessary to commit him to a county hospital for observation. A social study of the family and the findings of the hospital staff resulted in a recommendation that he be removed from home and placed in a treatment setting.

Frank was the third of four children. At the time of commitment both his older sister, twenty-six, and older brother, twenty-four, were married and out of the home. The family consisted of father, mother, Frank, and a girl two years younger than he. The father, a truck driver on a transcontinental route, was absent from home for weeks at a time, and since his trips were frequent he spent very little time with the children. He was described as an easygoing, ineffectual, quiet man who exercised little control over his family. The mother, on the other hand, was authoritarian, tyrannical, promiscuous, and a chronic alcoholic. Frank had witnessed at least one episode of sexual intercourse between his mother and one of her paramours. During one of the prolonged absences of her husband the mother "settled down" with one of her "boyfriends" in a more or less permanent relationship. Upon his return, the husband gave her a choice between himself and the other man. She decided to return to her husband.

One of the persons who had had an influence on Frank's early life was his maternal grandmother, who had been very protective of Frank and favored him greatly. She had been in charge of the home while the mother was at work, but this arrangement no longer prevailed when Frank was committed as the grandmother had died in the interim.

Frank was an unplanned child and his mother had been extremely upset when she discovered her pregnancy. She had attempted to abort, and later claimed that her drinking bouts began at the time of his birth. One of the significant events in Frank's life was his brother's marriage when Frank was eleven years old. This brother and Frank had shared a room, and after the brother's departure from home, Frank developed a fear of the dark which persisted for several months and necessitated that a light be kept on in his room. During an interview in the community clinic, after describing the beatings he received from his parents, he stated that the brother had protected him against the mother's cruelties. But at the termination of the interview, when he was leaving the room, he turned back and said, "I don't like my brother, John, best; I like my dog, Rex, best."

Frank's adjustment in the Village[1] was described as "decisively poor." The noisy, uncooperative, pugnacious behavior which he had manifested in school before coming to the Village reappeared. He was described as being "provocative, manipulating, scornful, contemptuous, and condescending." He was "cynical, pedantic, pseudointellectual, with grandiose attitudes, and aroused universal antagonism among his cottage mates." Toward adults he was "sarcastic, critical and demanding, and provoked punitiveness from them in return." His female case worker made every effort to establish a relationship with the boy; she even saw him daily at first because of his extreme separation anxiety. But the outcome after a year's effort was disappointing. "While there was some superficial understanding," wrote the case worker, "there was very little basic change in Frank over the period of a year of individual case work treatment."

---

1. Children's Village, Dobbs Ferry, New York.

Frank, now fifteen and a half years old, was placed with several other boys in an analytic therapy group which met for a period of six months. This was the first group in our project to test the response to group therapy of court-committed boys in residential treatment. During the first six sessions of the group there were the usual gripes against the institution, the staff, and adults in general. Frank, among others, expressed suspicion that the group was being watched and the conversations recorded. He was the most aggressive and the most disturbing member in the group. During the third session he screamed at the therapist: "I don't like you, I never would and never will like you!" At another time he threw an ashtray into the therapist's lap. His all-out efforts to create disturbances were resented by the other boys, who suggested that he be dismissed from the group. However, Frank's behavior was accepted with tolerance by the therapist, a fact that surprised the other boys greatly. After the third session, Frank asked to stay with the therapist for a while and revealed that he was very upset because his mother had been drinking heavily again and was very ill. It must be noted that when the mother drank she remained in a stupor for days on end, lying about sloppily on a couch, screaming vituperations at anyone who approached her.

When Frank came for his fourth session, he took a seat next to the therapist. When one of the boys mentioned sexual urges toward women, Frank suggested that "we leave sex out of this for awhile." This session, like the preceding ones, was characterized by a great deal of restlessness and complaints about adults taking advantage of the boys.

During a discussion in the seventh session, Frank revealed that he had recently been bothered by the thought that something was going to happen to his brother. He dreamed about his brother getting hurt. He had had this dream twice before, and once his brother actually did get hurt. As he was saying this, Frank became very anxious and restless and walked aimlessly around the room. When this distractability was called to his attention by the therapist, Frank said, "I am angry because they won't let me call my brother," and he continued his roaming around. This type of behavior was characteristic of Frank and was in striking contrst to that of the other boys. They also had resisted treatment for a long period, but they expressed their resistance verbally. Frank, however, was given to much greater anxiety than were the others and was the only boy who acted it out motorically.

Frank's complaints about his mother reappeared frequently during the group discussions. In the eleventh session, when the boys talked about stealing and homosexual activity, Frank remained silent. At another session he spoke of his acting up in the gymnasium because he felt "kind of miserable inside." He said that one of the coaches had slapped him, but he seemed to accept this punishment with equanimity. He said, "You know where you stand [when one is punished], and that is okay with me if I cross the line."

A degree of calm became noticeable in Frank as the group sessions proceeded, but in the thirteenth session Frank became very upset and attacked two of the more passive boys. His restlessness increased even more when the group started talking openly about their parents. His distractibility and disruptiveness mounted and he moved up and down the room. At one point he drew his cigarette lighter from his pocket and threw it out of the window. It landed on the slanting roof, and Frank attempted to crawl out through the dormer window. Because of the danger involved, this was prevented by the therapist, who promised that after the session he would help Frank retrieve the lighter. Frank quieted down, but when the other boys began to speak, he vehemently pounded on the table with the blade of his knife. Concerned that the knife might ricochet and hurt someone, the therapist suggested that Frank be careful. But Frank ignored this, screaming that the Village was a jail and that he was in it for punishment. He repeated that he hated the therapist, used abusive language toward him, and carved the letters f-u-c-k into the polished top of the table. This startled and upset the other boys. The therapist attempted to encourage Frank to talk about what was bothering him, pointing out that this behavior must stem from some inner turmoil. Frank burst out that he felt like running away and proceeded to narrate how he had received a letter from his mother with a newspaper clipping about an unmarried girl who had become pregnant and that he was angry because this was a girl he could have "gotten into." The girl, recently released from an institution, was the daughter of a woman who had accused Frank's sister of being a whore.

When the group left, Frank remained to retrieve the lighter, and the therapist took this opportunity to talk with him. Frank began by referring to the mother's letter but proceeded at once to discuss his fears about his brother. The brother had not come to visit him and he was afraid that the brother was angry with him.

In the next session the therapist found Frank to be much quieter. During the early part Frank commented that he didn't like his haircut and added that the therapist, too, needed a haircut. Another boy was discussing his mother whom he had hardly known and who had abandoned him when he was a small child. The boy said, among other things, that he would beat her if he ever saw her. Frank said he didn't think the boy should ever do anything to his mother. When asked why by the therapist, he said, "After all, my mother was drunk all the time and it is just something I have to live with. I used to knock the shit out of her, but that didn't do any good." When the boys questioned him, he corrected himself smilingly, "Maybe I didn't really hit her, but I wanted to at times." He proceeded to say that sometimes he thought it might be better not to have a mother around; he had one and she had not done him any good. He could not understand the attitude toward mothers because his mother drank and did not give him anything, "so why should there be anything in return?"

As the discussion progressed the therapist commented that sometimes people cling to feelings of guilt. Frank was the first to agree with this statement and elaborated that he always felt unhappy when he saw his mother drunk and that at times she accused him of doing things that "made her that way." At other times he felt guilty because his family worried about him because of his behavior.

It should be noted that Frank now invariably chose a seat next to the therapist.

At the fifteenth session the conversation among the boys led Frank to confess that he had stolen money from a boy in his cottage. He claimed that he did it in retaliation for the theft of some objects from his personal locker. On the basis of previous discussions as to why people steal, one of the boys explored with Frank other reasons for his stealing, but Frank repeated that it was a retaliatory act. The effort on the part of other boys and the therapist to explore further the meaning of his act did not prove fruitful.

At one point of emotional tension generated by the discussion, Frank said, "I know that I was mixed up and maybe I am getting unmixed, but it takes a long time, and it is hard to stay away from your family." When the therapist responded that the aim of the institution was to help the boys with these problems, Frank, for the first time, spoke favorably of it. He said, "Some people in the Village are all right and maybe they want to help us, but it is still a long way from home." He then turned to the therapist and said, "Do you remember when I tried to give you some money to hold?" That was the money I stole. You did not report me, but somebody heard me asking you for the money and that is how I got caught." After a brief silence he added, "Changing takes a long time and sometimes moves too slow."

At the close of this session, as at many of the others, Frank lingered on after the group had left, but when he saw that another boy wished to talk to the therapist, too, he left the room.

The free chosen theme of the next session was parents and the boys' relationships with them. Frank said resentfully, "Kids shouldn't feel that way about things." He stalked up and down the room and again proceeded to open the window. He conveyed his great yearning to go home during the holiday vacation that was coming. He revealed that during the previous week he had lain awake at night, unable to fall asleep; he had roamed around the cottage, occasionally meeting the watchman on his tour. When asked by another boy why he couldn't sleep, Frank answered curtly, "It's obvious: home." Another boy asked Frank why he didn't talk about it because, "when you talk you don't feel so tense." Again Frank burst forth with preoccupations about his mother being drunk, especially since the father would not be home this time of year. He said that he felt guilty about his mother and recalled that she always blamed him for her drinking. She never drank when the other children were born; she took to drink after his birth, she said. "I always think about it, and when I think about it I feel rotten inside," he declared. Several of the boys expressed sympathy with him and one of them suggested: "You know that it isn't true." Silence fell upon the group. When the group left Frank remained behind to tell the therapist that he would stay with his brother on his visit home if he found his mother drunk.

The next session was held after the Christmas visit home. Frank came in particularly disturbed and immediately went to the window. The therapist warned him about leaning out. He challenged the therapist by asking: "What are you going to do about it?" The therapist told him that he would send him out of the room. Frank sat down at the table with the other boys, and during the discussion he talked about his brother for a minute and then about a spider he had brought in a tin can. The spider's name was Herman. At first Frank threatened to release Herman so he could sting the other boys, explaining that Herman was so poisonous. After a while he said that Herman was getting on his nerves and that he would burn him. He lit a match and threw it into the can, but the fire quickly went out. Frank then stuffed paper into the can and set it on fire.

Recognizing Frank's agitation, the therapist asked him to tell the group about his holiday vacation. At first he refused to talk about it and the therapist asked him, "Do you mean your mother was drunk again when you went home?" Frank exclaimed piteously: "I couldn't even get into my mother's apartment she was out [in a stupor] on the couch again, plastered, so I went down to my brother's house and spent the weekend there." He then proceeded to describe how he had gone back and forth between the brother's and the mother's apartments, but she remained in a continuous stupor during the three days he was home. Further discussion about mothers ensued as a result of Frank's narration, which was terminated by his saying: "I will just have to accept it and work out something for myself as long as it does not hurt me." After this, he grew less agitated but was apparently unable to continue talking. When the session ended he asked the therapist's permission to sit for a while in the waiting room downstairs, apparently to collect himself, before returning to his cottage.

For a number of sessions the boys' discussion had turned to girls and women, with some members of the staff being mentioned as possible sexual objects. When a boy jokingly spoke of a social worker with large breasts, another said, "She always seems to be walking around stretching her arms so that people can measure her to see how much she's got." Frank identified her as his social worker and said, "I could measure her any time." *Soon after this Frank declared that if his brother beat him up he would accept it "because it is in the family."* One of the boys changed the subject. Frank agreed with still another who wanted to return to the discussion of women and said, "Let's talk about women, it's a more interesting subject." At one point the therapist remarked on the naturalness of sexual urges in adolescent boys. Frank misinterpreted his statement with the following remark:

"You mean you really want us to go home and feel them [girls] up and do things to them?" When the group's laughter had subsided, Frank said: "I'll go around telling everybody that you told me it was all right for me to do it." Again there was an outburst of laughter. When the therapist questioned Frank if he really thought that this was what the therapist had meant, Frank said, "I was only kidding." Frank did not remain with the therapist at the end of this session.

In the next session an interesting episode occurred. Frank, who was a member of the ROTC, brought his boots and some shoe polish and proceeded to shine the boots in preparation for inspection. He asked the therapist if he could shine his shoes as well. The therapist asked him why he wanted to do it, and Frank's response was that he had some polish left. The therapist said that his shoes were new and did not really need a shine but thanked him for the offer. This incident is rather significant in tems of Frank's nuclear problem.

The next session, the twenty-third, Frank brought with him a book of pictures of nude men and women and loaned it to another boy who wanted to look through it. The matter of sex was brought up again, along with the fact that living in an entirely masculine environment caused some of the boys to be preoccupied with sex. Frank said, "Well, you know what to do about it," and made a motion with his hand indicating masturbation. When the discussion turned to homosexual intercourse, the therapist explained the function of marriage as a means of satisfying the sex urge and ended by saying that he was aware that boys always wonder about these matters and the feelings involved and that they sought means of doing something about it. Again, Frank said that he knew what to do and indicated by his hand the act of masturbation.

One of the boys volunteered that his father had once caught him masturbating and was very angry with him. Frank suggested that the father may have thought that it was something wrong and harmful to the boy. This remark was probably the result of a discussion in which the therapist had conveyed to the boys that masturbation, of which the boys were very much afraid, was harmless if indulged in moderately. When one of the boys introduced the subject of the cottage parents checking up on the residents of the cottage during the night, Frank said, "You know, there are a lot of queers around." The discussion seemed to have met some need in Frank, for he spontaneously said, "Well, we talked today."

In a supervisory discussion of the episode in which Frank offered to shine the therapist's shoes, it was suggested that the therapist's refusal be aired with Frank. The therapist, therefore, found an opportunity to ask Frank what he thought about the incident. The boy's response to this was that he tried to find ways of getting the therapist angry. One of the boys, Albert, remarked that Frank had made himself angry instead since he had been rebuffed by the therapist. At this point Frank lost his temper with the boy. The therapist intervened by saying that Frank was really angry with the therapist rather than with Albert. He further stated that Frank was trying to show the therapist that he liked him and instead the therapist had pushed him away. "Like you?" exclaimed Frank, "Enough to kill you!" However, the statement sounded more like, "I like you very much," than one of hostility. Frank again left with the rest of the group.

At the twenty-fourth session Frank once more appeared very disturbed and described a conflict he had had with his cottage mother because of her slight of a Negro resident. During this recital Frank touched one of his arms and said that he was getting "boils" again and that it was the cottage mother who was "giving them" to him. The therapist stated that the boils might be caused by his own mother rather than the cottage mother. This sparked Frank's exclamation that he knew his mother was drunk again and "it is driving me nuts!" He had received a letter from her and from the manner of her writing he was sure that she was in a drunken state, and there was no one to take care of her because his father was away again. "If she would only stop for awhile!" he screamed. "If I was only home to take care of her!" He added that if he returned home he would have to stay with his brother, who would take care of him. His brother would never hit him. As the discussion progressed, Frank remarked that he really didn't need his mother any more; he was just concerned about her because there was nobody around to take care of her.

The next session, the twenty-fifth and last for this experimental group, Frank was in a euphoric state. He chatted with people on the stairs and greeted effusively one of the group members who had been away for a few weeks because he participated in the varsity ball games. As the group was discussing these games, Frank jumped up and began to juggle ashtrays. The therapist suggested that he put them down and that his behavior seemed to show that there was something bothering him. Frank said that he was going to throw an ashtray at the therapist, and he looped it into the therapist's lap. The group was startled by this, and some of the boys reprimanded him for doing "such a crazy thing." Frank said, "I told him [therapist] I was going to do it. You dared me to." He then rose from his seat and moved to another close to the therapist. The therapist suggested that Frank was upset about something and that talking about it would make him feel better. While group members expressed indignation at his behavior, the therapist repeated that Frank probably had acted the way he did because something was disturbing him.

Later, the boys were discussing termination. One of them, a new-comer, asked about having candy and ice cream. The therapist asked what they sounded like when they asked for candy and ice cream. "Babies," said Frank: "we are babies when we want candy." He then proceeded to nag the therapist to swap wrist-watch bands. "I want that band," he said, and then rhythmically repeated, "I want your wrist-watch band; I want your wrist-watch band; I want your wrist-watch band." The therapist told Frank that he could not have his band, since it was a gift, and several members of the group told Frank to "shut up," but he continued. The therapist asked Frank what it was he was trying to tell the group by his behavior. Instead of answering, Frank said, "I will count to thirty, and at that time I am going to take that band from you." A self-conscious hush settled over the group. One of the boys broke the silence, telling Frank that he better not try anything on the therapist. Nonetheless, Frank began to count, and the therapist turned to John, asking why he wanted to protect him. John said that no one should throw things at the therapist since he "didn't do anything to anybody." The therapist asked him what he thought Frank should do about his conduct. At this point Frank stopped counting, smiled, broke into laughter, and said, "Fooled everybody. I wasn't going to do anything to Mr. S."

Having broken through Frank's anxiety, the therapist again asked what was upsetting him. Frank said, "I am in trouble again." His grandfather had died and he had gone home on a weekend pass. At his uncle's home he convinced his small cousin to sell him a wrist watch for a couple of dollars. The wrist watch was worth much more, and he was sure that when his uncle found out there would be trouble. He knew that his cousin had gotten it from his uncle as a present and, therefore, he wanted it. John said, "But this is no reason for going around throwing ashtrays at people." Frank agreed and said he just did not know what to do with himself. He had gotten into trouble with his cottage parents the day before and a few days earlier. He struck his hand against the table in a manner that obviously hurt him. The boys minimized the importance of the events and tried to console Frank.

Later, when some of the boys asked the therapist for help in getting discharged from the Village, Frank said that he wanted to be around his sisters because "they are nice to me and take care of me." James said, "When Frank grows up and meets some girls, he will not always be talking about his sisters. There will be other people." Frank grew livid with rage, grabbed James' shirt at the neck, and threateningly shouted, "Buddy, don't ever say that again!" Questioned by the therapist, Frank responded, "I have no such ideas about my sisters and it is a dirty thing to say." James broke in and said that he had had nothing like that in mind at all and elaborated that, as Frank grew up, he would get married and would be thinking about his wife and family and "everything else." Frank, however, remained crestfallen and dejectedly murmured: "I just can't stand it any more. It is not the watch that is bothering me; it is what happened on the weekend." He grew very quiet, his face became very tense, and he said: "It is my brother. When I went home for the weekend I told my brother that I got smacked by the cottage father and he said that he'd take care of the cottage father for me." But when, later, the brother and Frank were at the cottage, the brother said to him, "Straighten up!" Frank said: "My brother didn't give me a chance. He just told me to straighten up, and he didn't listen to my side of the story." Frank again violently banged his hand against the table, screaming, "My brother betrayed me!" Questioned by the therapist, he asserted that his brother was "the one person I could trust, the one person I could turn to. Now I have no one to turn to," and proceeded to blame himself for everything that occurred in his life. When the therapist said, "You blame yourself for everything that happened and maybe when something like this happens you get yourself in trouble at school, throw ashtrays at people, hoping that someone will eventually hit you. This seems to be what you are doing to yourself now because of what your brother said."

The boys attempted to persuade Frank that his brother might have meant well. The therapist added, "Perhaps your brother in his ignorant way tried to help you." Frank burst out in intense rage, screaming, "Don't say that about my brother! He is the smartest man in the world!" The therapist explained that he had used the word in a different sense than it sounded. He meant to say that his brother did not have all the facts. John now began to quiet down.

Frank grew more cheerful toward the end of the session. As the boys were leaving, Frank was with Charles, the most recent arrival and toward whom Frank had been very antagonistic at first. They went out together, talking about Charles' brother who once beat him severely, but whom he now loved because he felt that his brother was interested in him.

Symptoms and Functioning after Twenty-Five Sessions of Para-analytic Group Psychotherapy

The cottage parents described Frank as more direct, less evasive, and less manipulative in dealing with them. He was less provocative with his cottage mates and was capable of acquiring and sustaining friendships. While six months before he had been described by his cottage parents as the "lowest of the low," they now spoke of him favorably and thought that he had carved out for himself a "niche in the cottage group." He frequently took responsibility for the conduct of the whole cottage and even for the cottage parents' children.

Similarly, the school reported that he caused "much less trouble than in the past" and that he was willing to wear glasses to correct his unilateral strabismus, something which he had vehemently resisted before. He was still distractible and finished his tasks only with considerable difficulty. He still provoked other boys occasionally, but this had been greatly reduced in frequency, intensity, and duration.

The female case worker who saw Frank during and at the termination of group treatment (not the same whose report was quoted) stated:

Frank is now freer and more open in his expression of anger toward his mother and is able to accept the fact that she neglected him. While in the past he denied this, he now recognizes more objectively his mother's personality and problems as separate from his own. His verbalizations and attitudes reflect more trust of adults than prior to group therapy. He is now able to speak in a more factual way of "being wanted" at home and to say that he was "not too unhappy" at the Village. He recognizes Children's Village, not as a punitive agent, but as an instrument for help with some of his problems at home. The group acted as a catalyst for individual therapy.

The case worker's findings were confirmed independently by the group therapist, who found evidence in Frank's productions in the group that he now recognized that his acting out was a result of inner turmoil rather than being due to purely external circumstances. He permitted himself positive feelings for the therapist and recognized himself as being "mixed up" and having an unfounded mistrust of adults.

A memo from a top administrative staff member who spoke to Frank before his discharge from the Village a year after termination of group therapy stated:

I think you will be pleased to know that before Frank left I asked him what he thought counted most in his stay at the Village. Somewhat hesitatingly he stated: "My cottage parents and Mr. G. [the Protestant chaplain]." We explored with him what was important to him about his association with these staff members, but he was quite unclear on the subject. After we shook hands, I said, "Good luck," and he was walking out of my office when he turned back and added, "It was really the discussion club with Mr. S. that was the most important thing." Frank then explained this by adding that the "kids could really talk about their real problems to each other, with those who understood them best, and it wasn't adult-dominated."

Discussion

There is plenty of evidence of the parents' neglect of Frank and of serious prenatal and postnatal rejections. The mother tried to abort him, considered him very ugly, and refused to believe that he was a normal looking baby. She seemed incapable of tender feelings toward him, blamed him for her alcoholism, beat him, and finally placed him in an institution. Despite all this rejection, Frank was strongly tied to his mother. She was a focus of his libidinal strivings, and she created a void in him which only she could fill. At the same time, he felt himself responsible for her rejection of him and saw himself as unworthy of her love. This contributed to his weak ego organization and his incapacity to mobilize resources to meet the demands of his life. His distractibility derived from this, as well as from his deep inner yearning for love and from the tensions generated by unfulfilled needs, which he vicariously satisfied by petty stealing from his mother.

Equally clear is his lack of identification with and support from his father. Because of the father's long absences from home, Frank was unable to achieve the identification that would permit internalization of the masculine traits of his father and his ego strengths, whatever they were.

Only one person seemed to play a constructive role in Frank's life, his brother, who was seen by the boy (in actuality or in fantasy) as one whom he "likes." Even this, however, he denied by the feelings toward his dog. An important factor in this relationship may be the fact that Frank and his brother shared a room. It is not known whether or not they shared the same bed. The boy's reactions to his brother, his continued reference to and dependency upon him, would point to a homoerotic or even homosexual tie. The circumstances of this patient's life favored such a development from every point of view. The castration by, and masochistic submission to, his mother, the lack of opportunity for identification with his father, the mother's preference for her daughter, and the physical proximity of the brother at times of affect hunger, all would favor such an eventuality.

This hypothesis is supported by Frank's adjustment to life. His provocativeness with peers which led to rejection and physical punishment was a continuation of his masochistic submissiveness to a (sexually) castrating mother. His placating and devious approach to adults as stronger persons can be understood as sexual submission, and his aggressiveness and attack upon the group therapist can be seen as a defense against his homoerotic feelings toward him. Frank usually stayed after the sessions so as to have at least a brief time alone with the therapist, and his offer to shine the therapist's shoes can be construed as his assuming the submissive, catering (female) role in relation to a strong (mature) male. His intense restlessness during the sessions, evidenced by frequent and impulsive standing up and walking around the room (the only boy in our analytic groups who did this), lighting matches, burning paper, scorching the table, carving on it, throwing things out of the window and perilously leaning out of it (symbolizing an attempt at suicide), all point to a homoerotic panic which gradually subsided.

That Frank came to terms with himself to some extent is evidenced by the report of the case worker: "There is even more telling confirmation of this in his behavior and relatedness in school, the community, and case work. These changes can be attributed to the help he received from the group in overcoming his guilt and emerging from the tragic sense of life that was his." This was achieved by universalization and reduction of guilt, objectification, and reality testing. It was also sponsored by ventilation of feelings, discharge of hostility, and by being accepted. There were improved feelings of self-worth and an improved self-image. Group therapy thus affected ego strength and personality integration both structurally and behaviorally. What is yet to be established in this case is the libidinal modifications effected by group therapy.

Here we need to view the problem both from its nonsexual and sexual aspects. The centrifugal flow of the primitive libido brings expansion and growth of the personality in numerous directions, but only if there are appropriate stimuli and opportunities in the environment. The capacity of the child to utilize opportunities for growth is derived from the support he receives from key persons in his life. They can either enhance his growth, restrict it, or block it off. When not too crippling damage has been inflicted upon the growth urge in these primary circumstances, it can later be reawakened by stimuli from extrafamilial sources, such as school, friends, and other individuals and groups. But if the restrictive and crippling forces in the home have been of great intensity, the personality becomes impoverished, and compensatory and defensive adaptations and behavior patterns arise. One of the forms this took in Frank, for example, was stealing.

The comments of the various staff members pointed to unmistakable improvement in this boy's social adjustment and capacity for relating to other people, but at the time of his leaving the institution, we noted that this improvement was only partial and might not be sustained under the inordinately stressful circumstances of his life at home. This prophecy was based upon our recognition that Frank was acting out a "transference neurosis" developed in the group. This transference neurosis stemmed from his homoerotic (or homosexual) tie to the older brother, displaced (transferred) upon the therapist. A transference neurosis cannot be worked through in group therapy; its resolution requires an extensive libidinal transference upon an individual therapist.

Our prophesy unfortunately came true. Shortly after Frank left the institution, he experienced a traumatic event which added to his distress and ego strain. His father took him along on a cross-country trip, and upon arrival at their destination, introduced his son to his common-law wife and asked Frank to live with them as a member of this duplicate family unit. Frank instead returned to New York and obtained a job in a spray paint plant where his brother was employed. He stayed on that job for several weeks, after which he tried to enlist in the Navy but was rejected because of his defective eyesight. He then returned south, where he worked on a part time basis in an amusement park and lived with friends of his father; we do not know whether this was the woman involved or whether it was a family of the father's acquaintance. While there, he met a girl and decided to marry her. He was at this time between seventeen and eighteen years old. Not having any funds, he returned to New York with the intention of earning and saving a sufficient sum of money so that he could go back and marry the girl.

Unsuccessful at obtaining the kind of job that he wished and that would pay him enough, he broke into an office building, stole some money, and later passed a bad check, apparently on a blank acquired during his illegal entry into the office building. When he learned that he was being sought by the police, he started south, hitch-hiking and stealing on his way. He was apprehended and returned to New York, where he was sentenced to a four-year prison term on a charge of unlawful entry. All this transpired within one year of his discharge from the Village.[2]

---

2. This patient was a member of a group of delinquent institutionalized teenage boys described *in extenso* in [62].

PART THREE

An S.R. Slavson
Bibliography

Articles on group psychotherapy which are of primary importance but which for reasons of space have not been included in the present collection are indicated with asterisks. For full bibliographical data on items appearing in this volume (chapters 1–49) the reader is directed to the sources and credits section beginning on p. 812.

Books

[50] *Science in the New Education* (with Robert K. Spear). New York: Prentice-Hall, 1934. (In which Mr. Slavson first described his Search-Discovery educational technique which he evolved in 1918. See also [4, 161]. This book was one of the Ten Best Books of the Year selected by American Publishers Association.)

[51] *Creative Group Education.* New York: Association Press, 1937.

[52] *Character Education in a Democracy.* New York: Association Press, 1939. Also in Braille. (This book was one of one hundred selected by the American Publishers Association. It also received an award from *Parents Magazine.* The phrase "group dynamics" was for the first time introduced in this book, Chap. 4.)

[53] *An Introduction to Group Therapy.* New York: The Commonwealth Fund, 1943. New York: International Universities Press, 1952. Also set in Braille.

[54] *Recreation and the Total Personality.* New York: Association Press, 1946. (The only book ever published on recreation in the light of psychology and para-psychoanalysis.)

[55] *The Practice of Group Therapy*, (ed.). New York: International Universities Press, 1947.

[56] *Analytic Group Psychotherapy.* New York: Columbia University Press, 1950.

[57] *Child Psychotherapy*, New York: Columbia University Press, 1952.

[58] *Re-Educating the Delinquent: Through Group and Community Participation.* New York: Harper & Brothers, 1954.

[59] *The Fields of Group Psychotherapy*, (ed.). New York: International Universities Press, 1956.

[60] *Child-Centered Group Guidance of Parents.* New York: International Universities Press, 1958.

[61] *A Textbook of Analytic Group Psychotherapy.* New York: International Universities Press, 1964.

[62] *Reclaiming the Delinquent by Para-Analytic Group Psychotherapy and the Inversion Technique.* New York: The Free Press-Macmillan, 1965.

[63] *Because I Live Here: The Theory and Practice of Vita-Erg Therapy with Deteriorated Psychotic Women.* International Universities Press, 1970.

[64] *Group Psychotherapies of Children: A Textbook* (with Mortimer Schiffer). New York: International Universities Press, 1975.

Books in Other Languages

[65] *Rieducazione della gioventi disadattata.* Rome: Roprieta Riservata, 1959.

[66] *Einführungs in die Gruppentherapie.* Gottingen: Verlag Für Medizinische Psychologie, 1956.

[67] *Einführung in die Gruppentherapie von Kindern und Jugendlich.* Gottingen: Verlag Vanderhoe und Ruprecht, 1972.

[68] *Psychotherapie Analytique de Groupe-Infants, Adolescents, Adults. Paris: Presses Universitaires de France, 1953.*

[69] In Japanese: *Creative Group Education.*

[70] In Japanese: *Introduction to Group Therapy.*

[71] In Japanese: *Analytic Group Therapy.*

[72] *Lehrbuch der Analytischen Gruppenpsychotherapie.* Frankfort-Main: S. Fischer Verlag, 1976.

[73] *Tratado De Psicoterapia Grupal Analitica.* Buenos Aires: Editorial Paidos, 1976.

Chapters in Books

* [74] The Group in Development and in Therapy. In *Proceedings of the National Conference of Social Work.* Chicago: University of Chicago Press, 1938.

[75] Group Dynamics. In *Character Education in a Democracy.* New York: Association Press, 1939.

* [76] The Dynamics of the Group Process. *Ibid.* and in *Readings in Group Work*, ed. Dorothea E. Sullivan. New York: Association Press, 1952.

[77] Some Psycho-Social Foundations of Group Work. In *They Say About Group Work*, Union Settlement of Hartford, 1940.

[78] Character Training. In *Mothers' Encyclopedia*, vol. I. New York: The Parent's Institute, 1942.

[79] Group Therapy with Children. In *Modern Trends in Child Psychiatry*, eds. Nolan D. C. Lewis, M.D. and Bernard L. Pacella, M.D. New York: International Universities Press, 1945.

* [80] The Integration of Case Work and Psychiatry with Group Therapy. In *The Case Worker in Psychotherapy*. New York: Jewish Board of Guardians, 1945.

[81] The Fields and Objectives of Group Therapy. In *Current Therapies of Personality Disorders*, ed. Bernard Glueck. New York: Grune & Stratton, 1946.

[82] Surveys of Group Therapy Literature. In *Progress in Neurology and Psychiatry*, ed. Ernest Spiegel. New York: Grune & Stratton, 1946.

[83] ——— (with Saul Scheidlinger). *Ibid.*, 1947.

[84] ——— (with Saul Scheidlinger). *Ibid.*, 1948.

[85] ——— (with Emanuel Hallowitz). *Ibid.*, 1949.

[86] ——— (with Emanuel Hallowitz). *Ibid.*, 1950.

[87] ——— (with Emanuel Hallowitz). *Ibid.*, 1951.

[88] ——— (with Emanuel Hallowitz and Leslie Rosenthal). *Ibid.*, 1952.

[89] ———(with Emanuel Hallowitz and Leslie Rosenthal). *Ibid.*, 1953.

[90] ———(with Emanuel Hallowitz and Leslie Rosenthal). *Ibid.*, 1954.

[91] General Principles and Dynamics. In *The Practice of Group Therapy*, [55].

[92] Activity Group Therapy with Character Deviations in Children. *Ibid.*

[93] Contra-Indications of Group Therapy for Patients with Psychopathic Personalities. *Ibid.*

[94] Treatment of a Case of Behavior Disorder through Activity Group Therapy. *Ibid.*

[95] Interview Group Therapy With a Neurotic Adolescent Girl Suffering from Chorea. *Ibid.*

[96] The Group in Child Guidance. In *Handbook of Child Guidance*, ed. Ernst Harms. New York: Child Care Publications, 1947.

* [97] The Individual and Society: Discussion. In *International Congress on Mental Hygiene, Published Proceedings,* vol. IV. London: H. K. Lewis, 1948.

* [98] Social Reeducation in an Institutional Setting. In *Advances in the Understanding of the Offender.* (Yearbook of the National Probation and Parole Association), ed. Marjorie Bell. New York: 1950.

* [99] When Is a Group Not a Group? In *Readings in Group Work,* ed. Dorothea P. Sullivan. New York: Association Press, 1952.

* [100] Problems of Research: Discussion. *Ibid.*

* [101] Extrafamilial Influences in Pathogenesis. In *Social Science and Psychotherapy for Children,* ed. Otto Pollack. New York: Russell Sage Foundation, 1952.

[102] Group Psychotherapies. In *Six Approaches to Psychotherapy,* ed. James L. McCarry. New York: Dryden Press, 1955.

[103] Symptom Versus Syndrome in Group Psychotherapy. In *The Fields of Group Psychotherapy* [59].

[104] Group Therapy of Unmarried Mothers (with Beryce MacLennan). *Ibid.*

[105] Group Therapy and Community Mental Health. *Ibid.*

[106] A Bio-Quantum Theory of the Ego and Its Application to Group Psychotherapy, *International Journal of Group Psychotherapy,* vol. 9, no. 1, 1959.

[107] A Group of Problem Girls. In *Great Cases in Psychoanalysis,* ed. Harold Greenwald. New York: Ballantine Books, 1959. New York: Jason Aronson, 1973.

* [108] Individual and Group Therapists Look at Each Others' Modalities: Discussion. In *Topical Problems of Psychotherapy,* vol. 2. New York: S. Karger, 1960.

* [109] Historical and Developmental Trends in Group Psychotherapy. In *Proceedings of the Third World Congress of Psychiatry.* Montreal: McGill-Queen's University Press, 1961.

* [110] A Critique of the Group Therapy Literature. In *Acta Psychotherapeutics,* vol. 10. New York: S. Karger, 1962.

[111] Groups in Guidance and Treatment of Adolescents in a School Setting (with Haim Ginott). In *Professional School Psychology*, vol. I, ed. Monroe E. and Gloria B. Gottsegen. New York: Grune & Stratton, 1963.

* [112] What is the Meaning of Aggression? In *Why Report: A Book of Interviews*, ed. Lucy Freeman and Martin Theodoles. Purchase, N.Y.: Arthur Bernhard, 1964.

[113] What is Group Therapy? *Ibid.*

[114] Types of Group Psychotherapy and Their Clinical Applications. In *The Challenge for Group Psychotherapy*, ed. Stefan de Schill. New York: International Universities Press, 1974.

[115] In press: Vita-Erg Psychotherapy, *Psychotherapy Handbook*, ed. R. Herink.

Chapters in Books and Journals in Other Languages

[116] Einige Merkmale der Analytischen Gruppen-Psychotherapie. In *Gruppen Psychotherapie*. Bern, Switzerland: Verlag Hans Huber, 1956.

[117] Gruppenpsychotherapie. In *Die Psychotherapie in der Gegenwart*, vol. II, ed. Eric Stern. Zurich: Rascher Verlag, 1958.

[118] Emergence de Facteurs Dynamiques Psychoanalytiques dans une Psychotherapie de Groupes d'Entretiens Avec Adultes. *Revue Francaise de Psychoanalyse.* Nov.–Dec. 1958.

[119] La Que Es Y Lo Que No Es La Psychoterapia de Grupo. *La Revista de Psychiatria Y Psicologia Medica*, de Europa y America Latinas, Tomo IV, Num. 5, 1960. Barcelona.

[120] Vorwort. In *Analytische Gruppenpsychotherapie, Grundlage und Praxis*, ed. Hans. G. Pruess. Munchen: Urban und Schwartzenberg, 1966.

[121] Unterschiedliche Psychodynamishe Prozesse der Activitat- und-Aussprachengruppen, Sur Gruppenpsychotherapie mit Kindern und Jugendlichen. *Ibid.*

[122] Meine Technik in Psychotherapie mit Kindern. In *Handbuch fur die Psychotherapie mit Kindern*, ed. Gerd Bierman. Munchen: Ernst Reinhardt Verlag.

[123] Die Arten der Gruppenpsychotherapie und Ihre Klinische Auswendung. In *Psychoanalitische Therapie in Gruppen*, ed. Stefan de Schill. Stuttgart: Ernst Klett Verlag, 1971.

[124] Types de Psychotherapies de Groupes et Applications Clinics. In *La Psychotherapie de Groupe,* ed. Stefan de Schill. Paris: Presses Universitaires de France, 1971.

Psychotherapy Papers in Periodicals

* [125] Re-Educative Activity for Delinquent Youth. *Jewish Social Service Quarterly*, June 1936.
[126] Personality Qualifications for Workers in Group Therapy. *Proceedings, National Conference of Jewish Social Work*, 1937. See also [59, 133].
[127] Values of the Group in Therapy. *News Letter of the American Association of Psychiatric Social Workers*, Winter 1943–1944.
* [128] Some Elements in Activity Group Therapy. *American Journal of Orthopsychiatry*, vol. 14, no. 4, 1944.
* [129] Values of the Group to Adolescents, Presented at a Leadership Training Course for the B'nai B'rith. *AZA Leader*, 1944.
[130] Group Therapy at the Jewish Board of Guardians. *Mental Hygiene*, vol. 28, no. 3, 1944.
[131] Chronologic and Clinical Considerations in Group Therapy with Children. *Nervous Child*, April 1945.
[132] Group Treatment for Individual Problems. *Better Times*, vol. XXVIII, no. 36. New York: Welfare Council, May 1947.
* [133] Qualifications and Training of Group Therapists. *Mental Hygiene*, vol. 31, no. 3, 1947. See also [59, 126].
* [134] Advances in Group and Individual Therapy: Discussion. *Proceedings of the International Conference on Medical Psychotherapy*, vol. 3. London: H. K. Lewis, 1948.
[135] Report of Commission of Group Psychotherapy to the World Federation of Mental Health, S. R. Slavson, Chairman, 1948. I. Group Treatment of Pre-School Children and Their Mothers; II. Group Therapy for Children in Latency; III. Group Therapy of Adolescents; IV. Group Psychotherapy with Adults: A Review of Recent Trends and Practices; V. Group Psychotherapy in Institutions; VI. Summary Conclusions and Recommendations. *International Journal of Group Psychotherapy*, vol. 2, no. 3, 1952.

[136] Group Therapy in Child Care and Child Guidance. *Jewish Social Service Quarterly*, 1948.

[137] Discussion on Group Therapy. *Annals of the New York Academy of Sciences*, October 1948.

[138] Some Current Practices in Group Psychotherapy. *Journal of the Brooklyn State Hospital*, April 1948.

* [139] Group Bases for Mental Health, *Mental Hygiene*, vol. 33, 1949.

* [140] Children's Activity in Casework Therapy. *Journal of Social Casework*, vol. 30, no. 4, 1949.

[141] The Dynamics of Analytic Group Psychotherapy. *International Journal of Group Psychotherapy*, vol. 1, no. 3, 1951.

[142] Group Psychotherapy. *Scientific American*, vol. 183, no. 6, December 1950.

* [143] Current Trends in Group Psychotherapy. *International Journal of Group Psychotherapy*, vol. 1, no. 1, 1951.

* [144] Some Problems in Group Psychotherapy As Seen by Private Practitioners. *International Journal of Group Psychotherapy*, vol. 2, no. 1, 1952.

* [145] Remarks on Group Psychotherapy and Community Mental Health. *International Journal of Group Psychotherapy*, vol. 4, no. 3, 1954.

[146] The Freudian Roots of Group Psychotherapy. *Guide to Psychiatric and Psychological Literature*, vol. II, nos. 8–9, April–May 1956.

[147] Psychotherapy in the Light of American Democracy. (Unpublished) 1956.

* [148] The "Adolescent Crisis" and Mental and Community Health. Presented at the Tenth Annual Meeting of the World Federation of Mental Health, Copenhagen. Published Proceedings, 1957.

* [149] Can Group Psychotherapy Be Effective? *International Journal of Group Psychotherapy*, vol. 8, no. 1, 1958.

* [150] A Bio-Quantum Theory of the Ego and Its Application to Analytic Group Psychotherapy. *International Journal of Group Psychotherapy*, vol. 9, no. 1, 1959.

[151] What Group Psychotherapy is and What it is Not. *Topical Problems of Psychotherapy*, vol. 3. Basel & New York: S. Karger, 1960.

* [152] Prospect for Group Psychotherapy. *International Mental Health Research Newsletter*, vol. 2, nos. 3 & 4. New York: Postgraduate Center for Mental Health, 1960.

[153] The Scope and Aim of the Children's Village Group Psychotherapy Project. *International Journal of Group Psychotherapy*, vol. 10, no. 2, 1960.

[154] Group Psychotherapy in the Service of Mental Health. Presented at Congress of the World Mental Health Association, Paris (read by Wilfred C. Hulse, M.D.). Published Proceedings, 1961.

* [155] Group Psychotherapy and the Nature of Schizophrenia. *International Journal of Group Psychotherapy*, vol. 11, no. 1, 1961.

* [156] Psychodrama and Group Psychotherapy: Discussion. *Berkshire Farms Monographs*, vol. 1, no. 2, 1963.

[157] Group Treatment of Adolescent Offenders: Discussion. *Berkshire Farms Monographs*, vol. I, no. 2, 1963.

[158] The Relation of Content and Process in Group Psychotherapy. Presented at the Annual Conference of the American Group Psychotherapy Association, 1965.

[159] Three Decades of Group Psychotherapy: 1934–1964, An Historical Fragment. Presented at the Annual Conference of the American Group Psychotherapy Association, 1965, unpublished.

* [160] On the Treatment of Adult Criminals. *International Journal of Group Psychotherapy*, vol. 16, no. 4, 1966.

* [161] The Integration of Mental Health in Classroom Practice. Presented at the Seventh International Congress on Mental Health, London. Published Proceedings, 1968.

* [162] In the Beginning.... *International Journal of Group Psychotherapy*, vol. 25, no. 2, 1975.

* [163] Address: Jewish Board of Guardians' Institute on the Fortieth Anniversary of Children's Group Therapy, in Honor of S. R. Slavson. New York, 1975.

[164] Book Review: *The Life and Work of Sigmund Freud*, vols. I and II, by Ernest Jones. *International Journal of Group Psychotherapy*, vol. 6, no. 4, 1956.

[165] Book Review: *The Life and Work of Sigmund Freud*, vol. III, Ernest Jones. *Ibid.*, vol. 10, no. 3, 1960.

[166] Book Review: *Free Associations: Memoirs of a Psycho-analyst*, by Ernest Jones. *Ibid.*, vol. 12, no. 3, 1962.

Education, Recreation and Group Work

[167] Creative Science Teaching. *School & Home*, New York, January 1924.

[168] Science as Experience and Attitude. *Progressive Education*, October 1931.

[169] Liberty Has Limits. *Progressive Education*, December 1931.

[170] Integrated Science for Young Children. *New Era* (London), January 1932.

[171] Character Training Through Educative Activity. *Jewish Center*, June 1934.

[172] Creative Group Education. *Christian Citizenship*, December 1937.

[173] Changing Objectives in Group Work. Proceedings of the Connecticut Conference on Group Work. New Haven, April 1938.

[174] Values of Laboratory Experiences. *Childhood Education*, April 1939.

[175] Group Education for a Democracy. *Journal of Educational Sociology*, December 1939.

[176] Democratic Leadership in Education. *The Group*, December 1939.

[177] Aims and Conditions of Group Work. *Christian Citizenship*, March 1940.

[178] A Plan for Group Education in the Elementary School. *Journal of Educational Sociology*, May 1940.

[179] Foundations of a Club Program Within a Democratic Framework. *Christian Citizenship*, 1941.

[180] Character is What We Make It. *Parents Magazine*, March 1941.

[181] Leadership and Democracy are Compatible. In *Group Work in a Year of Crisis. New York: American Association for the Study of Group Work, 1941.*

[182] People in Time of War. *The Group*, March 1942.

[183] Next Step for Group Workers. In *Group Work and the Social Scene Today.* New York: American Association for the Study of Group Work, 1943.

[184] A Group Plan for Classroom Teaching. *The Group*, January 1946.

[185] Leadership and Recreation. *Recreation*, March 1946.

[186] Group Work and Mental Health. *The Group*, May 1949.

Films

[187] Activity Group Therapy (52 min.). Film Library, New York University, Washington Square, New York, New York, 10012.

[188] Views and Comments—Interview with S. R. Slavson (70 min.). American Group Psychotherapy Association, 1995 Broadway, New York, New York, 10023.

About S. R. Slavson

[189] Klein, A. He Lets Them Grow. *The Survey*, vol. 85, February 1949. Also in *Courage is the Key*. New York: Twayne, 1953.

[190] Spotnitz, H. In Tribute to S. R. Slavson. *International Journal of Group Psychotherapy*, vol. 21, no. 4, 1971.

[191] One Hundred Most Important Leaders in the World of Health. *Family Health*, vol. 4, no. 3, March 1972.

[192] Rachman, A. W., S. R. Slavson: A Personal Reaction. *Group*, vol. 1, no. 1, 1977.

Sources and Credits

[1] 1976, Unpublished paper. [2] Presented at a National Symposium on Psychotherapy, Temple University, Phil. Pa., 1964, unpublished. [3] Presented at the Second International Conference on Group Psychotherapy, Zurich, Switzerland, 1957, in *Acta Psychotherapeutica*, New York, S. Karger, Vol. 7, 1959. [4] 1975, unpublished paper. [5] *International Journal of Group Psychotherapy*, Vol. 3, No. 1, 1953. [6] *International Journal of Group Psychotherapy*, Vol. 5, No. 1, 1955. [7] *International Journal of Group Psychotherapy*, Vol. 9, No. 4, 1959. [8] *International Journal of Group Psychotherapy*, Vol. 6, No. 4, 1956. [9] *International Journal of Group Psychotherapy*, Vol. 4, No. 1, 1954. [10] *International Journal of Group Psychotherapy*, Vol. 10, No. 1, 1960. [11] *Ameri-*

can Journal of Orthopsychiatry, Vol. 15, No. 2, 1945. [12] *International Journal of Group Psychotherapy,* Vol. 6, No. 2, 1956. [13] *International Journal of Group Psychotherapy,* Vol. 19, No. 1, 1969. [14] *International Journal of Group Psychotherapy,* Vol. 16, No. 1, 1966. [15] *International Journal of Group Psychotherapy,* Vol. 20, No. 1, 1970. [16] *International Journal of Group Psychotherapy,* Vol. 7, No. 2, 1957. [17] *The Psychoanalytic Review,* 38:1, 1951. [18] *International Journal of Group Psychotherapy,* Vol. 16, No. 4, 1966. [19] *International Journal of Group Psychotherapy,* Vol. 3, No. 1, 1953. [20] *The Psychoanalytic Review,* 37:1, 1950. [21] *International Journal of Group Psychotherapy,* Vol. 22, No. 4, 1972. [22] *International Journal of Group Psychotherapy,* Vol. 6, No. 1, 1956. [23] *International Journal of Group Psychotherapy,* Vol. 13, No. 2, 1963. [24] *International Journal of Group Psychotherapy,* Vol. 15, No. 2, 1965. [25] *Psychiatric Quarterly Supplement,* New York State Department of Mental Hygiene, No. 41, 1967; also in *Social Psychiatry—Special Aspects,* S. Karger, N.Y., Vol. 9, 1969. [26] *International Journal of Group Psychotherapy,* Vol. 5, No. 4, 1955. [27] Presented at the First International Congress on Social Psychiatry, London, England, 1964, McGill–Queen's University Press, McGill University, Montreal, Quebec. [28] Introduction to the *Fields of Group Psychotherapy* ([59]), paperback edition, New York, Schocken Books, 1974. [29] Presented at the Annual Conference of the AGPA, 1971, also in *Psychiatric Spectator,* 6:6, 1971. [30] *Journal of Contemporary Psychotherapy,* Vol. 6, No. 2, 1974. [31] *Mental Hygiene,* Vol. 24, No. 1, 1940. [32] *American Journal of Orthopsychiatry,* Vol. 13, No. 4, 1943. [33] Presented at a Conference of New York Psychologists, 1968, unpublished. [34] *The Nervous Child,* Vol. 4, No. 3, 1945. [35] *American Journal of Orthopsychiatry,* Vol. 13, No. 3, 1943. [36] *American Journal of Orthopsychiatry,* Vol. 15, No. 4, 1945. [37] *The Nervous Child,* Vol. 9, No. 2, 1950. [38] *The Nervous Child,* Vol. 7, No. 3, 1948. [39] *American Journal of Orthopsychiatry,* Vol. 17, No. 2, 1947. [40] *The Nervous Child,* Vol. 4, No. 3, 1945. [41] *American Journal of Orthopsychiatry,* Vol. 9, No. 4, 1939. [42] *International Journal of Group Psychotherapy,* Vol. 1, Nos. 1 & 2, 1951. [43] *Psychotherapeutica Psychosomatica,* Vol. 13, 1965; also in *Pathways,* New York City Board of Education, Vol. 6, 1964. [44] *The*

Nervous Child, Vol. 6, No. 4, 1947.   [45] *The Journal of Educational Sociology*, Vol. 24, No. 1, 1950.   [46] Yearbook, International Probation and Parole Association, New York, 1948, also in *Bulwarks Against Crime*, Proceedings of the National Probation Association, 1948.   [47] *International Journal of Group Psychotherapy*, Vol. 12, No. 2, 1962.   [48] Presented at the Annual Conference of the AGPA, 1968, unpublished.   [49] *International Journal of Group Psychotherapy*, Vol. 12, No. 2, 1962; also in *Case Studies in Psychopathology*, Louis Diamont, Columbus, Ohio, Charles E. Merrill Publishing Co., 1971.

INDEX